Also by James Andrew Miller

Running in Place: Inside the Senate

*Live from New York: An Uncensored
History of "Saturday Night Live"*

Also by Tom Shales

On the Air

Legends: Remembering America's Greatest Stars

*Live from New York: An Uncensored
History of "Saturday Night Live"*

THOSE GUYS HAVE ALL THE FUN

INSIDE THE WORLD OF ESPN

JAMES ANDREW MILLER
AND TOM SHALES

LITTLE, BROWN AND COMPANY

LARGE PRINT EDITION

Little, Brown and Company
Hachette Book Group
237 Park Avenue, New York, NY 10017
www.hachettebookgroup.com

First Edition: May 2011

Little, Brown and Company is a division of Hachette Book Group, Inc.
The Little, Brown name and logo are trademarks of Hachette Book Group, Inc.

The publisher is not responsible for websites (or their content) that are not owned by the publisher.

ISBN 978-0-316-04300-7 (hc) / 978-0-316-17810-5 (large print)
LCCN 2011925202

10 9 8 7 6 5 4 3 2 1

RRD-C

Printed in the United States of America

For Elizabeth Miller (1959–2010)
with love

"To love what you do and feel that it matters—
how could anything be more fun?"
— *Katharine Graham*

Contents

Introduction

It is the 27th day of August 2009, and a happy horde has gathered in remote Bristol, Connecticut, to celebrate — with equal parts sentimentality and pride — the thirtieth birthday of a television network. Not many broadcasting companies inspire this level of devotion, but this one is different.

The sun smiles down obligingly on ESPN's sixty-four-acre "campus" — the rolling, semiverdant site on which ESPN's buildings sit and from which its twenty-seven treasured satellite dishes suck signals from the sky, spewing others back into the ionosphere and out through much of the world. The grass all but glows green, something that couldn't have happened thirty years ago, when this place had less in common with a university than with the LaBrea Tar Pits, except that Bristol's primordial ooze was just plain miserable mud.

The thirtieth-birthday festivities are going to be much more understated than celebrations for the twenty-fifth. Then, cars full of ESPN stars motorcaded through Disney World, and even if you couldn't get to Florida, you could probably score one of the 1.3 million bottles of Gatorade produced in a special flavor called "ESPN"—or grab one of 300 million Bud Light cans with ESPN's twenty-fifth anniversary logo printed on the label. In the weeks leading up to the celebration, network nabobs chose what they thought were the top sports moments of the previous twenty-five years and aired a series of specials keyed to the anniversary—all the hoopla climaxing in one of the hottest tickets in the company's history: a blowout at the ESPN Zone restaurant in Times Square.

Because 2009 is turning out to be a brutally cruel recession year, ESPN's president, the unflappable George Bodenheimer, wisely elects to tone things down this time around. In a brief state-of-the-clubhouse speech, he looks to a rosy future before an audience that includes many of the company's senior executives and about fifty members of both old and new media.

So self-confident are the leaders of ESPN at this point in their history that they have even invited the head raccoon of *Deadspin,* the maverick and sometimes mean-spirited blog that has long considered the merciless ongoing examination of ESPN to be one of its public duties.

Deadspin editor A. J. Daulerio felt he couldn't

handle spending the entire day cozying up to ESPN's big kahunas, so he dispatched "Blazer Girl," the blog's answer to Lois Lane, to cover the event. If Daulerio is hoping she will go all Woodward and Bernstein on ESPN, however, he's going to be disappointed; Blazer Girl goes soft among the ESPN cognoscenti, especially when she gets to pose for a photo with the network's longest-reigning superstar, Chris Berman.

After lunch comes a celebration within the celebration: homage paid to forty-three people who, like Berman, started with ESPN in the first year of its existence—and are still on the payroll as the first decade of a new century ends.

It's part of the mythology of the place that many an ESPN employee doesn't just date the company but marries it. Longevity is the norm. Over the years, occasional employees leave because they don't fit in; some leave because they simply can't take so-called life in lonely Bristol; and still others leave for better pay and more ego stroking elsewhere. Lastly, though there have been notorious examples to the contrary, it usually takes a lot to get fired by ESPN.

Of the forty-three stalwarts being honored with their own stars on the ESPN "Walk of Fame" on this super summer afternoon, Berman, practically the network's avatar, and Bob "The General" Ley (pronounced Lee), the network's best journalist, are not only the most recognizable ESPN personalities but among the most recognizable guys ever to have a mic pack jab their rear ends. The two soak up the admiring applause of several hundred in the audience—other honorees, ESPN employees and family members, press, and guests.

In a moment that is somehow pure ESPN, Bob Ley looks down at his star and does a double take when he sees "Rob Lee" spelled out in gold lettering, a double whammy of a blooper that causes colleague Bill Shanahan, standing next to Ley, to explode in guffaws. Some might consider this a perfect reminder that through the years, ESPN management has never liked its personalities to become big names anyway; big names demand big bucks. They prefer keeping the talent humble.

Bodenheimer handles the officiating with presidential aplomb alongside Sage Steele—born seven years before ESPN was—as his mistress of ceremonies. Bodenheimer had rejected the organizing committee's first suggestion of an emcee and made the outstanding choice of Steele—who represents everything you could ask for in an anchor—himself. Berman and Ley speechify, then join other honorees posing for photos next to their stars and also with Bodenheimer, who on this day seems more benevolently paternalistic than ever.

Then they all adjourn to the ESPN Café and eat cake to commemorate the spectacular growth of the past three decades. ESPN was a funky little seat-of-the-pants operation in 1979 when it started, in a town so dull that employees worked eighteen-hour days to keep from dying of boredom outside. ESPN now encompasses six domestic U.S. cable networks, forty-six international networks, ESPN radio in North America and syndicated radio in eleven other far-flung countries, plus online operations, broadband, magazines, books, interactive media, wireless, CDs and DVDs, video games, and restaurants, all helping to pump coverage of more than sixty-five different sports into television sets, computers, and mobile phones in more than two hundred fifty countries.

Once a bastard stepchild filed, along with "almond groves," under "other" among the holdings of Getty Oil, ESPN is now the most important component of the Disney empire, worth more than the entire National Football League, worth more than the NBA, MLB, and the NHL put together.

This book pursues the mystery of ESPN's rise to stratospheric heights from subterranean depths. It reveals how a crazy idea grew into one of the most successful media enterprises of all time.

"Those Guys Have All the Fun." The men and women you will meet in these pages spend their days and nights talking and thinking about sports. Hard as they work, ESPNers toil in an environment that most folks would consider pure pleasure. And when they aren't working, ESPNers still have all the fun, or at least most of it. At ESPN, partying is a varsity sport.

What follows is not the history but *the story* of ESPN. It would take a dozen or more weighty volumes to provide an all-encompassing account of ESPN's innumerable hours of nonstop broadcasting through more than thirty sports-saturated years. More time and space would be needed to fully chronicle the many thousands who have come and gone — or come and stayed — over the decades. Still, many of those who have entered ESPN's orbit are here, and here in their own words. To write this book, over five hundred fifty people were interviewed, and the words you read are their own. In some instances, their quotes have been cleaned up (removing, for example, the "umms" and "uhs" that accompany most conversation); and certain discussions for the sake of clarity and exposition have been moved or compacted. But otherwise, what you read is precisely as it was told to us.

One thing that can be stated from the start is that the odds of ESPN happening just the way it did are somewhere in the neighborhood of a zillion to one. All sports, all the time — 24/7 and 365 days a year? When the notion was hatched back in 1978, it was liberally ridiculed — even though logic and precedent tell us that eventually, somehow and somewhere, someone would have looked at the tremendous growth of sports and sporting events in the United States, noticed the morphing of athletes into superstar celebrities, taken stock of the wide-open explosion in the number of potential cable networks, and realized that tens, even *hundreds,* of millions of dollars were lying around waiting to be made.

But it was hardly inevitable that anyone else's long-and-windy road to fruition as a media superpower would have started in a hamlet as unkempt, unlikely, and unheard-of as Bristol, Connecticut.

Maybe it all goes to prove that some higher power is a sports fan. Surely someone or something intervened to help see ESPN through the sometimes dark, sometimes bleak, occasionally slapdash early days. Today, lowly little Bristol has been transformed into the world headquarters of a globally branded, dominating presence.

Turns for the better were the results of crucial decisions made by six different men (and many others who worked for them or oversaw them). The men who at different times ran the company wound up being both the right guys for the job and, perhaps more important, the right guys for the eras in which they served. So much so that if, along the way, someone were to have started messing around with the exact order in which these men took charge, it could well have knocked ESPN off its trajectory. The company and the network that are ESPN might not even exist (much less be bookworthy), might have stumbled ignominiously into oblivion, if not for the exact sequence of these decision makers and of the decisions they kept making.

There were many more people involved, of course, than just executives and owners. In the chapters ahead, you'll meet them—people who worked at the company or who dealt with it from outside its cloistered campus. They all have stories of their own—happy, sad, adventurous, timid, wholesome as pie, or lurid as pay-per-view porn.

ESPN's playing field has been populated with winners and losers, champions and chumps, cads and catalysts, heroes and, for lack of a better word, villains—and theirs is a shared story of struggle, defeat, more struggle, losses, and victory.

The story began decades ago, but in a way, it's a saga that's just getting started. As, indeed, are we....

THOSE GUYS HAVE ALL THE FUN

1

Blood: 1978–1979

"A fanatic is one who can't change his mind and won't change the subject."
— *Winston Churchill*

It all started with a $9,000 investment, the purchase of a "transponder" by a father and son who had never seen one, and the suicide of a famous playboy.

BILL RASMUSSEN, *Chairman:*

I was fired as the communications manager for the Hartford Whalers in 1978, and then fired as executive director for Howe Enterprises. Gordie Howe was playing for the Whalers at the time, and the Enterprises job was just a way to do some things for Gordie and the boys. The way I was dismissed was intriguing. It was Memorial Day weekend, that Saturday morning, and I was getting ready to play golf. The phone rang and it was Colleen Howe, Gordie's wife. She said, "I don't have much time and I really wanted to see you because I didn't want to do it this way, but we're terminating you at Howe Enterprises. I have to catch a plane, so good-bye." It was a surefire way to ruin a good round of golf.

SCOTT RASMUSSEN, *Executive Vice President:*

My dad was in broadcasting my whole life. We have a close relationship, but it's complicated.

We would broadcast high school hockey games together, and when he was with the Whalers, I filled in with a pregame talk show a few times. I had taken a year off after high school, then went to college for two years and dropped out. I don't think my dad was surprised. School and I weren't the best of friends.

Then my father and I did a TV show on Channel 18 in Hartford—which was a religious station then—called *Sports Only,* which basically was *Sports-Center* in its earliest form. It was around that time that my dad and I started batting around ideas, but none of them were quite right.

Years before, in 1950, Bill Rasmussen had the opportunity to play in the Detroit Tigers Class D farm club; he would have grabbed at the chance, but like many others of that era, he felt he had to attend college—in his case, DePauw University—to hang on to a draft exemption that would keep him out of the Korean War. Sports remained his true love, however, and now, in 1978, with his forty-sixth birthday approaching, Rasmussen

*decided that the time had come to actually do what he
dreamed of doing.*

*While working for the Whalers, Rasmussen had met
an insurance man named Ed Eagan, who was working
at Aetna but really wanted to be in television. Eagan
had wanted to talk to Bill about the Hartford Whalers
being the centerpiece of a monthly cable show about
Connecticut sports.*

BILL RASMUSSEN:

I called Ed Eagan right after Colleen's call and told
him, "I don't think it's a very good idea to talk to me
about the Whalers since I'm not there anymore," but
he said, "Come on in, and we'll talk about something
else." We ended up thinking we should do what I was
going to do with the Whalers but do it independently.
As the conversation continued we thought, why not
do UConn basketball, and then we thought, if we can
do UConn, why not Wesleyan, why not Yale, why not
Fairfield, and Southern Connecticut? One thing led
to another. Ed even had the idea for the first two
shows: hot-air ballooning and a game from the Bristol
Red Sox. Ed said we would tape a show every month
with a sports topic of interest to Connecticut, and take
these big two-inch reels of tape in his car to cable systems. We could do shorter distances on bicycle.

*Rasmussen knew virtually nothing about the cable TV
business, but he wasn't alone: in 1978, there were just*

over 14 million homes receiving cable—less than 20 percent of all TV households. HBO had gone on the air in 1975 but offered limited programming and signed off at midnight. A year later, Ted Turner uplinked his then-piddling Atlanta UHF outlet to a satellite, thereby creating the country's first "SuperStation," but one that delivered more Braves games than original programming. The next year, televangelist Pat Robertson launched his 700 Club on satellite, and in 1978, despite the fact that HBO reached only 1.5 million homes, Viacom fired up its slow-blooming imitation, Showtime.

Regionally, cable was beginning to make some inroads. In Reading, Pennsylvania, a pioneering cable system acceded to demands from the local American Nazi Party to lease time on its public-access channel (regulations prohibited turning anybody down). On the other extreme, New York's Glenn O'Brien's TV Party provided a crazily kinetic TV home to punk rockers, subterranean semi-celebrities, and exploratory artists like Andy Warhol, Jean-Michael Basquiat, and David Byrne. Among the lyrics to the show's theme song: "We've got nothing better to do than watch TV and have a couple of brews…"

Beginning in the summer of 1978, Bill, his son Scott, Eagan, and Eagan's buddy Bob Beyus, who owned a video production company, sought the backing of cable operators and potential investors for a new sports channel. They had originally wanted to name it SPN, the

Sports Programming Network, but something called the Satellite Programming Network had already laid claim to those letters. Bill knew they'd have a tough time filling hours with only Connecticut sports and argued that they'd have to include some entertainment programming. Thus was it born: ESP, the Entertainment and Sports Programming Network.

On June 26, presentations began. ESP invited twelve representatives of Connecticut's cable operators to a rented conference room at United Cable in Plainville, Connecticut. Only five showed up, and those mostly out of deference to Bill Rasmussen's contacts in the industry rather than out of breathless anticipation of the new enterprise. Skeptically, they listened to far-fetched proposals about delivering Connecticut collegiate sporting events, amateur sports, the Whalers, and "entertainment" programming to cable operators via an interstate network. The reaction was a double shot of bad news: implausible, the cable crowd said, and too costly.

Undaunted that the presentation bombed, the quartet of entrepreneurs pushed ahead, holding a press conference days later to spread the word. Of the thirty-five reporters invited to attend the grand announcement of ESP, a mere four attended, and none of them were particularly impressed. Neither was Beyus, who had thought it complete folly to hold a press conference without any contracts, but was outvoted by his partners. Immediately following the press conference, he officially flew the

coop. Still undeterred, the Rasmussens and Eagan for-
mally incorporated ESP Network on July 14, 1978, for
a fee of $91.

BILL RASMUSSEN:

When Scott and I talked with Jim Dover over at United Cable, he told us about something new coming along called satellite communication and said it was going to be the wave of the future. A couple guys over at United helped us try to figure out what the satellites did, but nobody really had any idea. Then someone said that RCA was doing a lot of this stuff in Europe and we should talk to those guys. We called in the middle of the afternoon, and a young guy named Al Parinello answered the phone.

AL PARINELLO, *RCA Manager:*

In 1978, I was one of two people hired by RCA to penetrate the cable-television marketplace and basically convince new emerging networks that satellite distribution of their television product — as opposed to terrestrial distribution — was the wave of the future. RCA had launched a satellite called SATCOM 1, but no one understood that this thing was real, that it actually existed. Think about it: you couldn't see it, you couldn't touch it, and there was no way to demonstrate that it really was up there 22,300 miles above the equator. So it was a concept sale.

The first deal that I made was with a reverend who

called me and said he wanted to buy one or two hours of satellite time. I said, "Sure. Where is the uplink going to be?" He said, "We'll use your New Jersey uplinking facility," and I said, "Okay, great. Now, where do you want us to bring the signal down? We have facilities in Los Angeles, San Francisco, Miami, wherever." And he said, "What do you mean?" I said, "Well, where's it going, where do you want the signal to go?" He said, "I want it to go to God." I said, "What do you mean you want it to go to God?" He said, "This is a program that my parishioners and I have put together. It's our message to God, and we want to send it to him by satellite. It's just going out there; it's not coming back." So I said, "Okay." It was a $1,200 or $1,300 deal. That was the first order that was ever on RCA SATCOM for cable television usage.

BILL RASMUSSEN:

Al wanted to get together and asked us where we were located, but we didn't have offices. We asked Jim Dover at United Cable if we could rent the conference room there and he said, "Give me a $20 bill." So that was the rent, and Al came and showed us all these diagrams of satellites and how this happens, and how that happens.

AL PARINELLO:

We're talking pewter ashtrays, a big oak table, and china dishes that lunch was served on. Bill said, "This is our headquarters." Little did I know that he had rented this beautiful room.

My first question was "What kind of programming are we talking about?" And the answer was we're talking about regional sports programming—UConn sporting events, and so forth. I was confused. I'm like, "Bill, you need to understand that when you utilize satellite communications, your signal is going to go up to a geosynchronous satellite orbiting 24,300 miles above the equator. And because of that, anybody with an earth station anywhere can get your programming. So it seems to me that you shouldn't just be talking about Connecticut sports, why not think in terms of doing something a little bigger?"

That was the moment I saw Bill and Scott look at each other like I had just hit a nerve.

BILL RASMUSSEN:
Wow, what an eye-opener.

AL PARINELLO:
I can still remember the conversation. Bill said, "Let me get this straight. You mean to tell me, for no extra money—for no extra money!—we could take this signal and beam it anywhere in the country?" And I said, "That's right." And then he asked again, *"Anywhere in the country?"* And I said, "Anywhere." I remember we went back and forth like this a couple

times. Bill and Scott were looking at each other, and they might have been getting sexually excited, I'm not sure. But I can tell that they were very, very excited.

BILL RASMUSSEN:

Al had been talking about us buying a transponder on the satellite for nightly stuff on an hourly basis, but then he said the fateful words: "We used to have another one that was twenty-four hours a day, but no one bought it so we took it off the market." We all just looked at each other for a moment. So then I asked him what that would cost. He said, "$34,167 a month."

SCOTT RASMUSSEN:

I was only twenty-two at that point but I could figure out that $1,143 for twenty-four hours was a better deal than 1,250 bucks for five hours, so there was no question we should sign up for the full service. We were able to send a satellite signal around America for less money than it cost to send the same signal around Connecticut via landlines.

BILL RASMUSSEN:

Before Al got in his car, Scott said, "We should get three of those," and I said, "We don't have the money to buy even one." But we called Al the next day and said, "We'll take one." And Al says, "You'll take one what?" We said, "We'll take one of those twenty-four-hour ones that you've never sold before."

AL PARINELLO:

Bill's first goal was to convince me, as the representative of RCA, that I should go back to corporate and recommend this new venture as a viable candidate, and I was convinced. I was absolutely blown away by these two. They were good people. They were smart. They were savvy. And they listened intently. I went back to the home office and said, "I think we have good people here who we can trust. I can't vouch for where the money's coming from, but if we don't have a check by X date, we'll throw this deal away." It was that simple.

BILL RASMUSSEN:

What we didn't know was that there was going to be a column in the *Wall Street Journal* the day after Labor Day saying the wave of the future was satellites at RCA. They got a ton of applications after that, but we already had our transponder reserved.

SCOTT RASMUSSEN:

All of a sudden we had this distribution technology, but we had no idea about anything else.

BILL RASMUSSEN:

It was August 16, 1978. Scott and I were driving to the Jersey shore from Connecticut. We were on our way to see my daughter, who was working down there for the summer. It was her birthday; we couldn't miss it, we had to go. So we had a blue stick-shift Toyota, no air-conditioning. It was going to be a hot day, so we started driving early in the morning because we had to drive at least four hours. And as we approached Waterbury, just east of route 84, traffic just stopped. I bet I could place us within a hundred feet of it if we were driving right now. We were just sitting there in traffic and it was real hot. So we started doing a lot of brainstorming.

SCOTT RASMUSSEN:

Putting the two of us in a car was a sure recipe that all we were going to talk about was the business and what we were going to do with the transponder. We were having arguments, creative arguments, and they got pretty heated. At some point—we were on I-84 in Waterbury—I just got really fed up and turned to my father and said, "I don't care what you do with it, show football all weekend, see if I care." And for the first time all morning he didn't yell back at me. He said, "That's it! Not football, but sports!"

From that moment on for the rest of the day I was scribbling notes on a pad. We showed up at the Jersey shore but ignored my sister on her birthday. We were coming up with all kinds of ideas, estimating cable penetration, and trying to figure out how many people we would need. We talked about the cable subscribers and what kind of deal we could offer them. We talked about coming up with programming, and that we'd have one anchor sportscaster and then hire a bunch of other people for next to nothing. I probably filled every piece of paper on that pad. That night we couldn't even get to sleep.

BILL RASMUSSEN:

In one single day we decided that we would do sports twenty-four hours a day, have a half-hour sports show at 6:30 every night, which would be the sports center, that we would go out and hire sportscasters, and buy a fleet of trucks that would roam the nation covering sporting events.

SCOTT RASMUSSEN:

The next day we got in the car and talked all the way home. The plan was born, I won't say fully hatched, but the big parameters were already in place before we got back to Connecticut that night.

When we got in the house it was well after midnight and we couldn't think of anything more to talk about, so we decided to design a building, you know, what's our building going to be like? We took out a ruler that was marked off in eighth-of-an-inch increments and so we decided that one inch equals eight feet in our scale. I think the initial size was 96 by 64 and we made it two stories. We put in the executive-office corner, and we put in the studio. And we're rearranging and drawing and it's probably two in the morning and my dad just roars back and starts laughing. He says, "It's funny, we've got to have a tape room!" He took an eraser and erased the outside wall, made the building eight feet longer, and we had a tape room! What we sketched out that night *is* what was done. The executive offices, the control room, everything.

I can't fully describe the excitement of those two car rides. We were thinking we had the greatest idea in the history of the world and needed to guard it really carefully because people were going to want to steal it from us. It took us a little while to realize most people were going to laugh at us when they heard it, so eventually we got over that initial paranoia.

Then RCA called. They were concerned because they didn't have our financials on record to back up our order. I basically said, "You know I can't believe you're even asking this question. You haven't sent us an invoice. If you have concerns, send us an invoice and we'll pay it." Then they probably thought, "All right, well, it must be okay, and we'll send them an invoice." Fortunately they didn't send it for ninety days.

BILL RASMUSSEN:
At first, I was just using my own money—about $9,000 that I had put on a credit card, but that was no way to finance a business. So I went to my family

in Chicago—my sister, my brother [Don], my mother and father—and put together $30,000.

DON RASMUSSEN, *Regional Manager:*

I was a junior high school principal in 1978, and on December 14 my dad called and said, "Your brother Bill's here and he wants to come down and see you." I said, "Okay, have him come on down." When I got off the phone and told my wife, she said, "Bill wants money." Now, you have to understand that my wife and I had been married for twenty-two years and Bill had never been to our home. So this was really something.

There's a dynamic in our family that was either intentionally or unintentionally cultivated from the time we were kids—it impacts us to this day and had a big impact on the creation of ESPN. My brother Bill is five years older than I am. We had another brother who was less than a year older than me, who was killed as a naval navigator in a plane crash. And we have a sister who is three years younger than me. There was never any affection in the family at all. Now, as we grew up, Bill was the king of the roost, the child with talent and intelligence, and everybody else came in second. No matter what I did, it never measured up to Bill and all his successes.

Only twice in my life can I recall Bill challenging me. The first time was when I got out of the air force and he invited my wife and me to work at his factory during the summer. Somehow we got to digging deep holes in his basement because he was having problems with flooding. He started clowning around and said, "You're a big judo man in the air force, I want to see if you can throw me. Come on." I said, "Bill, you don't want to go there. I don't want to do that." He said, "Well, you're going to have to, because I'm going to come at you." And he did. So I took him down and broke three of his ribs, unintentionally. I wasn't trying to hurt him. After that, he never bothered me physically again.

The second time he challenged me resulted in a lawsuit over ESPN.

BILL RASMUSSEN:

When we were growing up, Don was always the third brother and it was tough for him. He was five years younger, so there's no way he could compete—but he wanted to. And more power to him. But we've always had a most distant relationship.

DON RASMUSSEN:

Now, during the time that he was at our house, Bill said, "The reason we've come to you is simply because we want the family involved." I didn't really know him all that well anymore, but my dad did and my sister did, and he told me, "Dad has committed to give us $10,000, Vivian, our sister, has given us $15,000, and we need another $10,000 from you to give us a little bit of a bridge until the big money starts rolling in. This way you'll be a part of it, and for your $10,000, you'll get 2 percent of the company."

I said, "Bill, I've got four kids I'm raising, I'm a junior high school principal, and I don't have $10,000 to just give you," and he said, "Well, can you get it before Monday?" And I said, "Yeah, I've got some friends I could probably talk to and they'd give me $10,000, but I'm not sure I want to do it." Then he went back to the big story about it being a family business and so forth, and I said, "Okay, I'll get you $10,000 by Monday." He said, "Okay, but we have to have it as soon as the bank opens on Monday."

I told him okay, but "if I get you some money, I want to join the company" and reminded him that I did have a background in play-by-play, radio, and I could learn other things. So he agreed that if I got the money, I could join the company. No specified duties were discussed, except he said, "You will never, ever be on television with us." I said, "Okay, that's no big deal." I just thought, well, he's the TV guy, and if that's the way he wants it to be, that's okay with me. I should have suspected some personality conflicts at that point, but I didn't.

So I talked to a friend who had a lot of money and he turned it down. Then I talked to the number two on my list and he said, "Sure I'll give you $10,000 and whatever comes out of it, half of it's yours and half of it's mine." He wrote me the checks and said he would cover them first thing Monday morning so I could wire them to Bill. And that's what I did.

BILL RASMUSSEN:

I jokingly say that ESPN was built on a dump, but that's what the Bristol redevelopment was, they took a dump, put fresh grass over it, and called it prime real estate. It was pure luck that we ended up on that spot. They couldn't give these parcels away, and we agreed to buy one right then. We started in Plainville. They could have had ESPN there. We had an address, 319 Fifth Avenue. But they had an ordinance against satellite dishes, and they successfully kept us out. I think things turned out okay for Bristol.

Since we had no knowledge of how satellites worked and what kinds of specifications we would need, we called Scientific Atlanta, the supplier of satellite installations, to see if we could put a signal up to a satellite from there. We had to be careful because there are certain angles that prevent the signals from getting through. They told us we could not have picked a better place. The signal is supposed to be ten and a quarter degrees above the earth to hit the satellite, and we were right there. If it had been another quarter degree off, we would have been out of luck. You know what we paid for that first piece of land, that acre plus? $18,000.

We still needed more money, and a friend I knew told me to call a guy named J. B. Doherty, who had

an investment firm named K. S. Sweet outside Philadelphia. He listened to my story and asked me if I
could come down to his office the next day to talk
with me some more.

J. B. DOHERTY, *Venture Capitalist:*

We took a security interest in the transponder
rights and were comfortable with the fact that if the
business was not going to get further financing, we
were going to get our money back by releasing the
transponder to someone else.

SCOTT RASMUSSEN:

My father and I were amazed when we got the
down payment from J. B. Doherty and K. S. Sweet
Associates. We thought he'd give us $35,000 so we
could pay a few other bills—but they gave us the
exact amount, $34,167.

*No matter. The transponder had been purchased, and it
was now the new network's most prized possession. Over
the coming years, it would become the Hope Diamond,
Holy Grail, and best asset for ESPN, the critical factor
in making so many of the possibilities the Rasmussens
discussed a reality.*

*Bill and Scott Rasmussen's decision to buy a tran-
sponder on RCA SATCOM 1 in 1978: Step Number
One in ESPN's rise to world dominance.*

J. B. DOHERTY:

Bill and Scott were floundering around trying to find a permanent financing source while we were funding the thing on an interim basis. We were looking for the big institutional investor and talked to various venture funds and insurance companies. We went to six or seven places but they all said no.

We were responsible for overseeing one of our insurance company's institutional-investor clients who had an investment in a hotel property in Hawaii, and Getty Oil was involved. Getty had a division that held all the non-oil parts of Getty, like hotels, nut groves, and other very strange things. It was run by a guy named Stuart Evey, and we took the idea to him.

Jean Paul Getty had five wives and five divorces, so his money suffered, but there always seemed to be "more where that came from"—meaning the ground. Oil made Getty a millionaire, starting in 1916, when a million bucks still meant something, and it made him a billionaire within a few decades, especially once his oil holdings were extended to encompass wells in Saudi Arabia.

Six sons were born to Getty over the course of his five marriages, but only one—the first—was named after Jean Paul's father, George. George Getty II was deeply troubled in the way rich men's sons are widely expected, and some perhaps doomed, to be.

On the evening of June 5, 1973, the son reached his breaking point. That night George had been especially upset and irritable, downing many a beer, two bottles of wine, some pills, and talking bitterly about the desirability of death. Eventually, he managed to get hold of a barbecue fork and poke an inch-deep gash in his gut. As blood spewed, George threatened to shoot everyone in sight, then locked himself in his bedroom. When none of the family could coax him to open the door, the family decided the only alternative was to summon George's executive assistant and family confidant, Stuart Evey, who rushed over in the middle of the night to take charge. The first thing Evey did was send two Bel Air security guards away; Evey was determined to keep this a private matter.

Cleaning up family messes and keeping them out of the papers was unofficially part of Evey's job. But this was personal, too, since George had, in fact, been Evey's mentor at Getty Oil.

STUART EVEY, *Vice President, Getty Oil:*
George Getty was not a big daily drinker. He was impulsive. Every once in a while, about every four months, he might go on a kick where he'd drink like a sieve, you know, ten, twelve beers at a time, but then he wouldn't have anything for six months or so. I was loyal to him, but I was also close to his wife, Jacqueline. She had a separate schedule, and we spent a lot of time together. I dated her for a while when George

was still alive. I was still married, but you know, kind of on the outside of it.

George and his wife had had an argument earlier and he'd taken a barbecue fork and punched his stomach. He tried to kill himself, I think to spare her, I know him that well. George's wife called me about midnight and said that George was not doing well and could I come over. So I went to the house and found out that he was in his bedroom and that he wouldn't open the door. I could hear snoring as loud as I've ever heard in my life. So I tried to be gentle, but then finally he just wouldn't come to the door so I called the doctor, our house doctor, if you will. He was a private practitioner but he was on our payroll and he had done a lot of stuff with George. He came to the house, we broke the door down, went in, and George was lying on the bed. He was in his boxer shorts only and there was blood, a wound in his stomach. But he was breathing and snoring loud so I said to the doctor, "What's wrong with him?" And he said, "It sounds like he's drunk." So I said, "God, I don't want this getting out."

Now in retrospect, we should've taken him across the street to UCLA, but I took the doctor's advice and we went to another hospital, which was farther away but more discreet. I was protecting the company and J. Paul from this potential scandal, you know? Again, protecting George, I registered him in the name of Glenn Davis, who at that time was a very

close friend of mine, a former Heisman Trophy winner from West Point. The whole night went on with
George in ICU, and then I went with him into his
hospital room, where I elected to sleep that night.
About three hours later, a herd of people came running in—apparently the monitors went haywire.
They rushed him out of there and within an hour
they pronounced him dead. Well, there I was with
nobody knowing, only me. So I tried to gather myself
up, then went into the office in the morning. I called
J. Paul Getty and told him George was in a coma,
that he hadn't died yet, but it didn't look like he was
going to recover in a reasonable fashion. I knew he
had died, but I didn't want to shock the old man first
off. Then a little later I called back and said, "Mr.
Getty, it's hard for me to call you like this, but I must
tell you that George has passed away." He didn't say
much, quite honestly.

Then J. Paul Getty called me back and asked,
"Who do you think should be temporary executive
vice president?" And I said, "You will recall, Mr.
Getty, that George had written you recently about
the company's management and he was very high on
the current vice president of finance, Sid Peterson."
And I said, "You know, if you'd like to follow George,
it seems to me that he would recommend Sid Peterson." He said, "Would you issue a statement to that
effect in the company?" So I gathered our top executives together and told them that George had passed

away and that Sid Peterson had been named to succeed George, not in an official capacity, because that
action would take the board of directors, but that Mr.
Getty—J. Paul—had recommended that Sid Peterson act in George's absence.

*The following fall, tragedy struck the Gettys again: J.
Paul's grandson was kidnapped by the Mafia in Italy.
When J. Paul announced he would pay "not one penny"
of ransom, the kidnappers chopped off the boy's ear and
sent it home. Eventually the rest of the boy followed—alive—and when it was time for the young
man to go to work, it was Evey who would get the call to
find him a suitable job within the company.*

*For favors rendered, for doing his duty well beyond
the call of it, Stuart Evey would be rewarded with what
could only be called a glamorous position at the firm,
vice president of non-oil operations, put in charge of
everything Getty was involved with other than oil.
While other Getty executives spent their time crunching
numbers or traipsing through dirt to see if wells were dry
duds or potential gushers, Stuart hung out at a luxury
resort in Mexico, at wineries, or wherever Getty had
investments.*

*As yet another desirable perk, Evey spent time with
athletes and movie stars in Hollywood, magnetically
attracted as they were to the Getty name and connection. This earned Evey envy, if not outright jealousy,
from those other executives. But they knew what Stuart*

knew—that his power came from on high. After all, he was the one who had told J. Paul who should be the president of the company.

GEORGE CONNER, *Finance Manager, Getty Oil:*

I was hired by Getty in Los Angeles to be the finance manager. We had responsibility for the J. Paul Getty castle in England, the Getty Museum, the automobile fleets in Los Angeles, pistachio groves in Bakersfield, and some vineyards for wineries. People knew Getty Oil had money, so they would bring a lot of crazy ideas to us hoping that Getty would say yes, we'll invest in it. We had just brought in Jack Nicklaus to look at installing a second eighteen-hole golf course at the Kona Surf hotel in Hawaii.

Stu Evey was not your typical conservative oil company executive. He was Hollywood. You'd be in his office and our senior secretary would come in and say, "Mr. Evey, Mr. Hope's on the phone." Stu would hit the speaker button so everyone could hear and it would be Bob Hope. He ran with that crowd.

STUART EVEY:

I was a big-time person down in Acapulco because I represented Getty. I'd come walking into the hotel after arriving and the band would switch to play my favorite song. The jet-set people always wanted to buy me drinks and stuff like that because they wanted to get close to the owner, you know. So I played that pretty good. I spent six years in and out of there, building the hotel and building the golf course, and I would make deals with foreign photographers who wanted to come and use our facilities for free. Well, they'd bring all of these gals, and I got brochures for our hotel free. The women part of it is kind of interesting. I mean, it's hard for me.

I had a trusting relationship with the family. I helped George with a lot of problems, even with his kids in their younger ages. And I kept it all quiet. He did some damage around the house with his first wife — he got upset with her during their turmoil, so I quietly had some doors put back on.

J. B. DOHERTY:

My take is Stu was sort of this jock sniffer or wannabe. This sports venture satisfied his ego to the point where I think he got himself one of those jackets like the on-air guys wore back in the early days. He was the kind of manager that could only survive in a fairly unprofessional corporate environment, and Getty Oil at that time was still run like a family business.

STUART EVEY:

J. B. asked me if I'd meet with this guy who had been everywhere trying to sell his idea, and would I have any interest at all in talking to him because they were no longer going to finance him. He had run completely out of money and struck out everywhere.

I told him I'd meet with him because I believed "you never know."

Bill came to my office very disgruntled because he knew, in his mind apparently, that there's no way an oil company would ever be interested in what he had in mind.

GEORGE CONNER:

In December of 1978, I was in my office in Los Angeles, and Stu calls me up to his office and says, "George, I have something I want you to look at." This was pretty early in the morning, maybe nine-ish. He said, "Bill Rasmussen just left my office" — of course I didn't know who Bill Rasmussen was at that time — and he said, "George, why don't you take a look at this business plan and I'll call you in the middle of the afternoon." It was maybe ten or fifteen pages in a clear plastic folder. I told Janet, my secretary, Stu must be pretty excited about this to want an answer so fast. Sure enough, at 11:30 he calls and says, "George, I'll meet you at the L.A. Club," which was a private club on top of our Getty Oil building at Wilshire and Western in Los Angeles. So we go up to the bar. He has a Scotch and water and I have a rum and Coke, and he said, "George, what do you think?" I said, "Stu, I think it looks pretty interesting. Let's look at it." He says okay. And about five minutes later, he said, "George, only one problem. Bill has to have a yes or no answer by December 31," which was three weeks away. And I said, "Stu, you know as well as I do that Getty can't say yes to a project of this magnitude in three weeks." He says, "Okay, just start on it." So I went back to my office and the only thing I worked on from that point until the end of December was the ESP Network project.

STUART EVEY:

I liked the prospect of it for about two weeks. Then I saw the stumbling blocks and recognized that we hadn't spent nearly enough time researching it. Most of my investigations about ESPN came from people that I knew. I was responsible for George Getty's thoroughbred business, breeding, and horse racing; in that capacity I got to know an awful lot of people, including the chairman, at that time, of Time-Life Books. I called him and he introduced me on the phone to the guy who was running HBO back then. I talked to him about what he thought of this idea we were considering, and he said, "There's no way anybody will ever watch sports twenty-four hours a day."

GEORGE CONNER:

The initial proposal from Bill was for $10 million, and what Bill wanted to do was build some studios in Bristol, Connecticut. I knew where Connecticut was; I didn't know where Bristol was. He wanted to build four state-of-the-art television production trucks with the most expensive equipment that there was to be built by Compact Video in Burbank; he wanted to hire some very expensive on-the-air talent; and he wanted to pay the NCAA, I don't remember the exact number, but something like $450,000 for the first contract to rebroadcast NCAA events and show them over and over and over.

I was trying to learn about transponders and Nielsen ratings and all that. I needed to get up to speed so I could properly evaluate it and make a recommendation for Getty to invest or not.

A friend introduced me to Tex Schramm, who was the general manager of the Dallas Cowboys at that time. I told him we were looking at doing a venture that would have sports on television twenty-four hours a day. His comment was "There's already an awful lot of sports on television."

BILL RASMUSSEN:

Getty had this thing where every investment has a best outcome, a probable outcome, or a worst outcome, and Stu would ask us to come out and present details about the cable industry and our business. I remember the topic of the day once was where will the cable industry be at the end of the 1980s, and how many subscribers would we have? There were 12.5 million cable homes in 1979, and we put together a presentation that said 30 million homes in ten years. Stu was really upset with us and told us that number was way too high and irresponsible. Turns out, at the end of the eighties there were 60 million homes.

We had somehow managed to pay ourselves $1,500 a month, but we were running out of money and we had to have an answer by the end of the year, which was twenty-two days away. I was worried because most companies can't make that kind of decision that fast.

GEORGE CONNER:

So the end of December comes—the 27th, 28th, or something. Stu called me in and asked, "George, what do you think?" I said, "Stu, if Bill has to have an answer today, we have to tell him no, but I kind of like the idea and I think you do, too. Why don't we fund payroll and some other expenses until we can finish looking at it." When we told our response to Bill, there was a long pause, but then he said that sounded pretty good. I mean, he had been turned down by seven other companies, he was up to his limit on every credit card he had, and the venture capital fund in King of Prussia, Pennsylvania, had said they weren't going to put any more money in it. This was the best offer he had.

SCOTT RASMUSSEN:

Then we had the situation with the Bristol development commission. We had "bought" the land but hadn't paid for it. They told us, "If you don't have financials at our next meeting in February, we're going to give the land to somebody else." My dad was out West pleading with Stu to find a way that we could give hints to others that Getty was going to invest, but the word from Stu was absolutely not. They hadn't committed anything; they weren't going to let their name be associated with it. So my father called and said, "You're going to have to do what you can. Go to the meeting and buy us a month." I sat there, kind of depressed, trying to think what I was going to say that night. Then I watched as it began to snow. The storm became so bad, the meeting was canceled. By the next month Getty was in. Had it not snowed, I don't know what I would've said, or if we would have found a way to buy a month. We might have lost Bristol.

Eight thousand, seven hundred, and sixty hours to fill. To realize his dream of a 24/7 network, Bill Rasmussen would need a much better recipe than the motley stew he'd prepared to air so far: Australian rules football, slow-pitch softball, Irish bicycling, and, also from Ireland, Munster hurling—which has nothing to do with vomiting cheese or trying to heave Herman, Lily, or Grandpa across a barroom floor. (Hurling is an Irish variation on rugby, with the same shirts and slightly different rules. For many years it had failed to take America by storm.) Rasmussen knew there was no way he could afford TV rights to any big-ticket pro sports. But college sports? That might work, he reasoned, and with the right ones, maybe he could persuade Getty Oil to fork over more dough. In Connecticut, NCAA basketball was king, and Rasmussen believed that this game — fast-moving, flashy, energetic — had the potential to woo new viewers. And a juicy contract with the league could do more than spike viewership; it could be the major, critical coup to give ESP legitimacy and stature.

Rasmussen made a sales call on the National Collegiate Athletic Association headquarters in Shawnee Mission, Kansas. A presentation filled with enticing generalities had been hastily cobbled together and rushed to a printer; even Rasmussen was surprised at how well it turned out. Plans for the new twenty-four-hour sports network included a major role for the NCAA, league leaders were told. Rasmussen also argued that their annual basketball tournament was getting insufficient attention from the current rights holder, NBC, and that there was great untapped potential in the tourney's early rounds. Those games, he said, suffered from severe media malnourishment. By airing the beginning of the tournament, ESP, as it was still known, could attract more fans for the NCAA while at the same time, and not incidentally, enticing viewers to sample ESP's other offerings.

Fortunately, the name Getty carried clout, and it helped ESP get taken seriously by the NCAA, at the bargaining table and elsewhere. Rasmussen was, in fact, cleverly playing both sides against the middle: he convinced the NCAA of the network's importance by dropping the name Getty every chance he could, and he enticed Evey and the Getty hierarchy to be more generous to ESP every time by dangling the prestigious acronym NCAA in front of them.

BILL RASMUSSEN:

In our negotiations with the NCAA, we talked about doing all the championships. For example, CBS was contracted for college football and for a one-minute highlight of the lacrosse championship game to be shown on the *CBS Sports Spectacular,* which was their Sunday afternoon answer to ABC's *Wide World of Sports.* Our presentation proposed complete live coverage of not only the lacrosse Final Four, but also Soccer Final Four, Hockey Frozen Four, and the entire College World Series from Omaha. They actually gave us their logo to put on the side of our trucks for the first year on the road. That was a real coup because they guard that so jealously. We were talking about doing every game that the networks didn't do during the basketball tournament, which was, like, all of them, except they did weekend games and that was it. I remember Walter Byers said to me, "Do you mean if Weber State and Lamar Tech are playing, you're going to televise it?" "If they're in the tournament, yeah. Every game. We mean every game." You know, if you go back and look, who played in March of 1980, Weber State and Lamar Tech played. I don't know whether that was rigged or whether it was just the luck of the draw, but that's just such a coincidence. It's very difficult for me to believe that wasn't a test.

As talks continued, one thing became clear: if ESP was going to get NCAA basketball, it would have to show interest — sincere or not — in the NCAA's seventeen other sports as well. So the network pledged that "the entire spectrum of NCAA sports will be included in the ESP package," including hockey, soccer, lacrosse, and the collegiate baseball "world series" from Omaha. A deal was forged: "A two-year agreement for the exclusive national cablecasting of a series of NCAA championships, as well as college and conference regular-season events in 18 sports, has been reached by the National Collegiate Athletic Association and the Entertainment and Sports Programming Network, Inc., of Plainville, Connecticut. . . . With the exception of specific events and sports programming already committed to other networks, ESP's cable coverage will be designed to include each NCAA national championship in the Association's three divisions."

BILL RASMUSSEN:
Getty wanted to see the results of a meeting we had scheduled with the NCAA. Walter Byers himself had said let's talk, and I went back and forth to the

NCAA's headquarters in Kansas City a few times. Everything came together on Valentine's Day. I was in Kansas City and they were agreeing to put this contract together. I also got a call from George saying that Stu had decided to go ahead and wanted me to fly out to L.A. after my meeting. So on the 14th of February, 1979, both the NCAA and Getty verbally said yes.

The final, binding document was signed on March 14, 1979. ESP was still six months from going on the air, but what happened that March would turn out to be a rousing endorsement of ESP's strategy as well as a terrific bit of timing.

Rasmussen may have been bluffing about the latent potential he claimed to see in the tournament's early rounds, but he was seen as a Nostradamus of the NCAA almost immediately. The 1979 tournament turned out to be the most exciting ever held up to that time — and for years thereafter. The final game, on March 26 — two weeks after the NCAA and ESP signed their contract — kept 24.1 million viewers superglued to their couch cushions, enthralled not so much by the matchup of the teams as by their two electrifying star players: Indiana State's Larry Bird and Michigan State's Magic Johnson.

Future ESPNer Michael Wilbon wrote that the 1979 tournament "launched the popularity of college basketball and began the Golden Age of professional basket-

ball" as well. It's been said that the final game was the most-watched in basketball television history, and that it played a greater role in the start-up and eventual success of ESPN than any other sports event. Cable systems found themselves flooded with requests from fans demanding "that channel that has all the basketball."

STUART EVEY:

While it's true that before Getty was officially involved the NCAA indicated that they would look at Rasmussen's proposal, they didn't commit to it until I made a personal visit to the then-director, Walter Byers, evidencing our commitment to proceed. And let me tell you, that deal was probably one of the key reasons ESPN survived.

SCOTT RASMUSSEN:

A small part of Stu's money started coming in February of '79, but I consider a meeting with Getty that happened in May to be the most significant. They had given us $5 million to tide us over while they kept looking at things, and in May they had to make a go, no-go decision. They had my father and me come out to Getty in California, and we sat at this huge table at the Getty complex. It was kind of like a horseshoe, or a boomerang-shaped type of table. We were on the inside and there were a whole bunch of Getty folks on the other side and they were trying to be intimidating. They were very good at it.

Sid Peterson, the president, was there and so was Harold Berg, the chairman. There were legal counsels there too and, of course, Stu. I didn't understand the corporate politics that Stu was playing, but it was clear that he had gotten to the point where he had to sell it again for that go, no-go decision.

GEORGE CONNER:

I'd never come across anyone who was more of a master politician. If Stu decided he wanted to do something, he would line his ducks up with the board members behind the scenes before a board vote. He always knew what the outcome was going to be.

SCOTT RASMUSSEN:

Somebody asked a question about our revenue projection through 1988. I gave an answer that was terribly imprecise and totally worthless.

Sid Peterson basically took command of the meeting then and said, "Look, he doesn't know what the revenue is going to be in 1988 anymore than we do. We have a decision to make. If we believe in these underlying assumptions that people will watch a channel like this and that advertisers will support narrow casting and all the different assumptions that are built into it, this is going to be a big win for all of us. If it's not, it's going to be another dry hole. We make decisions like this in the oil industry every day. Let's decide." My father and I were then asked to leave and they had their discussion, and we were told after lunch that they voted to fund it.

It was in theory a commitment for $100 million, but the actual allocation was probably about $15 million. But more than the specifics, more than the numbers, Getty was embracing and committing that they were going to fund this and make it go.

Bill and Scott Rasmussen had been to more than half a dozen potential suitors before Evey, and all had said no. Chances are they wouldn't have found another investor, certainly not someone willing to risk millions. Whether it was Evey's love of sports and his love for star athletes; whether it was the idea of doing something in George Getty's name to make his mentor proud; or whether it was just egomania, it was Evey's Getty money that brought the Rasmussen dream to life.

Getty's investment of $15 million in May of 1979: Step Number Two in ESPN's rise to world dominance.

STUART EVEY:
I was laughed at in the company, in a kind of a kidding way. They even called it "Evey Sports Programming Network," not ESPN. My whole business reputation was put on the line. Nobody had any idea the risk I took. But I had done so many things from the hip that had turned out so successfully, from a golf course in Acapulco to giving a big investment to the government in Africa for a boondoggle which we

took a huge tax loss on, but more than made up for when we discovered oil in the North Sea.

There's absolutely no way Getty would have gone into ESPN without me. None. I was given that opportunity to take the risk for past performance perhaps, but also for personal relationships. I did this primarily because I thought George Getty would've liked it. I know that sounds ridiculous, but it's not. George Getty always wanted to get involved with a business that didn't have his father's name tacked to it, a successful business, and that motivated the hell out of me. He had died in '74, and this idea didn't come along until '78, but it was still almost like in his memory. If he didn't get to do it, maybe I could. I was surrounded by oilmen who were using money to drill oil wells; shit, I was using money to build a new TV network.

SCOTT RASMUSSEN:
There were times when I thought that one of the reasons we got approved is some of the people at Getty wanted Stu to fail. I think some people thought funding ESPN would be a way to take him down a peg or two when it went under.

BILL RASMUSSEN:
You really didn't want to negotiate with Stu. The whole time we were going to do this thing it was for an 80/20 split, and just as we're about to close the

deal, Stu said, "I've been thinking about this and I want 85 percent." He wasn't asking, he was telling. It wasn't like there was a rational reason for the change. But we couldn't say, "Forget it, we're going somewhere else," because there was nowhere else. We wouldn't have had anything.

J. B. DOHERTY:

Stu had the morals of a rattlesnake. There were all these signals about doing the deal without us and I had to remind them that we were prepared to sell the transponder rights to the highest bidder and that we weren't going to roll over. Stu and Getty were so busy taking steps to basically screw the minority shareholders that we actually put up a $50,000 retainer with Skadden, Arps just to send a signal to Getty that we weren't going to sit around passively and let him completely ignore our interests. Stu was a guy without a moral compass.

In May 1979, Anheuser-Busch signed the largest advertising contract in cable history with ESP for $1,380,000. Bill and Scott Rasmussen celebrated the contract by drinking a Budweiser; a few six-packs would have supplied their staff. Rasmussen knew the network needed more sponsors and recognition. Ever mulling, he came to the conclusion that a four-letter acronym would help distinguish ESP from the Big Three three-letter networks and give ESP more promotional potential. So on

July 13, 1979, he added the word "network" to the name and an "N" to the monogram, and the ESP Network became ESPN-TV. Rasmussen brought it to printer Guy Wilson, who dropped the "-TV," which sounded like a local station's call letters anyway, changed the logo's type font, and added an elliptical circle around the bold letters "ESPN."

Stuart Evey, meanwhile, was following his money. While Bill and Scott pushed forward to a planned September launch, Evey decided it was time to supplement the executive ranks. He called his pal Hollywood super-lawyer Ed Hookstratten, known ominously around town as "The Hook," and put him on the case. Evey informed Rasmussen too, and Good Ol' Chairman Bill set out in search of a president who would report to him, with Scott holding on to the title of executive vice president. Evey's plan, after all, sounded reasonable enough . . .

DICK EBERSOL, *Chairman, NBC Sports:*

I had been fired by NBC as head of comedy, variety, and specials in January of 1979. [Legendary programmer] Brandon Tartikoff said at the time, "Dick then backpacked in his Porsche." I can't remember whether Bill Rasmussen made the first phone call to me himself or whether there was an intermediary, but ultimately I was talking to him. Bill and I had at least two meetings, and he seemed very, very intrigued by the idea of me coming to ESPN. Bill told me that I would be hearing from a guy named Stu Evey; I didn't know who Stu Evey was at the time.

STUART EVEY:

Dick Ebersol was Bill Rasmussen's idea. He gave me his name as a possibility for president because of his *Wide World of Sports* experience under Roone Arledge. But I never spoke to Dick Ebersol personally.

DICK EBERSOL:

Stu invited me to a meeting in late June of 1979, and we met late in the afternoon. I was well-read enough as a kid to understand that these people were to the right of the Reichstag. This was no great middle-of-the-road American institution, this was Getty Oil! I found it so odd that they were really going to fund this wacky idea where you get a satellite and people everywhere could watch Connecticut sports. But you could see it was growing from that; I mean, they had already done this NCAA deal with Walter Byers, which I give Rasmussen a lot of credit for. That doesn't get remembered. Evey seemed almost overly large; he more than filled the room. He was very clear about letting me know it would be him and not Bill making the decision. He did say, "You're Bill's first choice for this role."

Anyway, Evey seemed intrigued by me but I didn't hear anything for four or five days, so I called him up late one afternoon and said we should have another conversation. We met at a restaurant on Ventura Boulevard in the Valley that was a favorite of his. Except for maybe some college escapade, there was more alcohol poured that night than any other night in my life. I'm not a drinker, but he just kept pouring and pouring. It's one of only two times in my life I went in the bathroom and put my fingers down my throat to throw up so I could go back and take more of this while this guy went on.

I was very much intrigued by the job.

STUART EVEY:

The major player who had the most to do with our broadcasting end of the business was Ed Hookstratten. Ed had a reputation of being the most powerful man, agent-wise, in broadcasting. He represented the major on-air personalities in the network business. Ed and I crossed paths at many social events. As executive assistant to George Getty, I traveled in a crowd like that, and Ed was a personal friend of mine. Getty hired him on a consulting basis for procuring our on-air talent and all of our other management talent.

ED HOOKSTRATTEN, *Attorney*:

I saw pictures of him with Arnold Palmer and Bob Hope, and at first I thought, how did this guy meet all these people? But Getty Oil was a big thing. And he was their outside man. We became good friends, but we didn't socialize together. I had a lot of respect for him and his business ability. He was taking on a lot of responsibility, throwing a lot of the company's dough at this thing.

DICK EBERSOL:

The guy Stu was talking to said I was absolutely wrong, too young, and too opinionated for the job. I put A and B together and figured out who was saying these things—Hookstratten—but I couldn't get him on the phone. He didn't know me. So I called Dick Martin from Rowan & Martin, who was a personal friend, and told him, "I think there's a great opportunity for me which would allow me to go home to Connecticut. Can you help me with Hookstratten?"

He called Hookstratten and said I love this kid, been around him for the last three or four years, he's terrific, blah, blah, blah. So I went and saw Hook, and he, of course, said, "No, I'm not saying anything about you at all." He wouldn't own up to it. A day or two passed and I called Bill Rasmussen and I said, "I just don't see how this can go anywhere, it's clear to me that Evey has bought whatever Hook has told him." So I'm exiting stage right from this whole thing. I'm going to guess this might have been the third or fourth week of June.

STUART EVEY:

At that time, Dick Ebersol and his wife—I forget what her name is, but she was an actress—had recently been married on the beach in bare feet and swimming trunks and they were part of the wild culture at that time. I don't know quite how to explain it, but I could not see him with that kind of publicity working with and for Getty Oil Company.

DICK EBERSOL:
Then Don Ohlmeyer, who has been my lifelong friend, told me he wasn't getting along with Chet Simmons and that Simmons was talking with Evey's friend Hookstratten.

As the 1970s ended, NBC Sports looked like a successful and prestigious operation to those on the outside. Inside the glass house, though, things were not going smoothly, much to the consternation of the division's senior executive and sports-TV veteran Chet Simmons. His nemesis, NBC chairman Jane Cahill Pfeiffer, wanted to impose her own "new ways of doing things" even though she had little knowledge about the old ways and what made them work.

Chester "Chet" Simmons was one of a handful of pioneers who could claim credit for inventing sports television in the United States. He graduated from the University of Alabama in 1950 and earned a master's in communications from Boston University a few years later. In 1957, Simmons joined an outfit called Sports Programs Inc., which would become the standard setter for sports coverage on TV and eventually evolve into

ABC Sports. Simmons was instrumental in developing Wide World of Sports, ABC Sports' flagship broadcast, and he also helped make ABC's coverage of the Olympic Games a big-time national event. Simmons had been lured to NBC in 1964 and began shooting up its corporate ladder, but now, in 1979, he knew his days at NBC were numbered.

STUART EVEY:

Ed knew very well which people were reaching the end of their careers at the networks or were soon to be let go. That's how Chet Simmons came to light. Chet at that time was running NBC Sports, and Ed seemed to be aware that there were going to be major changes and that Simmons may be interested. Now he'd been a long time at NBC Sports, with a good reputation.

CHET SIMMONS, *President*:

I got a call from this big-time guy in California, Ed Hookstratten. We chatted a little bit and he asked, "How would you like to meet with Rasmussen?" I said, "I'll meet with anybody, I enjoy talking with people who have ideas." We had a meeting in New York, then Bill asked if I wanted to see the place. I lived in southern Connecticut, and so one Saturday my wife and I took a ride to Bristol. As we drove into the town, she turned to me and said, "Not on your life. Not on your life."

It was almost like a bombed-out shelter. All the

buildings were desolated, the windows were broken. Then all of a sudden in drives a white four-door Cadillac with the initials ESPN1, and out of the car bounces Bill Rasmussen. He is the hardiest soul you've ever met. He has got a smile on his face all the time he's hustling.

We made a date to go to California and meet with Stuart Evey. He was the bagman for the oilman's son and dealt with his suicide. Stu had a lot of ghosts in his closet; to get rid of all of them would be impossible.

I don't think NBC knew about any of these meetings, but I don't think NBC was happy to have old Chester at the network either. I think they figured I'd been around the world a little bit, knew what was going on in the business, wasn't the most dynamic creative guy to walk on the sands of NBC, but a very dedicated employee. I think honestly if I looked into their heart, if they had one, I'd see that they'd wanted to get rid of me. If I went out on my own, that would have been fine, and if I stayed, they would just work around me.

They had already started ESPN — there were some things and people in place. I thought that would make it more difficult. But when Stu called and made me an offer to run the company, I said, "Okay, I think it's a pretty fair opportunity." We talked some dough and I got a lawyer because I wanted to get covered six ways from the moon. The only thing Stu didn't give me was the one thing I really wanted: one or two points in ESPN that I would sock away and keep.

STUART EVEY:

I went through a series of long negotiations with Chet. He's kind of a personable fellow, yet he was almost afraid, if you will, to see the future of ESPN. I convinced him nevertheless.

What mattered most to Simmons at this point in his career was the opportunity not merely to be present at the creation of something new but to be completely in charge of it. Evey assured him that Rasmussen wouldn't stand in Simmons's way, which made the position even more attractive. Of course, that promise wasn't shared with Rasmussen.

Simmons was announced as president of ESPN on July 18, 1979, immediately enhancing the network's reputation.

Very quickly, Simmons brought a trusted friend and colleague with him from NBC: Allan B. "Scotty" Connal, who'd gotten his start where future NBC chairman Grant Tinker got his—in the legendary NBC mail room. Connal was a TV legend himself: in 1968, his pleas not to cut off the final moments of a big Jets–Raiders game (running a few minutes past its allotted air time) went unheeded by engineers who insisted that a scheduled network kiddie flick begin precisely at 7:00 p.m. Eastern.

The long-notorious "Heidi" incident represented an argument that Connal lost at the time but which history would soon declare him indisputably the winner of. Nobody ever pulled a "Heidi" again, Connal having struck a blow on behalf of the importance of sports (and especially football) to network television and to the American ethos.

Together, Simmons and Connal prepared to lay the groundwork for ESPN to get on the air, get taken seriously, and, most important, to survive.

CHET SIMMONS:

They could have hired a lot of people, but they needed to hire me because of both my management and production background. My first desk was in a small room with two other desks. I didn't even have an assistant. I was back-to-back with Rasmussen so our chairs hit each other—and his son was at the third one against the wall. You could hear every word everybody was saying. I could've left at that moment. I could've just said, "Stu, it's not what you told me, I'm getting out of here." But I didn't.

SCOTT RASMUSSEN:

When Chet came on, he didn't want to speak to me very much, so I didn't have a lot of direct conversations with him. He dealt with my father mostly, even though I was the executive vice president.

CHET SIMMONS:

I walked into the back of this building my first day and there was a whole bunch of people sitting at desks doing what is called ESPN, but nobody knew what the hell that meant. Now I could have roared, "Who are all these people?! Where did they come from? What do they do?" But what I did was, I walked in, said a little hello, walked around and shook everybody's hand, and asked them: "What do you do, young man, what do you do, young lady?" And while I'm doing all this, mentally I'm deciding whether to keep them, let them go, or put them somewhere else.

The big question was, would my personality be able to deal with Evey? I handled Stu as good as I could. I dealt with him the way I did because it was to the advantage of the company—my arm around him as we walked through the streets of New York or sitting at a bar: "You want to talk about ladies?" "Yeah, I'll talk about ladies." "You want another drink?" "Sure, I'll sit here and have another drink with you." I was doing that just to get the guy to understand what I wanted to do.

Am I a whore? Sure, I'm a whore. Evey had the money and we needed more of it. His number one thing was to deal with members of the board. God knows what he had on them.

CHUCK PAGANO, *Executive Vice President of Technology:*

Evey reminded me of Ted Knight in *Caddyshack,* with the freaking plaid sport coat, the ascot, and the hair slicked down.

ANDY BRILLIANT, *General Counsel:*

Stu had this place out near Palm Desert or Palm Springs, and we used to go out there for meetings a couple of times a year. There was a lot of drinking that went on there, a ton of drinking.

STUART EVEY:

I don't have any excuses, but circumstances at Getty Oil Company were such that drinking was part of our work. We would meet for lunch upstairs in the private club, and we'd have a couple martinis. And when we'd have our budget meetings, we'd set up a hospitality room with all the booze and everything else. So it was a natural thing to be exposed to. When I was with ESPN, I went to all kinds of those things. Drinking was part of the deal there too.

CHET SIMMONS:

One of the things that really turned my stomach to bile was when we got over to the business side and I sit down with Rasmussen and their sales manager and they started to talk about how many homes are we selling? And one of them said, "Well, you know, we've given a guarantee of one million homes," and I turned to that guy and I said, "Where?" And he couldn't show me. I knew that they were lying. Then I'm sitting there with Anheuser-Busch ready to make this big buy, and I have to tell them that we ain't got a million homes; maybe we can get five hundred thousand, maybe.

STUART EVEY:

Rasmussen trod on waters that were not acceptable, not only to me and my company, but to Chet Simmons. There was nothing operating-wise that he was needed for, and he tended to hype up "our huge bankroll" everywhere he went. My lawyers were very upset about that, and Chet Simmons was very upset that Rasmussen was getting all the publicity but not doing any work.

CHET SIMMONS:

There were a number of things that Rasmussen had already done, before me, that were really awful, including his plans for the actual launch of the network. He had begun planning a huge extravaganza, going so far as to hire Marty Pasetta to produce it. I mean, Marty did the Oscars and a bunch of really famous and costly openings, and here we were not able to identify any cable customers. I had to go talk to Pasetta and tell him there was no way that was going to happen.

ED HOOKSTRATTEN:

Stu was asking me, "What do you think of this, what do you think of that?" I said, "Let's grab somebody good to lead our sports coverage." I thought, we got Chet, a real sports guy running the place, now we need a real broadcaster.

JIM SIMPSON, *Announcer:*

I was with NBC, doing sports. My wife and I came home from being out somewhere about eleven o'clock at night, and one of my daughters said, "Mr. Hookstratten called and he wants to talk to you. You can call him back anytime because there's a three-hour difference between the East Coast and the West Coast." And I called Ed back and he told me about being on a plane going somewhere into California with the people from the Getty Oil Company. They were going to start a twenty-four-hour cable sports network, and was I interested?

And I said yes, but I was really not paying too much attention to him. When he hung up, I told my wife what it was, and she said, "What do you think?" I said, "If ever cable makes something, I'll consider it, but hell, I'm working for NBC."

Evey then began a campaign. When I was home,

not on the road, every night the phone would ring at 5:30 and the kids would yell, "It's the Getty man!" He talked to me every night for about three months, I'm not kidding, and sent me all kinds of things from *Broadcast Magazine* and other magazines about cable, about the possibility of ESPN.

So finally, to be quite frank, all of our kids, we had five, were going to be gone, the last was going off to college. I said to my wife, "We can be like older people and wait for our kids to come home and see us sometime. Or we can do something different." So I said to Hookstratten, "Let's look into this."

I was picked up in Hartford by Bill Rasmussen and driven down to Bristol. When you've been at NBC Rockefeller Plaza and you go up to Bristol and see this building still under construction with a parking lot of mud, well, you don't know what to think. It was not very impressive.

DICK EBERSOL:

ESPN needed an A-level announcer, and Hook got Simpson a three-year, $1 million deal. Can you imagine, a three-year, $1 million deal in 1979 for cable? I don't think anybody had come close to making that kind of money.

CHET SIMMONS:

Evey had no idea what compensation was like in the television industry.

STUART EVEY:

Jim's a great guy. He and I worked fairly close. I gave him a lifetime contract. He tell you that? I think it eventually got taken away from him—I don't know how.

CHET SIMMONS:

It was becoming clearer and clearer to me that I needed help. Scotty Connal had a pretty good-size family that he had to support. He wanted to know if I could get the kind of deal for him that he would need, but also if the challenge would be enough. He had been at NBC forever. What would be the impetus for him to leave? Well, for one, there was the fact that [Don] Ohlmeyer came and got an NBC job title that Scotty very much wanted. The people at NBC were in awe of Ohlmeyer because of his Olympic background. So I felt it was the right time to pounce on Scotty and I did. A lot of hiring Scotty was due to his wife. She had an awful lot to say in the construction of their family, and I finally worked the two of them to the point where this became a very, very appealing job for him. I knew once I got Scotty, I would get a couple of very, very good people to come along with him. And we did. I can't tell you what I would have done if he hadn't come.

BRUCE CONNAL, *Producer:*

My dad started as a page at NBC and was there for thirty-two years. He had done everything there, but the face of NBC Sports was changing. They had brought in a whole new regime for the Olympics under Don Ohlmeyer and Geoff Mason. It was a pretty bold move to leave the stability of an NBC Sports and go with this upstart that nobody heard of, and when people did hear, they said, "It's impossible. It will never succeed."

STUART EVEY:

Scotty Connal had a great reputation but he was kind of getting over the hill, and he came on board and brought with him many NBC employees. Bristol, Connecticut, gained the reputation of being the NBC of the North.

CHET SIMMONS:

I remember my first visit to the board of directors at the Getty Oil Company. I was going to give my first financial report. Well, you know, you gulp a few times in this kind of a scene. So I get up and said, "This is what we're going to do," and I pass out some papers, "and this is what it's going to cost," and it was $12 or $15 million a year. They sat in silence until one of the guys started to chuckle. I said to myself, "Oh, shit, here we go."

And then one of the other guys chuckles too, and I said, "Excuse me, why are you laughing?" And they said, "What you have just asked for is the cost of one dry hole. Let's move on." So that went well, I got my money. But I'm sure it was a setup to some degree with Evey, because he was great at that.

BILL CREASY, *Vice President of Programming:*

Chet and I knew each other from the 1950s. He came to New York and went to work for a small company called Sports Programs, Inc., on 42nd Street. I came to New York at the same time and ended up working at a company called Sports Network, a production-oriented outfit. We did a lot of stuff together—Big 10 basketball, Southwest Conference, Atlantic Coast Conference. Chet and I liked and respected each other.

His path took him to ABC and then on to NBC, where he had a top job. My path took me to CBS, where I produced Super Bowls I and II. Super Bowl I came at a time when there was a lot of competitiveness between NBC and CBS—NBC doing the AFL, CBS doing the NFL. Pete Rozelle made a deal that Super Bowl I would be produced by CBS Sports people, and NBC would take the feed and have its own booth with its own people. Each network would have its own pregame show, and we would share the feed out of the winners' and losers' locker room.

As the producer of the show, I ran the first production meeting we had in Los Angeles, but there was a lot of tension in the room. Nobody was really talking to each other. Finally, Chet spoke up. "I want everybody in the room to understand that Crease is the boss. What he says goes." That was a great thing for Chet to do. We then proceeded to make chicken salad out of chicken shit.

Chet and I stayed in touch over the years. I left CBS to become president of a hockey team in California. The owners of that went bust. Then I came back, formed a little company of my own, did some shows for Time-Life films, did a show with Dick Monroe, who was then publisher of *Sports Illustrated*—we put it on CBS. Chet was at NBC and offered me a job to take over weekend sports, and a show that was quite successful in England called *Grandstand* where you go off to different sports events. At that time, I was, and continue to be, a serious horse race fan, and I had produced half a dozen Derbys and Preaknesses and Belmonts and did all kinds of stuff.

So I got home one day and on my phone is a message from Jack Dreyfus of the Dreyfus Fund, who was chairman of the New York Racing Association and who for me was a god of horse racing. He said, "Bill, do you think you would find a moment to come out to the racetrack and talk to me about something?" Yes, sir, I'm on my way. He offered me the job to be senior vice president of radio, television marketing, and advertising, reporting directly to the chairman. So I got Chet and his great NBC offer here, and I got Dreyfus with that offer there. My God, what am I going to do? Three days later, I decided to go to work at the racetrack. It was a once-in-a-lifetime offer to work for someone so incredible like Dreyfus in a sport that I just fucking love. It was hard when I said no to Chet, and he was unhappy for a couple years. Then Chet called and wondered if I would be interested in coming up to Connecticut and help him start this cable network, so I went up to Bristol. What a shit hole. I mean, what were they thinking? But I liked challenges, and this was certainly a challenge.

GEORGE GRANDE, *Anchor:*

I worked in New Haven doing radio and television, then got a job working for the local CBS affiliate WCBS in New York. During the week I ran the sports news feed that went out to all the affiliates every day at five o'clock, and I'd compile the sports news and then little by little I worked my way into doing pre- and postgame interviews with CBS Sports. During my travels, especially at Giants Stadium, I'd run into Scotty Connal from time to time, and I think Scotty saw the way I worked, the way I operated. One of my strengths has always been in situations that are free-flowing, ad-lib, seat-of-the-pants kind of situations, and I think he saw that. When he and Chet left NBC to go to ESPN, Scotty called to ask if I'd be interested in doing the opening weekend. They were worried they weren't going to be able to get Jim Simpson out of NBC in time. I went to my people at CBS and said, "Do you mind if I do this?"—because I had a contract with them—and they said, "Hell no, no problem." They had no idea what this thing was.

BOB LEY, *Anchor:*

I went to Seton Hall and was on WOR radio. Then TV3 started suburban cablevision over in East Orange, New Jersey, just a couple of miles from where I went to school, and they needed somebody to do high school sports. So I started doing per diem work there and eventually they took me on for a full year, and I was a sports director. This is a time when there was no local cable in North Jersey, no local programming, so we were giving them stuff they'd never had before. We were even giving them election returns. I was producing all that and anchoring a lot of games. After about three years of doing that, I got a tip about an article in April of '79, *Sports Illustrated,* about a network that was about to start. So I sent a tape up to Connecticut and got a letter back on this blue bizarre logo stationery—I must have one of the few copies that's still in existence of the old logo, the ESP Network. It was from Lou Palmer, an anchor, who was a fellow Seton Hall alum, writing back.

So I'm asleep in my apartment, it's a Monday

morning, probably had been out late the night before, and there's a phone call in the kitchen. Could you come up to Connecticut for an interview? I'm not thoroughly awake, but I say, "Yes, I'll be up there this Friday. I'm sorry, your name again?" And the guy says, "Scotty Connal." Well, my jaw dropped. I knew of Scotty. I said, "My God, you're a legend. I'll see you Friday."

A couple hours later the phone rings, and New Jersey Public Television wants me to come in for a job there. I interviewed with ESPN on Friday of that week, and Scotty basically offered me a job as he was walking me to the door. The next day, I had an interview with New York Public Television in Newark, and they offered me the job as their number two sports guy, where I would anchor on weekends out of New York and Philly, then report three days a week.

I was twenty-four. I had two job offers on consecutive days. And I had a day to make up my mind in eighteen hours. The fact that Scotty was there was a big deal for me. The biggest.

I went back a couple weeks later to find a place to live, and Scotty introduced me to Chet. Chet sat me down in the office, told me, "We're hiring you for what you know. We're hiring you for your opinions." I was sitting there thinking, "I'm talking to this guy who was the head of NBC Sports, who was the boss of Curt Gowdy. What the hell do I know? What opinions do I have that they care about?"

LEE LEONARD, *Anchor:*

Right before ESPN I was at NBC Sports for four years doing a show called *Grandstand* with Bryant Gumbel. It was a typical Sunday wraparound show between sporting events. Basically, during football season it was like the *NFL Today,* which I had done for a year at CBS, then I worked with Chet and Scotty at NBC. But I didn't give up NBC Sports, NBC Sports gave me up. One day there was this big guy roaming around our studio, and I said, "Throw this fucking guy out. He bothers me." His name was Don Ohlmeyer. He was my new boss. So when my agent said, "Do you want to go up and talk to these people?" I said, "Sure."

They hired a bunch of guys like Jim Simpson, a real professional play-by-play guy, and they had some young guys who wanted to do play-by-play, I guess, but nobody wanted to be in the studio. Chet said to me, "You know how to do a studio show. We want you to anchor our studio show." So I did.

There was no running water in the building, and you had to go out to a port-o-san in the parking lot. Technically they didn't really know what they were doing; they had rented a truck which acted as a control room, and there was no way they were ready to go on the air.

CHRIS BERMAN, *Anchor:*

John Wilkes Booth was born on my birthday and so were a couple of other assassins. I was bummed when I heard that. Willie Mays and Joe Namath were heroes, but so was Lincoln.

I knew what I wanted to do when I was fourteen. Although I played varsity basketball and varsity soccer, I didn't play football. Big boy but didn't play football. I was tall and skinny. Varsity bowling. I played some soccer, which was barbaric in the early seventies. Played basketball. We had a little radio station and I announced the football games to two hundred people on Friday afternoons. I was loud, probably too loud. We didn't really need a transmitter.

Then I went to Brown. I majored in history because I knew that's what I wanted to learn. That didn't change the fact that I knew what I wanted to do. I was the voice of the Bruins at Brown and am very proud of that.

Summer of my junior year, I somehow had an interview with NBC Sports number-two man Scotty Connal. Don't ask me how, but somebody knew somebody. Oh, my God, it was the most nerve-racking interview I ever did. He liked me, said, "We're starting this new job called *Grandstand* Coordinator," which was their traveling football show. Each of the cities they were going to go to needed a college kid, and "We got a kid for Buffalo seven games. You can be our Patriot-game guy. We'll pay you fifty bucks cash." I would have done it for nothing. At any rate, whenever NBC Sports came to New England, I was their runner.

Senior year, I sent out about fifty or sixty résumés. I had a few interviews, then got hired in Westerly, Rhode Island. It was a little radio station. I didn't do sports, did everything else. But in the summer of '79, I got a weekend sports job at the NBC affiliate, Channel 30, in Hartford. It was just on the side, like Saturday and Sunday nights. I got $23 a show. I was only there about a month and then I heard about this new thing going on. It wasn't on the air yet.

GEORGE CONNER:

From day one, Bill Rasmussen wanted to be on the air September 7, 1979, at exactly 7:00 p.m. So that's what we were working on, but probably a month or just three weeks before we were scheduled to go on the air, Stu calls me from L.A. and says he just got a call from Chet, who said, "There's no way you guys are going to get this thing on the air for September 7." I said, "Stu, Bill and I are very comfortable that we're going to go on the air when Bill projected. We'll make it." So I think Stu called Chet and told him it was a go and Chet wasn't too happy about it.

SCOTT RASMUSSEN:

I couldn't tell you how we came up with it other than in those days new television series debuted in the fall. It was a Friday night. It seemed like for a sports network, the weekend was a good time to start.

I think, to be honest, we just had to pick a date and get started.

MARC PAYTON, *Director:*

I actually started at ESPN two weeks before they signed on the air. As far as I know—I'm not positive about this, but I'm pretty sure the event I directed was the first event that ESPN ever taped. I taped the American Legion World Series in Greenville, Mississippi, in August of 1979, two weeks before they signed on the air.

So we taped it—we had a mobile unit rolling there. I think I had four cameras, only one of my four camera men had ever shot baseball before, the remote truck was an old converted school bus, and we rolled in there and no one's ever heard of ESPN because obviously we weren't on the air yet. And we recorded the event on two-inch tape, and then the tapes were shipped back to Bristol, and then after the network signed on the air two weeks later, it was among the first programming that they aired.

It was really primitive. In fact, our home-plate camera position—which you know from shooting baseball is usually up high at home there, usually behind home plate up in the press box—well, this field didn't really have a press-box position. The home-plate camera was shooting behind the screen at field level. That was our play-by-play camera—shooting through the screen.

BILL SHANAHAN, *Vice President of Program Management:*

At that time ESPN was based on the unfinished second floor of a local cable company's business office, which is where I went for my interview. It was just a madhouse over there, every day. Folding tables, folding chairs, unfinished floor, and unfinished ceiling—you could actually see the insulation between the rafters. I joined ESPN about a week before we went on the air. There were twelve of us who were hired to be part of *SportsCenter* and work for Chet and Scotty: six producer-directors, six associate producers, of which I was one.

One day over lunch, the question came up, have any of you seen the studio? No! Four days to air and we hadn't even seen the facility that we were going to be working in. So we drove over to Bristol, and it was a construction site in every sense of the word—guys in hard hats, plastic tarps hanging where there were supposed to be doors, mud parking lot, Porta-Potties, delivery trucks. It was busy as hell because they had to make a deadline too. We wandered around for a while and someone came up to us and asked, "What are you guys doing here?" We said, "We're supposed to be doing shows out of here in about four days; we thought it might be nice to take a look at the facility." It didn't matter to them. They told us, "You really shouldn't be here," so we didn't get back in there until launch day.

CHUCK PAGANO:

I still have the footprint of my father kicking me in the ass when I told him I was leaving a Tiffany network affiliate to come to Bristol. "You want to go where? Are you out of your fucking mind?" But I liked the idea of uncharted waters.

We had September 7 on our dashboard as the launch date, so we didn't have time to smooth out any wrinkles. We were working eighteen-hour days, usually seven days a week. Conditions were rough. One day, Fred Muzzy and Ralph Eno, a guy who had joined us from Channel 3, had come back from a late lunch. I remember Muzzy had this brown Mustang that they pulled into the lot, but when they did, the ground underneath became weak because it had rained so much. So Muzzy's parking where he thought he had left his car before, but as soon as Ralph stepped out of the car, all of a sudden the damn sinkhole in front of the car erupted and the freaking Mustang went into the mud pit. Ralph went into the sinkhole trying to get Fred out, which they did eventually. It was comical as hell. Fred had mud up to his chest. It looked like he was wearing brown fishing bootleggers.

BILL LAMB, *Vice President of Engineering:*

I got a call on Friday the 7th, which was the first day that ESPN was on the air, asking me, "Do you know anything about production switchers?" I said, "Yeah, I spent the last ten years behind production switchers." He said, "You're kidding me. I need you to come up tomorrow morning as soon as you can get here and relieve a guy named Chuck Pagano, who'll be switching all night long since about six o'clock." I said, "What time do I need to be there?" He said, "Well, how about 6:00 a.m.?"

CHET SIMMONS:

Scotty was a somewhat emotional guy; we were very close, but we fought like God-knows-what over the simple fact of who should announce what the first night. We came to an agreement, because we always came to an agreement. It was sheer bloody exhaustion.

SCOTT RASMUSSEN:

That twelve-and-a-half-month experience of going from the idea on August 16 to on air September 7 was incredible. There were days, lots of 'em, when my father was convinced it was going to die. There were days when I believed it was going to die. But there was never a single day when we both believed it at the same time.

BILL RASMUSSEN:

Right before the first show, Scott and I went out for a walk. Of course, there was no grass, it was just a construction site. I'm guessing it was after six o'clock, within an hour of going on the air, and it came to a point where we stopped and said to each other, "Can you believe what we've done and what's going to happen here in the next hour?" This was going to go all over the United States. It was just an amazing feeling. We stood there for a few minutes and hugged each other.

SCOTT RASMUSSEN:

As we got closer to air, Stu wanted to get a picture of everybody and got my father and Chet and looked over and called for Scotty to get in the picture. I knew he meant Scotty Connal, who was right behind me, but I jumped in anyhow. I don't think he liked that, but we got a nice picture out of it.

GEORGE CONNER:

The night we went on the air, they were running the last cable from the control room down a hallway to the studio where we were going to do our first *SportsCenter* show. That was our connection up to SATCOM 1, and I plugged it in I think maybe five minutes before airtime. We cut it pretty close.

GEORGE GRANDE:

Just before we went on the air, we didn't have any of the live shots available at that point, and I asked the Creaser how we were doing. He says, "Well, strap yourself in! Get ready. We're gonna rock-and-roll!" I looked at him and he looked at me, and his eyes kind of rolled; he knew what we were in for. But as long as I live, I will never forget the sight of sitting on that set and looking into the control room where Chet and Scotty were, and it was like being in a maternity ward watching the parents watching the birth of a baby.

In 1979, television was still living through the "three-network era," with ABC comedies Laverne & Shirley *and* Mork & Mindy *topping the ratings. When ESPN officially went on the air on September 7, ABC was airing* Fantasy Island; *NBC had* Diff'rent Strokes *followed by* The Facts of Life; *and the CBS prime-time lineup consisted of* The Incredible Hulk, The Dukes of Hazzard, *and* Dallas.

At 7:00 p.m., a small band of bickering pioneers, along with a determined supporting cast, managed to beam a signal from its ten-meter earth station in Bristol up to RCA's SATCOM 1. There were 1.4 million homes available to witness the first image of the evening: a barren set and the face of Lee Leonard, who welcomed viewers to the new network by promising, "If you love sports . . . if you REALLY love sports, you'll think you've died and gone to sports heaven." Of the opening night's offerings, only SportsCenter *was truly auspicious, and even it looked a little tacky at first blush. Leonard introduced it by promising to bring viewers "the pulse of sporting activity," whether through interviews, play-by-play, or commentary — or, when in doubt, highlights, highlights, and more highlights. Then he turned to an area only a few feet away in the makeshift studio — ESPN's one and only studio at the time — and handed the reins to SportsCenter's first anchor, George Grande.*

Grande, done up in a yellow jacket and yellow shirt (a style that did not catch on except among bees), peered through the glass separating the studio from the control room and saw Chet Simmons, Scotty Connal, Stuart Evey, and Bill Rasmussen peering right back. The first result he announced was Chris Evert's victory over Billie Jean King in that day's semifinals of U.S. Open action. The show lasted a half hour and consisted mainly of videotaped highlights culled from the established broadcast networks.

Also joining the ESPN lineup that night were wrestling, college soccer, and a World Series game; no, not that World Series, but a critical matchup being played to determine — hang on to your hats now — the slow-pitch softball championship of the world. Lee Leonard refreshed the audience's memory about softball: "We all play it on Sunday when we drink a little beer." Speaking of which: the two teams competing were the Kentucky Bourbons and the Milwaukee Schlitz. Unfortunately, it wasn't Schlitz but Budweiser with whom ESPN had signed its first monster sponsorship deal.

On the very first night of programming, ESPN had managed to tick off their only sponsor.

In addition to the softball game, viewers saw an interview, live from Denver, *with University of Colorado football coach Chuck Fairbanks. There was one little glitch: no audio from* Denver. *The whole interview aired in silence.*

An estimated 30,000 viewers saw that first night of programming. Not coincidentally, perhaps, one of the year's big disco hits was Gloria Gaynor's anthem of assertiveness, "I Will Survive."

BILL CREASY:

I produced the first show and it was a technical nightmare. Everything was fucked up. It was dark in the truck and you couldn't see what you were doing. We carried a god-awful night game of slow-pitch softball from Milwaukee, at eight o'clock which was then seven o'clock out there. The lighting was just abysmal. You could hardly see the goddamn game. Then we went to interview Fairbanks, who was then the football coach at the University of Colorado.

CHET SIMMONS:

"Now we take you live to Colorado," and all I could see to my everlasting disgust was Simpson's mouth going and nothing coming out of it. I turned to the guys in the control room and said, "What have we got?" And they said, "We got nothing." I said, "Good, let him stand there. Maybe some people who can read lips will have a good time with this sucker."

And we sat there for whatever the interview was, eight minutes, seven minutes.

GEORGE CONNER:
My heart sank.

GEORGE GRANDE:
We had trouble getting feeds in, and we were supposed to have three live shots but didn't end up with any of them.

BILL SHANAHAN:
I ended up being a floor manager with my headset, and all you heard were these people screaming at each other, swearing at each other, and it went on and on. So Lee Leonard is sitting there patiently waiting and says, "May I ask what the delay is?" So all I had to do was lift up one of the headphones from my headset and he could hear this string of invectives come out. And he says, "Ah! I understand."

BOB PRONOVOST, *Director*:
I was walking down the hallway to go into the truck for *SportsCenter* and Creasy's coming down the same hallway on the other side. As he passes me, he goes, "Don't worry, young man. It can't be any worse than that. You got no place to go but up from there."
When we got on the air, there was even a bull-

dozer still going in the parking lot. People in back of me were saying, "Oh, he's getting awful close!" And I'm hearing this while we're on the air. The bulldozer was making so much noise that it became difficult for me to hear what George and Lee were saying, and I needed to hear them to change the graphics. It got to the point where I couldn't hear anything, so I had to guess what they were saying by reading their lips.

Then the bulldozer actually tapped the remote truck and shifted it a bit on its side. It knocked some of those phones off, which created a little more anxiety, because when you knock them off that means you're calling someone and that means somebody's calling you back. So now the phones are ringing in addition to the bulldozer roaring. It was pretty wild.

Lee Leonard had an IFB which was loose, and it pulled out of his ear at the last second, but I figured I didn't have time to worry about any of those types of things. When I walked out into the hallway, Scotty was there and I wanted some approval about all I had just done, and he looked at me and said, "If I ever see an IFB hanging out of a talent's ear again, that's the last day you'll ever work here." It kind of ruined the whole thing for me, but what I learned that day was that Scotty was right. He didn't want the audience seeing something sloppy, and all the audience ever sees is what they see on television. They don't care about our problems behind the scenes.

SCOTT RASMUSSEN:

We had the Milwaukee Schlitz playing in the very first event on with all the Anheuser-Busch people standing in the room, and we joked about that with them. We told them not to worry, nobody was watching anyhow.

BRUCE CONNAL:

My father called afterward and he said, "What have I done? What in the world am I doing here?" He was really questioning the move he made.

CHET SIMMONS:

When we were finished with the first night, which went from seven to midnight, everybody gave a big cheer, and there was some champagne. I rapped on a glass and got everybody's attention, and I said, "I just want to thank you for your efforts tonight; I know you're exhausted, and you've gone through the first night, but I want to tell you something: you've got to do this sucker every night, seven nights a week." And then Rasmussen makes the announcement— without checking with me—that we're going to go twenty-four hours a day within the next couple of weeks. I could have strangled him right there on the stage. That was the way he operated. It was still his business as far as he was concerned. We were as ready to go seven full days a week as I was ready to become the king of France.

BILL RASMUSSEN:

Two days after we went on the air, Stu told me point blank, "You don't have anything to do with ESPN, Chet's in charge, he reports to me, and stay out of the way." He wasn't firing me, he just told me to get out of the way. I had become a real burr under his saddle. The media kept calling me and not him. I was a little guy and this was a big idea. In one instance, one of the big magazines had called when Scott, Chet, and I were crammed into this tiny office and the secretary said there was a reporter on the line. Chet said, "I'll take the call," and the reporter said they wanted to talk to me instead. Well, that didn't go over very well with Chet. Another time, there was an article in *Sports Illustrated* and it didn't mention Stu's name, and he let me know he was really upset.

BOB PRONOVOST:

One of the first nights of *SportsCenter,* there was a car that hit a pole across the street right in front of the building. It knocked all the power out; we couldn't go on the air. A guy had actually died in the accident, and they left him in the car longer than they should've because he was right on the line between Bristol and Plainville. There was a jurisdictional thing between the police departments and it took much longer than it should've, so we stayed off the air for quite a bit of time.

BILL SHANAHAN:

Outside what was then the main entrance, there were construction trailers—the standard kind of blue metal mobile trailers that you see at construction sites—and ESPN was using two of them: one as our tape library (it had no shelves on it; you just put the tapes on the floor) and the other was the quote-unquote executive office. If you've been around those trailers, you know that you need to reach up and open the door and step up the high steps to get into the trailer. When they were paving the parking lot, the crew that was responsible for that came in and graded the whole area that was going to be paved, but left these two trailers up on this, like, four-foot dirt bluff, so the only way to get into the trailers afterward was to stand on a five-foot ladder.

The other trailer, the tape library, had no real archive system. We were just building it every night as we did events. We didn't do that much live because our contracts said so much of our programming came in on tape. Like all the NCAA football games couldn't air until after midnight on Saturday, and they'd be delivered via courier, big one-inch or two-inch tapes, and they'd be stored in this trailer up in the bluffs. When it rained the trailer was deemed unsafe, so we weren't allowed to go in and get the program reels. We would think, "Okay, what are we gonna do—the tape is in there and it needs to be on the air in a couple of hours."

But maybe best of all was the fact that we didn't have indoor plumbing for at least a month, so if you had to go, you had to go outside and find one of the construction company's porta-potties. Now, during the day that's one thing, but at night, when it's raining, and you're out in the mud with a flashlight, that's something else. The few women we had working there at the time really were like, "Oh my God!" I think Pagano will probably tell you that he and a few others found another suitable—hmmm—"outdoor site." Oh, man!

There weren't many doors, because things were still under construction. Flies would come in. It was awful. They were all over the place. I remember being in the newsroom one afternoon. It was noisy. In the hallway, we had these old wire machines—AP and UPI—and they're clacking away. There's no furniture outside of the folding tables, so the wire copy is piling up on the floor, and they're clacking away at these typewriters and finally Lee Leonard says, "Okay—listen up, everybody—fly break!" And everybody knew what it meant: you'd grab the nearest newspaper and roll it up like a bat and everybody would walk around—*bam, bam, bam, bam*—killing the flies on the wall. And then after a little bit, everybody would go back to work.

GEORGE GRANDE:

At the end of the first weekend Scotty said, "When are you going into work?" I said, "Tomorrow," and he said, "Can you come in and see me before that?" So I went in on Monday morning and he said, "Would you come and join us, be our senior announcer and put together an announcing crew?" I went home and talked to my wife, Joanne. I loved CBS, I loved the people I was working with, and I was right on the precipice of moving to a position where I would start to get some pretty good assignments. But this was something that, whether it lasted three months or three years, it was too good an opportunity to pass up—because of what it possibly could be, and because of Chet and Scotty, who were the best in the business. So after talking with Joanne, I agreed to do it.

When I went to cover the baseball postseason that year, I called for credentials, and Larry Shank said, "Sure, no problem, CBS, right?" And I said, "No, no, I left CBS. I'm at ESPN now," and he said, "What's that?" I said, "It's a cable operation, we're just starting up and we're going to be covering all sports." He said, "Look, I'll give you credentials this time, but you've got to come up with something more definitive next time."

BOB LEY:

I watched the first show on a black and white TV the size of a tape recorder. If you've ever seen a tape or disk of it, think of a toilet in a Holiday Inn that's been sanitized for your protection, because all of the gaffes and all of the inevitable technical challenges have been edited out. I was sitting there and watching this thing and thinking, "Oh, my gosh, I'm committed. I'm going up there." The next day, I went out to my car, which was packed full of all my crap that I wasn't shipping, and drove on up.

Once I was working up there, I found out they didn't have teleprompters, nobody had computers, and they only had old wire machines. I was soon wondering if I could get my old job back. I thought, "Holy crap, are all the days going to be like this?" I began to fall into this manic pattern of just trying to survive. And oh, by the way, we had no idea who, if anyone, was watching. But I was working probably 10:00 a.m. to 2:00 a.m., and they mandated that on every show, somebody had to be wearing a garish red sport coat because Getty wanted their color out there. And those things were made of pure polyester. Put them near a flame and you'd die.

CHRIS BERMAN:

In my interview with Scotty and Lou Palmer, I said, "Look, I'm just starting in TV, but this thing is just starting too. I'll tell you what, rather than me send you a little clip reel so you can see the best five minutes I ever did, why don't you turn on Saturday and Sunday night? You live here. Watch it for two weeks and see if you like it. If I fuck up, I fuck up. Just tell me what you think." And Scotty Connal called me about a week or two later, late September, and offered me a job.

STUART EVEY:

One thing you did get as a perk if you were a vice president of Getty, because they didn't have many, you did get a new Cadillac of choice or whatever for two years — every two years. Bill and Scott Rasmussen should not have gone out and gotten matching Cadillacs with the stupid license plates. They shouldn't have done it. They're in a start-up! And so here the chairman of the board of Getty had a worse car than the goddamn guy that didn't have any money that we bailed out, you know.

SCOTT RASMUSSEN:

You've got to remember we had the cars before we knew Getty, before we even met Stu. My dad and I each had white Cadillacs. We were promotion minded and that's why we had the license plates we had — my dad's was ESPN and mine was ESPN1. I've still got mine somewhere. Stu really was unhappy about that.

STUART EVEY:

Chet was doing anything he could to piss them off so maybe they'd run away. He had nothing to do with them. He didn't want them out in front taking credit for everything Chet was doing. I actually think this is beyond the personal, they were in the middle doing deals that were incredibly detrimental to the future of the company. Scott Rasmussen was his father's number one guy, I guess, but Scott at that time did not really have any experience with a network, if you will, or a business of that complexity. The only thing I know is that there was no place for him in the formation of our staff and management when we took over. Chet wanted nothing to do with them.

CHET SIMMONS:

All the Rasmussens I could lay my hands on, I fired. I made Stu a part of all that because these are the original guys that he had dealt with. Why take up space with somebody who was there just because they had been there at the beginning, and was the son of the founder? Why should he have the job when he was not really capable of doing it? I wanted experienced people in those roles. So I just brought my case to Evey and said, "Look, I'm going to do this thing and another." I felt that it was necessary for him to have a say in what I did with them. He never disagreed.

BILL RASMUSSEN:

They just wanted Scott out of there. Chet said to me one day, "If he was my kid, he wouldn't be driving a Cadillac, he'd be driving a Toyota stick shift." I wanted Scott around, but I couldn't do anything about that.

SCOTT RASMUSSEN:

As I think back, I have a different interpretation of Stu's role now than I did then. As I think back on the meeting I probably wasn't as jaded as I'd like to think. But Stu began the conversation by saying, you know, I can't think of what wording he used, but there were some problems between us and he wanted me to know that he always thought highly of me and really wanted me to be a part of the Getty family, and he spent a little bit of time talking about the enormous benefits that someone like me could have staying with Getty Oil forever.

I kind of knew what was coming. In fact, my father was mostly concerned that I not be too hotheaded, that I listen carefully to Stu, and not say anything I'd regret. He offered me the same amount of money to leave as I would get if I stayed, plus I got to keep the car. If I stayed, I gave up the car and got whatever that role was. After he went through and described it all, I played it back to him as best I could understand just to make sure I had understood what he said. Then, thinking about what my father warned me about, I calmly said, "I'll give you a call and let you know what I decide." I walked down the hall, went to George Conner's office, and called my father and said, "I'm out of here." My father was stunned because he said, "Stu just called and said you had a nice talk and he thought you were going to stay." I described what happened and that was a little strange, and so then we went back and had a lawyer write a letter to Stu saying neither option was acceptable and that they needed to negotiate something for me and a new contract for my father to stay.

Stu then called my father and said that he better disassociate himself from the lawyers and that I was already fired. Actually, he suspended me from pay while we worked things out, but I knew things were ending. I went from Stu's office to the beach in Ocean Grove, New Jersey, and hung out there while my lawyers argued with Stu over how much money I was going to get paid. I really enjoyed that stretch because I was suspended but with pay, so I just kept getting a paycheck every couple of weeks and stayed at the beach. It turned out to be a couple months.

I'm much more of a dreamer and an entrepreneur. I like to get it started and move on. The notion of staying with Getty or with ESPN for an entire career would have never in a million years entered my mind. Would there have been better ways to have made the transition or the exit? Probably.

I believe that I am the single biggest beneficiary of the ESPN experience of anybody out there, period. Not financially, but I was a twenty-two-year-old college dropout who learned a lot of hard lessons, who got to walk up to the treasurer of Getty Oil and say, "The Olympic Committee says we need three quarters of a million dollars in deposit if we're going to put in a bid," and he said, "Okay." That's an absurd experience to go through! So I don't look at it as a negative. My payout came in an entirely different manner.

BILL SHANAHAN:

Berman came in October and replaced a guy who was filling in temporarily. The 2:30 a.m. show was supposed to be a sports recap after the last event. We'd come on and it was just meant to be five or ten minutes wrapping up late scores. Well, as time went on and Chris began to realize something, I remember him asking me one night, "So, we don't really have to be off at any certain time?" And I said, "No, I don't think so." He says, "Oh, okay." So these short updates started getting longer and longer. He was solo, talking for twenty or thirty minutes straight, and he became very entertaining. It finally got to the point where the master control operator was saying, "Can you just pull a commercial break together for us?"

On another night, after the eleven o'clock crew went home, the only production people who were left were just Chris and me. I got a call from the master control operator who says, "Uhh, yeah, I don't know how to tell you this but — the [taped] football game?

We started with the second half." So I told Chris, "We gotta go down and just sit on the set, just quickly explain to the folks what happened, and we'll get them back to the first half of the game." So Chris comes out on the set, I go into the control room, and I yelled out at the engineers, "Okay, take us." We came up on Berman—and I still remember his line. He looks into the camera and says, "No, you didn't pull a Rip van Winkle; you didn't miss anything. It was our fault." Then he said we were going to go back to the first reel of the game.

CHUCK PAGANO:

At the end of the late *SportsCenter,* one of my responsibilities was to make sure I had an ice chest with beer in it. After the conclusion of the show, I'd open up the trunk of my car and we'd have beer and just look at the stars and bullshit. Well, one night we all had a little buzz, probably not quite a six-pack each, and I had to go somewhere to take a whiz and decided to go for a tree but I couldn't see my way back because it was freakin' foggy, and I couldn't find the path back. So I asked Chris to yell so I could figure out where everyone was, and Chris yells, "Chuckles, over here!" They called me Chuckles, it was like in *Animal House* when they gave those guys the freakin' names like Otter. So when I got back, I said to him, "Your voice is so freakin' boomy, your name from now on is Boomer."

LEE LEONARD:

Boomer was loud but he didn't know what the hell he was talking about at first. He was just a young kid in the candy store.

BOB LEY:

We had a lot of time to fill, and we were sometimes desperate. After we were on the air for maybe two months, Bobby Knight had a run-in with a Puerto Rican policeman at the Pan Am building, so that was a gift that kept on giving. We talked about that for hours.

OREL HERSHISER, *Baseball Broadcaster:*

I was in the minors when ESPN was born; that's when I came across it. I would come home from a game and couldn't gear down. It was unbelievable that there was sports on at two in the morning, so I'd get a pizza and watch bowling or billiards or any of the minor products they would just grab to fill time. It was awesome. I thought, this is the greatest thing ever.

GEORGE CONNER:

I knew with Getty money we could solve most problems, but one of my fears was the satellite, because we couldn't control that. We'd been on the air for maybe three weeks and I got a phone call. "We gotta take you off the bird" —which was the satellite. And I said what? The guy said, "We have attitudinal problems with F2, which is SATCOM 2, the military satellite, and it's unstable. You guys have a transponder and we're going to need it for military traffic during the daytime. You guys aren't on twenty-four hours a day, so it won't be a problem. We just hope we get it stabilized. I'll keep you informed." My heart almost stopped that night because my worry was the Russians might shoot the satellite down or it would just stop working. I didn't feel we could get in a vehicle in Bristol, Connecticut, and drive up 22,000 miles above the equator and take out tool kits to fix it. He called me a couple days later and said F2 was still unstable. I was really alarmed. But then he finally called the next day and said, "George, we have F2 stable. You guys are good to go."

CHUCK PAGANO:

We were working eighteen freaking hours a day and they were serving us this crap from a place called Dexter, which was right up the street. You can only eat so many grinders and soup after a while, so I think it was early December and we went to Kentucky Fried Chicken to get some freakin' chicken. Just as we sat down on our ass in the hallway, everything went to snow on the video. You couldn't see anything. Bill and I were sitting there eating our chicken and we both looked at each other and said, "Fuck it, we're gonna stay here 'cause we put enough time in here and all we want to do is enjoy one goddamn meal."

DICK VITALE, *Analyst:*

I got fired by the Detroit Pistons back in — actually, I remember the date: November 8, 1979, and I didn't know where I was going to go with my career. Then all of a sudden the phone rang about two weeks later, and a fella by the name of Scotty Connal said, "Hey, Dick. I was the producer of the last game you coached when you played number one in the country, Michigan, in a tough game in the Sweet Sixteen. I heard you speak to your team before the game at a practice and I wrote your name down. I wanted to get you involved in television if you were ever available. I just saw you were let go by the Pistons and I'm in charge of a new network and our very first national game is going to be DePaul and Wisconsin on national television, and I'd like you to do the game." I said to him, "I'm not interested. No desire. I know nothing about TV. I want to get back to coaching on the college level." But he called me again a week later and said, "Come on out and try it." My wife says, "Go do it." So I said to Scotty, "Well, who do you represent?" He says, "I'm with a new network called ESPN," and I swear I said something to the effect like, "That sounds like a disease. What is ESPN?" I'd never heard of it.

I actually did the very first game that was a

national-caliber basketball game, DePaul and Wisconsin, the first week of December of '79. I went into it with no idea of what I was getting into. I mean, I came out of a locker room, I knew nothing about television, and somebody just gave me a microphone.

Scotty told me after the first game, "Look Dick. You've got three things we can't teach: your enthusiasm, your knowledge, and you're not afraid to be candid. But you have no clue about the world of television, how to get in, how to get out, how to be concise." He said, "I'm going to assign you a giant, an absolute giant." I was a sports fanatic, so I obviously knew about Jim Simpson over the years, Orange Bowls and tennis and all that, so I was honored. Jim said, "You listen to me. I will try to help you because Scotty tells me you got great potential." In our first game together I was talking so much that he told the producer, "Cut his mic off. I've got to teach this guy a lesson."

LEE LEONARD:

It was shortly after the very first show and it was the first football game we were going to do. I think it was Oregon and Oregon State. I remember we had this beautiful picture and no sound, and they said to me, "Well, Lee, you have to do the play-by-play." And I said, "Well, who's wearing the black shirts and who's wearing the white shirts?" I had no idea which team was which. There was another time when they had no sound or picture and I was trying to explain why and I remembered this article I had read about satellite transmission, that it was really just a big mirror in the sky and you shot something up there at an angle and shoot it back and catch it. So I tried to explain to the audience how that worked. I don't know if anybody quite got it.

JIM SIMPSON:

One of the first games I did on ESPN was a Nebraska–Iowa football game, and Tom Osborne, the Nebraska coach, came to me and said, "When will this be on the air?"—because he knew it was taped. And I said, "Why do you want to know? Do you want to see your own team?" He said, "Hell, no, I want to tell all of our possible recruits to watch us play."

BILL SHANAHAN:

I think being in Bristol, Connecticut, was a blessing because we weren't in a major-media capital, we weren't surrounded by industry "wisdom"—"Oh, you have to do it this way" or "You can't do it that way." We were just a bunch of younger guys making it up as we went.

JIM SIMPSON:

Chet asked me to give kind of a motivational speech at the first Christmas party, in '79. At that time I think ESPN had maybe sixty employees and most of them—except for those putting tape on the air—gathered at the local Holiday Inn. My little speech was, "This is the beginning. You're in on the ground floor and those of you who stick it out are going to be glad you did." I believed it. I told them, "I know there's a lot of newspaper people, radio people, and media people who are saying this thing isn't going to work. They're wondering, "Who is going to watch sports twenty-four hours a day? Who is ever going to watch this thing?" I told them, "Nobody in their right mind. But if they want sports, they'll know where they can get it."

2

The Utility of Daring: 1980–1986

"If there is no wind, row."
— *Latin proverb*

SAL MARCHIANO, *Reporter:*

I did a lot of stuff with Muhammad Ali when I was at ABC. Cosell was his guy, obviously, but I still managed to do a bunch of interviews. The greatest assignment I ever had in my career was going to the Thrilla in Manila. Cosell wasn't enthusiastic about traveling internationally—he picked his spots, but he certainly wasn't going to go to a country that was under martial law. So I got the assignment and spent ten great days there.

Now we jump forward to when Ali fought Larry Holmes in Las Vegas in October of '80. I was there with ESPN. I was in the coffee shop and Angelo Dundee comes up to me and says, "I understand you videotaped Larry Holmes today at his workout over at Caesars Palace." I said, "Yeah." He said, "You know, maybe the champ would like to take a look at that tape." So I said, "Really?" He said, "Yeah." So I said, "Well, maybe I would like a one-on-one interview with the champ." He said, "Well, let me go ask him if he'll make a trade."

Dundee comes back down and says, "He'll make the trade. Can you come up this afternoon?" I said, "Yeah." So I go with Tom Reilly and Jeff Israel up to the suite and they tell us where to set up in the living room. While Riles and Jeff are setting up, I bring the tape into the champ's bedroom, where Ali is getting a massage on the trainer's table. We put the tape in the deck and he watches Larry's workout. The sparring is what he wanted to see; he was obviously looking at it for timing. So he watched the whole thing quietly and then he said, "Put it back at the beginning." We put it back at the beginning, where Larry is sparring. All of a sudden, Muhammad gets up— he's naked—and he starts to shadow box against the movements of Larry Holmes. His dick is flapping in the air and I can't believe that I'm seeing this. When he finished, he said, "I'll be out in a minute. I'm gonna take a shower." He came out and we started the interview.

In the middle of the interview we hear someone banging at the door, so we have to stop. In walks Bundini Brown, his so-called trainer, stinking drunk. He comes over and gives me an open-mouth kiss. Ali sees him do this, rips his microphone off, gets up, slaps Bundini in the face, drags him to the door, throws him in the hallway, and fires him. Then Muhammad comes back, puts on the microphone, and we start up again. But throughout the rest of the interview, in the background, we can hear Bundini whimpering in the hallway. Somehow, he wound up working the Holmes fight. As a matter of fact, Bundini was the only guy in Ali's corner who wanted the fight to continue. What did he care? He didn't have to take the beating.

ESPN didn't air the actual Ali vs. Holmes fight; Marchiano was there just doing reports for the network. Indeed, except for a few rowdy NHL games and nightly SportsCenters, the ESPN programming schedule that kicked off the network's first full decade consisted mostly of random and eclectic events, many of which were prerecorded and re-aired. Whatever ABC didn't want for Wide World of Sports, *or CBS didn't need for* Sports Spectacular, *or NBC didn't use on* Sports World, *ESPN pounced on. There was an occasional merciful surprise—like the tennis challenge match that featured a very young John McEnroe going up against Roscoe Tanner in Miami, Florida—but generally speaking, only the least demanding of viewers could have mistaken ESPN's quotidian output for some grand new Golden Age of Sports TV.*

Perhaps the only bright spots in the lineup were men's and women's college basketball and hockey games—results of the deal Bill Rasmussen had signed with the NCAA on March 9, 1979. ESPN had the rights to broadcast all NCAA championship events that were not legally committed to other networks. That meant ESPN could televise the early rounds of the 1980 NCAA Men's Basketball Tournament. Those early rounds were available for two main reasons: one, NBC, which had the final rounds of the tournament, didn't want to give away precious soap opera afternoon hours and valuable prime-time slots to the early rounds; and two, the whole idea of slotting early-round games on air was dismissed as a foolhardy notion by supposedly Smart Guys in the network TV sports business.

BOB LEY:

I know March Madness is a copyrighted phrase, but through the 1980s, our network created college basketball. Yes, you had Magic and Bird the year before, but you can argue that was more an NBA-maker than a college-maker. NBC, then CBS, had the Final Four, but they were standing on the shoulders of this cultural phenomenon that we kept creating, reinforcing and embellishing night after night through the winter and during the tournament. ESPN was the seminal impetus for creating what that tournament was.

LOREN MATTHEWS, *Vice President of Programming:*

The first Thursday afternoon of the tournament we went on the air around noon, and we did more than twenty-four hours of games. One game was live, but we'd bring in another game that was going on at the same time, tape it, then turn it around for air. We had to stop, I think, at noon or one o'clock on Saturday afternoon because of the NCAA's deal with CBS, but in all that time, we only showed one repeat. There were a lot of us who didn't even go home for those two days, but I remember looking at the screen and saying, "My God, there's something here. We might make it."

STEVE ANDERSON, *Executive Vice President:*

ESPN couldn't go regional. Unlike the networks, we only had one feed, so whatever we were showing was national. While we could only show the country one game at a time, it was important for us to keep people up to date with whatever else was going on in the tournament.

BILL FITTS, *Executive Producer:*

Chet came over to me and said, "I want you to cut in with reports on the other games." I said, "Chet, we don't have anybody near those other trucks. How am I going to do that?" and he says, "That's the problem," then walks away. So I put Bob Ley in the studio and just cut into games. I'd try to pick times when they almost had to give the score—there were no continuous scoreboards back then—and I'd say, "Okay, Bob, now!" Since I had nobody to coordinate with in the other trucks, sometimes I would cut in and they would never give the score or they would throw to a commercial as soon as we joined them. Those weren't good times to get in at all.

STEVE ANDERSON:

I read an article about the three networks criticizing ESPN for this notion of live cut-ins, which said: "They don't get that when people start watching a game, they want to see the whole game." And I'm just saying to myself, "That's not true." If we were doing a game and it was in the second quarter, but another game was near the end and it was close, it seemed obvious to us to go to that other game.

ROSA GATTI, _Senior Vice President_ _of Corporate Outreach:_

We kept publicizing that we had these games, and alumni, along with a lot of students, wanted to see their teams play, so they rented out hotel rooms that advertised, "We have HBO and ESPN."

BOB LEY:

After our coverage of the early rounds, Jeff Israel, David Shepherd, and I went to cover the Final Four tournament in Indianapolis. Jeff had a huge Hitachi camera with tubes; he had taken an ESPN bumper sticker and used a razor blade to cut the logo out so he could put it on the side of his camera. We were at the open practice that Friday, Iowa was getting ready for their game against Purdue, and I hear, "Hey, ESPN, we watch you guys!" We looked over and three guys who went to school at Iowa had come down to the top of the steps. We just looked at them and said, "You watch us?" Shortly thereafter, we began to hear stories of people who had actually rented out hotel rooms that had cable so they could watch our games.

CHET SIMMONS, *ESPN President:*

We created college basketball. The attention we gave to the early rounds changed the tournament. Nobody else was televising those early rounds, and nobody else had the time to do what we did. Word even got around to the coaching community that we were doing all these games, and we became a very important part of coaches' scouting.

ESPN was still bleeding money by the millions, and Simmons, desperate for more resources and better programming, was unable to spend lavishly, as he'd done at NBC and ABC. The ESPN president found himself pressured by company owner Getty on the inside and mocked by many colleagues in the sports business.

If anyone needed to be reminded that Simmons's stature in the business was still lofty, they'd only need to hear him dealing with longtime NFL commissioner Pete Rozelle. The two were buddies from way back, and yet if Simmons hadn't had such an enviable track record, Rozelle might have laughed him out the door—especially when he heard his old friend's latest, and wildest, idea: live, protracted TV coverage of the NFL draft.

The NFL draft was hardly considered spectator material. Just the opposite: it was a particularly insular affair, generating interest about the top picks but little if any about all the others. Some years, the draft was barely reported, much less covered. Simmons knew that as a TV show, it could be hobbled by long waits between selections and many a less-than-riveting moment when general managers and scouts huddled together in sessions of top-secret analysis. But he envisioned an NFL draft liberated from backstage cloisters and thrust into the open air of national spectacle—and of course, it would fill the hours. When Rozelle asked Simmons why in the world people would want to watch the damn thing, Simmons just smiled a wily smile and said, "Let that be my problem."

And so, on April 29, 1980, it happened: the first televised NFL draft, live on ESPN.

BILL FITTS:

It was February when Chet told me he wanted to do the draft in April. I said, "Chet, there's nothing there, there's just some people on the phone, and they're not even football people, they're just relatives—relatives of relatives! How can I do an all-day television show?" And he says, "Well, if you have to sign off early, that's okay," and I started to say, "But, Chet," and he stops me and says, "Look, you don't understand something. It's the NFL. Figure it out."

So I got some production assistants and said, "We've got to get some highlights." Fortunately, I knew Frank Ross from the NFL. He rubbed a lot of people the wrong way, but he was very helpful. I said, "Frankie, you got to help me here," and he started calling some general managers and getting some information for me. It was pretty damn good. I had background on everybody in the first two rounds. Then we called the universities, and said, "Look, we need highlights on these guys, and we don't want to spend a lot of time editing. Just send me the best forty-five seconds." Some of these schools had their own production crews so it was real easy.

BOB LEY:

Once it became apparent we were going to be able to do the draft, they bought this ad, which said, "See the Draft," which nobody had ever seen before. I still have it at home, buried in the files — a huge, full-page ad in the *New York Times* with ESPN and the NFL shield together. Chet said that was the most important thing, to align ourselves with the NFL, the Gold Standard of American television.

I think we went on the air at eight in the morning. The network had been on the air for just seven months, and we were basically doing what we had been doing all that time—making it up as we went along. We'd switch back and forth between Bristol and New York, and before you know it, it was four o'clock in the afternoon. Eventually it became apparent that we weren't going to realize Chet's worst nightmare—which was that it was just going to be a god-awful mess.

VINCE PAPALE, *Pro Football Analyst:*

I was shocked that I was asked to participate, but it sounded cool. Everything was done on the fly, and even though I played all the sports I've played, being a sportscaster was not a religion to me, so when it came to recalling names and facts, I wasn't that great at it. I was pretty much overwhelmed. It was the longest day I ever had on TV, totally exhausting.

GEORGE GRANDE:

We had about thirty people doing the draft, and a friend from CBS came over, and said, "Where is everybody?" and I said, "This is it." He said, "Well, if we were doing it," meaning CBS, "we'd have 130 people here." But that was the joy of it. It was us against the world, us against all the odds.

We sat down at 6:30 to go on the air at 8:00 a.m. and I didn't get up till eight o'clock at night. I didn't go to the bathroom from 8:00 a.m. to 8:00 p.m.

We all realized this was the start of something, a major step for us. Chet and Scotty would say,

"Someday we're going to have a Super Bowl. We don't know when that will be, but we're going to have the NFL, we're going to have Major League Baseball, the NBA, and we're going to have the NHL, but right now we have to build on a solid foundation with visions of getting there at some point in time." And I think that first step into the big time was the NFL draft.

CHET SIMMONS:

Every day was a different challenge. Every day was a battle to survive. The NCAA tournament was great for us, but it came and went. The draft put us in business with the NFL, and that was huge. We were starting to get a little bit of attention, but we still needed more ideas, more money, and good people.

BILL CREASY:

Before I got to ESPN, I was working on a project for Warner Communications. A fellow named John Lack hired me. They were doing this new channel called QUBE and trying to get more subscribers, and thought Ohio State football would help. So I was sent out to Columbus to get the rights to games, which we would tape and then show Saturday night. Steve Ross, who ran Warner, decided that even though I knew television, I should go with someone who really knew football. So he had Allie Sherman, the former head coach of the Giants, go with me. He was a legend, very famous, and very intimidating.

We get to the local station that's going to do the production with us, and there's this overweight, bearded, young guy with an afro there with his boss, who says to me, "Say hi to my head of production, Steve Bornstein." So the meeting starts, and Allie, in his acquired Southern accent, having graduated from Brooklyn College, launches in. "Boys, I'll tell you what we want. We're gonna need eight cameras, three tape machines, audio at four or five locations"—I mean, he goes on and on about what he wants. I was shocked by how strong he was coming on and all he was asking for. All of a sudden, over here to my right, young Steve with the afro and beard looks at him and says, "Mr. Sherman, with all due respect, this is what you're going to get: Only three cameras, one tape machine, and one truck. And that's it." I looked at him and said to myself, "I love this fucking guy."

STEVE BORNSTEIN, *Chairman:*

I always liked sports but was kind of a hacker. When I left college, I wanted to be a television sports director, but I ended up being really inadequate. Ultimately I couldn't watch twenty monitors at the same time, which is a pretty key component. So I decided to get into management and programming.

BILL CREASY:

When I got to ESPN, I offered Steve a job right away as one of my guys in the Programming department.

I said, "You gotta come with me." But it was a tough sell. It wasn't easy getting people to go to Bristol, no matter who Chet, Scotty, and Crease were. But Steve finally agreed. I got him for something like twenty-five thousand bucks and he started in January of 1980.

CHET SIMMONS:

Steve was hired by Creasy. He needed an assistant in programming, and here came Steve. It's a perfect example of how a senior guy can take a junior guy and teach him the industry, teach him the business, and have him be successful. Steve learned very quickly. He was the kind of guy you could turn loose and know he'll be very good.

Steve Bornstein hoped to attend Berkeley after graduating from Fair Lawn High School in New Jersey, but his father, insisting on driving his son to college, refused to take him any farther west than the Mississippi. So Steve wound up at the University of Wisconsin, which he had decided was the most "fun" school within Dad's borders.

He was certainly at home among the liberals of Madison. Back in Fair Lawn, his parents had long been prominent political activists, especially Mom, a legend in those parts. She was, by all accounts, a most formidable presence, and Steve inherited that quality, as well as the bonhomie of his indefatigable dad, a venerable

life-of-the-party businessman who owned a textile man-
ufacturing plant that kept the Bornsteins comfy.

Little wonder, considering his heritage, that Born-
stein wasn't intimidated by the fabled Allie Sherman
when their paths crossed. With his gruff manner, big
Raymond Burr eyes, and a bass voice known to boom,
Bornstein bespoke formidability himself. He could
hardly bark or bluff his way through his new set of chal-
lenges, however; Bornstein was entering a programming
department at ESPN that was struggling for survival.

ANDY BRILLIANT:
I had been at HBO for four years, and when I got
to ESPN in January of 1980, it was just a mess. There
was no organization; they had no idea what business
they were in. There were a lot of horrible programming deals. The NCAA had a stranglehold over us.
Yes, we got the early rounds of the men's basketball
tournament, but we paid a lot for them and the agreement also said the NCAA could put all these second-
ary sports on ESPN. The only rights we had for
football were for two- or three-day delays, and from
conferences that no one really cared about. The deal
was onerous and expensive, and it kept us from
accessing the kind of content we needed to drive the
business. One of the first things I did when I arrived
was to go out to Kansas City to try to renegotiate the
deal with the head of the NCAA, Walter Byers.
We used to have meetings almost every weekend

in Chet's basement, and his wife would serve coffee and danishes, and Chet would be saying, "Well, should I pick up the phone now and just tell Evey it's all over? We can't run this business—this is just not going to work." And we'd all have to give him enough encouragement to keep it going another week. Week after week we had these silly meetings. And he would bemoan the state we're in and say, "I'm used to doing the Olympics and now I'm running Ping-Pong tournaments and slow-pitch softball games. The cable operators just don't have any respect for us. We're running out of dough. Should we call Evey? Should we just end it? Shall I pull the plug?" This happened almost as soon as I got there. So it was a bit discouraging at first.

STEVE BORNSTEIN:

I thought it was crazy to always be in commercial at fifty-eight after the hour. It drove me up the wall! So pretty soon after I arrived, I came up with the idea that we wouldn't do commercials in between shows. Nobody else was making those kinds of decisions. It wasn't all "I-I-I" by any stretch of the imagination, but you made up the rules as you went along.

LEE LEONARD:

I hosted *SportsCenter* and we did a thing on the show called Lee's Lip, where I would talk about anything I felt like for a few minutes at the end of each show. It was like a closing monologue. Sometimes it had to do with sports and sometimes it was just whatever I could think of that day, like a little editorial. Nobody seemed to care. As long as we filled up the time, that was the important thing.

But I went to work for them with the understanding that the "E" for Entertainment in ESPN was really going to be something. I was tired of sports. So when it became obvious to me that there wasn't going to be any entertainment, brilliant me, I thought this thing was never going to work. So my agent called me and said, "There's this crazy guy, Ted Turner, who's doing a news network," and I thought to myself, "Well, people might want to watch news twenty-four hours a day." I asked, "Where am I going to work if I go to work for them?" And they said Los Angeles. And I said, "Oh that's pretty nice." I'd play golf in January. So I grabbed the offer and left. I wasn't at ESPN very long — six months maybe.

LOREN MATTHEWS:

I was doing PR with the Mets for most of the seventies, and when the Mets were in the '73 World Series, I was their liaison with NBC. I wound up meeting Scotty Connal back then. Once I got interested in ESPN, I had to go down to my in-laws and watch, because they had cable.

I joined in January of '80 as a one-man broadcast promotions department, but at a certain point I was saying to myself, gee whiz, did I make a mistake? I didn't know anything about television. I had told Chet and Scotty right up front. I know how to promote and I certainly know sports, but I don't know anything about TV. And Scotty said, "Don't worry, we'll teach you television."

But you have doubts. At one point I was getting on an elevator to go down to Scotty's office and say to him, "Look, they haven't filled my old job with the Mets yet, maybe this wasn't the right idea. I think I should go back to New York." As I'm getting on the elevator, Scotty's getting off, and I said to him, "I'm just heading down to see you." He said, "Well, I just want you to know that I think you're doing a heck of a job." One sentence. That's all I needed at that point. I stayed for seventeen years.

BILL FITTS:

When we moved into our house, we didn't have cable, so we called United Cable. The cable guy comes out and asks, "What do you want cable for?" I said, "I'm working for ESPN," and he says, "Ah! Don't worry about them, they'll be gone in a year." And this was the cable company telling us!

BILL CREASY:

It was a big deal when we hired Bill Fitts. He had tons of experience and I really wanted him up there with us, but in all fairness to everybody involved, some people were concerned about his drinking. He assured me that he was fine and then I assured them. He became our head of production, and he didn't go back to drinking. But I bet he was close to returning to it many times because it was a very trying experience being up there in Bristol. He had virtually no money to spend on shows, and it was never easy.

BILL FITTS:

At CBS, a lot of our meetings were held in bars, restaurants, ad agencies, et cetera, and we certainly drank. Almost nobody went back to work after lunch. I had stopped drinking while I was looking for work, and when I went up to ESPN, I still didn't go back to hard liquor, although there were times when I had beer and wine. Yeah, there were some times when I wish I hadn't, but it was a bigger problem for me at CBS than it was over at ESPN. Then I quit for twenty-five years.

DREW ESOCOFF, *Director*:

Bill Fitts was the greatest boss anybody could ever have, and the greatest guy. To be able to have him as your first boss was magical. He was hysterically funny, but more important, he instilled a kind of work ethic, a creative ethic, and a free-thinking ethic with everyone who worked for him that you try to continue for the rest of your career and pass down to the people who are now working for you. It means you start with a blank slate on every show you do. It means you don't rely on things that have worked in the past, because they may or may not necessarily work in the future. And it means you have to be forthright with people in terms of your critique, but to try to keep it as fun as you can, because you know what? You're doing television. It's sports; it should be fun.

There were people who would move up to Bristol and didn't have an apartment yet, and Bill and his wife, Fran, would say, "Just come stay with us for a while." People would end up staying there for months.

I haven't worked for Bill now in twenty years, but I could go to him right now with any favor, and he'd say yes.

JOHN COLBY, *Composer:*
Bill had a lot of pressure on him and was a very volatile guy. You could always gauge his level of agitation by the size of the sweat rings under his arms.

TERRY LINGNER, *Coordinating Producer:*
I was working for ABC at Lake Placid and played hooky from the Olympics a couple of times in February of 1980 to go down and visit Scotty Connal in Bristol. After the games were over, I interviewed with him and was able to get a gig, so I didn't even have to go home. Frankly, I thought ESPN was going to be a better fit for me. I was tired of all the screaming and yelling at ABC. They had this saying, "Did you get

tattooed?" and ostensibly that meant, "Did someone scream at the top of his lungs and dress you down on the headset?" I guess they had fun with their own egos. It was just mind-boggling to me. It made me think, "I may be learning from the best people, but this is not the way I want to work."

Bill Fitts was the brightest guy I've ever met in the business. I consider him my mentor, almost a father figure. He once told me there wasn't one aspect of our business that he didn't like. He didn't care if he was pulling cable or writing for Summerall or Musburger. He just loved it all—top to bottom.

FRED GAUDELLI, *Senior Coordinating Producer:*
Bill was the type of guy that you really didn't want to ever disappoint. He inspired you to do good things and actually to try to do great things. Scotty believed in specialization; if you were a football producer, you should be doing as much football as possible. If you were an auto-racing producer, you should be doing as much auto racing as possible. Or if you were an event producer, you should not be producing *SportsCenter*. Bill believed the total opposite. He didn't think there should be any specialization. He thought that such specialization would inhibit your development as a production person. He never wanted you to work on the same thing more than two times in a row. He wanted you spread across the spectrum doing as many different sports as possible.

I'll never forget something he said once in a meeting about our written reports. "When you guys finish your shows, take that file and throw it out. Do not keep one piece of paper, because next year when we have to come back and do this again, it will force you to rethink everything you did, not just pick up from where you left off and implement the same procedures and production elements that you did last year." And he was 1,000 percent correct about that.

STEVE ANDERSON:

We knew how good CBS, ABC, and NBC were, and we realized we weren't as good. Part of it was their resources, part of it was their talent. They had guys in the trucks who had years and years of experience; we had guys like myself, who were just starting out. Bill expected us to work like dogs, and we knew it. He wanted us to take a lot of pride in what we did and keep in mind that we could do what we needed to do with less.

GREG GUMBEL, *Anchor*:

I don't know how they heard about me other than the fact that both Chet Simmons and Scotty Connal had previously worked with my brother at NBC Sports. I kind of freely admit that they probably needed a face with color on the air, and I don't deny that probably played a part in why I was hired. Now I'm awfully quick to point out that that's not the reason why they keep you.

I wound up living in the town of Simsbury, on Climax Road. The local people couldn't even bring themselves to pronounce it "Climax"; they pronounced it "Climix." I said, "Well, it must hurt the hell out of you that the next big crossing street is Bushy Hill."

The nice thing about going to ESPN back then was that sports was not just important, it was the only thing going on there, so you didn't have to fight for time.

ANDY BRILLIANT:

The town was nothing but a broken-down shopping center. Most of the stores were closed. I remember there was shattered glass all over the place. That was about all there was to the town. I remember the last Christmas I was still at HBO, they used to have these annual Christmas parties at like Studio 54, and they were pretty incredible affairs. In 1980, just after I landed at ESPN, we were invited by Chet to a function in Bristol where we had a table. I guess we were being honored by the Lions Club. My wife wound up sitting next to Chet's wife, Harriet, and Harriet was telling her that she had to go to the local Marshalls store and buy these bolts of cloth so she could make a dress for $15 — and this was the president's wife!

Then this one guy's girlfriend was evidently this Cuban whore who sat at the table with us, so it was kind of a very strange set of circumstances. I had to console my wife on the way home; she was just absolutely in tears: "What have you done to me?"

BILL CREASY:

Chet and Scotty owned homes in the Hartford area, and Chet really pushed me to buy a house and be part of the community, to prove my allegiance. They arranged for real-estate agents to take me around, and I'd go look at little three-bedroom ranch houses, all that kind of crap, but the truth is, I didn't want to live up there, and they didn't want to keep paying for my room at the Holiday Inn. Chet wrote me a personal letter—very laudatory—about how much they couldn't have accomplished if I hadn't been part of the team, and a lot of other good stuff. Then four months later, he had Scotty tell me that we'd come to the end of the rope. I had to buy a house and live up there or I had to go. I left.

STEVE BORNSTEIN:

I thought Bill kind of abandoned us, and he became persona non grata to Chet and Scotty after turning them down. They felt betrayed. But he wasn't about to give up his lifestyle.

BOB GUTKOWSKI, *Vice President* of *Programming*:

I'd been working at NBC Sports for twelve years, and it's May of 1981. Chet makes me an offer to become head of programming and I was struggling with what to do. At NBC, Ohlmeyer's temper was really starting to get to me, so I sat down with my wife and told her, "I'm gonna do this ESPN thing, but I'm not going to tell anybody until after Wimbledon so we can get another trip to Wimbledon." We loved going to Wimbledon, and I figured when I got back, I would resign.

So we go to Wimbledon, and word starts to get out that Gutkowski is going to be leaving. I figured, we're here now, let's tell them. So I tell my boss, and he doesn't try and convince me not to do it, but warns me, "Don't say anything until we get back, because we don't want Ohlmeyer to find out." They thought Ohlmeyer was starting to become fond of me, and he would've gotten pissed if I left. So I said, "All right, fine, I'll keep my mouth shut."

So on the final day of Wimbledon, my wife and I are walking in the park there and we see Don and his wife. I say to him, "Don, I'll see ya. Take care." And he says, "Yeah, I'll see ya next week." And I said, "No, I really mean, see ya. I resign." And he goes, "You can't do this. You have to give me a chance to talk to you." So my wife and I take the regular flight home, and Don takes the Concorde. By the time I get home that evening, there are four messages: "You have to call Don Ohlmeyer." So I call Don, and he says, "You have to see me tomorrow in my office at nine o'clock in the morning." So I go to his office, and he says, "I don't want you to go," and he offers me the vice presidency of NBC Sports programming, and I'm thinking, "You gotta be fucking kidding me." He says, "I don't want you to go. We'll move Geoff Mason over here"—this, that, and the other. Then he said I shouldn't go, because he was single-handedly going to kill ESPN. So I walk out, I close his door, go to the elevator, but say to myself, "I gotta work for Chet, I'm gonna give it a shot." So I turned Ohlmeyer down. We were never really friends again after that. Ohlmeyer was always pissed off at me for leaving.

By the way, a couple years later, he wound up coming to ESPN as a consultant and working out a deal to buy a piece of it.

BOB PRONOVOST:

They tried to bring in people from New York to organize and schedule us; management was trying to get control of the asylum. It was a cuckoo's nest. We were completely out of control.

We had this producer, Fred Muzzy, who was about 350 pounds and looked like Jackie Gleason. He was hanging out in Rhode Island at a clambake one day—he had a tendency to drink and was a great partier—and realized he had to be at work at 3:15 to do a show, and it was already 2:45. So he hired a helicopter and landed it outside the building in the mud. One of my funniest images of working at ESPN is of Fred strutting in through the parking lot, covered in mud up to his chest, walking into the newsroom, barking out demands like there was nothing wrong.

Another time, Fred went out and got drunk at a restaurant on the corner called Hamps, which we used to call Cramps. It got close to airtime and he hadn't shown up, so I started to realize that in addition to my directing duties, I would have to start producing if we were going to make it on the air. Then all of a sudden, I see some PA is wheeling Fred down the hall in a chair and he's barking commands all over the place. He came into the control room and was totally drunk. We wound up switching back and forth with producing and directing duties, and at one point, the TD [technical director] says, "I'm not putting up with this shit," and walked out.

CHUCK PAGANO:

The most anxious day of the week was payday because you ran to the bank up the street to make sure the damn check cleared before it bounced. We were bleeding red. Everybody sort of kept their engine running just in case they shut the doors. Our desire was just to make product, get the fucking thing out of here, and figure out what the hell we had to do next. None of us were what any normal organization would ever hire—we weren't refined enough. I guess we were like Vikings just trying to clear the forest.

CHRIS BERMAN:

The first year I still had a mustache, long hair, and long sideburns. Chet was president of the place, knew everybody's name, and I mean every camera man who worked at eleven at night. I remember one time he passed me in the hall, turned, and said, "You still got that mustache, huh, Chris?" Now, I'm not a dumb kid, so I ask, "Does it bother you?" He says, "Let me explain something to you about TV. You're pretty proud of what you say, aren't you? You want people to listen to you, don't you? So, if you wore a loud tie, 20 percent of the people are noticing this aggressive orange tie, and might not hear what you say. Suppose 10 percent of people, while not offended, are distracted by your mustache and are trying to decide should you have it or not, does it look good or not? They're not listening to what you say. That would be a disservice, wouldn't it?" I said, "I'm going down the street to buy a freakin' razor right now. It will be off tomorrow, never to return." That was my Chet. He didn't order me to take it off. He put it in terms of me hurting myself.

STEVE ANDERSON:
I was lucky enough to be teamed with Chip Dean as a producer-director team. At the time, the networks were doing a great job, so all we wanted was to be as good as them. We watched everything they did. We knew what they did, how they did it, why they did it. So, part of it was to make sure that no one could say we weren't as good. And then we tried to do things that were better.

We mostly did basketball, but we did a lot of other

things together too. We got five cameras for the big games and were thrilled. We were trying to do off-the-ball isolation, which nobody was doing in those games. We were taping the guys without the ball, so Chip and I had it worked out: we would follow Chris Mullin, for example, before he got the ball and hit that jump shot. I don't remember us getting any kind of credit for it.

ELLEN BECKWITH, *Director of Production:*

When Jim Simpson was in the booth with Dick Vitale, he did a thing to get Dick to stop talking. He had gotten tired of telling Dick to stop talking and poking him in the arm, so he would take a white napkin or handkerchief, put it in front of Dick's face, and just drop it. And that meant, shut up, Dick.

DICK VITALE:

One night we had a game that I didn't think was that big, and Jim Simpson said to me, "It's a big game to those kids and coaches who are playing." And I always try to keep that in mind and make sure I make every game special. That really came home when I realized people were paying attention to what I was saying.

I believe it was Michael Jordan's sophomore year. North Carolina was playing Virginia, which was number one in the country. Virginia had Ralph Sampson, who had been the player of the year for three years in a row, and they were a super basketball team. They were up maybe seven or eight points with about two minutes to go, and all of a sudden, Jordan goes out of his mind, making one great play after another for an incredible comeback. I said something to the effect of, "Forget about Ralph Sampson! My player of the year is the magnificent Michael Jordan." A bit later, I went to Virginia to do a game down there, and Ralph Sampson looks at me and says, "Here comes Michael Jordan's PR agent."

JED DRAKE, *Senior Vice President of Production:*

Jim Dullaghan was one of our top financial guys and a former Marine Corps drill sergeant. He had a sign above his desk that said something like "I'm the meanest son of a bitch in the valley." He offered me a contract, a $45,000 to $55,000 three-year deal. I quickly said, "If you factor in my overtime, I'm making more money than that right now." He just looked at me and smiled. "Overtime's not guaranteed; if you don't sign this contract now, then it's off the table." That's when I knew that I was going to be here for three years.

We were single and young. We used to go out at night and hang out together. We were together all the time. I ended up marrying somebody who worked for ESPN.

JEFF ISRAEL, *Camera Man:*

One of the odd things back then was that even though our service was satellite based, we didn't have a lot of money to spend on uplinking. When we were covering our first Masters, we would finish the day's stories, then drive them to this small airport in Augusta to put them on a plane for the 11:00 p.m. show. Well one day, I was on Seve Ballesteros, and he had this great shot. I had followed the flight of the ball as it hit the green and went in the hole. Obviously that was a big part of our story for the day, because that was the shot that put him ahead for the tournament, and he actually won a green jacket. So we drove that to the airport. The next day, CBS came to us and said, "We'd like that footage to put in our preview show," and they couldn't understand why we couldn't give them the tape and had to turn them down. It was because it wasn't in Augusta; it was in Bristol. They couldn't imagine us not using satellite technology to get that stuff up to Bristol.

Throughout most of 1980, and despite previous promises that it would be a nonstop operation, ESPN's programming was decidedly not nonstop. Apart from early rounds of the NCAA men's basketball tournament, after each weekday's final SportsCenter, which aired between 3:00 and 5:30 a.m., ESPN simply signed off until it signed on again—at 6:00 p.m. On weekends, the televised day wouldn't begin until sometime between noon and 2:00 p.m.

In 1979, Bill Rasmussen had promised that ESPN would soon air 'round-the-clock, leaving Simmons furious because he didn't think there was any way that they were ready for it. Nevertheless, Don Rasmussen, Bill's brother, working on affiliate relations out of his basement in Peoria, Illinois, had been passing word along to Simmons that cable systems were getting antsy and wondering if ESPN was an outfit that didn't, or couldn't, live up to its promises. There was also the danger that ESPN would lose the channel space if it didn't expand.

And so it came to pass, on September 1, 1980, that ESPN began broadcasting 24/7, finally making good on Rasmussen's pledge. Simmons remained unhappy about having to fill up acres of additional airtime. As was so often the case, money was more than incidental to his gloom. More hours would mean more programming and higher labor costs.

For his part, Evey was achingly aware of all the Getty dollars going, going, gone with the wind—$1.5 million a month, after deducting minuscule revenues, just to keep the lights burning and the satellite dishes turned on, and this was in addition to the $35 million Getty had already invested. "Revenues" were ad dollars, but even at a modest selling price of $1,000 per thirty seconds, half of ESPN's available ad time went unsold. (While ESPN was charging advertisers pennies, the established broadcast networks were getting $50,000 for the same thirty seconds of ad time on sports shows, and $300,000 for events like the Super Bowl.)

Chet Simmons turned to his friend Mike Traeger for life-support money, and Traeger turned to an old friend and benefactor of ESPN's, Anheuser-Busch, the ever-

booming Bud brewer who'd been ESPN's first real big-time sponsor. Together, Simmons and Traeger skillfully negotiated a $25 million deal over five years that granted, among other things, brand-name exclusivity to Anheuser-Busch, making it the only beer bottler whose commercials would be seen on the network for the duration of the contract. Michael J. Roarty, Anheuser-Busch's marketing VP, proclaimed, "This is the largest sponsorship commitment in the history of America's budding cable television industry." In a cable universe now seventeen million viewers strong, ESPN's audience, Simmons said, had gone from a piddling 1.5 million subscribers to more than 6 million in just over a year.

Simmons ballyhooed as "awesome" a cable advertiser's ability to target its "key audience" via ESPN, as exemplified by the Anheuser-Busch deal—"especially," he said, "if you realize how sports can reach beer drinkers." Roarty added, "This new multiyear package is different; we know what ESPN can do—deliver the people we need to reach."

Evey was thrilled. "It's an endorsement, really, a complete endorsement," he proclaimed. ESPN, now a flag-bearer for the whole cable industry, capitalized on the good news. Simmons noted that ESPN would sell between $6 million and $7 million in advertising during the year. While not nearly enough to cover the network's costs, it was an impressive figure considering that all of cable television had sold only $7 million in ads the year before.

Among other companies purchasing ads on ESPN: Hertz, Pontiac, Subaru, Mobil, Sears, and Magnavox. Not surprisingly, Getty Oil had bought time too — and so, in this election year, had Ronald Reagan's campaign, even though ESPN would be running tape of an old Michigan-Indiana football game on Election Night, when most other networks would be feverishly reporting results.

BOB GUTKOWSKI:

The Busch deal absolutely saved ESPN. It was a lifesaver. But even that deal became a problem after a while. As ESPN started to gain traction, the exclusivity was too restrictive. If ESPN was really going to become a viable entity, it had to have other beer companies. Eventually they had to change it.

According to ESPN's original business plan — to use the term "plan" rather loosely — the all-sports network was expected to break even in its second year of operation, and to be pleasantly profitable, with around five million satisfied subscribers, by its third or fourth year. Getty's cumulative investment in the business — to get it to the break-even point — was supposed to top out at $25 million, but Evey and his crew had gone through $25 million in just their first seven months of operation. No longer comfortable trusting the Rasmussen vision, Evey turned for advice to McKinsey & Company, a consulting firm that had worked previously for Getty.

And so, in 1980, twenty-nine-year-old wunderkind Roger Werner, straight out of central casting's crop of well-spoken Classy Guys, rode into Bristol with his University of Virginia MBA. Along with coworker Sharon Patrick, Werner set out to investigate just what the hell was going on at ESPN.

ROGER WERNER, *Chief Executive Officer:*

Remember, at the time, there was really no cable programming industry. There was HBO and there was Ted Turner's WTCG, even before it was WTBS, but it was essentially just a regional broadcast television station. CNN and MTV had both been announced, but the cable industry was no more than seven to ten million subscribers nationally—it was still a tiny industry in search of a business plan. So we had to model the development of the cable television industry, literally try to predict what rate of penetration those wires would achieve over time and, based on that projection, what kind of programming industry might be generated. Essentially, we were asked to look at the business and determine the feasibility of developing an all-sports network.

I quickly figured out Stu Evey had covered up a lot for George Getty, and it seemed to me that Stu also had a lot of dirt on a lot of guys that still worked there. He was owed a lot of favors. That may be one of the most serendipitous factors in this early story, because while all this money was going out the window,

Stu's support at Getty gave us the opportunity to take three or four months to look at the development of the industry and write a blueprint for an all-sports program network.

The biggest fundamental flaw was that by the time we got involved, in the spring of 1980, the founders of ESPN had signed distribution deals with all the major cable companies promising them the service for free. They had looked at the successful guys—NBC, ABC, and CBS—and said, "Well, they pay the station groups to carry the programming, they make tons of money, we should do the same thing, be just like them." So they effectively replicated the broadcast television business model, where the affiliate got paid a little by the network to carry the network program. We understood this would be the Achilles' heel for the foreseeable future, and we had to build a business plan that was advertising-sales only in the near term.

I will remember this as long as I live because we had a meeting at McKinsey & Company's office on Park Avenue with a number of the Getty guys, including Stu, and it was the day after John Lennon's assassination. We showed them a liquidation option and the dollars they would get from that. Then we talked about another option, which was to stay in the game. We gave them a business plan, a model of what the cable industry might look like over the next five to ten years, what might be doable in terms of programming, even ratings that might be produced and ad revenue. It was a rather thorough presentation.

I don't know what my colleague at McKinsey, Sharon Patrick, thought about this, but I certainly felt like I had stuck my neck way out. As a young guy, this was my first high-visibility assignment as a management consultant in a business I'd always wanted to be in, the television broadcasting industry, and here I was, recommending to Getty that they not give up and proceed with the network.

ANDY BRILLIANT:

I'll just never forget this — they had affiliate contracts written on parchment paper, a little longer than legal size and folded in three, and essentially it gave the operators the right to do as they wished with the signal. They could cut it up, use it as filler material in their own local sports channels. They didn't have to report subscriber numbers, there were no fees basically — and that's what we were dealing with.

ROGER WERNER:

This thing was now getting much bigger and way more complicated than Bill Rasmussen imagined it would be. It was like he was the most successful Dairy Queen operator in Bristol, Connecticut, doing the best he could, but what he had been doing was grossly inadequate and really damaging to the company.

It's sad in a way. Bill was still referring to it as the

"entertainment and sports programming network" and from time to time he would ask, "Shouldn't we be doing movies for women on Saturday afternoon?"

It was clear to Getty and Chet that you just literally had to retire him and his brother as gracefully as possible and get professional management people into the business. We at McKinsey completely agreed.

STUART EVEY:

When we took over the company, I made Bill chairman but in no way did I want to give him any responsibility. To him, it looked like a lot because he was the chairman and that was above the president. Well, that's not what I intended. I was getting all kinds of heat from Chet about Bill's involvement, and I was annoyed as well, so I'm telling you, it was really wearing thin. Chet having the ego he had—and rightfully so, he earned it—was not going to take a backseat to all of the stuff Bill was throwing around. Chet was there building the broadcast center, building the network, hiring employees. Having Bill Rasmussen play a significant role was just not part of the deal.

CHET SIMMONS:

The problem was, Bill didn't have much to do. I don't even know what he expected to do. I had no confidence in his ability to go beyond having come up with the idea. He was very good at that stuff. But he was only an idea guy, and the idea had already been formulated.

ANDY BRILLIANT:

Try and follow this: Simmons didn't like Evey. I think Evey scared the living bejesus out of him. And Evey didn't like Simmons. Rasmussen didn't like Evey, but no matter, because Evey didn't respect Rasmussen. Of course Simmons wanted nothing to do with Rasmussen, and Rasmussen didn't like Simmons.

BILL RASMUSSEN:

A lady reporter from a news magazine called our office, where Chet and I sat, and the receptionist in the hallway said so-and-so was on the line and she wanted to speak with me. But Chet said, "I'll take it," and got on the line. The reporter said to him, "If I wanted to talk to you, I would have asked for you," and told him to put me on the line. Chet was really upset. Stu would get mad too if people didn't mention his name when they were interviewed. I would try to mention Getty, but people didn't care about that. They knew Getty had money.

GEORGE CONNER:

I was in Bristol once, and Stu called me. He said, "George, did you see that article in *Sports Illustrated*? Why wasn't my name mentioned?" He was really upset. Chet was the same way. He wanted to do the interviews and he wanted his name to be the one associated with the company. It became a very significant conflict.

CHET SIMMONS:

I didn't want to deal with Bill. At that point, we didn't like each other. I felt he got his nose into it when he didn't know what he was talking about. We had a couple of screaming arguments where I screamed and he listened. I can scream with the best of them. Eventually, recognizing how I felt and recognizing how Stu felt, I think he knew his days were numbered. And they were.

BILL RASMUSSEN:

Basically they were paying me $100,000 just to sit there. Eventually, it just didn't make any sense, and I went into Chet one day and said, "It's time to go. Obviously I don't have anything to do anymore." So I initiated it, even though Stu initiated the idea that I would no longer be involved with anything. It was December 1980. So I stayed around for fifteen months after we first went on the air.

While I was leaving, Stu said, "I'm going to give you"—I've forgotten what the number was, maybe $50,000—"for all your stock, and you're going give it to me." I said, "No, I'm not. I would not do that." He wanted our stock. He wanted everything. He said, "Well, all right, I'll make it a quarter of a million." I guess he was thinking we were so naive or so poor we would take it. Then Stu brought up the car again—the Cadillac. For such a small item, Stu was just bananas over that stuff. Flipped out. I was supposed to keep it. That was part of my leaving. He said, "You need to give me a $5,000 check for the car." So I had to pay him $5,000. My father had never had a nice car in his life, so I was just giving it to my father. As a matter of fact, he kept that car until the day he died. He was ninety-four years old—so that would be 2002 or whatever—and he had a classic Cadillac in his garage until he died. I still have the license plate hanging on my wall.

J. B. DOHERTY:

I have warm feelings for Bill and Scott, but it's a good thing for ESPN that it sort of evolved as it did, and I think it's arguably a miracle that it survived the Rasmussens—and Evey.

STUART EVEY:

I admire Bill, but ESPN became more than he ever envisioned because of the efforts of a lot of other people. It still gripes me when people say, "Wasn't Rasmussen the guy who started it all?" He was to the extent that he brought it to me, but it's different from what he brought. And thank God I got the guys in there that made it different. I guess that's all I can tell you.

BILL RASMUSSEN:

Some people had gotten a pretty heavy-duty plaque with my name on it, with "Founder." It was going to be a surprise for me. They were coming to put it up, but Stu intercepted it—"No way is that going up, get it out of here." They said to take it to the dump! That was extremely petty on Stu's part. So I put it in the trunk of my car. Probably five or six years later, I had some guy in Florida make it into a coffee table. It's an interesting conversation piece.

There are two things you can do when something like that happens: you can be bitter the rest of your life, or you can say, okay, this is just part of a new day, let's start over. Because of ESPN, I've had a pleasant thirty years. I speak at a lot of places; people still want to hear the story.

DON RASMUSSEN:

The company announced on September 30, 1980, that Bill was leaving. He called me earlier that day and said, "I didn't want you to hear it through the grapevine, I wanted to call and tell you myself—I'm leaving ESPN." Then he said, "And you start preparing yourself because they're going to get rid of you, too." I said, "Uh, okay." A little while later—I don't remember where we were going, but Chet and I were going someplace—Chet said to me, "Don, just know, in our eyes, you are not connected with Bill. Bill has no impact on you." When Bill called me the next time, I told him, "Chet talked to me about my position at ESPN, and he says I'm okay." Bill said, "Don, you are so naive. That vote of confidence means he's getting ready to fire you. It's like the baseball manager who gets a vote of confidence from the GM and then two months later, he's fired."

So about a month later, Bill calls up and tells me he and Scott were founding something called Enterprise Radio—an all-sports radio network. He then says, "Don, they're going to fire you, you need to resign before they fire you, and we've got a job for you. Come to work for Enterprise Radio." I said, "Well, I've got a good friend I've worked with at ESPN and I want to talk with him." He said, "Are you talking about Jim Bates? We'll hire him too." So I talked to Jim and we both submitted our resignations to go work at Enterprise Radio in mid-January. We were due at ESPN for a bonus, but as soon as we resigned, that bonus was canceled. I wasn't real happy that Chet canceled my bonus, but I figured he was going to cancel it anyway, since Bill said he was the one that supposedly was going to fire me.

Well, I wasn't gone more than a couple of weeks when I got the word through the grapevine that ESPN had planned to move me to Connecticut with a big raise and put me in charge of affiliate relations. And I thought, "Oh, boy, Bill led me down the primrose path." I had this thing ingrained in me since I was a kid, that Bill is 100 percent honest and trust-worthy, and if Bill says it, that's the truth. I took Bill at his word. I went to Enterprise Radio, and within five months Enterprise Radio was bankrupt and out of business. So I was up the creek without a paddle. I had been had. I'd been had by my brother.

I called Stu after the Enterprise Radio thing fell apart. He said he would love to have me back, but he wouldn't hire me back unless I sold him my stock, and I told him I couldn't do that, so we just parted ways.

I didn't confront Bill because I knew that if I did, there would be no more relationship, and I felt that at some point he and I were going to be all that's left of the family. For a long time, I made it a point to call him every year just to tell him he has a brother, and in more recent times, I've called him more often because he's getting older and I have a little more knowledge than he does in certain areas that can be beneficial to him. Basically it boils down to I've for-given him, but he can't forgive me for knowing that he did these things.

Years later, members of the Rasmussen clan would cash in big on their initial investment in ESPN. The family had originally invested a total of $39,000. Bill individually put up $9,000 (on a credit card), and thereby owned 12.32 percent of ESPN until cash-out time came around. But when the hour arrived for the cutting of the big fat *check, at least nine claims had been filed representing other parties' interests, most of them banks, who sought to recover money loaned to Scott or Bill Rasmussen. The final Rasmussen payout would reach a total of $3,414,866.51 — not bad for a thirty-nine-grand investment, and according to Bill Rasmussen, an obscure IRS tax law led the family to receive even larger sums in a second payout roughly two years later. Nevertheless, Don Rasmussen was none too pleased with his allocation. Years of pre-payout strong-arming by brother Bill meant that as early as December of 1978, Don had effectively lost control of his 2 percent stake. When that $3,414,866.51 check arrived, Don's share was a mere $403,337.*

And just like that, the Rasmussens were no more at ESPN.

GEORGE BODENHEIMER, *President:*

I wrote a letter to Jim Dullaghan about a job, and he said, "Sure, come on up." He walked me down to the head of human resources at ESPN, Barry Black, who literally interviewed me without looking up. I had an economics degree from a good-standing university in Ohio — Denison — and he looked at my résumé and said I was qualified to be a driver. Then he asked me if I would mind shoveling snow. I said, "Not if you tell me where you keep your shovel."

My dad and I went out that night to a very famous restaurant in Greenwich called the Clam Box. We had some beer and clam chowder and he gave me some great advice that I always mention to kids looking for work. He said, "If you think the sports-television business would be a good career, then if they call you, you should accept the job. It doesn't matter what the pay is or what the job is. You should make a career decision, not a money decision." So we agreed there at the bar at the Clam Box that if ESPN called with an offer for a driver position, I would take it. Ten days later, they called.

One of the big parts of the driver job at Bristol in those days—and I'm not sure if it's still that way—was you were constantly making two or three trips a day to the Hartford Airport, not only to pick up Federal Express packages, which had our programming, like tape-delayed college football, but you were also driving talent, executives, and producers back and forth to the airport. I quickly figured out this was a great opportunity because I had you for forty minutes in my car. I remember I would really pepper executives and talent about what they did and if they liked their jobs.

I was also in the mail room, which once again ended up being a fantastic opportunity for me. As someone in charge of delivering the mail, moving boxes, or whatever else needed to be done, I had an opportunity to meet everybody. I never had trouble mixing up with new people, so, for me, it was actually a magnificent opportunity to learn what they did. There was zero formality, and there were about 150 people here at the time.

DICK VITALE:

George Bodenheimer was my driver, and he used to pick me up at the airport all the time. Even for such a young guy, there was something great about him. But he was worried about the future. He would always say, "Where am I going with this job? I got a great college education, but I'm working in the mail room, and driving to pick up guys like you." I used to tell him, "George, be patient, man. Someday you are going to make it big."

GEORGE BODENHEIMER:

Australian rules football was one of our bedrocks and we put up a graphic on the screen that said, kind of in ESPN style, "We don't know the rules either. If you would like to know the rules, send us a postcard." And we got fifty thousand postcards.

CHRIS LaPLACA, *Senior Vice President of Communications:*

It was crazy. Some kids in Florida started an Australian rules football league in their hometown, they liked it so much.

BOB LEY:

When Johnny Carson did his first joke in the mid- to early eighties about Australian rules football on ESPN, I said, "Oh, man, it's a crossover moment.

Carson's watching, which is nice, but also it takes you to a whole other realm."

GEORGE GRANDE:

We were doing reports in '81 from Super Bowl XV in New Orleans. One night, we were rushing to get to the airport to send the tapes back, and Fred Muzzy and I didn't have any packing material. I said, "Muzz, get some paper," because we didn't want the tapes to rattle around or break, and he says, "I don't have any paper, but hold on." He goes off to another room, comes back, and closes up the box. I said, "What did you put in there?" He said, "My underwear." I said, "Was it clean or dirty?" He said, "Dirty." So we sent the tapes back to Bristol with Muzzy's dirty underwear and socks in there so the tapes wouldn't move around. I told the guys when I called, "When this box comes in from the airport, open it very slowly!"

TOM ODJAKJIAN, *Director of College Sports:*

The day I started at ESPN was the day Major League Baseball went on strike in 1981. So ESPN, which of course didn't have the rights to the majors, said, "Let's do minor-league baseball." And since I didn't have any assignments yet, they said, "Let the new guy jump on it." So I became the minor-league expert and picked all the games. I tried to find some hook, like Yankees versus Red Sox minor-league teams, or Cal Ripken Jr. highly thought of as a minor-league player. We got a lot of attention for doing live minor-league baseball to fill the fans' needs during the strike.

It was also my job to outline the twenty-four-hour schedule. Back then, we aired so many things that had been taped, and we repeated a lot, so live events weren't driving the schedule. In order to keep track of what was on, I did weekly charts, and I would literally color them with Magic Markers. I remember red was boxing for blood, brown was rodeo, green was golf, and blue was swimming. There wasn't that much original programming.

GEORGE BODENHEIMER:

I spent about 90 or 120 days in the mail room before I was promoted to the videotape library. And I remember vividly that my first shifts there were 4:00 p.m. to midnight and then midnight to 8:00 a.m., so I saw all the different sides of the place. But I remember sitting in the tape library one afternoon, minding my own business, when a producer barged through the door and says, "You! You know how to run camera?" And I'm like, "Well, no." He says, "Good, come with me." And, like, two minutes later, I'm operating a camera for a college football program. But I quickly came to the conclusion that my interest was more in sales and marketing than in television production. And then I went to meet the heads of those areas and because of the informal nature of the place, you could easily ask, "Can I come by and have a cup of coffee with you?" So I met the heads of the sales and marketing groups and basically concluded that I would take whatever opportunity I could get to move into either the affiliate area or the advertising sales areas.

CHRIS BERMAN:

In '83, the ABC affiliate in San Francisco was looking at me to be their sports guy. The GM loved me. They'd changed news directors and they were worried. They wanted me. I don't know if many people know about this one: Giants, 49ers, the whole bunch. I wasn't from there, but man, did I love that city. I always imagined that's what I'd do.

SAL MARCHIANO:

He said, "I got an offer to go to KGO, ABC's owned and operated station in San Francisco." And he says, "They offered me $100,000." And I said, "Well, what are you making here?" He says, "Well, I'm making $35,000." I said, "How old are you?" Now, I think he said twenty-seven. I said, "Chris, you know, this is gonna be bigger than KGO, and if I were your age, I would never leave here. I don't care what they're offering you. This is gonna be bigger than KGO."

CHRIS BERMAN:

It was me and another guy. They picked the other guy. They wound up being afraid I was too hard-core about sports. Had they picked me, I was going. But I wound up being in San Francisco for the game that changed the history of pro football. I was there for the catch. Montana. Clark. Unbelievable. The game's over. The place is erupting and we're running on the field to get interviews. One of the greatest moments in my career. Then I have to ask Tom Landry good questions after a one-point loss. This shit isn't easy. I'm twenty-five.

So now, everybody's interviewed for the first time in the brief little history of ESPN, and we're going to drive like frickin' Steve McQueen in *Bullitt* up to the city of San Francisco to KRON, Channel 4. I'm writing the piece in the car, and they're going to give us an editor who we've never met to get it on the 11:00 p.m. show, which was 8:00 p.m. where we were. We run in there, and it's about 6:35. We sit down with tapes and interviews, and we're going to edit a piece for five minutes, including footage of the game and shots from down in the field. You have five seconds to make a decision. ESPN never attempted anything like this. We got it done at 7:51. It was a brave new world for us.

BILL FITTS:

Chris showed some talent early on, but the funny thing was, he kept on wanting to go out in the field. I told him, "Chris, we got a million guys out there, you don't want to be out there, you want to be here, where you're at an anchor's desk." I could tell he didn't agree with me, and so we tried to get him out there from time to time, but at some point I remember he did come to me and say, "I guess you were right. This is where I wanted to be."

STEVE SABOL, *President, NFL Films:*

We had an x's and o's show that was turned down by all the networks. It was a convention-puncturing idea, because no one thought at the time that you could use coaching film, showing all twenty-two [players]. But Allie Sherman was really good; he could explain things and simplify them. Chris Berman was like the host, and I was sort of like a trained observer in there. I remember when we started, Chris was just sort of developing his shtick, and I thought it was really funny, but Allie couldn't stand it. Allie thought that the show should be really serious about football, and of the three of us, he was the only one qualified to do it. But it also couldn't be *entirely* all that, and anytime Chris would interject any of his personality, whenever we took a break, Allie would stand up and say, "Chris, come here, I want to talk with you." And he'd take him into the men's room. And lecture him. And he'd say, "People don't care about what you have to say about football. I'm the expert. They want to hear me. You are just here to tee it up and send it over to me." But I was also the producer of the show, and I would pull Chris over and say, "Hey Chris, keep doing what you're doing. It's great, we love it, don't let Allie intimidate you." So I felt bad for Chris because he was getting two different types of instructions.

CHIP DEAN, *Director*:

I worked the overnight with Tom Mees and Chris Berman. I'm not sure there was ever a better team on *SportsCenter* than those guys. They were probably two of the more knowledgeable sports guys I've ever met, and they were passionate about what they did. They had personality. They sort of rubbed off each other. They sort of hit on each other on air. And they could wing it. Back then, we had a lot of young people working on the show; things weren't perfect. It wasn't the glossy *SportsCenter* of today. It was more a pure fun kind of experience, and those guys were witty and fun. We used to do the 2:30 show and have beer waiting. To us, the 2:30 show was seven o'clock at night. We lost track of time. For two years I worked from 7:00 at night to 4:00 in the morning. It didn't matter. My wife was working during the day and I never saw her. But the show was a blast.

GREG GUMBEL:

At one point, they cut the eleven o'clock *SportsCenter* down to fifteen minutes, of which the first seven and a half were going to be live for the West Coast and the other part replayed from the earlier show.

That's how insignificantly they thought of *Sports-Center* at the time.

Scotty fought the advent of teleprompters. His argument, and he turned out to be entirely correct, was that if it was up there on the prompter, people were going to read it even if the stuff was wrong. And that's exactly what happened sometimes. The guy who really tried to keep things on the straight and narrow was George Grande. He voiced our complaints and took the brunt of the criticism for the other anchors. He knew how to do things the right way.

BOB RAUSCHER, *Vice President of Production:*

At Super Bowl XXIII in Miami, with Montana passing against the Bengals in the second half, I remember sitting there in the press box and realizing my eyes were closing. I had been going nonstop for a week plus, and I was exhausted, but I was telling myself, "Whoa, here I am at the Super Bowl, you gotta wake up."

BILL CREASY:

I lived at 80 Central Park West, 68th Street, right up from ABC, and Evey called me one day around noon. He was at the bar at 21, and told me to get my ass down there. We were alone at the bar, and he had been drinking, and he said, "I'm going to fire Chet. It's over. Do you have any names?" I gave him three names, one of which was Bill Grimes. I didn't know

Bill Grimes personally, but while I was at CBS, Bill had run CBS Radio, and I always admired the way CBS Radio was run.

ROGER WERNER:

Chet was a programming guy who bought rights and made decisions about producing games, and he was very good at that, but he wasn't the manager of a start-up business. Bill Grimes worked at CBS Radio, was a very bright guy, so as part of the consulting work, we recommended that he come on board. Getty hired him.

BILL GRIMES, *CEO*:

I was living in Darien, Connecticut, working at CBS Radio, and Richard Duffy, a marketing consultant, said to me on the train one morning, "I just got a call from a headhunter for a job opening as the number-two guy at ESPN, and I'm not interested, but I gave him your name." I vaguely remember seeing something about the company in *Ad Age* but didn't really know anything about it. The headhunter called me later and we met. Then I met Roger Werner's boss at McKinsey, Carter Bales. Then it was time for Stu Evey.

Stu told me to come meet him at an apartment on the East Side of Manhattan at nine o'clock in the morning. I had never met him. So I rang the bell, and a voice comes on and says, "Come up to the fourth floor." I went up, and the door was slightly ajar, so I pushed it open. The first thing I saw was a table with empty pizza boxes and beer bottles and I think some whiskey bottles. It was obviously the remnants of a party the night before. Then I heard some voices, and this guy comes out, and he's buttoning his shirt. This was Evey. And here I expected, because it was an oil-company executive, to have a real formal-type meeting. So we're sitting in this living room stinking of stale cigarette smoke and booze, and Evey produces this folder and says, "We know all about you. Are you interested in the job?" And I said yeah. That was the interview. He didn't ask me one other question.

I was thinking, here Stu was, offering me a job reporting to a guy that I haven't even met yet.

CHET SIMMONS:
Stu and I both hired Grimes. After I met him, I had to get Stu to sign off on it.

BOB PRONOVOST:
Stu Evey was dating this woman who everybody thought was a stripper—and he used to show up with her, and everybody would kind of ogle when she would walk in with him, because here is this big shot at an oil company, and it was kind of a maverick thing to have a guy who owns a big chunk of your company show up with a woman who looked like a hooker—or, excuse me, a stripper. It was kind of odd.

CHET SIMMONS:

I quickly realized that Stu and Bill were spending a lot of time together, and I think they were forming a relationship that worked to both of their benefits. Bill was one of the few guys that could stand Stu and work with him for his own benefit.

BILL GRIMES:

The first time I went to L.A. for a meeting with Stu, it was at the Getty Oil Building on Wilshire. Stu said, "Be over tomorrow morning at 11:00," and when I got there, we chatted for a while, then got into the elevator to go upstairs. I asked him who we were going to meet with, but it turned out the company bar was upstairs, and it opened at 11:30. As soon as we sat down, a waiter came over and poured Stu three fingers of vodka straight up into a tumbler. Stu would have his periods where he'd lose his train of thought, but most of the time in a business setting he could function pretty effectively.

As for Chet, he had been involved in television programming; I came up through radio and sales. I was from CBS; he was from NBC. Chet had populated ESPN with lots of NBC people, and it was kind of uncomfortable for me. And in meetings with Chet, Scotty Connal, and Bob Gutkowski—and I forget the affiliate guy at the time that I later fired—I always felt like a bit of an outsider, and I think the resentment built a little bit.

ROGER WERNER:

I spent a couple months riding the commuter train with Bill. We used to ride home at the end of the day and have a couple drinks in the bar car and go over the issues and numbers and where we thought the business could go. He and I became friends, and he asked me around January, February of '82, could I come on board and become COO and take on some other operating responsibilities, and I agreed. In March of '82, I left McKinsey and came on board full-time. By that point, I had fallen in love with the company, so it was not a difficult thing for me to say, hell, yes, I'll leave McKinsey and join up and be the COO at ESPN. It was something I was wedded to at that point emotionally and psychologically.

BILL GRIMES:

In my opinion, it was the best thing that happened to ESPN during my tenure.

ROGER WERNER:

The company's biggest challenge was top-line revenue, selling advertising and fixing our distribution deals. Bill and I created an executive office in New York, but we worked in Bristol those early years one to two days a week when we weren't on the road calling on customers.

When it came to revenue, ESPN was wide open to opportunities — even if there wasn't a ball, bat, or racquet in sight.

DENISE AUSTIN, *Fitness Instructor:*

I went to the guys up at ESPN and said, "I can give you a trim-and-travel TV show," and they told me I needed to find a sponsor who would pay for production and pay me, and then they'd air it. It was like a barter situation.

Since I was kind of like the first spokesperson for Reebok, I went to [Reebok chairman] Paul Fireman himself and said, "Paul, I have a great opportunity to do a travel exercise show. It will broaden the base of people who might want to watch aerobics because they'll also want to see beautiful locations." He said, "Oh, my gosh, this is great, sure." ESPN was really impressed that I had found my own funding, and we went on the air. They aired it twice every morning, 5:30 and 11:30, and every week I would come from a different resort. I wound up going all over the Caribbean. We had this amazing following; over a million people watching every week. Some would follow along, some would tune in to check out the place where we were coming from, and some just wanted to see what I was wearing.

One of the coolest things that happened to me as a woman in this business was when I found out I was pregnant. I went up to ESPN to tell them and was really nervous about their reaction, because here it is, this guys' channel, and I was afraid they wouldn't want me in that condition. But Steve and the other guys were so sweet. They just said, "Are you kidding, of course we still want you." I filmed my shows pregnant, and then, you know what? My ratings shot up after I had the baby. People wanted to see how I looked after giving birth, and they wanted to see how long it would take me to flatten out my stomach again. I spent ten years doing those shows for ESPN in the morning.

MIKE SOLTYS, *Vice President*
of Communications:

My favorite thing about Denise was that when she was introduced to people, within a short time, she would say, "Touch my tummy," as a demonstration of her steel abs. I got to experience that firsthand.

SAL MARCHIANO:

When Stallone starred and produced the movie *Rocky III,* the night before it premiered, Stallone bought two and a half hours of time on ESPN and staged his own fights at Caesars Palace. About a minute before we go on air, he freezes on me. He told me, "I can't do this." I said, "What?" He said, "I've never done live television." And he really freaked. I said, "Just calm down. Just listen to me. All you have to do is answer a couple of questions. I'll lead you." We got through the opening, and he even came back between some rounds.

TOM ODJAKJIAN:

We did an auction of Elvis Presley's car, and we did a fashion show that aired at midday for a few weeks. Budweiser had a lot of influence in those early years. As part of their exclusive deal, they actually had the right to put on a number of events, I think it was ten a year that had the Budweiser name on it. So we did Anheuser-Busch horse jumping, and even Bud Light hydroplane racing.

These were wild and rowdy days. ESPN was like a mining town in the Old West—the Gold Rush days of basic cable complete with drinking, carousing, and copulating. Adultery was practically an indoor sport. When one husband contracted a venereal disease from an extramarital fling, he had little choice but to confess to his wife—who decided not to leave him.

BILL GRIMES:

I remember Roger Werner coming in and saying, "We gotta get rid of this apartment on 47th Street"—which was a remnant from Getty—"because the mail boys got a couple of our secretaries hooking over there." Hooking! That's what he said. I said, "What are you talking about?" He said, "They're making money after work when no one's there. It's getting out of control."

ANDY BRILLIANT:

It was an apartment that Evey kept, but we all had access to it and it was well stocked with liquor. Oh, my God, that was amazing! And whenever Evey was there with his entourage, they would destroy the place with liquor, drugs, hookers, and whatever else they were doing. They had to replace furniture half the time. Everybody used the apartment for one thing or another.

There was a time when all the senior executives working in New York—a lot of us were there at Lexington and Third—were all in competition with each other to have the best-looking secretaries. And I must say, mine was the best by far; she was absolutely drop-dead gorgeous. My secretary started off very well kept and dressed and professional, but she was a lot of fun and we had a lot of fun together. Then I noticed toward the end, she started getting more and more disheveled, and she'd come in sometimes with what looked like a modified sweat suit on. Her performance was really falling off, and I was about to let her go, when she came in one day to say she'd met some lawyer in a bar and he was offering her much more money than I was paying and unless I was going to match, she had to leave. And I said fine, I can't match it, go.

About six months later, she called and said, "Do you want to have lunch?" I said sure. And I went out to lunch, and she said, "Do you know where I've been all this time?" I said, "No, where have you been? I thought you were working for this other law firm." She said, "No, I've been in a detox facility." I said, "What are you talking about?" She said, "You didn't know I was addicted to coke?" I said, "No, I had no idea. How in the hell could you afford it on your salary?" She said she was doing tricks. I said, "What are you talking about?" She said the mail-room guy was keeping the apartment for these girls, and all these good-looking girls were turning tricks in the apartment. It was going on right under our noses. And the receptionist was a really good-looking girl, and she was blowing FedEx delivery guys in the bathroom after work hours.

About the same time, one of the executives found a vial of cocaine on the floor of his office, and Werner walked into the conference room once, and all these girls were in there. One was cutting the other's girl's hair, they were playing some kind of music really loud, and there were a couple girls on the conference-room table. That's basically where it all started falling apart. It was amazing what was going on with these girls.

The company would have Christmas parties up at some horrible place in Bristol. A couple of them were drunken orgies, but who could blame these people out in the middle of nowhere? It became like a big frat party. There were a lot of drugs being done in the bathroom. There was quite a bit of screwing going on afterward, a lot of it extramarital. But everybody went back to business the next workday.

ELLEN BECKWITH:

When I went to ESPN in 1980, there were eighty people in the company. We worked all day and into the night. We had no social life because we worked all the time. So, what we did is we became social with each other, because who else had the same hours? And we became very social. Very social. There were a lot of interoffice romances going on because you didn't have a chance to meet anybody else. People were working seven days a week, so it was no fun. People who you never thought would get divorced were getting divorced, and a lot of those guys didn't have any regard for women.

GAYLE GARDNER, *Anchor:*

When I first got there, it was kind of small, and I was the only woman at the time on most of the assignments. I was put on *SportsCenter* and did cut-ins during events. We had to work really hard back in those days. We would do three *SportsCenters*—the seven o'clock, the eleven o'clock, and then the late one, too, at two o'clock in the morning. We worked these horrific hours. They really got their money's worth.

SAL MARCHIANO:

Bornstein once took a trip with me to a *Saturday Night Fight* in Detroit, and I'll never forget that when we were coming back that Sunday, he said, "You do this every week?" I said, "Yeah." He said, "This is tough." I said, "Yeah, I know. I gotta tell ya, it's ruining my marriage." And eventually, it did.

One time I went into a meeting, and Scotty Connal said to me, "I just had a woman, one of our employees, leave here complaining that she has no sex life." And Scotty said, "How do I answer that?" I didn't want to tell him what was really going on. This woman must have been very proper, because there was a lusty sex life going on there. There was screwing in the hallways.

Okay, maybe not in the hallways, but there were a couple of stairwell stories. There's a couple stories in the office late at night. I did not hang out there. I was gone. I didn't go to the condos where people lived and had the parties. There were drugs in the building, that I knew. There was one guy who dealt pot. But I stayed away from everybody. I just came and went.

FRED GAUDELLI:

There was a lot of betting going on in the early days of ESPN. There'd be people saying, "I got ten on the Giants today" or "I've got twenty on the Colts today" or "I've got so-and-so in a parlay." I mean, all that stuff went on. There are people there now in some pretty high positions who ran the gambling operation back then, or who were a part of it.

BILL SHANAHAN:

Here you are in this start-up, it's very loose and you're making it up as you go, and I look back and I realize that those who were into betting on sports were working at a place where the only other place you could be where that much information was coming in about games was Las Vegas. And here these guys are, handling all this information and spending their whole workday, along with the talent, talking about it, and analyzing it. Who could resist?

Oh, man, it almost took over for a while. You had to be in on the culture, but the references that would show up on air! Just very subtle things like, Chargers-Giants and the Giants won, and you could hear the tone of voice and the sigh, and "no, they didn't cover," and what's going on in the studio is one anchor and another shaking his head, you know, and directors getting into their ears and saying, "Yeah, it killed me." We actually ended up doing a show called *NFL Line by Line,* and it was exactly that. Chris was the main anchor, and Paul Maguire was on it, and Fred Muzzy produced it, and it was nothing but a half-hour analysis going into the weekend of what the point spreads were. We dropped that show when we really started competing for an NFL contract.

BOB PRONOVOST:

There was a promotion going on in San Diego one time, and the game started half an hour before it was listed on the wires. Some of the guys who used to bet realized the Giants had scored six runs in the first inning before the game was supposed to start. So everybody got on the phone and called their bookies. Now the great moral of this story is that 6–0 Giants became 7–4 Giants, and then it was tied and actually went into extra innings. The Padres wound up winning the game and everybody lost.

Berman was doing *SportsCenter* that night, and I was the one who had to tell him in his ear that the Padres had beaten the Giants. I think he said something like, "And in a game that had a little less than passing interest around here, the Padres have beaten the Giants." You could hear the whole place go, "Oh, my God," as they said good-bye to their weekly salary.

Were we stupid? What can I tell you? You learn your lesson and move on. But that was something. It's like going to Vegas and being told you're going to get a twenty, and the only way you'll lose is if the dealer has a twenty-one. And that's what happened.

SAL MARCHIANO:

There were nights when they gave partial scores because guys had bet on games, and there were a lot of times when there were second and third meanings to the scores, like if a guy had bet on the game and he had the right side, he would be giddy, or if he was behind, there would be some ribbing that the audience couldn't get. I heard, and don't know if it's confirmed, that the Connecticut State Police actually had recordings of people betting using the office phones.

ROGER WERNER:

The company was on a razor's edge—liquidation or continuing operations; what's it going to be? It was almost a coin toss. We did the analysis on both sides, and I concluded there was a business there but it was going to take five years, and over $100 million to make it work. There were no easy fixes. Miraculously, the Getty board said okay. Stu Evey may have been a character, but to his credit, he kept the cash flowing from the Getty board. He kept the whole thing going.

But when we went out to board meetings in L.A., we would literally be on call 24/7. I would get calls at two in the morning, and Evey would say, "Roger, goddammit, you're the worst manager I've ever had. You fucked this up, you did that...," you know. He'd get raw, and launch into some tirade immediately. He'd wake you up out of a sound sleep and say, "Ah, hello, who is this?" I mean, it was just ridiculous. But that's what Chet lived with for that first year and a half. It was ugly.

STEVE BORNSTEIN:

Evey was a difficult man. Impossible. I didn't work directly for him, but I certainly heard from him, and he was always difficult. I don't think he speaks well of me, because he thinks I ignored him and I don't give him the credit he thinks he deserves. I did ignore him, so that part's accurate.

I always used to say Bristol was an hour too far away—from everywhere, particularly New York City. I had made a deal with Evey that the day that we actually turned a profit, when the company was no longer hemorrhaging money, he would buy us a helicopter. Until then, I ended up doing a barter deal with another Connecticut-based company, Timex, which was outside Hartford and had a helicopter that went back and forth to New York twice a day. I gave them ad inventory to sell watches, and they gave us a certain amount of access to their helicopters. We had just concluded this deal, and Evey made a little state visit to Bristol to review what was going on business-wise. It was a big deal. Grimes was president at the time, and we did this massive presentation to Evey and a couple other Getty executives.

After the meeting, we put Evey and the Getty guys on the chopper to take them back to New York. Evey was, of course, drunk as a fuckin' skunk, and he opened up the helicopter door while it was flying. The pilots then had to do an emergency landing, which is, I guess, the regulation. Needless to say, they reamed out Evey. He was just basically being Evey at five o'clock on any given day. So they go up again, and sure enough, Evey starts fucking around and opens up the goddamn door again, and they have to make another emergency landing. They totally ream him out again and go up a third time. And here's where my facts get blurred. I don't know how many times they did it, but it was more than two; it could have been three or four times that Evey opened it up. Needless to say, the next day I get an irate fuckin' phone call from my counterpart at Timex: "The fuckin' deal is off! You can never use the helicopter again."

STUART EVEY:

Ted Turner came to me in '81 or '82 at a cable convention and said he wanted to meet with me privately, so we went to his hotel room, where he had all these papers spread out about how great CNN and ESPN would be together. I knew he had a reputation as a character, a very bombastic guy, and he was planning some ridiculous moves — offering bids on rights to college football games that were just sky-high and things like that. He just threw money away because he didn't care about debt — all he had was debt. The cable companies were supporting him along the way to keep his programming, but I knew I couldn't sell his plan at Getty.

In 1982, ESPN found itself with the chance to finally air live football, when a previously unavailable package came to the market from the NCAA. Even though the games were only from Division II schools, Simmons was desperate to buy them. But Ted Turner, among others, was salivating as well, and he had deeper pockets—plus a willingness to empty them.

BOB GUTKOWSKI:

The only college football we had was on next-day delay. It was never live. Chet had a very good relationship with Walter Byers, who ran the NCAA, and this was going to be an important bid for us. We worked really hard on our presentation—NCAA football, Division II, Saturday night. There were three of us bidding: USA Network, ESPN, and TBS, which was Turner's Superstation. Now, Chet, because of his relationship with Byers, had an agreement with Walter that if it wasn't going our way, Walter would call us and give us a heads-up. So we give our presentations, and we sit in a suite, and Chet gets the call, hangs up, and says, "Walter said you're not even close, you got to come back." So we worked up our numbers, and we wound up eventually bidding $7 million for the two-year package. But this is how crazy the cable business was: USA bid $900,000 and TBS bid $17 million! They outbid us by $10 million for no rhyme or reason. We believed Turner bid seventeen because in Atlanta he was Channel 17. Regardless, they outbid us by $10 million, which back then was like $250 to $300 million. It made no sense. We later heard they lost $10 to $12 million on it.

STUART EVEY:
Fast-forward to a party at the Playboy mansion that I was at with my daughter. We were waiting for our car, and Ted came up to us. I guess we'd both had a couple drinks. Ted motioned to the woman he was with and said, "I'd like you to meet my wife." I knew it wasn't his wife, and he gave me a chuckle. I said, "Well, it's nice to meet you, and I'd like you to meet my daughter." Now, my daughter was very good-looking, and Ted said, "Yeah, sure, your daughter." Well, things weren't going too well with me at home, so that didn't sit well with me. I didn't punch him, but I grabbed him by the collar in a fit of immediate anger. We didn't get into a fight, but some people had to separate us.

In February 1982, Stuart Evey made a play to acquire TV rights to the new USFL football league. New league plus still-new network; it sounded like a natural fit, and Evey would look brilliant if the USFL eventually posed a serious challenge to the mighty NFL. But the USFL's asking price was $6 million, with apparently no wiggle room, and the Getty board had approved only $5 million for Evey to make the buy. In search of $1 million, Evey turned back to Anheuser-Busch.

In thinly veiled desperation, Evey made the call. He talked Anheuser-Busch into pitching in half a million, but he had to make concessions. Among them: he agreed to guarantee that ESPN announcers would mention Budweiser every five minutes during USFL telecasts—in addition to running regular paid commercials. Buoyed by this near-success, Evey went back to the USFL and told them they had a deal, even though he was still half a million short.

Although the board let his little discrepancy ride, Evey was increasingly paranoid about the millions of Gettybucks he was spending—and losing. ESPN was becoming a sinkhole. Getty had already gone $50 million beyond its original $10 million investment. Then there was something called a "burn rate"—$8 million per month going out that was not covered by revenue coming in. At this pace, Evey calculated, losses could reach $150 million by the end of the year. Meanwhile, Chet Simmons was interested in the new football league for non-Bristol reasons.

CHET SIMMONS:

I got a phone call from my friend Mike Trager, and he told me about a new football league that was being put together. Then we talked about my discomfort with Evey; it was something that was beginning to gnaw at me. I still didn't have control of the thing the way I wanted.

STUART EVEY:

Chet never quite understood the pressure I had at Getty. When he was at NBC Sports, he was just responsible for the on-air look at NBC. But at ESPN, he was responsible for everything: human resources, contracts, purchasing of programming, hiring and firing, on and on. I represented the parent company, with me as head of ESPN. Chet never appreciated that. He was told a number of times that my people could not get timely information from him in which to incorporate our budgets and planning. He was very difficult to get ahold of when we called him, and he did not like his people talking directly to Getty. So it became a major problem.

CHET SIMMONS:

I got a package one day and there were these portraits of Evey and the president of Getty. So I told my assistant, "Get Evey on the phone." I said, "Stuart, I got these lovely, lovely portraits, what do I do with them?" He said, "Well, you hang them in the lobby." And I said, "Why?" And he said, "Well, every part of the company hangs these two pictures—the guy who's the chairman of the company and the guy who runs that division." I said, "So I should take down the picture of the great shortstop and put you up?" "Well," he said, "everybody has it." When I hung up,

I turned to my assistant and said, "Please put them in the closet."

We were in Vegas at one of those industry shows, and we had a room where we invited advertisers and other buyers to come have a drink and hear about ESPN. We even had a mock layout of what ESPN was going to look like in a couple years. I saw Stu across the room, and he looked really angry. I went up to him and asked, "Hey Stu, what's the matter? You look like you're pissed off." And he said, "Arrrgh," turned around, and left! I jogged after him and said, "What's going on?" Then he said to me, "Well, you're introducing everybody to everybody else and you haven't paid one bit of attention to me."

He just couldn't keep his hands off things. I began to realize that this toy he had was so important to him that he would do what he wanted to do, irrespective of other people's opinions. He'd hire people and make suggestions to other people around me by calling them directly. The force of his will and his position made it difficult for people to stay away from him or avoid him when he would come and talk to them. I just had to sit back and let him do it and try to undo whatever problems his involvement generated. He liked me to talk to him every day and tell him everything that I was doing— everything. And I refused to do that. It wasn't anything I was keeping secret, but I had work to do, and the work was not to be on the phone with him 24/7.

ROGER WERNER:

Chet used to complain to us bitterly through the year and a half of consulting—1980 right on through the end of '81—quite bitterly about Stu's midnight phone calls and verbal abuse. It was a pretty strained relationship. Chet obviously was trying to protect himself from a boss who had a volcanic temper and was rather unpredictable.

Getting panicky, in early 1982, over the mounting millions in ESPN losses and what the Getty board might decide to do about them, and knowing he needed even more money to bid on cream-of-the-crop programming, Stu Evey decided the best course was to spread the absence of wealth around, to sell a minority interest in ESPN to the highest bidder. Evey's first move was to once again get Ed Hookstratten to circulate rumors of Getty's intention to sell ESPN. Evey's plan to pit ABC's Roone Arledge against CBS ultimately succeeded. (NBC was not included in the effort to avoid a conflict of interests given that many of Hookstratten's clients— including Tom Brokaw, Bryant Gumbel, and Don Ohlmeyer—worked there.) ABC agreed to purchase at least 10 percent of the company within the next two years; it also had an option to up its stake to 49 percent in five years. CBS would not match the offer. A key in the negotiation was Evey's insistence that the deal include a programming association between ABC and

ESPN, which would help with inventory. The two sides subsequently argued fiercely over the fees ESPN would need to pay to obtain certain levels of programming, with lower-level programming remaining free. That dispute stemmed primarily from ABC's tardy realization that it had been "outnegotiated": Evey had overvalued ESPN.

STUART EVEY:

I pulled a hell of a deal with ABC Sports to buy 10 percent of the company. A hell of a deal. That was the biggest thing that probably saved ESPN—when I worked CBS against ABC, with them having no knowledge that I had any interest in selling it, other than a rumor that was planted by Ed Hookstratten. That did not sit well with Chet, nor anybody else in Bristol, but having the money responsibility, it sat perfectly well with me and obviously it became the turning point in the initial acceptance of ESPN.

CHRIS LaPLACA:

We had a horrible, horrible snowstorm up in Bristol—this was soon after ABC's initial investment—and because our generators were outside, they froze and the power went off. So we were off the air. They called this crusty old engineer who lived on a mountain and told him we needed him to get us back on the air. He had this old truck and somehow made it through the storm. He surveyed the scene, then took out a pair of jumper cables and started up the generator. He essentially jump-starts the network! Now if you're a publicist like I am, this is a great story, so I go crazy with it. The next day, there's a big headline in the *New York Post,* I think it was, "Engineer Jump Starts Network."

Then I get a call asking me to come to the office of the guy in charge of engineering, and I'm thinking he's going to say to me, "Thanks for giving my guys some love." Instead, he's upset and asks me why I talked about it to the press. He says, "I didn't tell anybody at ABC that we were off the air for three hours, and they didn't know until they read it in the papers."

CHET SIMMONS:
I decide I'm going to meet the people from the United States Football League. And we had a nice meeting. God, every one of them just oozed money — I mean, really big-time money.

STUART EVEY:
One of my closest friends before and during ESPN's start-up was Bill Daniels. Daniels Communications became a real powerhouse when cable companies began to expand, and he owned the Los Angeles Express when the USFL was started. Daniels called me after a meeting of the United States Football League owners when they first were formed and said, "Stu, I hate to call you about this. But a number

of the owners know I know you, and they wanted me to talk to you about Chet Simmons and the USFL commissioner's job." I immediately said, "Jesus Christ, Bill, cut it out. You know we're right on the cusp of making this thing work, and, my God, that would take the heart out of me." Well, that was bullshit, but I continued anyway. "Look, I can't stand in the way of his career, and I certainly won't."

BILL GRIMES:

It was just awful, very, very difficult for Chet. I was very empathetic. Getty had a management meeting up at a place called Silverado up in Napa Valley. So Stu invited Chet and me to come and spend a day there. The idea was to meet the Getty people. But once we got there, you couldn't say good-bye to Stu in between sessions, after sessions, even after dinner — you had to hang with him. So he told Chet and me to join him for drinks, and right in front of me, he began to berate Chet. It was awful. It was a bad, bad, bad situation. And I felt horrible. And either the next day or later that night, Chet said to me, this is not your fault, and I just hate this prick.

CHET SIMMONS:

So I'm coming to the end of my contract and all this stuff comes at the same time, which is good and bad. So we go to a bar — figure that out — we're going to have a chat: Am I going to stay, am I going to go, what's going on? I said, "Stu, look, I love this company, I love this job. If you want me to stay, these are the things that you gotta do. Number one: get out of my hair. I know I've got to communicate with you, but get out of my hair. And you've got to make me an offer to stay that's incentive-based."

And after seven hours, eight hours, going over the same crap hour after hour after hour, he would not move on any of the conditions of re-upping me except that he'd stay out of my hair, which was bullshit, and this and that and little things, but he wouldn't do the big things. It was clear he wanted me to go, and I wanted to get rid of him. I put my hand out and said, "It's been great and I wish you luck."

I knew the USFL was having a meeting—I think we were in Chicago—and I walked from the bar to the hotel where they were having the meeting, and I walked in, and here are all these owners sitting around a table, and I said, "I accept your offer to be commissioner." And that was the end of that.

STUART EVEY:

When I met with Chet, it was very short and sweet. I expressed my disappointment that he was leaving, but the truth is, it relieved me a great deal. Bill Daniels couldn't have given me a better opportunity. I told everyone I was disappointed, but deep down, I wasn't.

Chet always had a chip on his shoulder for me, but

that's fine. No problem. You notice, however, that he lasted only one year as commissioner at the USFL.

CHET SIMMONS:

We had a party. Everybody had a couple of beers. I felt for every one of them. These are the kids that had helped me make this company. I gotta tell you, it was a very, very exciting part of my life, those two years up until the end, when all the crap came down on my head from Evey. And if you ask me, the greatest part of my life, it was ESPN. Without question.

BILL GRIMES:

I got a call from Stu—maybe in the middle of the night, and he was drunk, in my opinion, calling from Los Angeles. He said, "I'm firing Chet and I'm going to name you temporary head of ESPN." So I wrote him a letter and said I wasn't interested in being an interim anything. I told him I wasn't about to sit there while he went out to interview a lot of people, then bring somebody else in. And he responded very quickly—it may have been the same day or the next—and said, "The job's yours."

ROGER WERNER:

In those early days, we would go to Getty for board meetings and present our results. Stu would often suggest that we stay at his home, or close to his home, because we were essentially on call. We'd be presented with screwdrivers with three fingers of Stoli at seven o'clock in the morning, you know, to start the workday, and then we'd be dragged out to lunch somewhere for another two or three martinis. Then by 3:00 or 3:30, everyone's concentration would be wandering, and it would be time to go down to the country club and pull up a chair at that point. There was very little sober deliberation going on. We were kind of taking a sip and, you know, dumping stuff in wastebaskets, because we couldn't function this way. Stu was literally physiologically dependent at that point. He wasn't eating any food. All of his calories were coming right out of the bottle, and he would start at breakfast and go right through the day. He would get progressively harder and harder to deal with as you got closer to four o'clock in the afternoon, when the serious drinking would start up.

GEORGE GRANDE:
There's no way to overstate the legitimacy that Chet and Scotty brought to the company both inside and out. Give Bill Rasmussen the credit he is due—he had the idea—and Stu gets credit because his influence secured the Getty money. But Chet Simmons and Scotty Connal, in my mind, were a unique combination in sports television. Chet was brilliant, had great foresight, and could meet in a tank with sharks to battle them tooth and nail. Remember, the businesspeople in the sports profession can be very tough.

And then on the other hand, you've got Scotty, and nobody was ever better at running the production side. Without these two men, people would have looked at ESPN in the early days and said, "This is a lark; it's never going to make it." And in that case, that might have been right.

BILL GRIMES:

The dynamics of ESPN changed dramatically when Chet left to go to the USFL. All of a sudden it became New York—me, Roger, and Steve—against Bristol—Scotty, Bill Fitts, and a couple others. We all banded together. There would be no ESPN if it weren't for Scotty Connal and the people who surrounded him, but there was a line drawn between us and them, and after Chet left, that's when I began to say it's probably going to be time for some people to move on.

ABC's initial investment in ESPN introduced ABC executive Herb Granath to the small executive gang in Bristol. Granath, who had a strong bond with ABC founder Leonard Goldenson, would now become a key player for Evey, Grimes, and Werner. Granath understood the largely uncharted world of cable more than most broadcast executives did; he had been involved in several of ABC's joint efforts with cable already. He was more cautious than the ESPN guys, however, and very protective of what he considered the proper channels of communication.

The relationship between Granath and Grimes would be a pivotal one for both ESPN and ABC, and it would be a powerful reminder that first impressions not only matter but often have huge consequences.

BILL GRIMES:

Stu said to me, "ABC owns a piece of this thing now and the person you are going to be working with is this guy Herb Granath at ABC, and I want to get you two guys together." Now, to put this story in perspective, you need to know that I lived in Darien, Connecticut, and there is a line that divides it from the next town, Norwalk. Darien is kind of an upscale Waspy place, and Norwalk, to the east of Darien, is a blue-collarish kind of a town. This might sound completely trivial as you hear this but when I get to the point of the story, I think it makes a more significant point. So I go see Herb Granath, and we have a lovely, nice chat about things. Blah, blah, blah. There's a little pause, and I say to him, "Oh, by the way, where do you live?" And he says, "I live in Darien, Connecticut." I said, "What a coincidence! I do too. Whereabouts do you live?" And he says, "I live on Maywood Road." I said, "I'll be darned. I live on Maywood Road too." Now I see him clench up a little bit and his smile went away. And that's because there are only four or five houses on Maywood Road that are in Darien, and I lived in one of those houses; the rest of the houses — it's a street about a mile long — are in

Norwalk. So I said, well, what house are you in? We must be across the street. Oh, he says, "Oh, I'm at number such and such," and I just said, "Oh, yeah, you're in Norwalk." So he looked at me really, really annoyed, cold, angered, embarrassed that, on a simple thing like where he lived, he had to say he lived in Darien because it was more prestigious. The chances of me living on the same street and knowing that he really lived in Norwalk were ten thousand to one. But he knew that he had told the tiniest lie and he knew I knew it. It was a little thing. For all I know, I may have done the same thing myself. I'm not so much knocking what he did, but he told a little bit of a lie, and I think that caused him discomfort. I never ever brought it up again but that moment kind of established the tone of our relationship from then on.

Many of ESPN's initial contracts with cable operators were about to end, and a big game of chicken was about to begin.

ROGER WERNER:

Early on, some of the cable operators did have a nominal fee in the neighborhood of one or two cents that they paid to ESPN. Rasmussen's right when he says there were some of those. The problem was, those contracts also included other payments going the other way. So net, the essence of the contract, was we were paying them to carry the service. We ran the business as an ad-sales-only business for all the rest of 1980, '81, and '82.

BILL GRIMES:

Whenever I would look ahead, I would say, we're not going to be able to get enough ad revenue to make this thing profitable. We were buying more programming, and the ad revenues weren't coming. Then we're paying more nickels as every new cable subscriber came on in America. It won't work. Getty is not going to be patient forever.

ROGER WERNER:

The failure of CBS Cable was one of those watershed dates that opened a big window of opportunity for us. Cable stocks fell dramatically within one or two weeks. It was an obvious reaction, and the press was almost universally negative and predicting bad things for the cable industry. If CBS can't make it as a cable network programmer, how could anybody else like ESPN hope to succeed?

So a number of our affiliates, I think, were worried that another failure by another leading cable programming network in 1983 or '84 would be a terrible thing.

GEORGE BODENHEIMER:

About fourteen months after I started, this position was open for an account executive in Dallas, and much to my benefit, I was the only person inside the company who applied for the job. I had no sales experience, and on the flight down to Texas for the interview, I was reading trade magazines to try to pick up a few buzzwords and learn about the business. I guess I came off reasonably well at the interview, and I got the position. A week later, I'm driving around Texas, Arkansas, Oklahoma, Louisiana, Mississippi, selling this new crazy cable channel's twenty-four-hour sports to mom-and-pop cable operators in the Southwest.

I was the negotiator for hundreds of contracts throughout those five states, but we were still basically giving it away for free. But we were establishing the precedence of paying on a per-subscriber basis. If you were a cable operator with five thousand subscribers, we would say, "Pay us on a hundred subscribers at four cents a subscriber a month," which times twelve months is $48 a year times five years—we'd do a five-year deal—was how we got the $240.

Obviously that's not a significant amount of money, so we were still giving it away, but we were establishing the precedent, which was new at the time, of pay us a per-subscriber fee. Who wouldn't sign a contract for $48 a year for five years? It's like buying a shirt.

ROGER WERNER:
We went to the market with this sort of survival pitch essentially as follows: If you come in voluntarily

and do a new deal with us, we'll start your rate at four cents in 1983 or '84 and then we'll go to six cents the next year, then eight cents. Either rip up the old contract and have some protection for whatever the term of your new affiliation agreement is going to be, or pay the prevailing rate when your old deal expires. There was the specter that if we were still around—and we intended to be around—we'd be a much more expensive service.

BILL GRIMES:

We were thrown out of offices. I flew to Denver once to see a company called United Cable that TCI later bought. It was run by a guy by the name of Gene Schneider. He was a guy about my age who had been in the telephone business and then became one of the early cable founders and made big money. I had made an appointment with his secretary to see him, and I sat in a room for two hours waiting to see him, but he refused to see me.

ROGER WERNER:

J.C. [Sparkman, COO of TCI] kind of told us to get fucked and that TCI would never pay us a penny.

BILL GRIMES:

Cablevision was the first cable operator whose contract had expired that we were trying to get to be the first cable-system company to pay a fee. It was, in many ways, the worst operator to start with because they had some sports programming! Dolan was a tough guy. We had to threaten to turn ESPN off.

ANDY BRILLIANT:

It was an all-day negotiation that Bill, Roger, and I conducted with the Cablevision people on Long Island. They all got really pissed. There was a lot of walking out of the room and throwing stuff around. It got to the point where we really thought that there wasn't going to be a service.

BILL GRIMES:

There was yelling and screaming. We took quite a beating early on. They had five guys, and all of them were tough. But Andy played our tough ass, and Roger was the smart, brilliant guy. Dolan hadn't said a word. He kind of sat there. Roger called him the Buddha.

ROGER WERNER:

Essentially we were saying, guys, if you're not interested in paying a fee and you're really not interested in stepping up to the plate in the near term, tell us now and we'll pull the plug.

Nobody really wanted to deal with the idea that they were going to be paying for a product that had been free, but actually my recollection of this is that it was very stress-filled, it was very contentious.

ANDY BRILLIANT:

But at the end of the day, they blinked and agreed to pay us a dime per household. We breathed a massive sigh of relief. It was the first time we actually received validation that our service was worth something to the cable operators. I think that really put us on the map for good.

BILL GRIMES:

I'll never forget. We got in the car and stopped at the first bar we saw. It was a Mexican place. I know I had at least two margaritas. Then we called Evey on a pay phone. We didn't have cell phones. I said, "Stu, we got it. We got the toughest one. We got the deal." And from there it was not easy, but that was the start of it all.

STEVE BORNSTEIN:

Bill recognized we needed to make the change in order to survive, and Roger had the balls to roll up his sleeves and take on the cable operators. I'm telling you right now, it was those two guys who figured out the business. There were no ifs, ands, or buts. 'Cause nobody else was doing it. Nickelodeon wasn't doing it. MTV wasn't doing it. Nor was CNN.

They were the Butch and Sundance of cable's early years. Or maybe the Lewis and Clark. What Bill Grimes and

Roger Werner did was a little like the opening of the West in cable terms, because they enabled cable to become a big business. The beauty of it wasn't in the simple awareness that two revenue streams are better than one. A smart junior high school student could probably have figured that one out. No, the beauty was their realization that without the second stream, there was no business. Just a money-losing ego trip. ESPN would never have survived if it had been forced to rely only on ad sales for revenue. Several colleagues—among them Andy Brilliant and Roger Williams—contributed to the effort, but the whole enterprise would have crashed on the rocks and sunk without the inspired work of Grimes and Werner, disciples of the profit motive and unsung heroes of basic cable.

The advancement of a dual revenue stream in March of 1983: Step Number Three in ESPN's rise to world dominance.

BILL GRIMES:

Roger had something I didn't have—an MBA. I learned a lot from Roger. He thought in a wonderfully strategic way about all aspects of the company. And here's an example: This was, like, '83; at that time we had boxing one night and skiing, tennis, and a whole bunch of other stuff on the schedule. We were talking one day about the fact that there was a lot of college basketball becoming available. I said, "You know, we could get basketball six nights a week.

Our weekly ratings in prime would really go up." But Roger said, "That's true, we could probably get a better rating. But they're only numbers. We're now in the business of subscriber fees. So what we want is as diverse programming as possible. Even if a program like skiing or auto racing gets a lower rating, there are people who will never watch a basketball game. So we should now think a little bit differently." This was totally contrary to what I had grown up with in the business—rating, rating, rating. Get the highest ratings we can get. But Roger was right. We didn't want all our ratings from one thing, because it's only those hundred people who watch the skiing event that'll yell like hell if the cable operators ever do decide to drop ESPN. His belief that sacrificing a little bit of ratings to have greater variety was going to create more rabid fans of ESPN was absolutely right.

ROGER WERNER:
The cable-programming business wouldn't be what it is without the development of a two-revenue-stream business model. Because of it, ESPN has fueled the growth of sports overall, the inflation of player salaries, the cost of thirty-second spots, and the cost of tickets to games. It's all interlinked. We in some ways opened a Pandora's box. We certainly aggravated an inflationary situation that was already there.

GEORGE BODENHEIMER:

I was driving through Holcomb, Kansas, which is where *Cold Blood* occurred, and I remember thinking, "This isn't really a good omen." The hotel I checked into there—I had never seen it before that night—had a huge sign behind the front desk that said, "No Pheasant Cleaning in the Rooms." I told them not to worry about that. I was probably twenty-four or twenty-five, and I had to go and debate a guy who was twenty years older than me and very well connected in the town. He ran the cable system and we wound up in front of three hundred townspeople on whether or not he should pay twenty cents or something like that for ESPN.

I was nervous, but it turned out the night had nothing to do with my debating skills. The people really didn't want to hear anything about his business strategy or hear his protestations about paying twenty cents. They just wanted their sports. They wanted college football and Kansas hoops. A week later we signed that guy and he got back on the cable system.

While Grimes and Werner dealt with the business issues, Connal and Fitts handled production, and Gutkowski and Bornstein figured out programming, the men—and a woman or two—in the trenches were doggedly plugging away at improving the product and polishing the air fare. The work was paying off; by year's end, ESPN would be America's largest cable network only four years into its existence. Occasionally, thanks to divine providence or fate or dumb luck, its progress got an unexpected boost. So in mid-March of '83, two months into the network's newly revised financial arrangement with cable operators, lightning struck. ESPN's innovative policy of cutting simultaneous basketball games—from game to game to game—paid off spectacularly at that year's NCAA tournament.

Viewers saw three perfect buzzer-beater finales within hours of one another: Maryland's Len Bias helping to strike down Tennessee-Chattanooga; Ohio University's Robert Tatum ending Illinois State's run; and Purdue's Steve Reid breaking the hearts of Robert Morris. It was a brilliantly orchestrated Hallelujah Chorus of sports—the director in the control room making just the right decisions on which game to cut to, and when to cut to it. Fans were dazzled, and ESPN's reputation burgeoned.

By October of 1983, ESPN could claim the title of America's largest cable network, its signal reaching 28.5 million homes. Ad revenue rose 60 percent to $40 million—and yet that was still not enough for the business to show a profit.

SAL MARCHIANO:
I was in my rental car and heard the lyric "happiness was Lubbock in my rearview mirror," by Mac

Davis. Next time I went back to *SportsCenter,* I introduced "Bristol" instead of "Lubbock" to the guys, and it became such a common phrase in the building that at night when we used to split, we'd be in the parking lot and just yell out to each other, "Happiness." That's how common the phrase was.

Chet had given me a good deal, and in fact, my nickname to the young guys at *SportsCenter* was "Six Figure Sal" because I was the only guy at *SportsCenter* who made six figures. But I was also doing boxing on their Thursday-night show, which was the reincarnation of those glorious Friday-night fights that used to be on NBC and the *Pabst Blue Ribbon* series of CBS. I was the only one on *SportsCenter* who went on the road, and one of my two days off was always a travel day. So now I'm dealing with Scotty Connal, who was great at production but had no people skills. He was a very angry, impatient man. My three-year deal was up, and Connal was making my renegotiation very difficult. My agent, Jimmy Walsh, who also represented Namath, couldn't make a deal with him, and so I said, "Oh, I'll go in and talk to him." Scotty was very abrasive and started the meeting by talking down to me. I said, "Listen, I'm not some prep-school kid and you're not some dean. Let's make this adult." Of course, he had never heard anyone talk to him that way, but I had a background and I had a lot of experience. I said, "Do you want to make a deal or don't you?" So Connal said, "You're too expensive for

SportsCenter. The most I pay these guys is $35,000 a year and you're making over a hundred thousand." Actually I was making $195 including the boxing, which was extraordinary money back then for anybody there. So he said, "Boxing is great, you're terrific at boxing. How about you just do boxing and then you don't have to come here and do *SportsCenter*?" I said, "That's fine with me." And so we had a handshake on the deal. He said this to me on a Thursday but added, "You're still on the schedule this weekend for *SportsCenter*," and Sunday was a big-deal show, so I said, "Yeah, no problem. I'll be in Sunday night." So I came in, did the show, and at the end, Bob Ley, who was the co-anchor, said, "We have to explain something. You're going to be here, but you're not going to be here." So then I explained the situation, that I wouldn't be doing *SportsCenter* anymore, that I'd be doing just boxing, and after my explanation, he said, "Well, I guess there's only one thing left to say," and he thought I was going to say good night, and I ad-libbed, "Happiness is Bristol in my rearview mirror."

It was the first time it was said publicly, so they were falling out of their chairs laughing in the control room, and I had one guy tell me he fell off his couch laughing. The next morning, Jimmy Walsh calls me and says, "You know that deal you made with Scotty?" I said, "Yeah." He said, "Well, he's taking it off the table because of that remark about the rearview mirror. Connal said you 'shoved it up everybody's ass who worked at ESPN,' so he doesn't want you back." I tried calling Connal, but he wouldn't take my calls. Barry Frank at IMG tried to help out by telling Connal, "Nobody heard it. It doesn't mean shit," and even suggested a suspension, but Connal just said, "I don't want him back." Jimmy was able to get copies of the *Bristol Press* for the thirty-one days after the remark, and he went over it with a fine-tooth comb, and there was no reference to my ad lib in the local newspaper. So he went to see another attorney, and he told us that we could in fact sue for a year's salary because of the handshake, since it wasn't disparaging enough to be in the local paper. But when Jimmy and I went to see John Martin, who was VP to Roone at ABC Sports, he said, "You'll win your litigation, but no network will ever want to hire you again. My suggestion is that you just eat it and go on." And that's what I did. I got a great-paying three-year deal from Channel 4 in New York to back up Marv Albert, and I must admit, I was glad when I heard that Jerry Solomon, who was responsible for Budweiser ads, just ate out Scott for losing me, because they had lost apparently one-half of their ratings after I left. When Bill Grimes became president, he took me to 21 to try to get me back, but I stayed at Channel 4.

BILL GRIMES:

One day I get a call from Sid Peterson, who was running Getty at the time, and he said, "I have to tell you something in confidence. Things are happening here, things that you are going to read about. There's going to be a big change here at Getty." I found out they were going to be bought by Texaco. I knew the general counsel of Texaco—he lived in my town, and our kids were at the same school—so I called him and said I knew they were buying Getty and that there was this little thing called ESPN, and I'd like to come with one of my guys and tell you guys why you ought to keep it. Roger and I felt if Texaco kept ESPN, we would get better compensation and maybe a piece of the action. So we go to Texaco. There were fifty people in the room, and they listened and asked some questions, but I got a call from them later, saying they couldn't keep us, the fit was wrong, and they were going to sell us. That day, I got a hold of the Texaco annual report and looked at the list of directors, and I see Tom Murphy's name, the head of Cap-Cities. So I went and saw Murphy. For three hours over lunch I outlined the entire ESPN business plan, what our prospects were, why we thought we were going to make it, and kept pointing out to him that because they owned cable systems, this would be a terrific fit. Murphy said to me—I remember this very specifically—that although he trusted us, he couldn't buy ESPN because they were thinking about larger acquisitions at the time. Of course, shortly after that it was announced that CapCities was buying ABC.

Anyway, so Evey came to town not knowing that I had spoken to anybody at Texaco, not knowing that Roger and I had met people there, not even knowing I had talked with Murphy. He said, I'm going to try and set up a contract with you at Texaco—for you, Roger, and Steve. I told him it wasn't necessary, and that I had already talked to Texaco, and that he didn't own us anymore. We were sitting real close, and Stu had big hands. And he took his big finger and pointed it right at my face, real close, and said, "You will never work in this industry again." With that, I got up, ran out, and made the 10:05 train to Connecticut. That was the last time I saw or spoke to Stu Evey until ESPN's twenty-fifth anniversary.

J. B. DOHERTY:

Our venture-capital firm still had a piece of ESPN from our initial investment with Bill Rasmussen back in 1978. Getty was trying to screw us out of the deal from day one. We heard about the CapCities deal and thought it was sort of an inside job. We had to hire Skadden, Arps to represent our interests as minority shareholders. We were concerned that such a deal wasn't going to deliver fair market value. In fact, we were actually instrumental in getting competitive bidding going between Ted Turner and ABC. We called up Turner's vice president of corporate development and said, "Aren't you interested?"

ROGER WERNER:

We had one meeting with Ted Turner in Atlanta. Ted just sort of sat Bill and me down and proceeded to wander all over the room, screaming and hollering about how he was going to put us out of business if we didn't sell to him—the usual bullshit. Typical Turner; he figured we were just a couple of middle-management corporate suits, and he'd bring us down to his inner sanctum and threaten and cajole us for an hour or two and we'd divulge company secrets and help him find a way to acquire the company.

That was in the days before he was professionally medicated. He was modulating his bipolar problem with Wild Turkey. So you'd get very strange behavior out of the guy from time to time. Sometimes he'd be as nice a guy as you'd want to meet, and sometimes he'd just be weird. But we listened to him, had a few laughs, and said, "Hey thanks for the turkey sandwich," got on a plane, and went home.

In January of 1984, ABC upped its stake in ESPN to 15 percent of the company—with house bean counters predicting the sports network would reach the break-even point in the first quarter of 1985. Getty's stake sank to 70 percent, with 15 percent still in the Rasmussen camp, mostly Bill's. Meanwhile, though, the natives at Getty Oil were more than restless. Heirs to the Getty family fortune and managers of the company squabbled end-

lessly, and with takeover predators Pennzoil and Texaco circling, Getty's directors sought to lighten the debt load by trying to dump part or all of ESPN, still considering it a liability and a nuisance.

Before 1984 was a month old, Texaco bought Getty Oil for $10 billion, and since Texaco had no more interest in nurturing a sports network than Getty did, it happily sold ABC the 85 percent of the company it didn't yet own for $188 million, with ABC in turn selling 20 percent to RJR Nabisco (based on Don Ohlmeyer's recommendation to honcho Ross Johnson).

STUART EVEY:

My involvement with Getty came to a close with the Texaco takeover. We would not have sold ESPN had Getty Oil not been sold. But one of the younger Getty sons put the company in play and it was sold. Never in our history would anybody have ever thought this would happen. But it did. ABC exercised its option to buy ESPN, and that was that.

ROGER WERNER:

Ross Johnson's point man on the ESPN investment was Don Ohlmeyer, who had worked for Roone at ABC Sports, and Don had a production company that operated basically inside Nabisco. At that time, Nabisco had a tremendous number of sports sponsorships—it seemed liked everybody from Arnold Palmer to Billie Jean King to A. J. Foyt. Everybody was on the payroll of Team Nabisco. They were basically Ross's traveling companions and goodwill ambassadors. He'd go to the Masters or he'd go to the Indy 500 or he'd go somewhere else, and he'd have half a dozen of those guys on the plane. And Don was the point guy running that sports marketing, sponsorship stuff.

Because of Don's background in sports production, he became Ross's surrogate on our board. So we basically interfaced with Don and his number-two guy, John Martin, who was also an ex-ABC Sports guy and Arledge protégé. They ultimately got paid by ABC for consulting services as a part of ABC's sale of 15 percent to Ross and Nabisco. They ultimately made a lot of dollars with very little effort, honestly, very little. But those were the times, and the ESPN acquisition, a $230 million deal, was at that time the biggest deal in the history of ABC. It seemed Leonard Goldenson was quite nervous about it, and so being able to lay off 20 percent at a profit reduced his risk. I'm sure that having Don and John on board reduced his perception of that risk even more.

HERB GRANATH, *Chairman of the Board:*
ESPN wasn't my first involvement with sports. I was the field executive in charge of *Monday Night Football.* If something went wrong, I was the one who fixed it. *Monday Night Football* was a traveling freak show, like the circus coming to town. One night,

Howard [Cosell] called, and said, "I just got a call from the chairman of the board!" I said, "[ABC chairman] Leonard [Goldenson]?" He said, "No, no, Frank! Sinatra! He wants to sit in the booth." I said, "Howard, you know we have a rule, nobody inside the booth except for our announcing team and statistician." He says, "For God's sake, it's Frank!" I said, "All right, but no entourage, it's just him alone." So I had nothing to do and wound up sitting with Frank Sinatra for two and a half, three hours, yapping away. Afterward, because we were on the West Coast and the game was over at nine o'clock, he and Howard said, "Let's get something to eat," and we went to Trader Vic's in the Beverly Hilton. Merv Griffin was there, and everything was hotsy-totsy. But some drunk came over and started to give Frank a lot of shit, so Frank gets up and punches him in the mouth! I thought, "Oh, my God, that'll be on Page Six," but I never heard another word about it.

Another time, Howard called and said, "I just heard from John Lennon. He wants to sit in the booth. He's an American-football fan." So he sat in the booth. Afterward, we went back to the Beverly Wilshire, to a little bar there called Hernando's Hideaway. Hernando saw us coming, shoo's everybody else out, closes it, we sat there until one or two in the morning talking, whatever. I had to admit to John that I had been a Beatles fan when I was younger, and when I went back to New York, there was a case waiting for me from him with every record the Beatles had ever made. He was a terrific guy.

Ted Turner knew how to overpay for TV rights, but he also realized just how effectively he could help drive costs up for other stations — like ESPN — for TV rights he allegedly had no legitimate interest in acquiring. Turner had outbid ESPN by an absurd $10 million for rights to Division II football in 1982, and whether or not it truly was due to an arbitrary and incomprehensible bid by Turner, the bidding for the second USFL deal in June of 1984 featured a Turner who was dead set on making ESPN pay dearly for the USFL. And so ESPN did.

Turner believed ESPN needed professional football for its programming and would be willing to top any bid he could make. When bidding began for the United States Football League's new three-year cable contract, Turner kept raising his bid, offering the league $62 million for the next three years. By the end, Turner had forced ESPN and ABC to bid $70 million on a three-year package with an estimated worth closer to $50 million. ABC exercised its option for 1985 at $14 million. and when it came time to negotiate for the next contract, ABC, having experienced high ratings with the league, offered the USFL $175 million over four years in addition to ESPN's $70 million. The league, however, because of mergers and shutdowns, turned down the money.

LOREN MATTHEWS:

Chet had always been adamant about not having professional wrestling on ESPN. He would say, "We're a legitimate sports network, we're not going to do that." But Grimes came in and decided we needed to get into the pro-wrestling business ASAP because it was the highest-rated sports product on cable. USA and Turner were getting huge numbers. Remember, back then, the NFL wasn't on cable yet. So Grimes calls me one day and says, "Tell me about wrestling," which I actually knew something about because I had the typical eighty-year-old grandmother who watched it three times a week when I was a kid.

I told him there were three federations and Bornstein had actually met with Vince McMahon a while back and had used us to sweeten his USA Network deal, so that was out. And I told him Turner was in bed with Jim Crockett, so we can't get in there. He asked what the third-best federation was. That had to be the AWA out of Minneapolis. Bill told me to set up a meeting with them, and it turned out they were coming to do a show at the Meadowlands. Bill got very excited and asked me when the meeting was. I told him, Tuesday night, and he said, "Perfect. I got a board meeting Wednesday morning. I want you to get a deal done, and I don't care how late it is, just let me know the deal is done so I can announce it at the board meeting. And oh, by the way, assuming you'll get this done, send me a little cheat sheet with their famous wrestlers that I can use to tell the board." Now this is the ABC board here. We're talking about Roone Arledge and a bunch of heavyweights. So no pressure there.

My meeting lasted for hours and hours, but we got a deal. I called Grimes that night around ten o'clock at home and said it was done. Signed and sealed. He said, "That's just great." So he told me later that he goes into the board meeting all fired up about our deal. He announced it, and there was just silence. Nobody said a word. So he takes out the little cheat sheet with the names on it, and tries to get them enthusiastic, telling them they've got wrestlers like the High Flyers and Sgt. Slaughter. And all of a sudden, one of the directors says, *"We got Slaughter?!"* And all the other directors, including Roone, just turn and look at him like he's absolutely crazy. So the guy gets real embarrassed, and says, "Uh, well, uh, my kids watch it."

TOM ODJAKJIAN:

I was originally against us doing wrestling, but I finally got on board with it when Loren said, "Ideally we're going to saturate TV with it and kill off the sport. Or, we're going to jump on the bandwagon and benefit from it."

CHET SIMMONS:

One of the things that happened between this new guy who was then made president and Evey was to get rid of everybody who really was associated with me, people who were really close to me, Scotty being very high on that list. And there were others.

LOREN MATTHEWS:

Scotty ended up interviewing all the members of the programming department one-on-one to ask about Steve and what we thought should be done with the department. He left me till last, and, candidly, I didn't know if I was being set up or what here. Scotty and I were very close at the time. It was a very uncomfortable situation. And when he asked me, I looked him in the eye and said, "Steve deserves the job."

He just looked back at me and said, "Okay, this meeting's over." Our relationship was pretty much over after that.

GEORGE GRANDE:

I saw the handwriting on the wall well before they moved Scotty down, and it was at that point in time that I started to think about moving on. I loved my time there, I loved the people there, but at the same time, I didn't want to be part of what direction everything was heading in. Chet Simmons and Scotty

Connal were ESPN. Scotty was still the heart and soul of production, the heart and soul of what the essence of ESPN was, but he was in Bristol, and with Chet gone, he had no ally in New York. Chet had always had his back. When Chet left, little by little, Scotty lost the protection that he'd had among the suits in New York.

STEVE BORNSTEIN:

Scotty ran production for a year or so, and then Bill made me head of production and programming, and that was sort of the end for Scotty. He had to report to me. I tried to work with him. He was not incompetent, but clearly there was this whole cabal of his supporters making things such a soap opera up there, and I wasn't about to allow myself to get sucked into it. Ultimately, I had to get rid of Scotty.

BILL GRIMES:

Scotty didn't like Steve; I don't think he felt comfortable with him, and I think Steve looked at Scotty and thought his time had come and gone. There definitely wasn't a good feeling between the two. Steve was doing a great job, and if he couldn't live with Scotty anymore, then I was going with Steve.

ROGER WERNER:

Ultimately Scotty had been around there a long time and was a good guy in many ways and made a big contribution in many ways. So what we tried to do—what I tried to do—is arrange as graceful a transition as we could under those circumstances, and that meant a kind of retirement as opposed to a termination, and it meant a fair bit of lead time and a reasonably kind of humane approach to it, I think. If Scotty were alive today, he might contradict me. I don't know.

GEORGE GRANDE:

Ohlmeyer came in as a consultant, and I'll never forget, right after we had gone to the Olympics, he said, "You guys did a pretty good job with the Olympics, what did you spend?" So I took out my Olympic folder and looked. Our whole Olympics coverage—pre-Olympics, Olympics, post-Olympics, everything—came to $242,000. And he looks at the thing and starts to laugh. "Two hundred and forty-two thousand dollars?" He says, "I spent that much on limos when I was at the Olympics with the network."

ROGER WERNER:

Obviously Steve was a protégé of mine and so I was trying to keep peace in the valley. Scotty would come to me and complain, so I'd sit and listen and then give him four or five good points about what Steve was doing and tell him to try to get along. Then Steve would have meetings with me and say Scotty's undermining him and he's sabotaging me and he's doing this, that, and the other things.

CHET SIMMONS:

I thought they treated Scotty like a slave. It was awful.

BILL GRIMES:

I can't even remember how Scotty left. Did we fire him or did he quit? Either way, we picked the right horse, that's for sure.

In 1977, sixty-two NCAA football powerhouse programs from five conferences—including the Southeastern Conference (SEC) and the Big Eight (now the Big 12), plus a few independent teams, joined forces to form a college football association (CFA) to challenge the NCAA and cash in on rights deals from broadcast networks. By 1981, CFA members were chafing under the NCAA's tight grip on TV rights. According to NCAA policy, teams like Oklahoma, Alabama, Texas, and Penn State received the same revenue from a televised game as did teams with little national prominence. In addition, broadcast networks were required to schedule games in which at least eighty-two different NCAA teams appeared during a two-year period, but no team could appear nationally more than four times, and those appearances had to be divided equally among the net-

works. The whole point of the CFA was to wriggle free of NCAA restraints. It found a potential ally in NBC, which offered the CFA a four-year $180 million rights contract. Ever anxious about threats to its power, the NCAA threatened sanctions that would affect other sports in addition to football, and squashed CFA's efforts to cash in.

By 1984, increasingly apoplectic over what it saw as the NCAA's unreasonable restraint on trade, the CFA— led by Oklahoma University's Board of Regents—filed suit against the NCAA in a case that would go all the way to the Supreme Court.

The Court ultimately determined that the NCAA was in violation of the Sherman Antitrust Act and affirmed a Court of Appeals' judgment that the NCAA plan was "an unreasonable restraint of trade" because of the plan's "price-fixing and output-limiting aspects." The ruling held that the NCAA could no longer "limit the number of games that are broadcast on television" or contract for an overall price that has the effect of setting the price for individual game broadcast rights."

Thus freed from NCAA shackles, teams and conferences were able to negotiate their own TV contracts. Now there were better games and more money to go around. So it would be that ESPN, boosted by its association with ABC Sports, landed the rights to broadcast forty-eight games in the 1984 season. College football finally aired live, all season long, on ESPN.

LOREN MATTHEWS:

Nineteen eighty-four was our first full year of tele-vising live college football, and if you count Sunday, which was a travel day, I was on the road Labor Day until December 10 with a total of only three days off. I would fly in to where we had that week's game on a Thursday or a Friday, meet with the athletic director or conference commissioner, stay for the game, and fly back on Sunday. We'd pick our games on Mon-day, and start the whole thing again.

MARC PAYTON:

Paul Maguire is without a doubt the most fun character I've ever known in my life. We did college football at ESPN together, then we did USFL games. In those days, pretty much all the teams were in the South, so we were in Florida, Alabama, and Texas a lot, where the weather was warm. The first thing Paul would do when we'd get into a town, even before we checked into the hotel, was stop at a 7-Eleven and buy a Styrofoam cooler with beer so we could have our production meeting at the hotel pool, drinking beer. He would even travel with a blender so he could make frozen drinks for everyone.

STEVE BORNSTEIN:

In the early eighties again, there was a big effort to challenge ESPN. Multimedia, which was a big cable operator, TCI, which was at the time becoming the biggest if not already the biggest cable operator, and Anheuser-Busch all formed a sports network to take on ESPN. And Multimedia, based in Wichita, Kansas, was the first one that dropped ESPN and was going to replace it with this new thing—I forget what they called it—SportsVision or something like that. We immediately scheduled an Oklahoma prime-time football game for the following Saturday. Roger Werner and I flew into Tulsa, and it was the first time I felt like a rock star, because, as soon as we landed, the local Tulsa television stations were at the airport, filming us arriving. It was a big town-hall meeting in Tulsa. People wanted to know what Multimedia was doing dropping ESPN. There were four or five hundred people and a town council up there and some executives from the local cable operation. There were these guys in the back of the room with chain saws threatening to cut down the telephone poles carrying the cables unless ESPN was restored to the cable system so they could watch NASCAR races.

LOREN MATTHEWS:

We flew from the Texas–Texas A&M game on Thanksgiving night over to Oklahoma State in Stillwater, and when we landed, we heard on the radio there was going to be a big storm that Saturday night with ice and snow. We were hoping they were wrong, because they were going to be playing the game at night, but they weren't wrong. It was horrendous. The field was covered with ice. They played because it wasn't like there was lightning, but it was in the most miserable conditions ever. We were losing cameras and camera men; it was just awful. Finally the game was over, and our guys had to tear down everything. They're still working about an hour after the game, and they see these two people sitting in the middle of the stands up there in this horrendous weather. So they go up and see what was going on. Apparently the woman had been drinking at the game and had gotten so drunk that she'd peed her pants and she was now frozen stuck to the metal bleachers. And the guy with her, who was also drunk, couldn't free her. He was trying to pour hot coffee around her to get her out. So now, our guys had to literally chip the lady off the bleachers and get her home.

TERRY LINGNER:

We had a pretty major role in NASCAR's ascension and growth, and everyone could see it. When we started covering them, there was nobody in the grandstands. I had come from ABC, where they had standards and practices and never would let you show even the Miller beer logo. So, when I came on the ESPN scene, I clearly remember going to all the drivers and saying, "Hey, we're just a fledging cable network and we have no standards and practices. We want to be your friends. We want you to be successful. So, if you want to mention Miller beer in your answer, go for it." Then I said, "I'll shoot you wide if you need to show your sponsors while you're thanking them." I felt like it was vital for us to get the drivers and their teams on our side, 'cause if we did, it would make us fairly popular fairly quickly.

RICHARD PETTY, *Race Car Driver:*

ABC's *Wide World of Sports* would give us five or ten minutes between mud wrestling and marble shooting, you know what I mean? That was about the only coverage we had. Then ESPN came on and started picking things up. I can remember when they first started. They were new and kind of crude, but they were quick learners and their people were pretty knowledgeable. Every now and then you'd run into one of them who would come up with something totally off the wall or ask a stupid question, but you'd try to help him because you're trying to help yourself. We had to remember that this guy was trying to help racing.

What ESPN did was create interest all over the country. Before ESPN, we were still a Southern sport. They took us all over the United States. At first, we couldn't see the effects, but all of a sudden, there were more photographers, more interview requests, more newspapers around us, more local TV stations. We woke up and said, "Golly, look what's happened."

They covered our sport like nobody else had ever done it before. So, as far as I'm concerned, they set the pattern for everybody else to follow.

How much the fans came to see racing, and how much they savored the inevitable crashes that sent flaming cars climbing walls and soaring into the air, can't be known, but the action was thrilling, and putting it on ESPN civilized the sport without diminishing its sheer kinetic power.

MIKE TYSON, *Boxer:*

ESPN helped me a lot in the beginning. There were many people who saw me fight for the first time on ESPN, and it was great because it was national television. So anybody could see me. It turned out to be a great showcase for me. I don't think many of the fighters back then realized they could really make a reputation by being on ESPN. I did. I would try to be on every card. I said yes as much as I could. It was "you shake my hand, I'll shake yours" with them because we helped each other, 100 percent, 100 percent. And when I experienced it myself, watching ESPN, I had never seen highlighting like that before. They did a great job, not just with boxing but with all the other sports. They were pretty awesome at that time.

FRED GAUDELLI:

Right after the '84 Olympics, we acquired the rights to the U.S. Olympic Festival, which was basically a way for the USOC to develop their Olympic teams during the next four years. They were all summer sports—swimming, diving, track and field. At that point in time, ESPN was not nearly sophisticated enough from a technology standpoint to pull this thing off. We were basically a bunch of young kids being taught by Bill Fitts. But Bill had us going in there like we were doing the Olympics.

After one snafu after another, with Bill producing and in master control in the truck, the truck—I kid you not—catches on fire. So the head engineer rushes into the truck and says, "Okay, everybody out of the truck!" But Bill says to the guy, "We're on the air! We can't go anywhere!" And the engineer says, "Did you hear what I said? The truck is on fire. Out!" So Bill says, "Okay, everybody out except me and the guy who's pushing the buttons." And that guy looks at him, and says, "Me?" Bill says, "Yeah, you. We'll wait until we go to commercial and then we'll be able to leave." And that is Bill Fitts in a nutshell.

ROGER WERNER:

Jack Gallivan was kind of forced on us through the Don Ohlmeyer connection. Don was lobbying hard for him. Jack's family was very wealthy and owned television stations, including an ABC affiliate, I think, in Salt Lake, and Don had some connection there, some reason to want to do Jack a favor.

Jack was in charge of *SportsCenter,* and his vision

was that he wanted it to be, in his words, "the news source of record in the sports world." He saw that in very serious journalistic tones, and his vision was kind of *New York Times*. Nothing wrong with that, per se, but where it started to create a real issue, and why I ultimately had to sit down and fire him, was that he was trying to get Chris Berman to stop using nicknames and the shtick that Chris had developed over the years, and he tried to do the same thing with Tom Mees and every other talent. Essentially he wanted everybody to be Edward R. Murrow.

My feeling on *SportsCenter* was that journalistically it ought to be the top-quality source for sports news—no question the source of record—but that the whole sports area was the fun and games section of the journalistic world. I felt personally there ought to be a high degree of tolerance for colorful personalities, for gags, for shtick, for whatever worked—for whatever made a sports fan tell his buddy at the water cooler the next day, "Hey, I saw Chris Berman" or whoever—Dick Vitale or any of our guys—"and he said an amazingly funny thing," or "he had a different take on something." That's where Jack got himself into trouble.

I thought that if you're lucky enough to be running and building a product like a sports network, then the job had better be a lot of fun for everybody. 'Cause if it isn't, something's horribly wrong. People had better treat each other with respect and make it a healthy, exciting, fun place to work, or get out. And we gave him a fair bit of rope and a fair bit of time to try to get on the team and be one of the boys and kind of do it the ESPN way. So I had to let him go.

HERB GRANATH:

In 1985 Leonard Goldenson, the ABC founder, was looking around at all these major conglomerates that were "diversifying" and buying up a lot of properties. Leonard was eighty, and he did not want his baby to be gobbled up by some faceless conglomerate. He wanted a broadcaster to run the company. So Leonard went to see Tom Murphy and Dan Burke of CapCities and basically said, "Tom, I want you to buy ABC." Tom choked and said, "That would be the ultimate min- now swallowing the whale, there's no way we could afford to do this." And Leonard said, "Yes there is. Warren Buffett is on a plane heading here from Omaha and he's got"—I'm trying to remember the number, I think it was—"$3 or $4 billion that he's going to put up to buy ABC stock. And he's also going to give irre- vocable voting rights to either you or Dan as long as either of you is CEO of ABC, which will give stability to the company." Warren joined the board because he was one of the major shareholders of the company. And that's the way it was done.

When it was first announced, in March of 1985, the purchase of ABC by Capital Cities Communications was *a shock to the entire broadcasting industry and to many more-than-casual observers. CapCities paid $3.5 billion for ABC, even though ABC was four times bigger than CapCities when the deal went through. It was financed in part by busy billionaire Warren Buffett, chairman of the exclusive Berkshire Hathaway investment company, and for his resourcefulness and troubles, Buffett now had a 25 percent stake in the new combined company.*

Much of the scuttlebutt about the deal concentrated on the fact that CapCities was a very conservatively run, by-the-book company. Speculation spun about what the effect would be on ABC's operations. Together, the new company owned more TV stations than FCC rules allowed, so lawyers and executives set about deciding which stations were expendable (read: less profitable). Some radio stations with overlapping signals also had to be jettisoned.

Almost forgotten at the back of the room: ESPN, the same network that Murphy and Burke heard so much about from Bill Grimes when he was trying to get them to buy during the Texaco takeover of Getty. ESPN wasn't very prominent in news stories about the CapCities deal, but make no mistake: Murphy and Burke had a very strong sense of what it was, and what it could become. And they proved it when they turned down an incredibly attractive offer to sell it.

DON OHLMEYER, *Ombudsman:*

In early '86, after CapCities had closed on its purchase of ABC, I approached Ross Johnson with a wild idea. "Look, these guys are carrying ESPN on their books at $220 million or whatever. I don't know if we have the balls for this, but I think we should take a look at it. CapCities is basically into stations and local broadcasting. Absorbing a broadcast network is going to be a tough nut to swallow, and running a sports cable network is not exactly their cup of tea. I've done the homework. We could go in and offer them $500 million. That would double the money for them and could be one of the great investments of all times for us." Ross thought about it and said, "Go ahead and see where their heads are at."

So I met with Dan Burke. We chatted for a while, and then I got to the point. "Dan, I want to talk to you about ESPN." That seemed to perk up his interest. I said, "I don't know what your thoughts are, but I know you guys have always been focused on the station business and now you've got a network to digest. We'd be prepared to offer you north of $450 million for your interest in ESPN." There was a moment of silence, then he said to me, "You know, I'm sure that is an extraordinarily fair offer, but I have to explain something to you. Tom [Murphy] and I are buyers, not sellers. In our entire history in business together, we've never sold anything other than something that we had to divest because of a conflict — like some of our stations when we bought ABC. We just don't sell. I'm sure it's a very fair offer, and I'm sure in ten years I may come back and say, 'How foolish, if only we'd taken that money,' but I'm afraid we're just not, and never have been, sellers." A fairly brilliant "no interest" from them, as it turned out, leaving us disappointed but with an ever-appreciating minority interest and a consulting contract.

In its first few years of existence, "ESPN" was something short of a magic acronym. If you worked there and tried dropping the name, you were more likely to receive a blank stare of bewilderment than a delighted smile of recognition. But ESPN had been beaming its highly specialized, increasingly polished product into more and more homes, clubs, and corner bars, and staff could console themselves with the anticipation that a breakthrough had to be right around the corner.

Thus, every bit of recognition was somehow gratifying—just a sign, just a moment in time, whatever form that might take...

FRED GAUDELLI:

A couple weeks before the Big East championships—this was the great '86 tournament, where St. John's beat Syracuse—Jeff Israel, Mo Davenport, and I were sent out to shoot scenics for the tournament. We went to Brownsville, Brooklyn, where Pearl Washington was from, then we went to the South Bronx, where Walter Berry came from. We were going all around the city in the freezing cold of winter trying to get what we could. Now it's about eight o'clock at night and we're in Lower Manhattan. So we go, "Hey, let's try to get on the roof of the World Trade Center and get some great shots." We go there and get in the elevator and head up to Windows on the World, which I think was the last floor, and we ask them, "Hey, can we get up to the roof? We want to take some shots of Lower Manhattan. We're with ESPN." And they told us that we needed to get prior clearance to get on the roof, that we just couldn't walk up there. So I asked, "Is there anybody we can talk to about it?" And they say, "There's a security guard over there, try him." We asked the security guard, "Can we just go up for twenty minutes," and I think Mo had an ESPN hat on, and next thing you know, we're giving him the hat and he's letting three guys with no clearances and a camera on top of the World Trade Center. We were standing right next to the big antenna!

STUART EVEY:

One night, I thought I'd have a cocktail, and then after I finished it, I decided to have a cup of coffee. Next thing I knew I put some liquor in my coffee, and it went on and on. I had about three or four of those—all night—and I wasn't drunk. But I knew the time had come. I couldn't even enjoy a cup of coffee without the stuff. So finally we went to the Betty Ford clinic. They say a miracle happens in A.A., and I think this was a miracle. They introduced me, and everybody stood in a line and hugged me, "Stu, it's great to have you," on and on and on. The last guy was a little fellow. He worked for the Denver Broncos. They didn't know what I did. He had been in there for a while and was going to leave the next day. He put his arms around me and he said, "Goddamn you smell good, Stu," because he could smell the alcohol. I had nobody to blame but myself. And I'll tell you what, I haven't had a desire to have a drink since.

3

Ripeness Is All: 1987–1991

"But the real glory of science is that we can find a
way of thinking such that the law is evident."
— *Richard P. Feynman*

DENNIS CONNER, *America's Cup Skipper:*
How would you like to have someone come into
your bedroom with a camera while you were fucking
your wife and she was screaming? Unless you were
ever part of a team sport, you would never know what
it's like to work for thirty-six months together, training all the time, and then have someone intrude.
Because the last thing in the whole world you would
want is to have people you don't even know onboard
hearing you say "fuck" or "shit" or "what the hell is
happening here." That's not including all the gear on
the boat, production people coming and going in our
compound, and having people tell us where the cameras should be. Having ESPN on board with us was a
big distraction.

Of all the sports that could make a difference in the pro-file and identity of a sports network, most were bread-and-butter: football, baseball, basketball, hockey, tennis, and soccer would all likely make the grade. Yacht racing, if it made the list at all, would probably tag along after, say, poker or bowling. But not at ESPN.

GARY JOBSON, *Yacht Racing Analyst:*

I went to Dennis and said, "Look, we want to put this onboard camera on the boat," and Dennis said, "I don't know about this. I don't want to give up my secrets. The competition is going to watch and know how we do everything. But I'm a fair man. Come back at seven and you can present your camera, tell the crew what you want to do, and then we'll take a vote of the crew." Now, these were guys I knew really well, went to college with, and raced with in the ocean. And no one in the crew voted yes! I was crushed, and the only thing that came out of my mouth was "Okay, Dennis, I guess you're the swing vote on this." He kind of laughed and he said, "I'll tell you what; we'll do this for one day and if we don't like it, we're done. We won't do it again." And to his credit, two days later for the race, he put in the onboard camera.

DENNIS CONNER:

I knew TV would help us raise money in the future. Make no mistake, though, it certainly wasn't going to help us win the America's Cup.

GARY JOBSON:

After the race, the crew had the next day off, and every one of those guys on that boat heard from girls—old girlfriends, new girlfriends, and wannabe girlfriends. They suddenly realized they were heroes being on live television. So the next crew meeting I got invited to, the vote was unanimous in favor of the camera. They told me, "We like this camera. This is going to work out just fine."

BILL GRIMES:

About a week before the races were going to start, I got a call from Geoff Mason, who was down there producing the America's Cup for us. He said, "We got a little problem. We want to put a camera on board and Dennis Conner wants $50,000 for it." We were already over our production budget, so I said, "Is this really, really going to make things better?" and he said, "Yes." I paused for a minute, then told him to go ahead and do it. Then I quickly called the guy who was in charge of spending for Anheuser-Busch and got him to spend the extra fifty grand. We got some great shots and great publicity from that camera.

On the afternoon of the final race for the 1983 America's Cup, ESPN was airing an old tape-delayed football game when phone calls from viewers pleading or demanding that ESPN air the race began to flood the switchboard. With a responsiveness unusual for any American TV network, ESPN ditched the football game and switched to live coverage of the race, taking a split from a local Rhode Island TV station.

That year, the longest winning streak in international sports history was broken. Having held on to the America's Cup for more than twenty challenges spanning an amazing 132 years, the New York Yacht Club lost the race—and thus the Cup—to the Australia II, owned by Aussie business tycoon Alan Bond. Even though sailing could hardly be labeled "America's Pastime" or the country's most popular sport, the loss resonated throughout the land, as if some foreign interloper had marched in and somehow managed to win the World Series or the Super Bowl.

With the Cup in new hands, many in the TV sports business saw the America's Cup of 1987, the next time the event would take place, as a huge opportunity for new challengers that would radically heighten popular interest in the event.

ESPN's top trio of Grimes, Werner, and Bornstein looked at the spectacle from a practical point of view. They believed strongly that corporate America would solidly support the race, that this epic underdog story would attract unprecedented millions of American viewers, and that national pride was clearly and dramatically at stake.

ROGER WERNER:

We had to go to our parent company, CapCities, and ask for $650,000 to get the rights again and mount a major production. The basic proposition was "Guys, we want to make this commitment to America's Cup and we're going to light up the screen with it, do this thing big-time." They agreed, but then months before the whole thing started, we still hadn't sold a dollar's worth of advertising. It was not a good situation. So we concocted a package of incentives and prizes for advertisers and affiliates to piggyback on the thing.

BILL GRIMES:

Roger had a fabulous idea. We invited one person from every one of the top cable operators to come down to Australia with us for a two-week junket. The invitation was nontransferable. We chartered a Qantas jumbo jet and took them all down to Perth. There were big advertisers too, like the president of Coca-Cola, whom I knew. We had a great time, and it was a big success.

GEOFF MASON, *Executive Producer*:

Was it challenging? You bet. Was ESPN used to supporting such a project? God, no. Did we break new ground in terms of how ESPN approached new events by doing that project? Absolutely. What do you do for the viewer who is watching live coverage of a sailboat race for the first time? How do you keep them involved? First, we pegged it on personalities. I had learned that at ABC from Arledge. We didn't do television about games, sticks, or balls; we did television about people. So we focused our coverage heavily on white hats and black hats: Conner, the Aussies, the French, the Italians, and the Kiwis. We had a ton of stories to tell because the people who were involved in the competition were a wild group. Second, we had to educate viewers on the sport, so we had Gary Jobson—the best who ever lived in terms of articulating what the sport means—get into a pool for an entire day with little model boats and we shot about twenty pieces on the rules of the game.

GARY JOBSON:

I actually sailed in the America's Cup ten years before, so I looked at America's Cup that year with very wide eyes. A lot of curves crossed in favor of ESPN on that magic event. By 1987, the country had been dealing with another recession and was just not feeling great at that moment. We had lost the America's Cup in 1983, a shocking loss to many. You don't want to lose an American icon after 132 years. At the same time, the movie *Crocodile Dundee* had just come out, and the Cup was happening in summer in Australia, which is winter in the U.S. You could watch the races live and get onboard the boats, which had never happened before. It was windy and exciting every day. So the combination of patriotic fervor and strong winds matched up perfectly with an outcome very much in doubt.

I had done some racing with Walter Cronkite, and we had become friends. I went to him and asked, "What should I know about commentating for the America's Cup?" And you can hear Walter's voice, "Well, Gary, here's my advice: Make every word count." Pretty good advice. Then I had one other friend who was in television, Ted Turner, because I had been his tactician in two of my America's Cup campaigns, and Ted was very helpful to me too. His advice was simple: "Have fun and just do what you normally do. Explain it to others like you explain it to me. You'll love it." And U.S.A. won 5–1 in that final's best-of-nine series. In other words, it was exciting television, it meant something to America, and people were watching.

Steve Bornstein once said that the America's Cup was "the essence of cable TV. You could find something there that you couldn't find anyplace else."

JED DRAKE:

The west coast of Australia was like the Wild, Wild West, and we were in Fremantle and Perth for many months. I was thirty, and we had the time of our lives. It was the best event I've ever done. We even got a cable from David Letterman, whom we were going head-to-head with because he had just started doing late night. It said, "I think you've really got something with this TV yacht racing. It could be bigger than wrestling. Keep up the good work. All my best, David Letterman."

DENNIS CONNER:

There was a great group of young people who worked for ESPN, and they had a very wonderful time hanging out with all the crews at night. You know, the guys were fucking all the girls. Not our actual crew—we were there to win the cup. But I certainly wasn't keeping track of where all my one hundred employees were every night and what time they went home.

GEOFF MASON:

We had a bunch of kids who liked to work hard but also have a good time, and my goodness, did they do both. We had a break during Christmas and New Year's, and it was just party down. I mean, it was absolutely amazing.

GAYLE GARDNER:

I had one big moment of total panic. It was the end of the race and some of the reporters who had been covering it were supposed to join me in the studio to talk. We realized we couldn't get anyone off the boats because everything was jammed up, so I had no one to talk to and just started talking about the nice boats and pretty pictures. They told me, "Just keep on talking." My heart was thumping. I wound up talking on my own for forty-five minutes.

GEORGE BODENHEIMER:

I got a call from a cable operator who sounded quite serious and annoyed. He said to me, "I've got a bone to pick with you." Now, in those days, this was not an infrequent call to get. There were a lot more cable systems back then and they all had their own issues. I asked him what his problem was, and he said, "I didn't get any sleep last night. I was up watching the sailing all night." We then had a good laugh over that. It was obvious ESPN was really beginning to break through.

ROGER WERNER:

You want to talk about a high-water mark? How about when our America's Cup coverage made the front page of the *New York Times*. That's when we believed we had finally made it. We had taken something as obscure as yacht racing and made it into something entertaining enough to attract a broad spectrum of viewers. We even made money on that event, and when we were having our discussions with NFL owners like Art Modell, several of them said how impressed they were by our coverage.

STEVE BORNSTEIN:

Herb Granath, our chairman, never paid me enough, but I love him dearly. So get this: we had just done the America's Cup from Australia and had even been mentioned in the *New York Times*. We got the Television Critics Award for our coverage, and it was the first time that a group of people looked at us as other than a chickenshit operation. And we were up for a CableACE Award. Turns out it came down to us or the Discovery Channel. They had done a week's worth of programming from Russia. Now, Herb was actually the chairman of this Golden ACE committee of twelve people, and he decided to abstain from the vote. And guess what? We lost by one fucking vote. It was going to be a huge deal for us, but we never got that acknowledgment. On the other hand, what the fuck is an ACE, right?

What a high point it was for ESPN — luring new viewers to the network who might never have tuned in before, and demonstrating the network's ability to improve dramatically on the production techniques of the previous Cup four years earlier. Pride was becoming a commonly used word, and employees didn't have to constantly repeat the name of the network when people asked where they worked.

Coverage of the America's Cup challenge in 1987: Step Number Four in ESPN's rise to world dominance.

DAVID HILL, *Fox Sports Chairman:*

The guy I worked for at the time in Australia, a guy called Kerry Packer, had been offered ESPN for $80 million in 1987. I was told to get on a plane and to have a look at this thing. The cable industry back then was all mom-and-pops; it hadn't been consolidated. It was one or two people stringing a wire between two telegraph poles and controlling a certain area. Everything had to be negotiated. So I was sniffing around ESPN in Bristol, Connecticut. It wasn't obvious at all that ESPN was going to become what it is today. Then there was a real downturn in the market and we stopped even thinking about buying it. Nothing was obvious. It wasn't like we were going to be looking back in twenty years going, "Holy shit, why didn't we see it?"

Yacht racing wasn't the only big-ticket item for ESPN in 1987. As the NFL's five-year, $2.1 billion contract with ABC, CBS, and NBC wound down in 1986, it was estimated that over the life of the contract, ABC, CBS, and NBC had lost a combined $75 million televising the games. Naturally, then, their first question was "Where do we go to sign up for more?" It's not that the networks were masochistic; TV rights to NFL games were almost always a prize package no matter what, the prestige consistently outweighing the drawbacks. And yet, change was lurking around every *corner. Multimillions in losses were starting to matter more than they usually did to network executives, who were being forced by evolving realities to learn the importance of parsimony across the board. Make no mistake: they wanted the NFL; they were just a bit reluctant to spend as freely as they had in the past.*

For its part, the NFL now had an eye on the future of telecommunications—and an ear to all those prophets of profit who spoke of "the end of the three-network era"—and thus began to see wisdom in perhaps placing some of its inventory on cable. For ESPN, this created an opportunity filled with considerations not only practical but also somewhat mystical. The NFL had always been the network's big dream. Despite the fact that it was now steadily growing, ESPN could never be considered top tier without an NFL presence.

In the spring of 1987, it looked as though ESPN might finally have a chance.

It would not be easy; ESPN was up against the broadcast networks, the pay-cable giant HBO, and basic cable channels such as Ted Turner's "SuperStation" WTBS. There was the USA Network, an initially sports-intensive channel known as Madison Square Garden Network when it signed on in 1977, which then became USA Network two years later, the same year ESPN went on the air. In addition to these individual contenders, a consortium of cable system operators had banded together to negotiate as the Cable Football Net-

work — its sole goal being the acquisition of an NFL package for cable.

BILL GRIMES:

Steve had been spending a lot of time with Val Pinchbeck, who was the number two guy at the NFL under Pete Rozelle. Val called and asked if I was going to the Super Bowl, this was '87, and I told him yes. He said that Mr. Rozelle and Art Modell, the owner of the Browns, would like to meet with me. So I went to the Bel-Air Hotel, where they had this massive suite, and it was just the three of us. They said, "As you know, we're going to add a fourth network to our next television contract, and we've talked to HBO and Turner. We know you guys have talked to Val, and we want to hear more about ESPN." So I gave him my ESPN pitch, including that we were in more homes than HBO. They were concerned about our commercials, so we talked about that. At the end, they said, "We don't know the guys at CapCities very well, but what do you guys think you could pay?" I forget the numbers they mentioned at that time, but they said ABC was paying X, and asked if we could pay Y. I said I didn't know but I could find out quickly.

I called Dan Burke, the CEO of CapCities, at home and explained what Rozelle and Modell had told me, including that we could get the Sunday-night package and you guys would get the renewal of

Mondays on ABC. Then Burke says to me, "Why are you talking to those guys directly? Where are the ABC guys on this?" He said he wanted it to be a team thing.

HERB GRANATH:

Don't forget, in those days we in the cable world were second-class citizens. We would say to the cable operators, "Hey, if you want to be big-time, if you want to compete with the big boys, the NFL is the name of the game. We can't afford it on our own, but if you all put your money where your mouth is, we can go and buy an NFL package." So our plan was, buy the rights, and whatever those rights cost, charge that back to the cable operators. It became about convincing the operators that they had to pay us for those rights.

ROGER WERNER:

We had rolled all the affiliation deals over. The operators were paying us fees now — the base rate was around fourteen or fifteen cents per subscriber. So in 1986 we said to them, we're hoping we're going to acquire rights to the NFL and we will guarantee you that there will be no more than a thirteen-cent surcharge the first year. At an industry convention in 1986, we showed a group of them a business-plan projection where we assumed that 60 to 70 percent of the industry complied and 40 percent stiffed us. We discussed the plan and said, look, if 100 percent of you take it, the surcharge gets smaller and smaller, and that meant we ultimately got everybody. When we went out and started making those pitches in '86, we hadn't made more than three or four before the cable industry banded together and decided to create their own consortium to make sure we didn't get the NFL rights and couldn't come to them with a surcharge. They would get the rights and allow any interested networks to compete for the right to carry it.

Their problem was they had no guaranteed network vehicle to display those games on, they didn't have a credible management team, and they couldn't reassure the NFL that games would get cleared in syndication in the home markets so no one would be denied access to a home team.

BILL GRIMES:

Roger and I met with this consortium that had been put together, and they told us they had decided they didn't want us to bid on the NFL games; they wanted the rights. But they said if they won the rights, they would guarantee the games would be produced by and televised on ESPN. We were quite surprised, but we were firm: "Negotiating for and obtaining sports rights is our business, not yours." The meeting ended acrimoniously, which was nothing new with many of our meetings with cable system executives.

ROGER WERNER:

It was an ugly meeting. We were pissed off. I couldn't believe after doing all the hard work to convince the NFL that this had merit, building the business model, and showing the operators how much money they could make on local ad sales and how many subscribers they would gain — all we got from the operators was them going behind our backs to try and create a competitive bid. We got up and walked out.

BILL GRIMES:

At the first CapCities/ABC/ESPN management meeting since the acquisition, there were more than a hundred participants, and it was indicative of how unimportant CapCities thought we were — and how feeble Herb's support of us was — that I had tried and failed for Steve Bornstein and Andy Brilliant, our counsel, to be there. Herb told me we would have a private lunch with Tom Murphy, Dan Burke, himself, and Warren Buffett. I can't remember whether Fred Pierce and Roger were there. Anyway, we went into a private room of the Phoenix Biltmore and I reported on our negotiations with the NFL and then the details of the day-before meeting with the cable-system companies' consortium. Murphy and Burke asked numerous questions. Herb remained as quiet as he could until Murphy asked him what he recommended we do. He said, "It's a tough call. The cable guys are our customers. I am worried that if we compete with them we will have continued problems. We could do this deal and still make money with them owning the rights."

Buffett finally spoke and wanted to know my opinion— "the guy on the firing line"—and I stressed that cable operators were distributors and we were content creators and producers. We didn't want our distributors to be our competitors in this business. Buffett said he thought buying it for ourselves would certainly make it simpler and agreed with me. Murphy agreed as well, and we were off and running.

ROGER WERNER:

The cable operators fought us down to the wire, but they didn't have enough solutions that served the NFL's interests, which were not just economic but also political. The NFL didn't want to present their product in a way that would be embarrassing to them. They wanted guarantees about the level of presentation and promotion. They felt comfortable ESPN could deliver on that. There were a lot of little wrinkles that had to be built into a plan to satisfy the NFL, and at the end of the day, the cable operators just couldn't get their act together.

We brought the NFL cost and the surcharge in at eight or nine cents versus that thirteen-cent ceiling.

We created an incentive for everybody to play along, for everybody to kick in, and we divided the rights fees pro rata on a per-subscriber basis. That was the premise on which the NFL was sold into cable.

GEORGE BODENHEIMER:

We set a deadline and we told everybody there was a benefit to committing to us then, but those who didn't sign by midnight of the deadline date would pay a higher price. I remember pleading with one particular cable operator who was my account who said he wasn't going to agree to sign on. His name was Leonard Tow.

BILL GRIMES:

Tow was a PhD in engineering, a real hard-assed guy, very successful. I said, "Look, I live in the next town. Why don't I come see you tomorrow for breakfast?" So I go to his house. It was a mansion that was just being finished. Incredible landscaping; there must have been twenty-five Mexican workers out there. I ring the bell, and a butler opens the door, takes me to this gigantic room. "Tea, coffee, sir?" Then Leonard comes in, and you know what the first thing he says about the deal was? "We can't afford to do this." I said, "People not seeing the games aren't going to like it." Leonard said, "I know football's popular, but we're already paying you guys a subscriber fee. We'll just put on some other local programming the night of the game." I reminded him that if he changed his mind after tomorrow, he would have to pay a 20 percent incremental fee, a premium, but he just kept saying nope. On the way out I said, "Leonard, look, we're really successful now and we're going to be more successful in the future. It would be awful not having you a part of this, but I really believe you're going to wind up changing your mind. Just wait until people find out you won't have the games." He disagreed and we said good-bye. One week later, he called and signed on. And, oh yeah, he paid the extra 20 percent.

From the time that ESPN made its initial presentation to the NFL to the network's first game, almost two years had gone by, along with dozens and dozens of meetings. It would be time well spent.

ESPN won the rights to nine Sunday-night games, two exhibition games, and the Pro Bowl, all part of a three-year deal that would cost ESPN $153 million—an audacious expenditure for the company at the time. From their base rate of approximately twenty-seven cents per subscriber, the network wound up adding an NFL surcharge of eight or nine cents per subscriber.

CHRIS BERMAN:

Man, do I remember our first preseason game. Chicago Bears at the Miami Dolphins, August 10, 1987. Every engineer we had who'd ever plugged in a plug was on duty that night — just in case something went wrong. I tripped over the guys getting in the studio, there were so many of them. I bet we had every technical person on the payroll that night working to make sure this game got on. We did a little pregame thing. I got Marino. Then I thanked all the viewers. I think I said, "You've been with us for the Wonder-bread years; that's all about to change. I now present on ESPN for the first time, the National Football League." I'm going to tell you right now, I almost cried.

ESPN aired its first regular season NFL game on November 8, 1987. It attributed about 700,000 new subscribers to the NFL package; indeed, by the time ESPN started airing games, the Bristol upstarts had found their way into 45 million homes, becoming the first cable network to achieve 50 percent penetration in the U.S. television market.

Bristol wanted to look like a big-time operation, not cheesy in comparison to the broadcast networks the viewers were accustomed to watching. Accordingly, big-time talent was signed up. Guest commentators for the 1987 season would include Larry Csonka, Jim Brown, Ed Marinaro, Tom Jackson, Roger Staubach, and O. J. Simpson. And on December 6, 1987, when ESPN aired Chicago at Minnesota, the network was rewarded with a 14.4 rating, humongous for cable. Indeed, it was the highest rating ESPN had scored in its existence, and it would remain the network's record holder for years and years to come.

A new chapter was beginning. The story was getting more complex and less predictable. This was, in every sense, the Big Time.

Garnering television rights to NFL games beginning in 1987: Step Number Five in ESPN's rise to world dominance.

STEVE BORNSTEIN:

Televising the games was a big deal, but I got something else from Rozelle that year which would wind up being incredibly significant as well. We made up this tape of the way we did highlights and asked him to give us unlimited minutes of highlights, which meant he had to carve that out of the network deals, because there were always time limits on how much you could show. He agreed, and so now we would have a great highlight show on Sunday evening before our game that night. Thus was born *NFL Primetime.* Then all I had to do was convince Chris Berman that he shouldn't be doing play-by-play of the games, and instead anchor that show. That turned out to be harder than getting the highlights out of the NFL, but once Berman agreed, *Primetime* became a huge profit center for us.

BOB RAUSCHER:

When we did *SportsCenters* before we got the NFL, there were always footage restrictions by the

NFL on how much we could show. But once we got the NFL package, we could go as long as we wanted. We were showing three, four, five minutes of highlights! The conceit was, don't just show me Emmitt Smith's touchdown, show me the key block that sprang Emmitt's run as well. One game had twelve straight completions; we showed all twelve. It was an opportunity to really take people inside the game, give them a sense of how a game unfolded. It was a revolutionary time.

On Sundays, people tuned over to see our show after the earlier games ended, and the numbers grew as we got closer to our game. They had a re-air slot at midnight. Players watched it. Coaches watched it. And Chris Berman was the perfect person to host. His passion and his love of football came through. He's a true fan at heart. In January 1987, we had been outside the Rose Bowl in Pasadena, where the Giants beat Denver in the Super Bowl. In those days, we had a really scaled-down operation, so we ran out to the truck for Chris to voice all the highlights, which would be rolled from Bristol, but there was no net return, no video coming back to us, so Chris couldn't see any footage. Chris wound up doing the highlights of the Super Bowl sight unseen and nailed them. He did it from memory and from his understanding of the game. We had a producer in Bristol who was in his ear telling him what was on the screen, and Chris was then basically embellishing those plays as he delivered that highlight presentation. That always stuck in my mind.

Then in 1988, *NFL GameDay* with Chris Berman, Tom Jackson, and Pete Axthelm—I was producing at the time—won for best studio show. It was the first ESPN studio show that won an Emmy. I was very proud of that. We all felt as if we had really made it, and made an impact with what we were putting on the air.

TOM JACKSON, *Pro Football Analyst:*

I had a very good relationship with the media when I was a player. I enjoyed talking to them, I think, as much as they did with me. The last game I played in was Super Bowl XXI, where we lost to the Giants, but I sat in that locker room afterward and gave anybody who wanted an interview. I was actually the last person to leave the locker room. I announced my retirement from football in the spring of '87, and within a week I got a call from NBC, who asked me to come in to New York for an audition. After I did it, I was literally marched into the next room and asked if I'd like the job. Now here's the weird thing: my dad always told me, when you're going to make a big decision in life, geographically, professionally, whatever, if you can, take a week and really think hard about what it is that you're going to be doing. So I asked NBC if I could have a week to think about it. During the course of that week, ESPN called. They wanted me to come up to Bristol for an audition, because they wanted an analyst to work on their studio show. That's actually when I met Chris, and there was something between the two of us that just clicked. I know that sounds a little bit intangible, but it's true.

The highlight package is the lifeblood of broadcasting the NFL—next to the games. Nothing takes the place of the games, but in lieu of that, the next thing that I really believe you have to have is a highlight package that shows in a smaller context, microscopically, what the game was about. I was very fortunate in that—and I sensed it right away—and I would put this to the test of anybody who wants to argue it: there is nobody who does highlights ever, and maybe there never will be, like Chris Berman. My ability to quickly analyze and to know when to get in and out was key, because you never want to take away from what he is doing. So I began to understand my role—get in and out—and allow that highlight package to flow.

BRENT MUSBURGER, *Sportscaster*:
When *Primetime* first began, those of us at the broadcast networks didn't pay a whole lot of attention to it. We were still wondering what ESPN meant, and where they got that name. I knew they had some games up there, but rarely did I watch the show after. Then Chris Berman caught my attention, and I was

even a little jealous of the fact that they had such a long time frame for postgame highlights on Sunday. When they got their NFL deal, they got permission to use our highlights and NBC's. We could only really use highlights at halftime, so we couldn't tell the full story like Chris and those guys did. I remember some of my colleagues doubting ESPN could have much success with the NFL or thinking it was going to be more regionalized, but pretty quickly, they changed their minds.

JOE THEISMANN, *Pro Football Analyst:*

When I got hurt in '85, I went to work for CBS, and in 1987 I was at the Charlotte airport and ran into Mike Patrick, who had just started to do the NFL for ESPN. Mike and I had actually done Maryland basketball together in '76, and we were sitting there—I remember this like it was yesterday—and I said, "Wouldn't it be great if we could work together again?" and we both sort of chuckled and said, "Yeah, that'd be terrific." Then the experiment at ESPN with multiple different analysts didn't seem to go very well, and so I believe there was a decision to make between O. J. Simpson and myself regarding joining ESPN and doing the telecasts. From what I understand, it was Steve Bornstein who decided that he would go with me, and it was much appreciated, trust me. I certainly appreciated the opportunity to be able to stay around the game of football.

JIM GRAY, *Reporter:*

This will make me sound like I'm talking about myself, but I did an interview that was long credited by many people for putting ESPN on the map in terms of a news-gathering organization. I broke the Eric Dickerson trade from the Los Angeles Rams when he was holding out and owner Georgia Frontiere wouldn't pay him. She wanted to give him new furniture for his house, and he wanted $1 million a year, and this was after he had broken the single-season rushing record with 2,105 yards. I was the only reporter he would talk to through that period in 1987, and he had decided not to go down to the Rams facility. So he said, "If you want to see me and talk, you can come to this Halloween party I'm going to." Well, about two hours before the party, he called and said, "You better come over to the house. I'm not going to the party." I said, "Why?" He said, "Just get over to the house as soon as possible."

I got the directions and went over to his house. It was there that he told me he that coach Ron Meyer had called him and that he was being traded to the Indianapolis Colts. There was going to be a press conference in New York to announce it, because they were playing the Jets that weekend. So as we were talking, Eric was getting into his car to go to the airport. I said, "Eric, can you let me do an interview with you in the studio in downtown Los Angeles before you go? This would be big for me and we could announce this trade right now." He thought about it and said, "Okay." So I drove his car to the studio. I didn't have any clothes to be on camera, so he gave me a coat, a tie, and shirt of his to use; the neck was just huge on me. We had a certain window that we could only do it because it was 1987, and satellite time was limited. So we went speeding down the 101 and got there with about two minutes left. We jumped out of the car, ran up, and Eric did this ten- or fifteen-minute interview. Tom Mees was anchoring that night, and we broke the story on the air.

So in 1987 we had a scoop comparable to LeBron James in 2010. Eric Dickerson had his own fifteen minutes on the air when nobody else knew, and it was very, very newsworthy. Eric was the biggest player in the NFL at that time, and there was no Internet back then, so the next day it made the back pages of the big papers. The whole thing just exploded, and I was very proud of that. Tom Mees, Chris Berman, George Grande, and even Herb Granath said this was the night ESPN arrived as a news-making operation, and *SportsCenter* went from playing yesterday's highlights tomorrow, to an organization where you could look at them as being a real news-gathering operation.

Although the Eric Dickerson interview brought much-needed and much-valued attention to ESPN, it had come about because of a reporter's close relationship with a player—not because ESPN's news-gathering operation was such a miracle worker. For ESPN to prove itself as a serious, credible, solidly professional news operation, it would have to grow up and make key changes in the way it did business. Fortunately for everyone involved and for ESPN's evolving reputation, the leadership now recognized this.

Steve Bornstein didn't know exactly what he was getting when he hired John Walsh as a consultant in July of 1987. The two hardly knew each other, and Bornstein had actually rebuffed Walsh's attempt, through mutual friends, to join ESPN once before, telling him, "We're not ready for you yet." But things had moved fast since then, and with NFL games coming to ESPN in the fall, the network was entering a new era. Why not have some new names and new expertise?

Back then, Walsh was known by many names. To some friends and colleagues he was "John A."—in the vein of "the Great John L.," nickname of nineteenth-century heavyweight champ John L. Sullivan—and to legendary editor Ben Bradlee, Walsh's boss at the Washington Post, *he was "Whiteman." To a select few who knew him well, he was "the world's most dangerous albino"—as christened at a New York bar by the founder and lead singer of Kinky Friedman and the Texas Jewboys after Walsh was invited onto the stage to sing a few numbers with the group.*

MIKE McQUADE, *Vice President of Production:*

There were no car services for people at ESPN. Either they drove themselves to and from the airport or we went and picked them up. That was my first job there, a driver-messenger. I would often go to the airport to pick up employees, analysts, and highlight tapes that had been shipped overnight.

KEITH OLBERMANN, *Anchor:*

Mike McQuade used to delight in telling this story: His first day working in the mail room, they sent him to a hotel in Hartford, where a consultant for ESPN named John Walsh was staying. This is before he was the John Walsh of ESPN. And McQuade, I don't know, twenty-one, twenty-two years old, says, "How I will know who he is?" And they all said, "Don't worry, he's like nobody you've ever seen before. Picture Santa Claus at the age of forty-five. Keep that image in your mind and you'll recognize him immediately." Obviously they used the A-word here; he's an albino. Okay?

And he drives up to the hotel and there is a banner hanging outside, "Welcome National Association of Albinos." And it is wall-to-wall Edgar Winters. There is nobody who does not look like Santa Claus at some age. And Mike's just trying to find the needle in the haystack. Somehow, after half an hour, he and Walsh hooked up, and Walsh is breathing heavily and says, "In my whole life, I've only seen about ten people who looked anything like me, and now it's a hotel full of me. People coming up to me congratulating me on a speech I gave, and I don't even know what the speech was about!" That's apparently the only time anybody ever saw Walsh completely disheveled. I love that image. I reveled in that when he told me that story.

Walsh was born in Scranton, Pennsylvania, and grew up above his father's "store," a funeral home. Like his twin albino brother, James, he inherited the genetic distinction via the "autosomal recessive" route from carrier parents who themselves showed no outward signs. In boyhood, Walsh developed intense loyalties to certain people, places, and institutions, and it was also where Walsh launched a Zelig-like life beginning in his twelfth year, when he attended Don Larsen's perfect game at the 1956 World Series between the New York Yankees and the Brooklyn Dodgers. Just eight years later, Walsh was on hand when Philadelphia Phillies pitcher Jim Bunning cranked out another perfect game, the first such National League game in eighty-four years.

When it was time for college, Walsh couldn't bring himself to leave his cherished hometown, so he attended the University of Scranton. Afterward, he broke away to the University of Missouri for a master's degree in journalism. His first few big editing jobs were outside the sports world—first at Rolling Stone *and then at the* Washington Post's *Style section, but in 1980, his passion for sports finally dovetailed with a professional opportunity when he was named editor of* Inside Sports *magazine. True, the magazine flopped in the early eighties—losing $30 million for his beloved patron, the legendary Katharine Graham—but it established the viability of sports journalism for the literate, civilized, and worldly, not just chest-painting yahoos or compulsive gamblers. Walsh became an expert at distilling the essence of sports, stressing the beauty and poetry and exhilaration that go way beyond scores and rankings and even drug and sex scandals. Even in failure, Walsh's* Inside Sports *took the standards of sports print journalism to new heights.*

Upon his arrival in Bristol, Walsh instantly won "most unforgettable person I ever met" honors all around. Colleagues learned about his background—his adored nun sister, his friendships with gonzo journalist Hunter S. Thompson and actor Bill Murray, and perhaps most significantly, his strict and deeply rooted Jesuit values. His trademark quirks ranged from wearing "funny" hats to ordering "Heineken keck-tails" to compiling what may be the world's largest Rolodex (in multiple volumes) to his annual good-natured stints playing Santa, white hair and beard both real, of course.

The big question was, how would a man who had never worked in television, who had to be within six inches of a TV screen even to see it (being legally blind), fit into the world of television? How would the Bristol troops react to this very visible outsider?

JOHN WALSH, *Executive Vice President:*

When *Inside Sports* folded and Westinghouse bailed on a regional sports net, I was broke and looking for likely consultantships. This wasn't anything new, because when I left *Rolling Stone,* I was in debt. I was out of work four times and in debt three of those four times. I learned firsthand how to scramble for money, and I always had confidence I'd find something. I went to Steve Bornstein, but he said, "We just aren't ready for you; it's too early." Then I went to *US News & World Report* with Shelby [Coffey], who was then the editor. My days with Shelby were great because it was a terrific learning experience about not being in charge. I had known enough about being in charge, but being one of the second guys is different. Three years later, I went to Bornstein again, and this time he said, "We're ready; you can do a consultantship with us."

I began by watching *SportsCenter* every day. I wanted to know everything about what they were doing—what was on the screen, at least. Then I wrote a thirty-two-page memo to Bornstein, saying, "Here's what I think the network should be." One of the recurring themes in my memo was that in the media, you amass a certain amount of material—data and other types of information. At a place like ESPN, every hour of every day you have editorial choices to make and you have to be selective. You need to say,

"I'm going to communicate the most effective part of this to reach the largest possible audience for the longest possible time." And that's one of the important things that I was concerned with back then—making the best choices that are conducive to the presentation. The fact that I was now talking about television instead of print meant that I now had to consider the most effective way to use moving pictures. I didn't know much television when I got here, but I knew news, and I knew sports pretty well.

JANN WENNER, *Publisher,* Rolling Stone:

John had energy and enthusiasm, and lots of ideas. He was a charismatic guy; we all really liked him. He was here for about six months or so. He was too much energy for *Rolling Stone.* It was almost like we were too small a field for him. He'd come from *Newsday,* where there were like thirty or forty people, and here we had six or eight in editorial. But he moved us into a more modern era—started a copy desk, proofreading, systematizing all that kind of stuff. He really liked Hunter [Thompson], and he made a lot of lifelong friends here. He's quite the talent.

BILL CREASY:

During those days, I was consulting for Steve [Bornstein], and he says to me, "I'm thinking about hiring this guy, John Walsh, and I want you to work with him, teach him everything you know, so you're going to have to spend more time up here." The first time I'm with Walsh, I was in his office and we were talking about what the place needed. He was sharing his thoughts and I was sharing mine. It gets to be like 5:58, and he says, "Crease, I gotta watch *SportsCenter.*" He gets up from his desk, goes up to the wall, basically puts his face up against the TV screen, and squints his eyes. And I thought to myself, "Holy fuck, the guy can't even see the goddamn set."

STEVE ANDERSON:

Hiring John Walsh was a risk because he was a print guy with very little TV experience, but that's what the entire place was about then. We wound up being a great team. John needed me, and there's no way I could have done it without John.

JOHN WALSH:

The consulting gig became a full-time job in January of 1988. It was a leap of faith on Bornstein's part to hire me, a big leap of faith. The first day I was officially on the job, I couldn't go into the office because Bornstein didn't tell the guy I was replacing that I was coming in to replace him. So I actually went to work on Tuesday, January the eleventh.

The very next day, Steve Anderson said to me, "You and I and Al Jaffe" — who was then running part of the news operation — "have to sit down together because we have to hire some new on-air people. We don't have the bench strength that we need." It was late afternoon. Al begins by saying, "I have some tapes of people," and the first tape he put in was of this guy named Keith Olbermann. The first tape. Everything about it was brilliant—point of view, knowledge, the playfulness, the whimsy, combined with seriousness when he had to be serious. So I turned to Al and Steve and said, "Man, this is going to be easy." Thus began a recruitment drive to get Keith. We didn't get him for four years.

In the coming months and during the next year, we looked all over the place for talent. ESPN was hiring women before I got there, and of course CBS had hired Phyllis George, who was a real firecracker and made a big impact. Lesley Visser was the first woman who made an impact on the sidelines, and she made the Andrea Kremers of the world possible. You can't overstate how much credit these women deserve. But Gayle Gardner was also incredibly important. She showed the world that a woman could anchor every day. That was a huge achievement. So that standard had already been set.

The network had also already distinguished itself by hiring Pete Axthelm and Beano Cook, people who were not necessarily first choices for a visual medium, but who were first choices because they knew what they were talking about.

We looked at the people at CNN. Remember, in those days, CNN *Sports Tonight* was out-rating

SportsCenter, and so we looked at Fred Hickman and Nick Charles. But there was this guy that was also on their air, Dan Patrick. We all liked his writing ability, so we flew him in, and I thought he was very strong and that he could be a number one with us instead of being a number two behind Hickman and Charles. So we eventually hired him.

And Al Jaffe had this woman in Atlanta named Robin Roberts who he had met a couple years earlier, but she wasn't ready for a national audience yet, and now he thought she was, so she came in. Then one time we sat down and looked at a tape of this kid just out of Syracuse, Mike Tirico; we said, "That's like a no-brainer; we'll hire him." I thought we should try to get a deal with Peter Gammons. I had read him in the *Boston Globe* and *SI* for fifteen years, he knew the most about baseball, so I wanted him and that worked out. Recommendations came from all over. Steve Bornstein came in with a note from his liquor-store owner, who said this guy, Charley Steiner, who was a radio announcer, was now available. He had just been fired by the Jets as their play-by-play guy on radio, so we hired him. Jimmy Roberts had been a producer for Howard Cosell and Dick Schaap at ABC Sports, but never on air. Jimmy had a tape of pieces he had written and produced for others; he had gone back and reshot them all with stand-ups of himself. We hired him. And Andrea Kremer, from NFL films, had never been an on-air reporter before either, but she was an incredible news hound.

PETER GAMMONS, *Baseball Analyst:*

I was purely a print guy when John Walsh hired me. I don't think I had ever even thought about going into television at that point. I was the lone print guy at the time, and it was really nail biting. They helped me understand that I should think of it as talking to a bunch of people who were interested in what I was interested in, who were interested in what I was doing. Once I figured that out, it made the transition a lot easier.

In 1988, we had the great Orel Hershiser year, the Hershiser playoffs and World Series. Jim Kaat was my partner, a brilliant baseball guy. We would do a lot of talking before games and then interviews. Hershiser was on this incredible run and he kept pitching, so I remember asking him, "Don't you worry what this is going to do to your future?" He looked at me and said, "Lookit, I don't care, 'cause I may never be in this place again in my life. This is what I set out to play baseball for. So you don't worry about whether you get hurt or not. You worry about enjoying the moment." And of course he did blow out and his career was never the same. But it was a great moment for me to understand how athletes think and why certain athletes have so much passion for what they do.

JIMMY ROBERTS, *Reporter:*

All you need to know about my career is I was hired to do television by a blind guy. John Walsh hired me, and I started the first ESPN bureau, in New York. But I have to tell you—and I'm not being falsely modest—I had never been on camera before, and I wasn't very good at it. So those first few years were painful. I was just fortunate to land at a place where they let me be as bad as I was and learn on the job.

I had been hired in June of 1988, and my first assignment was to work the Tyson-Spinks heavyweight championship fight in Atlantic City. I was terrified because I was going to have to be on live television. I wasn't going to narrate something on tape—that I could do a hundred times till it was right. I was going to be on live television. I had to do an interview with Robin Givens, and our coordinating producer at the time was Barry Sacks, who is a very rough kind of New York guy. He says, "This is the way we're going to do this. Jimmy, I think you've got to ask her about the miscarriage. You've got to ask if Mike's hitting her caused the miscarriage." And I told him, "You know, Barry, I don't feel comfortable asking that question." So he says, "No, you have to ask that question. It's what everybody wants to know. We're going to ask that question." We went back and forth, and I remember finally I said to him, "Barry, unless you're a fucking ventriloquist, those words aren't coming from this mouth."

CHARLEY STEINER, *Anchor:*

I was the oldest guy in the newsroom and a rookie—a lethal combination. I was a short, dumpy, almost-forty-year-old with a beard who'd never done television. Who would hire me to be on camera? Nobody, except John Walsh. Look at the people John hired during those early years; none of us had ever done live television. On my first day at ESPN, September 1, 1988, this guy comes up to me, looks at me, and he says, "You're the new guy?" And I said, "Yeah." Then he says, "This fuckin' place," shakes his head, and just walks away.

A couple hours later, a producer comes up to me and says, "How's it going?" And I said, "I'm feeling really overwhelmed." He said, "Well, don't worry. We're putting you on an airplane tonight; you're going to Vegas tomorrow for the press conference to announce the Sugar Ray Leonard–Donny Lalonde fight." Okay. I'd covered a lot of fights in the eighties, when I was doing network radio, and I knew Leonard a bit. And from that point on, I became the boxing guy. It was an interesting time. Don King, Bob Arum, and others were starting to figure out that in order to have pay-per-view audiences, you wanted cable television, and if you were a sports fan, you needed ESPN. So we were granted unbelievable access to all these guys—Leonard, Hearns, Bowe, Holyfield, and Tyson. I became pretty good at tapping into what these guys were thinking and feeling. I was able to differentiate between confidence and false bravado. It got to the point where I was reasonably confident, after spending the final day or two before a fight studying the fighters, that I could pretty well tell you who was going to win and who was going to lose.

GREG GUMBEL:

I have never gone to a place with the idea of moving on to somewhere else afterward. Now I won't deny that every subsequent job that I took paid me more money. At ESPN, I was doing *SportsCenter* Monday through Friday and hosting a weekly NBA show. I was working with guys in *SportsCenter*—George Grande, Tom Mees, Lou Palmer, and Bob Ley—who all had a desire to do play-by-play. But the one thing Chet and Scotty really, really denied some people was the ability to let them leave the studio and go out and call games. And it wouldn't have been that big a deal, because these guys were so happy and wanting to do it that they would have done it for practically nothing. Yet they were forbidden to do it. I never really had a desire to do play-by-play, but Bob Gutkowski had left ESPN for Madison Square Garden and asked me not only to be the host of various shows at the Garden, but to also occasionally call New York Knicks and New York Yankee games. So I kind of felt my way into the play-by-play thing by accident. I won't deny that Madison Square Garden offered me a lot more money than I was making at ESPN at the time.

At that time, I think there were a lot of people who saw ESPN as a building ground, a place to learn your craft, because you had to learn how to do highlights on the fly, you had to learn to ad-lib, you had to think on your feet. Sometimes we'd be out of material three minutes before the end of a show. Not everything was scripted. That's probably why I came away from ESPN much more self-confident, simply because of the way we had to do things. ESPN proved to be a great training ground for me.

BILL WOLFF, *Producer:*

We had this overnight anchorwoman who used to be on the sauce, and she would just lose her shit. I remember she called James Donaldson of the Dallas Mavericks "Sam Donaldson." I mean, are you kidding me? Rick Tocchet was "Rick Toe-shay." She was very proud when she called Wayne Gretzky "Wayne Gretzky," 'cause it was like, "Aha, I'm getting the hang of this hockey stuff." She was a disaster.

One time we were doing the tale of the tape between, I think, Razor Ruddock and Mike Tyson, and there was a ten-inch reach advantage, and she says a "ten-inch advantage." Then her mind goes to the gutter, and now she can't collect herself. She can't stop laughing because she's making a dirty joke about Razor Ruddock's ten-inch advantage over Mike Tyson. And this is happening on TV. Don't forget, this was mom-and-pop cable operators, and here she was laughing her ass off.

It was kids putting on a show in the backyard. We didn't know shit from shit. We were there in the middle of the fucking night, a bunch of twenty-three year olds and maybe one twenty-nine year old. You think John Walsh was there? Hell, no! He was sleeping like everybody else.

STEVE BORNSTEIN:

One of my biggest contributions to the network was that I recognized that the *SportsCenter* franchise was really valuable but that it had no direction. It was a little bit of the inmates running the asylum. I'm looking at a business that basically cost nothing to produce other than the people I hired to put it on the air. There were no rights fees. We're making all our profit out of *SportsCenter,* so I needed more *SportsCenter* on the air. But all I had was a bunch of kids at 2:00 a.m. on the weekdays, an average age of twenty-two and a half, trying to figure out what to put on the air based on what they used to watch in their dorm rooms at Syracuse a year and a half earlier. I mean, this was insanity.

BILL WOLFF:

It was the Wild Wild East. There was no union, no managers, no supervision, and certainly no ombudsman. There was one girl on staff for every twenty guys. Part of ESPN's success was there was no place to go, so there were no distractions. It was like being on Parris Island. You were working in this box all the time, and your whole life was that. Then it was like three o'clock in the morning, let's get the fuck out of here. You went back with your roommate, who also worked there, hopefully somebody had bought a six-pack of beer before eight o'clock when the liquor stores closed, and then whoever came to the apartment that everybody from work was at, you split six beers 'cause there was no getting any more.

STEVE BORNSTEIN:

I needed a grown-up. We had personalities like Chris Berman and Bob Ley, but I can't have them running it, and no twenty-two-year-old is going to tell those guys how to do their jobs. So I needed someone who was intellectually capable of handling some very bright guys who were shooting from the hip. I had to bring in somebody intelligent, smarter than the talent, and in the case of Bob Ley, that's not an easy thing to do. If Walsh wasn't smarter, he was at least their equal. *SportsCenter* needed to get under control.

JOHN WALSH:

In addition to hiring talent, I did two big things: first, I went traveling with two marketing-research guys. The head of marketing was Dana Redman, and he hired a marketing consultant named Ed Wolf. Ed Wolf was made for ESPN, a sports nut, and he went out and did field research. I went with him all over the country. In the first year we saw upwards of seven hundred or eight hundred people, two or three days at a time, watching focus groups. We talked to the viewers about what they were looking for from ESPN. The second thing I did was to sit down with everyone so I could figure out what wasn't quite right with what they were doing. Fifty to seventy people, on-air producers, even PAs.

STEVE ANDERSON:

The decision was made that John was going to run *SportsCenter*. What John instilled was this notion that we need to be journalistically sound, we need to be a news organization, we need to think about *SportsCenter* as a franchise. Part of it was as simple as rethinking how we formatted the show. CNN was doing a score-and-highlights show. In those days, they would start with baseball and you'd do all the American League, and then the next segment would be all the National League, and then the third segment would be the NBA. Once you started a sport you had to finish it off. Now, when John came in, he said, "Let's look at the first segment as the front page of a newspaper." He was using information differently, thinking about our viewers as fans, and really thinking about what is it they want from us as opposed to here's what we're going to give them. He totally changed the way people thought.

I used to say John was a fountain of ideas; they'd be just popping up all over the place. So my other job was to catch the best ones and figure out how we were going to execute them.

NORBY WILLIAMSON, *Executive Vice President:*

One day he's sitting there reading a paper, then two days later it's like he's in charge. Why the hell would we reinvent *SportsCenter*? It's not broken.

FRED GAUDELLI:

SportsCenter was undervalued by people within ESPN. It had gone through ever-changing leadership. There was a new executive producer seemingly every eighteen months. It did not have a lot of internal respect, and people working in remote production felt like they were superior to *SportsCenter*. But Walsh came in with a definitive plan and a definitive structure. And the more you heard him talk, the more you knew. Slowly and surely, you either jumped in or you jumped out. It was clear he had the vision, and it was clear he had the power.

MIKE McQUADE:

Walsh was called the Antichrist. He was not well received at all. It's hard to accept a guy who's legally blind and who's working in television for the first time. A lot of people had problems with him. The DNA of the show became very different. It used to be very much "here are all your baseball items; here are all your hockey items." The show was laid out that way. It wasn't until John got there that it became more of a "here are the top stories of the day."

ESPN suddenly became more of a business. There had been a lot of talented people working, but there was just chaos. Now we were getting serious. John wanted to know what everybody did—the APs, PAs, even the producers. And to John's credit, he spent countless hours there. It's not like he said, "Okay, this is what you're doing tonight," and left. He was there.

JOHN WALSH:

Remember, the first three or four years of ESPN, the highlights were coming into Bradley Airport and being shipped overnight to ESPN. That's what they had to put on the air. They couldn't worry about breaking news. They had Jim Gray on the West Coast break the Eric Dickerson trade story; that was their big news scoop. They covered press conferences.

The kids were all sports fans so they lived by the highlight. I was a huge sports fan. I wasn't saying don't do any highlights; I was saying, hey, make the highlights better. Let's try to do a nonchronological highlight. Let's put some journalism or storytelling into a highlight.

After we started to think about how we lined up the show and the highlights, we wanted to put together teams. We made a decision in the first couple months of '88 that we would put together both broadcast and production teams so that the same producers and the same talent would work the same shifts. We wanted to move Bob Ley into *SportsCenter* full-time. I think he was doing *SportsCenter* but also doing college-basketball wraps; he was a premier journalist and we thought journalism would rule at seven o'clock. Then other pieces just began to kind of fall in place. Chris Berman and John Saunders were the eleven o'clock team when I started and they were very good, but they had been doing it for years and were ready for a transition into other sports-specific programming. That opened up the eleven, and we saw Dan Patrick as a host right away and we paired him with Bob Ley.

DAVID HILL:

Steve Bornstein deserves all the credit in the world for taking one of those beautiful gambles, which is what the great hits in life are all about, rolling the dice, and bringing in John Walsh to run *SportsCenter* and turning it into what it has become today.

JOHN WALSH:

People weren't accustomed to going to meetings; people were accustomed to just gathering around people's desks. I said, "No, we want to get everybody's attention in a meeting where we're talking only about the show." At first, I had to literally go around and ask people to come to a meeting, then I finally got this idea from working at the *Washington Post,* where every afternoon at three o'clock, Ben Bradlee went out and rang a bell, and everybody showed up at the meeting. So I got myself a bell and I rang it for every meeting. It drove people out of their minds. John Saunders called it the Cattle Call.

JOHN COLBY:

In the early eighties I had been working for Ken Burns, producing music on his documentaries, playing in bands, and writing industrial music. I used to watch *SportsCenter* late at night when I came home from gigs. Like a million other musicians, I thought I could make better music than what I heard on the air. In late 1983, I cold-called ESPN, looking to write and produce music for the network. Somehow I got through to Bill Fitts, who oversaw all production. That was lucky, because he was a history buff and knew my work. I got hired as music coordinator in 1984.

At the time, the way ESPN handled music was starting to be a problem.

Producers would just pull cuts off records and air them. The network was still under the radar and nobody noticed, but the legal department saw the time coming when ESPN couldn't continue to use music without either licensing it or producing it.

I was there at the right time, and started to write and produce more music than I ever dreamed of; by 1986, I had written just about every theme that was on the network.

All the while I was weaving in four-note logos. I wanted to create ESPN's version of the NBC chimes, but nothing stuck.

By 1989 it was time for a new *SportsCenter* package. John Walsh — man of many hats — suggested that we go in a *Saturday Night Live* direction. To me that translated into a sax-driven R&B feel, and so the theme package was written and recorded. I loved the way it rode out on the sax solo and capped — this time I didn't even address the elusive four-note cap. It went on the air and I thought no further of it — on to the next project, you know.

Next thing I remember about it is about a year or so later, and I walk into the office, and Charley Steiner says, "Holy shit, man, do you see what's going on with this *dah dah dah* thing." I'm like, "What are you talking about?" It went viral, as they say. Not only did those notes identify ESPN but they became a catchphrase of any play that was so good as to make the highlights on *SportsCenter*.

When people find out who I am, they say, *"Dah dah dah, dah dah dah."* I'm always asked if royalties from *SportsCenter* have made me rich, but there are no performance royalties on music aired on ESPN. All music on the network is either a work for hire, licensed per program, or library music. Brilliant business on their part. I've got no regrets playing it, believe me.

CHUCK PAGANO:

We began doing more graphics than the networks. Our graphic development helped tell stories better, define the *SportsCenter* product more clearly, and serve the fans better. Serving the fan means you have to bombard them with information in one form or another. NBC was primarily doing sport events; they weren't serving the fan. They were filling time in between entertainment television; the same with CBS. We were satiating viewers' appetites for stats and information. We even won a Sports Emmy Award for our graphics work.

SCOTT ACKERSON, *Coordinating Producer:*

In the late eighties, *SportsCenter* was an hour show on Sunday, the only *SportsCenter* that was an hour long. One week, I had a hole in the show that was about seven minutes long, because it was the British Open and we just had that and baseball. So I said, "Let's have Cliff Drysdale interview Jack Nicklaus, and talk to him about anything *besides* the British

Open. I don't care about the British Open, I just want to talk to him about the state of golf." And the interview was really good. He talked about the state of the game and where he thought golf was going in the future. I called it "the Sunday Conversation," because I think you ought to title everything so it resonates with the viewer.

The next week, ESPN was televising the Davis Cup, and we did the same thing with Mary Carillo interviewing John McEnroe about the state of tennis. That was great too. So now, from a producer's standpoint, I'm thinking I'll have seven minutes' worth of coverage I won't have to worry about. So the next week John Walsh sees me and goes, "Hey, I noticed the last couple of weeks you've done this 'Conversation.'" I didn't necessarily know what he was going to say, but then he says, "I really like it. Do you think we can do more of these?" I replied, "Well, yeah, I don't see why not." So the next week we did one with Peter Ueberroth from Cooperstown.

I can't say it was any grand vision I had to start "Sunday Conversation" on *SportsCenter;* it's just how a lot of ideas in the early days of *SportsCenter* came up. "Hey, let's try this. I got three minutes here or five minutes here; let's give this a shot." And sometimes you hit and sometimes you missed. When you hit, it's great, and when you miss, you say, oh well, it's one show out of 365 days—there's another one tomorrow.

After that, I left to produce *NFL GameDay*. Then the guy who took over for me, producer Steve Vecchione, comes up to me and says in a kind of joking fashion, "I hate you." I said, "Why?" He says, "Because now we are going to have to do these 'Sunday Conversations,' and the first three you rip out are Jack Nicklaus, John McEnroe, and Peter Ueberroth. What I am I going to do?" I kind of felt bad for him having to follow that lineup, but c'est la vie.

CHRIS BERMAN:

I didn't do many *SportsCenter*s in the nineties, but in the late eighties, I was doing *SportsCenter* with Tom Mees, and that was one of the most fun things I've ever done at the network.

MATT SANDULLI, *Senior Coordinating Producer:*

Back then, if you wanted to know what was happening at that moment, you had to rip wire copy off the machine. Production assistants were literally assigned to a desk where you would answer the phone and rip the wires. In August of '88, I was filling in that day and a wire crossed that Gretzky had been traded to the Kings. It was like a bomb exploded in the newsroom. The greatest player in the game had just gotten traded. People started running around going crazy. When the press conference started, I was assigned graphics, which wound up being incredibly exciting. It was an unbelievable night, and we were there, watching it unfold right in front of us, and we felt like we were the only ones around. We were using TSN from Canada, but there was no Fox, there was no Comcast. We were the place to go for that kind of stuff, and it was really cool when those big ones happened.

CHARLEY STEINER:

The first couple of months, I was doing the 2:30 a.m. show — 11:30 Pacific time. I would go home after the show was over and pop in a videotape, like a quarterback watching plays unfold. I was constantly critiquing myself. I'm only there a few months, and Walsh and Anderson take me to this little restaurant in Bristol and ask, "Well, how's it going?" And I said, "Well, I don't like this nine p.m. to five a.m. shit. I don't need to be in Bristol, Connecticut, and I don't know how much longer I can do this. If you are planning on keeping me on these hours, I'm going home." They said, "Well, what do you mean, 'home'?" "I mean I'm going home!" And to their everlasting credit, they said, "By February first, we'll have you on the seven o'clock show." And that's where I stayed for about twelve and a half years.

BOB LEY:

John doesn't drive, so I would drive him home. We'd be leaving there 12:30 at night, because I was doing the 11:00 p.m. *SportsCenter*. He'd been there all day. I can recall him slamming his fist down in frustration, because people weren't listening. I had to educate him. I told him, these people have just gotten out of prison. They just had a very tough period of time being managed by someone who didn't have great people skills. They saw people fired. Now another guy is coming through the door with a lot of changes. Meanwhile, CNN was beating us in the ratings. It was a tough time.

CHRIS MYERS, *Reporter:*

I didn't get to ESPN until about a year after Walsh had gotten there, and I was assigned to cover the All-Star game in Anaheim. I was with my producer on the way to the game to talk to athletes and stuff, and — this is something you just can't make up — we hear that Tim Burke of the Expos, who was scheduled to pitch, had just found out that he and his wife had gotten the paperwork approved to adopt a child in Guatemala. They hadn't been able to have a child on their own, and now there was a certain time frame at an adoption center in a village down there in Central America. They had to get there in a certain amount of time or somebody else would get into the rotation. So both Tim and his wife needed to be there, something to the effect of signing the papers. When I talked to Tim, he said, "Hey, I've got to leave tonight, the late flight out of L.A. down into the jungle where this adoption center is." I said, "Well, I hate to be rude, but if I could go along, would you mind?" And he said, "Sure, you could come along. But I don't know exactly how it's going to all turn out."

So I asked Walsh, who was my boss at the time, if I could do it, and he says, "Go for it. This is a great story." We got a camera crew lined up. Lasorda used him early, he pitched in the All-Star game, and he left while the game was going on. We got on this plane, flew into the jungle, and landed at the airport like you see in the movies, complete with weeds on the runway. We walked with him to the adoption center; his wife was there. Our camera man Rick Telles and our producer John Hamlin captured the moment when they first saw their child, with all the emotion and the excitement. It was incredible. But the story didn't stop there. We flew back with them, and his wife took the baby home, and Tim had to go to a game in Cincinnati. We landed there while the game was going on. The Expos rallied to take the lead, Buck Rogers, Montreal's manager, uses Tim in the ninth inning to pitch, and he saves the game for the Expos! As he's walking off the field, Buck says something to him like, "That may be your second-best save ever." We quickly put all the pieces together, and the story was on the air within a few days. We won ESPN's first reporting Emmy.

JOHN WALSH:
There was one incident which occurred in September of '88 that really got to me. It was a Saturday

in September. I was in touch with the *SportsCenter* guys pretty much all day about what the lead story was going to be, and I had been talking to them about it being a big audience on Saturday night after college football. I was out with the kids somewhere and I got a phone call at six o'clock that they had canceled *SportsCenter* that night. I couldn't believe it. I said, "What?!" They said, "We've got to replay a golf tournament." I tracked Bornstein down at a restaurant, and I just went nuclear. I was very animated and very angry. It was a very heated discussion. Steve tried to defend the action, but I said, "I can't do this job this way. These kids have got to care about this show; you can't treat *SportsCenter* like this; and you have to be devoted to putting this show on every night." After that night, it never happened again.

DAVID HILL:

John Walsh should be in a house living next to Bill Gates right now, because the Disney Company should get down on their hands and knees and pay him a boatload of money. He was their secret weapon back then.

BILL GRIMES:

In 1987, we had been looking for a new CFO, and we hired a headhunter who found someone they wanted me to interview. So I was on a business trip to California, and I'm sitting next to a guy who's reading. I look over and see my picture in a *Forbes* magazine article about ESPN. So that caught my attention. The next thing I know, I see he has the ESPN business plan. So I don't know what to do. I don't whether to say something to him or not. So I got off the plane, thinking maybe there was some mistake. I mean, I did have a drink or two on the plane. The following day my secretary says one of the candidates from the headhunter is here. I'm sitting at my desk, and the guy who was sitting next to me on the plane walks in! So now I have to ask him, "Where did you get that plan?" He said, "I got it from Bob Wright over at NBC; Don Ohlmeyer gave it to him." Now, Don Ohlmeyer was on our board, and I just flipped. I called Herb Granath and said, "I want to see Burke and Murphy." Well, Granath shitted at this. I got a meeting, but Murphy wasn't there. It was me, Roger, Granath, and Dan Burke. I just said, "This guy should be thrown off our board." And you know what Burke said? He just said, "Jack—meaning Welch—must be having a midlife crisis if he's having guys like Ohlmeyer bring him competitive business plans."

When it acquired a majority stake in ESPN in 1984, ABC management reached out to television guru Don Ohlmeyer for some consulting. Ohlmeyer, who had recently left NBC Sports, founded and ran the Ohlmeyer Communications Company with funding supplied by *his friend Ross Johnson — he of Barbarians at the Gate fame and head of RJR Nabisco. The consulting deal with ESPN was $2.5 million for five years, but when Johnson heard about it, he asked Ohlmeyer, "Why don't you demand some equity?" Ohlmeyer went back to ABC and asked, but they weren't about to give away a chunk of the company for nothing. So Ohlmeyer Communications, with Johnson's funding at its back, bought 20 percent of ESPN for $60 million. It just so happened to be the same 20 percent that Texaco had inherited from Getty, and in which they had lost all interest. As part of the deal, Ohlmeyer got a seat on the ESPN board and a stake in ESPN. Indeed, once Nabisco got the "average return on investment" from ESPN it enjoyed with other business deals, Nabisco and Ohlmeyer would split the remaining profits. As it happened, ESPN wasn't making any profit in 1984 — but Ohlmeyer was playing long ball and was in no rush to cash out.*

BILL GRIMES:
The entire Ohlmeyer thing was crazy.

I remember I once got a call from Granath, and he said, "Bill, I understand you guys aren't going to put that bathing-suit show on that was pitched to you." I said, "No, we don't want that show." He said, "Well, it's Don's show; he's producing it." I told Granath I didn't care if it was Don's program — I had already talked to Steve and Roger about it and we didn't want it. But he just kept saying, "Oh, Bill, it's Don's program." And we ended up putting the fucking thing on because Ohlmeyer got in Granath's face and I got huge pressure.

When Ohlmeyer wanted something, he would never go to me with it; he would go to Steve and work on Steve and then he'd go directly to Granath. I really didn't exist in Ohlmeyer's mind, but I had to be careful because his business partner, John Martin, was running the ESPN board! And those board meetings were awful. They would start by yelling, "We don't like the fact that the anchor guys are wearing different ties; they should all be the same, with blue sport coats that say ESPN on them. And why don't you do this, and you're 22 percent over budget." His name never appeared in our directory, but Ohlmeyer was a big presence at ESPN during my time, believe me.

STEVE BORNSTEIN:

Don Ohlmeyer made more money out of ESPN than anybody else. Hey, he's a smart guy.

BILL GRIMES:

I knew Johnson had bought a piece of the company and he and Ohlmeyer were close buddies, but I thought he was just given handsome compensation. I didn't know Ohlmeyer had actual equity. Oh, goddamn it, that's awful. That's going to push me toward my evening cocktail. When I get to that part in your book, I'm not reading it. It just makes me sick.

ROGER WERNER:

At the end of 1987, I was still the COO of ESPN, reporting to Bill Grimes, and I got called into Tom Murphy's office, not knowing why. He said, "Here's what's going on at ABC. I want to put you in there as the executive vice president and John Sias's [ABC network president] understudy. I want you to spend a year or two learning the business, then run the TV network business for us." I was kind of dumbfounded, but you can't say, "Let me think about it," when a guy like Tom Murphy offers you an opportunity like that. You have five, maybe ten seconds to reflect. I just said, "Gee, Tom, when do I start?"

ESPN was now on a pretty nice trajectory, and I knew Bill would have Steve there for him. There were still a lot of challenges, but they had bigger problems at ABC. I started almost right away. For a young guy learning the network business, we had a fun development season that year. We launched a couple hit shows—the Roseanne Barr show, *Coach* with Craig Nelson. But the fundamentals of the network business had huge structural problems: out-of-control costs, declining ratings, declining ad sales, all kinds of legacy problems. Tom had asked me to go in and change all that—essentially, I think he saw me as the guy who could help create a new paradigm for broadcast television, a new business model, if you will. He saw what I did at ESPN and thought maybe I could apply that kind of McKinsey logic and managerial skill to this big battleship. I had three divisions reporting through to me. Dennis Swanson was running the sports division—where a guy named Bob Iger was working for him; Brandon Stoddard was running entertainment; and Roone Arledge was running news. You would have thought Roone and I would be close, given that I was coming from ESPN, but he was a little distant.

The ESPN era in television sports followed another: the Age of Roone. For a quarter century, Roone Pickney Arledge Jr. was the dominant figure in electronic sports coverage, a dazzlingly prodigious pioneer who revolutionized the medium with such shows as Monday Night Football *and* Wide World of Sports *("the thrill of victory, the agony of defeat"), and who personally produced ten marathon Olympic broadcasts. He was mentor to such key figures as Dick Ebersol, Don Ohlmeyer, legendary reporter Jim McKay, and the indefatigable, the incorrigible, Howard Cosell.*

ESPN grew up in Roone's shadow and, once it became connected to ABC, within his grasp. Since he wielded such immense power, many expected him to be all over ESPN, obsessing about every detail of production and programming. He did sit for a time on the ESPN board. And yet, mysteriously enough, ESPN was for Arledge mostly a hands-off deal. Why? On the surface, it just didn't make sense. One had to look closely, and dig down, to learn the reasons.

DON OHLMEYER:

Roone and I had often talked about the notion that if somebody's really busting their balls on something, after a certain period of time, all the good new ideas they have in that area are pretty much drained. And I think that's how Roone came to feel about sports. He felt he'd accomplished just about everything he could. Roone wasn't a normal person motivated by the things that drive most people. He was truly a renaissance man with a really brilliant mind that was constantly curious about new things. He knew all about cooking, was fascinated by plants — he could even sit and talk about Middle Eastern philosophy. For him, sports had become a little too much "been there, done that." Most of the time, he would have an excuse for not coming to the ESPN board meetings. Even when he did come, I could see he wasn't really interested, and so could everybody else. I think he made it a point to let everybody know, "Don't count on me — my plate's already full fixing news.... I've moved on."

Bristol was revving up, but in New York, ESPN president Bill Grimes was grinding down, feeling hassled by his boss, ABC honcho Herb Granath, and chafing at the knowledge that while he was producing beaucoup bucks for the network and for corporate parent ABC, he personally wasn't becoming as rich as he felt he deserved to be. In the five years of his presidency, this rough-and-tumble swash-buckler from West Virginia had gone from reporting to Stu Evey at Getty, to Granath and other ABC executives, and then to the CapCities crowd. In addition, he was clearly expected to heed the counsel of board member Ohl-meyer. Of the entire gallery, Grimes really respected only Murphy and Burke. If he could have reported directly to them—at double or triple his salary—he would have been batting a thousand, but no one gets to bat a thousand. Grimes felt trapped by the status quo.

BILL GRIMES:

It all began to deflate me after five years. Things began to slowly disintegrate, mostly because of Granath. He gave me a lot of autonomy most of the time, but he was a guy who looks out totally for himself. He doesn't support his people. I almost lost my job twice by going over his head. He didn't fight for anything we needed.

My biggest frustration was that Granath was not supportive within ABC of my requests for compensation increases for those of us at ESPN. I was tired of feeling we weren't properly compensated for the value we created. Look, I grew up in West Virginia. My father left home and then my mother decided she didn't want to raise children, so I was raised by my grandmother. I didn't grow up around a lot of money, and when Getty hired me, I thought I was so lucky to be making $150,000, but I had no equity.

My attitude at ESPN from the start was "I'm going to support my guys and we're going to do what we think is right. If any of that gets me fired, so be it." Very quickly I began to feel we weren't getting paid what we should. When I got to ESPN, we lost like seven or eight million that first year; when I left we had $300 million in revenues and $100 million in profit. And after many years of creating a couple billion dollars' worth of wealth for CapCities shareholders, I think I had a net of a million and a half bucks worth of CapCities stock. When the Hallmark Channel called and offered me the job of president, I thought it was a better chance to make some real money.

They gave me a wonderful going-away dinner party at 21. Roger and Steve arranged to have a note sent to me from more than fifty employees who had something that they remembered, and they put it together in a book. I still have it.

STEVE BORNSTEIN:
I was thirty-six when Bill left. I knew what I knew—programming strategies and production, particularly in our reinventing of *SportsCenter*—and knew what I didn't know—the revenue side—either ad sales or affiliates. I was really unfamiliar with much of the business end. So I knew they weren't going to give me Bill's job and felt pretty comfortable when I heard Roger was coming back. Christ, he couldn't wait to come back.

ROGER WERNER:

When Bill called to tell me he was leaving, it was quite unexpected. He said he had a terrific offer from Hallmark and thought he could make some real money. I didn't blame him. Bill Grimes was an extremely visionary guy in terms of seeing the potential future of the cable industry. He saw that big-league programming was going to produce big games for cable, and his decision to go to the cable operators when he did and ask for fees was incredibly important. He had a huge impact on ESPN.

As soon as management heard about Bill's departure, Tom Murphy asked me if I was interested in going back to ESPN, and I couldn't say yes fast enough. At ABC, I had felt like I was an alien microbe in that organization and they were throwing antibodies at me as fast as they could. Nobody in that place really wanted to change the way they did business; frankly, even Tom and Dan had such a personal connection to the broadcasting industry—after all, these were business models they helped build—that they didn't want to rock the boat that hard either.

It was real exciting. I came back in the fall of 1988, and from the start I told Steve that I would develop a succession plan for him. We had a solid game plan going forward. You know, I thought I had crossed a bridge and left my baby behind, but here I was, going right back.

I was in Bristol one day a week, sometimes two, but I felt I had a pretty decent handle on what was going on up there. My door was open when I was there, and the guys knew they could call me any time day or night or, if needed, come and see me in New York. But I relied a lot on Steve for programming and production issues. My involvement in those areas was more strategic. I was not focused on day-to-day micromanagement; I delegated. I wanted to look at how we were going to spend our money and the major decisions that followed from that. We certainly had some personnel-management issues — the Steve versus Scotty struggle was a difficult one, and some people had difficulties with how some of our other managers treated the staff. We certainly had our share of infighting. Even though the company was quite a bit smaller then — we're talking less than around five hundred people in the late eighties — I can't tell you that I was aware of all of the personnel battles going on.

At the start of 1989, ESPN became the first cable network to surpass 50 million subscribers, covering 55.5 percent of all U.S. television households. ACNielsen reported that ESPN had been the country's largest cable network since the late summer of 1983.

And it wasn't letting up. ESPN even televised the North Atlantic Conference basketball championship, which was played in the Hartford Civic Center — despite the fact that literally no fans were in attendance, because there was a measles epidemic in the conference and the tournament was under quarantine. It didn't matter to ESPN. Siena won in a squeaker over Boston University, 68–67.

For some, it was the best of times—working at ESPN in the rowdy years when it was still a fairly wild and crazy workplace. For others, however—especially the women who were making a bold but frustrating attempt to move into what was still mainly a man's world—it often seemed the worst of times.

Management probably should have seen it coming. Here were dozens of young guys working long hours (sometimes through the night) in a male-oriented business, located in the middle of nowhere, doing work that for eons had been considered "guy" work, and the women on the job were likely to be the only women they would meet. Such factors combined to make the place a giant petri dish in which misconduct could breed and thrive.

Sexual harassment took several forms: women would be hit on or hooted at or touched inappropriately, or sometimes men would propose offering workplace privileges in exchange for sexual favors. Guys would share photos from girly magazines or look at pornography on house monitors and laugh among themselves at the discomfort they caused women nearby. Women could object and be ignored, or play along and be compromised. Up to this point, there wasn't even a viable human resources department to turn to, so anyone who complained of *sexual harassment in those early frontier days risked being labeled a troublemaker, being passed over for promotions, and generally having her workdays made miserable. Even male executives who wanted to help were inhibited by the fear that other guys might look upon them as sexual traitors, or as giving aid and comfort to "the enemy."*

Enter Karie Ross, a talented and hardworking new hire with a serious background in journalism. The fact that she was incredibly attractive made her a natural for on-camera work but also, unfortunately, a target for much unwanted attention from more than a handful of men at the network. The work environment clearly had to change, and it was Karie Ross who decided, when she simply couldn't stand it anymore, to take aim not at individuals but at the system itself.

KARIE ROSS, *Anchor:*

I grew up in Clinton, Oklahoma, population eight thousand, in an avid University of Oklahoma home. My dad took me to the Oklahoma football games when I was in diapers. We were huge OU fans and we never wore orange, which was the color of Texas and Oklahoma State colleges. Of course I went to Oklahoma and majored in journalism, where I received an award for one of my writings. I worked at a daily newspaper during the summer, and I took TV courses as a minor. Then I entered this competition called "Maid of Cotton," where I had to do several interviews and give a speech, and I won the darn thing. The prize was traveling around the world. So I went to China, Hong Kong, Korea, India, Thailand, Spain, and Italy. And I was on television everywhere I went. That was really what got me hungry for television.

My first job was in Oklahoma City, working in the sports department at KOCO, an ABC affiliate. Then I went to WBNS, a CBS affiliate in Columbus, Ohio, for four years and got a lot of experience doing sports. Once, at the university basketball game, I saw Dick Vitale. I walked right up to him and said, "You are one of my favorite people," and introduced myself. He handed me the mic, and said, "Okay, Karie, interview me." And I interviewed Dick Vitale for the guys back in the truck, I guess. But anyway, someone took a picture of that—me with an ESPN mic and interviewing Dick Vitale. Then, lo and behold, this is really weird, I heard that Steve Bornstein was visiting his in-laws in Columbus and offered to fly me in for an interview. That's how I got my job at ESPN.

The very first day on the job, I got attacked in my hotel room. A guy tried to strangle me. Not many people know this. I had reported for duty, came back to get changed, and this guy was in my hotel room. I was just so innocent and naive, I was like, oh, maintenance is here fixing my bad sink or something. But then he looked at me and immediately I knew it wasn't good. He slammed the door and he had me in there for, I don't know, ten minutes or so, trying to strangle me. I don't know how I did it, but somehow I got out. They say you get the strength somewhere. I just clawed my way out and started screaming at the top of my lungs. They never caught the guy, but it was pretty traumatic, 'cause I had to stay in that same hotel until I found a place.

Still during my first week, I was writing at my desk, really focused, and I just felt this feeling that there was something going on, so I looked up, and the Playboy Channel was on, with naked people, from the monitor right above my desk. I looked behind me, and there were like twelve to fifteen guys standing there just to see what my reaction was. I think I disappointed them because I just looked back down and started typing like I could care less. So that was sort of my first surprise.

You have to remember that back in those days, we weren't a politically correct nation. This was before Anita Hill, and ESPN was almost all men. Gayle Gardner and I were about the only females there. Maybe there were a couple females in marketing, but it was definitely a locker-room atmosphere. There was just testosterone everywhere.

HOWIE SCHWAB, *Coordinating Producer:*
When I first got here in '87, the Playboy Channel was up on one of the monitors, but that changed within a year. There were a couple of bad people who

just weren't good human beings, well, one in particular that I couldn't believe what a jerk he was. He was a coordinating producer and got fired pretty quickly. He was harassing women. One time there was a baseball trade, and John Saunders and I were standing there and he goes, "Wow, three blacks for two whites." I just looked at him and said sarcastically, "How the fuck did you figure that out that so quickly?" I was glad he didn't last very long.

GRACE GALLO, *Assistant:*

There really wasn't a cafeteria. We had this woman, her name was Carol and she had a southern accent, who would have a lunch cart and she would literally make your sandwich for you. You had an option of ham, turkey, tuna, or chicken salad. And we had vending machines that would carry a whole bunch of junk for your sugar highs. But that was it. It was ridiculous. And Bristol back then was nothing. The biggest thing to hit town was when a McDonald's was built. We thought we hit the jackpot.

We were so tiny, so provincial, it was really like living on a small college campus. ESPN was like a little biosphere. That's why we became so close and were such a family, but you were limited to the people who you could meet. There was no one to date.

I think the majority of women I would talk to would complain mostly about not being treated equally to their counterparts. A female producer would maybe not get an assignment that a male producer would get, that kind of thing. But it was a rough environment for women, I will say that. I mean, they all cursed and acted crazy, especially as a show would get closer to air. A half hour before the seven o'clock show, people would go nuts. There were a lot of testosterone tantrums that women had to witness.

JULIE ANDERSON, *Producer*:

They were hiring some young PAs who were very cute. It was the first wave of cute young girls. Or maybe I was a cute young girl when I was there; I have no idea. There was this one girl, really skinny and very pretty, and she felt very threatened. It's not a nine-to-five place, so when you're on a show, you're there with your people on that show all the time, at night, on weekends, and the higher-ups were there from nine to five, right? There was no supervision. It was really hard for management to keep an eye on what was going on. And then, if you're in production and on the road, my God, the road. Everything happens on the road.

KARIE ROSS:

There were two particular people who had been trying to pursue me, and even though I told them I had a boyfriend, I had no interest in them, and I wanted to just keep things professional, they just wouldn't take the hint. I learned that when stories were being assigned and my name would come up, those two guys would shoot me down, saying I couldn't handle it.

GRACE GALLO:

I myself didn't see a lot of sexual harassment, but it was very easy to get away with bad behavior, let's put it that way.

STEVE BORNSTEIN:

We were hiring these kids right out of college, and all of a sudden we're paying them to do what they used to do for nothing with their friends in the frat house. We had a bunch of twenty-three-year-old bosses of twenty-two-year-olds with absolutely nothing else to do up there. So there were a lot of issues, and we had some high-profile ones.

KARIE ROSS:

I wrote an anonymous letter—I certainly wasn't going to put my name on it; that would have been a career killer—to *USA Today,* saying we were going through a lot of sexual harassment at ESPN. I basically explained the situation. I was hoping and praying that this columnist, Rachel Shuster, would call somebody about it or report the story. But they didn't do anything about it, maybe because I didn't put my name on it.

The things that I remember were guys patting the girls, telling them they looked sexy in that dress, and a lot of verbal stuff. I don't think a lot of these men knew what they were doing was illegal, but they should have known that using the influence of their position to date or get sexual favors from these girls underneath them — who had no power whatsoever — was not right.

The younger women started confiding in me because they felt like I was the only one that had any clout at all, I guess because I was a female on air. It was getting harder and harder for women to work there. They were just out of college and getting hit on and harassed like crazy. They were put in such horrible situations. There were guys trying to trade editing time. It was a big commodity, and there were only a few of these edit booths. You had to get the time to put your pieces together. They were saying to the women, "Look, I've got the editing time you need, but I'll swap it with you if you'll go out with me." I could slap these guys upside of the head and say, "Absolutely not, buddy!" but these girls couldn't. You weren't taken very seriously.

FRED GAUDELLI:
In Connecticut the bars closed early. Most of the time, they closed before we got out of work. A lot of times the best-looking women you were going to find were sitting right next to you in your office. We were

all very, very young, and this was pre–Anita Hill, so the corporate culture in America was much different than it is today. You might see a guy rubbing a girl's shoulders or telling her, "Hey, you're looking pretty hot today," something like that. But you're twenty-three or twenty-two years old. You're not thinking like this person might not want this, you're thinking, "Hey, I'm still in college and this is not a big deal." Again, you're working with a bunch of guys, you all love sports, and you wound up doing things that jocks like to do. That was the atmosphere really, until Karie stood up.

KARIE ROSS:

There were no women around in upper management for us to talk to. No one was going to talk to an upper-management male because then they'd be the female that was causing trouble. Finally I decided the only way to get my point across was to stand up in front of the whole place. I wasn't thinking, "Okay, I'm going to shake this earth and bring this company to its knees." My only point was to tell these guys to quit harassing these poor girls.

There was a company meeting in what we called the cafeteria, and I don't know exactly how many people were there that day, but maybe it was 200 or 250. It was a lot. It was practically the whole building. I was so nervous. I remember shaking. I'd never done a live shot or TV show where I was shaking that badly.

I stood up and said, "Look, this behavior has got to stop. This is crazy. You guys can't be doing this. Guys, you must stop sexually harassing these women. Don't be trading edit time for a date. Quit making all the lewd comments. Just let us work in peace." And then I said, "I know it's illegal." My voice was shaking as I spoke. After I finished, you could hear a pin drop.

Immediately afterward, I got called in to the office; it was John Walsh and I can't remember who else. He was very concerned and said, "Okay, Karie, what's going on?" I told him I wasn't going to name names, but that he had to do something at this point. And he said, "Okay, we'll handle it." Later, they brought us all in to a meeting and we were supposed to tell our stories. But a lot of the women were uncomfortable telling their stories in front of these management people—I think there was one man and a woman from marketing. I actually told the man that I'd feel a lot more comfortable if he left the room, which he then did, and some of the women started talking a bit.

Once the cafeteria speech was made, I received a lot of letters from the girls saying, "Thank you so much for standing up. We could have never ever done that on our own."

JULIE ANDERSON:

I worked with Karie a lot. She was beautiful and slightly high-maintenance. Some of the guys were intimidated by her or respected her because she was the beautiful girl "who I'll never get" kind of thing. But she also got trashed and harassed. When she stood up in the cafeteria, the guys were stunned. Stunned. I knew it was going to happen and sat next to her. She was mad. John Walsh and Steve Anderson were in the front of the room and they knew there had to be an acknowledgment. There was just too much going on. Too many girls were talking about it. A lot of people were really upset.

So sometime after Karie's speech, they finally said, "You should feel free to go to HR." Actually, we were invited to go to HR as a group or on our own, so we could say whatever we wanted about guys in the company, and they would put stuff in their records. Of course, nothing ever came of it. Nothing happened. We were all mad because nothing happened.

JOHN WALSH:

Until Karie Ross made her speech in the cafeteria (really a vending-machine hall back then), we were really not aware of what was going on. And then, when we found out, we dug in and started really acting on it, doing the best we could. All this stuff cropped up and you had to deal with it. It's something I had never experienced in my life, so I didn't know how to handle it. The human resources department for all intents and purposes didn't exist back then. The guy running it had left the company. Steve

Anderson and I wound up doing these interviews and later Jim Allegro got really involved. The interviews were no fun. It was people with different versions of a story and it was hard to find out what actually happened.

FRED GAUDELLI:

Karie was the first woman to bring it all to a head. We lived together for five years, and we had some discussions about what was going on. I remember she told me she would be at her terminal typing up the *SportsCenter* show she was about to do, and her desk was in front of a big wall of monitors. Guys would come in, turn on the Playboy Channel, pull up seats behind her while she was working, watch the Playboy Channel, and do the play-by-play: "Hey, look at this, look at that," that type of thing. I told her, "Look, I'm no shrinking violet here, but that doesn't sound cool to me at all. It sounds like they're way out of line."

She stood up in a meeting and said, "Guys, you know what, all this bullshit's got to stop; we're trying to do our jobs just like you are, and this is preventing us from doing our jobs." She ended up going to human resources to report two guys that I was pretty friendly with, but at the time, neither guy knew that Karie and I were dating. I remember both of those guys being hauled in, but I never talked with them about it. They were not fired. They were given a warning.

CHRIS BERMAN:

I was not at the cafeteria meeting, but Karie was right, I'm sure of that. I liked her. She was a great-looking woman; still is, the last time I saw her.

As far as the women were concerned, I will say this: we looked out for each other. If somebody had a problem, a couple of the guys took care of it. If I talked to someone, I would say, "Take it easy. We're all still friends. Don't make anybody uncomfortable here." If someone was uncomfortable and they came to the right people, it was "Cut that shit out." If there were a couple of the camera ladies having trouble with some guys, they would let the right people know about it and it was policed. The right guys didn't stand for that. But maybe I was naive.

BILL CREASY:

We did have some women on the air and on staff, but we certainly were looking for more. I'm a great believer in having a lot of women around you while you work. That was my track record at CBS. I like the idea of having female talent and female executives. I know it's quite sexist, but when you have a pretty girl around the office, it's a little bit happier than having an ugly girl. And if that pretty girl is good, then you've just sort of added to tree of your growth. I firmly believe that.

FRED GAUDELLI:

I give John Walsh and Steve Anderson credit. They said, "Hey look, what Karie said is 1,000 percent right, this crap has got to stop right here, right now." And there wasn't any wavering on their part.

STEVE ANDERSON:

We used to do research, focus groups and things like that, to have a better understanding of what people wanted. In all the discussions over the course of years, we would get over and over, back to 1988, "I don't know why you guys put women on *SportsCenter*. Nobody wants to get their sports from women." You would hear that all the time. And then we hire Robin and within two years, "You guys just don't get it, you shouldn't put women on *SportsCenter,* women don't know about sports—except Robin Roberts." Whatever it was, Robin was able to connect with those guys who believe that they don't want their sports from women. She was an original in that way.

KARIE ROSS:

Drugs were very prevalent back then. One time I was out on the road with a producer and camera man, and they pulled out some marijuana to start smoking. I just came unglued. I said, "You guys can't do that; you just cannot do that. Cannot, cannot, cannot. We are driving. We're on the job." And I just said that if we get pulled over right now, it won't be your name in the paper, it'll be mine. I was so mad that they put me in that situation. And they never did after that. Something like that could be a career killer.

I'd actually never seen a bong in my entire life, then I walked into this party and there's potato chips, dip, beer, and I said, "What's that?" Well it was a bong, and they all started laughing at me because they couldn't believe I didn't know what a bong was. I just said, "I have to get out of here," and I left. In fact, any time there were drugs at all, I wound up leaving right away. We all know it's guilt by association.

GAYLE GARDNER:

George Grande tried to talk me out of going to NBC, but I had put in over five years at ESPN and was ready to go. It was a very small place; you kind of knew everyone who was there, and Bristol was a small place to live if you didn't have a family. Single people were lonely up there. It was very hard. You had no social life, there wasn't anything to do, and that combination was hard on you. I wanted to get back to New York, where I had grown up and was really happy. So when the opportunity came along, I took it. It wasn't that I was unhappy with the work or anything like that, it was just that you couldn't have a real life there.

When I got to NBC, I had less work. You actually

had less to do. There were fewer events. Everything was geared toward the weekend. You were taken care of. Everything was essentially first-class. They drove you everywhere. You had all the perks of being at a different place. I felt like Cinderella.

PETER ENGLEHART, *Director of Program Planning:*

In all candor, it was a guy's culture, so most women didn't even apply. To be a production assistant was a real guy kind of thing. And then Jaffe put in the test to answer trivia questions as part of the hiring process. It was pretty arduous. You had to go to sleep with batting averages in your head to answer some of these questions. And that's how they would weed out the thousands of people who would apply. Hell, I couldn't have answered some of that stuff.

ROSA GATTI:

Young people weren't as skilled and experienced yet to deal in a workplace environment. Many young guys never really learned or were never trained in college. So we ramped things up, diversity and sexual harassment training. By the way, *sexual harassment* was not a term used in society in those early years. I talked with women all the time. When women joined the company, I would take them to lunch. Then it got so big I couldn't do that anymore. I would coach women who came to me, but if there was a serious matter, which was rare, I would direct them to human resources. As an officer of the company, I had an obligation to do that. I coached many men too.

You always want to look at the individual and you want to handle matters the best way possible for all parties involved — all parties. As a senior leader, I was asked to sit with women so they could comfortably describe situations. Women would come to me, and part of what I tried to do is to help them understand how you handle certain situations. We had young people dating each other because they didn't know a lot of people outside the company. Sometimes you would meet someone in the workplace and you would get to know them as a friend first, which can be a very good foundation for a relationship. But in some situations not everybody does the right thing. That's not an anomaly for ESPN. This happened at many, many companies.

STEVE BORNSTEIN:
I think part of the sexual harassment stuff was location. Bristol, Connecticut. It's one hundred miles from real civilization, and you got the kind of testosterone, jock mentality, frat house approach that's pretty much a recipe for stupid decisions being made. If I could go back in time, would I have been more diligent? Yes, but it was part of the hand that we were dealt, and I think we did become better about managing it.

KARIE ROSS:

I think I had been termed a troublemaker after all that happened, so they put me on the 2:00 a.m. show and then took me off *SportsCenter* altogether. Then they put me on *College GameDay*, where my face was never shown. I just felt they didn't want me anymore, so I had to leave. In fact, before the cafeteria meeting, I had a meeting with Steve Bornstein, and he said they wanted to renew my contract and they had only missed the renewal date because they were so busy with one of the new contracts. "We're talking to your agent; it'll get done," he said. I told him that all sounded fine, but after the cafeteria, my contract was never renewed.

I've often wondered if I regretted standing up, but leaving Bristol eventually got me to Miami, where I met my husband, so everything worked out for a reason. I look back with no regrets.

A few men were disciplined for infractions in the late 1980s, and such remedial efforts as awareness classes and a more liberal open-door policy were instituted. But there was no rapid, dramatic change in the workplace. Karie Ross had stood up and fought to make the workplace "safe" and achieved some measure of success, but in the end, she didn't get to benefit from the very improvements she helped bring about. She did have the satisfaction of knowing she'd taken a stand, however, and by doing so had maybe helped those already there and those who would follow.

As Bristol tried to regain its footing after all the upheaval, Roger Werner and Steve Bornstein were still in acquisition mode. By now, ESPN had the NFL, college basketball and college football, but the end of the '87–'88 season marked the end of its contract with the NHL, and there was still no pro basketball or baseball on the bill.

Baseball was most important to the network's inventory. Summers on ESPN had been too quiet. The network had been covering the U.S. Olympic Festival—an amateur competition for potential Olympians—and in 1982, began carrying the College World Series, which capped off coverage of collegiate baseball in June, but then the wind stalled. Major League Baseball was clearly the best live product to acquire for the summer, and it, along with the other sports ESPN had rights to, would mean the network would be in good shape for ten of the twelve months of the year.

Broadcast rights to Major League Baseball were coming to the market again, and the suitors were lined up around the block. If ESPN could bring this bounty home, it would become a high-profile force in Major League Baseball at last. Not that college baseball hadn't provided a nice surprise or two along the way....

LOREN MATTHEWS:

Tug McGraw was a friend of mine from my Mets days, and I always thought he would make a great broadcaster. We weren't doing major baseball on ESPN yet, but we were doing college baseball, so I talked him into doing a game for us — Mississippi — the Ole Miss. He wasn't sure if he wanted to do it or not, and told me he didn't know anybody, so I said, "Look, I'll fly you in, we'll spend some time together, you'll do the game, and you'll see if you like it." So we're in Oxford, Mississippi, and he says, "Well, we have to go to dinner early because my son's coming into town tonight, and I have to meet with him." Now, I knew Tug's family, so I said, "Oh, Mark's coming to Oxford?" And he said, "No, no, no. This isn't Mark. You don't know about this son 'cause I just found out about him not too long ago myself. It was a spring training fling years ago." He said he didn't even know he had fathered a child way back then, but the kid was college age now, and he wanted to become a country music singer. Now, I'm not sure I want to get involved in all this, so I tell him I don't think I should come along. "No, no," Tug said. "I want you to help me break the ice; I barely know this guy." So we go to the Holiday Inn in Oxford, and sure enough this beat-up old eight-cylinder jalopy comes chugging in, and a nice-looking young guy gets out. Tug introduces me to him. Then the kid says he wants Tug to listen to some of his music, so he puts a cassette of his into this old car. Afterward, I pulled Tug aside and said, "Look, Tug, I don't know anything about music, but I have to say, it sounds like this kid's got some talent." He said, "Yeah, he is pretty good, isn't he?" Long story short, obviously it was Tim McGraw, and he and Tug later became close, but I'll never forget being in that parking lot, listening to Tim McGraw play his cassettes from this old beat-up jalopy. I mean, who knew?

When ESPN landed the NFL in 1987, it was the debut of professional football on cable television. That, combined with football's popularity, had enabled ESPN to hit up cable operators for a surcharge. But baseball was different. Because baseball had been on cable in the past—Ted Turner had been airing Atlanta Braves games since 1979—the deal that ESPN made with Major League Baseball held no such prize. Baseball was actually perceived as a cable staple and thus not surcharge-worthy. Besides, there was no way ESPN would be able to ask for an additional surcharge on top of the one already demanded for the NFL. As a consequence, the baseball deal had to be totally ad supported. The result was economically brutal.

ROGER WERNER:
When Bill was still president, he and I, along with Steve, had spent a good amount of time thinking about baseball rights. We had talked with Peter Ueberroth early on, and I had drinks with him at the Waldorf when the deal was just opening. I have a lot of respect for Peter, and I think he played all of us potential buyers like a Stradivarius. It was a deal that

involved more than a hundred games per season, not because any of the bidders wanted that big a volume, but because Peter very cleverly structured the cable-exclusive baseball package in a way where it would be absolutely critical for an ESPN or a would-be competitor to have it. He made it so big, so heavy, that a competitor could have been launched around that package. If Ted Turner's TBS had had that package, it would have made them much more competitive as a sports service. If Cablevision's Sports Channel had gotten that package, they would immediately have become a nationally competitive sports service. And don't forget cable operators like Malone and Dolan, who could have started a national sports network around it. That's how big this thing was. Peter understood my commitment to being the leader and being dominant. He knew we were pretty hungry and wouldn't let that go without a really tough fight.

I remember vehemently arguing in favor of getting the deal done, not at any price but almost at any price, with our parent company guys—Tom Murphy, Dan Burke, and Herb. Dan was a huge baseball fan, so that certainly helped, but we had some very heated debates. I kept stressing that there was enough programming volume there to start another channel. I remember really sweating bullets on that deal until literally the last night. It was a big-time nail-biter. On the night of the final bidding, Dan Burke, Steve Bornstein, and I hung out at the bar at 21, waiting for Ueberroth to call back with the final decision. It didn't come down until probably midnight, and we all sighed a sigh of relief and had a bunch of drinks to celebrate. I didn't get back to the hotel until after one a.m., and we had to do a press conference at eight that next morning. The deal cost us $400 million for four years. Peter had played it well and got absolute maximum value out of ESPN. Arguably we did overpay, but I would say we had to, and in retrospect it was absolutely the right investment to make. I rank it a close second to the NFL deal.

STEVE BORNSTEIN:

We paid a lot of money for baseball, so much so that it had a negative impact that first year on Cap-Cities' bottom line. We misjudged the value of the property. At CapCities you could make mistakes, you just had to make honest mistakes.

CHRISTINE DRIESSEN, *Chief Financial Officer:*

The first baseball deal was not a good deal. It was for a lot of money, and the league brokered a real tough deal which came during really tough economic times. Basically, as soon as we signed it, the economy tanked, so we were really struggling with ad sales. That was a difficult time.

STEVE BORNSTEIN:

We felt a lot of pressure. We had to pay a ton to get Major League Baseball, but now that we were losing money on it, we were going to have to find a way to fix it.

In June of 1990, Capital Cities / ABC Inc. posted its earnings for the second quarter — a dreary 1.5 percent rise in net income. It also had to warn Wall Street that the current quarter would probably be even worse — below last year's. According to the Wall Street Journal, *the company blamed, among other factors, "the new baseball contract at its 80 percent–owned cable channel, ESPN." The announcement saw CapCities / ABC shares crumble by almost 9 percent. There were more than a couple movers and shakers — inside and outside of ESPN — who thought the MLB deal was the worst in the company's now decade-long history.*

Although the deal may have cost too much, and the rotten economy made ad sales for the games particularly difficult, the value of the baseball contract at that time had to be measured in other ways. The combination of the NFL deal and the MLB deal meant that ESPN had attained a virtually unassailable lead in cable sports. The NFL deal was incredibly important on its own; when combined with the baseball deal, it meant that all other competitors in the cable universe were severely disadvantaged, now and for the foreseeable future. You want to compete with ESPN on cable? Fine. Even if you could get a ton of money together, you'd still have to find enough inventory to fill the hours. ESPN now had a burgeoning share of sports programming and of the faithful fans who watch it.

The $400 million, four-year 1989 Major League Baseball deal: Step Number Six in ESPN's rise to world dominance.

ROGER WERNER:

The first season of baseball on ESPN was nothing but headaches. We had people within the baseball organization arguing about blackouts and game selection and start times and how many appearances per team and everything. There was a huge menu of problems. I was going out to San Francisco to talk with Fay Vincent, who had just recently become baseball commissioner after the tragic death of Bart Giamatti. I remember driving on the lower deck of the Nimitz Freeway and thinking to myself in the back of the limousine that this just doesn't feel right. I asked the driver to pick a different route.

I had my meeting with Fay, where I asked for help on a variety of issues, then flew back to New York. Got off the plane, got home, flipped on the game from Candlestick, and watched the whole earthquake, saw the Nimitz Freeway pancaked, and was just chilled.

JOE TORRE, *Baseball Analyst:*

We were way up in the third deck behind home plate at Candlestick, waiting for the game to start. Then they had a flyover, and we felt the vibrations. I had never been in an earthquake before, and I thought that initially it was the vibrations of the jets, because they were really low. But then all of a sudden that vibration didn't stop and then the second vibration came, and the top deck started moving to my right, and then it just came back. Then the third time it moved I was waiting for it to just go down. It moved a little bit farther to the right, the top deck came back, and then it seemed to stabilize. All of a sudden, everybody started cheering. People who live in California may have experienced this before, but I certainly hadn't, and it was surreal for me. We were so high up, I could look over the top of the stadium and I started seeing smoke in the Marina area. I turned, saw Boomer, and said, "Boomer, let's get out of here." He said, "What do you mean?" I said, "There's not going to be a game; let's get out of here."

It was during ESPN's pregame show, at 8:26 p.m. Eastern time, 5:26 Pacific, October 17, 1989, that the rocking and rolling began, and it was then that ABC's all-star team of Al Michaels, Jim Palmer, and Tim McCarver vanished from view, just as Michaels said, in that brilliantly distinctive voice of his, "I'll tell you what, we're having an—" The audio went dead, the screen went black, ESPN was knocked off the air, and it became pretty easy to figure out what that missing word was.

JOE TORRE:
It looked bad. We finally got down and decided the safest place for us to go was probably onto the

field. Everybody had lost power except ESPN, and ABC had Al Michaels, who was doing the game, using our feed for their broadcast. We stayed there till about ten o'clock at night doing interviews and reports, but I gotta tell you, it was really weird. It was just about as strange of a situation as I'd ever been in.

CHRIS MYERS:

I was the field reporter and the only one of our bunch who had experienced an earthquake, a minor one, when I lived down in L.A. But this one sounded different and looked different. I remember this vision of the field looking almost like ribbon candy.

BOB LEY:

You heard it before you felt it. I was seated five rows from the top of the stadium—auxiliary press seating—row 17, section 1—and suddenly it all started to move. It was like trying to stand on a water-bed, except it was concrete. The lights in the stadium were whipping back and forth like weeds in the breeze. It lasted about twenty seconds, long enough to start a Hail Mary, not quite long enough to finish it. They had TVs throughout the section, and it was all dark. There was no power. Then I looked at the field. The scoreboard was out. I ran back to the production truck. Everybody at that moment knew without being told: "Do something important. Get on the air. You do this, you do that; don't stand on ceremony." Joe Torre was working with us as an analyst on that series, and to this day, I remember Joe saying, "Give me a camera. I'll go out and see what I can get." He went out and started getting Q&A. I think he might have gotten Willie Mays.

PETER GAMMONS:

It still cracks me up that Rene Lachemann, the As' third-base coach, and Walt Weiss, their shortstop, were in the outfield doing their pregame running when the earthquake hit, and never realized there was an earthquake.

ABC stayed on the air briefly, broadcasting live from the stadium — the first "live" telecast of an earthquake ever — but then its equipment failed. (ABC was there to televise the entire game; ESPN was there to offer coverage but not play-by-play.) ESPN producers had shown the foresight to bring along a backup generator, however, and so the sports network was quickly back up again, and soon it had the live coverage. Its team of sportscasters was drafted into service as newscasters, a reminder that the qualities required to be the best at either job are largely the same. ESPN's team was supplemented by Joe Torre, Chris Berman, and Chris Myers at the stadium, with Bob Ley joining them eighteen minutes in — as fast as he could get from row 17 of the upper deck to the ESPN booth.

"It was my first earthquake," Ley said later, as if recalling a wedding or a graduation or some other rite of passage — which, in California, an earthquake sort of is. This quake was formidable; it would take sixty-three lives, cause injuries to 3,700 people, and do $6 billion in damage to structures in the Bay Area.

It was a source of considerable pride at ESPN that it proved its mettle at this hypercritical moment and that ABC would have been up a creek without ESPN and its faithful backup generator.

JEFF ISRAEL:

Joe Torre and I went out to the field and talked to players and their families — all of it was seen minutes after the earthquake happened. ABC didn't get up for a little while longer after that. We had power. So in a tragic situation, things were coming up roses for us.

CHRIS BERMAN:

We were still little ESPN then, and ABC was getting credit. They did a great job, but they weren't really on. It was our power. Even the police used our generator. We did a good thing for the city. Everything was out. We were the only ones on. We looked across the bay and saw the fires in the refineries over in the East Bay, then we heard about the bridge and other fires. Oh, this is more than just a little earthquake now. This is a pretty big earthquake. And every five or ten minutes we were learning more and more about it all. There were ten or twelve of us, doing what we were supposed to do. We weren't trained by management on how to be newspeople, but we were doing a great job covering this news story.

BOB LEY:

We had the only two phone lines in a twenty-mile radius that were working. We gave one to the police so they could have it, and we kept the other one for ourselves.

SCOTT ACKERSON:

I was in Bristol. We were no longer a sports network, we were a news operation.

MIKE McQUADE:

I remember at one point I looked up and saw ABC's *World News Tonight* and *Nightline* had used part of our coverage. That was kind of a watershed.

CHRIS BERMAN:

At the end of the night, as appreciation for what we had done, we got an escort into town by the police, because the drive in to San Francisco was without lights. I thought of London during the bombing in World War II and Churchill. This is what it must have been like. The lights were all knocked out for the night. The Germans were bombing. Oh, shit. A whole dark city on fire. When we got to our hotel, we needed candles to walk up the stairs to our rooms. Thank God I wasn't big-time then; I was only on the fourth floor. They would put me on the thirty-fifth floor now, and I don't think I could make that anymore.

Which reminds me. Nobody really knows this, but one of my favorite people in the world—Bob Lurie, owner of the Giants—had taken me to lunch at 21 in '88. One of my goals in life was to do play-by-play for the Giants, and he offered me the job. I certainly didn't know that was coming, but I was honored. Then I said, "Do you think I can make enough difference in your attendance to pay me what you're going to have to pay me?" In '88, I was making, it might have been six figures. He said, "Yeah, of course. That's why I'm asking you." He asked if I needed a day to think about it, but I knew then. I had two kids, one and two years old, and we had just gotten the NFL the year before. I told him, "You've come to me a year or two too late." Years later, he said, "You were a very smart young man with that decision."

PETER GAMMONS:
This was obviously a piece of baseball history. I stayed in San Francisco for two weeks. They wanted me to go do a piece with Bob Welch, who actually

lived in San Francisco, in the Marina. In order to go there, you had to go line up at the middle school to get a permit to enter that area. It turned out that Bob's wife had already done it for us, but as we were passing the middle school, who was standing on line, unshaven and in a windbreaker? Joe DiMaggio. So Bob says to me that we should go say hello, but I said, "I don't think Joe DiMaggio wants anyone to speak to him when he's unshaven." So Bob let it go. A couple of years later, I told that story to DiMaggio, and he actually thanked me. He said, "Even then without knowing me you knew me," and I said, "Well, I had a pretty good idea, Joe."

JOE TORRE:
  I didn't know it at the time, but I was getting toward the end of my broadcasting career. The following August I started managing the Cardinals. I had been broadcasting for the Angels since '85, but to get that national gig with ESPN was real fun. The point is never lose your connection with the game. You play it, you get to manage, you become an analyst. The only thing missing in the broadcasting part is you don't know if you won or lost.

By March of 1989, Peter Edward Rose had long established himself as one of the greatest players in baseball history. When he retired from the Cincinnati Reds as a player in 1986, he had logged 4,256 hits, a baseball record. He'd also served as manager of the Reds from 1984 until 1989. But on March 27 of that year, the world of baseball and of sports was shocked by the news, in a Sports Illustrated cover story, that Rose had been charged with gambling on baseball, including many of the games in which his team had played.

Some compared the resulting scandal to the notorious Black Sox mess that befouled the 1919 World Series. Baseball Commissioner Bart Giamatti, who conducted the three-month investigation into the charges against Rose, had lamented pointedly that "baseball almost died in 1921" in the wake of that scandal and said, "The act of betting on a game you are involved in ... is to place your desire for monetary gain ahead of the team."

After the investigation was concluded in August of 1989, Rose reluctantly accepted a lifetime ban from the sport. Rose conceded the ban was based on factual reasons in exchange for Major League Baseball making no formal findings against him; he technically did not admit to gambling as part of the agreement.

But Rose's troubles had only begun: the IRS and a Cincinnati grand jury had been investigating him on possible tax-evasion charges, an allegation that was first made public only a week after Rose accepted lifetime suspension.

In the end, it was the Feds that got him, at one point serving him with a lien for back taxes totaling $973,000 and change — money "earned," at least partly, betting on horses at the track.

On trial for tax evasion in April of 1990, Rose became a daily fixture on ESPN, which provided extensive coverage of the proceedings—extensive partly to demonstrate the network's commitment to sports journalism, and perhaps partly to show that it would not suppress or downplay bad news about sports or sports figures no matter how bad it was. In the case of Pete Rose, it could hardly have been worse.

JOHN WALSH:

The Rose story presented itself almost as a gift-wrapped box. We had essentially decided we would put people on it full-time, and we had big plans for "Decision Day": we would get the Dowd Report, and everybody would come into work and read it very quickly and do the coverage. We had a lot of practice before we did the actual-day coverage. We had three or four false starts after hearing, "Oh, it's going to be tomorrow," and everybody would come in and then all of a sudden it was "Oops, it's not going to be tomorrow." The driving force was "We have a chance to cover this story unlike anybody else. Let's just get on it, throw everything we can at it, and let us use every resource we can handle"—Jimmy Roberts, Charley Steiner, Dan Patrick, Chris Myers, and of course Bob Ley, who being the whiz that he is, was on top of it all.

We set up an ambitious plan for when the news would break. We had a reporter ready in Cincinnati, we had a reporter ready on the streets of New York, and we knew Jimmy Roberts was going to go to Cooperstown.

Then all of a sudden the report came out, and Bob came in and read it in his usual, like, three-and-a-half minutes and knew every question and every nuance of the report, and so we were in motion for the next day. The one thing I did was at that point the seven o'clock *SportsCenter* was a half-an-hour show, and I had negotiated with programming that we would be an hour. And I do remember that we did forty-two consecutive minutes of Pete Rose. I will never forget that number. We started at 7:00 and went to 7:42 on Pete Rose. The other thing I'll always remember is a phone call I got. "I've never met you. My name is Don Ohlmeyer, I'm in this business, and I want to congratulate you because that's what *SportsCenter* should be." That was a great call to get.

BOB LEY:

The night we broke the Pete Rose story in '89, our legal correspondent, Jim Zucker, had the tip and got it to us that the terms of the suspension were going to be the next morning. We broke that. The computers were crashing in the newsroom one by one. So when I started typing the story, I had to go from computer to computer. When the Dowd Report was released, everybody ran for the narrative; I ran for the foot-notes, and all these people were named, including who the witnesses were who had talked to Dowd's people. I flew out to Pennsylvania to talk to this guy who had overheard a conversation where Pete made bets. Dan had some sources too.

The next day was an eighteen-hour day. We were on the air in the morning, did a special report, the press conference from Giamatti, the press conference from Rose, then for the six o'clock show, we had reports from all over the country. Heck, somebody even went to Cooperstown. We were on till midnight. In thirty years of the network, it was one of the ten best days for news that I've ever been involved in, because we had this thing nailed. There was no cogent doubt on the part of anybody who worked that story that summer here that Pete had bet on baseball. I've talked to Pete a number of times since. Once, I spent an hour and a half with him at the Hard Rock in New York, and he continued to give me his rap of why he was innocent. He never stopped trying to make you believe his story.

NORBY WILLIAMSON:
We weren't trying to be Woodward and Bernstein, but we were asking questions that would get us to the second, third, and fourth levels of the story. And that was John's and Steve Anderson's influence journalistically. What did this mean to baseball? Is this more pervasive than just the Pete Rose situation? What do we really know right now? What did the owner

know? Is there any cover-up of the investigation? I think we asked more questions than we answered, but we were smart enough to ask the right questions.

CHARLEY STEINER:

When the Pete Rose thing was happening, I was sent to Ohio to try and find a fella named Ron Peters who was making bets for Pete. My producer and I walked into this dark, woody bar in Hamilton, where the gambling money came and went. Feeling like a cross between Inspector Clouseau and Mike Wallace, I asked this one guy, "Do you know Ron Peters?" He replied, "Who are you? Wait, I know who you are. Well, he ain't here." I gave him a business card and my hotel phone number. Not to be impolite, the producer and I hung around, had a beer, but not a word was uttered in the saloon the whole time. The next day at the hotel, I got a call from that same guy at the bar. *He* was Ron Peters. He was Rose's bookie.

CHRIS MYERS:

I can't reveal how I came across it, but one of the breakthrough moments for me on these gambling charges was when someone got me some paperwork in an envelope—I didn't pay for it—and some audiotapes, cassettes, of someone talking to Pete Rose—let's just say of a mob-type nature, you know, threatening, "If you don't pay up, this could happen, that could happen." My God, I debated on what to do. I went to ESPN and said I got them by digging around—I didn't steal 'em, I didn't pay for 'em—and it became their decision on what we could put on the air and what we couldn't. And Pete, I remember him being very cordial and friendly with me. I watched John Gotti later about the way he had handled things in front of the courts and the media, and I think Pete felt he was bulletproof; that's just my perception. You loved the way he played the game so you hoped it wasn't true if you were a baseball fan. He thought it was going to go away, that it wasn't that big a deal.

I remember interviewing Bart Giamatti; I believe it's one of his last interviews before he died from a heart attack, and I think it's unfair, although some people still claim that the stress of the Pete Rose situation had an effect or had something to do with that for Bart Giamatti. But I remember him even off-camera, and he was a very smart guy but also a very passionate baseball fan. I could really see his angst when he said, "I don't want this to tear up the game. I wish Pete would just step up and own up to this and we can get through it, but these constant denials, we have to take a stand on this; it's the code of baseball." I think it really just tore him up personally. He was so happy to be the commissioner of baseball and loved the game, and then something like this comes up. I think it was a very difficult thing because he really appreciated the baseball skills of Pete Rose.

ESPN's broadcasting of Major League Baseball began on April 9, 1990. The event wasn't attended by as much hype and hoopla as was the arrival of pro football in 1987, and CapCities and Bristol bean counters were still aghast at the price tag, but many others were thrilled to have this great American game on the network. There's no fan like a baseball fan, and as if to reward them, it wasn't very long before baseball rose to the occasion: on June 29, 1990, in two separate ESPN games seen the same day, both Oakland's Dave Stewart and the Dodgers' Fernando Valenzuela pitched no-hitters.

JON MILLER, *Sportscaster:*

ESPN was the first national network with the Sunday night game to cover regular-season baseball as if it were the postseason. We would bring, as the technical people inside ESPN call it, the "Full Monty" production team, and to this day, nobody does that until the postseason or the All-Star Game. We have maybe sixteen to twenty cameras and eight replay machines, and the whole thing is like a military operation.

When we first started back in 1990, I was doing the Orioles games all week long, so I would tape the Tuesday night game of one of the teams we'd be seeing on Sunday, because generally speaking the guy pitching on Tuesday would be pitching again on Sunday. I wanted to look at that team and the pitcher to get an idea of what kind of pitches he threw. Then, on the plane on Monday, as I flew off to wherever the Orioles were going to be playing, I'd watch a tape of the previous night's game so I could critique myself. About a month into the season I started thinking to myself, "What am I doing? I can't keep doing this. I can't keep broadcasting a game seven days a week and watching these other games that I'm taping." I was starting to dream about baseball. It was like the only thing happening in my whole life, and I was like, "Man this is not good. This is a little bit out of control here. I need more balance in my life." So I finally just decided that I was just going to have to give up on all my reviewing.

Timing is a major issue in baseball. In football, the timing is a given. They come up to the line, they snap the ball. The play-by-play guy does the play-by-play, then the guy gets tackled and then the analyst comes in and they start showing replays and dissect the play. It's easy. Football is the easiest. I'm not downgrading anybody who does football, but I think it's the perfect made-for-TV sport. In baseball, there's a pitch thrown every ten to fifteen seconds, roughly; sometimes it's a little bit longer if there are men on base. There's a tendency for people to think that nothing's going on in baseball until the ball gets hit. That's a fallacy. That's a real misunderstanding of what's going on. You have the signal from the catcher to the pitcher; the signal from the shortstop to the second baseman about coverage; somebody might be signaling the center fielder if he can't quite see the catcher's signals; and don't forget, every defensive player needs to know what every pitch is supposed to be. Every pitch in baseball is akin to the snap of the ball in football.

OREL HERSHISER:

ESPN helped me with my understanding of baseball. It brought scouting to another level. Before, when you only had a game of the week, you only saw one game on television. But as soon as ESPN started doing games in locations on multiple nights, we had more of a library of what players were doing around the country and in the game, and so we were able to start plotting and scouting and analyzing. I would grease-pencil the broadcast to see a hitter's eyes move. I would look at defenses and slow-motion replays to see a guy hit that pitch, and then he pulled it to the shortstop, so we would change the positioning of the defenders. ESPN definitely helped us. The moment that more games were broadcast than just a game of the week, the game changed scouting-wise and ability-wise.

JEAN McCORMICK, *Coordinating Producer:*

In the spring of 1990, I was in my first months as the first female studio producer at ESPN. While people had for the most part been kind and supportive, I was constantly being tested on knowledge.

One afternoon, something came up about various records for scoreless innings in pitching. I mentioned that Babe Ruth had pitched the most number of consecutive scoreless innings in the postseason (twenty-nine and two-thirds) for the Red Sox from 1916 to 1918; a record wasn't broken until 1961 by Whitey Ford. This led to a conversation about the 1918 World Series, at that time the last year that the Red Sox had won the World Series over the equally cursed Cubs.

At some point someone asked me, again most likely a test, who the star pitcher was for the Cubs. When I said Hippo Vaughn, the group said almost in unison "Ah, Hippo Vaughn." Everyone dug into his career and statistics as if he were going on the mound for the Cubs that night. Vaughn had pitched in the famed double "no-hitter" of 1917, where neither team had a hit in the first nine innings. The remarkable thing about this conversation was that *it wasn't remarkable for ESPN*. Pitching stats from 1917 and 1981 were analyzed in as great detail as those from the previous night. When you participated in conversations of such high caliber, it was and still is often hard to discuss sports with "normies" who didn't work at ESPN. I often wondered where people would have worked, myself included, if ESPN hadn't been created.

After that particular conversation, a male production assistant followed me out of the newsroom and said, "Sometimes I think that you may know more than I do about some things." I later commented that nowhere else in the work world would an assistant several rungs lower have said that to a superior, even a female one. And the response was something to the effect of "Oh, he would have said that to a male superior. People take enormous pride in their sports knowledge. That was a huge compliment."

BILL WOLFF:

At ESPN, the code of the place was you don't root for anybody; you just want your game to end quickly. You lose your team allegiances. You just don't care. Whatever. Did the game go quickly? Okay, I can cut thirty seconds of highlights. They get handed to Bob Ley. Can I go home now? It sort of sucked the *joie de sports* out of it. That was part of the deal. But not always. The greatest night I ever remember at ESPN was February 11, 1990. I was only an entry-level guy, but it was incredible.

Tyson versus Douglas. Eric Clemmons was the reporter. He had to con management into letting him go to Tokyo. "Buster Douglas? We're not sending anybody." Remember, Tyson was Tyson; people forget—he was unbeatable, he was the man, nobody was close. Clemmons told them, "But it's the heavyweight champ of the world. You gotta send somebody." So they said, "All right, Clemmons, you go." Clemmons goes. We're watching the fight back in Bristol. I'm in graphics that night. Wow, this isn't a knockout. Oh shit, it's the third round, it's not a knockout. Oh shit, it's the fifth round, he's not knocked out. Douglas's mama had just died, and he was saying, "This is my time. Fuck all of you — I don't care who I'm fighting." We just didn't know that before. And Douglas wins the fight! He did it, man. So here's this fucking Buster Douglas from Columbus, Ohio, becoming heavyweight champ of the world. I thought I came up with one of my proudest moments. We had built, "Tyson Wins," but now we had to say "Douglas Wins." So I build one, it was a *Ghostbusters* slash through a picture of Mike Tyson, and the slug said, "Tysonbuster." It was one of my proudest moments. I was like, "I'm the greatest twenty-four-year-old currently walking the face of this earth." Tysonbuster? Tysonbuster! Unbelievable. I thought *Sports Illustrated* would mention it, but no one ever said it again.

Anyway, I thought it was the greatest upset in sports history. People talk about the miracle on ice; I don't think so. I think it was Tyson-Douglas. It was off-the-board in Vegas. Forty-two-to-one, I heard. It was the greatest night in my history at ESPN. We were all high-fiving. We all knew we had just seen something that would never be forgotten. It was shocking. And despite the fact that we were all made of lead, we couldn't be moved by sports — you were uncool if you were moved by sports — we were moved. We were moved by Buster Douglas. Anyone who says he wasn't is lying to you. People couldn't help themselves. I remember walking down the hall, fucking high-fiving: "Did you see that fucking fight! High five!" That was a night I'll never forget.

CHARLEY STEINER:

The same year Douglas beat Tyson, he fought Holyfield. The weigh-in for the fight was unbelievable. Here's Buster, who had just pulled off arguably the greatest upset in sports history: right out of the journeyman ranks, he knocks Mike Tyson into the ozone. So he's getting like $25 million for his first defense, and it's going to be Holyfield. Now, he weighed around 215 or 220 for Tyson, but he's been training on beer and pizza! So the weigh-in happens, and when Douglas takes his shirt off, Ray Leonard, who was on the set with me, says something like "Oh, my God!" Buster was near 240 pounds, with a belly that was bigger than mine! As soon as they announced the weight, there was a rush on the Vegas bookies like you've never seen. All the money went to Holyfield.

ANDREA KREMER, *Reporter*:

Before I got to ESPN, I was at NFL Films, and as I was getting prepared to start being on camera there, I basically asked the producer, "What should I look like?" And then he uttered the immortal words to me, "Friendly, fuckable, and informative. It's like they want to be fucking you while they're talking to you about football." Now I'm staring at him, just in total shock. Understand, this was 1987. If it was 1997, he probably wouldn't have a job if someone had overheard him saying that. But he's still one of my closest friends, and we still joke about that comment to this day.

I always wanted to look professional, but it wasn't something I spent a whole lot of time on, because there was so much else to be concerned about. I was at ESPN when Doug Collins was fired and they were announcing Phil Jackson as their next coach. It was 101 degrees in Chicago, and I went over to the Bulls' offices, where they were having a last-minute press conference to introduce Phil. I'm wearing a little dress and it's sleeveless, but I'm okay with that because I am thoroughly athletic and muscular for a small person. But ESPN freaked that I was showing my arms. So I said, "Well, number one: it's a hundred-some degrees, and number two: the day you start buying me clothes is the day you can start telling me what to wear." And guess what? They started buying me clothes! So I actually had a clothing deal before it got put on my contract. I'm serious. And ever since then, I've always had clothing deals.

Back then, there were only three bureau reporters—I was in Chicago, Jimmy Roberts was in New York, and Chris Myers was in L.A. We didn't have computers and we didn't have BlackBerries. We didn't even have cell phones. We were lucky we had phone cards. We all had our own producers, but at that time, I had infinitely more field-producing experience than they did, because that's how I started off at NFL Films. So there was no opportunity for me to learn how to get better from a producer. I was basically teaching them the job. In some respects they were to me like production assistants—setting things up, making sure they went smoothly. I never, ever, ever had anything written for me, never anything handed to me, no questions, no preparation, nothing. It was all on my own. And that became my level of expectation for producers. It's very simple. We're working on deadline, and if you can't carry your load, well then, I don't really have a lot of use for you. I'm just going to do it myself because I'm darn well not going to take my time to do it for you. They were always concerned that I would be too hard on the producers because I had high levels of expectations, but what was happening was that everybody wanted to work with me because I came prepared in a totally different way than anybody else. And I was doing a lot more writing than anybody else. But I constantly had to tell these people to stop saying things were going to get fixed in the editing room. Who gives a shit what's happening in the edit room? You can have all your bells and whistles but don't worry about style, worry about content. Get your elements. Make sure you're organized.

One day, Jim Cohen and Bob Eaton, my bosses,

took me to some local Italian place, and we're sitting there talking about my work. They both have really good bedside manner, and I never questioned for a minute if they had my personal and professional growth in mind. They were very supportive. But we're sitting there and they're basically telling me, "Look, you're really hard on producers and it's hard to deal with." It wasn't like I was in trouble or anything, but I can still remember having a lot of emotions built up where you kind of want to cry because you're semi-angry and semi-hurt. I felt a lot of resentment, anger, sadness, everything. But I was trying to keep my composure and certainly not turn defensive but try to use it productively. After they made their spiel, I said to them, "Just answer me one question. Would we be having this conversation if I was a man?" They looked at each other and then said no. Well, that pretty much told me all I needed to know.

TERRY LINGNER:

Rich Volger probably won more sprint and midget car races than anybody on ESPN, and that's including guys like Jeff Gordon and Tony Stewart. He was one of our early stars, although Gordon was quickly becoming one. Rich was not sophisticated, just kind of a blue-collar guy, but an unbelievable racer. We were in Salem, Indiana, a rickety old half-mile-high banked track. Rich was scheduled to make his Winston Cup debut in Pocono, so he was flying back and forth trying to qualify in Pocono, but came back to Salem to race that Saturday night. It was kind of a career weekend for him because he was going to make a nice step up to the big leagues, if you will, and he was running away with the race. He was so fast, he had Gordon and everybody just completely buried. I had a theory that he wanted to have such a great race, to almost spit in Jeff's eye, like, "Not only do I deserve to go on NASCAR, but I'm going to kick your ass here on live TV." A lap and a half from the end of the feature race, he ran up over the top of another guy and hit with such force that it actually threw his helmet off, which was really scary to see. It was a horrible accident and he was killed. It was a really sad day for me—that's the sad part of getting to know these guys really well.

RICHARD PETTY:

The thing about crashes is everybody wants to know what's going on and if you're really hurt. One time I got hurt and I was just lying in the infirmary, watching the replays over and over again on TV. You know a little bit, but you really want to see what happened. I had family and fans wanting to know as much as possible, and TV's helpful at times like that. ESPN would cover the good, bad, and indifferent, which was good for us. The more attention we got, and the more the drivers and crews cooperated, the better chance we had getting to new fans. The way they covered us really worked out well for us, and them. It certainly helped us grow.

JEFF GORDON, *Race Car Driver:*

Racing on ESPN turned my career around for me—not turned it around, but really took it to that next level, because I'd been racing sprint cars on a lot of different tracks, and the next step was probably go to outlaw racing, and somebody talked me into going and racing a midget the night before the 500 and said, "Oh, by the way, it's on ESPN, live on ESPN, so it's good publicity as well." And I went, won, and set a track record. All of a sudden my phone starts ringing off the hook after that 'cause everybody saw it. I was like, "Wow, this is unbelievable—one race on TV and look what happens." So we really started focusing on the ESPN TV races, even out west.

Larry Newberry, who was working the broadcast booth for those events, he and I had become friends and he was helping me with advice on career options. He brought up NASCAR to me, and I told him I didn't really know a whole lot about it, so he said, "Well, go down to Buck Baker driving school in Rockingham and just give it a shot. See if you like it." And so he kind of worked it out with ESPN for them to follow me down there, and they brought some cameras down there and filmed a little bit of it for *Saturday Night Thunder.* I enjoyed the heck out of stock car, I liked it a lot more than I thought I would, and the tracks were cool 'cause they're type 8 tracks and ovals, and that's what I grew up on. I met a guy there that had a Busch Grand National car, and he showed some interest, and the next thing I know, I'm being talked to about driving a car.

JEFF BURTON, *Race Car Driver:*

ESPN made us relevant. Even back then, people were looking to ESPN for things that were relevant in sports, and their coverage of our sport made the basketball fan, the football fan, and the baseball fan stop and say, "What is this? Is it a stereotypical southern sport?" So ESPN brought to the sport a lot of people who otherwise wouldn't have paid attention.

BRIAN FRANCE, *Chairman, NASCAR:*

I think that our sport, maybe more than any other for ESPN, at least in the early days, had the biggest influence because we had quality programming available that wasn't picked up at that point by network television. Finally, there was a sports channel that was widely distributed. At least it got to be widely distributed. The interest level in our sport was very robust, but a lot of our fans had no way to consume it. So ESPN became the home for NASCAR in the early days, and it just worked for us through the years. We gave them a large bulk of quality programming that they could actually put on and draw ratings with, not just fill up time, and it scored out pretty high for us.

And when it became known that live start times were on ESPN, that was something special that took off for us and them. Their growth directly tracked the popularity of our sport.

In 1990, Roger Werner, one of the smartest and classiest people ever to cash an ESPN paycheck, chose to leave; around the same time, KKR, having picked up a 20 percent slice of ESPN when it gained control of RJR Nabisco in 1988, decided it didn't want a piece of Bristol cream pie after all. In the ensuing sale, CapCities / ABC had the first right to buy the remaining 20 percent but, partly under advisement from consultant Warren Buffett, it passed on the opportunity to become sole owner. Billionaire Buffett later said it was one of the worst business decisions he ever made.

CapCities hired Steve Rattner of Lazard Frères to go chase down a buyer. Don Ohlmeyer and Ross Johnson, meanwhile, had little cause for complaint; they would each more than double their $60 million investment in the sale. Obvious questions arose: Who would replace Roger Werner at ESPN? And who would buy KKR's share of the network?

ROGER WERNER:

One of my biggest frustrations was that Tom didn't buy that remaining 20 percent. CapCities didn't want to write the check, basically because they said, "Hey, we've got a lot of issues with our broadcast network; its profitability is declining. We've got a 20 percent interest that has no vote that's completely passive interest. We don't know why Leonard would have sold it to Ross Johnson. We don't know why Ross Johnson would have bought it, except that Ross liked to hang out with athletes and fly around on his airplane." There's no compelling reason why anyone would want to be a passive investor in a kind of dynamic high-growth situation that admittedly could be very valuable in a few years, but would you really want to have no votes and no liquidity, no ability to get out, and no ability to influence policy as a partner? So Tom looked at it and said, "Anybody who wants to buy it, we'll sell it to them."

Once he decided not to buy the rest, my strong conviction was that we ought to bring in a strategic partner so that we had a little leverage with our distribution. I set up a dinner at the Four Seasons restaurant with Ralph Roberts, Brian Roberts, Tom Murphy, and me, to talk about Comcast buying the 20 percent. I think Tom saw the wisdom of that, and that deal did not fall apart because Tom didn't want it to happen. He thought they'd be a good ally on the distribution side, and we might encounter less resistance in terms of additional fees for additional high-product acquisitions. What happened was, frankly, the Comcast guys, I think it was Brian maybe more than Ralph, demanded too much in terms of voting rights and veto rights with certain important decisions. They tried to drive too hard a bargain. Brian is a very tough negotiator. In this case, he didn't get a deal that would have been unbelievable for Comcast.

FRANK BENNACK, *Hearst Corporation:*

As [we were] the largest of ABC affiliates, Tom Murphy and Dan Burke knew us to be good partners. Good partnerships prove themselves out. Many times, you have to defer to the judgment and to the needs of a partner. We had a very strong association with them already by our having started what is now A&E, Lifetime, and History channels together, so because of my association with Leonard, we were approached by Lou Gerstner. He was looking for a buyer at a price well above what we thought it was worth at the time, so we told them we were interested but not at the levels they were talking about.

Lou and I engaged in a negotiation and we ended up making a deal. People talk about how prescient we were to have bought it when we did buy it, and while I think almost anyone would have seen some future in it, certainly at that time, it was not a robust business that would bear any resemblance to what it looks like today.

Even after a decade on the air, even after signing contracts with the NCAA, NASCAR, the NFL, and Major League Baseball, even after turning a profit by establishing the dual revenue stream, still no one wanted

20 percent of ESPN—not until the Hearst Corporation stepped up with its checkbook open. And it could be argued that Hearst's interest was piqued less by ESPN's potential than by the fact that the company held a tax certificate, soon to expire, that could be used to save Hearst millions of dollars (the 20 percent cost about $175 million; the certificate brought that down to $140 million). So now the company was owned by CapCities and Hearst, with Steve Bornstein in charge, reporting to Burke and Murphy.

ROGER WERNER:

I thought the Hearst people were great guys, but they didn't really bring anything to the dance. I wanted some leverage out of that deal somehow. We didn't get it.

By 1990, I'd watched all of my peers on the distribution side become billionaires, and I'd never been with any company long enough to even have a 401(k) plan. We went through so many management changes, changes of ownership, not management, but guys that we reported to during the eighties. It was Getty, and then Getty/ABC, and then Getty was acquired by Texaco, and then Texaco put all those assets on the block and the company was acquired by ABC. Then ABC immediately spun off 20 percent to Ross Johnson and RJR Nabisco. Then RJR Nabisco was acquired by KKR in that *Barbarians at the Gate* saga. Then CapCities came in and acquired ABC. That was my decade. I don't know how many changes of ownership that was, but I spent probably a third of my time while we were trying to build the company making presentations to new owners and telling them what the hell we were trying to build, literally. And none of them gave us the equity ownership that should have been there.

STEVE BORNSTEIN:
You weren't going to make real money working for CapCities. We were always paid significantly less than our colleagues at HBO or CNN. Time Warner and Viacom always would pay them more. We had no contracts at CapCities. You took what they gave you. To their credit, both Dan and Tom Murphy took a lot less money out of the company than their colleagues would in similar circumstances.

ROGER WERNER:
Bill Daniels was a cable industry pioneer from Denver. He had become a mentor of mine and was one of ESPN's earliest cheerleaders. His health was failing, and he asked me to join him to help him with a bunch of regional sports networks in partnership with John Malone. They had networks in Southern California, Texas, Colorado. They had a piece of the Sunshine Network in Florida and some other stuff. It was all losing money, tens of millions of dollars. I got equity and a cash guarantee, so I left the company and joined Bill on a personal-services contract to fix his

sports TV stuff, build it up and find new owners for it; that was the mission. And I did that in spite of my love for Tom Murphy and Dan and the company and everything else, simply because I was forty years old at that point and had literally made no money from a decade that I created something that everybody said was worth $2 or $4 billion. I just said, you know, I can't get a major financial whack out of the deal here. I'm going to stay here, be an executive buried in this huge corporation making good money, but never having any independence. I felt like I had to exercise control over my future, and it was time to leave.

So the early management at ESPN all reached that point where they saw the value of what had been created, but they hadn't shared in the ownership of any of that value, got frustrated, and left. In retrospect, I wouldn't trade my time at ESPN for any of my money. As you get a little older and wiser, it's not about the money. That's not the scarce resource.

When I had my conversation with Murphy and Burke to tell them about my decision, I said I had been grooming Steve and he should be my successor. It wound up being a very smooth transition upon my departure. They understood Steve was the right guy, and Steve understood he had lots to learn.

STEVE BORNSTEIN:
People think I was disappointed that it took eight days or ten days or whatever it did to announce

my promotion. It would have been nice if they had done it instantaneously, but it was not fair to some of the other contenders—primarily that knuckle-head Roger Williams. He was running affiliate sales for ESPN at the time. He deserved to maybe be considered. But I was glad when they finally made it official.

FRANK BENNACK:

I was a bit disoriented, because when I made the decision to make the investment in ESPN, Roger was heading up the company, and I knew him well and respected him very much. He was a world-class guy. And then all of a sudden, he's not there. So I have this new, important investment and it was being run now by Steve, who I really didn't know well. It was a difficult time for me, particularly since, in my own shop and among my own board, I had a lot of detractors. A lot of people had been saying, why do you want 20 percent of this thing—tractor pulls and all the other pejoratives that can come out from one's advisers. So I was not pleased, even though I had heard Steve was a talented guy.

TERRY LINGNER:

I love Steve Bornstein. He did a lot for guys like me, Anderson, and Wildhack. He started paying us better, including trying to beat the system by giving us outside contracts. But, by the same token, he didn't make it easy to work for him, nothing like working for Scotty Connal or Bill Fitts. There was always a lot of second-guessing. When you would go up to the third floor, you weren't sure if you were getting feedback from him, Ohlmeyer, Creasy, or whoever else was consulting at the time.

I kept a notebook a lot of times in meetings, and it really annoyed Steve. I would write everything down, which is not my nature at all—I actually hate it—but too often I would get specific instructions in the morning and then in the afternoon I would get a complete 180 from what I was told in the morning. I once said, "Jesus Christ, Steve, I mean I got it right here. You told me to do this." And he said, "Well, I've changed my mind." I can't tell you how many times that happened.

But sometimes I could get away with what I wanted. This is kind of a funny one. Steve was not a fan of Lee Corso's. I had hired Lee for *College Game-Day,* and every Monday it was like, "Fire Corso. I can't stand him, blah, blah, blah." I said, "I'm not doing that. I can't do it, Steve. Tell me somebody better." And we'd go at it. I called Corso on his twenty-fifth anniversary at the network and said I'm glad it worked out.

In the early days, Bornstein, Creasy, and I did a fair amount of hanging out together after hours; we were bonding pretty well. It was clear Creasy was very, very high on Steve and Steve felt the same way about Bill. They fed off of each other and they were both programming guys. I was in the production department, and we'd be at a bar, and they would say to me, "You ought to slide over to our camp. You better start learning programming, because this is the path you're going to have to start taking." All I could think about was I wanted to learn more about production than I did about Nielsen ratings and trying to schedule programs.

It certainly crossed my mind that I could become president of ESPN, but I wasn't prepared to do the things I would need to do in order to get it. I refused to play the cards the way they needed to be played to get there, particularly the politicking.

I left ESPN April 1, 1989, but stayed with the company as an outside contractor-producer. I really didn't want to have a policy manual, and I wanted to do as much with auto racing as possible. It coincided with Major League Baseball coming to ESPN, which, I think, this is probably another good reason why I shouldn't run a sports network. I despise baseball. I can't watch it. I can't even make believe that I enjoy it. And I knew that was sacrilegious in the sports world. But the thing is, if you cut me right now, I'd still bleed the place.

CHARLEY STEINER:
At the Christmas party the year before he took over—back in the days when a Christmas party had

about two hundred people and everybody knew each other—it was getting late, maybe two, three o'clock in the morning, and Bornstein comes up to me and says, "You know, in a perfect world, we would have *SportsCenter* with robots. But you, Berman, and Saunders fucked up my master plan." We had all been interchangeable parts, which was perfect for him—perfect financially and for his vision of what *SportsCenter* would be. He was so clairvoyant about the future of sports and ESPN; where he was a little slow to the dance was the appreciation of the guys who delivered the news, which was what made it so fascinating. But maybe his attitude explains why we were the last ones to realize that ESPN was becoming a big deal. To us, it was the sports station on cable—no more, no less.

JED DRAKE:

I was walking one afternoon with Bornstein and John Wildhack, and something either Wildhack or I said triggered the latest rendition of "You fucking guys," which was said with that inevitably all-knowing sly grin that Steve always had when he was trying to be a bit fatherly. So he says to us, "You fucking guys...Here's the deal: I can't make all the decisions myself. What I do is put you guys in place, guys who I think are pretty smart, who will make the right decisions most of the time. Now, I know you're not going to make the right decisions all the time, that you're going to screw up sometimes, but that's okay. I just have to be able to trust you." Wildhack and I, heads looking somewhat downward as we continued to walk with Steve, nodded our heads, but we glanced at each other, each with slight grins, knowing that this was actually a major signal from Steve that he really believed in us, and that we were indeed going to be called upon to make major decisions on our own. That was the Stevie B. speech: all about putting the right people in place to make decisions that Steve would likely make himself.

BEANO COOK, *College Football Analyst:*
Bornstein had a temper; Roone did not have a temper. Bornstein yelled; Roone never yelled at people in public. In those early years, Bornstein had a lot of Roone in him in terms of programming. But things get really different when you're no longer hidden behind the guy in charge. Once you take over everything, things have a way of changing.

In the beginning, Bill Rasmussen took a wild idea and got it going with Stu Evey and Getty. Chet Simmons came on board to put the network on the air and give the company legitimacy and a patina of professionalism. Then Bill Grimes and Roger Werner constructed the all-important dual-revenue stream, solidified relationships with cable operators, and secured powerhouse programming acquisitions. Thirty-eight-year-old Steve

Bornstein had been around for virtually the whole trip and had played an incredibly aggressive role. But now the company was his, and the question became, how would he leave his mark?

STEVE BORNSTEIN:

People forget, but we had a business show that ran in the mornings. I always wanted to get rid of it, but neither Grimes nor Werner would ever let me do it, because they didn't want to piss off the Chamber of Commerce, which produced the show. Well, as soon as I became president, I decided to bite the bullet, take them on, and end our contract with them. This was right around the time that I was starting to get really conscientious about my health, and I started working out in the mornings. So it was great to have *SportsCenter* on as I worked out; I could watch that instead of the business show. As I got more in shape, I was able to work out longer, and that became the primary reason why I expanded the show from thirty minutes—which it was back then—to sixty minutes.

GARY MILLER, *Anchor:*

I came over to *SportsCenter* in 1990 from CNN. We had been well aware of ESPN through the years and it was a real rivalry. It was pretty much neck and neck, but after ABC bought them, Ted Turner did something to piss them off, so they wouldn't let us use any ABC footage. That actually influenced my decision to leave CNN and go to ESPN. We had to cover a World Series ABC had without using any footage from games, and they had the Kentucky Derby, and we had to shoot it from on top of Churchill Downs. Besides, Turner didn't have any rights besides the Goodwill Games and the Braves, and they still sucked at that point.

Once I arrived, I realized I had no concept of what a wasteland Bristol was, especially back in 1990. It's unimaginable, especially because I was single and I was coming from Atlanta, which might be the greatest city on earth to be single in because it's a 4:00 a.m. town, and we were pretty heavy partiers in the CNN days. So the social life in Bristol was almost impossible.

Dan [Patrick] and I used to have fart wars upstairs. We'd type in our little cubicles, then go down to the newsroom and battle. I actually did it to him once on the set, but normally I didn't engage him because he was deadly. I was more about sound; he was more about fury.

There was a Double-A minor-league team around there, the New Britain Cats, and we would see them and yell at opposing players and coaches and stuff, then we'd end up meeting with them because they were staying at the Ramada, which is the only hotel in New Britain. One night we were sitting there drinking with them after the game, and somebody on the other side was having a bridal party, and Dan and I decided to moon them as they were opening gifts. They basically looked up, then just went back to opening their presents. So then we were sitting with this coach—and I swear to God this happened—and the guy was a tobacco chewer. The coach for the Harrisburg Expos, or whatever the Harrisburg team was called. And he had a spit cup about a quarter full and he started betting Dan that he wouldn't drink it. But sure enough, Dan sat there and drank it all. I think Tirico was there that night; he had just come to ESPN and that was one of the first things he saw. It was like, "Oh, you want to hang with the big boys? Better be ready."

But my favorite Dan story from back then was from while I was interviewing, and I was following him back to his house in my rental car. We're taking the I-84 freeway back to West Hartford, where he lived, and Dan's going sixty miles an hour, then slows down just a bit. I'm thinking, "I'm following you; what are you doing?" and I pull up beside him, and while he's cruising down Interstate 84, he moons me right through the driver's-side window.

PETER GAMMONS:

One of my most enjoyable moments ever was before the '91 All-Star Game, which was going to be played in San Diego. I went down to Florida, to Ted Williams's house, to do a big interview, which we wound up using in about eight to ten different pieces. When I was six, my parents gave me a little plastic statue of Ted Williams, and I still have it to this day. Ted was so great. He had everything set up. He had even brought out a picture of himself with Babe Ruth so it was right behind me when he was sitting and facing the camera.

After about an hour and twenty minutes, he brought me, the producer, two camera men, and two soundmen into the kitchen, where he had fixed all these trays of crackers and cheese, hors d'oeuvres, and iced tea. Ted Williams was actually setting up snacks for us because he was afraid we would be tired, hungry, and thirsty after listening to him for an hour and twenty minutes. That was amazing.

CHRIS MORTENSEN, *Pro Football Analyst:*
I actually had a mustache for about twenty years before I joined ESPN in '91. It was part of my identity. And the night before my first *NFL Countdown* show, Steve Anderson called and asked, "What would you think of shaving off your mustache? I looked at the tape, and I think it makes you look a little meaner." So being a team guy, I thought, "What the heck?" As soon as I shaved it off, I looked in the mirror and said, "Oh my God, what have I done?" Then I go in the next day and the makeup lady wants to mess with my hair. Now, I'm a beach boy from Cali-

fornia; I've never even combed my hair before. After the show, I got a lot of phone messages saying, "It was your voice, you did a good job, but it sure didn't look like you."

Normally the breaking of a big news story energizes and excites journalists, but the story that broke on November 7, 1991, truly tested the journalistic mettle of ESPN. This was the day that Earvin "Magic" Johnson, thirty-two but looking younger, faced cameras and microphones in Inglewood, California, to tell the world he was HIV positive and was bidding good-bye to basketball, the game at which he had so spectacularly excelled.

"Because of the HIV virus that I have attained," *Johnson said, calmly and soberly, "I will have to retire from the Lakers today." He'd played twelve spectacular seasons with the Los Angeles Lakers by that point—twelve times an All-Star, three times league MVP—and everyone watching had to process the shattering news that Magic's career as a player was now over.*

As is often said of momentous events, there was a haunted, surreal quality to the day—a sense that it couldn't really be happening. The television cameras and microphones validated something that everyone wanted to deny. In fact, Johnson had taken the HIV test twice more after testing positive in the hope that the first positive was a false one; unfortunately, the answer kept coming back the same.

Johnson's declaration immediately became one of the biggest sports stories of the age, as well as one of the most affecting. For many ESPN reporters and producers, covering it dispassionately was difficult; Magic was one of the best-liked and most affable athletes around, on and off the court. Indeed, the room in which the press conference was held was all but awash in tears, many from supposedly hard-bitten reporters. For his part, Johnson had never been a press-basher; he included journalists among those he thanked that night.

"I will miss you guys," he said, looking out at the crowd.

The story tested the professionalism of the ESPN team, requiring everyone to stay cool even when emotions ran high. Heading up the coverage, Bob Ley kept viewers informed and involved with his gravitas and empathy—and no hint of sensationalism.

Public interest ran high, and so, apparently, did public trust in an improved ESPN. The network's Thoroughbred Digest, usually seen in the 6:00 p.m. time slot, had averaged a .6 rating; Johnson's press conference, at 6:10 p.m., earned a 2.0, and ratings continued to build through the evening, with the seven o'clock SportsCenter garnering a highly unusual 2.3.

November 7, 1991, would be, then, a day of culmination, when all the elements and improvements in the ESPN newsroom came together; when the changes made *in the years leading up to this date—in process, standards, personnel, and other areas—had strengthened the news operation and got it working like the proverbial well-oiled machine.*

Newfound parity with "the big guys" at long-established networks was apparent in what ESPN did, not in what it said about itself. Magic Johnson's press conference had been available on many other channels, including the all-news kind, but for many viewers, ESPN was now the source of choice for a story such as this. Competitors, take note.

4

Manifest Destiny: 1992–1994

"The difficulty lies not so much in developing new
ideas as in escaping from old ones."
—*John Maynard Keynes*

JOHN WALSH:

We were ready to make Olbermann an offer, go
full board to get him, and Steve Anderson and I told
Bornstein, who says, "You got a tape of this guy? Let's
see him." We pull the tape off the shelf and put it in.
I swear to God, the tape is on maybe fifteen seconds
and Olbermann's got one of those looks in his eyes,
and Bornstein pushes the pause button and says,
"Take a look at that." We looked at Olbermann's face
and then Bornstein says, "Good luck," and walks out.

*Have Keith Theodore Olbermann spend a few seasons
working at your television network and see how you
feel. Sort of like Kansas after a twister. Olbermann long
ago established himself as a living, fire-breathing force of
nature, not only on the air, where both his brains and*

his style are his meal tickets, but also off the air, where he bedevils and infuriates many a manager or coworker who runs afoul of his biblical-size wrath. If Olbermann hadn't been so brilliant and talented, few of those managers or coworkers would have put up with him. But he is.

It is said that Olbermann decided what his career would be when he was eight years old: he'd be the game announcer for the New York Yankees. And with that decision out of the way, he continued and eventually completed his childhood—most of it lived within the beautiful confines of Hastings-on-Hudson in Westchester County, an affluent bedroom community north of New York City. Lore has it that a company that manufactures baseball trading cards "published" Olbermann's first book, The Major League Coaches, 1921–1973 *(well, a friend made one hundred copies of the manuscript) when he was fourteen. Olbermann has a talent that can't be taught. He can relate to people on the other side of the camera and, indeed, relate to the camera itself, in a way that comes across as second nature. And yet he once told an interviewer that on some level, he's always making fun of television: "Like, 'look how ridiculous this is, me sitting here and you sitting on the other end, watching me—what are you doing that for?' I think that's always been my attitude."*

Olbermann's father was an architect; his mother was a teacher and lifelong Yankees fan. Even as a child, Olbermann was a baseball fanatic, listening to

games on the radio in his room at night when his par-
ents curtailed his TV viewing and shut off his bedroom
light.

If you're going to write a book at fourteen, you might
as well enter an Ivy League university two years later,
which is what Olbermann did. He enrolled at Cornell
and, being no slouch at academics, graduated in 1979
at the age of twenty. While at Cornell, he anchored a
daily sportscast on a commercial ABC-affiliate radio
station run by some of his fellow students. Olbermann
wore a number of hats at the station, including sports
director, newscaster, vice president of training, and
operations manager.

Olbermann first found regular employment as a
sportscaster at UPI Radio Network (1979–80) and
later at RKO Radio in New York (1980–1982), where
his boss was none other than Charley Steiner. Even in
small-time jobs, Olbermann gave off sparks that made
him an unusually compelling figure on the air—but he
also polished his image as a backstage bad boy who
rebelled against management and saw almost any criti-
cism as persecution.

In 1981, Olbermann got his big break when CNN
hired him as a sports reporter in New York, replacing a
woman by the name of Debi Segura who moved to
Atlanta to be with her husband, Lou Dobbs. While at
the pioneering news network, Olbermann was subse-
quently promoted to anchor and earned a considerable
amount of attention, but he quit after only three years,

spending the rest of the decade bouncing among local stations in Boston and Los Angeles.

ESPN had first approached Olbermann way back in 1982, but shortly after his arrival in 1988, Walsh began his own pursuit. He offered Olbermann the 11:00 p.m. SportsCenter, *cohosting with Chris Berman. Olbermann declined. After the Major League Baseball deal was completed the following year, Walsh and Steve Anderson asked Olbermann if he would fly from Los Angeles to Bristol every weekend to host the new* Baseball Tonight, *but again, the answer was no. Finally, by August of 1991, Olbermann agreed to come to ESPN the following spring as an anchor for the 11:00 p.m.* SportsCenter. *In the last year of his contract with KCBS—which they chose not to renew—he had been making $475,000. His starting salary in Bristol would be just over $150,000.*

KEITH OLBERMANN:

There were no jobs open in any of the big markets. I wanted to be back East to be closer to my family. I had no doubt of my skills and knew ESPN would only enhance my earning capacity later—even if I stayed there forever. Besides which, $160,000 or whatever it was went a lot further in Bristol than something like $450,000 did in Beverly Hills.

When I was at CNN, we used to look at ESPN as our comic relief because, for a long time, the first three or four years that both of these networks were on, in terms of sports news, CNN was a ten-times-better product than ESPN. I used to look at my old friend Berman sweating away in the studio without a teleprompter trying to read his notes—one night at 1:45 a.m. and the next night at 9:30 p.m., and it was never the same thing twice. I thought, "Thank God that there's somebody on the air in worse shape than we are." And then I finally figured out how they survived for nearly a decade with basically no funding: they were in the middle of nowhere. Across the street was a McDonald's, what was always reputed to be a toxic waste area, and cows. So, unless you're clearly a freelance dairyman, there was no place else to go. If you committed to them, you committed to them. There was no chance you were going to jump to some other television outfit across the street.

STEVE BORNSTEIN:

By the time Walsh and Anderson told me they had closed a deal with Olbermann, I had become familiar with his work. He was really good and really legendary. I remember telling them, "Be careful what you wish for. He's pure genius, but he will be a bucketful to handle." And he was, from the day he got there to the day he left.

BOB LEY:

I still remember the lunch when John and Steve were deciding whether they were going to hire Keith.

I said, "You're aware of his reputation, aren't you?" They said, "Oh, it's not going to be like that. He's not making all that much money." I said, "It's not a function of money. Know what you're buying." When he arrived, Keith had one thing in mind: it was Keith. That's fine. Nothing wrong with that.

STEVE BORNSTEIN:

I had an epiphany shortly after I got to be the CEO. I had been number two under Roger Werner for two years, and number two or three for Bill Grimes. In a way, I thought I ran the place because those guys were running off doing what they were doing and I was operating the pedals, right? But now that I was actually formally in charge, I felt this incredible burden for the first time. All of a sudden, I realized I was responsible for my friends' kids' college education. I couldn't screw this up. I didn't get depressed, but it forced me to really think about what I wanted to do with this job. And I decided that I wanted to make sure ESPN wasn't just a network anymore. It had to be a way of life for people, with as many angles into their lives as possible. I wanted ESPN to replace the word "sport" in the dictionary. And the only way to do all this was to be everywhere.

Steve Bornstein didn't wait long to mobilize his expansion plans for ESPN. For his first big move, he decided he would launch in January of 1992 an all-sports national radio network with ESPN as the call letters. If that sounds like a fairly simple proposition, it wasn't. For one thing, precedent was not on Bornstein's side; of three previous attempts to start national sports-radio networks, two ended in ignominious belly-flops, and the other was something less than a raging sensation.

As chance would have it, The Enterprise Sports Network had been started and operated by Scott Rasmussen. Despite the pedigree, Rasmussen's ESN (sound familiar?) lasted only from January to September of 1981. A second sports network, the small-time RTV Sports, had launched from Mashpee, Massachusetts, in 1987; by 1988, it was out of business. Bucking the trend, the Sports Entertainment Network was now managing to survive under the name Sporting News Radio in Houston.

ESPN announced that its new radio network would run in tandem with ABC Radio, the first significant example of synergy with parent company CapCities. The initial agenda was to operate first only on weekends, with a limited schedule of live news, game updates, interviews, and magazine-style feature pieces. The plan was to expand from there with drive-time reports on weekdays, and to move to round-the-clock service as quickly as possible.

Although obviously not the first sports network in American radio, it was the first and only bearing the auspicious ESPN brand. The name ESPN now spoke more loudly; scarcely had plans for the network been announced when twenty-five stations in the top fifty markets eagerly signed up. Much as it had done in television, ESPN started off its radio network with a minimal expenditure and a skeletal staff putting in sometimes torturously long hours — not so much because of passion for the project as a management demand that they couldn't refuse.

Keith Olbermann was one of three main on-air personalities signed at the start. The other two were the explosive Tony Bruno, who'd become a highly popular radio star in the sports-crazed Philadelphia market, and Chuck Wilson, least outspoken of the bunch. The radio network was jointly run by ABC Radio's Shelby Whitfield and ESPN's John Walsh. For Olbermann and Walsh, it would be the start of a long, winding roller coaster of a relationship.

On January 4, 1992, the ESPN radio network signed on. Luck on timing paid off pronto. By the second night, it had already broken a national story. Eventually ESPN Radio would encompass five owned stations and dozens more affiliates.

JOHN WALSH:

I remember Bornstein calling me into the office and basically putting me against the wall and saying, "Look, I want to do radio, and I don't want to spend any money. You tell all these guys that they're going to go on radio and we're not going to pay them anything

extra, and if they don't want to go on they can leave."
And so radio launched. We started with fifty-one
stations and it was on Saturday from 6:00 p.m. to
1:00 a.m., Sunday from 7:00 a.m. to 9:00 a.m., and
Sunday from 6:00 p.m. to 1:00 a.m.

JIM ALLEGRO, *Executive Vice President*:

Steve brought me in as his number two in 1990
and I was not well received. A few of the people up
there thought that I was coming in as a spy for Cap-
Cities—that was absolutely not the case, but there
was definite coolness there.

I had final approval for *SportsCenter* hires and
John Walsh came to me with a bunch of people, one
of whom was Keith Olbermann. He was willing to
sign on with us for a greatly reduced salary to prove
his worth, so we took the gamble. I did his contract.
There were a lot of constraints and outs. He had been
kind of a renegade out in California and, to be truth-
ful, he was making a lot of money out there and not a
lot of people wanted to pick him up. We did, at a
very, very cheap price. But one of these deciding factors was that we had decided to launch ESPN Radio
and Keith had a good background in that area.

KEITH OLBERMANN:

The deal I reached with ESPN in '91 was very specific: no radio, and no TV other than *SportsCenter*. I
was going to take a couple months off to go to Hawaii

and sit on a beach before I went to Bristol, and then we were going to start up *SportsCenter* with Dan Patrick in March or April. About a day after New Year's Eve, there was a frantic phone call from John Walsh to my agent, Jean Sage, saying that they were starting the radio network that Saturday night, but they only had two hosts, needed a third person, and they didn't have anybody who had enough radio experience to help it. Could I possibly come back for just a couple weeks? Well, for some reason, I decided to cancel my Hawaii trip and instead I went to Bristol in January to do radio for them. My reward for being a team player: I had to keep doing one night per weekend and take split days off well into 1993.

On the first night, there was one seven-hour-long show done by Tony Bruno, Chuck Wilson, and me. On the second night, January fifth, we realized that [right fielder] Danny Tartabull was cancelling visits to potential signing teams. All of us, producers included, had worked the phones and I had narrowed it down to a couple of teams when it suddenly dawned on me that I still had Tartabull's home number. I reached him around 11:00 p.m. and we were able to scoop it: he'd signed with the Yankees. They had to redo the late *SportsCenter* and suddenly radio wasn't an afterthought.

TONY BRUNO, *Host:*

I was doing a radio show in Philly, so I would do my show, then jump in my car and drive to Bristol before Friday afternoon when we would begin our meetings. ESPN loves meetings. John Walsh was totally unfamiliar with radio; he came from the structured newspaper and magazine world so the meetings were still part of the whole print way of doing things. We'd have a meeting and then have another meeting and then producers would come in and we'd have another meeting. I mean ESPN is the meeting capital of the world. Everybody knew what they were doing, but when you're doing a free-flowing seven-hour radio show, you can't time everything out. After a while, John, to his credit, saw how good we were, and pretty much started letting us do our thing. It was definitely the radio that people remember to this day — maybe the best weekend programming ever available.

HOWARD KATZ, *Executive Vice President:*
When we ventured into talk radio on ESPN, it was a very difficult time for John, because prior to this, all anchors were created equal. Okay, Chris Berman was a little more equal, he got away with a few things, but generally, everybody did their own writing, and their own research. And everyone was held to a very high standard, with John the taskmaster.

When radio launched, it obviously needed to be a personality-driven genre. And John had a terrible, terrible time coming to grips with that. We hired Nancy Donnellan, best known as "Fabulous Sports

Babe," for example, and she was all about herself. She wasn't about ESPN, or the work ethic of the place. But I said to John, "To be in this genre you've got to accept the fact that we're going to have to build personalities who people will want to listen to, and they may not act like everyone else." He wrestled with that a whole lot. In fact, I don't think he ever got comfortable with it.

TONY BRUNO:

Every Friday night, Keith and I would go out to dinner. That was our ritual. Actually, we would buy baseball cards because Keith was a big collector and then go to dinner. We'd go to the same Italian restaurant, Pallaci's. I stayed at the Radisson Hotel across the street—for seven years. We would come in on Fridays. We'd all stay at the Radisson. Then Keith finally found a house, he didn't want to live in the Radisson anymore. So we would go to Keith's house on weekends and would have pool parties. After the show, I would have what we call "Bruno Bashes" in my hotel room. Saturday night, we'd come back to my room. Somebody would go out and buy a case of beer before the liquor store closed. I'd get ice and fill up my bathtub with beer and ice. And the whole staff would come over and sit in my room having a couple beers just talking about the show. It was more of the feel of like a fraternity. Keith didn't drive, so I would drive him home.

KEITH OLBERMANN:

Los Angeles was a buyer's market for cabs and even for rides. The drivers there were so amazed that there was actually somebody who didn't drive, they were happy to take me somewhere if I told them the story of why I did not drive. I hit my head leaping onto a train at Shea Stadium in 1980. Two years later, at the US Open, my eyes started doing a Marty Feldman. I was sent to the city's top muscle ophthalmologist, Dr. Renee Richards—still a friend—and she said the damage I'd done was to my inner ear. Essentially, I had no depth perception while traveling more than 20 mph. It took me several seconds to figure out where the other cars actually were. I still sometimes flinch as a passenger.

When I moved to Southington, Connecticut, the big town that adjoins Bristol, I found out that there was one cab company and that it only had three cabs. Walsh always had one on standby because he didn't drive either, and the state basically used the cab service to get all of its state-care medical cases to and from doctors and hospitals. So really there was one cab for everybody else. ESPN had this massive deal with a car service that was running shuttles to the airport, but they wouldn't let me use it. I finally said, "For God's sake, I'm asking PAs to give me lifts home on Sunday night at two o'clock in the morning. This is ridiculous."

MIKE McQUADE:

Southington Taxi, Keith's normal taxi service, raised their rates, and he refused to pay it, so he hung up a sign, "If you want to drive me home, I'll pay you X amount of dollars per trip." He put fliers in all the production assistants' mailboxes offering $6.25 to have the honor of driving Keith home after *Sports-Center*. I drove him home sometimes, and I didn't even live in that direction. Sometimes I would go into his house, we'd have a beer or two, and look at some of his baseball cards. There were binders and binders and binders of baseball cards. Sometimes we'd just talk shop—you know, how the show went, different ideas for the show, that type of thing.

JOHN WALSH:

Keith didn't drive and I had said to him, "Look, I have this wonderful guy named Forest who comes to my house, picks me up, and takes me home. He's terrific, he's retired, he's available all the time. You should use him." So for a period of time, Forest drove me and Keith; sometimes I would get feedback from him about how Keith was thinking.

CHARLEY STEINER:

I hired Keith Olbermann in 1980 in New York on the radio. Keith is one of the smartest people I've ever met. In those days, he was frustrated that the other kids couldn't keep up with him. So intellectually he was a genius and socially he was, well, a special-needs student. When I heard he was coming to ESPN I knew it would take some getting used to — on everyone's part. But when he arrived in '92, I was caught up in covering the Tyson rape trial. That was a really big deal for me and ESPN.

Before the Holyfield fight had been postponed, the producer Julie Anderson and I went to Don King's condo in Vegas to interview Tyson. It was about ten o'clock in the morning, and King answers the door. Instead of the hair going north and south, he's clearly just out of bed and it's going east and west. And his red silk robe is open. This is no way to start the day.

We go into the condo with two camera men, and immediately, King starts screaming at me. He couldn't believe we were covering the allegations. "False! False!" So while the camera guys are unpacking and getting set up, I'm off in the corner with King, and we're screaming at each other. I had no idea what was going on with Julie.

JULIE ANDERSON:
When we drove up there the first day, lined up outside the condo were five Mercedes-Benzes that Tyson had just bought for his entourage, and one of the guys was outside scrubbing them down. So we go inside, and in the living room, scattered all over the floor, were all these porn movies. All over the place.

Don King was mad because of something Dan Patrick had said on the air about Tyson that he thought was insulting. Charley said, "I'm not responsible for what Dan Patrick says," and then Don went on about the media and how the media was all these white men who were united against black people, Don King and Mike Tyson in particular. It turned into a real screaming match. They're both big personalities and I never heard Charley's voice that loud. I mean honest to God, it reminded me of being a little kid when parents would start screaming; they were screaming, screaming.

Meanwhile, the crew is unpacking; they're bringing things in and out of the house, so every once in a while a crew guy comes in and then leaves. It was decided that the first day, Charley would interview Tyson, and I would produce. Then I would go the second day alone and interview King and the entourage, because we were working on a huge Tyson piece. I was also doing his childhood, and we had even gone to Bed-Stuy and found his second grade teacher—that's how far back I went. So anyway, the crew is getting stuff outside, and Charley and Don King are still yelling at each other off in the corner. At this point, I'm really afraid they're going to get into a fight.

And on the couch, doing absolutely nothing, totally disconnected from everything, is Mike Tyson. He looks up at me and goes, "So, are you married?"

And I say, "No." And he says, "Why not?" And I say, "I don't know, I think I'm just working." And he says, "Do you have a boyfriend?" I said, "No." And still screaming, screaming, in the background. So then he says, "What are you doing later? How long are you going to be in Vegas? We should get together." It was crazy, it was insane, it was scary. So I'm just sort of backpedaling, hoping that Charley will save me and not get into a fight with Don King. I didn't know what to say to Mike. There was a tiny part of me — the journalist part — that wanted to say yes because I was working on this story and I knew if I went out with Mike Tyson, I would get more out of him than Charley would, but in a very different way. So that would have been interesting, very interesting, but I just couldn't do it.

The next day when I got to the condo, now scattered on the floor are all these biographies of great African American men in history, like Martin Luther King Jr. and Malcolm X. We went out in the backyard and I interviewed Don King, and during the interview, he kept stopping and saying to me, "I really like you a lot, and so does Mike. I think you'd be great with us. I don't know why you're working with ESPN when you really should be with us, we've got to find a place for you." I didn't say a word. He just kept talking off the one question, and continued to try and hypnotize me by saying, "You should really come join us, we'll find a job for you."

CHARLEY STEINER:

When the Holyfield fight was postponed, we thought: "What are we going to do with this great treasure trove of video that has never been seen before, all this wonderful biographical stuff, because it was supposed to be used for the fight?" So we decided to use it in our trial coverage.

The Tyson trial was one of the high points of my career. I remember one day we figured out that Mike would go home and watch TV coverage, go to bed, and wake up pissed off. I said, "Fuck, he's going to run. He'll train. Let's get a fucking crew out there!" Sure enough, the next morning, five o'clock, he's out there as if he's training. He's got the wool cap on, the parka, and the whole deal. And that night, we had this video, all ours. The next morning, there were half a dozen camera crews outside; they're bumping into one another, the neighbors are getting pissed off, it's utter chaos. We just sat back and roared. But we were getting seven, eight, ten minutes to cover the trial each night. I had to write like a son of a bitch in the truck every day, but it worked. And again, when the conviction came in, we were the first ones on the air with it. Guys from all over the world were carrying this thing in the Marion County Court House. The next day, I was on *Nightline, Good Morning America*—you name it, I was everywhere. And this Aussie guy comes up to me and says, "We have a

Nightline show, can you do it? We'll pay you a thousand dollars." Good! So I did the show, and I bought dinner for the whole crew and a bunch of others who had been covering the trial—all thirty of us at St. Elmo's steak joint, downtown. We were drunker than skunks the whole night. It was terrific.

We won pretty near all the awards that year, including the Clarion, which is a very highfalutin one. Steve Anderson and John Walsh accepted it. I was not invited. I actually went into Steve's office and said, "But it's my story—how can you do this?" I never got a reply. I felt it was a curious way to say, "Thank you for a job well done."

MIKE TYSON:

I was upset at the time by their coverage, sure. There was so much of it. But looking back on it now, that stuff doesn't bother me. I know they were just doing their jobs. Charley Steiner was great, and he, Max and Brian Kenny were all great students of boxing. That was important. I don't take myself that seriously now, and I don't hold any grudges against those guys. Whatever happened in the past happened.

In the 1980s, George Grande had worked wonders with limited resources to help guide ESPN's SportsCenter toward respectability. The show made its first appearance on the same night the network made its first appearance (September 7, 1979) and remained on the schedule from then on, but it was hardly considered the jewel in the network's crown. It was more like the rhinestone in its navel.

Tom Mees and Chris Berman had been the show's best anchor duo of the eighties, and the work done by Walsh and Anderson — along with fellow producers Scott Ackerson, Norby Williamson, and Barry Sacks, stats guy Howie Schwab, and the impressive reporting bench of Jimmy Roberts, Andrea Kremer, and Peter Gammons, among others — had all dramatically strengthened the broadcast. When a new era began late in the decade, the goals were straightforward: to make SportsCenter *as important as anything else in the* ESPN lineup — *if not more so — and to overtake CNN in the ratings.*

When Keith Olbermann and Dan Patrick took over the 11:00 p.m. edition on April 5, 1992, there was neither a massive marketing campaign to alert viewers nor a splashy PR strategy for landing their faces on other talk shows and magazine covers. Fanfare was minimal. Instead, Olbermann and Patrick showed up for work and just started doing their job.

DAN PATRICK, *Anchor:*

I had gone to Eastern Kentucky. I came out of high school totally confused, thinking I was either a professional baseball or basketball player, and it turned out I was neither. I transferred to Dayton, where my dad worked in computer science. Two older brothers had gone there, and then my younger brothers and sisters went to Dayton as well, so all six of us went there just 'cause my dad was there and we got a discount to go to school. They had a 50,000-watt radio station there, and my brother was on it, so without my brother being at WBUD in Dayton, I wouldn't have gotten on the radio. I don't know how I would have gotten into the business.

I sent Bob Ley and Greg Gumbel a tape of me interviewing Joe Garagiola, who had come through town, but they said I needed more time before going on TV. I couldn't get hired in Dayton, because I lost out to a guy who now drives a limousine. Then I went to Atlanta to visit a girlfriend and she said, "You should take a tape into CNN." I waited until the last day 'cause I didn't want to get rejected again. I asked to see the head of sports and when they told me to just leave the tape, I said, "I'm going back to Ohio tomorrow." They told this to Bill McPhail's assistant—he was the guy running sports—and he told her to ask what part of Ohio. I said Dayton, and it turns out he was from Columbus. He came out to see me, looked at the tape, and hired me that day.

I was making $50,000 a year at CNN and was now working in New York. You know who I had replaced? Keith Olbermann. I took his place as the sports reporter. We covered Philly, Boston, New York, D.C.—no matter what it was—Preakness, Belmont, World Series, the great Celtic games, the Garden, whatever it was in that area, we covered it. Then I had the audacity to ask for a raise as my own agent. I said, "I want $10,000 more," and they said no. So instead of understanding the negotiating game, I said, all right. I called John Walsh and I said, "You know who I am?" He said, "Yes, I do." And then he said, "When can you come up?" That was a Friday. I went up the following Tuesday, and he asked me if I would be willing to move to Bristol. I said yes, and then he hired me. I took whatever they gave me—I think it was $100,000. Didn't even bargain.

Six months in, I go to lunch with Steve Bornstein, and Stevie B. said, "I think you're doing a pretty good job. I'm going to tack two more years onto your contract." I thought, "Wow, fantastic. The president of ESPN thinks I'm doing a great job. I'm going to do the eleven o'clock *SportsCenter*. I'm on national TV every day and making more money than my dad did probably the last four years of his life." But what I didn't realize was that I had really shot myself in the foot, because agreeing to that extension really meant I wasn't going to be making any *more* money. I think he added a total of $10,000–$15,000 more for two more years, but now I was locked up for five years.

LINDA COHN, *Anchor*:
Before I got to ESPN in 1992, I was working in Seattle at a CBS TV station out there, so when I got the job at ESPN, I was a little nervous because even

back in '92, it was a bigger deal than working at an affiliate. You knew you had to step it up. You weren't doing four-minute sportcasts anymore, and there was a lot of pressure on me because there weren't a lot of women. I got on the phone with Dan Patrick, who is actually funnier off-screen than on, and I was so excited to talk to him. And one of the first things he says on the phone is, "Hey, Linda, I just gotta tell you, all the women before you have failed." So that was my roll-out-the-red-carpet type of thing.

KEITH OLBERMANN:
My first year there, they came to me and said, "Hey, we're going to have an expansion draft in the National League at the end of the '92 season — the one that created the Rockies and the Marlins — and we think it's a no-brainer but would you want to be the anchor?" And I said, "Well, what are you going to do?" "Oh, we're going to televise the whole thing." And I said, "You're gonna televise the whole thing?!" It was simply every baseball geek's dream just to attend one of those things. My friend — let the name drop, but just to give you an idea of what we're talking about — my friend, Jason Bateman, who is now in every movie that is being made, says his baseball drafts every year are the highlight of his year. Well, one year they weren't because his daughter was born, but to have a draft count and actually have it create real franchises, and be the anchor, was great. Some-

times I've been unable to sleep or having to fight for sleep the night before a big broadcast in anticipation of the anxiety. That night in November of '92 I just thought, "My God, I can't wait for this to get started." We were on the air about ten hours, twelve hours, and it was a feat that could not possibly have been achieved anywhere else.

DAN PATRICK:

I was there fourteen hours a day, spending more time with Keith and the people on the show than with my real family. I really enjoyed the staff. I talked to them and had fun with them because they were the guts of the place. I cared about those people more than I did anybody else in that building. But the hours I was putting in were mostly about the work, and insecurity was a big part of it. Insecurity has driven me my entire life, from a family of six where my mom also lost six kids at birth to a Dad who died at fifty-four. I never took anything for granted. I never wanted to ease off the accelerator and say I've sort of made it. I used to look at the tape of the show after every show I did with Olbermann—every single show. I would take it up right after it was done and I would analyze what I didn't do. Finally, Keith said, "Will you stop looking at the fucking air check! Relax, you got the job." It got to the point where I wasn't having any fun because I was so worried, and Keith really shook me out of it. He just said to me,

"Just be the fucking guy you are off the air when you're on the air." And I just said, "Okay."

There were two moments when I realized people were actually watching. One was talking to Jerry Seinfeld and he said, "I use your home-run line when I leave the set. I say, 'I am gone.'" And I said, "Wow, okay." And then a couple weeks after I had said on the air that one of the toughest things about coaching at Tennessee would be to find that color tie to go with all your outfits, Bill Murray grabbed an orange tie on an A to Z pub crawl in New York and said to me, "Here's your fucking tie. It's not that hard to find."

ROBERT WEINTRAUB, *Assistant Producer:*

Dan Patrick was first among equals in terms of star anchors being beloved, at least at my flunky, production assistant/peon level. One day, one of the senior producer guys was unloading on one of the new low-level guys, a production assistant, just taking him to task—I don't remember for what, but screwing up somehow, and Patrick just kind of sat there and watched it all for a few minutes, then calmly butted in, and started mercilessly making fun of the senior producer, mocking him for all manner of things so as to preserve a shred of dignity for the production assistant, who really appreciated what Dan did. Obviously that made him quite heroic in our eyes, even beyond his talent.

DAN PATRICK:

I didn't want separation between myself and the producer who was talking to me in my ear or the director or anyone else working on the show. I saw us all as being on the same team. That's why I had these guys, including PAs, over to my house. I even had them over for Thanksgiving, just because they had no place to go. And guess what? When I brought my son home for the first day from the hospital, you know who was there in the driveway? Three kids who cut highlights for me on *SportsCenter*. They just wanted to offer up any help they could. How fucking unbelievable is that?

So began a new era of serenity and tranquility, destined to continue for—oh, about five minutes. Indeed, anyone who'd thought there would be peace in the valley had to be kidding themselves—and forgetting, perhaps, that wars can ignite from the most unlikely of disputes.

KEITH OLBERMANN:

One night right after we started, swamped by the work and a little jealous that CNN was just a thirty-minute show and we were doing an hour, I said, during a commercial, off air, to Dan, "This is a BIG fucking show." He laughed, I laughed, and so I figured I'd get him to giggle on the air by saying, on the air, "…when this BIG…show continues." The next day a dozen people came up to one or both of us and said, "The big show!" Walsh may have even been one of them. So I started using it.

DAN PATRICK:

Keith's whole thought was, "Let's mock ourselves." We didn't know who was watching. And so it was, "Welcome to *The Big Show*." I remember we did it for a while and the guys on the six o'clock—Bob Ley, Robin Roberts, and Charley Steiner—didn't like the fact that we called it *The Big Show,* like we thought we were better.

KEITH OLBERMANN:

Charley and I always had gently gone back and forth with crap in every possible relationship between two guys who worked together and were in the same field for thirty years. It was never personal with Charley. I think Bob resented it and Robin couldn't have cared less. And management was saying, "We don't want you putting an individual stamp on your *SportsCenter*." I was thinking, "Yeah, right, that boat sailed already too."

Dan and I essentially tried to escalate it every week just to stick it to management.

JOHN WALSH:

We had one huge editorial blowout. Huge, huge, huge. It was the July Fourth weekend, I watched the show, and they were going off the rail, it was crazy. So we had a meeting, Tuesday morning. The genesis of the meeting was basically Keith was taking over *SportsCenter*, it was no longer *SportsCenter*, it was *The Big Show*; he kept calling it *The Big Show*. One of the points of the meeting was, "It's *SportsCenter*, it's not *The Big Show*. You can have your nickname but when you're going to break, it's not *The Big Show*, it's *SportsCenter*." So Keith said, "What do you want us to say, just 'This is *SportsCenter*'?" I said, "Yeah, that'll be just fine." So they started to say, "This is *SportsCenter*." It was Keith sticking it to us as management because he was going to promote it in the least promotable way: "This is *SportsCenter*."

DAN PATRICK:

My philosophy was: the bigger the room, the more trouble you're in. So we went into the big conference room with wood paneling all around. And it was Keith, myself, and Mike McQuade, our producer. And we got a tongue-lashing by management, pounding on the desk, the whole thing. "We're not going to put up with this, calling it *The Big Show!*" Walsh was pissed. He railed on us. "You will not call it *The Big Show*. From now on, when you're getting ready to go to break, you will say, 'This is *SportsCenter*,' and nothing else." I walked out of that meeting thinking—at the time I had two children, maybe three—and I remember saying, "Oh, my God, I'm going to get fired." We're three steps out of the conference room, and I ask Keith, "What do you think?" and he says, "Fuck them!" I said, "What?" And he looks at me and says, "Fuck them." And I said, "All right."

MIKE McQUADE:
So now, Keith decides, "I'm going to say the name of the show a hundred times." So he would say going into break, "Of course you're watching *SportsCenter*," or, "You are immersed in *SportsCenter*," or, "This is *SportsCenter*." He must have said "This is *SportsCenter*" four or five times per show for the next couple of weeks. I think at some point someone in marketing must have heard that and that's how it ended up becoming "This Is *SportsCenter*."

JOHN WALSH:
And it turned out to be the biggest ad campaign in the history of cable television.

KEITH OLBERMANN:
The Walsh Madness is accurate, but it had nothing to do with "the big show." Dan had been away for several weeks—I think vacation plus NBA Finals. Whenever he ventured away, he'd come back spunky. By his own admission he was just so happy to share our fun again that he'd overdo the silliness.

For some reason, this one time, this enraged John. He brought us in to Anderson's tiny office. I think

Steve and I sat. Don't know about John, but Dan was leaning against a wall. And he swore at us. "You're Nick and Hick. No, worse than that, you're god-damned local news!" I got mad but merely jousted with him. Dan was shaken. He thought we were going to be fired. Steve had to call him at home to apologize—and he said something to me in the office the next day. The irony here was that it wasn't the excess John was criticizing, it was the style, which was about to put the 11:00 p.m. on *TV Guide's* list of the top ten shows on the tube.

By the way, both catchphrases—"the big show" and "this is *SportsCenter*"—worked, and both made them millions.

There were two natural antagonists at the heart of the conflict who would never be able to peacefully coexist: Olbermann, representing talent, versus John A. Walsh, who personified management. It seemed likely there'd be calm in the Middle East before Walsh and Olbermann would be lighting each other's cigars.

DAN PATRICK:

It was all about who had control. We may have taken the seatbelts off a little bit, but they said, "We're locking the car. You're not getting out." It was their way of saying, "We don't care who you are, what you've done, how popular you are, or the feedback you're getting, we still control you." They figured, if we let them get away with things, then everybody else is going to want to do the same. Precedent setting is a big issue at ESPN. They're very concerned about that.

They never paid us much, just so you know. I don't think they liked making stars out of us. As Keith and I were told one time, "We don't need another Berman." That was a real concern. Chris had established himself as unique and passionate, bold and fun, and I think they were worried that Keith and I were sort of levitating above everybody else.

When Steve Bornstein surveyed his senior staff in early 1992, he saw stability, longevity, and, for the most part, harmony. And that was the bad part. Bornstein didn't like things to be too easy, and while he wanted things to run smoothly, he didn't want everyone sitting around the campfire singing "Kumbaya" and roasting marshmallows. Bornstein wanted a burst of energy for his network that he felt only internal friction could create. With encouragement from ever-present consultant Bill Creasy, he hired John Lack. He didn't hide Lack away, either; he named him executive vice president of Programming and Marketing, putting him in charge of a huge chunk of the company.

To the task at hand, Lack brought impeccable credentials, including being one of the creators of MTV, among the most innovative and influential of all cable networks and one with immense global impact. MTV

Music Television arguably changed both music and television forever. Lack identified with the adventurous audience that MTV was born to serve, and this sensibility set him apart from most others in the ESPN executive suites (actually not suites, just offices, and not particularly lavish ones, either).

There was more. As COO of Warner-Amex Satellite Entertainment from 1979 to 1984, Lack oversaw the birth not only of MTV but also of the Movie Channel—cable's first twenty-four-hour pay network—and the groundbreaking Nickelodeon children's channel as well.

From the moment Lack arrived at ESPN—he had offices in Bristol and New York—he became a major blip on the company radar screen. Tall, aristocratic in demeanor, and fascinated with such lofty concepts as "sports as a metaphor for culture," Lack never really did assimilate the Bristol milieu or the ESPN way of thinking, but then again, he didn't try. While George Bodenheimer (who reported to Lack) and others in New York spent many a lunch hour brown-bagging it at their desks, Lack had a table perpetually reserved in his name at 21. When he went to L.A., he could be found making poolside calls from the plush Peninsula Hotel in Beverly Hills.

Two things were clear as Lack settled into his new role at ESPN: first, he would actively try to dismantle the Bristol culture; and second, he wanted Steve Bornstein's job.

JOHN LACK, *Executive Vice President:*

I get a call from Bornstein one day who said, "I really could use some help over here." I said, "What kind of help?" He said, "You know the place is getting a little frayed and we don't really have an image. We're the sports guys, but it's like we're just sports fanatics. We're not broad enough. We're just not attracting a big enough audience. And *SportsCenter* really hasn't grown like I want it to. We think we should be marketing it but we don't know what to do." So he and I talked for a while and I said, "Well, I'll consult for you." I consulted with him for a month or two, then he said, "I'd really love you to come inside." I said, "And what?" He said, "We'll make a job for you. Why don't I give you all the operating units? We'll make you executive vice president of Programming and Marketing—you'll have all the revenue and programming. Finance, administration, and legal will still report to me, and you'll report directly to me." I said, "It sounds like fun." Then he said he thought we really ought to do a second network because the "must carry" regulation [FCC rule requiring cable systems to carry all local channels] was upon us and we needed to take advantage of it. So I had this double mandate. To clean up what we got, and then do the best I could to raise our profile, including adding a new network.

As soon as I got there, I was known as the MTV

guy. That was my fame and fortune. Forget that I was a journalist at CNN, that I went to Northwestern and had a PhD in communications at Penn. When I got to ESPN in early '93, they just didn't have enough personality—besides Berman—to grow the ratings. Women weren't going to watch and young people were watching MTV. So I had a strategy to create more personalities. Make talent more visible. Now this wasn't Walsh's strategy. Walsh was a guy where journalists had bylines and you never knew who they were. I said, "This is not journalism. This is television journalism. We need to have people be big and real and fun." I was the Antichrist, especially to Walsh. He knew why I was there and he knew that my charge was to make this thing more popular and less about sports fanatics. But he fought me all the way. Walsh was not a fan of mine.

JOHN WALSH:

Steve was always looking to see if there was somebody from the outside who would give the place a jolt, and he thought Lack was that guy. We were told he was going to be the guy to pull things together from the business side. He would have an interest in what the content was, but he was mainly going to focus on advertising and the affiliates.

Lack did change the culture. We had been through all the sexual harassment stuff and part of it was we had to have a dress code. Lack destroyed the dress

code that we established and came in and said everything's casual, nobody has to wear a tie. Well, one
day there was a twenty-seven-year-old guy at the news
desk with short shorts and a tank top on, and I just
thought, "Oh, my God."

*In terms of sexual conduct at the office, ESPN had
remained like a wild frontier town; when a "mission
statement" was posted on the wall, some members of the
night shift plastered it with tomatoes. As more women
arrived in Bristol, a handful of ESPN men continued to
misbehave. Women would find themselves being followed home at night by guys they worked beside during
the day. E-mail was still new in the nineties and its
illicit possibilities were just being discovered, including,
of course, porn as a come-hither ploy that often offended
rather than enticed.*

*No fewer than fifty cases of sexual harassment were
reported by women on the staff to ESPN management
in the first half of the 1990s.*

*It was by no means a simple matter of good guys and
bad guys. Two men in their twenties who were accused
of sexual misconduct also happened to be two of the best-
liked, hardest-working people in the production department. When executives attempted to impose punishment,
older workers protested. One of the most venerable cautioned an executive to make sure sanctions were imposed
equitably across the board—that is, the rules should
apply to the vice presidents as well as to the production*

assistants at the other end of the spectrum. The intent was fairness, but the implication was that offenders might not be found exclusively in the lower ranks.

One of the most notorious cases to arise was that of Mike Tirico, who became very unpopular with some of the women on staff. They said Tirico never took "no," or even "leave me alone," for an answer, and that some of his flirtations got way out of line—especially offensive, some argued, because Tirico claimed to be happily married.

One woman told of being approached by Tirico at a 1992 staff party with the come-on, "You are the most beautiful person I've ever seen." Even though firmly rebuffed, Tirico would not relent, and reportedly followed the woman to her car when she left the party, then reached in through the car window and thrust his hand between her legs as she attempted to start the engine.

Such incidents were hushed up at the time by the old-boy network, but Tirico got the equivalent of counseling from executives who more than once took him to lunch because they hated to see such a bright talent self-destruct—and because he seemed unable to handle his own urges. They also met with Tirico's aggrieved wife, Debbie. Finally, though Tirico insisted the charges were based solely on "misunderstandings," management had to take some kind of action: Tirico was suspended for three months without pay, during which time he did not appear on the air.

Some said the punishment was too harsh, others found it almost laughably insufficient. But at least management had acknowledged they had a problem, and although it would be overstating to say the floodgates flew open, there subsequently were enough sexual harassment charges to keep executives busy—in fact, to become a major drain on their time. A concerted attempt was made to keep the problems in-house, as when one of the managers in the radio division was charged with sending obscene e-mails to a female employee.

Eventually, though, the human resources people became inundated and outside counseling was brought in to help deal with the ongoing problem—a problem that would, indeed, continue into the next millennium, with some lurid cases becoming nationally notorious and helping earn ESPN a reputation as a nest of "horndogs" who had all the self-control of the fraternity brothers in Animal House.

JULIE ANDERSON:
Nobody was being reprimanded for anything. With Tirico it was obvious that they had to do something, so he was suspended, but then he came back and nothing changed. And then he got all these really big assignments, including *Monday Night Football*. I was mad that they didn't do anything to him. He was very flirty—and he was married—and he used to say things like "So when are you going to marry me?

When are we going to get married?" They didn't do anything about it. *Why* didn't they do anything about it? And it sucked. I would just laugh it off. I didn't really work with him.

They'd never fire an executive, but they fired a PA because he was e-mailing to another PA about a girl across the room. She was kind of a hot blonde, and the kid got fired because he was writing, like, "She's really hot," or "I'd like to fuck her," or something like that. And they fired the PA. He was just a kid, doing what kids do. At most they should have put a little note in his file.

MIKE TIRICO, *Anchor:*

Most of the people over time who have worked with me have enjoyed working with me. I hope they have. At least they said they have, and I hope they always will. I've worked with a lot of our people in remote production — the different sports, covering events — and it's given me a chance to interact with a lot of folks, and I'm pretty sure from what they've said that they've enjoyed their time working with me, and that they feel we have a common goal: to give the person at home the best show, and to enjoy the camaraderie of everybody along the way. And hopefully we've done that. That's what I hope my legacy is there, and I've done a lot the last eighteen years toward that. Hopefully.

GARY MILLER:

I wasn't in the screening room where a lot of this stuff supposedly went down, or around for the daily conversations. I imagine it had to be awful, because it was kind of like a locker room. But most of the girls that were working there then were kind of like jocks. They would tease and give the same kind of stuff, stuff that in today's world would get you sent down to human resources right away. And they might even initiate some of it, but it was so 90–95 percent male that, at the beginning, it wasn't even an issue. I didn't see any of the sexual harassment stuff right in front of my face. I knew the people that eventually—years into their behavior—got called on the carpet for it, but I would only see just the real icky stuff: He's wearing his shirt open, and doesn't he realize how cheesy he looks? Or: he's always paying attention to this person.

JOHN LACK:

The first thing I did to fix the place was I hired a lady that worked for me at MTV by the name of Harriet Seitler as vice president of Marketing. She was not a sports lady; she was the antithesis of sports. I brought her in to really get a sense of who we should be, and as I was bringing her in, I hired Wieden + Kennedy as our ad agency, which was a big deal. I had gotten to be very friendly with Dan Wieden and saw what he had done with Nike and making that company a cultural phenomenon that went way beyond box scores. We made a deal with Dan that he would never admit. I said "Dan, we really can't afford you. The culture here is such where hiring a big ad agency is not what we're about. So you gotta work the first year for no profit. We'll pay your costs but you can't make a dime on us, but we'll give you a three-year deal. If you do well the first year, you'll make a little money the second year and, hopefully, the third you'll be back up to what you should be making. If you can't do that, I can't make the deal." They wanted us so badly because of their experience with Nike and knowing what they know about sports that Dan finally said okay. He acquiesced. That hiring alone was a little bit of a shock to some in Bristol. Walsh looked at it and said, "Oh, we're going to be like Nike television now."

Harriet fought valiantly for all the right stuff. *SportsCenter* was good when we came, but it wasn't hip. Now it became hip. Spike Lee did a couple commercials for us. It was all really great stuff, and that was all Harriet. Walsh looked at Harriet as the Antichrist. He thought: "It was bad enough Lack was here, but now Harriet Seitler?" He wanted to kill her.

GEORGE BODENHEIMER:
I give John Lack a lot of credit for hiring Harriet. Her marketing acumen was not something that had regularly been seen at ESPN. She really involved

herself in the creative look, and her artwork was some of the best stuff we ever produced.

HARRIET SEITLER, *Vice President of Marketing:*

I had spent thirteen years at MTV networks. I started in affiliate sales and marketing and ultimately was the head of marketing and promotional development for MTV. I took the ESPN offer because the opportunity to play around creatively in an on-air environment and launch a new channel was significant. So, yes, it was a big opportunity for me to be able to create a new on-air environment and to really do on-air as well as brand building. A big opportunity.

JOHN LACK:

We were working really hard—six or seven days a week. My life was three days a week in New York with Steve; Bodenheimer, who was head of affiliate relations and worked for me; and Jack Bonnani, who ran ad sales and also reported to me. Then I was in Bristol two days a week. It was a pain-in-the-neck commute but it was much more fun for me in Bristol. I was a program guy. I'm a sports nut. So the more time I spent up there, the happier I was. When I was in New York, it was just frenetic.

STEVE ANDERSON:

When John Lack showed up, everybody just knew, at many different levels, he wasn't right for the place.

It was sort of obvious. It just didn't seem to work from day one. People have to buy into what ESPN is all about, and it's about the culture. When you're not willing to work hard, and not willing to be viewed as a team player, you're not going to fit in.

VINCE DORIA, *Vice President of News:*

Al Jaffe and I went out to L.A. on a couple trips. We were looking for potential anchors and for somebody to do a talk show out there that eventually became Jim Rome's. So they put us at the Peninsula, a very nice hotel. One day we walked upstairs just to look at the pool, and Lack was up there. He had a cabana all set up and he'd been there apparently for weeks. I'm not sure what he was doing—maybe he was doing God's work, I'm not really sure—but it had the appearance that he was sitting there spending the company's money. John was not shy about spending money. He used limos when almost nobody did. He was from the outside; he didn't really understand the Bristol way of doing things.

STEVE BORNSTEIN:

For a couple years I really wanted to launch our version of the MTV Awards because I thought we could own it, and nobody else was in that space. Walsh just kept ignoring it, or, to put it another way, it was not high on his priority list. So I finally went out and hired a couple guys to do it. That infuriated the DNA of John Walsh so much that he finally engaged in the idea.

I had only two edicts for the awards show: no black tie and not more than two hours, both of which they ignored.

JOHN WALSH:

When my magazine *Inside Sports* was folding, I was trying to come up with ideas for shows, and one of them was an awards show. Much to my surprise and astonishment, who decides he wants to come and look at the proposal but Dick Clark! Dick Clark came to the *Inside Sports* offices! My heart was beating so fast. When I was growing up, every day I came home from school and watched *American Bandstand* from 3:30 to 5:00. They came to Scranton, but my parents wouldn't let me go because rock-and-roll was dirty.

So anyway, Dick Clark passes on it and I take it over to ABC, where I meet this guy Bob Iger, who's in programming. I showed him the proposal but he passed on it, too. So I just threw it away. When I did my consultancy for ESPN in '87 before I was formally hired, I gave Bornstein the proposal, but I don't think he even looked at it. When Magic announced he had HIV in '91, we were in the board room and everybody was thinking he was going to die, so how should we honor him? Somebody said, "How about an awards show? We could call it *The Magics*." So I pull out my awards proposal and said, "We should do this show." At the same time, a group of people led by Ray Volpe and Ed Griles approached Bornstein about a sports awards show and the two things came together. Ed produced the first show, which was one of the top ten moments of my life both in terms of honors and horrors.

JIM ALLEGRO:

Once Steve had approved the concept for the ESPY Awards, he kind of bowed out, and it became my thing. And when I say mine, I mean I had the go/no-go, but the brain behind it was John Walsh. It was originally planned to be a two-hour show, but it grew and grew. I would ask Steve if he wanted to come to the biweekly meetings to review the progress, and he said, "No, you just keep going with it." About two months before the show, I went to Steve and told him I had some bad news. I said, "Steve, this thing is starting to grow," and he said, "I want a two-hour show, and that's final." Well, it had gotten to be three hours and twenty minutes, and we tried and tried to make cuts, and two nights before the show, I went to Steve and I said, "Steve, I got great news, I got it back to three hours." Steve looked at me and said, "You gotta be crazy. I don't care what you do, but get it under two hours." So Walsh and I worked all night cutting out things, but finally I called Steve and said, "Come and do it yourself. We can't do it."

Everything about the show was tense. Dennis

Miller was the host, and during the show one of the producers was trying to give him hand signals about what to do, and Dennis was giving him the finger. There wasn't a lot of harmony. Two days after the show, I wound up in the hospital with heart palpitations. It was a very, very strenuous event. But most enjoyable.

DENNIS MILLER, *ESPY Host:*

At the time I was friends a little bit with John—what is his name? Sweet man. I think he's an albino. You know the cat I mean? Anyway, he called me and said, "Let's have breakfast." I remember I had some eggs that were really good. He told me they were thinking of doing a play on the Oscars for sports and I said, "Oh that sounds like a cool idea," and he let me do the first one and I think I may have done the second. I actually think I did the first MTV Movie Awards, too—my kids can't believe I was hip enough to do that—and a couple of Emmy Awards. I had like a five-year period there where I was hosting all these things. But the ESPYs were cool. I'm a sports nerd so to meet some of those guys really meant a lot to me.

JOHN SAUNDERS, *Anchor*:

I'd known Jim Valvano over the years when I was covering basketball. When he got hired at ESPN, he was immediately the best analyst there ever was. He wanted to teach the game with a sense of humor. Right after the first game we did together we went out for a drink. There was a bar next door and I didn't know if he was a party guy or whatever, but a bunch of people came along because that's what Jim was like, he'd walk around and people would just follow him, people would just light up. So we go in and sit down at the bar and this very attractive girl and a biker kind of guy sitting next to her are talking and looking over at us. Finally the girl comes over and says, "You're Jim Valvano, aren't you?" He says, "Yes, I am." She said, "I think you're very, very cute and my boyfriend doesn't mind that I come over and talk to you." Mind you, this is his first day on the job! So he talks to her for a while, she goes back to her boyfriend, and then she comes back again and says, "My boyfriend says he wouldn't mind if I went home with you tonight." And Jim says, "That's very, very nice of him, and I appreciate that, but no, I'm going to have to pass." So she says, "Can I at least get your autograph?" She pulls down the top of her pants to reveal her underwear and says she wants Jim to sign it. So he looked at me, took the pen, and in big letters wrote, *DICK VITALE.*

Jim and I used to talk every day, and so one day he calls and says, "My back is killing me!" I told him, he had been on an airplane and it was probably just sore, but the next day he called me up and said, "John, I just got back from the doctor. I've got cancer. I've got less than a year to live." And I was instantly, literally in tears. Now *he's* trying to calm *me* down: "Don't worry, John, I'm going to find a way to beat this." He wanted to keep working, and he kept coming up to Bristol, and either his daughter or his wife would come with him. We would do our shows three days a week, and go up to a game, but he'd be in so much pain that it was just unimaginable.

JOHN LACK:

Several months before the ESPYs, I went to Bornstein one day up in Bristol and told him I wanted him to take a look at a tape from last night. It was a basketball show, college hoops. I think it might have been Digger Phelps or maybe even Vitale on with Jim Valvano. I said to Steve, "Look at Valvano. He's dying on our air. I think we should do something about it." He said, "Like what?" I said, "Steve, we don't give to anybody, except maybe a little money to the Special Olympics. With this huge juggernaut of a company, we make all this profit but we don't give anything back. Our guy is dying on the air of cancer. Let's start a foundation." Bornstein looked at me and said, "Well, geez, John, how do we do this?" I said, "I'll do it, you just gotta approve it." Then I told Steve I heard he was going to be doing this Arthur Ashe thing at the first ESPYs, and I thought we should give it to Valvano. He said, "He's certainly deserving of it."

So we called Valvano in that day. Steve tells him,

Not Much Joy in Mudville. The beginnings of the E.S.P. Network (later changed to ESPN) were nothing if not humble. Here a billboard welcomes visitors to Bristol, Connecticut, where ground was about to be broken for the first ESPN building, the Broadcast Center, in 1979.

Opening Night. It's showtime, or almost. George Grande (left) and Lee Leonard make last-minute preparations for the first-ever telecast of *SportsCenter* on ESPN's premiere night, September 7, 1979.

Chris "Boomer" Berman, twenty-six, with former New York Jets great Freeman McNeill (right), at ESPN's second annual coverage of the NFL draft in 1981. No one had thought to try turning the draft into a TV show until ESPN, desperate for programming, transformed it into a national marathon. It never went away.

A persistent fixture on ESPN in its early years was Australian rules football. With little money to spend and few big-ticket events within reach, ESPN scrounged the back alleys of sport for events that no one else wanted—perhaps had never even heard of.

Two Bristol Pillars. Former basketball coach Dick Vitale chats with Bob Ley on an early ESPN set. Vitale, who liked to be known by his child-like nickname "Dickie V," joined Ley within the first year of ESPN's existence, and both men remained. In fact, more than forty employees from ESPN's first year would still be there thirty-one years later.

Allan B. "Scotty" Connal served as executive vice president and CEO of ESPN after following Chet Simmons over from NBC. Connal started at NBC as a page in 1947 and became one of the most influential leaders of ESPN's pioneer days. He died of a heart attack at the age of sixty-eight in 1996.

It Wasn't All Games. Aerobics instructor Denise Austin needed to get her own sponsor before ESPN would air *Keeping Fit with Denise Austin,* her bouncy and friendly exercise-to-music series that stayed on the schedule for years. She even produced the daily program.

America's Cup '87. A triumphant moment for ESPN, when live coverage from Australia, including shots from cameras on board the boats, turned viewers on to the spectacle of yacht racing. David Letterman would send a telegram congratulating the team.

NASCAR and ESPN did a lot of growing up together and enjoyed a mutually beneficial relationship throughout the eighties and nineties—until NBC and Ted Turner stole NASCAR away with an irresistibly huge offer in the year 2000. Many ESPN staffers regarded the loss as one of the most devastating in the network's history.

The debut of the ESPY Awards in 1993 proved unforgettable, all because of this man: Jim Valvano, basketball coach turned ESPN analyst and the first person to receive the annual Arthur Ashe humanitarian award. Though suffering tremendous pain and exhaustion from terminal cancer and its treatment, Valvano stunned the audience with a true demonstration of courage—a speech that turned out to be his farewell. Cancer would take his physical abilities, Valvano told the tearful crowd, but "it cannot touch my mind, it cannot touch my heart, and it cannot touch my soul." ESPN established a hugely successful cancer research foundation in Valvano's memory.

Cue Talent! But first, Dan Patrick and Keith Olbermann, the funniest duo ever to host *SportsCenter,* have to check each other's "rouge" in a men's room mirror. The scene is not from backstage preparations at all, but a shot from one of the great, funny promos keyed to the theme "This is *SportsCenter*" as concocted by the Wieden + Kennedy ad agency and performed by the ESPN Players, with additional appearances by superstar athletes. The campaign was such a success and the promos so popular that ESPN showed a solid hour of them in prime time, back-to-back-to-back.

ESPN's version of *The Mod Squad:* anchors for the 6:00 p.m. *SportsCen-ter* in the mid-nineties. From left, Charley Steiner, Robin Roberts, and Bob Ley. While Dan Patrick and Keith Olbermann may have received more attention outside Bristol, on the inside these three were incredibly popular and much easier to handle.

Everything that had made *SportsCenter* smart and funny seemed to make *SportsNite* dumb and lame. An attempt to duplicate the style, and success, of the original show, *SN* was just one of the calamities to beset "The Deuce" on ESPN2. Keith Olbermann, who had been talked into wearing a leather jacket, was joined by newcomer Suzy Kolber and columnist Mitch Albom as co-anchors. Olbermann's first remark on opening night—not in the script—was "Good evening, and welcome to the end of my career."

Tom Mees, the much-admired and effortlessly amiable *SportsCenter* anchor, died tragically at the age of forty-six while apparently attempting to rescue one of his young daughters from a neighbor's backyard swimming pool. Anchors, producers, and even management wept upon hearing the news.

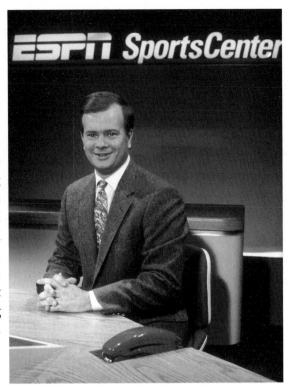

ESPN's *X Games* was a solid hit and thriving moneymaker right out of the gate, creating overnight stars like Tony Hawk, shown here in action, and later, Shaun White. Considering all the money that ESPN usually had to fork over for rights fees, it was a great relief to create a property of their own.

No executive in ESPN history had a more meteoric rise than Mark Shapiro (pictured here with anchor Dana Jacobson), who became head of both programming and production at the age of thirty-three. It was hard to find anyone who didn't have an opinion — pro or con — about Shapiro, or who didn't consider him the most powerful "No. 2" in all of television.

The *NFL Countdown* team in 2003, from left: Chris Berman, Chris Mortensen, Steve Young, Michael Irvin, Rush Limbaugh, and Tom Jackson. A remark from Limbaugh about superstar quarterback Donovan McNabb resulted in Limbaugh departing just three weeks into his first season.

At ESPN's twenty-fifth anniversary in 2004, all six of the network's head raccoons flashed congenial smiles despite extraordinary tensions among several of them. Somehow, the difficulties rarely got in the way of success. From left: ESPN founder Bill Rasmussen, Chet Simmons, Bill Grimes, Roger Werner, Steve Bornstein, and current president George Bodenheimer.

Well, at least "Jaws" is smiling: the *Monday Night Football* booth in 2007 (from left, Ron Jaworski, Mike Tirico, and Tony Kornheiser). Management's decision to add Tony Kornheiser, after turning their back on the team of John Madden and Al Michaels, was one of the most controversial moves in the history of the multibillion-dollar property. Kornheiser and Mike Tirico may have had a few laughs on the buses that took them from game to game, but on the air they were one of the least contented couples in sportscasting history.

Serena Williams found it shocking at best when host Jamie Foxx serenaded her at the 2003 ESPY Awards: "Can I be your tennis ball? You can smack me up against the wall." Although the quality of entertainment has varied radically, as has the comic prowess of the celebrity hosts, the ESPY Awards show has survived enough stormy seasons to emerge victorious—an annual established television event. (Kevin Mazur)

Before he made his own "Decision" during a much-ridiculed ESPN prime-time special, LeBron James cohosted the ESPYs with Jimmy Kimmel in 2007. The ESPYs remain a decidedly non-Bristol operation, with bigger budgets and more celebrity hand-holding and cozying up than anything else ESPN does. (Kevin Mazur)

Cross-Pollination. NFL star Terrell Owens hobnobs with NBA great Kobe Bryant at the 2008 ESPY bash. Most athletes who come to the ESPYs say they get a real kick out of meeting and getting to know stars from other sports. (Kevin Mazur)

Past, Present, and Future. Rob King (left), editor in chief of ESPN digital media, meets with John A. Walsh, creator and custodian of the network's journalistic DNA. While King spends his days tied to the smallest details and words of the empire's dot-com operation, Walsh operates on a broad canvas of big-ticket items for the future, supported by his devoted boss, John Skipper.

"College GameDay: There Is No Substitute." Yes, the NFL may get more attention from the Boys of Bristol, but Chris Fowler (left), Lee Corso (middle), and Kirk Herbstreit (far right) consistently deliver the best show on the network(s). Joined by Desmond Howard and Erin Andrews, they have an extraordinary fan base whose enthusiasm is uncurbed. Andrews was already determined, back in her college days, to become a part of ESPN.

Bumper Crop. Chief Technology Officer Chuck Pagano likes to call ESPN's crowded backyard "the Satellite Farm," where all the big dishes grow. This impressive spread, along with the company's $100 million–plus Digital Center, has made ESPN the high-tech envy of the broadcasting world.

The Campus. Once considered out of bounds by approximately everybody in the world (except for employees who *had* to be there), ESPN's Bristol, Connecticut, campus is now a destination in itself for athletes who want to appear in the clever and funny *SportsCenter* promos; for actors who want to plug new movies; and for many other celebrities willing to endure the rigorous "Bristol Car Wash," visiting all the platforms in one crazy, crowded day.

ESPN the Magazine was launched less because of its strategic value to the company and more because Michael Eisner wanted to strike back at Mouth-from-the-South Ted Turner and his aging *Sports Illustrated*. In a move so obvious that no one tried to hide or deny it, "The Body Issue" would become ESPN's answer to *SI*'s famed Swimsuit Issue, but with more exposed skin.

ESPN International involves more than two hundred countries situated on every continent. More than 350 million subscribers tune in to at least one of ESPN's forty-six networks, broadcasting in sixteen languages throughout the world. There are also thirteen local versions of *SportsCenter* produced in eight languages: Spanish, Portuguese, English, French, Hindi, Cantonese, Mandarin, and Japanese.

Where Content Is King, It's Good to Be the King—of Content. John Skipper (left) had virtually no television background when George Bodenheimer put him in charge of the most visible chunk of the ESPN empire. Here Skipper stands with humble but fearless standout Michelle Beadle and Colin Cowherd, one of Bristol's top alpha males.

On the lush lawn outside the ESPN Café, the countdown to the 2010 World Cup in South Africa looms large. Virtually every corner of the company was caught up in this, the most enormous effort in ESPN history. Some on the staff referred to it as "Skipper's Cup," after Skipper had made it his top priority, upon succeeding Mark Shapiro, to take the rights away from NBC.

"John wants to start a foundation for you." He looks at me and says, "You would?" I told him we wanted to call it the V Foundation for Cancer Research. "What do you think?" His eyes misted up and he rose a bit—by that time, his little body was getting thinner and thinner. He says, "I don't know what to say to you guys." I told him the ESPYs were in three months, and that he was going to get the Arthur Ashe Courage Award. He said, "I can't believe you guys are doing this for me." I said, "Jimmy, you are us, baby."

STEVE BORNSTEIN:

I had wanted ESPN to be significantly involved in a charity and when Lack and I, at the Radisson in Bristol, had pitched Jim and Pam on the idea for the foundation—and coming to the ESPYs—no one could have guessed how bad he would get and how soon.

DAN PATRICK:

After Jim did his last college basketball show for us, he was in the back of the newsroom over by the printer and I walked up to him and I said, "I want you to know that I've purposely stayed away from you the last couple of months." He's like, "Why, why?" I told him my dad had died of cancer. And the first thing he said is, "How long did they give him to live?" And I said, "Six months." He asked, "How long did he live?" I said, "Six months to the day." He told me,

"Look, do me a favor, when I die, make sure the picture you put above your shoulder on *SportsCenter* is a good one." He started crying, I started crying, right there in the newsroom. I hugged him—and never saw him again.

DICK VITALE:

My friendship with Jimmy V really developed when he came to ESPN. We were working together, and even though he had cancer, he was going to work right to the end. One night we were on the road, and I was in the restaurant. The girl said, "Mr. Valvano would like to talk to you," so I got on the phone and he said, "C'mon upstairs, we'll watch the show together." I think it was a show with Frank Sinatra. So I go up to his room, and I will never forget this—every time I hear his name I think of this moment. We're sitting there watching this show and then all of a sudden out of nowhere he jumps out of the bed and starts punching the walls, screaming, and crying about the pain. He said, "Take your worst toothache and run it through your body and that's what I feel." But he was determined to beat it. He kept saying to me, "They say 20 percent can beat it, and I'm going to be that number. I'm going to beat this." He exercised; he did everything they told him to do. And he couldn't wait for this big checkup to get some good news.

That night I called his house. I had just done an

ESPY rehearsal at Radio City. I called and his wife got on the phone. She was crying and I could tell, man, this is not good. She said, "He said he doesn't want to get on the phone with anybody." And I said, "You got to get him on the phone." He got on the phone and he just kept saying, "It's over, Dickie V, it's over." I tried to give him a little inspiration, but he said, "I don't want to hear any inspiration. I'm not going to see my little girl graduate college." Then I said, "You have to come up here, Jim. This is going to be special." I saw at the rehearsal what they had planned, unveiling the V Foundation, the Arthur Ashe award and all that stuff. He wound up coming with Mike Krzyzewski and his wife. The guy was throwing up, he was in a wheelchair. How he was able to get up here and how he was able to deliver that speech to this day is beyond me. If you had seen him that night before the show, you would have said there is no way in the world he would be able to deliver a speech.

JOHN LACK:

We flew him up to New York—he was living in North Carolina at the time—and he calls me from the hotel. He says, "I can't make it on the air. I'm too sick. I'm throwing up." I said, "I'll come and get you." He said, "No, Johnny, I can't do it. You've got to fill in for me." I said, "Jimmy, I ain't filling in for you, baby. I'm coming to get you." When I got to the room, he was still saying he couldn't do it, but I just wouldn't listen. He said he couldn't even tie his tie, so I tied it. Then I told him we were going. We wound up carrying him into the cab. When we got to Radio City, he saw the crowd and he began to gain his strength. I told him not to worry about the teleprompters.

CHARLEY STEINER:

In the green room that night, before he arrived, Dickie V and I were talking, and it was the only time I've seen Vitale nervous. He said, "Charley, I don't know what to say. What do I do?" I said, "Be yourself." So here's Valvano. There were stairs on the set and he had to be helped up to do the speech. You couldn't help but get chills. He did the speech, and there was this group hug. We all knew it was the last time we were ever going to see him.

STEVE BORNSTEIN:

I had been with Jim earlier in the day in his hotel room. It was really unclear whether he was physically going to be able to make it. I thought it was going to be sad and not what we had hoped for, but there was nothing we could do.

But when I saw him walk on that stage, twenty feet from me, I essentially saw—for the entire time he was on stage—the disease leave his body. And that was the most remarkable experience. He had always been a fabulous speaker and storyteller, but he summoned this speech up from deep, deep within. I've seen lots of television shows; I've never seen anything like that.

JOHN LACK:

Anytime you see the speech, it brings tears to your eyes. He was amazing. So afterward, he comes off-stage and falls into my arms. We went to this little reception area in the back, and everyone was around him. Then he said, "This is the greatest day in my life." I said, "Better than the championships?" He said, "Yes, better."

Upbeat and passionate, Valvano regaled the crowd with stories about his family, his coaching career, and his philosophy of living. When the producers flashed a red light to warn him to wind things up, Valvano responded, "They got that screen up there flashing thirty seconds, like I care about that screen. I got tumors all over my body and I'm worried about some guy in the back going, 'Thirty seconds'?" He kept right on rolling and closed by telling the audience, "Cancer can take away all of my physical abilities. It cannot touch my mind, it cannot touch my heart, and it cannot touch my soul. And those three things are going to carry on forever." The crowd gave him a standing ovation. He died less than two months later. His tombstone quoted advice he gave during the ESPY speech: "Take time every day to laugh, to think, to cry."

GEORGE BODENHEIMER:

Every year someone asks me this question: "Did you know what kind of significance this speech would have?" And of course the answer is no. You didn't know he was going to deliver that speech until you heard it. And it was such a powerful speech that you were almost left numb. The V Foundation is fully endowed now, and has raised over $100 million for cancer research. The foundation is run akin to true ESPN style—that is, in a relatively low-budget manner. No one is living high on the hog. I've talked about ESPN being run as a family operation, and unfortunately a lot of times when that is demonstrated is when people are ill. And unfortunately a lot of the illness is cancer. And so the V Foundation has played a tremendous role for us, not only in our ability to try to do some good things and give back, but specifically when we learn that an employee has been diagnosed with cancer, we have access to quick and highly professional medical staff who offer advice and resources. I'm enormously proud of the V Foundation and ESPN's contributions to its growth and positive impact.

ROBIN ROBERTS, *Anchor:*

I'm backstage, and while Jim was giving his great speech, I was looking out and seeing people in the audience crying. You realize it's an unforgettable moment. After he was done, I was the next one to have to walk out onstage, and I was thinking, "What do I do? What can I possibly say?" I wound up saying something like, "I've never been more proud of ESPN than I am at this moment." I think that was the night as a network that we realized, "Yeah, we can actually do something else, not just fun and games. This thing can be bigger than that." We found our heart in '93 at the ESPYs.

The glow of the ESPYs didn't last long for Bornstein. He was worried about competition from the outside—and rightfully so. Liberty Media was proceeding with its scheme to build a sportscasting empire of its own and mount a challenge to "the worldwide leader in sports." It started by buying out its largest partner, Bill Daniels, and increasing its ownership of Daniels's Prime Network regional sports channels by acquiring more of Prime's parent company, Affiliated Regional Communications Ltd.

As the sole general partner of Prime Network, Liberty snared the country's largest regional sports network— fifteen affiliates serving 26 million subscribers. Coming up in second place among regional networks was Sports Channel America, co-owned by GE through NBC and Cablevision Systems Ltd., reaching 18 million subscribers via ten affiliates. If you combined the two big regional holdings, you had 44 million subscribers, not far off the 60 million that belonged to ESPN.

Although the regionals had fewer households in the aggregate, they had higher viewership and higher fees than ESPN because of powerful local Major League Baseball and NBA games that they televised. Bornstein feared that if the regionals ever launched a competitive product, they would have a huge audience, particularly as a lead-in opposite what had by now become the greatest cash cow of ESPN—SportsCenter.

So it was that Liberty then set about the next logical step up its imagined ladder of success: attempting to acquire Sports Channel America and consolidate all those subscribers. ESPN, meanwhile, wasn't just dangling its toes in the water. It was already looking beyond its domestic success to make "worldwide leader" a literally true slogan. ESPN agreed to merge its partly owned European sports network, TESN, with that network's chief rival, Eurosport, thus creating the largest sports network on the European continent—a trilingual operation with a reach of nearly 40 million English-, French-, and German-speaking households.

But back in the United States, Bornstein was reminding Lack that one of his biggest charges was to mount a second network. Bornstein was adamant about digging the moat deeper around ESPN, and not letting competitors grab what he believed to be a ton of sports content that couldn't fit on ESPN. He declared that the debut of ESPN2 would take place on October 1, 1993, and for Bornstein, now obsessed with fighting off the competition, it couldn't come fast enough.

JOHN LACK:

Steve says to me, "Now what are we going to do with this thing? What's this second network going to be?" So we did a lot of research and I came back to him and said, "Look, we can't do another ESPN. These cable operators aren't going to carry it. They're bridling at the fact that they're paying us fifty cents for this product today; they'll never give us another nickel more for the same stuff." Now at this time, MTV had started this division there called MTV Sports. They had this good-looking kid who was doing all these celebrity baseball and softball games and some extreme sports. They were putting on a ton of reality shows, and they were climbing, climbing, climbing. They were beginning to nip at our heels, taking our young audiences right away from us. They were hot. And it became pretty clear that we were very short in the youngest demos.

I said to Steve, "Look, I got a little credibility in this demographic. I think we can do ESPN2 with extreme sports, with hockey—we thought it was going to be the first major sport we could put on ESPN2 because it was men, eighteen to thirty-four—and music videos. Then I brought in the sales department and asked them if they could sell that. They said, "Absolutely.""

JOHN WALSH:

We had an off-site in Greenwich with all of Steve's senior people—there were probably a dozen of us there—Steve, Creasy, Lack, Dick Glover, myself, and some others. Steve said we basically were not going to be able to exist and compete with just one network. We're going to have to do other things. So we went around the table and the big idea was to do a twenty-four-hour *SportsCenter* channel—basically ESPN news. There was vigorous debate over two days and then it came time for a vote and it was that we should do ESPN News or *SportsCenter* or whatever you wanted to call it. But Steve said, "No, we could do that anytime. We'll keep that in our back pocket for when anyone else decides to do that, then we can beat them to the punch. It might be our third or fourth channel."

SEAN BRATCHES, *Executive Vice President*:

We had a big sales meeting at the Sheraton in Hartford and gave out paper airline tickets to the team. Our objective at the time was to pitch a product that we called Sport TV, because the marketplace didn't want more ESPN; they wanted a differentiated product. One of the most salient learnings that I've had in my twenty-one years at the company came out of that time. In a two- or three-week period I was on the road to a lot of operators, and when I made my presentations they said, "Listen, we love what you're doing, we think it's great, we want the product, we want the content, but please put ESPN in the name—it's the brand." We were all hearing the same message from the marketplace, and it's a great example of why the creative side is in many cases driven by the sales side. And ever since that point in time, we've never launched another product without ESPN branding.

STEVE BORNSTEIN:

Those were the biggest balls I ever had at ESPN and the biggest move I ever made there. I bet my entire career on ESPN2. It was either going to work or not work, and the results would be on me. This was make-or-break for my career. It was fucking scary.

Had we not launched ESPN2, any one of these pretenders could take us on and be successful—a Fox, a TCI back then, a banding together of regionals, any other guy with a hundred million bucks that wanted to get into television sports business. There was just too much content out there.

But no one else wanted a second network. No one else believed in it. CapCities certainly wasn't saying, "Let's do a second network." They all thought programs on ESPN2 were going to be a bunch of beach volleyball games, but I knew better. I saw college basketball growing. I saw college football growing. I saw motor sports growing.

Emboldened by the success of launching ESPN Radio, Steve Bornstein reasoned—or just decided—that retransmission held the key to getting ESPN's new channel, ESPN2, not just on the air but into millions of homes. The Deuce, as No. 2 was soon known inside and outside the empire, was conceived as a hot and hip supplement to the still-young ESPN.

In the murky gray miasma of federal communications rules, bedeviling the broadcasting industry since 1934, the interrelated Retransmission Consent and must-carry policies of the eighties and nineties were among the most confounding. They had to do with the money that cable operators could charge broadcast stations for relaying their signals and thus expanding the stations' available audiences—or whether the broadcast stations could charge the cable operators for permission to retransmit their signals, thereby expanding the cable system's available programming. Cable would arguably flop, and flop hard, if subscribers couldn't see the network affiliates and independent stations they'd been watching for years.

Cable subscribers would end up paying through the nose, but that wasn't even the issue. This was a battle between titans in which the rich would get richer.

For Bornstein, the hardest part of the plan—and one of the toughest tasks he ever undertook as an executive—was talking his bosses at Hearst, ABC, and CapCities into forgoing one of their favorite things — cash — and accepting in its place signed agreements to carry ESPN2 on cable systems big and small.

STEVE BORNSTEIN:

The biggest fight I ever had was with Murphy, Burke, and even Buffett, trying to convince them that we should use retransmission consent to get value on ESPN2 as opposed to cash for their own stations. That was an incredibly difficult and arduous internal negotiation — one of my biggest battles ever.

Warren Buffett went along with it begrudgingly. He much preferred the cash, as did Tom Murphy, because that would have been better for the network — for the traditional broadcasting business. Our argument was you aren't going to get cash out of these operators. It was the biggest disagreement we had with CapCities since they had taken us over. CapCities didn't tolerate failure. That was a big bet. If it didn't work, I would not have been around.

It was an inspired scheme that quickly caught fire — with the October 1 launch date of ESPN2 looming ever closer. In August, CapCities / ABC, in conjunction with ESPN, signed a deal with three big cable operators representing 2.6 million homes that allowed their systems to carry programming from ABC and Hearst-owned TV stations in exchange for adding ESPN2 to their rosters. In the end, not only did ESPN2 get a "substantial rollout" on their cable systems, but the network even got a fee.

Unfortunately, the plan was so good that other networks and cable systems got into the act, including the Fox network. Much more worrisome to ESPN were moves by Liberty Media, the cable giant that sought to come from behind and grow large enough to challenge ESPN.

FRANK BENNACK:

I got this call from Dan Burke, who is at this time the head of CapCities / ABC, saying, "Frank, you know this is going to cost a lot of money and, if you guys don't want to go in it, you can stay in the original, you don't have to be in ESPN2." And I just said, "Dan, come on, you know I'm going nowhere."

JOHN LACK:

In looking for elements for ESPN2, I wanted a good sports talk show aimed at a younger audience. We didn't have much sports talk on ESPN because Walsh had never been interested in that genre; they all reminded him of Howard Cosell. They had Roy Firestone, who did interviews, but it was kind of bland stuff. So we looked around for a talk-show guy and the best ones are on the radio. On the West Coast, there was a guy named Jim Rome who had a hot sports talk show from San Diego that was just about to be syndicated on radio. His ratings were so high there that a syndicator—I think it was Westwood One—was just about to sign him up. So I went to interview him and liked him a lot. He was brash and young, and his dream was to be on someplace like ESPN. He wasn't a great TV personality at the time—he was kind of awkward—but he had that great voice, a great mind, and he had the respect early of the trash-talking black and Hispanic audience. I thought he was good-looking enough to be an eventual star on television.

So I told Walsh, "Look, he is by far the best available, and he doesn't have to quit his radio show, so he won't cost us a lot of money. We can get him part-time, we'll sign him to thirteen weeks, and if he doesn't work out, we can always get rid of him." John looked at the tapes and went gaga; he thought this was going to be Waterloo, and he was going to fight this one because he thought it flew in the face of the journalistic ethics of ESPN. I kept saying, "It's not about journalism, it's about young people, and getting involved in what they care about." He didn't buy any of that psychological shit. All he cared about was, "This guy is too controversial and I don't think that he's smart enough." And I said, "Look he's definitely smart enough." We went back and forth, I auditioned Rome, then sent him a contract, and all the time John is just boiling. One day, I got a call from Steve. He said, "You better get in here because John's going nuts and he says if you hire Rome, he's going to quit." Okay, whatever.

We schedule a meeting for the next morning. John comes, looks at me, and says, "You're going to ruin the journalistic integrity of this network, which we've built up all these years. We're finally getting to a point where we are the real deal in sports journalism, and this guy's going to blow it all in a week on the air."

And I said, "We're not impinging on the journalistic values of ESPN, the mother ship; this guy's not going to appear on ESPN, he's going to do a show in the afternoon on ESPN2, where our audience is very young—the main audience I want." Now Steve agreed with me as a programmer, but John was getting so heated up about it, Steve doesn't know what to do. So the meeting ends, Steve asks me to stick around, and says to me, "Can't we just find some other guy? It's not worth this fight with John." I said, "This is a guy who's going to cost us fifteen or twenty grand who could do a point-three or a point-four rating, which means we could make a couple of hundred thousand dollars on this show alone." So he says, "Okay. I'll tell John." I was told by Vince Doria, who was with Steve at the time, that Walsh said, "If Rome comes here, and Lack has the right to do that, then I'm quitting."

JOHN WALSH:
I never threatened to quit on the basis of any one decision. Throughout my career, I have always tried to make sure that I agreed with the vision, spirit, and collegiality of whatever enterprise I was involved

with, and if I didn't, that became my breaking point. I doubted Lack's vision, style, and experience. I, along with many of my colleagues at the time, knew he wasn't right for the company in so many ways, even though from time to time he would have a good thought or recommend a winning person, as he did with Harriet Seitler.

I trusted Jim Allegro's wisdom and guidance, so I went to him and asked if Lack's ways were going to become the pattern around here, and said if they were, I wouldn't find that comfortable. Jim assured me things would not continue like this, and the culture he and I endorsed would win the day.

DAVID ZUCKER, *Vice President of Programming:*
Was there contentiousness between Walsh and Lack? Of course. There was contentiousness between Lack and everybody. Lack is a brilliant, smart, creative guy, but just a loose cannon—a bull in a china shop. I don't know that he ever understood ESPN the way the old guard did.

In March 1993, things were definitely going Don Ohlmeyer's way. Scarcely had he been named to a new job as West Coast President of NBC—the top programming position at that time—than it was announced that ESPN was buying the sports programming and sales interests of his Ohlmeyer Communications Company, producers of sports and entertainment shows.

Terms weren't disclosed, but the selling price was north of $24 million—a nice piece of change for Ohlmeyer, who had bought out RJR's interest in ESPN after the sale to Hearst. Howard Katz, who had served as chairman of Ohlmeyer's ten-year-old company, was part of the sale to ESPN and got a well-deserved bonus from Ohlmeyer as well.

Also part of the deal: ESPN got The Skins Game, *a made-for-television event that Ohlmeyer had concocted and produced for ABC. It was part of some two hundred hours of sports programming that his company produced annually for various networks.*

VINCE DORIA:

Al Jaffe and I went out west to hire a small staff for the Rome show. The last hire was for a production assistant who was going to be the low man on the totem pole. There was a twenty-one- or twenty-two-year-old kid who was just out of college and who had done a little work for NBC. He came in and interviewed. You could see he was very smart, so I hired him. His name was Mark Shapiro.

At the same time we hired Mark, we hired a guy named Bud Morgan who had worked at NBC and ABC, where he produced *American Sportsman* with Curt Gowdy. We were really happy to have him because he was a real veteran. In the ramp up to the show, he would call me back in Bristol several times a week and give me updates. One day he calls me to run over things, and he says, "Listen, by the way, the kid that you hired as a PA, Shapiro, we have to get rid of him." I said, "What's wrong?" And he said, "He just can't stay out of everybody's business. Instead of paying attention to what he's supposed to be doing, I find him over here trying to get involved with this, or over here trying to get involved with that. He's got the assistants running off doing something that they shouldn't be doing. We just don't need this kind of hassle from the low man on the totem pole." I told him, "Look, do me a favor. I think he's a smart kid. Why don't you have a talk with him? Tell him what the problems are here. Give him another two weeks and see if he can straighten out. If he doesn't, then go ahead and get rid of him. But let's at least give him another shot." A couple weeks later, Bud calls me and says, "I had a good talk with Mark. He's back on track—very smart, lots of good ideas about the show, and he's developed a good relationship with Rome. We can definitely keep him." So that's how close Mark Shapiro came to not staying with ESPN.

Unlike their brethren in the news and entertainment divisions of ABC, the powers at ESPN were not particularly interested in developing celebrity anchors and reporters. Such luminaries might, it was thought, become more important or visible than the network itself—and stars have a nasty habit of asking for more money as their popularity increases.

JOHN WALSH:

Lack decided to go with the popular wave of the time, which meant wanting Keith to move over to ESPN2. His feeling was: If the company is betting so much on this new venture, why not get our most visible, popular, acerbic guy over to do this show? Some pointed out that if you really wanted to differentiate the show with topics that were going to be different, that really wasn't who Keith was. So that debate went on and on and on, but finally John got permission from Steve to talk to Keith, and then you had the courting of Keith by John.

KEITH OLBERMANN:

Walsh successfully broke up the Berman/Saunders partnership and did not want another strong team developing. He promoted Saunders to game work and especially Hoops. He thought he'd solved the KO/Dan problem by "promoting" me to my "own" network. When that failed, and I came back, he began to try to stave off the team's success. Long after Dan and I reestablished our unit, he remarked to somebody, "I've lost control of the talent."

JOHN WALSH:

I was torn. We had hit the magic formula with Dan and Keith. They had the act down really well and knew how to relate to one another in a way that was appealing to a large mass audience. We did understand that the two of them together were greater than each individual, that it was one plus one equals three. We had a debate about Keith going over. That's the way the place operates, you keep talking about it, asking questions: What's the best decision we can make? Who's going to get us more attention? Who's going to get us more publicity? I know at various points along the way, I had argued strongly that we had a successful thing here, and why would we want to break it up?

KEITH OLBERMANN:

The approach about ESPN2 came in the late spring of '93, so I had only been on the air doing *SportsCenter* for a year. Their target date being October 1 would have meant that I'd only been on *SportsCenter* for a year and a half before they moved me.

I was told it was going to be the younger, hip version of ESPN. My initial reaction to this was, "Are you sure you want me to do this, and do you want to break this team up?" Principally the idea was to have one dedicated to older viewers and another dedicated to younger. They were essentially splitting the audience in half—building another stadium next door, all these analogies. It was Walsh.

I had my doubts and would have more doubts, obviously, as time went by. But they said, "Would you do this?" I can be extremely argumentative when it comes to defending my point of view, and believe my point of view is as valid as any boss that I've ever had. Those are my terms, and I've always stuck with them personally, largely, I think, to successful ends. Having said that, and despite my reputation to the contrary, I am actually a team player. If I work for you and you ask me to do something and give me your reasons why, especially if it's an option to do it or not do it, I will usually defer. And ultimately, although I had a lot of misgivings about it, I said, "Okay, let's try it. But you can't seal me off. I can't not have a way back." And they said, "Well, we're going to ask you to commit to it for six months to a year." I said, "Okay, as long as when I come back, if I want to I can come back to the eleven o'clock *SportsCenter*." And they said yes. We put that in specific language in the contracts. I was not looking to get away from *SportsCenter*. I can say without question that Dan called me from the All-Star game in Baltimore on July 13 to tell me how many players asked him about me and how there was still time to go back to Walsh and turn it down even though I'd agreed a month or so earlier.

The guy originally put in charge of the project was John Lack. He and Walsh both said, "Look, this network needs a Berman, and we want you to be the centerpiece of the network. We want to build this around your personality and your approach. And in

addition to being on the air, we want your input as to
what the show should look like. You will be probably
the only veteran ESPN presence on this program; the
rest of the people will be outsiders. You will be the
continuity point. You will be the leader of the rest of
this group. You will be, in many senses, an on-air
producer."

The longer we got into this, the more that was
emphasized to me. And it sort of tapped into the
responsible Keith who, and I've always told them this,
if you put me in charge, I automatically get more
conservative because it's essentially my money on the
table in addition to yours.

Concomitantly, Walsh was telling us ESPN2 was
designed to get a younger audience. About a week
before we premiered, he asked me a weird question,
given that we were in the midst of a metaphorical
burning building. "Do you know which TV show
has the largest percentage of its viewers under the age
of twenty-five?" The number is a hazy memory, he
might have said twenty-one or even eighteen. I
guessed something on MTV. "Nope! The 11:00 p.m.
SportsCenter!" Needless to say, I was newly confused
about what ESPN2 was for. "I want to move that
audience over there and keep *SportsCenter* for adults!"
That wasn't my first hint of disaster but it was one of
the biggest ones. You do not "move" audiences. I did
ask—in fact we got it in the rewrite of the contract as
I went to ESPN2—that I be permitted to do some

play-by-play. "Some" turned out to be one Astros-Phillies game in September 1993 for which Buck Martinez and I didn't even have a monitor for the first two innings.

JOHN WALSH:

At that point in his life, Keith was seeking advice from anyone and everyone he could. I can't distinctly remember what I told him, but it was something about the fact that he was very successful and he should go to ESPN2 if he could get comfortable with what the show was going to be; that ESPN2 was going to attract a great deal of attention; and within the company, it was a big priority, so it would be front and center. That was always an attraction to Keith—whatever was going on within the company. He always wanted to be at the center of what people watching the company were paying the most attention to.

DAN PATRICK:

Initially I thought Keith was getting a lot more freedom than I was getting; Keith had an ability to make a job sound better than what it really was. But I think that was him convincing himself that he was going to be able to go over there and have his own show and have fun with it while I was somehow stuck on this sedate *SportsCenter*. This was not really reality, but I think Keith was selling it that way. Like he said, "Hey, I get to have all this fun for three hours."

Then I think it dawned on him, it was *three hours.* No matter how much fun it might turn out being, it was still going to be three hours.

I said to management, "You guys make the decision who is going to replace Keith because you're watching the show. You tell me who you like." It was a pretty tightly knit shop and I wanted everybody to have the chance at it. I didn't want to decide and then have people feel I had taken away their fair shot. I wanted management to pull the trigger. I think it was Steve Bornstein who ultimately made the decision that he wanted Kenny Mayne in there. And I wanted Kenny to be able to do what he wanted to do.

With Keith, we were probably equal in the stories that we would cover whether it was a serious story or a fun story. With Kenny, I would probably get more of the serious stories just because of Kenny's personality. When [NASCAR driver] Tim Richmond died of AIDS, for instance, I knew I was getting that story. I was becoming more of the straight guy. You have to be a chameleon sometimes and ask, "Who am I working with and what role do I need to adopt to do this show?" Kenny had a challenging role. He was following in Keith's footsteps. It's much easier to be the guy who follows the guy who follows the guy.

VINCE DORIA:
The studio programming for ESPN2 that I was charged with ended up being two shows—a show

called *SportsNight,* which was the Keith show, and the Jim Rome show out on the West Coast, a talk show. *SportsNight* was an always-evolving show; we were trying all kinds of things on it. Suzy Kolber was the first coanchor with Keith on *SportsNight.*

JOHN LACK:

Suzy came at the suggestion of Dan Burke. Walsh looked at her and said, "Jesus, she's cute, and she came from Dan, but I don't know." I said, "Let me have her. Let me get this girl in there because she's attractive and she's fun and she's got a sizzle, and we'll give her what she needs to let her come out of her shell." She had a fresh face and loved sports. That's what came across on ESPN2, and it wouldn't have come across on ESPN under Walsh. If she had started at ESPN under Walsh and played in that game for two years, she wouldn't be the Suzy Kolber you see today, in my opinion, because she wouldn't have gotten the chance to feel her own confidence and get to be who she was. I gave Keith another life. He fought me on it, and Walsh hated it. But Keith and Suzy were great together because the lack of chemistry or the inappropriateness of it all kind of worked in some ways.

SUZY KOLBER, *Reporter:*

How does it work out that an eight-year-old little girl sits and watches football by herself? I just loved it from the beginning. My dad's a great athlete and my whole family is into sports, so sometimes I wasn't watching alone, but I believe football was in my soul. I was one of the first girls in the country to play football, back in 1974. It was on the front page of the *Philadelphia Bulletin*. The league said if I played, they would suspend my entire team. So I never got to play in a game. But my helmet and mouthpiece are still in my workout room.

I had been working in West Palm Beach for a year and a half as a reporter and I got calls from both CNN and ESPN. The ESPN interview was so ridiculously stressful, I didn't go to the bathroom all day. That sounds like such a silly thing now, but I did so many interviews, with so many people there and they shuffled me from interview to interview, that I couldn't say, "Excuse me." I couldn't wait for them to drop me in the lobby so I could go to the bathroom but they walked me right to the car and I actually got in the car and went to the airport. I think I met with John Walsh twice, and had lunch with Al Jaffe, and then I met Vince Doria. But it was very stressful. The CNN interview was just the opposite. I just loved Bill McPhail and Jim Walton. We had lunch. We hugged. They offered me the job, and I accepted. A couple weeks later, Al Jaffe called and said, "We really like you, and we want you to come back for an audition for this new network we're starting, ESPN2." I reminded them that I had said I was interviewing elsewhere and then told them I accepted a job with

CNN. He said, "You didn't sign anything, did you?" I said, "No." He said, "Don't do anything," and wound up offering me more than triple what I was making.

KEITH OLBERMANN:

I think the answer to why I was shipped to ESPN2 is contained in this: In '92 to '93 Dan and I foreshadowed our real success and Walsh could see it coming and knew it meant only one thing: it would no longer be his show. Putting me on ESPN2 solved that—or so he thought. John Lack was coming up and whispering into my ear, "Ignore what the rest of them tell you, you're the producer of the show on the air, you do what you want to." My cohost had been selected, if I remember correctly, by the CEO of CapCities. Walsh told me Lack was in charge, but he was clearly heavily influential in what was being done. Lack told me Lack was in charge. Then they brought in Vince Doria because Walsh was apparently still pushing for ultimately making ESPN2, as he put it, "the *Christian Science Monitor* of sports." He was going in a totally different direction. I did not know that the *Christian Science Monitor* scored particularly well with the young demographic. But then Doria came up to me, maybe three weeks into it, and said, "Hey, you know I have just realized I don't know as much about television as I thought I did. Can I tap your brain on some of these things 'cause my instincts are not what I thought." I said, "God bless you. I'm happy to do it. I'll stay after class." But there were two other people who were "in charge"—Norby Williamson and Mike Bogad, who were the line producer and the coordinating producer, respectively, of the eleven o'clock *SportsCenter*.

In the middle of all this, just weeks before we went on the air, Howard Katz came in as an executive. So in addition to not knowing who was in charge, now there was a new guy whose title was, I think, executive vice president—a title that sounded bigger than Walsh's. So I went to him and asked if he was aware of this whole project, and he said, "Well, I'm in charge of it." I think it was around this time that I made this joke: "Let's stop people in the hallway and see how many think they're in charge of ESPN2." It was like the documentary about screenplays in Hollywood where you just stand outside a supermarket and ask people, "How's your screenplay?" And only 33 percent of the people that they stopped said, "I don't know what you're talking about; I don't have a screenplay." But the other 66 percent all said, "Well, it's in development, well, it's over at Metro." Little old ladies pushing grocery carts had screenplays. It was like that at ESPN2. I simply could not tell you who was in charge.

VINCE DORIA:
The truth of it is none of us knew exactly what we should be doing. There was much discussion in the

business of what was the need for a second all-sports network: Is there enough even for one all-sports network? What are they going to do with two?

I do know that if John Lack had ever gotten Steve's job, he probably would have paid off John Walsh and shown him the door. But at least Walsh would have left with something.

MITCH ALBOM, *Author:*

Walsh was a big champion of mine. He believed in good writing and he thought that I was a good writer. At least, that's what he said. And he thought that because I was working with college football and it was a young sport, I should be part of this new network. At the time it was like, "What is this, the minor-league ESPN? How can there be a second ESPN? It's just ESPN, that's all there is." So I was a little bit hesitant about if it would even reach anyone. And they brought us in to do this thing called *SportsNight* and what they told me was, "You're going to be working a lot, it's a long show and you're going to be on a lot." And I thought, "Well, all right, it's a lot of airtime and it's a lot of exposure, and it's a lot of work." I guessed it would be worth it because they were asking me to come and live in Bristol for three days a week. I already had a life and a girlfriend and I didn't know how that would all work out. But I would fly in on Friday mornings, stay at the Ramada across the street for three days, and do three hours a night of this show.

CHARLIE PIERCE, *Columnist:*

I was one of the people who was brought in to try out. This was one of the more preposterous exercises of all time. They called Bud Shaw, me, and a whole bunch of people and they kept rotating us through these tryouts. When I walked into the studio and saw Olbermann and Suzy, I thought, "This is really a chemistry experiment gone wrong here." And then Mitch Albom. I don't mean to sound like Jerry Seinfeld, but I don't know what consulting genius put those three together. I had known Olbermann for a while and I went outside and he was sitting on the hood of a car smoking an immense cigar, just shaking his head very, very sadly. I think they offered me some sort of *Crossfire* thing with John Feinstein to argue about college basketball, but I turned it down because I didn't want to argue professionally.

JIMMY ROBERTS:

Bornstein had let it be known that there was going to be this internal contest to come up with a nickname for ESPN2. I'm guessing this is September. I was in my office, which was where the corporate offices were, and I went into the copy room. There was this woman named Kitty, who was John Lack's secretary, and she was getting some stuff ready for John. She said, "He's going out to the Western Cable Convention. We're announcing the launch of

ESPN2." And I said, "Oh, you mean the Deuce?"
And she looked at me and I said, "Oh yeah. That's
what we call it around here," just kind of joking
around. And I didn't think anything of it. Sometime
later, close to the launch, I was watching the feed
from the press conference where Steve was introducing ESPN2. "But I'm going to let John Lack here tell
you more about it." And he says, "Well thanks, Steve.
Thanks for launching ESPN2, but around the office
we like to call it the Deuce." And I remember having that Albert Brooks moment—you know, from
Broadcast News? "Oh my God. I said it here, and it
came out there."

GEORGE BODENHEIMER:
   Those of us trying to sell ESPN2 were constantly
being asked, "How does it differ from ESPN?" So,
for instance when "Jock 'n' Roll" was conceived, that
was something important to us. We could tell affiliates that on ESPN2 we were going to be putting
sports highlights to rock music, which of course
hadn't been done before. And John Lack deserves the
credit for that. We were also able to say *SportsNight*
with Keith Olbermann was going to focus on action
sports. All of those things ultimately went by the
wayside, but they served a very valuable purpose in
helping us launch ESPN2 by creating a difference
from ESPN.

STUART SCOTT, *Anchor:*

I was hired for ESPN2. I didn't watch much TV in college, and my roommate and I had this little black and white, and we didn't even have cable. So I didn't watch ESPN. I had worked in news and then I got a chance to anchor sports on the weekends, but ESPN was my first full-time sports job. I don't think any of it ever came easy, but that's not to say it wasn't fun back then. Something can be difficult *and* fun.

VINCE DORIA:

Keith was standing outside the building one day in a leather jacket and Lack came running up to him and said, "You need to wear that on the set." It was that kind of a kneejerk, "Hey, this looks good," kind of thing. It's a good thing he wasn't wearing a mink stole.

KEITH OLBERMANN:

The reason I was wearing that awful leather jacket when we went on the air was that I had been wearing it in rehearsals because it was so cold. Suzy Kolber was so cold she was wearing a full blanket on her lap, because they had tied this state-of-the-art lighting system and the state-of-the-art HVAC system, never noticing that one of the air-conditioning monitors was directly under one of the back lights. So this monitor always read 212 degrees and kept pumping cold air into the studio all winter long. By October first, it had to have been 55 degrees in there. They had technicians in there every day trying to make it warmer. They couldn't do it. It was an icebox.

SUZY KOLBER:

My version is Keith was a genius who finished writing the three-hour show in about twenty minutes and he was outside smoking his pipe and he had thrown on his leather jacket over his goofy print shirt and John walked by him and said, "That's the look I want." They had given me so much money to go to New York and buy clothes, it was unbelievable. I had worn one of my favorite outfits from West Palm to a preview show and John Lack's comment was, "She looks like she's in West Palm." But at least we got makeup. They didn't even have makeup at ESPN until the start of *SportsNight* on ESPN2.

CHARLEY STEINER:

Shit, when I got there they had maybe ten anchors, if that. Now comes ESPN2 and they're adding more, and it's the next generation. They wanted to emulate a new ESPN attitude. See, all of us back on the original didn't have an attitude, we were just being ourselves.

The problem about the birth of ESPN2 was, you can't try and be hip; either you are or you aren't. It's that simple. Likewise, you can't try and be smart; either you are or you aren't. But putting poor old Keith in a black leather jacket like he's heading for a dominatrix studio, come on!

STEVE BORNSTEIN:

It was irrelevant to me whether Olbermann was wearing a leather jacket or a fucking tutu. All that creative stuff and tensions wasn't the battle. The battle was getting distribution. I was much more concerned about working with Bodenheimer to get TCI, Time Warner, and other operators on board. We needed to quickly figure out how we could leverage our service to make them distribute ESPN2. All I wanted was shelf space and more sub fees.

MITCH ALBOM:

They told us how to dress, which was the first time in my career that anyone ever did that. And they said, "Well we want Suzy to look a certain way, and we want Keith to look a certain way, and we want you to look a certain way." We were all going to have our own kind of 'way.'" I had to have the Don Johnson look: I had to wear sport coats with T-shirts underneath them, but I had to pull the sleeves up on my sport coat. Keith was wearing a leather jacket, and we were teasing him about being Fonzie; everyone was saying, "So we have the Fonz."

KEITH OLBERMANN:

Those who have that little touch of paranoia in them about a certain group—as I do about management—really are a little bit more—*comfortable* might be the right word—in a situation in which management is failing utterly. You don't have to say, "See, I told you so," because everybody is seeing it in real time. So my attitude was, "Let's see what we can do with this. I don't think it's going to work. But they said I could go back in six months if it doesn't."

As opening night for the new network and the launch of its flagship series SportsNight *grew closer, the atmosphere around ESPN2 was filled with doubt. If not doubt, then trepidation. A full dress rehearsal for* SportsNight *confirmed some of the darkest fears harbored by Olbermann, and on the morning after a September 26 dry-run that he considered a medley of calamities, he fired off a three-page, single-spaced memo on what went wrong. Since Olbermann is such an erudite and accomplished writer, the memo reads beautifully. It also says the show sucks.*

Olbermann found the show to be "neither hip nor particularly informative" but instead "purposeless," about the worst thing a show could be. "It is not an expansion on SportsCenter *but an apparent redundancy," he wrote. "Neither is it a new generation's version of* SportsCenter *but merely the prover-*

bial *fifty-year-old wolf in twenty-year-old sheep's clothing."*

"*From my previous experiences here and outside of ESPN,*" Olbermann lamented, "*the quality of this one show, which I thought was poor, could not be achieved on consecutive nights without inducing heart attacks in the booth and on the floor.*"

He divided the show's alleged flaws into technical and editorial—ten of each ("the top ten" of each, he said, indicating there were many more). Complaining that his role on the show "*has devolved into that of a glorified announcer or emcee,*" Olbermann said his coanchor Suzy Kolber, with whom he was not exactly chummy (she was mentioned only twice in the memo), nonetheless had his sympathy for suffering a similar fate. Since the show was a waste of his talents and skills, Olbermann complained, "*anybody with any broadcasting experience could have come in off the street and done all I was permitted to do*" and get away with it.

"*The show is over-produced,*" he wrote, adding that although the producers and executives had said they wanted a "loose" show with byplay, interaction, and ad-libbing among the assembled personalities—all of them under instructions to "have fun" on the air—the actual program was produced more like "a concentration camp." He also found it by turns "laughable," "pathetic," "gratuitous," "boring," and, in the case of one feature piece, "tasteless."

Olbermann wrote that the experience was akin to

"running ahead of an out-of-control locomotive" or "driving to work while leaning out the window, prying the hood open, and trying to repair your smoking engine."

KEITH OLBERMANN:

I did threaten to quit, and I did walk out, but I think it worked to the degree that it at least got us some idea of what the show might be like.

JOHN WALSH:

We never believed that Keith was going to quit. He was just always nervous about something new, especially if it took time.

VINCE DORIA:

I was never really worried that Keith would actually quit before the start of *SportsNight*. Where was he going to go? Keith and Suzy were certainly not a marriage made in heaven but they were much better compared to Keith and Mitch—*there* were two very accomplished, strong-willed and smart people with good-sized egos who clearly had gotten off on the wrong foot, and for probably no reason. I don't remember this exactly, but I think somewhere along the line Mitch came into the building and didn't notice Keith or didn't say anything to him, and Keith took it as a slight, which led to one guy thinking the other guy had no use for him and vice versa. I still think were you to get them out somewhere on the same page, they could have had some interesting byplay between them.

MITCH ALBOM:

Keith was temperamental, but it didn't throw me much because I thought of Keith as the TV guy and I just thought that's what TV guys did. He would go off with a pipe—I don't even know if there was tobacco in it—and sit in the corner, just looking off into the air. I would think, "I guess that's what TV guys do." I was a reporter; I was a journalist. I was there for credibility even though I had my sleeves rolled up. I was a serious journalist compared to Suzy, who was just starting out. She didn't have a body of work. I think they probably wanted a mix of male and female. I was just worried that if he did quit, I was going to have to do all his parts, because he would have these scripts that were a hundred pages to go through every night.

SUZY KOLBER:

It was pretty ugly. I was told I was the cohost and Keith believed he was the host and I was supposed to be more like the sidekick. I can't honestly say I remember being told, "This is what the show's going to be like." Keith quit a couple times before we actually went on the air. The weeks leading up to the launch were just horrible. I was talking it out with my boyfriend, and then I would talk to my mom every day.

The night before we went on the air, they were still making major, major changes. They were scrapping everything. We were all in this giant room while they were doing it, and I seem to vaguely remember Keith sitting on the floor in the corner.

I just felt that Keith was an unhappy person. He made a lot of people unhappy around him. I'm sure he made me unhappy.

GEORGE BODENHEIMER:

If I'd had a Bible handy, I'd put my hand on it when I tell you that on the first night we launched — October 1, 1993, at exactly eight o'clock to the second — as Keith Olbermann came up on the air for the official launch of ESPN2, you could hear the little beeps and clicks of my fax machine, and we could see the TCI signatures coming across. The timing was unbelievable. That agreement meant we launched with ten million homes, the largest cable launch ever.

KEITH OLBERMANN:

Lack came to me within no more than an hour before the first show and said, "Walsh doesn't know what the fuck he's doing." Which was true, but it was not inclusive enough. What I meant to say to him was, "None of you know what the fuck you're doing. I don't know what the fuck I'm doing. I don't know what I'm going to say in an hour."

It was tense. I've never seen anything like it. To this day, as chaotic as some things got with MSNBC the first time I worked there, CNN—either in its original incarnation when I worked there in the eighties, or when I went back in '02, when they had fifteen or twenty vice-presidents who had something to do with the show, I was guest-hosting and they all had an idea—as chaotic as those things were, nothing came close to what was going on at ESPN2.

MITCH ALBOM:

The network began on a Friday night. We were sitting in the dark waiting for the lights to come up and I remember thinking, "Wow, this is the start of a network, this isn't just the start of a show, this is the first time you turn the lights on in the building, this is the first time you turn the key to the house, this is the first time your ship sails and lands on the shore of an uncharted island. Who starts a network? Wow, I'm part of history here."

And with that thought in mind, the lights come up and Keith Olbermann, wearing a leather coat, says, "Welcome to the end of my career." Any grand thoughts I had about the significance of that moment went right out the window.

MICHAEL MANDT, *Production Assistant:*

I was working the teleprompter for that first show, on the set, and I can tell you that first line of Keith's was not on the prompter.

BILL WOLFF:

So we start ESPN2, it goes on the air, and the first words from our anchor, Keith Olbermann, are, "Welcome to the end of my career." We've got twenty-three-year-old guys making seven bucks an hour, working twenty hours a fucking day, killing themselves, and the guy in charge decides to mock the network. It was a killer, I mean a killer. So you had to have a pretty big sense of humor and you had to have a lot of perspective to understand Keith and to understand that some of it was hyperbole and some was done for dramatic effect. But not every twenty-three-year-old has that perspective.

GARY BETTMAN, *Commissioner, National Hockey League:*

I was the first live guest in the studio on ESPN2. I actually went up to Bristol, and came on during the very first hour. I think the big deal then was that I wasn't wearing a tie. That passed for big news in those days.

SUZY KOLBER:

To me, the launch wasn't that monumental. I don't think I ever grasped how big a deal it was until the night we were on and there was this massive party going on outside in the parking lot and we were in this stupid little studio out in the garage doing this show. I didn't go to the party. We were on the air for three hours. Afterward, I went home.

What a night. There had never been anything quite like it in the history of ESPN, certainly not on this scale. While it's true that back in the network's Jurassic age, some of the early gang's impromptu booze bashes got pretty raunchy, and ESPN Christmas parties of that era were both cherished and notorious, the party celebrating the launch of ESPN2 was a grand affair, held on-campus in a giant tent.

Many ESPN clients (advertisers) and friends were invited out from New York for the bash, marking the first time the huge gap between Bristol and Manhattan had been bridged. Attendees were liberally lubricated, which inevitably led to a relaxation of manners and morals. The big rented canopy was soon christened the "tent of consent."

Feeling no pain, once he got sufficiently sloshed, was ESPN president Steve Bornstein, who expected the Deuce to be another feather in his crowded cap. He drank with abandon—but "abandon ship" is what Rosa Gatti from PR urged him to do once things started getting wilder than expected. After at least one amorous encounter, Bornstein, reportedly so blitzed he collapsed into a clump of bushes, was said to have given at least two women the impression they'd be going home with him. Instead, he took his adviser's advice and called it a night—solo!

STUART SCOTT:
We did a three-hour show and had a big party. If you ask most people working the show that night, one of the things they will remember was that M.C. Hammer was there. I don't remember the show, I just remember M.C. Hammer being in a tiny little green room in Bristol, Connecticut. I think he was wearing some shiny big pants. But it was just past Hammertime, I think. Hammertime was '89 and '90; this was '93.

JOHN LACK:
I don't know how many buses there were that night leaving Manhattan, plus all the limousines for the ad agencies. So in that sense, it was a whole new experience for ESPN. They had never done any of that stuff before. No one had ever come to Bristol, including advertisers. It was a chance for the first time that I remember at ESPN for the people in New York and the people in Bristol who really lived in different worlds, I mean the employees, to really join hands as

a family and to launch something they were both proud of that was kind of fun.

Sales secretaries from New York were kissing Dan Patrick hello; traffic ladies were hanging out with production managers. It was all stuff that this company didn't do because Bristol was ninety miles away. So it was a joyous family occasion. And the ad community kind of got into it with us because they had been to lots of launch parties for other networks but had never been out of town in the middle of the woods at the sports place, where we were doing pop culture for the first time. So it was a great night. It really took ESPN from this sports journalism, the sports nobody wanted, to finally getting a couple of sports, to now "We are American sports culture." When I introduced Steve—and I worked hard to make it all look like his idea that night—he made mention of the fact that we were expanding our horizons and that it was the beginning of a larger ESPN culture that we all should be proud of. It was now sports as a metaphor for culture, not just a reflection of what goes on Saturdays and Sundays. From that standpoint, I think we were all very proud and everybody got a little bigger. We kind of moved from the pages of *Sports Illustrated* a little into the pages of *People* magazine that night.

RON SEMIAO:

Hell, yeah, I was at the ESPN2 launch party! I was with my buddies out there getting hammered—but not with M.C. Hammer, though I did see him around in a big limo out there. It was a good old ESPN party. You're working your ass off without any sleep for like two weeks and at the end you have a wrap party where everybody blows off steam and everybody tries to get laid. That's exactly what was going on. I started in '85 so I was at the Christmas parties where you knew 95 percent of the people there and things were totally crazy. But this was a hell of a lot more people. People at ESPN know how to party—or, I should say, knew how to party.

I did hear that Bornstein was hammered in the control room, and he and a couple others called like Dan Burke and Tom Murphy, the guys who run CapCities, and were yelling: "Yeah, we're on the air, whaddaya think?" Those guys were probably in their fucking pj's at home, having a cup of tea.

STEVE BORNSTEIN:

The party was legendary. There had been so much stress built up. We had started on July Fourth and ended on October 1, and we had done one thousand different contracts. Literally, you were doing ESPN2 distribution deals with cable operators, and there were over three hundred cable operators at the time. You were doing retransmission consent for the eight ABC stations, and you were doing retransmission consent for the, whatever, thirteen Hearst stations. Those were three different contracts with everybody, and it wasn't cookie cutter. Those were three hundred fifty negotiations with three hundred fifty different cable operators. We only had that period of about a hundred days to get all those deals done. And we did. So we had a lot of steam to blow off.

After George got the fax, we popped the Cristal, and I certainly did my share of drinking. At around midnight, I called Dan Burke to tell him, "Hey, we're on the air," and evidently a little bit more. Then, frankly, I don't remember much after that. All I can say is that I will forever be thankful to Rosa Gatti, who came up to me at that party and said, "Time for you to go home." She got me out of there and to the hotel across the street.

The next day, I get up, and the first thing I do is call Dan Burke to tell him that we had closed TCI, and that we had gone on the air, totally forgetting that I ever called him the night before. He couldn't have been nicer, saying, "Is this a different TCI than what you told me about last night?" I then realized I had just put my foot in my mouth because I had gotten so hammered, I didn't remember calling him, and then I wondered what else I didn't remember. I just kind of covered myself and said I just wanted to make sure he didn't have any questions about the deal.

DAVID ZUCKER:
We always had Christmas parties, but that ESPN2 launch party was out of the ordinary. It was a big

bash, which was pretty unusual for what had always been a tightly run, cost-conscious organization. We were rolling; we were making money.

JOHN WALSH:

We were ecstatic that we got it on the air. We felt as though we did what we set out to do, and it reflected all the thought, energy, and conclusions that we had put into it all. People were really ebullient that we did it. We launched something new. We had guests who made it to Bristol, and that had never happened before. But I was totally exhausted. It was eleven o'clock when we got off the air, and I think I went in and probably had one drink and was home by 11:30. It wasn't until the next day, when people were talking about it, did I realize what had gone on. It was pretty evident that some people were overserved.

Bill LAMB, *Technology:*

It was one heck of a party. It was under the tent, it was all over the grounds, it was just a great time. Yeah, I heard about Rosa telling Steve Bornstein it was time for him to go home—but was that after he fell over the railing into the creek, or before?

It wasn't just one party; there were also the after-parties. There were lots of them. They were nonauthorized, non-business-related. The one that I was at was maybe fifty people. You watched the sun come up, pretty much. We're a pretty good operation that work together and play together. You can imagine.

SUZY KOLBER:

Once we got started doing the show, things didn't become any easier. One particular circumstance that stands out about Keith is related to his love of fantasy baseball. We would do skits for every show. Some major leaguer had been there the day before and so we were playing off of that. The language I used in this skit was something about Keith being obsessed with fantasy baseball, and he got so bent out of shape that he threatened to quit. We were minutes from being on the show. He had seen the taping of the skit and he went to Norby's office. I think he said, "I'm quitting." And Norby begged him, "Don't quit now." So he didn't, but Keith wouldn't talk to me—throughout a three-hour show. I don't remember how long that lasted but he never discussed what happened, what was wrong. He just wouldn't talk to me.

The other instance that stands out to me was during the Nancy Kerrigan and Tonya Harding situation. Keith and Christine Brennan [columnist] had become very good friends, and Christine was all over that story. I had the lead on the show that night about the two of them and he knew a lot because he had spoken to Christine. But he didn't share any of it, and he let me go on and do whatever I did without giving me any information. I found that to be unacceptable.

MARK GROSS:

Man, I tell you, honestly, I don't know how Suzy got through it. There were times when I said, "My God," because Olbermann was being really tough. But he's also a genius.

TONY KORNHEISER, *Sportswriter*:

Whenever ESPN2 started, Feinstein and I taped about ten things in a day, sitting outside the Capitol, just two guys yapping for ESPN2. We were called the Wise Guys. They just wanted debate. I don't know if it was funny or not. We would debate an issue for about a minute and a half, then do another one. I never saw one of them; in fact, to this day, I've never seen any of them.

STEVE BORNSTEIN:

Now this move became kind of a legend in the business: About four months after we launched ESPN2, I put the North Carolina–Duke basketball game on ESPN2. I seem to remember it was a number one versus number two matchup—obviously a huge national interest game. And that was a really ballsy move that subjected us to a hell of a lot of political and other pressure. I always planned it for ESPN2 but I wanted to cause a consumer outcry so the cable operators had to televise ESPN2. There was great political pressure. Governors, everybody else, calling and saying, "Why don't you just put it on ESPN? My cable system doesn't carry ESPN2." Every citizen in North Carolina and every college basketball fan thought we did a bait-and-switch on them. But it truly established ESPN2 as must-have cable.

SUZY KOLBER:

At ESPN2, we were already the stepchild. Charley Steiner and Mike Tirico were the only two *Sports-Center* anchors who befriended us and who would come over to our area.

DAVID ZUCKER:

My job was to fill up the schedule, but a lot of the sports leagues that we dealt with, whether it was college or professional, were very resistant; they didn't want their product on ESPN2. Like with baseball, if we had a conflict and tried to move a game over to ESPN2, there was a lot of resistance. They even tried to sue us. We spent a lot of time working through that one.

Sometimes things actually work out the way they should—at least the way that common sense and simple sanity suggest they ought to. Such was the happy denouement for Olbermann in February 1994, as word came he would soon be liberated from the leather straitjacket and painful perch he'd grumblingly endured on ESPN2's SportsNight *and would return to his royal roost on ESPN's* SportsCenter. *It was precisely what Olbermann—as well as the network's fans, including many college and pro athletes—had been hoping for.*

People wondered whether ESPN executives had swallowed their pride and realized the mistake they'd made, or if it was just that they could no longer stomach Olbermann's demonstrable unhappiness over being exiled to ESPN2 and sentenced to cohost a show that he essentially loathed. Not only would Olbermann be back at his old SportsCenter *post on the mother ship, but he'd be reteamed with Dan Patrick, with whom he'd made* SportsCenter *a much talked-about hit. The change was seminal for* SportsCenter *in another way: ESPN announced that when Olbermann returned on April 3, the show would expand to an hour, airing 11:00 p.m. to midnight every night but Wednesdays.*

KEITH OLBERMANN:

The last ESPN2 show I ever did was after the show had been moved twice, furniture had been changed, segments had been changed, and we had shows where for three hours not one section of the show, one commercial-to-commercial segment, went on the air at the time it was supposed to. There was a C section of the third hour that became the lead section on the first hour and the B section of the second hour became the B section of the first hour. It went through this for three hours but we had no idea what was coming up next. "We'll be back with *something* after this." So this last show had a two-part twenty-minute piece by Tom Friend, a sportswriter from L.A. with long hair who looked vaguely like Richard Loomis, and a twenty-minute piece on a kid who did all of his college applications for basketball scholarships by mail and telephone and did not know until he showed up for the first class that he was the only white guy in an all-black conference. And in the studio, playing a portable Hammond organ, was Eddie Layton, the organist of Yankee stadium, who in the middle of the winter was playing "Take Me Out to the Ball Game."

It was like that from October to March. Every show was this kaleidoscope, as if all the people who were told they were in charge — literally eight or ten people were told they were in charge of the final product — it's as if what was left out of that was, "Yes, you're in charge for five minutes. Then you, you over there, you're in charge for five minutes. And you're in charge for five minutes." And you weren't allowed to know what the previous guy did. That's what it was like. It became such an unpleasant experience because I think everybody on it had the same sense, that "this is a minefield." Stuart Scott probably didn't feel that way because it was his first big break.

VINCE DORIA:

If the network had said, "You're going to stay here and that's how it's going to be," who knows what he would have done? Would he have left the network completely? Maybe. I don't know. It's all very hard to predict with Keith. But there was never an ultimatum. It was never, "Send me back or I'm quitting." It was just clear that he was unhappy, had been unhappy, and was growing more unhappy. Frankly, it wasn't a healthy situation for anyone. John Lack was in on it, John Walsh was in on it, even Bornstein. Everyone agreed it had gotten to the point where it was best for all for Keith to move back to *SportsCenter*. Stuart Scott took his place, which was a great opportunity for him and he thrived in the role. He also had a much better chemistry with Suzy than Keith did.

KEITH OLBERMANN:

I paid the ransom money—about $25,000—and got out of ESPN2. There was a maxim at ESPN that Howard Katz, who negotiated this, once admitted to my agent, "If you let them know what it is you want, they will use it against you in some way." Well, all I wanted was to go back and do *SportsCenter*. Remember, part of the promise was, "get this started for us and, if it's successful or if it's not, then you can come back, if you want to, or you can stay if you want to, whatever is your choice at that point." And they said,

"Well, you know, we're not going to pay you the same amount of money just to go back and do the eleven o'clock *SportsCenter.*" So really, faced with the option of being stuck on this show, whatever the demand was, $25,000 less per year, and add another two years to the contract, whatever it was, I had no choice. And I wasn't happy about it but I just said, "All right, let me just get out of it."

STUART SCOTT:

Suzy Kolber and I were hosting together and since it was ESPN2, we were supposed to dress kind of funky, not a suit-and-tie thing. So we both were wearing a very similar colored shirt and a tie kind of loosely knotted. Casual shirt, casual tie, similar color. And so when we went back to do our fixes for the show, we changed ties. We do fixes for different segments and if you watched the show—it was maybe just an hour then because it shrunk from three to two to one—but the first segment, second segment, third segment we have different ties, and about four or five viewers caught it. We did it just to see if anybody would notice.

KENNY MAYNE, *Anchor:*

Keith went crazy and went back to ESPN, Stuart moved up to sit next to Suzy, and so they needed one more guy. The funny part about coming to ESPN2 was I remember distinctly being told, "Don't have any great aspirations of being on *SportsCenter* or moving over there. It's not like you come here and you immediately go there or even anytime soon." I really didn't care. My checks still had ESPN on them; so what if I'm on their second channel?

BILL WOLFF:

Chris Berman was the first guy not to take it so seriously; he was the first guy to pull away the curtain and say, "Aaah, I'm just a big dumb sports fan." Like, "It's okay, I'm just having fun." And Berman really introduced fun to sportscasting, revolutionized it by introducing fun. Keith introduced satire and brains and rapier-carving, biting comment, first guy to do it, and he's the best they ever had. Much respect to Berman: Berman carried that place, Berman made that place, but the guy who made ESPN a household word, the guy who gave ESPN a brand, the guy who made ESPN mean something in the market to everyone, was Keith Olbermann. God, he was a genius. He just reinvented sportscasting by being the smartest guy who ever did it. And watching him in the mid-nineties was a pleasure. It was appointment viewing: What was Olbermann going to say that night? And it was largely him, it was his brain, it was his point of view, it was the way he approached it. He was the first super-smart guy just to do highlights every night—not the first super-smart guy to be a sportscaster, the first guy just grinding it out every night, doing the highlights.

MIKE McQUADE:

Sometimes his lead-ins to the highlights would seem interminable. It would be something about the Cleveland Spiders in 1899 that would go on for forty-five seconds! I said, "Look, the lead-in to the highlight cannot be longer than the highlight itself."

ROBIN ROBERTS:

My big Norma Rae moment was about offices—we didn't have any. We just had cubicles. And finally, we were like, "Dammit, we're important, we're big, we need offices!" So myself and Keith Olbermann went walking into John A. Walsh's office with all these demands and he looked at us like, "You've got to be kidding."

DAN PATRICK:

"Precedent setting" is a big deal at ESPN. They're very concerned about that.

They were worried that if they gave Chris Berman an office, we would all want one. Howard Katz initially told us that the fire marshal said they couldn't have any more offices, that the cubicles were more flame retardant. But if you were there for three weeks as a coordinating producer, you got an office. So we'd always joke, "Is the fire marshal here yet?"

Again, it was all about who has control and precedent. "If we let them do it, then everybody else is going to want to do it." So we would be in these cubicles and everybody would hear what you were doing and there was no privacy whatsoever. To get dressed, you'd go into a bathroom.

MIKE McQUADE:

I'd do the rundown and Keith would sit behind me, and I wasn't even done, but Keith had already written everything in the show. He'd say, "Are you almost done?" and I remember the first time I said, "What do you mean?" He said, "I've already written the entire show up until the point you're at." I said, "Oh come on." And he wasn't writing stuff like "the Knicks play the Nets tonight, let's go to the Garden"; what he wrote was well thought out. It was insane. In thirty-five minutes he had written the entire show. And that happened every day. See, for me, that was fun, because as long as you were, as he put it, "on the raft," you were good, meaning you were in with him. He had people he was constantly taking onto the raft and putting off the raft.

DAN PATRICK:

Was it the "raft" or the "lifeboat"? I think maybe it was "life raft," a combination of the two. I just love that expression. Keith would always say, "Who's in the life raft?" And I remember Gus Ramsey and Mike McQuade would always say—it was almost like semi-regular—"Are you still in the life raft?" If they had screwed up with Keith or he was angry with them, then they would be excommunicated. You didn't know from day to day—at least these guys around him—if you were on or off, and it was tough for them because they didn't have the power to be able to say to Keith, "Hey, stop; grow up, fess up."

Everything he did when he was in there was personal—how he wrote it, how he covered it, how he looked at you, everything was on his heart, or on his sleeve. And that was what made him great there. And if he felt like you had just turned on him, then you had actually turned on him, and that was something that was very, very deep to him. If he had your respect, you had that respect, and that was something that never wavered for me with him till the very end.

There'd be times when I had to say to Keith, "Hey, come on, it's okay, don't worry about it," or, "We'll get through it." You had these little reminders for him, because he would take it personally. Walsh was phony with it but eventually he would go through me, and they all went through me, to deliver messages to Keith—to which I said, "This isn't part of my job description." There was always a message delivered that seemed like it might have been to me but it was really for me to deliver to Keith. Everybody was afraid to say something to him. So I was Kissinger. But, God, was he entertaining!

KEITH OLBERMANN:

So little of what went into the 11:00 p.m. *SportsCenter* could be preapproved, largely because neither Dan nor I had any idea what we were going to say until it happened. The thing that in retrospect strikes me about the show and its success was that it was every night, and every night it was organic. It was essentially the same premise as improvisational jazz. We have a vague idea where we're going with this, we know which instruments we've brought out here onto the stage, but Lord knows who's going to play what and when. Very often it would happen that we would be in one of those situations—the highlight would play and we'd have no idea what was going on. We had not been provided with any information and basically had to guess while looking at a seven-inch-diameter monitor.

So it was obvious very early on that, once you get the mastery of how to deal with highlights dropping on your head like anvils, once you do that and, other than the prewritten on-camera intros to stories or highlight leads, nobody's approving it. They either approve of you or they don't. It was very difficult for a specific thing that was said or done to be criticized, because essentially everybody's goal was to get a great product out while surviving the experience—and there were lots of people who tried to do that but succeeded at neither. What was it Churchill said about, "Nothing is as exciting and makes you appreciate life more than being shot at without success"? I mean that's really how it was almost every night. So there was very little for them to approve. And again their approach had to be, "you're buying the whole package; you can't pick and choose what you don't like. If there's something you've seen on the air that you don't want me to do again, that's fine, go ahead and tell me that." The idea that I should be in some sort of trouble or Dan or anybody else would be in trouble for doing something when it was so spontaneous—I can't recall an occasion where they actually did that.

DAN PATRICK:

We never read each other's scripts because we always wanted to be surprised. We would go in there and he would always have issues but he could write a show in forty-five minutes and spend the rest of the day being upset about something or questioning something with management.

BILL FAIRWEATHER, *Coordinating Producer:*

It's the nature of the beast when you put competitive people together. John Walsh is going to butt heads with Keith Olbermann, or Bill Fairweather is going to butt heads with Dan Patrick over how we should do a story.

I had been there for probably three months, so I was the new kid on the block—"Who's this smartass from Boston who thinks he knows everything?"—and I was working with a coordinating producer who had been there forever, the kind of a guy that got on a lot of people's nerves and people had frustrations with. And I didn't care, I wasn't going to put up with any of his shit. So finally, on one of the overnight shows, we had it out. It escalated to the newsroom, then to the control room. Then it was like a scene out of *Good Will Hunting*. I said, "Well, we can just go outside." And I said, "I don't give a shit who you are, how long you've been here. I've been hearing from day one that people don't respect you, and you do nothing but hassle me on every single show." I called my girlfriend at the time—she's now my wife—and I said, "Look, I'm going to be coming home. I'm not going to make it past tomorrow. Once management gets wind of this, it'll be the end of me." Sure enough, first thing Monday morning, one of the management guys who actually hired me called me into his office. As soon as he said, "Bill, close the door," I just said, "Hey, listen, I'm really sorry but thanks for the opportunity here. The guys have been great. But I just couldn't take it anymore." But he said, "Bill, don't worry about it. You said something that a bunch of guys around here have been waiting to say. It's not something that we encourage or we want to have happen again, but we understand—or at least I understand—why you did it."

MIKE McQUADE:

One time, while Dan was talking on camera, Keith got really agitated—"why are we doing it this way, why are we not doing it this way," that kind of thing. I finally said, "This is how we're doing it. Shut up."

Then there was the night we were doing the show and, during a commercial break, I said to Keith and Dan, "Who are those people back there?" The guys turned around, looked, and said, "Uh, looks like some kids just walked in from a nearby school or something." And they were right. These guys had just walked into the studio! That's how lax security was then. I said, "Look, could you at least tell them to be quiet?"

It took me a good hundred shows to have full command of the show every day, and I should preface all of this by saying, I learned so much from those two in producing the show.

While Olbermann and Patrick were being lavished with attention—and loving it—for their ad-libbed hijinks on the 11:00 p.m. edition of SportsCenter, *the 6:00 p.m. triumvirate of Robin Roberts, Bob Ley, and Charley Steiner was, with fewer gags and antics, putting on their own solid, straightforward edition.*

Two shows, two different approaches. The Olbermann-Patrick team came across as smart, edgy, and full of attitude. They were in fact developing what could be called the new ESPN style, a smart-alecky outlook and flippant delivery that owed something to the comedy of Bill Murray and David Letterman. The six o'clock team was more old school, holding themselves to broadcast standards and styles of yesteryear—and doing a very good job of it.

At eleven o'clock, Olbermann and Patrick arguably had the most to work with—a huge trove of raw materials collected all day every day, and into the evening, from satellite feeds and other sources. That's in part why the six o'clockers' in-house cheering section maintained that their team had it tougher, because they had fewer highlights to show, fewer scores to report, and yet all that airtime to fill (a half-hour at first, soon expanded to an hour).

Indeed, when they signed on at 6:00 p.m., many of the day's games had yet to be played. Insiders also noted one more factor that made the earlier show harder to do: many ESPN executives were routinely still in the building at that hour and loved dropping by the studios to see how things were going; you couldn't get away with much mischief if the bosses were staring right at you.

Ley and Steiner were compatible on the air and off, despite their constant awareness that Ley, the conservative, and Steiner, the liberal, rarely agreed on anything away from a field. Ley got probably his most important early journalism experience in print, at the Passaic Herald-News *in New Jersey, while Steiner was working for such radio stations as New York's WABC, where he covered the Jets. Both men worked at New York's WOR for a time—but not the same time.*

Roberts had an unmistakable aura of authority, a true pro's unflappability when it came to crises and last-minute changes to the rundown, and an ability to coexist on an equal plane with "the guys," without trying to become one of them. Statuesque and tirelessly enthused, Roberts was recruited from her native Atlanta. Her father had been one of the original Tuskegee Airmen, a unit of African American flyers—the first ever in U.S. history—who served with honor in World War II.

But Roberts, who'd played basketball while at Southeastern Louisiana University, had to surmount obstacles facing two minorities—and years of built-up, built-in opposition—to become a star in what was, for an African American woman, a sometimes hostile field. Surveys repeatedly told ESPN that its audience did not—N-O-T, not—want to get its news from a woman. Even so, separate polls, with similar respondents, gave a big thumbs-up to Roberts for her performance; apparently if they had to have a woman, they wanted that woman to be Roberts, and they got her.

And they loved her.

ROBIN ROBERTS:

When I was hired by ESPN it wasn't because Gayle Gardner had left, it was just because they were looking to expand the roster. I appreciated the fact that I wasn't just being hired to replace a woman. ESPN has never done that. At the other networks, when they lost a woman, they replaced her with a woman; they didn't just hire a woman because they thought she was good, there always seemed to be something behind it.

I loved doing *SportsCenter* but it killed me. It was heavy lifting in a sense but many of us came from local TV, where we were given two minutes and treated like the stepchild of the news department — you know, "Sports is a necessary evil and you'll get two minutes in a thirty-minute show and be glad." So when you go to ESPN, it's 24/7 and it's all about sports.

We would try new things sometimes, like once we changed the music to this jazzy thing, and our switchboard really lit up with, "How dare you!" and, "My son can't fall asleep to that! He needs dah-dah-dah, dah dah dah!" That new theme lasted less than a month before we went back to the old one. I think that's when we realized people were actually watching. And then, athletes started saying, "Yeah, we'll probably get on *SportsCenter* tonight with that highlight."

Bristol was a big part of why it succeeded, there was nothing else to do. You didn't mind being in the building 24/7 because you almost didn't want to go home. There was nowhere to go, no one you were going to meet, so why not just work your tail off. We did get out sometimes. The White Birch was a little restaurant right nearby, and I thought I had hit bottom when I was there having Jell-O shots at two in the morning because there was absolutely nothing to do. That's when I was like, "What have I done? Why did I come here?"

CHARLEY STEINER:

We'd call each other the Mod Squad, only we were the negative photo of that. Instead of the black guy and white woman, we had Robin and two white guys. We worked together, Bob, Robin, and I, for six or seven years. Every day. The chemistry was just there. She used to call me Big Bro and I used to call her Little Sis. When Robin came over, the only big question was, "Okay, how are we going to configure the set?" So Robin and I were on the anchor desk and Bob had his own little set. The very first night we used it, I entitled Bob's set the General Store. We had a coordinating producer who told us we couldn't write that about the store, so I ad-libbed it.

MIKE McQUADE:

All the shows were competitive, and there was competition among producers. Now the ongoing joke was, "If news happened at seven o'clock, it was news to the six o'clock." But their show was a much more difficult show to do. Ours was just reacting to highlights. Just put them all in and figure out how to mix it up. But they got to go home at a decent hour and have a normal family life. We never had that option.

CHARLEY STEINER:

I was driving into work one morning and listening to WFAN, and they had like ten seconds of Carl Lewis butchering the national anthem. So I went in and told everyone I thought that would be a nice way to end the show if we could get a tape of it. So we get the tape in the morning, and I'm watching it and just losing it. I saw it maybe twenty-five or thirty times that day, and I'm figuring by the time I get on the air I would have laughed myself out. But when we go to it on the show, I'm feeling like the kid in the back of the class with the substitute teacher and trying to hold the laugh in. The more you hold it in, the more it's going to explode. So while the tape is airing, I'm laughing, the camera men are laughing, the teleprompter guy is laughing. And poor Jack Edwards, my coanchor that night, doesn't know what to do. The boogers are flying out of my nose, the tears are coming out of my eyes, and then I say, "That was the version written by Francis Scott Off-Key."

Now, the show is over and nobody has ever done that before—lose it so uncontrollably—and I go back up to the newsroom not sure if I've even got a job waiting for me. I walk into the newsroom and the whole place is on the fucking floor laughing. I didn't hear anything from management so I went home, not sure what my future would be after this unbelievable loss of composure. I turned on *SportsCenter* at eleven o'clock, and I think it may be the only time in the history of *SportsCenter* they actually repeated a segment from an earlier show.

JOHN LACK:

I was the guy who convinced Bornstein—and we almost came to blows about it—that he had to renew Chris Berman's contract, the first million-dollar deal. Steve was about to let him go. I said, "You can't. This is our franchise. You can't let him go. You're going to see him on CBS."

CHRIS BERMAN:

I told Steve he was nice to come to me two years early, two years before my contract expired. It was like the Space Odyssey deal. Steve was talking about a seven-year deal, and I said, "Seven years is 2000. Eight years is 2001—Stanley Kubrick." He says, "Good. We're done." We sent out the release and it was great. I was the first network person to be signed into the next century.

HOWARD KATZ:

Mark Shapiro and I go back a long way. I was at Ohlmeyer Communications, and then we sold the company to ESPN, and we had a talk show out of L.A. that Roy Firestone hosted. There was a guy that had worked for me for a long time, named Bud Morgan, and I said, "What I'd love you to do is spend a month observing everything at this talk show and tell me who's good and who's not." He called me one day and said, "You've got a real star here: this kid Mark Shapiro. He's a young Don Ohlmeyer; he's got Don's creative instincts and he's got Don's ambition." So we made him producer of the show.

ROY FIRESTONE:

Arthur Ashe was unbelievable. I really felt overmatched intellectually with Arthur Ashe. I mean he'd been all over the world, he'd seen all kinds of things, he had firsthand experiences on everything. And then when he announced that he had AIDS, not just HIV positive, but he was afflicted with the AIDS virus, it was world news, obviously. It was the first time that it had ever happened, and it really hit me because I had just interviewed him, and he looked very thin but I did not know and he did not want anyone to know. *USA Today* obviously did the exposé or whatever they called it. So I was shocked as I had just done this interview with him and I had called him and I said, now that it's come out, would you mind doing an interview again? And he said, "I can't do it right away; I promised I would do something else" — I believe it was for HBO. But he said, "I will do it soon." And we set up for New York City — I'll never forget this — on a Saturday. It was a hard-driving cold rain in New

York. And my camera crew couldn't find the place. And it was ten o'clock and I go into what I thought was going to be the studio, in a hotel, and there's no crew, there's no set-up. They got lost. As I see that, at five to ten, I see Arthur Ashe dripping wet. And he has AIDS. Dripping wet on a cold day in New York, he walks in, and I have the incredible pleasure of having to tell Arthur Ashe the crew didn't show up. Oh, God. So I walk up to him and I said, "Arthur, this could be the most humiliated I've felt in my professional life, but my crew's not here." He says to me, "Let's do it tomorrow." He goes back out into the rain, gets in the car, and drives home. The next day, there's a great interview with him. Now that, in and of itself, to me, elevates him to a level of his own. That's the kind of human being he was.

There were two things that really stuck out. He said, "The most difficult lesson I've learned about my life and life in general in all my travels, it was really hard for me to accept this, is that everybody wants to shit on somebody else. It doesn't matter what country it is. It doesn't matter what culture it is. Blacks shitting on other blacks. It's not just in America. It's all over the world." And he says, "It was really hard for me to accept the fact that everyone needs somebody to beat up on. And it really, really caused me a great deal of pain. And so I've devoted what life I have left to really focusing on that with which we can uplift each other, find some way to do it." Boy, it just really got me. And then he said, "I try to go from the global to the more immediate. I spend as much time as I can seeing my daughter." Her name was Camera, ironically, because his wife, Jean, was a photographer. "And Camera—the biggest pleasure of my day is to watch my daughter eat chocolate cake." And I said, "Why is that?" He said, "Because I can draw so much joy in my life seeing her joy, and to watch that child eat that chocolate cake with such abandon, with such love, and such joy, gives me the joy externally to see that."

CHRIS MYERS:

How I got *Up Close* was, I'd done some episodes of *SportsCenter* and *Baseball Tonight* at ESPN, but I really did want to live on the West Coast, and I kept offering, "Could we open up a late *SportsCenter* out there?" and heard, "No, no, that's never gonna happen"—which is funny because it finally did.

Roy Firestone owned *Up Close* at the time; he created it. But Roy was leaving and ESPN was taking over the show. They called me in and said, "We know you love the West Coast, we'd rather you stayed here to anchor *SportsCenter* or *Baseball Tonight*, but there's an opportunity if you want to go out there." And I said, "Absolutely." And they said, "Remember, don't think about this as a promotion or a raise or anything." ESPN had raised the profile of that show so it was kind of like coming in after a John Elway or replacing a Johnny Carson—not to that degree but in terms of the establishment of one guy with the show. That was the challenge ahead.

MARK SHAPIRO, *Executive Vice President of Programming and Production:*

Chris Myers, who they had flown in to take over *Up Close* when they parted ways with Roy Firestone, was as soft as you can be. Myers deep down wanted to be Johnny Carson or Pat Sajak. Those were his two favorite guys, Carson and Sajak. Every guy who came on the show, Myers wanted to befriend. So if you're Joe Montana, his goal was to befriend him and take him out to dinner so he could tell his friends that Montana was his buddy. He was so superficial and shallow. He couldn't hide it, and the audience quickly turned away from him after he took over for Firestone in 1996. The ratings dropped in half from what Firestone was pulling in. This was how I got my first big break. Howard Katz came to Los Angeles and moved me from Rome to Myers and *Up Close*. They made me producer and signed me to a three-year contract for fifty-five, sixty, sixty-five thousand. I was twenty-five years old so this was a big deal. On the other hand—a producer at NBC is making a buck-fifty at that time, so there is a price you pay. But my dad had said, "How long would it take to become a producer at NBC?" I said six years. So I stayed at ESPN and it took six months.

They told me, "We're going to either kill the show or you're going to turn him into a tough interviewer." I had the total support of Walsh and so I kind of became Walsh's project, if you will. He loved that I loved interviewing. He loved that I had a passion for research and journalism. He rewarded a hard work ethic. Whenever he was in town, we'd go out for a meal and just talk about the art of interviewing. We were both fascinated by it and we grew close during those one-on-one sessions.

After six months or so, the ratings went up significantly, almost doubled. Clearly people were taking a better liking to him, and it wasn't just because of better booking. Now don't get me wrong, I didn't change Myers, I improved him. I never succeeded in getting him to be a great interviewer, but by practically scripting him and getting in his ear a lot, he was much more structured and thoughtful. He would get pretty pissed off about it, because he thought I was trying to control him, but so be it. I had a mandate—or the show was going to be cancelled. I'm the producer, dammit.

And the turnaround success of that show opened the door for me to run *SportsCentury*.

BILL WOLFF:
SportsNight on ESPN2 was one of the more lavish and expensive failed experiments in the history of televised media. The restrictions couldn't have been fewer; the vision couldn't have been more blind; the

instruction couldn't have been more vague. There was *no idea*.

I went, around Christmastime '93 or '94, to St. Louis, my hometown, and I had three stories to do. One was a coach from the toughest, roughest, all-black high school in St. Louis — Central High, home of the Redwings. He was a big deal with a big Superfly hat in the seventies, very famous guy, but he had quit, and he was now coaching the Block Yeshiva High School, where the kids all wear yarmulkes. So it was hilarious. And they had become okay. They were now acceptable. They could play basketball because this Black Shadow had come to this all-Jewish school. So that was one story I told. And then the other one they sent me to do was that Brendan Shanahan, the hockey player of the St. Louis Blues, was reputed to know every single thing about *The Flintstones*, the old cartoon series. And I thought, "What am I going to do? What is this going to be? Two minutes on Brendan Shanahan? That is pure shit. In fact that's the stupidest story I've ever been sent to do and I'd been doing this for a while. This is the worst ever. What shall I do? What will I do?"

And, it's the night before I'm going to go, and I'm sitting in the breakfast room where I grew up, and I decide that I'm going to just make fun of the very fact that I'd been sent to do that story. And I'm going to be an over-the-top, super-self-serious idiot reporter, and I'm going to report the story that way.

And so my mother came up with the name of the reporter, Victor Star—"victor" meaning winner, and "star," well, speaks for itself. And so I went as Victor Star to do this super-drippy, over-the-top human interest story about a guy who likes *The Flintstones,* and I sort of told Brendan what I was doing, and he was a great guy, he was totally down with it and played it totally straight. And, in the meantime, I'm giving him the over-the-top Roy Firestone, Barbara Walters treatment about *The Flintstones.*

First we shot him being interviewed on mic, then we shot the cutaways, and there's one where I'm crying and another one where I'm gargling—and it's completely ridiculous. And I didn't tell anyone what I was doing. Then I went back to Los Angeles, where I was living, and I constructed this piece, the front half of which was over-the-top, idiotic, generic ESPN sports—"He's a wing-footed, bladed warrior fighting," all that crap. And then you get to the middle of it, you take a turn from the rock music into the drippiest possible piano funereal music, and the line is, "He's a complicated superstar." And then there's a closing stand-up where I'm standing on the ice at the arena in St. Louis and I was saying something about Brendan Shanahan and then they throw me a hockey puck and I catch it and I throw it back—it was to Keith Olbermann and to Suzy Kolber, they were the hosts, and I threw it back, saying, "Ken and Sally, back to you." And I sent it in—to my friend, Mark

Gross. He was the head producer on that show. And I said, "You're going to get this and, if you think it's wrong and bad, just destroy it, just don't fire me. It's not what you expect it's going to be." And I was nervous that they would say, "You're an asshole. You're out." So I sent it to him, then I waited and waited—like two weeks without hearing anything. I'm thinking, "I'm fucked. I got no job. What am I going to do? Am I going to move back in with my mom?" And then I got a call from him. He hadn't watched it right away and when he finally did, he said, "It's the greatest thing ever. We're going to send you around the country and you're going to do more of this. You're going to be Victor Star. And the first thing we want you to do is come to the second annual ESPY Awards."

I love John Walsh, and I have a fond feeling for ESPN. But I find the ESPY Awards objectionable. We already have awards. The World Series is an award. An MVP is an award. We don't need more awards. They make up this crap so they can fill time with it—the worst. And so it was the second annual crappy, shitty ESPY Awards. I went backstage with the assembled media, which was basically every small paper in Long Island, every small paper in New Jersey—that was who came to the ESPYs—and me, tuxedo, of course. Everybody else is just a schlub. There was no red carpet. There was an interview room after the guys would stand on stage and say,

"Here's the award." Then they'd come back and be interviewed. It was bad. "What a night it's been here at Madison Square Garden! Yes, it was the ESPYs. Extra special presentation—yes. Making it up. I'm Vic Star. Back to you."

I was sort of poking fun, I mean come on—human interest? First of all there is tremendous human interest in every single guy, right? Most of the guys who get there are amazing. They come from nothing and somehow they're so brilliant, they work hard, and they are great, and then they become stars. That's a great story. But it's a story that's utterly common. They all have that story. When they try to make these guys into complicated superstars, they're not that complicated. You know what they like to do? Play sports, make lots of money, and do lots of stuff. It's not that exciting. I mean they really don't have anything to say. Athletes generally, there are like a half dozen that—Charles Barkley is always fun to talk to but mainly, try Joe Montana as a football analyst, he was the biggest snore of all time. He's a brilliant football player and probably the nicest guy in the world, but he's a lousy TV analyst because jocks don't have anything to say. They're jocks. You can tell who the eight guys were who were great talkers; they're the ones who wound up on TV. The other ten thousand aren't worth talking to.

Then somebody had the bright idea that I should go to an Indy Car race at Nazareth, Pennsylvania, and give them the Vic Star treatment. So I was goofing around. And the guy who was announcing was the famous Voice of Indy Car, Paul Page, and I threw it back to "Page Paul," of course. And there was a vice president, a famous guy, a powerful guy who I don't really care to piss off, called Howard Katz. To this day I've never met Howard Katz. But apparently he was not a big humorist. He was very serious. And from what I understand he was a huge racing guy. He thought racing was the shit. And so here was this punk in November of 1994 making fun of NAS-CAR, making fun of Indy, making fun of everything. And so the word came down from on high: "No more Vic Star. I don't like this guy. Fuck him." If I weren't still a guy who needed to have a job, I'd have some choice words for Howard Katz to this day.

HOWARD KATZ:

I don't remember the exact event, but I do remember there was a point where I just said, "No more, no more. I can't take this anymore."

I don't think ESPN2 would've gotten launched when it did had it not been for John Lack's perseverance and his drive, and that was his contribution in—I think he was there under two years. It ultimately would've happened, but there was a sense of urgency and that is to his credit. But John acted as if he was the chief operating officer of ESPN and threw his weight around in ways that were not consistent with what others of us thought. John Lack was constantly trying to get me to fire John Walsh. He just didn't think very highly of John for whatever reason and he and I battled about that a lot.

JOHN LACK:

Steve, for all of his brilliance as a programmer, wasn't a great people-person, so I was also brought in to manage and develop people. What I'm the most proud of, I think, in my two, two-and-a-half years at ESPN, is many people that I nurtured have gone on to bigger and better jobs, not just Bratches and Bodenheimer, who were sort of on their way, but others as well. All these people had it in them but weren't getting the time spent on them to develop them as managers.

LESLEY VISSER, *Reporter:*

When CBS lost the NFL contract in 1993—they had televised the NFL since 1966—it was an enormous blow to all of us. Most people went to Fox, like my husband, Dick Stockton, John Madden, and Pat Summerall. I had always wanted to work, sometime in my career, for John Walsh. Everybody used to hang out at Runyons, a subterranean sports bar that had a literary feel—it was where Dan Jenkins wrote his "Ten Stages of Drunkenness"—and John Walsh was central to the party. Just about everyone wanted to work for him.

At the Super Bowl in 1993, John said, "Come on over to ESPN, with ABC. We'll have a buffet of things for you to cover and it can be in conjunction with a terrific contract with ABC." So it was sort of an end-of-the-rainbow opportunity for me because at ESPN I did college basketball, figure skating, horse racing, *SportsCenter*, *Monday Night Countdown*, and *NFL GameDay*. And on ABC, I got to do the Super Bowl, the U.S. World Figure Skating championships, the Triple Crown, the World Series, and *Monday Night Football*.

PETER ENGLEHART:

Bornstein would ask very pointed questions. Back then the budget was fairly large—seventy to ninety pages, just on the cost side, and everybody was responsible for a certain portion of it. You had to come in there so totally prepared that you would have to memorize a lot of stuff just to anticipate his questions. And it was pretty easy to get tripped up. He believed the cost side of the business had to be run frugally so that there was no margin, that it was essential you know it inside and out. So instead of looking at the bottom line of a race, he would want to know what the cabling costs were at North Wilksboro. "What percentage of your cabling costs went up?" Nobody can answer that question, and so he starts to roll his eyes. At that point, it was better to say, "I don't know, but I'll get back to you," than to try to make up an answer. That's when he would chew you out publicly. But what he was trying to get at was, we could not afford to spend more money than we had. Money was very tight back then and the bottom line of the cost side had to be managed so frugally.

LESLEY VISSER:

At CBS we had the ASCAP contract so we could use any music we wanted for pieces, and we would go out and shoot a lot of footage. When I first came to ESPN, features were more about the brilliance of the producer in the edit room than getting original material. Then, pretty soon after I got there, John Walsh developed this show called *Backstage,* which was very different for ESPN. I would focus on just one athlete and have one topic. Usually, there were five producers you had to serve, and a lot of things to go over. That wasn't the case with this. I went horseback riding with Emmitt Smith, and I went bowling with Jarell Benefi. I remember Curtis Martin collected art and we went through an art gallery; Chris Stolman, the defensive end for the 49ers, played the saxophone for me at night with the moon behind us and it was a beautiful shot. There were so many opportunities — it was a professional bonanza.

KELLY NAQI, *Reporter:*

I worked on a story with Bob Ley about a former Olympic swim coach who had a habit of sleeping with his swimmers through the course of his career. And I got some swimmers to talk to me about their sexual relationships with him. I scheduled an interview with him in Florida. But whoever it was in the Sports and Information Department who arranged it never asked me what the interview was about, which really doesn't happen any more these days. But this was back in the day, when they never asked. So we flew down, and were driving to the school, and between me scheduling the interview and us driving down there, I had interviewed a ton of the coach's former swimmers throughout his swimming career and some of what we discussed got back to the coach, and then Florida said, "What is this?" So they cancelled the interview. And did their own internal investigation and fired the coach—on the day or the day before our report aired.

JEAN McCORMICK:

Shortly before the 1992 presidential election, *Outside the Lines* aired a special on presidents and sports. There were all sorts of interesting stories: Gerald Ford was a major college football star; JFK was actually a better golfer than Eisenhower but hid it for fear of backlash; Nixon came up with a play for the Redskins. We submitted requests to the Clinton and Bush [senior] camps for interviews. Clinton had recognized the power of cable and its ability to reach highly targeted demographics. He had already played the saxophone on MTV. His camp agreed immediately and we shot the interview and promoted the show through the clips. The Bush camp initially turned it down because—well, because he was a sitting president of the United States, and sports cable did not seem fitting. To his tremendous credit, Bob Ley kept going back to them. And they kept saying no.

About two weeks before the election, when Bush was way behind in the polls, they started to see the Clinton ads. And someone in their camp realized that ESPN was an incredible conduit to a very sweet demographic for them, men eighteen to forty-nine. Bob Ley received a call on a Wednesday or Thursday from the White House, which basically stated, "You are doing this interview"—technically we had to because of equal access—and "it will have to be on Air Force One on Sunday," as they had no other time on the schedule. And so ESPN interviewed the president on Air Force One. While President Bush was extraordinarily gracious, a college baseball star, and an avid fan who had actually met Babe Ruth at Yale, the last-minute nature of the interview posed challenges. They had forgotten to schedule a makeup person; the harsh light was unforgiving. The Blue Jays had won the World Series the night before. They kept trying to set up a call between the president and Cito Gaston, the manager; the call kept failing while we kept shooting. Still, it was an amazing moment not just for ESPN but also for cable, as it recognized the ability of various channels to deliver targeted demographics. Today we live in a world where the sitting POTUS fills his brackets out on ESPN; then it did seem a bit extraordinary that they let our cameras on Air Force One.

MATT SANDULLI:

I was basically just a kid, been in the business for only three or four years. Having grown up a Mets fan, I was the guy who was given the assignment to produce Tom Seaver's Hall of Fame piece. So here I am, sitting in Tom Seaver's backyard in Greenwich, Connecticut.

I knew of his reputation, that he'd big-time the shit out of you and just throw you off in a heartbeat, so I wanted to make sure everything went perfectly. There were a bunch of different interviews scheduled, and we were the last one of the day. He was not particularly thrilled to keep going, but when we sat down, he said, "I got twenty minutes, guys, okay?" Well, okay. So I'm sitting there asking him questions and, long story short, we go like forty-five minutes. I've had the time of my life. And by the time we were done, the big-time edge had gone away and he was genuinely reminiscing about his career. Then it turned into the most bizarre thing, because the camera man started talking to him about his garden, and all of a sudden, we're in his garden playing with the squash that he was growing. Then Nancy Seaver asks, "You guys want some lemonade or something?" It was just surreal.

Within a month and a half's time after that, I get Pete Rose at a boat show, George Brett in Kansas City, and Frank Thomas who, at the time, was a young stud. All half-hour, forty-five-minute interviews. Talking baseball with Pete Rose, Tom Seaver, George Brett, and Frank Thomas. Are you kidding me? I was in heaven. It was why I got into this business. It was the greatest thing that ever happened to me.

JEAN McCORMICK:
Anyone who stayed at ESPN more than six months had to have a deep love of sports, and many times that transcended the gender stuff. That's the true beauty of sports. I was the first female studio producer, but honestly, it was a bigger deal for me to move to northwest Connecticut and out of New York than it was to be the first female producer. There certainly were some wonderful women who were in the newsroom. Having Robin [Roberts] start at the same time I did was fabulous.

At ESPN, you find the other people who cried when a team lost. If you had never cried when your team lost, you really shouldn't work at ESPN. You just won't get it. But if you cry like I did when the Bruins lost to the Flyers, which still hurts all those years later, if you're able to really touch into that feeling, then it's a dream job and a dream place to work.

KARL RAVECH, *Anchor:*

When I first started in '93, one of the first people I ended up doing the two thirty in the morning *SportsCenter* with was Craig Kilborn, who, of course, was as different as anybody that's ever been on this network. I recall going into a meeting with Steve Anderson, who was running *SportsCenter* after a particular show, and saying, "What is going on here? I really don't understand what he's doing and it strikes me that this isn't exactly what ESPN was about." But over a period of months working together, we developed a good friendship and I finally understood what his style was and it clearly appealed to a lot of people. He was always being his own self, but there was always shtick involved. What I realized in all of this was, you needed to have people who are funny and entertaining and kind of offbeat. Kilborn was one of those, but I certainly wasn't going to go there because I didn't have the authority to do it.

MICHAEL MANDT:

I had come from HBO, which was Monday to Friday, nine to five. We had a gym in the office. It was the country club of sports and a great place to work with lots of smart people. But it didn't own your life. ESPN is really a mentality, and unlike any other place

I've ever seen. People are very competitive, and it starts at the beginning. As soon as you start out, you have to make it, either you're good enough or you don't have a job. So right out of the womb, you're taught to compete, and do everything you can possibly do. Competitiveness and drive exist from the bottom up, and that's part of the culture. So people really care about what they're doing, and that makes for a very successful place.

The first highlight I ever cut was two weeks into the job: August of '93, Twins at the Royals. Totally generic, nothing special, not that important as a highlight. Unlike a lot of kids there who had majored in communications and had taken lots of TV classes, I hadn't taken anything. So this was the first time I would be doing anything—on national TV, for ESPN, and in a matter of minutes. This highlight was supposed to be forty-five seconds, average time, for somewhere in the middle of the show, around 11:15 p.m. Linda Cohn had the highlight. Now you could say, this should be pretty easy—isolation of a batter, isolation of the pitcher, a play, another play, a react, and you're out. But I had no clue how long a play would take and the first play I cut down was a triple and I never thought, "Wow, a triple will take up twenty-five seconds of the highlight." So my timing was all off, and I totally screwed up how the story was supposed to be told. Now I'm looking at the clock and we were always told highlights never miss air, and I'm getting a call from the producer: "Is it going to make it?" My editor slapped together a highlight that didn't tell much of a story, with shots that were not very good and weren't timed properly, and my writing was chicken scribble. It was arguably one of the worst highlights ever to air on the network; I'm pretty confident of that. Anyway, Linda does the highlight and did the best she could with it and, after the show, she saw me and said, "Hey, listen, I know it's your first day. But, kid, you gotta do better than that." Then she walked away. She was 100 percent right. I knew I had to do better. And that's the type of thing you start sweating about when you go home. There's a lot of pressure. To make matters even worse, when your highlight airs, all your peers are watching it and judging it, saying, "Oh, boy, that was really good," or "Who cut that? That was terrible."

Pretty soon after that, it was the first Saturday in college football that year, so we had baseball going on along with a million college football games. It was a really busy day and I was assigned to cut one minute of highlights for halftime at Minnesota at Penn State. Penn State had scored a touchdown and Kerry Collins was the quarterback, and I wrote on the shot sheet, "Kerry Collins to Mark Ingram," even though it was Bobby Ingram. I wrote "Mark" because I'm from Michigan and I'm thinking Michigan State. So Chris Fowler reads the highlight and says Mark Ingram. The second I hear it, I just cringed. It was like, "Oh, my God, did I write Mark Ingram?" And people were looking at me like, "You messed up." Chris came in talking pretty loudly—"Who did this, who wrote this"—and chewed me out in front of a lot of people for writing Mark Ingram instead of Bobby Ingram. But I had no problem with it. He was 100 percent right. Some people might get upset in that situation if they were being yelled at, but I didn't mind. I had done the wrong thing.

JIM ROME, *Anchor:*

I was doing live TV for an hour a night on ESPN2 without a net and I was coming in after a four-hour radio show every day that I was hosting by myself. The only way I was going make it in the business is if I was very straightforward and not afraid. When you're not a former athlete and you don't have a great voice, who cares what you think? Why would anybody hire you? And I used to think about that a lot. Like, if I don't come up with an answer to that question, I probably won't make it. So my style was, I wasn't going to pull any punches, I wasn't going to be afraid, and I felt like I had to ask the questions that people wanted to hear.

One night, this kid comes in after I'd been there for about a week and he says, "You probably don't know me. My name is Mark Shapiro. I'm a production assistant." He said, "Let me ask you something. If you do a four-hour radio show and then a one-hour

TV show, how do you prepare for the guest who is going to be on TV?" I said, "I haven't really figured it out yet, to be honest with you." He says, "Well, Warren Moon's going to be on tomorrow. Can I help you out with that—can I make a few notes for you?" I said, "Knock yourself out, kid." He comes back the very next day with this perfectly crafted ten-page research packet—questions, research, the whole nine yards. He says, "Look it over and tell me what you think." So I read through the thing, and it is unbelievably brilliant. It was perfect. So then he says, "Hey, listen, if that was all right, can I do it again?" I said, "Absolutely."

So then we were at the Super Bowl in Atlanta and we got this big interview with Jesse Jackson. Everybody was fired up that we had him. So I ask Jackson a question and he just starts to filibuster. And all of a sudden in my ear I hear this strange voice—not the guy who's normally talking to me—and the guy says, "Don't ask him another question, he's killing us!" I'm like, "Who the hell was that?" We finish the show, I go back and ask, "Who was that?" Shapiro says, "It was me." How's that for balls? I mean the guy was a PA. He'd been there for just several months, and he literally grabbed the mic in the truck and got in my ear! Everybody else was just excited we had Jesse Jackson, but Mark was thinking about what was best for the show.

It was an absolutely amazing time in both of our

careers, because we were both so young and hungry and pretty motivated, and we were out there and didn't have a lot of experience. We were both raw. We were both green and we're out there doing live TV for an hour a night. I mean these were really, really heady times, just amazing. Every single night we had an amazing experience. It was incredible. I remember calling my agent one day and telling him, "I just met the most remarkable kid. This guy one day will run this network." And I had an agent who was like, "You're probably going to meet a lot of guys like that as you get further on." I said, "No, you don't understand. This guy is about the most unique, different guy I've ever met. You have no idea the kind of charisma and presence this kid has at twenty-three. I've never seen anybody like him. I'm telling you one day this guy is going to run this network or more." And my agent just laughed at me—like, "Okay, whatever you say." But sure enough, that's exactly what happened. I mean, literally from day one, you could tell this guy was separate from the pack. Number one, he's the smartest guy in the room; number two, he's the most charismatic guy in the room; number three, he's the most loyal guy in the room. I mean, it's amazing. If he produced you and you had success, he was unbelievably ecstatic for you and the show and the team—which was a really unique quality even for a guy at that age. And he inspired incredible loyalty because he was so loyal to *you*. He was smart, he was loyal, he was incredibly ambitious, he was fiercely competitive.

I'm telling you, within a few months, he was producing the show and under contract. I called my agent one day and said, "I just met this most remarkable kid named Mark Shapiro. I mean, this guy one day will run this network."

MARK SHAPIRO:

Roy, who is a terrific interviewer, was the king of, "people will say," or, "one will say," where Rome would just say, "Here's why you're a malcontent. Tell me why I'm wrong." Say what you want about Rome but he's a tough interviewer. He'll ask anything, even if it gets him beat up.

JIM ROME:

After my contract with ESPN lapsed, I went to FX, which was just getting into sports, and I cohosted something called *The FX Sports Show,* which ran one season. Then I went to Fox Sports Net for five years. At the end of that, when my deal was coming up again, Mark Shapiro picks up the phone. By now he's running the whole place. He calls me up and says, "Jim, it's time for you to come home. It's time for you to come back to the family. You need to do this." It was really amazing considering where we started, what I had gone through, what he'd achieved. For him to pick up the phone and say, quote, "It's time for you to come home. It's time for you to come back to the family," was really amazing. So he came out to L.A. on whatever business he had. We met in a hotel — my agent, him, a couple other people. We sat down, and they negotiated the deal on a napkin in fifteen minutes and, just like that, I was back in the family.

JIM EVERETT, *Professional Football Player:*

I get a call from my agent right after I was traded to New Orleans. It was a quick conversation. He said, "Hey, you're going to L.A. and you're going to be on ESPN." I thought, *Great.* So I'm going to the studio thinking I was going to be meeting with Roy Firestone. By the time I get there, I find out that no, I'm going to be on ESPN2 with Jim Rome. So I ask, "What's going on here? Isn't this the guy that's been bad-mouthing me on radio the whole time?" So some guy sits me down and says, "Hey listen, this is a big show, this is Jim Rome, I know he's had some comments about you being like Chris Evert and I'm going to let you know, he told me he's going to bring it up, but he wants to move on, move forward, he knows you're excited about going to New Orleans, and that will be the focus. He promises." I'm like, "That's fine, I'm a big boy, I can handle it, I'm moving on, I got a great situation with New Orleans."

In the segment before me, he was dogging Gordie Howe, and I'm thinking, "How does someone who's never played sports dog Gordie Howe? He's a hockey legend!" I knew I was in trouble when I went out to the set to meet Jim, and he would not look me in the eye. And I was like, "Huh?" He finally says, "You sit here," so I sit on this chair, which was like a first-grade chair. I felt like I was sitting on some Vietnamese toilet.

JIM ROME:

I had been on the radio calling him Chris Evert. Mind you, this was not something I made up, it was something his teammates were doing behind his back. So I started doing it, and the next I know, he's booked on the show. My feeling was, I can't *not* say to a guy's face what I've said about him on the radio. I've said it. I'm going to own it. And I'm going to say it to his face. Of course my problem was, I *kept* saying it to his face.

JIM EVERETT:

I start turning my chair because I'm so uncomfortable at the table. The interview starts, nothing is planned, and then he just starts calling me Chris, over and over. I warned him, and then I warned him again, and realized, "He ain't gonna stop." That's when I went off. I'm like, "That's too far." I gave him the final warning—like, "take a station break," whatever. I thought he would take the hint but he was so immature at the time, he said it again, and I just went off on him. I hit the table and I start going toward him. I think it shocked him, and he starts backing off. Well, the stage is about eighteen inches high. So as soon as he gets to the edge, he falls down off the stage and I'm like going at him, and he curls up like a little bunny. And that's when you can't see him on the camera. I'm not doing anything to a guy who's down; he's all covered up, in the fetal position. And that's when all the camera guys and stuff come in and I'm just like, "Oh, my God." I don't ever do anything like that. This was just so unlike me but he put me in a position that—I think America can relate to it. It infuriates me when people say that was staged. Why would Jim Everett ever agree to that? No, it wasn't. I'm not an actor. I am so not an actor.

MARK SHAPIRO:

No, it was not staged. On my child's life, not a shred of truth to the idea it was staged. Not even a shred.

JIM EVERETT:

The next segment he came in on TV and said, "Yeah, I had the right to do that"—he kept going with this immature part. All I really wanted from Jim at some point in time is for him to say, "Hey, I'm sorry, I was wrong, went too far." But he never did. When it went down, I got a ton of letters from kids in classrooms about standing up for your own rights, and someone doesn't have a right to do that type of stuff. I had so much support.

JIM ROME:

The whole thing unraveled on me. That was something that got away from me. It was not a good thing. I'm not defending it in any way. This happened to me fifteen years ago and it always comes up and I have never once answered that question by saying, "You know what, that was a long time ago." Are we gonna beat this dead horse forever? Because I kind of resent that when athletes do that. It's part of who you are. You need to be accountable to it, responsible to it, and that's why I am.

It's like people always say, it's kind of trite and it's kind of clichéd, but you know who your friends are when that goes down. After it happened, I pulled aside Janet (who is now my wife, but wasn't at the time) and Mark Shapiro and told them, "This is going to get so much worse before it gets any better. We gotta dig in. We need to grind this thing out." I was a national punching bag. Katie Couric was talking about me, *Saturday Night Live,* I mean, everybody got in line to punch me in the mouth. And understandably so. But I should mention that ESPN didn't rip me off the air. They didn't fire me. They didn't suspend me. They didn't discipline me. They definitely stood by me.

JIM EVERETT:

There was a large U.S. corporation last year that wanted to use that film and they approached me and I'm like, "Yeah, go ahead, I'm good with it, let bygones be bygones, go ahead!" It was kind of good for what they were selling, and it would have been a good six-digit deal for Jim and for me. But he nixed it. And I'm like, "God! What's the problem? Why not?" Well, clearly he's recognized he does not come across well at all. It's amazing his career survived it.

JIM ROME:

Here we are now fifteen years later and I hate to still be known for that one moment.

SUZY KOLBER:

After the Rome/Jim Everett thing, it got even worse at ESPN2. I was horrified. And I just remember thinking, "This is going to be a bad day at work. This is going to make things difficult for all of us." And it did. We were fighting for credibility and respect. That was certainly not a way to build it.

JOHN LACK:

I thought it was fabulous. He told us he was going to do it beforehand and Everett really went crazy, and no one expected that. He really thought Everett was a pussy, for all the reasons he said, and to egg him on was right out of late-night talk-show stuff. It was like Andy Kaufman, David Letterman kind of stuff. No one got hurt. This wasn't the Indians and the Pakistanis here. But God, the press we got—and the press *he* got! That put ESPN2 on the map for a couple of weeks.

JOHN WALSH:

I thought it was a complete embarrassment. Exactly what I was worried about with this guy. Mark Shapiro called and got me out of my fantasy baseball draft in New York to tell me what happened. He just said, "Hey, you should know this happened. He walked off the set. There was confrontation. It was physical. The whole works. We gotta get PR in the room. What are we going to say? What are we going to do?" I don't think he was elated. I think he was nervous. This was a new experience for him, and he was a young guy, so he was kind of looking for what's the best direction here. We all got together and talked with Bornstein, and we decided we weren't going to suspend or fire him. I'm not going to give you what my opinion was on that.

GARY MILLER:

Whenever I think about ESPN2, I think about the American League Championship Series in '93 right after they started. We're at the playoffs in Comiskey Park. Toronto and the White Sox. We were going to give them some live stuff before the game. So I'm riding in the cab from downtown Chicago to Comiskey with Peter Gammons; his personal producer, Debbie Robeleski; and Matt Sandulli, who was field producing at that time with me. Peter's just ranting about this ESPN2—what a joke it is and John Lack is turning the place into MTV and he's just going off. So we get to the stadium and Peter's supposed to do an afternoon live shot for that *SportsNight* thing—you know, the one with Keith in his leather jacket? So they're getting ready to throw to Peter and Matty says, "Peter, they want you to take your tie off." And he's like, "I'm not taking my tie off." "Well, John Lack called and he wants you to take your tie off. This is ESPN2." So Peter goes, "Fuck this. This is fucking ridiculous. Why don't they just dress me up like a fucking clown?" And Peter could explode better than anyone I've ever worked with. I mean, he could blow a geyser. So he takes the tie off, and thirty seconds later they're live and he does this flawless, perfect, relaxed, conversational storytelling report. And then as soon as the camera's off and the live shot's over he goes back into his rant. So the next day, we get ready to do our thing and Matty and I are sitting there ready for Peter to go on, and as soon as they throw to him Matty and I turn around and we've got these big red clown noses on staring at him from the camera. Then we got a bunch more so that whenever we went out after games and stuff during that postseason, everyone had a clown nose.

SUZY KOLBER:

SportsNight only lasted eighteen months. I was really disappointed that they weren't going to give it more of a shot because I was hosting with Stuart, which I loved. *SportsNight* had changed five different times since it was launched. If we had wanted to be young and irreverent, we should have done it from someplace else. There had been rumors early on that we were going to do it in San Diego. That might have worked. I feel like there just wasn't a clear-cut vision — that there was never a clear-cut vision from the time we went on our first assignment and were told to just make it different.

STEVE BORNSTEIN:

Lack was a mistake. I love John Lack, but one of the things I learned with him was to be careful hiring people you like or people who are your friends. Not unlike MTV, we don't do well hiring outside of the culture. John had a different point of view, which I thought was more critical to establishing ESPN2 than John Walsh, so I empowered John Lack. John Lack probably gets more strikes against him than he deserves. As a guy that I could bounce ideas off and to keep me thinking big, he was the best. But managing people and trying to lead and galvanize the organization was not his thing. I quickly had to change that, but it had nothing to do with Lack or Walsh, it was the fact that we realized that ESPN2 was just another extension of ESPN. Originally, we thought we had to differentiate it.

At the end of the day, I did fire John Lack and it was the right thing to do. I forget how long his tenure was. I think he was there for all of three years. The mistake was in my hiring him. Look, he created MTV and deserves the acknowledgment. But he didn't *execute* MTV. He was incredibly important to me in keeping the focus that I had to launch ESPN2. Other than that, a mistake.

JOHN LACK:

It wasn't my vision that was running this company. It was my personality and a vision that I tried to get other people to share. At that level in business, as you know, you get things done through other people, you don't do them yourself. It wasn't my company. I didn't own it. I was brought in to develop it and they kind of let me do it. In two and a half years, I had very few confrontations.

BILL CREASY:

In my humble opinion, in the history of both ESPN and ESPN2, John's personality and his drive were a pretty big thread at that time.

I always firmly believed that if Steve left, John

Lack was the perfect president. I think in the end a lot of people wanted to like him, but Lack turned them off with his forceful personality. I always called John 1-A, so whenever he came by, he would say "1-A checking in," as in "the heir apparent." He hurt himself with his obvious, maybe self-deprecating "Oh, I'm just 1-A," but hidden in there, people would read that he really wanted to be president after Steve left—if Steve ever left.

JOHN LACK:

In the end, Steve was intimidated by me doing it, so he finally said, "Look, I'm going to get rid of this guy; I don't need him anymore." You're always going to have conflicts with people in business, but especially if you're not from the original culture. But I can't complain. I can't look back, nor should anybody else, and say, "Jesus, Lack didn't get a chance to do what he wanted." I pretty much did it all. I hired Keith and Suzy against all their objections.

HOWARD KATZ:

I think John came in there believing that the culture that existed at ESPN was not the right culture, and was a culture that John Walsh had built to a large extent in terms of the work ethic and the way you treat people, and John was just about results. John Walsh was very concerned about the way you went about things—and that was an enormous clash there. John Lack was a culture shock to what had been created at ESPN.

The year 1994 brought another major change for ESPN—this time, in the way the network promoted itself and its image. There'd been plenty of promos over the years, but nothing like the campaign about to be launched. Even the choice of ad agency was a break from conservative company tradition; ESPN called upon the maverick firm of Wieden + Kennedy, based in faraway Portland, Oregon, and globally acclaimed for its artfully soft-sell "Just Do It" Nike campaign.

In a sense, the campaign constituted a seismic paradox: the network that considered the star system to be anathema was going to be putting its performers in the spotlight over and over again, hardly a gateway to anonymity. But the hope was that the brand would be the real star of the campaign. It was unlike anything ever before attempted in Bristol, so naturally there was opposition and skepticism at first encounter.

JUDY FEARING, *Senior Vice President of Marketing:*

Wieden + Kennedy wrote this great white-paper and it became our mantra when developing advertising. We never look at ESPN as a television network; ESPN is a *sports fan*. We should always approach the advertising, whether it's of an event or of our own shows, like we are a sports fan talking about sports as opposed to a network promoting a show. And that was really front and center in everything that we did. Using Wieden's words, and trying to stay true to that, I think helped the advertising go from what had already been very good to something that I think was great. When I first got to ESPN, I went around and talked to John Walsh, Howard Katz, and Steve Bornstein, and one of the key things they told me was that the marketing organization needed to embrace sports and, in their opinion, promote some of our proprietary programming. We were promoting "tune in to sporting events," but it was really time to start making people aware of some of the home-grown programs that ESPN had—*Baseball Tonight, NFL GameDay,* which I think is now *Countdown.* So my team, along with Wieden + Kennedy, got together and said the real jewel is *SportsCenter* because it's on all the time. It's on all evening. It's in reruns in the morning. This was the one that we really should invest in and focus on.

So we sat in my office and brainstormed. And the guys from Wieden + Kennedy said, "We see it on TV, we just want to go there and hang out." So a group of creatives went and hung out in Bristol and watched *SportsCenter.* They watched it from the preproduction meeting. They watched the stories being written. They watched the guys put on their makeup. They watched the tapes being handed in at the last minute—this was back in the day of tapes—just in time to get on the air. And after they'd been there for a while, they had an idea. They said that for a sports fan, being in Bristol and watching *SportsCenter* being produced is the single best sporting event you can ever go to. It's mecca. Because you're watching all the highlights. You're watching guys talk about sports. You're watching guys debate what are the best events to put on for the night. You've got them trying to write their stuff. And then you've got the anxiety of trying to put it all together and put it on live and get it all down to ninety to sixty minutes, whatever the show's length was. It's the best thing that's on TV. And they said that helping the consumer see what goesintoputtingonthisshowisgold,andthattheywanted to create a campaign that gives the viewer an eye on what the making of *SportsCenter* is. And that was really the genesis of the idea. They said, "What we want to do is do it in a way that's a little bit of what we call the 'mockumentary.' We want to shoot it documentary-style, but we want to have some fun with it. We want to make people know that this is the mecca of sports, so that athletes might hang out at *SportsCenter*, even mascots might hang out at *SportsCenter*. But it's about the show and the guys who are at the anchor desk. And it will give consumers a little eye into what it's like to be there."

And that's how it started. I remember going with my compatriots Al and Mike and talking to John Walsh about it, and he loved it. I remember being in

Aspen at one of Steve Bornstein's staff retreats, sitting next to him at dinner one night, and him looking at me and asking if we were going to "make our announcers stars." And I said, "No, because it's about the show." He says, "No, that's what you're going to do—you're going to make Keith and Dan Patrick and Craig Kilborn stars." I repeated, "No, it's about the show." And he says, "Don't worry; it's a brilliant idea. But you're still going to make them stars and that's going to cost me money." And we were very lucky that Keith Olbermann and Dan Patrick and Craig Kilborn were among the anchors, because they could pull it off.

HARRIET SEITLER:

We focused Wieden + Kennedy on how do we build this emotional connection, and we identified *SportsCenter* as the secret sauce—and then, separately, how do we create this other identity for a network?

ALAN BROCE, *Director of Advertising:*

I had been an advertising director at Pepsi. When I saw that ESPN hired Wieden, I was a huge fan of Wieden and the Nike campaign, so I'm like, "God, man, I want to be a part of that." I love ESPN, and I love Wieden + Kennedy. I went down and met with Harriet Seitler and she said, "You seem really interesting and great—and I'm leaving." And I thought,

"Well, there goes my chance." But she forwarded my letter to Steve Bornstein, Steve brought me down, and I met with him, and we hit it off pretty well. He thought I was too young—I was twenty-nine or thirty at the time—but he hired me anyway.

When I walked into the situation, I expected that people were doing cartwheels down the hall about Wieden + Kennedy's work. But not everybody was thrilled with Wieden + Kennedy. Not everybody was thrilled with the shift to wanting to build a brand at the expense of just promoting a show, then telling what time a game is going to come on. And so it was a little rough sledding there.

JUDY FEARING:

We sold male eyeballs to advertisers. That's the business that we were in, and we sold at a price premium because men are hard to reach. Advertisers are not going to pay us a premium to reach women, they could get women much, much cheaper on other television networks. Men are more elusive. That's the value that we brought to the table.

KEVIN PROUDFOOT, *Executive Creative Director, Wieden + Kennedy*:

The *SportsCenter* campaign came about envisioning ESPN, as absurd as it seemed, as sort of the center of the sports universe. Because at that time, no one else was broadcasting sports twenty-four hours a day.

And so it seemed this was the twenty-four-hour, seven-day-week home of sports, and if it's the home of sports, it's the center of this universe that expands out to all these games and all these athletes and all these personalities, and doesn't it make sense that when you go behind the scenes at *SportsCenter* and you're in the hallways or you're in the cafeteria, that athletes and mascots and coaches are there too, wandering around, doing whatever it is that they're doing as they pass through on the way to the next game and whatnot? And so that was the impetus for that whole campaign.

They will come to us with athletes they think would be great to get in the campaign, but at the same time, people who work on it are huge sports fans. And if they have an idea of something that's happening in the world of sports right now, then we concept a spot and present it to ESPN. After we've presented a few rounds of scripts to them and decide on which ones we want to move forward with, ESPN will start reaching out to the athletes to see if they want to be involved in the campaign. One of the interesting things that's happened over time is that having your own *SportsCenter* spot as an athlete has become a little bit of a badge. These athletes come out, they come out of college, they're making a ton of money, and there's not a lot that they can't buy. But having a *SportsCenter* spot—that's your own, like being part of that, it's obviously a cool thing to have.

HANK PEARLMAN, *Commercial Director:*

I came up with *This Is* SportsCenter for the campaign. Obviously, they'd been saying "This is *SportsCenter*" for years, at the end of the show. The derivation was Spinal Tap — *This Is Spinal Tap, This Is* SportsCenter. We needed a line for the end of the spot that kind of cemented the idea that it was a fake documentary about *SportsCenter*, so you know, *This Is Spinal Tap* was the fake documentary about that.

I remember presenting the campaign in script form to a roomful of anchors up in Bristol, a room full of talent, before we'd shot anything, basically to get them on board. And nobody was laughing, nobody was smiling; it was tense. I got the sense that all the talent was thinking, How is this going to affect me? How many spots am I going to get? Is management going to let me do what I want to do? The very beginning, before we shot anything, none of them wanted to show up. None of them wanted to show up on their day off. None of them wanted to do it. After they saw the spots, there was never a problem again. I think they saw how good it was for them and for the show.

HARRIET SEITLER:

Lenny Kennedy came up with "This Is *SportsCenter*." I mean, maybe it was John Lack, but I think it was Wieden + Kennedy.

We really were focused on, okay, how can we create something that is a definitional place on ESPN? What one vehicle can we use to create a singular statement about ESPN that would change the way people think about ESPN? And because *SportsCenter* was on so much and because there was so much to mine within *SportsCenter*, we really focused on that to say, "This is ESPN — *SportsCenter* is ESPN."

HANK PEARLMAN:

When they first showed the early *SportsCenter* commercials to all the talent, Keith Olbermann's reaction was, "When is the Craig Kilborn action figure coming out?" I think it was because we'd done a lot of Kilborn commercials the first round and I think Olbermann was taking notes and I think he was very conscious of who got how many commercials. A lot of people didn't want ESPN to do the campaign. There was a fear from the beginning that it was going to put too much emphasis on the talent. That was Bornstein's thing: "You're going to make stars out of these guys and then they're going to think it's all about them." And he was right — to a certain extent.

For better or worse, the talent kind of fell into roles. Bob Ley was a great straight man to deliver the setup, like the documentary-style interview. In one of my favorite spots, it's about the kid who comes out of school too early and then becomes a *SportsCenter* anchor and then Bob Ley sets it up: "We grab the kids right out of high school, you know." Bob Ley is the ultimate straight man.

Charley Steiner was one of my favorite guys. I loved him. He was a go-to guy in terms of comedy. He knew it and he was good at it. He knew we could cut to Charley either wearing or doing something silly. Then Dan and Keith understood the comedy really well and they could do both things; they could set up a spot or they could act with one of the athletes. Dan was great in all the spots. We did a "we are the world" kind of thing. We did a spot in the first round where he's confronted in the stairwell by professional wrestlers who are mad because they never show professional wrestling highlights on *Sports-Center*, and Dan did some funny improv with these seven-foot-tall professional wrestlers. Dan was great, I loved Dan.

Keith was injured in the Gordie Howe spot. He let us know the next day that Gordie Howe had stick-checked him in the back and he was a little upset about that. We just kind of heard that he had gotten hurt doing the spot. I wasn't privy to the conversation he had with management. Keith had opinions about the spots, but he also got it. He understood the sense of humor. He's a big Monty Python fan, and he understood comedy pretty well. But he did think Craig got too many spots in the first round. A lot of people felt that.

CHARLEY STEINER:

I remember the first time in particular that I got recognized after the commercials started airing. It made me laugh and pissed me off at the same time. I was running through the airport and—you remember that Holyfield commercial, "Come get your whopping"?—I had this five-year-old kid, who came up to my knee cap, tap me and say, "Come get your whopping!" I wanted to drop-kick him through the goal post of life.

But my personal favorite spot was being traded to *Melrose Place*. I was traded for Andrew Shue. He was the young buck who became the big star on *Sports-Center;* I became Bobby the pool boy. It was the only time in my life where I wore a sleeveless shirt, and I thought it was so cool being out there. Of course, the woman I did the commercial with had no idea who the fuck I was. She was thinking it was the end of her career.

JUDY FEARING:

I knew we had struck gold when one day I was on the phone with a friend of mine, John Shue, who was in L.A. to see his sister Elizabeth at the Academy Awards for *Leaving Las Vegas*, and he says to me, "I'm with my brother Andrew. He's interested in doing the spot." Then my assistant came in and told me Bill Cosby was holding for me on the other line. I thought it was a joke, but I said good-bye to John, picked up the phone, and it was Bill Cosby. He said, "I have some ideas for you for your *SportsCenter* commercials."

I went to John Walsh once and asked him if he knew when Roger Clemens, who was with Boston at the time, was going to be in town because we wanted him for a commercial, and without looking at anything, John went through the Red Sox's schedule and rotation out loud. In a minute he was able to tell me when Boston was going to be at home and Clemens wouldn't be pitching. Roger wound up doing a couple really good ones.

HANK PEARLMAN:
In the first round of spots I think we ended up with thirty spots finished. The one that felt right for me just from the start, it was so simple, was Grant Hill playing piano in the lobby. Dan Patrick walks by and just kind of hangs out and talks to him and puts some money in his jar. It was so simple that it sort of crystallized the idea of the athlete's role. The other one that happened that same round that felt right to me was Jason Kidd coming in on the helicopter with the highlights and Dan and Keith ran out to the helicopter and got the three-quarter-inch tapes—that was when we were still using three-quarter-inch tapes—and you know, Jason Kidd showed up with

his highlights. And Jason has a line, "Check out the third quarter; I think it's pretty good."

JUDY FEARING:

We wheeled a baby grand piano into the lobby for one commercial on an afternoon during working hours and filled it with smoke. Then we had Michael Buffer announcing anchors as they were coming to work. Howard Katz called me and said, "Judy, you have thirty minutes to get everything out of the lobby. We run a production company here." So I called him back and said, "The good news is we got everything out, but the bad news is that the van with the piano is stuck under the catwalk." It had lodged into the side of the building and it couldn't move. Nobody could get into the facility until they were able to lower all the tires.

ALAN BROCE:

We had no idea which athletes were actually going to show up for this. There were a lot of unknowns. Before we went to Bristol and shot, we had to present scripts or ideas, and I would say, of the fifteen scripts that we presented, we probably shot four. And the rest was all stuff that kind of happened spontaneously. I knew we were on to something great, and the potential was great, and I trusted Hank and I trusted Wieden. I think that was one of the best things about the overall ESPN relationship with Wieden—how much trust we had in each other. And so then we set the date and the script started to get more form, and we started going after talent. And that job sort of fell to me. I would send out letters to agents first trying to describe to them what we were doing, which is hard to do because it wasn't like a storyboard or script, and then I'd follow up and talk to people. A lot of times I would send them the hockey spots or other ESPN work that we had done. People had started to sense that ESPN was doing good work and interesting stuff. And people were inclined to want to be involved. But then I said, "What we need you guys to do is fly to Hartford, and we'll pick you up at the airport and drive you to Bristol and we'll shoot it there." And usually there was like a five-second pause—like, "Wait a minute, you want us to come to Bristol—to Hartford? And no money?" I said, "We'll make a thousand-dollar charitable contribution on your behalf." So it took a ton of convincing. It was hard. It wasn't convenient for *anybody* to come to Hartford and do that.

It was tough to get talent in the beginning, and a lot of people we didn't know if they were going to actually show until the day before, or a couple days before. And we got up to Bristol that first day and, I think, as much preparation as we had done with Norby and John Walsh and everybody on what was coming—the circus that was about to blow into town—I think that when the truck actually rolled in with the amount of people, it totally freaked everybody out. Because they were very clear with us from the beginning that, well, their show was going to go on: "We're not stopping work for you."

JUDY FEARING:

This is not the easiest place to get an athlete, so what we would try to do is to look at the calendar and we would block, let's say, two to three major shoots during the course of a year. And we would try to look at when we thought athletes were going to be in the area or when we could get an athlete to commit to being in the area. And as soon as we could get one or two big guys to say, "Yes, I will come on X, Y, and Z dates," okay, now we had a party. So we just started bringing more and more people.

ALAN BROCE:

One of my favorite *SportsCenter* stories was — it was actually at the second shoot, when we all stayed at the Radisson in Bristol. And one night, in the middle of the night during a shoot, the fire alarm went off. So everybody had to come down and go into the lobby and go outside. You have all these traveling salesmen in the hotel and then you got like three Harlem Globetrotters and Mary Lou Retton and the Oklahoma State Cowboy mascot with a giant cowboy hat going outside.

JUDY FEARING:

We had Keith doing a job interview with Bill Bradley to be either an anchor or production assistant, and he asked him if he had any experience talking to large audiences. And Bill Bradley says something like, "Well, I've delivered the keynote at the Democratic National Convention." And Keith looks and says, "No, I mean to a really large audience." And his timing was just brilliant.

Keith is a very, very smart man. I think he knew that these spots were very good for him. Keith thought—I don't think he ever wanted people to know he would play well with my guys. We needed Keith to do one of the spots on his day off. And Keith was making a huge thing about doing it. And I got a voice message in my mail box from Keith saying, "I'm gonna do it, I'm actually going to do it, but I can't let anyone else know that I'm going to do it willingly," or some words like that. And to me what that always said was that he understood the game. We were there to help promote his show—*SportsCenter*. We were always going to make him look good. He knew people loved his spots. He knew it put him in a good light. And he was going to do them. But he could never let people know that he worked with the production group.

HANK PEARLMAN:

We knew athletes were familiar with the spots. Mary Lou Retton was in that first round and we did some stuff with her where she's just kind of flipping down the hallway and she was teaching some of the anchors how to smile. Another one was where Mike Richter did some stuff where he was talking to the talent about putting him in more highlights and sweet-talking them to get more exposure.

The good thing about getting them to come to Bristol, Connecticut—'cause everybody thought, like, "You're crazy, you're never going to get athletes to come to Bristol, Connecticut"—but what happened was, as a result, the people who came to Bristol, Connecticut, were there because they really wanted to be in the spots and they liked the idea. Getting Grant Hill was hard but we got guys from Boston, guys from New York. Mary Lou Retton, I remember talking to her, and she got it, she'd made fun of herself in movies and things like that. And the athletes, I think, liked the idea that they were going to just be themselves and we weren't going to give them a bunch of lines to memorize and they would not have to perform like actors.

ALAN BROCE:

I point to the seminal moment where I think people first really got a sense of, "Okay, this is going to be really funny," which was when Dan and Keith did the makeup spot in front of the mirror, and they had the conversation. They were talking about hockey and what represents old-school hockey and stuff, and then Keith says, "You need more rouge." People around the set were watching on playback monitors. And they saw that, and they're like, "That's funny! I get it. I get what this is going to be."

HANK PEARLMAN:

We'd talk to management and then we'd talk to talent, and you start to get a sense of how from management's point of view the spots were about how the show was produced and the journalism part of it—the part that John Walsh brought and a lot of the other guys there, how good they were as journalists. Then you talk to the talent, whether it was somebody like Craig Kilborn, who was very irreverent, or Keith Olbermann, who was very opinionated, or Dan Patrick, who was just a great guy to hang out with—a lot of great personalities there. And it was great for me to sort of sit back and say, "You're both right"—the fact that *SportsCenter* does have this credibility and you've got the journalism thing going for it, it allows people like Kilborn, who I was watching a lot, to be very irreverent and just have fun with it. You could tell the guy just wanted to do comedy basically; in a certain sense they let him, because it was a 2:00 a.m. show.

ALAN BROCE:

We'd have to watch every night after we shot, we would sort of get together in a small conference room and go over, like, here's who's the talent, the athletes, that are coming in tomorrow; here's the basic idea that we're going to shoot; and here's where we're going to shoot. So every day was like a new adventure. And I shuttled back and forth between that core creative team and usually Norby or Vince or John Walsh's office or somebody in operations saying, "This is what we want to do." They're like, "You want to do *what?* You're going to land a *helicopter?*" And they were always flying by the seat of their pants.

GARY MILLER:

Keith would actually show up to these things in, like, a robe and a pipe, like he was on the set of a movie or a sitcom or something. I mean, he was in almost all of them. And Dan too, obviously, 'cause they were the main anchors. I didn't try to influence the producers or anything, but I know Keith did. Management wouldn't let talent do commercials. People would come to them with offers, but it was always, "Oh, no, you can't advertise a product." And I don't know if it was Keith's Boston Market commercial that broke the ice or Dan's Coors stuff or whatever, but eventually they had to cave in, and I think the "This is *SportsCenter*" campaign is what really changed everything, because it made us look human.

There'd been many "cool" and funny TV commercials and promos over the long history of the medium, but the dryly witty ESPN campaign was unique in the annals of on-air promotion. This was not the kind of thing networks did to advertise themselves—especially unlikely, one might have thought, from a channel devoted to sports for a broad mass market. The spots were anything but the artsy indulgences of some elite boutique outfit; they were there to raise brand consciousness and encourage viewer loyalty, two very practical concerns being dealt with in a gratifyingly smart, original way.

The campaign was certainly a creative extension of the smart-alecky, softly self-mocking humor practiced by ESPN personalities. That helps explain why some of those personalities took so naturally to performing in the promos and contributing ideas. This was ESPN "attitude" raised to an inspired new level.

Not every spot was a thing of genius, but more than a few had a cockeyed comic sparkle that made viewers glad to see them pop up—so glad that more than once, ESPN filled an entire hour of primetime with nothing but spots back-to-back. Viewers who'd missed them could catch up; others could laugh again at old favorites. Yes, people sat there and watched a solid hour of nothing but network promos.

Wieden + Kennedy's "This is SportsCenter" campaign: Step Number Seven in ESPN's rise to world dominance.

MEL KIPER Jr., *Pro Football Analyst:*

Back in 1994, Freddie Gaudelli was producing the NFL draft and he said to me, "We're coming back to you to get your reaction to what [Indianapolis Colts VP] Bill Tobin just said about you. He was ripping you back in Indianapolis." Among other things, Tobin had said that I had never been offered anything in the NFL, which was not accurate. Ironically, I was offered a position with the Baltimore Colts back in 1983, right before I got the offer to go to ESPN. Had I gone to work for the Colts that year, I would never have been at ESPN.

So Tobin criticizes me for saying the Colts should have taken Trent Dilfer, and then Trent ends up coming to Baltimore and winning the Superbowl with the Ravens in 2000.

BILL CLEMENT, *Hockey Analyst:*

My job was to be objective and I prided myself on professionalism. In every city, local people are used to listening to their local broadcasters. They're used to hearing their local call where there's nothing objective, at least there wasn't then. So in every city I was criticized for favoring the other team, but I would get it from both sides. If I was doing the Rangers-Flyers series, I would be accused by Rangers fans of favoring the Flyers and I would be accused by Flyers fans of favoring the Rangers. The truth is, I actually cheer for players more than I cheer for colors. As a former player, I'm not as invested emotionally as a fan is. I cheer for good people. Over the years as a broadcaster, you get to meet so many good people on so many teams that you've got a lot of different allegiances. I had friends on every team. It's hard because you're still part of the fraternity and you have to be able to separate yourself from the fraternity and still be able to be critical. You have to adjust to and get used to it.

I once got a call from the late Roger Nielson, who was a really classy guy, but he was upset because of something I had said on the air after he had been fired by the New York Rangers. Roger heard that I said he should have been fired. I said, "Roger, that's not what I said at all."

What I said was that it was widely understood that Mark Messier had a hand in his dismissal. I said if Roger Nielson was fired because of some things that Mark Messier wanted or Mark Messier said or because of the influence that Mark Messier had on that division, Mark Messier was just doing what they brought him to New York to do, which was be the consummate leader. And leaders, if something is not right, and they don't think they're going to be successful, status quo doesn't do it. I said if Mark Messier had anything to do with it, then he was only doing what he was brought to New York to do. I wasn't agreeing with the player's right or the duty to do it. I was pointing out what leaders do. When we had the conversation, he said, "That's not the way it was explained to me." He understood it at that point.

JED DRAKE:

It was the 1994 World Cup. I was in charge of the project, and the short of it is that because it is soccer, you don't run commercials and hence you have to have commercial sponsorship come off the miniboard, the scoreboard. The first game was at Soldier Field and we had all kinds of miniboard problems; graphics and logos would not get up there on the screen, and so I was screaming at people, "We've got to get this fixed now! It's not right." The next game, Italy versus Ireland, game two at Giants Stadium, I'm in the truck there, but now I've put backups in place. We have two systems working online in the truck, and we had two backups in Bristol. We get to the first quarter and we can't get the scoreboard up. And I'm like, "Guys, this is impossible. It is incomprehensible that out of four machines we cannot get a scoreboard on the screen! What are we going do?" So at halftime I'm on the phone to Bristol. "Guys, I'm going to lose my mind." They said, "No it's working now, we've tested it. Everything will be fine." The second half starts, and machines one and two in the truck go down. Then machines three and four in Bristol go down. I said, "Motherfucker!" and I took my hand to the side of the truck and I just punched it as hard as I could. And I felt it go. My hand went numb. And everybody in the truck was mortified. Then one of the guys says, "Oh, my God." It was then that I realized I had broken my hand.

Now the game is still going on, but there was silence in the truck for, like, fifteen seconds. Then everybody got back into it and we did get the clock on about three minutes later. After that, they took me down to medical. The guy said, "Yeah, oh yeah, it's definitely busted. It's a boxer's fracture." It's a bone that still sticks out to this day. So they put it in a splint, taped it, gave me ice, and I walked back to the truck, still overseeing the whole thing with my hand in the air with a bag of ice.

When I got home, my wife had no sympathy at all. She just said, "You just take this television shit way too seriously." We're no longer married.

LINDA COHN:

I thought I was doing quite well. Then my bosses called me in—John Walsh and Steve Anderson. I remember because it fell on a big day for me and for the New York Rangers. It was 1994, and they were playing the Devils. I just finished doing the six o'clock *SportsCenter*, and I wanted to rush home to see game seven. They call me into the office and I had no idea what they wanted to talk about, and they basically said, "Hey, Linda, we like you, you're a delight, you're this, you're that. You're great with the troops around here, blah, blah, blah. And we know that you know sports, but you're just not showing it like we thought. So we're not going to pick up your option but, because we like you, we're going to let you stay for six months to see if you improve. And, if you do, we'll keep you." That was the first kind of feedback I really got, but it was negative and I was almost fired. It was a big learning experience for me, but it obviously put a lot of added pressure on me. I was either going to shrink or I was going to say, "OK, I'll show them!"

They helped me, actually. They hired a consultant. She was working with some other people. I said, "Yeah, okay, I'll do whatever it takes. You want me to see her, I'll do that." I would meet with her maybe, like, once every couple of weeks. We'd look over my tapes and the greatest advice she told me was to slow down during my highlights and pause. Let the viewer digest, not make it one run-on sentence. And that really helped.

You know what's interesting? I could see that with some others, they would fake their way through conversations about sports, but with me it's natural, because, and this is true, I'm always talking sports. You can go to anyone in that newsroom and ask them.

Americans over a certain age may never forget where they were on the night of June 17, 1994. It was a big sports night, in terms of volume, at least: the Knicks were playing the Rockets in Game Five of the NBA Playoffs, Arnold Palmer swung his way through the final round of the U.S. Open, World Cup soccer games were under way in nine U.S. cities, and New York was cleaning up after a ticker-tape parade that celebrated the New York Rangers' victory in the Stanley Cup final, their fourth since the competition began. All very exciting—but nothing compared to the most gripping, most talked about, most mondo bizarro unscheduled event of the year, a kind of nonsanctioned NASCAR competition in which the cars moved at a mysteriously pokey, rush-hour rate. The "race" boiled down to two vehicles, basically; the one in the lead was a white Bronco driven by Al Cowlings, a friend of O.J. Simpson, football player turned actor turned murder suspect for the killing of his ex-wife Nicole Brown Simpson and her friend, Ronald Goldman.

For ESPN, the immediate course was clear; this was the biggest story in the country at that moment and it involved a sports figure. "Truth really is stranger than fiction," Craig Kilborn said as he and Karl Ravech began that night's edition of SportsCenter, *which would be unlike any other night's edition of* SportsCenter. *But a snap decision had to be made: to cover the O.J. chase in the same depth as other networks or to push it to the sidelines and treat it as some lunatic oddity in the news?*

BILL FAIRWEATHER:

There was a complex where a bunch of guys from ESPN lived and we were all hanging out in the afternoon, talking about the show that night. I said, "Oh, the show's gonna be a piece of cake for me because O.J.'s turning himself in and all the pieces on O.J. will already be done for the six o'clock. I'll take all the features that were done plus a couple basketball highlights and that will fill up my show." We all sat around and laughed about what a piece of cake the 11:00 p.m. would be that night.

I show up in the newsroom and the whole place is in a scramble. Nobody knew what the hell was going on. O.J. didn't show up.

SCOTT ACKERSON:

I happened to be walking by the control room and there were all those people watching O.J. in the Bronco. Once I realized what was going on, I said, "Everybody out of here, we've got to get on the air." I got Jack Edwards, who was still around from the previous *SportsCenter,* and we basically just stole feeds from whichever station was up. Whoever had a better shot, we'd cut to them. Jack did a great job.

STEVE ANDERSON:

It was so bizarre. Once we understood what was happening, it became very obvious that this was something we had to cover, but we had no rulebook. We were making it up as we went. A week before, if someone had asked if ESPN would ever cover a police chase, I don't think anyone would have ever imagined that it would be something we should or would ever do.

JUDSON BURCH, *Producer:*

The O.J. Simpson car chase was unbelievable. I was too young and too inexperienced to know all that was really going on as we covered it, but I knew I could take a step back from it and say to myself, "Just watch. You're going to want to remember this someday."

I remember vividly how challenging it was to find a satellite feed of the NBA finals because NBC was on O.J. Simpson. So the guy whose job it was to screen the NBA finals that night was sitting there knowing the game was going on but he couldn't see it. The anchors were out on TV for a very long time that night and were getting kind of fried. At one point, Gary Miller did one of the TV techniques where he said, "If you don't want to know the score, turn away from the TV," and he gave the score, but it wasn't for the basketball game, it was for a World Cup game. He wasn't sure what he was doing.

NORBY WILLIAMSON:

We had some passionate Knicks fans here, so when NBC went to the double box, they were like, "Are you kidding me? We're in the finals! Let them chase him some other time!" That's what this place is. It's a different mix of people.

I think we did a smart thing on O.J. We didn't overplay the sports angle. We basically admitted to everyone we were going to cover it because he was a big sports figure, but we didn't go crazy and make fools of ourselves by reminding everyone all the time that he rushed for two thousand and three yards. No one cared about that. This was a murder case.

SCOTT ACKERSON:

Pretty soon after the O.J. deal, I got a call from Fox and met with them on a Tuesday. They made me an offer and told me I had to decide by Wednesday whether I was going to take the job. I had been at ESPN since '86, it wasn't so easy a decision, but I went and told my good friend Barry Sacks that I was going to take the Fox job. We called down to where Anderson, Wildhack, Walsh, Creasy, and Bornstein were. It's my understanding that the vote was two to two on whether they should let me stay or escort me out immediately and the person who cast the deciding vote was Creasy, who said they had to get me out of there. So they called back and Barry said, "This isn't me, but they told me you've got to get out. You've got forty-five minutes to get your stuff together." So I said, "Let me get this straight: I don't have to stay here tonight till 3:00 a.m. like always?" I wasn't the first employee to be escorted out. It was what it was. I don't harbor any bad feelings and am happy with the way things worked out.

By the end of 1994, ESPN was in 63.1 million homes, the most of any cable network. To Steve Bornstein's dismay, the network was now very much in the business of breeding stars, and he knew all too well what would happen next: the people on the screen would want to get paid in proportion to their popularity with the people at home. Adding to the pressure was the advent of the five-hundred-channel digital universe and all the other attendant new technologies. Heavy expenditures would be required to keep ESPN relevant and competitive. ESPN2, meanwhile, may have worked its way onto cable systems, but it was still struggling to get all those hip and youthful eyeballs it had been designed to seduce.

On the plus side, SportsCenter was thriving; the newsroom staff felt like there wasn't a story out there that they couldn't handle; and football and baseball were front and center. In the broadcasting business, rumors swirled about CapCities merging with, or being acquired by, some other entity. And, of course, there was Ted Turner. Having been rebuffed in an attempt to buy ESPN, he was now determined to squash it, or at least slow it down. What might he be up to, and could the Bristol brigade fight him off?

5

Jonah: 1995–2000

"Poor man wanna be rich, rich man wanna be king,
And a king ain't satisfied till he rules everything."
— *Bruce Springsteen*

Suppose ESPN were a human being—let's call him Espin—instead of a company. And suppose it's 1995 and feisty Espin has managed to survive a birth and an infancy in which his life was threatened more than once; navigated wild and raucous toddler and childhood years filled with poverty and mishaps; and careened through an adolescence marked by expansion—in his size, reach, and vision. Having reached the age of sixteen, he is preparing for collegiate years ahead. Will he overindulge in wacky frat antics, or get serious about encroaching adulthood and its opportunities for further growth, industry, and success? Can he pull off the neat trick of managing both? From his current late-adolescent viewpoint, he can foresee the glorious possibilities but not, perhaps, the pitfalls.

ROY FIRESTONE, *Host:*

Cameron Crowe had written the script for *Jerry McGuire* and called my producer to say he'd like some ideas about casting a Roy Firestone–type person. And the guy said, "What about Roy Firestone?" And Cameron literally said, "You mean we could get Roy Firestone to do the Roy Firestone interview?" He said, "Hold on a second," and handed me the phone. Cameron couldn't believe he could get me, but I of course couldn't wait to do it. Sony Pictures asked ESPN to use our set for the scene, and they turned them down! God only knows what their reasons were. So the studio literally had to reconstruct the *Up Close* set piece by piece, along with the photographs. The truth is they did a better job with the set; it was more multidimensional than the real one. When the film was wrapped, they destroyed it. It was the craziest thing. Metaphorically speaking, it was like doing the White House better than the White House, then destroying it after you make a movie.

I told Cameron years later I didn't even read the freaking script because I thought my scene was just going to be cut out of the movie anyway. I couldn't believe the scene made it to the final cut, because so much other stuff was cut out. But there I was, and there it remains. It's become a calling card for me and it will probably be my epitaph. Being in that movie turned out to be a huge piece of business for me. To this day, there isn't a single airport, there isn't a single hotel lobby, there isn't a single sporting event, there isn't a single line I'm in every single day of my life, where somebody doesn't say to me, "Don't make me cry, Roy." Not a single day. I even titled my second book *Don't Make Me Cry, Roy.* It's a wave I've ridden happily.

PAM OLIVER, *Reporter*:

When I was reporting for ESPN, I remember Emmitt Smith looked me in the face one day and said, "You must have no life." And I said, "What do you mean? How can you say that? You know I have a life." And then I thought, 'Hey, he's right. It's true.' I was never home because I was always working, and I had gotten into that creepy area where you're single and working nonstop around athletes on television. That's a double whammy for some insecure men who I didn't really want to be messing with anyway. But it was definitely a long dry spell. I don't think I even had a boyfriend when I was at ESPN. It was a three-year drought.

BILL MAHER, *ESPY Presenter*:

Of all the award shows, the ESPYs have got to be the dumbest award show there is. First of all, award shows in general are sort of silly and ridiculous and we know they're just for creating publicity, but at least it makes some sort of sense within that framework to have an awards show for movies, or television, because there is no way with those to know which is the best. But when we're talking about sports — *they actually play the game.* We don't have to give an award to the best team. We know who the best team is — they've already won! That's the great thing about sports, there's a built-in objective mechanism by which we can ascertain who the winners are. But no, you have to win a second time in a tuxedo, and a spokesmodel has to hand you a trophy; that's what's important.

DAVID STEINBERG, *ESPY Writer:*

I did a lot of writing for the ESPYs, and we really tried to push the line, never play it safe. We'd always be going at it with management, battling about what could be included. The year they had the baseball and hockey strikes — do you remember that John Kruk had testicular cancer? Well, I wanted Kruk to come on the show and just say, "And the count is two strikes, one ball." Okay? That was the joke. So we called Kruk's lawyer at the time and he said, "I'm sorry; he will not make fun of his situation. He just won't come out in a tuxedo and do that." I called him back and said, "No, no, no. You don't get it! We're not making fun of his one ball. We're celebrating the remaining ball."

John Walsh was totally in favor of the sketch, but Kruk didn't do the show.

BILL MAHER:

There's a narcissism contest going on right there at the ESPYs, with jocks and models in the same room. Have you ever been in one of those highfalutin nightclub scenes where everyone is either a model or a jock and you feel like Billy Barty in *The Wizard of Oz*? Well, I'm five foot, eight inches tall, and that's how I felt at the ESPYs. You're meeting people and constantly raising your hand above your head to just shake hands while you say, "Hi, how are you, Amazon woman?" Or "Hello, Amazon sir." You're in this forest of giant bodies, and you're only coming up to everybody's navel.

DAN PATRICK:

The night my daughter was born I obviously missed the show, but I tuned in and saw that Keith has his glasses off and he's wiping away tears. And I went, "Oh, no, he finally did it. This is it. He cashed in his chips. He's gone crazy. He's Howard Beale." I couldn't find out what happened because he was just laughing so hard. So I call the newsroom and they tell me, "Levy was talking about a guy with a bulging disc and he said the guy had a bulging dick." And I just went, "Oh, no." I thought to myself, "Steve wouldn't be in this position if I had been able to do the show."

STEVE LEVY, *Anchor:*

The good old bulging-dick reference. Sort of my claim to fame.

KEITH OLBERMANN:

All I could think of was, "I have to follow this; I better say something funny before I lose the ability to talk." So as he came to the end of this video of NFL carnage but before I was to come on camera I mumbled, "Thank goodness you didn't have video of that first injury," only he wasn't finished. Unbeknownst to me he had a graphic of still more injuries, all groin pulls. Only then did Steve lose it. I took the glasses off because of the tears. I kept them off because I suddenly realized if I couldn't see anybody else I might not dissolve. And amazingly I didn't.

LINDA COHN:

There's a lot of pressure to do catchphrases, and I was talking with a friend of mine in North Carolina, who played for a coed softball team named the Master Batters, okay? And she says to me, "When someone hits a home run, why don't you say, master batter." So I'm like, "That's brilliant. It's subtle enough, and I don't think anyone will get the whole innuendo, and if they do, then they'll laugh."

So of course I did it during a highlight that night: "Mike Piazza, master batter." *Sports Illustrated* did a blurb on it, so I thought it might catch on. But Norby, who was overseeing *SportsCenter,* called me into his office that same week and asked, "Did I hear you right? Did you say Mike Piazza, master batter?" I told him I thought it would be cute, but he said it wasn't funny and was inappropriate. Then he looked at me and said, "Don't do it again." So that was the end of Master Batter.

CRAIG KILBORN, *Anchor:*

When Reggie Miller was jawing at Spike Lee in the front row, I had that highlight. Now, most people would have said, "Reggie tells you to sit down or shut up," but mine was "And Reggie looks over at Spike Lee and says, 'Hey, Spike, develop the female characters in your movie, man.'"

There were always catchphrases and jokes; sometimes the producers would even pitch some to you. I'll tell you maybe the most irreverent one I did was when I was shooting the breeze with my brother, and told him I was working that night and Hakeem [Olajuwon] was coming back to play after being out a few weeks with anemia. My brother is a very bright guy and says, "His red cell count must be up." I said, "Oh, that's cool. Give me another word related to blood," and he said, "Hemoglobin." I said, "Thanks, buddy." So that night, I'm on camera. "Hakeem's back with the Rockets tonight after being out two weeks with anemia. Let's go to the Summit. First quarter, underneath to Hakeem, oh, the red cell count is up! They go right back to him, next time down: oh, hemoglobin!" Some guy from the NBA called me the next morning and said, "I fell off my chair when you did that."

BRETT HABER, *Anchor:*

Kilborn, Ravech, and I were one day marveling at the influence that catchphrases had and how much people got into them. We'd hear them repeated and you'd see people holding up signs that said *"Sports-Center* is next." I think it was Kilborn who I bet that we could invent a catchphrase that meant absolutely nothing and that if we used it a couple days in a row it would catch on. We were sitting around eating Mexican food and someone said, "Let's make it *salsa*." So Craig said he'd do it, and for the next couple of nights, he'd be doing highlights and someone would have a mass dunk and Craig would go, "So-and-So . . . Salsa!" He did it for like three nights in a row, and on the fourth night we were watching a game and sure enough, somebody in the crowd was holding up a sign that said, "Salsa—*SportsCenter* is next."

RECE DAVIS, *Anchor:*

The first show I did with Kilborn, I guess he was just testing me. You know, the rookie coming in, let's see how he holds up, see if he can handle the pressure and all that kind of stuff. So I'm doing the first highlight, and he reaches over and grabs my leg, not in a perverted way, just to distract me, just to see what I would do. I just kept going. But after, I said to him, "Keep your hands to yourself." He just basically acted as if it never happened. He was just showing the Kilborn style. He did a lot of clever writing and pushed the envelope. I think he was actually starting to put together segments of his Comedy Central show.

We caused a little controversy with one catch-phrase. It was a rip-off of the *Seinfeld* line "No soup for you." Actually, a guy from another network thought that he had said it first and wanted me to stop saying it. Well, Keith and Dan got wind of this and they actually did a show later where they just emptied the barrel. It was, "No beef-barley for you, no minestrone for you, no Manhattan chowder for you." It became a much bigger thing that caught on. Then I did a whole bunch of glove-and-love puns: "Addicted to glove," or, when a guy made an error, "Glove stinks." When a guy hit a home run, I tried, "It's not the size of the stick, it's all about finding the sweet spot." I look back on those now and think to myself, What were you doing?

CHRIS BERMAN:

In '95, I did the Swami standing on the corner in Winslow, Arizona. I mean, we actually went there. Tommy was there too. We did the whole thing, even had a babe get out of a flatbed Ford and say, "Take it easy." At first, we were told we couldn't do it. "There's no acting allowed," and "It will make it look like you're hitting on her"—that type of thing. Up and up the appeals went, then Howard Katz said no as well. So I told the guys I was going to make one call and we'll see what happens. I said, "I like my chances." So I called Bornstein and said, "Steve, what the fuck?" Less than five minutes later, I had his approval. When we aired it, I loved it, and the reaction was fantastic.

GARY MILLER:

It was a great time to be at ESPN. By '95 we were pretty much the dominant force in studio sports, so we would get the first interview. In the early days, you just had to be aggressive, grab somebody, and try to make friends with the PR people. By '95, they were bringing everybody to us.

When the Braves won the '95 World Series, it was just great. I had met a lot of those guys when the Braves still stunk and a bunch of us from CNN, where I worked before ESPN, would go to the games and there'd be like only four thousand people in Fulton County Stadium. Back then, they had Chief Nokahoma fire-breathing on the mound, then running to his tent in the left field bleachers. They even introduced a second character, "Princess Winalotta," who was pretty attractive, came to a few parties, and had a fling with one of the CNN anchors. But now they were World Champs, and I was at ESPN interviewing people like [Tom] Glavine and [David] Justice live right after their victory. It was kind of poignant because I could remember and they could remember seeing me back when they were losing a hundred games.

TONY BRUNO:

When Arkansas was in the Final Four, we got an interview with President Clinton. Now, the White House protocol was that we had to send questions in advance; you really can't do anything impromptu to throw the president off. So we had sent lots of sports questions in for the president, including, of course, Arkansas basketball. I remember vividly when I introduced the president. I said, "People listening to the show know that we always have fun here, and people think I'm always trying to pull a fast one on the American public, but right now, ladies and gentlemen, I wanna tell you, we're not pulling a fast one on you. Ladies and gentlemen, for the first time on this show, the president of the United States of America, Mr. Bill Clinton." And then he comes up and says, "Well, you know, people out there always think I'm trying to pull a fast one on the American public too," and that wasn't in the script. I was really impressed; he came out strong right out of the gate and even responded to impromptu questions. He was brilliant and it was a lot of fun.

BONNIE BERNSTEIN, *Reporter:*

The first thing that really put me on the map was during football season my first year at ESPN, back in 1995, and it had to do with Lawrence Phillips being suspended at Nebraska for having an altercation with his girlfriend. My boss at the time was Jim Cohen, and he called me after eleven o'clock on a Sunday night and said, "Are you seeing this stuff about Lawrence Phillips on *SportsCenter*?" I said, "Yeah," and he said, "I want you on the next plane to Lincoln, 'cause I want you to go interview Tom Osborne." So I got on the plane and met up with Kelly Neal, who was one of our producers, and we went on a manhunt for Tom Osborne. I remember I kept calling the sports information director, Chris Anderson, but I never got a call back.

We got a tip that Osborne was speaking at a booster luncheon that afternoon, so Kelly and I went over there and waited for him to finish. He came out and I introduced myself, but he just kept walking. So I just kept walking right along with him, followed by Kelly, our camera guy and sound boom guy in tow. Next thing I know, he's walking down a spiral staircase, and as he does, he asks why I didn't try to set up an interview with the Sports Information department. I said, "Well, I called Chris Anderson, but he never got back to me." Now, it turns out that "he" was actually a "she," and she was right next to him, which was kind of mortifying. But I kept going and started asking him about Lawrence Phillips. So he gets to the bottom of the spiral staircase and there's an elevator. He gets in the elevator thinking he's been able to escape me, but I just jumped right into the elevator with him, along with Kelly, and our camera and sound guys. We wound up getting the most significant sound bites from Osborne going down in the elevator, and I got major kudos from Bristol for that. It was the first time that Rudy Martzke of *USA Today* had ever written about me, because I hadn't been there that long. I think after that interview, people realized I had the tenacity to handle the job, and that meant a lot to me.

AL JAFFE, *Director of Recruitment for Talent and Production:*

I felt like the dean of admissions at Harvard. There was a huge pool of people who wanted to be here, and as a result, I could be very selective. We had started a production assistant program in the late eighties, that's the entry-level job here, and the number of applicants was growing and growing. We wanted to make sure people were qualified, so during their interview with me, I came up with something that came to be known as "the Quiz." It wasn't trivia like "Who hit more than forty home runs in 1950?" It was more about the current scene, so I could have an idea of whether the person was knowledgeable enough to work here, because in addition to being a good writer and needing to be creative, they had to have a thorough understanding of sports on a national level.

I'll give you an example: "Let's pretend you're the general manager of the Dodgers and we're doing this interview in December. It's the off-season. What do you need to do to improve your team? Which free agents would you go after?" If somebody said they were from Los Angeles, then I would ask about the Cardinals or the Red Sox. Then I would ask, "Tell me about the strengths and weaknesses of *SportsCenter,* and be candid," or "If you were to come to ESPN, pitch me an idea for a longer story." These are mostly kids coming right out of college, although we've had older people apply too, but if they said, "Oh, geez, we don't have cable in the dorm," well, that was a problem. It's amazing; there are a lot of people here who came through that process that now have big jobs. Mark Gross is senior vice president of studio production, and he started as a PA. It's cool for me to walk through the halls here and see people who passed the quiz and have gone on to succeed.

JUDSON BURCH:

When I interviewed with Al Jaffe, I went off on a five-minute dissertation about why Craig Biggio shouldn't be a lead-off hitter. I think that gave him a general idea that I was a baseball fan, and I remember thinking afterward that this had to be a cool job if part of the interview was getting to assess Major League lineups.

KEITH OLBERMANN:

My mother had gotten used to this attention-garnering thing of mine fairly early on. I was never in a group. I've never been a wallflower. And so there was a lot of this for her beginning in the third grade. Obviously a smaller group, but the teachers would all come over to her and go, "Sooo, you're Keith's mother," with a combination of awe and pity. By, let's say, '95, my mother would somewhat wearily say, "You know what, I was writing a check somewhere or buying something, and somebody recognized the last name and said, 'Oh, what a great coincidence. You have the same last name as my favorite sportscaster,' and she would just wait for it and then have to explain that she was, in fact, my mother. And there was this pride overload. "It's okay. I get it. He's your favorite sportscaster, and he's this guy's favorite sportscaster and he's this next guy's favorite sportscaster. That's great. Thanks a lot. Can I just have my sandwich now?" It was like George Carlin's line: "Thanks for wishing me a nice day; now can I have my fucking change, please?"

BRETT HABER:

I had done the 2:00 a.m. *SportsCenter* and then had to fly the next morning to Philly to do a story. So

I get to the clubhouse at the Vet around 11:00 a.m., and the guys were all watching *SportsCenter* on the big screen in the locker room with me anchoring, but there I was standing right in front of them. A bunch of the guys looked at the TV, then looked at me, then looked back at the TV. They couldn't quite get their arms around the concept, you know, a "What are you doing here?" kind of thing. They were having this out-of-body moment. I guess a lot of people didn't realize *SportsCenter* was repeated.

LESLEY VISSER:

My husband and I were in the Far East, this had to be in the mid-'90s when I was working for ESPN, and I remember we were taking the Star Ferry from Kowloon to Hong Kong, and we looked up at the TV and they had ESPN playing! It was already becoming a global player, and their penetration was getting enormous.

JODI MARKLEY, *Senior Vice President of Operations:*

In 1995, I was in Brazil, where we were working to launch a new ESPN network. It was a big, complicated project, and it took several years to get it really going right. As ESPN was not a known entity in any manner in Brazil, the logistics of hiring top-notch talent both in front of and behind the camera, while having to explain what ESPN actually was, turned out to be quite an adventure. We cobbled together a pretty good team, crossed our fingers, and went for it. Fast-forward a few years after we started, and I was getting off a plane in the small city of Curitiba, Brazil, and all of a sudden I see this kid wearing an ESPN T-shirt. None of us had given it to him to wear, so he must have gotten it from somewhere else. And I don't know why this image meant so much to me at the time, but it was one of the most fulfilling moments I've ever had.

JEFF ISRAEL:

In '95, we were going to do a pregame show and a *SportsCenter* the morning of a Giants game at the Meadowlands. When we pulled up to the stadium, it was almost as if the game wasn't going to be played, because no one had cleared the snow. I immediately said, "This is going to be a problem." So we did our stand-ups and reports from the stands, where the snow was up at your ankles. I couldn't imagine fans coming there and sitting in snow, but they did. This turned out to be the infamous snowball game where everyone was throwing snowballs. I noticed that people in the end zone were firing snowballs at people along the sideline, and then people on the sideline were firing snowballs at people that were near the end zone. My crew and I walked across the end zone figuring no one would fire at us, but we were really pelted. I couldn't keep my shots steady because I didn't have my camera on a tripod; it was on my shoulder. There was a still photographer from a newspaper standing next to me, and he got hit with a snowball at the top of his head. He went to his knees and I looked down. I said, "Are you all right?" And the next thing I know he was just folding over. They had to take him away from the game because he was knocked unconscious.

Steve Bornstein's epiphany upon becoming CEO in 1990 was that ESPN shouldn't be just one single TV network; it needed to be a brand that branched out and communicated on a variety of channels and platforms. He had first put the theory to use with ESPN's expansion into radio, then with the creation of ESPN2. At the same time, ESPN was becoming more aggressive internationally. But now a new big juicy world was starting to open up — the Internet — and the ultracompetitive Bornstein was not about to lag behind others in the broadcasting business. He wanted to establish an online beachhead for ESPN as soon as possible.

STEVE BORNSTEIN:
By the mid-nineties, we were making serious money, but we weren't the only game in town. We were just getting started on the Internet, so I was buying a bunch of data businesses like Sports Ticker, which to me was all about the digitizing of the assets. That was our next big opportunity, and that's why I

hired a guy named Dick Glover to head up our exploration into the Internet area.

DICK GLOVER, *Vice President of Acquisitions:*

Steve never said much to me in terms of direction, he was just very encouraging. I did a lot of research and met with the folks who were running Prodigy, CompuServe, and AOL. I would go to a cable show, sit with Steve Case, who was there trying to meet people, and no one had any clue who he was. Anyway, I came back to Steve Bornstein and said, "Let me show you some things," at which point I discover that Steve had an e-mail account and it was like SteveB@aol.com. I believe Steve Case was Steve@aol, so Bornstein, without ever having said a word to me, sort of acting like he didn't know much about it, was probably one of the first thousand users of AOL. All this time that I thought I was the evangelist and I was the guy blazing the trail, in reality, Bornstein knew absolutely more about it than I did.

After everything was looked over, it came down to Prodigy or AOL. Prodigy was offering to buy $10 million of our advertising time in addition to operating a little ESPN site on Prodigy and pay us a royalty, or really a share, of revenues that were generated. Steve Case said, "I don't believe the way to promote these services is through TV advertising. I'll buy some, but my plan is to get AOL software disks into everybody's hands, basically give them out for free, so

I can't make an advertising commitment to you. But I'll tell you what: I'll give you warrants in our little company that's just gone public."

Bornstein and I liked the way AOL worked better than Prodigy, but ultimately, we said $10 million in advertising was something that we could really use. It was a very bad decision. We went with the wrong guy. A few years later, I think those AOL warrants we turned down were worth $200 million.

The good news was that the deal we did with Prodigy was only for a year. The year was not a particularly happy or successful one, in part because we always felt AOL was better. Ultimately the decision we made was to partner with Paul Allen's Starwave. They saw the world as we did; they were huge sports fans and they were as comfortable in Bristol as they were when they were at their own headquarters.

Starwave had actually built a service called "Satchel," after Satchel Page, and then they said that they wanted to call it "Sportszone." So we said, "What's the point of doing an ESPN service that isn't branded ESPN? That makes no sense; we'll never do that. Nor does it make sense for you." So we agreed that it would be "ESPNET SportsZone," and that if we broke up we would own "ESPN Net" and that they would own "SportsZone." So that's how it got named.

But the real key was Bornstein: he set the direction, and everybody in the industry knew we were marching to his beat. Inside the company, we would have a once-a-year big off-site gathering—not the entire company, but around 100 to 150 important managers. One of the last things was a Q&A with Steve, and somebody asked the question, "What are the one or two things that you see as being keys to our future?" And everyone in the room was certain that number one would be ESPN2, and number two would be sales, and Steve without hesitation said, "The Internet and international." From that day on, I was important.

On April 1, 1995, ESPNET SportsZone was launched in Seattle, during the NCAA Final Four men's basketball tournament, to coincide with both the tournament and Paul Allen's location. "Microsoft is thrilled that ESPNET SportsZone will be part of the Microsoft Network when it debuts later this year," said the GM of the online services group at Microsoft, Russ Siegelman. The group was bragging that Satchel Sports had already logged 150,000 fans and over a million hits a week.

PAUL BROOKS, *Senior Vice President of NASCAR:*

In our sport you have forty-three teams on the same field playing together at the same time. So there's this constant action and interaction between these teams, and the data and information that is collected is just mind boggling compared to any other sport. We had timing and leader feeds that were very significant; we thought if we could just get those feeds on the Internet, and people could turn on their computers to get running orders and see the same screen that the pit crews were using at the racetracks, that would be the best thing in the world.

Bill and Brian France asked me to lead our effort in that area, and after making the rounds, we thought our smartest bet was to follow the lead of our partner, ESPN, so we put together a partnership with Starwave. ESPN quickly learned that some enterprising fan out there had already registered NASCAR.com, but thankfully he was a NASCAR fan, so I think all it took to get it in our hands was two tickets to the Daytona 500, some pit passes, a few gift bags, and meeting his favorite driver. We got the URL transferred to us in a matter of a couple days. Thankfully this was before all the crazy auctions; just another six, eight months later, that would've been a very expensive transaction.

These were busy times. Less than three months after the Internet launch, ESPN began a new venture, and this time there wouldn't be any need for a partnership, other than advertisers. ESPN gave birth to the Extreme Games (later shortened to the "X Games"), which were almost entirely based in Newport, Rhode Island. The event was an ad sales department's dream, with seven major sponsors: Advil, Mountain Dew, Taco Bell,

Chevy Trucks, AT&T, Nike, and Miller Lite. Nearly 200,000 fans would attend the first games.

Athletes would compete in twenty-seven events in a variety of warm-weather sport categories: the Eco-Challenge, a weeklong, multistage endurance race, mountain biking, in-line skating, skateboarding, BMX, sky surfing, sport climbing, street luge, windsurfing, kite skiing, and bungee jumping.

The Extreme Games had no real blueprint, but ESPN once again became the ultimate "What if" company: "What if we tried this? What if we tried that?" The network placed cameras on participants' helmets, on the walls of ramps, and throughout the racecourses. And a lot of other ideas passed through gatekeepers who would have shut them down at other companies.

RON SEMIAO:

When I got hired in programming, all I heard about was how much they wanted ESPN2 to be different, and to focus on younger audiences, particularly those with interests in "extreme" or "action" sports. So I went to the Barnes and Noble in West Hartford and found out there was no such thing as a *Sports Illustrated* for extreme sports. But there were all these individual magazines for skateboarding, snowboarding, climbing, BMX, and I bought 'em all. Here's what stuck out to me: Tony Hawk was as good at his sport as Michael Jordan was at his, and all these guys had their own look, their own wardrobes, their own music, and were having big influences on the culture. Mainstream companies were using images from these sports in their commercials because they wanted to associate their product with something cool. I thought they would attract the exact audience we were all going after for ESPN2, but it became clear to me that while these sports were doing okay vertically, there was nothing going on horizontally, nothing bringing them all together. So I started to think that the whole would be greater than the individual parts, and rather than program them all separately, we should bring them all together under one umbrella. So I came up with the idea to create the Olympics of Extreme Sports, an event that would showcase both the lifestyle and the abilities of these athletes. It would be like creating a Superbowl for ESPN2.

PETER ENGLEHART:

It was Ronnie's idea. I told him I thought it was fantastic, and that he had my one hundred percent backing, because I thought it would really help differentiate ESPN2, and the sales guys would be excited to sell it. He said to me, "Well, what do you think we should call it?" I said, "I don't know; I'll schedule it, I'll help you get it through, we'll budget for it, and we'll get some meetings going." Then he asked me, "What are you going to put it on the schedule as?" I said, "Right now I'll just put it down as X Games," and that's how the name came about.

RON SEMIAO:

The pitch made its way up to Steve Bornstein, and he took a straw poll among his senior executives and it was quite polarizing. I was told there were a lot of senior executives at this company who didn't think we should do it, but perhaps most importantly of all, Creasy loved it. You know, he's *the Guy*.

STEVE BORNSTEIN:

Semiao gets a lot of credit for it; I suspect he deserves most of the credit, but as with everything, it became a collaboration. Once the idea got to my level, I green-lit it immediately. It was an equity opportunity and a growth area. But it was very expensive — $12 million! I still remember the price tag. We had never done original programming like that before. And $12 million was a big commitment back then. That would've been a hockey contract.

RON SEMIAO:

We then somehow needed to identify the best athletes in these sports. I felt like Lee Marvin in *The Dirty Dozen,* when he was trying to sign up guys for a suicide mission. I got sucked in a few times, like when I saw a really cool fuckin' picture in *Details* magazine of this guy kite skiing in Seattle. He wore special water skis and this special harness so he could do all these tricks as the wind blew him along. The article explained that his dad was an engineer on the original Boeing 707. I tracked him down and asked if he could get the ten best kite skiers in the world to compete. He was like, "Absolutely!"

What he didn't tell me was that the only two people who really knew how to do it were him and his brother. But ten people showed up, and it looked like a Wile E. Coyote cartoon. One guy got blown face-first into the rocks, and another guy didn't know how to turn and the wind took him so far down the shore that he disappeared. He ended up making land and calling a taxi, where he put his kite ski in the trunk and rode back to the venue. We never put the event on the air.

My first idea of where to do the games was San Francisco. I thought that'd be a really cool place to do it because of its whole history of counterrevolution and incredible geography. But we couldn't get past a pay phone at a 7-Eleven with the mayor's office to have a meeting. Fortunately, through Red Sox Fantasy Camp, I was friends with a guy who was running the state of Rhode Island's newly formed sports council, designed to bring in sporting events for economic development. The town council of Newport loved tourist dollars; they just didn't like tourists. We couldn't get a permit, and it kept on getting tabled for a vote. Finally, my buddy from the head of the sports council talked to a couple of guys from an organization with a long history of influence in

Rhode Island politics and we got our permit by a four-to-three vote.

BILL FITTS:

Ron was always asking me, "Can I do this? Can I do that?" Most of the time I said yes, because that's what we were all about then: making it happen. Sometimes we could tell pretty fast something wasn't going to work, so we tried something else.

RICH FEINBERG, *Vice President:*

Getting from the words "sky surfing" on a piece of paper to actually trying to come up with a concept to broadcast it live was a challenge. How about people jumping out of an airplane and falling to earth at terminal velocity, 120 miles an hour? How are we going to put it on the air? Should we have an audience at the drop zone? What do they look at? What if we had a JumboTron? But what happens if the wind blows them off course and they don't land in the drop zone? One of the cool things about motor sports is in-car cameras; let's get the guy who does in-car cameras for NASCAR or Indy and see what he thinks about some of this stuff. Let's talk to our guys who know a lot about RF transmission and see what they think about sky surfing. We went through that creative process on all the sports.

We built a broadcast center outdoors at Fort Adams, which was an eighteenth-century fort in Rhode Island, and we wanted to build a set looking back into the bay of Newport, so the best view we could find was on top of the walls of the fort. Well, we never really gave a whole lot of consideration to what it would mean to put 600-pound cameras and lighting grids on something that was built in the 1800s. At some point, we decided we'd better hire a structural engineer.

SUZY KOLBER:

There was no running water or bathroom at Fort Adams. I would allot myself one trip to the Porta-John a day, and as it got hotter, there was dirt everywhere, even flying around and getting in the tapes. When it came time to get dressed to go on the air, there was no place to go, so I would just tell Chris Fowler or whoever else was in our trailer to turn around so I could change.

STEVE ANDERSON:

We were a wreck the whole time. It was the first time a lot of these athletes had people telling them what to do or how to do it. One of the groups, I think it was the skateboarders or the Rollerbladers, decided it was becoming too commercial and they were going to walk away. Somehow Ron got them to come back so we could do the show.

RICH FEINBERG:

There was an uproar about scoring, and some of the athletes wanted us to let them rescore the event.

And they said if we didn't let them rescore the event, "We're not going to compete tomorrow. We're not going to show up." Long story short, we accepted their reason, whether we believed it or not, that the mistake was more mechanical than judging. So the judges sat in the truck till three or four in the morning watching all the competition again, rescored it, and then we had to come back on the air the next day and say, "Remember those results we gave you going into the finals? Well, the judges made a mistake and miraculously, So-and-So's back in the finals!"

FRED GAUDELLI:

You have to keep in mind that no one in the company, and probably not in the entire TV sports business, was ready to stage and produce an event like the X Games. In addition to having to make up new competitions and rules, it seemed like every hour brought a new major issue, either with the athletes, the facilities, or the weather. We were always putting our fingers in the dikes, and it felt like ten days of crisis management. But I do think we were so concerned about making everything legitimate, we ended up taking it all too seriously in terms of how we produced it.

I'll give you an example: for the skating and bike events, the judges were kids or adults who never grew up and were stoned the entire time. They had never even used any type of electronic equipment and were either too stoned or not inclined to figure it out. So we had huge delays and major controversies, especially when the number-one in-line skater, a guy we had hyped out the yang, didn't make it out of prelims. It was blasphemous to us, but that's where we got caught taking ourselves way too seriously.

We could all tell right away that Tony Hawk was not only a very special athlete, but a legitimate star. There was no one else like him. But the top two in-line skaters and athletes we incessantly promoted were Arlo Eisenberg—"the prince of darkness"—and Chris Edwards—an avowed born-again Christian. God versus devil. Arlo didn't have the goods as a skater, and Chris, the guy who couldn't get out of prelims because the judges were stoned, got injured in the half-pipe, and we had to get an ambulance to take him to the hospital. Now, in the lead-up and in the games themselves, we were running pieces on this kid preaching the word of God and all his goodness. When he got injured, we put a camera in the ambulance to ride to the hospital with him. As the door is closing he looks at the camera person and says, "Please don't shoot this. My wife is going to see this, and this girl next to me is my girlfriend, and my wife will figure it out."

SUZY KOLBER:
While we were on the air it was great fun, but overall it was unbelievably stressful. I had nightmares

for two weeks after the games were over that we didn't make air, or that we weren't done yet.

TONY HAWK, *Professional Skateboarder:*

I thought it was a little misguided at first that they wanted to group *so* many different sports together. We felt like we didn't have a connection with bungee jumpers or rock climbers, you know what I'm saying? They were saying you're either into all sports, or you're into extreme sports, and that means that you skateboard, you ride motorcycles, you Rollerblade, you bungee jump, and you sky surf. I didn't do any of those other things, and it was a hard thing to convey to people that all of our sports are very, very different. Just because someone has labeled them extreme doesn't make them all similar.

But somehow because of the way it was presented and the way people perceived things, it wound up working. The X Games had a huge influence on our sport. Up to then, the only people who enjoyed skating were skaters themselves. Nobody else understood it that well or wanted to. The games brought a fan base to skating that didn't necessarily skate but enjoyed watching it, and that in itself set a foundation for skating in terms of popularity. ESPN not only came with a new audience for us but they were informative enough to allow everyone to understand the intricacies and difficulties and obviously the passion of the skaters themselves. All of a sudden we had kids who understood what a 360-flip is and the mechanics of what was involved.

I did feel that they were only focusing on a very select group of athletes, and more guys deserved coverage, to show their personalities and have their stories told. After the games, they set up an athlete committee to help refine it and make it more representative of how we perceive our sports. They picked athletes from each different discipline, and we had a lot of input. I also got to understand better what had been going on behind the scenes and some of what Ron had to deal with in terms of costs and programming issues. All this became really helpful for improvement through the years.

RICH FEINBERG:

There was some discussion about us doing it once every other year. Bornstein had a meeting with us before the games were even over and said, "I love this; it's so different, so great, and I'm getting unbelievable reactions." Next thing we know, he was holding a press conference where he said, "We're going to do this every year."

BILL FITTS:

The X Games led to the Outdoor Games, which did really well and made ESPN a lot of money. It also allowed them to buy [sporting goods retailer] Bass later on. So there was a whole new "outdoors" component to ESPN, and even though I wasn't an out-doorsman, I was really proud of all that.

RON SEMIAO:

We were all feeling great after it was over, and I got a lot of nice feedback. They bumped my pay up and after I'd gotten that big raise, there was something almost better. [ESPN executive John] Wild-hack called me one night and said, "Ronnie, I'm having dinner with Bornstein and Creasy tonight; they want you to come." Well, that's the fucking honor. This was Don Corleone and Luca Brasi inviting you to dinner. I'm serious. I was a fuckin' foot soldier, and all of a sudden I'm in the Pentagon! We were walking into Scores, and Steve said, "Semiao, didn't I just approve a big raise for you? Okay, the night is on you." It was like fifteen hundred bucks! They had to put it on my credit card.

But you know what happened? I couldn't handle success. Here I was getting all this great attention for coming up with the X Games, I'd become the director of programming, and I'm hanging with the big boys. But it was a disaster for me in social situations. Nothing at work, just afterward. Creasy could sit there and sip his scotch, but I'm drinking four to his one. Next thing you know, I'm slobbering all over the place. I had gotten crocked at this one event and basically someone had to put me to bed. The next day, Wildhack, my boss, is calling and saying, "You stupid shit, you fucked up. You gotta call Creasy and apologize." And that was one of the worst fuckin' calls of all time. Creasy's like, "You motherfuckin' cocksucker, after everything we've done for you! You're fuckin' it all up for us! So you're not getting your promotion right now." I got held back on things until I straightened out. Creasy was right. They had given me more professional responsibility and I wasn't acting very professional. Their credibility was taking a hit. Now when I go to these functions, I drink club soda. It's all good now.

It was the rare kind of day when the unstoppable flow of news seemed to stop, when a piece of "sports news" trumped almost everything else happening in the world, when even SportsCenter *trashed its own routine and forgot about trying to be objective and unemotional. August 13, 1995 — the day "the Mick" died.*

DAN PATRICK:
Some people talked to us about how the *SportsCenter* model meant that we had to do the Mantle story up top and then do a retrospective later on in the broadcast, but Keith and I went, "No, no, no." We told them we needed to go straight through from the beginning. There was nothing that could be put between that would complement Mickey Mantle dying. Anything would be such a non sequitur that we couldn't do it. Keith and I wanted to let a differ-

ent generation know the magnitude of Mickey Mantle's life, and we fought really hard to get our way. So we wound up dedicating the first eighteen minutes of the show to him. It was one way to show everyone that he was more than just a great baseball player in New York, and that he represented a lot of different things to many different people. It was the right thing to do.

BILL FAIRWEATHER:

It was my responsibility to produce that *Sports-Center* show. I said to Keith, "Obviously, you have to write the obit for Mantle, and he said, "Yeah, no problem." We went through the rest of the meeting, Keith leaves the room, and by the time I make it back to the newsroom, about fifteen minutes later, Keith calls me over to his desk. I say, "What's up, K.O.?" and he says, "Hold on a second, I'm almost done." And he had written a complete five-minute-and-thirty-five-second-long obituary! I know that because the computer would tell you how long the actual version would be on tape. So he handed it to me and here was this obit with when Mick had come into the league, what he had hit in particular years, home runs, and the dates of important milestones. Now, Keith did have a little reference guide next to him, but let's face it, how much time did he actually have to look up a lot of things if he wrote the whole thing in fifteen minutes? You know what I mean? And don't forget that he types with one hand, but it's probably faster than anybody who types with two. So whatever you think about Keith—and everybody always has many different opinions—if you're a producer, this guy's hitting grand slams for you. Who else do you know who could sit down and do that?

The newscast that night was incredible, but I have to tell you, after producing two hundred *SportsCenters* a year, the eleven o'clock show after the seventh game of the World Series, being in the chair for O.J., and in the chair when we found out an hour before airtime that Jordan was going to retire from basketball, those were all big, but Mickey Mantle's funeral, to me, was almost a responsibility. This was why I was working for ESPN. We were the ones producing the live event, and it was important that it was done right. There wasn't going to be a second chance to produce Mickey Mantle's funeral, and there was no way it was going on my résumé that I had screwed it up. From a producer's standpoint, covering that funeral was like doing the Super Bowl. This is the guy who everybody looked upon as their boyhood idol for generations, and I was the guy who was in the chair to produce this. From the moment I walked into the control room, and right throughout the coverage, I was determined that it was going to go right. And it did.

As I prepared, I remembered when I was twenty-one years old and working at this local station in the sports department and Mickey Mantle came by as part of a promotional tour. He came into the sports office and wound up sitting there while the PR guy was doing some other stuff. So we're in this room together, but I'm not going to bother him. He's Mickey Mantle, right? The office had TV screens with different feeds and games that are going on, but one of the screens had the live feed from Boston Garden. So now it's like 4:30 p.m., and the lights are not even on at the Garden, but Larry Bird is out there shooting, as is his pregame ritual. He would always be out there hours before anyone else, shooting a half an hour or an hour by himself. Not even anyone retrieving the ball.

So Mantle sits back and starts watching Bird shooting, and two minutes go by, and I notice Bird hasn't missed a shot. Two more minutes go by; Bird still hasn't missed a shot. And I see Mantle start to sit up, to get on the edge of his chair and get more and more intently focused on watching this. No joke, Bird has probably taken a hundred shots in a row and not missed one. Mantle is just totally amazed by what he's seeing, and I'm watching him watch Bird. I'm getting a real kick out of this because I'm seeing this guy, one of the greatest baseball players of all time, watching one of the greatest basketball players of all time, all the while knowing that there are only two people in the world who are aware of what's going on now, and it's me and Mickey Mantle.

I think Bird was shooting for close to ten minutes without missing a shot, and finally Mantle gets to the point where he has to say something. He's just so amazed by what he's been seeing that he looks at me and says, "This boy doesn't miss." And I looked at him and I said, "Yeah, but you're Mickey Mantle."

Cal Ripken Jr. debuted on August 10, 1981, for the Baltimore Orioles. He would end his career with 3,184 hits, nineteen All Star selections, eight Silver Slugger Awards, two Gold Gloves, two AL MVP Awards, and the 1983 World Series championship. But ESPN would broadcast his most notable individual accolade on September 6, 1995, when he broke Lou Gehrig's record and played in his 2,131st consecutive game.

Ripken had come close to missing this moment on two occasions. In 1985, he sprained an ankle, but thanks to an off day was able to play the following game. In 1993, he twisted a knee and thought the streak would be over. But like always, he managed to get ready in time.

Chris Berman and Buck Martinez called the record-setting game for the network. When the final out of the top of the fifth inning was called, amid cheers throughout Camden Yards, Berman boomed, "And let it be said that number eight, Cal Ripken Jr., has reached the unreachable star."

And then Berman, known through most of his career for his boisterous voice, his glib nicknaming of athletes, and his rapid-fire delivery during highlights, stunned the national television audience by actually staying silent (Martinez following suit) during the twenty-two-minute celebration that ensued. Berman tactfully let viewers witness the spectacle, the elated cheering of the crowd, the unveiling of the record-setting number on the front of the B&O Warehouse, without interceding or interfering. He let the scene speak for itself and didn't try to upstage the pictures or sound with his own patter. It was a classy gesture, and it drove home the point that ESPN was the place where momentous things happened in the world of sports; that, indeed, it was the world of sports in all its facets, its fantasies, its realities.

CHRIS BERMAN:

It wasn't like I was going to flex my muscles and get that game for myself. The record-breaking game was supposed to be on another night, so it wouldn't have been on my schedule, but the season started two and a half weeks late because there was a short strike, so it got changed. Around early May, when I saw that it was going to fall on a Wednesday, I just said to myself, "Holy shit, what do you know, that's my night." But there was still time, a lot of shit could happen, rainouts, whatever. It's baseball. You can't say in May that a particular September day will be game 2,131.

In early August, I started reading a book on Lou Gehrig, which I thought would be a nice way to prepare. Nobody told me to do it; that was my contribution, all by myself. I just wanted to tell some Gehrig stories that weren't really known, not just that he gave a great speech on July 4, but stuff beyond that. Two weeks before the game, I told Howard Katz, "I view this telecast as a semi-announcerless game." He went, "What do you mean by that?" I actually didn't know exactly what I meant, but I gotta give myself a little credit. Knowing ahead of time that would be the best strategy was pretty cool, particularly because by that point, we didn't know that there was going to be a spontaneously planned twenty-two-minute celebration where Cal was going to slap the hands of every man, woman, child, security guard, and player in the park.

I thought America should learn a little bit about Lou Gehrig. I'm a history guy, and I was bringing with me one of the best, Buck Martinez, one of my dearest friends. The perfect guy for it. If anybody would understand what was going on, it would be Buck—in Major League Baseball for twenty years and knowing what it was like to go to work every day for fourteen years and never call in sick. He broke a leg and still made a tag at the plate.

Now it's the night before and I can't sleep. Oh, my God, this is going to be unbelievable. Everybody is going to be tuning in to see that moment after Anaheim bats five times, and 2,131 comes down. We interviewed Cal when he got to the park. I looked him straight in the eye and said, "Cal, do you think you might get in tonight?" And he just lost it. Cracked up. He goes, "I hope so. I haven't seen the lineup card." He thanked me later. I'm the only one who put him at ease the whole couple of days — not that that's what I was trying to do.

Joe DiMaggio — representing Lou Gehrig — was there; Brooks Robinson, Earl Weaver, and the president, they all came by. The president [Clinton] showed up an inning earlier than we had heard he would, sat down, and it was the easiest inning we did. He talked about work ethic, America, even our forefathers. Before the game, I had said to Buck, "See left field? See that scaffolding over there? See that guy up there? Look at that third window over there." He says, "Okay, you got me. What are they all about?" I said, "Do me a favor. If a pen falls while the president is sitting in here, don't make a quick move to get it. Those are sharpshooters up there."

So then it happened. 2-1-3-1. It was unbelievable. It was America.

CAL RIPKEN JR., *Professional Baseball Player:*

Chris had asked me if I had listened to him do any baseball games and asked me for my thoughts. I don't think he had been doing baseball long, and I think he was trying to figure out what he was going to do when it became official. I certainly didn't tell him what I was going to do, because running around the field never crossed my mind until Rafael Palmeiro and Bobby Bo [Bonilla] pushed me out of the dugout, so there was no

choreography known in advance. I just surrendered to
the event, which is what my wife had advised me to do.
It was, Okay, whatever happens, happens.

CHRIS BERMAN:

As Cal was running around the park, we were crying half the time. We couldn't have spoken. We were
crying. So it was twenty-two minutes of quiet. We
wanted America to just see this.

CAL RIPKEN JR.:

People commented on the fact that they thought it
was really cool that the action was all by itself with
no commentary, but I didn't really have much of a
perspective on it besides what people were telling me.
For the longest time I wouldn't even look at the tape.
I wanted to preserve it and remember it how I experienced it, not looking from the outside, but looking
from the inside out. When I finally looked at the
tape, I didn't realize so many things were happening
at the same time. And I got to see great glimpses of
my dad and the rest of my family while it was all
going on, because the camera was on them quite a bit
during that time. That really opened up and broad-
ened the entire event for me.

*By 1995, ESPN had been shunted through a maze of
majority owners and co-owners. What started with a
family loan and Stu Evey writing a Getty check led to*

partial ownership by ABC, then varying interests held by RJR Nabisco, CapCities, Hearst, and even Kohlberg Kravis Roberts, the famous private-equity firm. Michael Eisner, who had been busy building Disney into a Goliath, was running out of big moves. Now, in 1995, he looked at CapCities and its 80 percent ownership of ESPN as a new golden path. It wasn't the first time he'd thought about it either.

MICHAEL EISNER, *CEO, the Walt Disney Company:*

When ABC first bought ESPN, everybody thought it was a joke, not a serious acquisition. In 1984, we had looked at buying all of ABC for $2 billion, including ESPN, but we were considering NBC before General Electric bought them. Later I heard rumors that investors were circling ABC, but Leonard Goldenson [ABC chairman] told me, "We want to be independent; we don't want to sell." So I said, "Okay." Six weeks later he sold it to Tom Murphy and Warren Buffett, so I guess I was the dodo there. I believed him.

But, of course, almost a decade later, in '93, I've got Tom Murphy and Dan Burke wanting to sell the company, and Dan is sending me information as part of the negotiating process. It turned out the information was low as to what ESPN was doing. That's how fast ESPN was growing; faster than even Dan could follow month to month. In fact, the ESPN financials were pretty awesome, but I didn't have the right figures.

Mine were lower than the reality. So I called Tom and I said, "Tom, this doesn't add up; we can't do it." He said, "Michael, that's the price, tell me you want to do it now, or the company will be off the table." I said, "Tom, we can't pay that price." So the deal fell apart.

Three weeks later they came out with their earnings, and ESPN was probably, I'm guessing here, 60 percent higher than what Dan Burke had sent me. I called him up and said, "Dan?!" He said something like "You know what, Michael, I think I read a figure wrong. It was a two, not a one." I think if he'd given me the right figures, we would have bought it then.

I was still on the hunt to find an acquisition that would add a new dimension to the Walt Disney Company. *Lion King* was about to come out; I knew it was going to be a giant hit, but I knew our movies beyond that, I knew how far we'd pushed our parks, I knew how Euro Disney was doing. I knew that we were going to grow but not at a high enough percentage rate for the next ten years. The only way I could see that kind of ridiculous growth would be with a new leg on our company, something like ESPN. So here is what happened. I made a deal to buy Capital Cities / ABC with the CEO Dan Burke. I felt the deal was done, and of course it included ESPN.

So [Disney president] Frank Wells, Sid Bass — our major shareholder — and I go to Dan's apartment in New York, and we're sitting there with Dan, Tom Murphy, and Warren Buffett. Sid and I think it's too quiet, and we're here to celebrate the deal, so I made a joke and said, "Where's the champagne?" And Tom Murphy says, "What's the price?"

I said, "What do you mean, what's the price?" Tom says, "What's your offer?" I said, "Well, Dan and I have agreed at X dollars," and Tom says, "Not enough." And I said, "Tom, your CEO and I have made a deal." He says, "It's not enough." And Warren's not speaking, so two things became very clear to me: Tom Murphy was the boss—I don't care that he didn't have the title CEO—and Warren Buffett was Tom's real partner in this kind of decision, the owner, so to speak. So I learned a little bit about business that night. I had been dealing with the wrong guy. Dan ran the company, he was fantastic, he was Tom's partner for decades, but he didn't make that kind of decision. And he was sitting there in the chair saying nothing.

I was pissed, but I didn't say anything. Frank and Sid were annoyed as well. Instead of saying, "Okay, let's still do the deal," because they didn't want that much more, let's say (I'm making all this up) it was $17 billion and they wanted $200 million to $500 million more. But I was not going to do it. And neither was Sid and neither was Frank. So we walked out. We didn't get the company. They repurchased their stock on Dutch auctions.

Now it's two years later, and I run into Warren Buffett and Tom Murphy in the parking lot at Sun Valley. They still wanted to sell. They didn't believe they had all the management they needed. Charlie Munger [Berkshire Hathaway vice chairman] hates the entertainment business, and they had just had a ten-year ride. They wanted out and thought we were good management. So I said, "You know what? I'm going to step up." So Warren walks me to the end of the parking lot and says to Tom, "Michael wants to finally step up and buy the company; we should do it." Tom says, "Yeah, good. What will you pay?" I said, "Well, why don't we talk about that on Monday?" Then I walked another fifty feet and, surreal, I bumped into [CBS CEO] Larry Tisch and his wife. And I said, "God, the strangest thing just happened. I just made an offer for Capital Cities / ABC at the other end of the parking lot." And Tisch said, "Buy CBS instead." And I said "Maybe we will. Maybe that's better." So he started negotiating with me, really suggesting strongly that we buy CBS. In the same parking lot. So I had at least some leverage when I went back to Tom.

PETER ENGLEHART:

Bill France Jr. represented seven races at the time; this was before we made all the deals through NASCAR. But when we negotiated the deal, we did contracts for only six races because it was Bill France Jr.'s fervent belief that the seventh race be done on just a handshake.

I said "Bill, really? You know Steve [Bornstein] likes things to be buttoned up." He said, "You tell

Steve the reason we're doing this is because you'll work harder based on your handshake to be a good partner for me, regardless of what's in any contract. Your word is more important than your contract." So when Disney was buying the company, their lawyers were going through the audits and they asked, "Where's the seventh contract?" I said, "That's a handshake with Bill France Jr." And they looked at me and said, "You're telling us that this race, which is making ESPN a million dollars, is based on a handshake?" I just said, "Hey, call Mr. France."

MICHAEL EISNER:

There were a lot of people, including some financial people at our company, who wanted us to do CBS because it was only $6 billion compared to the $19 billion that CapCities/ABC was going to cost, but I had no interest in CBS. For me and Sid it was all about ESPN, and only ESPN. The valuation that we at Disney made for the ABC network during our due diligence for the acquisition of all the CapCities / ABC assets was zero.

HERB GRANATH:

That's total bullshit. What he [Eisner] wanted was ABC. He wanted that network because that was his dream; he started his career there. In fact he was there while I was there. So when they bought it, he asked me to come out and meet with him. His CFO was there, and he had papers in his hand, and he said about ESPN, "Well, it's looking like you're making a profit, but I don't know if it will ever be a big business. It's going to be a good diversification for us."

STEVE BORNSTEIN:

He did not value it at zero. He appreciated the asset of ESPN, but he never valued ABC at zero. It was making too much money. It was the number-one network! The TV stations and the network were probably throwing off a billion dollars. When they did the acquisition in '95, I can tell you the exact date they announced it, July 31, 1995, and I can promise you that in 1995, ABC was a profitable entity. For him to say in hindsight, fifteen years later, that they were only buying it for ESPN is bullshit. He appreciated the asset of ESPN, but he wanted to run a network.

FRANK BENNACK:

Getting control of ESPN was a major motivator for Michael Eisner in the takeover. I don't want to say it was the biggest factor, but clearly Michael saw ESPN's upside and all the opportunities surrounding ESPN at that time.

STEVE BORNSTEIN:

Michael Eisner will turn any circumstance into why he was a prescient genius.

CHRISTINE DRIESSEN:

When Disney bought ABC and all the assets, we [ESPN] were a diamond in the rough. At that time, ABC's television network profits were at probably an all-time high; then the world fell apart the next year.

BILL FAIRWEATHER:

There was the closed-circuit feed coming in so we could see the press conference with Eisner and the CapCities guys. Eisner was talking about what a great acquisition it was, going through all the properties and giving everyone their due. You have to realize here we are, hearing this thing in this small building in this small town in the middle of nowhere, right? And here's Michael Eisner running the Walt Disney Company and he's going on and on, and everybody's kind of half listening. And then there was a line that came out that I can still remember, and will for the rest of my life. He says, "I really consider the crown jewel of this acquisition to be ESPN." We all instantly thought, what ESPN is he talking about? He can't be talking about this little building!

STEVE BORNSTEIN:

Tom Murphy is a legend and I loved working for him. CapCities was the greatest company to work for because they led by example. They gave you a long leash, they were there when you needed them, and they rarely second-guessed you. But Murphy didn't want the remaining 20 percent of ESPN, and he'll tell you that was the biggest business mistake of his career. And there was a bunch of other stuff that he turned down. He would never support me in any of my regional pay businesses that I really wanted ESPN to get into. And CapCities focused on capital expenses like you would not believe. In 1994, when we wanted to buy computers for ESPN, we had to fly to Omaha and explain why to Warren Buffett, because the Cap-Cities guys didn't want us to buy them. When Disney took over, we were certainly looking for some relief from those types of things.

FRED GAUDELLI:
You were now starting to have Disney people attend your meetings to kind of see what your show was about, who you were reaching, and what you were doing. And they were there, ostensibly, to try to figure out how they could latch on to you and get their initiative promoted. I didn't consider them to be spies, because some of them were just nice, regular people. But we had to go to movie screenings to figure out how you were going to get this movie into your telecast. I'll never forget when they said, "We need you to attend an early screening of the animated film *Hercules* so you can determine how you can get *Hercules* into all the shows in remote production." So I went to the

screening. The movie was only about 50 percent complete. There were still drawings in a lot of it, but you always knew you had to give them something or else it would only get worse. So we came out of it saying, "You know what? This music is really *championshipesque*. We'll play the *Hercules* theme for a lot of our championships." That's kind of the way it went.

BOB LEY:

Early on in the Disney era, there was a decree that we had to announce the results of this yacht race. Somebody there had an interest in this yacht race, whether they knew somebody that was in the race or not, I don't know, but I distinctly remember we had to report it. We buried it in the show.

FRED GAUDELLI:

I remember at ABC doing Rose Bowls where at halftime you had to do a feature on the teams visiting Disneyland. You know, things that were just blatantly, journalistically wrong, you were forced to do because Disney owned the company and if they wanted a feature on the Trojans and the Buckeyes visiting Disney World they were going to get it. One year there was even talk about moving the Pro Bowl to Disney World. That was an awful idea.

The ESPYs were a better fit because it's a celebrity night. They like to get in bed with Hollywood.

BOB LEY:

People started wondering if they were going to move us to Orlando, and I said, "We ain't going anywhere. Look around. We've already got millions in the ground here. I don't think they're going to jerk us up, move all this to Florida, and turn this into a theme park."

JACK EDWARDS, *Anchor:*

There was an effort by Disney to monopolize all intellectual property that came out of everyone's head while they were working at ESPN, and I'm not sure, but I believe the boilerplate of the contract came out of the Disney Animation Studios, where they're so afraid that some brilliant young artist working in the sawmill there is going to come up with a tremendous idea and make a gazillion dollars off of it that wouldn't help the price of Disney stock. They thought that they could send the same contract to the people in the *SportsCenter* newsroom. The problem with that, of course, as anyone who has ever worked in a newsroom understands, is that it's a completely different environment, and people in newsrooms, at least people who have good minds in newsrooms, when given an authoritative order with no rationale behind it, their first reaction is to question authority.

Most people, when they were given the contract, just signed it and returned it, and gave up intellectual property rights to literally everything they'd thought of. Actually, the way the contract was worded, if you left ESPN and later wrote a memoir about your days at ESPN, Disney still owned it. I directly called the general counsel of Disney, who had sent the contract around, and I said, "Look, I have a personal-services contract with you, but that's the entirety of our agreement; there's no other part of it. I'm not going to sign anything that supersedes it." And the general counsel said something along the lines of "Well, yes, you are going to sign it," and I said, "No, actually, I'm not, and if you want to have me assign my intellectual properties to you, my price starts at $700,000 a year, so we can just go on from there." He got so angry that he actually started swearing at me over the phone. I just laughed at him because there was no way I was ever going to sign that contract.

So Olbermann and I challenged it, and it just went away. They never followed up on it because they had no grounds. Olbermann and I were the only guys in the newsroom who stood up and said, "You're an idiot if you think we're going to sign this thing." But that was the way Disney operated. I mean, they have this ridiculous top-down mentality that I think is a highly destructive element.

JUDY FEARING:

Disney was all about synergy. In its purest form, synergy can help both sides. So an example of good

synergy is when ESPN takes a week where they telecast from Disney World. We would go down and do
a lot of live remotes, whether it be radio, dot.com, or
SportsCenter. It made for a great backdrop. We also
did promotions to get fans to go to Disney, and I
thought that worked well for each other. But when
one division tries to get the upper hand, then it's out
of whack. Right after the takeover, some people at
ESPN were trying to figure out a way to help Disney
but they weren't staying true to our brand. If there's a
movie about bugs, you can't start looking for them
on a baseball field for promotion. When you compromise what your brand is like that, you only have yourself to blame.

When we were acquired by Disney, there was a lot
of concern about what was going to happen to us, but
I always thought Steve was our greatest buffer. A lot
of people out in Burbank were afraid of him. Not
Eisner, but a lot of his staff, and as much as he could,
Steve wasn't going to let anybody push him, or us,
around.

STEVE BORNSTEIN:
Bob Iger, for all his accomplishments and successes, is a very insecure guy. One of the reasons he
survived under Eisner was that there was a certain
meekness where he would actually never stand up to
Eisner. Other executives stood up to him, guys like
Katzenberg, guys like me. You remember *Sports Night*

[ABC sitcom], don't you? Well, early on after Disney's acquisition of Capital Cities, we were down in Orlando at Disney World for our first annual budget meeting with the Disney guys. All the executives get into this room, like thirty of them, and it's kind of an inquisition where you go into all the financial numbers. One of the ideas Eisner had, because he was always famous for inventing synergy, was that he wanted to put *Sports Night* on an ESPN network. I had absolutely no interest and did nothing about it. So a while later, he brought it up again, and for the second time I said that I didn't think that it was a good idea. Well, then he suggested it again, practically demanding that we do it. So I finally said, "The real reason I won't put *Sports Night* on ESPN is because *SportsCenter* is funnier than *Sports Night*." It was a pretty sarcastic, pretty negative comment. It may not sound that way today, but the way I said it, and the way it came out, just stopped him in his tracks. Iger kind of looked at me like it was my funeral. But that was the type of executive I was and I stood up to Michael. I think I made my mark standing up to Michael.

By the way, I didn't put it on, and I turned out to be right about that one.

MICHAEL EISNER:
The fact that ESPN was in Connecticut led to a more stable executive pool. At Paramount or Disney,

you'd have a hot executive and next thing you know, twelve companies would be competing for him, so his price went up. At ESPN, you either lived in Bristol or you didn't.

I liked the culture in Bristol, and I liked the economic model. They were in a Days Inn mode. They were not chained by seventy-five years of Hollywood labor practices—not only unions, but the New York and L.A. cost of living. They weren't on the star system because there was no star system.

Steve Bornstein had never forgotten his idea for an ESPN news channel—he had put it in a back pocket to save for another day. That day came in March of 1996, when Time Warner's CNN and Sports Illustrated *joined forces to announce that their awkwardly named CNN SI channel would launch on December 12 of that year—all sports news, all the time. ESPN was not about to sit back and let anybody else blaze a trail in TV sports.*

JOHN WALSH:

A couple hours after the CNN SI announcement, Bornstein gathered everyone in the newsroom and said, "Okay, here's the drill: they're going on in December, and I want us on the air by the end of October, so get your asses in gear."

Usually Steve was obsessed with graphics and sets, but ESPNews had to be done on a shoestring budget and be done fast. He kept telling us, "Just get the goddamn thing on the air. I want us to beat those sons of bitches."

For our first broadcast, we decided to go with Don Barone's great investigative piece on the Russian Mafia. We wanted to show CNN SI that we could do any and all of the stuff they were planning on doing.

Few reasonable people would expect to find the Walt Disney Company, ESPN, the National Hockey League, and the Russian Mafia all in the same sentence, or even on the same page. But there they were, soon after the Disney takeover, strange bedfellows indeed, with NHL star Pavel Bure, "the Russian Rocket," prominent in the controversy.

His story was produced in conjunction with an Outside the Lines *hourlong special on Russian Olympic sports five years after the collapse of the USSR. Since its premiere in 1990,* Outside the Lines *had established itself by mid-decade as the network's version of* 60 Minutes *and a perfect vehicle for Bob Ley, who brought gravitas and estimable journalistic skills to the program, and investigative reporter Don Barone. Their work, and that of others on the show, had helped* Outside the Lines *win six Sports Emmys by 1995.*

ESPN launched an eight-month investigation into Bure's life off the ice as a corporate officer for the so-called 21st Century Association, considered a front for the notorious Russian mob. Head of the company was Bure's longtime pal Anzor Kikalichvili, described in FBI documents as a "major Russian Mafia kingpin," reputedly into money laundering, extortion, and drugs. Asked to respond, Bure said vaguely, "I heard about this. But I don't think that's true."

The story attracted more than casual interest from the NHL, which tried to get it killed outright, but it was more complicated than that. Potential conflicts of interest for ESPN included TV rights to part of the NHL season and Disney's ownership of the Mighty Ducks hockey team of Anaheim, California, home of Disneyland.

Nevertheless, Ley and Barone were determined to pursue the story.

DON BARONE, *Investigative Producer:*

There was a whole backstory that the Russian mob was somehow involved with players in the NHL. What would happen is that Russian players would come over to America, they'd make all sorts of money, and the Russian mob back in the Soviet Union would say, "Listen, we want 10 percent of your money or we're going to kill your family." It was like taxes. So the players were paying. But the part of the story that was interesting to us back then was that some of the players were alleged to be connected to the various Russian mobs over there. They would know the salaries of the other guys, and they would know their weakness.

One of those guys linked to a mobster was this dude Pavel Bure, who was playing for Vancouver. We were told not to fly there because of safety issues, so Bob and

I flew into Seattle, drove at night into Vancouver, got a hotel room, showered, shaved, and put on new clothes. We went to the rink where Pavel was and confronted him about his friendship with a known Russian Mafia guy. We told the camera guy, "Whatever happens, don't stop rolling." When Pavel said he didn't know the guy, we pulled out a picture, a Polaroid of this Russian mobster eating borscht in a Moscow restaurant, and he wasn't real happy about that.

I had gotten the picture in a scene right out of a James Bond movie. I was standing by a certain dumpster in New York City with a backward baseball cap on, and this person walks up in a trench coat, reached in their pocket, pulled out an envelope, handed it to me, and walked away. I was a crime reporter way before ESPN, and I had sources in various federal agencies in America helping us out with it. Law enforcement was helping us out too. And this wasn't just some dude off the street.

So Pavel says the guy was just a friend, but as soon as we started to push him, he would say, "I don't understand English." If I remember correctly, we were in the locker room, and there was a guy sitting next to him. He got upset and then Pavel got upset and then the whole thing was kind of over.

HOWARD KATZ:

We knew we had our facts right and had a good story, but it wasn't necessarily flattering to the National

Hockey League. So I called Gary [Bettman, NHL commissioner] and said, "Here's what we're going to do; we'd like your side of it," and Gary said, "You can't do that." So he called Michael [Eisner] and said, "You gotta kill this." Remember, Disney owned the Ducks. But Michael told him, "When Disney bought ABC and ESPN we built two moats, one around ABC News and one around ESPN *SportsCenter*." He told us, "If you feel like you've got the right story, you should run with it."

As many times as we were forced to do promotion for Disney things that didn't necessarily fit, when it came to *SportsCenter*, we were given tremendous independence and autonomy. They never messed with our editorial content.

DON BARONE:

We wound up with stand-ups in Red Square, Washington, and Vancouver. After it aired, several people wrote stories on the report, and I heard from several newspaper guys who were pretty impressed by the thing.

BOB LEY:

The story did much to embellish the *OTL* franchise, and it set the stage for *OTL's* report two years later on sneaker factories in Vietnam. That one had some people around here a bit uncomfortable, given the fact that Nike was a rather big advertiser. We also wound up doing follow-up reports on the Russian organized-crime influence on the lives of several NBA and tennis players.

My deal at ESPN was coming up just as CNN SI was coming to be, and ESPN and I were going through a tough negotiation. Meanwhile, Jean McCormick, who had worked at ESPN and had gone to CNN SI, wanted me to join her. So I went down to Atlanta and talked with Jim Walton and a couple of other people. They put an offer together, but then ESPN stepped up and that was that. There is an ethic that pervades at a moment like that. There's the comfort level of not having to uproot. There is the fact that your thumbprints are in the concrete of the foundation. You're in the DNA of the place. And I knew I could walk into anybody's office at ESPN, put my feet up on the desk, and talk about anything. If you have a problem, you can get it dealt with. You understand who you're dealing with, and you have the ability to call on that shared history. That counts for something.

LINDA COHN:
I'm not married now, but I was for twenty-two years. I remember when I was pregnant, it was the first time an on-air woman was pregnant here. I was seven-and-a-half months pregnant and I felt big, okay? And some of the guys would make comments like "When are you going to drop that thing?" And

I'd say, "I still got some time here, folks," or "Hey, give me a break," and "You try walking around like this." But it was all in fun, because these guys meant no harm. Most of them had wives, and most of those wives were pregnant. I did a *SportsCenter* thirty-six hours before the baby was born.

CHRIS MYERS:

I got a call from one of O.J.'s representatives saying "O.J. watches your show [*Up Close*] and thinks you're very fair with people. He'd like to come on your show, but he'll only do it if the show is live." I said, "Oh, that'll be no problem." Barbara Walters had wanted to talk to him, but since he'd only do it live, she said no. So this was going to be the first live interview with O.J. after the criminal trial and the wrongful-death lawsuit.

We had a conference call with our producer, management, and one of his representatives ahead of time. I wanted to be clear that if we were going to do this, I had to be able to ask whatever I needed to ask. To my recollection, the only restriction was, "Can we leave his kids out of this?" And I said, "That's fair."

When some people heard we were going to have him on, I actually had death threats. People said, "How can you put this killer on the air? You're going to glorify him." I never told anyone this before, but I talked to Bob Shapiro, who defended O.J., and he told me, "I'd stay away from him. Anything connected with O.J. is bad news, is trouble, so I wouldn't do the interview." Bill Murray, whom I had met at the ESPYs and become friends with, recommended a book to help me out, with a title something like *How to Talk So Kids Will Listen and Listen So Kids Will Talk*. Vincent Bugliosi, the guy who put Manson away and a prosecuting attorney, was also very helpful.

When O.J. came to do the show, I believe we had police protection on the street because there were protesters. He is the only guest whose hand I never shook. In the first segment, we talked about his wife being murdered and how he was going to find the real killers, and then, as soon as we hit the break, his PR woman came out of the green room screaming, "You can't ask these questions!" And O.J., to his credit, said, "No, I can handle it. Let him ask whatever he wants."

Then, still during the break—this just tells you something about the guy—he turns to me and says, "Hey, I have a tee time at Riviera next Tuesday, if you want to play a little golf." I was just stunned. This was a guy I felt eerie about, and I just kind of went, "Naah, no thanks, but we'll pick the show up here again in about a minute." When we came to the second break, which is where we were supposed to finish, the executives back at ESPN said, "There's sports scheduled, but this is too good, let's keep going," so we went from what was going to be a half-hour show to fifty-plus minutes.

I asked him, "Are you capable of killing?" and "Did you do it?" I didn't expect him to confess, but if you watched that interview, your mind would be made up about what happened there. After the interview, he was sarcastic and said, "Well, it was great talking sports with you," since we never talked sports. I said, "What did you think we were going to do, talk about your Heisman Trophy?" And then I walked away.

I think it was a breakthrough moment. I heard people say, "We gathered around the TV set; we stopped everything at work." You know, Wall Street, wherever, they watched closely. Jay Leno used something in his monologue about it; so did Tom Snyder, who was on after that. To me it was legitimate news from a major story, and yet it was on a sports network that was continuing to grow.

RICH EISEN, *Anchor:*
I was working in Redding, California, at KRCR-TV, the ABC affiliate there, and an agent named Henry Reich from William Morris called and told me he had heard that my tape was being watched by everybody, and I was "one of the hottest up-and-coming sportscasters in America." I said, "If you say so, 'cause I gotta take my three-quarter-inch equipment and drive out to a small town called Burney and shoot girls' high school volleyball for tonight's broadcast in my Men's Wearhouse jacket with a hole in it."

He asked me to send a tape to him. I said, "No problem," then I hung up. Five minutes later, another long ring-ring, and I sarcastically said, "Watch, this is ESPN on the phone; I'm such hot shit." And it was Al Jaffe, who told me they saw my tape and wanted me to fly out as soon as possible to audition for *Sports-Center*." I said, "You gotta be kidding me." I had watched Berman, Dan, Keith, and Kilborn, so there wasn't any of me saying that I could shoot higher. No, this was it — *SportsCenter* was the end-all and be-all.

When I first got there, they had you observe for three weeks. I wound up observing Chris Berman, who only did like three or four *SportsCenters* a year back then, and I noticed he was saying stuff in meetings, and if people laughed, it wound up in the show. He was trying out material, if you will; playing Peoria before going to Broadway.

They had these ESPN banners hung up in the hallways for the higher talent to sign for charity. People would say, "This is for such-and-such charity, and can you please sign this banner?" So I'm now doing a Sunday six o'clock *SportsCenter,* and Berman is doing *Baseball Tonight* right after it. The two of us are in the same makeup room; he's in the chair. I had chatted only briefly with him before this, and I asked him, "Chris, you're Mr. ESPN, let me ask you: how many shows do I have to do before I'm banner-worthy? You know, to sign those banners for charity. Is there a certain fail-safe point?" And he goes, in his big voice, I'll never forget this: "You do a show here?" I'm like, "Yeah." He goes, "Fuck it, sign the damn things."

BRETT HABER:

Gary Miller and I were doing a *SportsCenter* in the studio; we were on the air, and all of a sudden the lights went out. The studio became pitch-black. They couldn't see us on camera, but they could hear us from our microphones. We just laughed and tried to carry on.

GARY MILLER:

I just kept going with the highlights, and that shows you how much we hated doing the re-airs if we were the last show of the night. We figured if we kept going, they could just add the video in later.

CRAIG KILBORN:

I would come in at seven to do the 2:00 a.m. show. I used to eat a lot of carbs back then. There was this unbelievable pizza place right outside of Bristol, and they had this clam pizza that had a white sauce, red and green peppers, garlic, clams, and a bit of bacon. I used to go berserk on that.

RICH EISEN:

It was all very exciting. This was what I really wanted. But on the flip side, I wasn't getting living in Bristol. It's the ultimate humbler, if that's a word. I don't want to bash the town, because it's like low-hanging fruit for people who always hear about ESPN. In fact, it's a nice community, but it's not the place for a guy who's twenty-six years old, single, and reaching a professional level that was a dream. It was always difficult to get much of a social footing. I would go to a bar, and a free drink would wind up in front me, and I would look up for the fattest guy in the bar, and sure enough, he would be the one raising the glass. That's the way it goes, man. Then again, I did meet my wife there.

CRAIG KILBORN:

You ever heard of a "Bristol Day"? A Bristol Day is where you come in, you're off, you're not working, you just come in and hang out in case they need you. They might need you to voice something over for the six o'clock or something else, but you don't have to write and host a *SportsCenter*. Everyone had Bristol Days, but I never had one because, man, I liked working five nights a week. It was exciting, right? So in my last year, after working at 2:00 a.m., getting to bed at four or five, and being unhealthy, I decided for my health's sake that I would rotate with different guys on my 2:00 a.m. show. I worked five days a week, another guy might work three, and another guy two, okay? And I loved that. But then I said, "Can I have a Bristol Day? Because I'm getting a little worn out." I just wanted to work four days a week instead of five. And I was declined. I wasn't surprised.

Then they said, "You don't have to do *Sports-Center;* you'll go to ESPN2, not on camera, just to do voice-over wrap-arounds for college basketball games. They'll come to you and you'll do scores. You just say, 'Craig Kilborn breaking in, and Xavier is up by fifteen in the first half.'" But my thing was, I'd never been on ESPN2 before and some of the guys were giving me shit. So this is me, ready? "Kilborn on the Deuce, let's check some scores." I said "Kilborn on the Deuce," right? And they suspended me for a week! I was just being sarcastic. That's called good-natured ribbing. I don't dislike them; I just think they were overreacting. They take themselves *very* seriously.

JOHN WALSH:

I'll never forget, Steve Anderson was doing day-to-day *SportsCenter,* and Kilborn was doing the 2:00 a.m. show with Haber. That was a real load to manage. Mark [Gross] came in to me one day, totally flabbergasted, and said, "John, I don't know what to do. Basically Craig Kilborn told me he's not interested in anything except basketball, that he doesn't want to do any stories except basketball, that his career was going to go somewhere else."

DAN PATRICK:

I never thought Craig was a knowledgeable sports guy as much as he was great at delivering something from somebody who was a knowledgeable sports guy.

He loved the NBA and knew it well, and he loved the Minnesota Vikings. But I give him credit: he took a Dennis Miller delivery and made this hybrid with a catchphrase or two. He had his own vernacular, and he pulled it off. He was very, very entertaining.

JOHN WALSH:

There was a big argument about the overnight show, which had always been from 2:00 a.m. to 2:30 a.m. Steve Bornstein wanted it to be expanded to an hour, and we were all holding out for it to be half an hour. He wanted it to be our decision; he was very smart about this, but he was practically on his knees begging, saying, "Guys, if it doesn't work after six months, we'll go back." So we did it, and Craig Kilborn came in and demanded twice the salary because it was going to be twice as long. He's now in L.A. somewhere.

STEVE LEVY:

Listen, guys come here to be famous. They want commercials and endorsements and cameos in movies, all those kinds of things. I've always just wanted to be a sportscaster, you know what I mean? I like the games and I like reporting on the games. If the other stuff comes, that's fine, but I think Kilborn *wanted* to be a TV star. Not necessarily a sportscaster star. And by the way, he went on to do it. Not too many people leave here and go on to bigger and better.

CRAIG KILBORN:

I don't have that strong desire to be the center of attention or be in the public eye. I love leading kind of a quiet life.

LINDA COHN:

Sports was not Craig's number one passion—well, maybe basketball, because he played—but while everyone was watching late games, he was busy watching David Letterman every night. That's where he wanted to be, and I admire that because he was honest about what he wanted. They loved him here and offered him a lot of stuff, from what I've heard, opportunities other than *SportsCenter,* because of his comedic talents, but he followed his dream. He went with that, and good for him.

BILL FAIRWEATHER:

Craig loved Hollywood, he loved show business, he loved the supermodels, and he loved Letterman. He wanted to be a television star. ESPN came to him and wanted him to do *NBA Tonight,* which they were starting up, but Craig didn't want anything to do with any of that stuff; he knew that the whole world was seeing him over and over and over again because his 2:00 a.m. show was repeated all morning. He was smart in that regard; if you wanted face time, then that was the show to be on.

I remember talking to him when he told me he was going to go to *The Daily Show,* and I was like, "You don't even know who the vice president of the fuckin' United States is and you're going to be doing a show about current events?" But obviously he had the support system that he needed. I thought he was brilliant in that late show.

SAL PAOLANTONIO, *Reporter:*

I had just come to ESPN, and Peter Gammons was not available for some reason, so I got called at literally the last minute by Jim Cohen to do an interview with Marge Schott of the Cincinnati Reds. The producer was Kelly Neal, and even though I got quickly prepped through my own research, nine-tenths of the legwork had already been done by Kelly. Mostly we were going to interview Schott about the controversies over the umpires. Among other things, I think she recycled some flowers and sent them to an umpire whose wife had died.

She did a couple of things right away that suggested she was quite eccentric, to put it mildly. She wanted to know what my full name was, so I told her it was Salvatore Anthony Nicholas Paolantonio and that I was born on St. Anthony's Day, June 13. She said she had a St. Anthony medal in her drawer, and when she opened it, believe it or not, she had swastikas in there. She pulled out the medal and started rubbing it on my arm for good luck, and I just thought, "I obviously have to ask her about Hitler." She said of Hitler, "Everyone knows he was good at the beginning, but he went too far." I specifically remember her saying that and thinking to myself, "This is the end for her. She won't survive this." And I just shut up and let her continue talking. Once she gave the answers that she gave, we knew right away that this was going to be a big story. *SI* had done a take-out about her where she intimated something about Hitler that was positive so my interview was not exactly the first time she said something positive about Hitler, but this time it was on camera, so it had more potency.

Kelly and I called Bristol right away and had the tapes couriered back there. Within a day, I had E! Entertainment trucks on my front lawn, and people from all over wanted to interview me about the interview. I remember being on the cover of *USA Today*. At that point, my wife and three children had no idea (A) what I was really doing, because I went from newspapers to TV, and (B) how important ESPN was. I certainly didn't understand the power of ESPN either. From that point on, I did.

Of course they wound up banning Schott from baseball, and I went to Riverfront Stadium to get the reaction. I got into the elevator there, and one of the security guards looked at me and said, "Do you have a credential?" and I said, "Yes, sir, it's around my neck." And he yanked it off my neck and said, "You don't have one anymore," and kicked me out of the stadium. I had to talk my way back in through the PR department. I would say the hostility toward me there was palpable.

CHRIS MYERS:

In 1996, I'm doing the *Up Close* show, and we took it to Atlanta for the Olympics and taped interviews after *SportsCenter*. One night they asked me to stay late and do an Olympic recap, and this was the middle of the summer in Atlanta, and it's so ridiculously hot that I actually put on shorts. You can't see them behind the desk, just my coat and tie. We had an outdoor location right downtown in the heart of it all, on the top of the Chamber of Commerce building, and a balcony where we were looking out over the city. That's where we would do the broadcast. There were people down below making noise, but you're trained as a broadcaster to work right through things, get the story out, don't be disrupted by a horn blowing or a fan hollering. So I'm reading these boxing results and all of a sudden I hear this loud BOOM. I thought it was fireworks or something, because there weren't any events going on at that hour.

Then I looked out below and saw people scurrying and knew something was wrong. I heard sirens, and then one of our guys said a bomb went off. Then they said, "They don't know if it's terrorists, or if there are more bombs. They want everybody out of the downtown area." I remember talking over the headset and saying, "Leave the camera man here with me and I'll see what I can get." A policeman from whatever military squad came up and looked at me kind of funny in my coat, tie, and jacket with Bermuda shorts and sneakers, and I told him, "It's okay, I'm with the media." He said, "Well, it's not safe; you're going to have to get out of here." So we moved around the building and watched as the National Guard blocked off streets and put up barricades. We wound up being the only media that stayed in the downtown area. Whenever someone came up to me, I stretched the truth a little, saying, "We're supposed to be here reporting on what's going on." We were able to do a kind of play-by-play of how security and the Olympic Committee were handling the situation and clearing everybody out for safety—except us, of course. As soon as they were able to determine that it was a bomb, a Code Red went into effect. I stayed on the air, and the last report I did was at eight in the morning. ABC News and *Nightline* carried us, along with local stations too, because there was no other news source that was there while it was going on.

JACK EDWARDS:

The six o'clock *SportsCenter* on the night after the Olympic bombing reported that Richard Jewell was in the "first circle" of suspects. Every single network chased the tail of the *Atlanta Journal-Constitution*, which jumped to its conclusion based on a hypothetical psychological profile of the bomber and came up with Richard Jewell, and the *Journal-Constitution* in spectacularly irresponsible fashion identified him. I'm sure you remember the campout at his condo as all the law-enforcement people went in there. We had a tremendous investigative producer who had an unimpeachable source, and we went on the air and said that Richard Jewell was no closer to the center of the FBI's "first circle" than any other suspect. We never varied from that, even while everyone else was identifying Jewell. I'm pretty sure I'm the anchor who said this first.

For me, that was *SportsCenter*'s greatest moment, because we were the only, and I do mean only, news agency anywhere that was not pegging Richard Jewell and putting him in the electric chair. And then lo and behold, years later, it comes out, no, it wasn't him. It was that freak who was bombing abortion clinics, not Richard Jewell. Tom Brokaw had gone on NBC and said, "No one has told us that he is not the guy," a double negative. And NBC I believe ended up writing a big check to Richard Jewell. And the poor guy had all kinds of psychological problems and stress issues for the rest of his life, and died way before his time. I lay his death right at the editor's desk at the *Atlanta Journal-Constitution;* it's on them. That was terrible journalism. But we did it right.

An August weekend in 1996 turned out to be one of the saddest in ESPN history because of two unexpected deaths. Even as the hour drew near for a memorial service honoring Allan B. "Scotty" Connal, the former executive vice president of ESPN and TV sports legend who had died earlier in the month, Bristol was shaken by the news that Tom Mees, forty-six, a sportscaster with the network from its beginning, had died in a drowning accident, apparently while trying to save his four-year-old daughter, Gabrielle, who survived. Mees also left behind his wife, Michele, and another daughter, Lauren.

Mees had been one of the network's first on-air personalities. Behind the scenes, he was described by more than one coworker as "the life of the newsroom." Boyish and, considering his profession, unusually humble, he had an unquenchable love of sports and an especially infectious enthusiasm for hockey. His dedication to the "Frozen Four" NCAA Hockey Championships helped it grow into the national event that it remains today.

Connal, who died of a heart attack in an Atlanta hospital, was sixty-eight, and Mees was to have been one of the speakers at his memorial service. The wake for Mees was on Friday, the memorial service for Connal on Saturday. Connal's family asked Bob Ley to mention Mees in his remarks eulogizing Connal, and he did. Chris Berman spoke in memory of Mees at his funeral on Monday.

It is hard to say what ESPN would have looked like if Connal had never gone to work there, but it would have certainly been different. Connal established many *of the production standards for the network, and he and Bill Fitts were probably the two greatest mentors of ESPN's first decade. Although Chet Simmons considered Connal indispensable, once Simmons had left, Connal found himself on the losing side of a power struggle with Steve Bornstein. He nevertheless remained at ESPN for several more years before forming his own production and consulting company.*

BOB PRONOVOST:

In 1983, I went into the bathroom at ESPN and Tom was in there putting on his makeup. Back in those days, that's where anchors had to put it on, because there was no other place. Tom was complaining about his agent and how he was getting screwed on his deal at the time. Thirteen years later, I bumped into him at a Mobil gas station, and I said, "Tom!" He went, "Bobby!" And the very next thing out of his mouth was "My agent is screwing me over." Thirteen years later, the exact same thing, the same conversation. He picked it right up like it never stopped. We talked for a bit and he said, "Bobby, my life now is all about my wife and my kids. Can you come over for dinner?" It was a day or two before I was supposed to go over that he died.

CHRIS MYERS:

Tom Mees was viewed as kind of a renegade to management. He'd been there a long time. He was old-school but very talented. He had a tough exterior but was a very warm soul. I had never lived in the Northeast, and my wife's from the South, so he had us over for dinner and talked about the operation there. I remember him specifically saying, because he knew I was from Florida and swam a lot, that he didn't swim and that he wanted to make sure his daughters had swimming lessons so he didn't have to worry about that. And the tragic irony that he would drown was obviously very sad.

CHRIS BERMAN:

I had taken my family to the Sky Dome in Toronto. I'd made friends with the people up there when I'd covered the Blue Jays a few times. It takes an arm and a leg to get one of those rooms, but we went up for two games when they were playing the Red Sox. No one knew where we were, and I checked my voice mail. I hear about a dozen messages, not "Here's what happened" but "Chris, you need to call me," or a few old-timers from work saying, "I'm so sorry to hear about Tom," or "I don't know what to say about Tom." So I kept hearing "Tom" or "Tommy," but nobody ever said a last name. I have three great friends at ESPN: Tom Mees, Tom Jackson, Tom Riley. One of the three of them was dead. I didn't know which one. I don't know who I was rooting for. Which one of these three was I rooting to be dead?

ROBIN ROBERTS:

I remember that day vividly. Tom had stopped by the studio earlier that same day. It was so great to see him. It had been a while since I had seen him, because he was doing so much hockey on the road by then. When they told me the news, I kept saying, "You're wrong. He can't be dead! I just saw him. You must be mistaken!"

CHARLEY STEINER:

It was around three o'clock in the afternoon, and we were called into the newsroom for an emergency meeting. Vince Doria came out of his office and said, "I don't know how to say this any better than what I'm about to say: Tom Mees just died." That night, I was co-anchoring with Robin, and it was my task to write the story. I was in shock. We had lost a family member, and I was in mourning, but here I was having to talk to the Bristol police and hospital personnel for the story.

There was much internal debate about where to place the story, and we decided it would be the last story because, had it been the lead, we would never have been able to make it through the half hour. Robin with her elegance had some final words after the story, and that was the end of it. But it was brutal. The next day we got questioned by the *New York Post* for "burying the story." We took turns saying, "Are you fucking kidding?"

BOB LEY:

In a vacuum, sure, not leading with the story was the wrong call, but there's also that part of our DNA that thinks, "Is any one of us that important?" Maybe it's presumptuous to think that the horrible death of one of us would be that important to lead the show.

Obviously it was the wrong call. The national reaction to his death was stunning. We couldn't believe it. I had toll takers on the Tappan Zee Bridge stopping me for months afterward, saying, "I'm sorry about your friend Tom."

CHRIS BERMAN:

I gave the eulogy at Tom's funeral. I wrote it. Tommy was never going to be a star for whatever reason. Not that he wasn't good enough; he *was* good enough, but Tommy had long been bypassed, if you will, on the fast track. Early on, he and I actually were charter members of the B team. We had T-shirts he made for the overnight crew that said "The B-team." You know, we're not good enough to be on before frickin' midnight. So he always had the fake chip on his shoulder, I think, but he had long since been comfortable with "I'm not going to be 'this,' but I'm really good at what I do."

I say this with love: he was kind of the whipping

boy, just because you knew he could take it. And he was such an Eagles fan. If they lost, he took it so hard. He and I used to bet beers on things like the All-Star Game. We'd have the whole crew out in the parking lot at 3:00 a.m. downing beers after the show.

DAN PATRICK:

When I first arrived at ESPN and was the new kid on the block, Tom didn't like me because he got moved down the totem pole. And I said to myself, "You know what? I'm going to make him like me." And I remember going over to see a boxing match at his house and I realized that he had this veneer, this facade, and when I got behind it, I realized he was scared. He had kids, and he was just scared about his future.

As soon as you walked into the funeral home there was a big picture of Tom, and I broke down immediately. Then I took a right, and Tom's casket was right over there. John Saunders came over and put his arm around me and I said, "I can't do this. I can't do this." I walked over to Tom's wife and said, "I'm sorry, I can't do this," and then I walked out. It just crushed me.

Keith and I went to management and asked if the newsroom could be named after Tom, but we got pushback because they said it was too precedent setting. But to this day, I don't know why they didn't do it.

Of the many permutations to Disney's taking over ABC, one of the most complex and troublesome was the relationship between ESPN and ABC Sports. Asking these two to get along wasn't quite like expecting Israel and Iran to co-exist within the same borders, but it certainly didn't lack ferocity. The cheeky upstart and the venerable champ had begun their dislike-hate relationship virtually with the birth of ESPN, and things never got any chummier. The challenge now was to have peace break out before civil war did.

SEAN McMANUS, *President, CBS Sports:*
I remember very well when Dennis Swanson was running ABC Sports, and they really were very condescending toward ESPN, extremely condescending. And I remember Bornstein coming in and saying, "Hey, why don't we do college football together? If we bid together, we could be much more powerful." But the ABC Sports guys completely looked down their noses at ESPN. I think that was never lost on the senior management of ESPN, the way they were treated. I remember I did a Big Twelve negotiation for cable and network rights, and if ABC had been with ESPN, they would have clearly wiped anybody else out. I said to the ABC Sports college guy, "Why don't you guys get together? You could get this deal." He said, "No, our guys don't want to compromise with ESPN." All it meant was compromising and sharing a couple of picks. They just didn't want to do

it. It was like negotiating with two separate companies: you'd do an ESPN discussion, then an ABC discussion. It was the damnedest thing. So we ended up doing a deal with Fox Sports.

GEOFF MASON:

The ABC Sports culture was one where we worked harder than most, but we found time to play as well, probably more than most. Parenthetically, that ultimately contributed to my having to go away to the Betty Ford Center to treat a severe alcohol problem. I just couldn't stop. It wasn't the best job for preserving marriages; our divorce rate was pretty high.

The ABC corporate lawyers were very nervous about exploring areas of cooperation with the non-union shop of Bristol. And who could blame them? But it was more than that. There was grumbling all around. There was complete and total mistrust. People don't like change.

HOWARD KATZ:

When I joined ESPN in 1993, it was difficult to get people at ABC Sports to give us what we felt was proper respect, and there was clearly a very difficult, dysfunctional relationship between Steve Bornstein, the president of ESPN, and Dennis Swanson, president of ABC Sports. It was ugly. Steve resented Dennis, and Dennis resented Steve. Not a very good situation.

JOHN SAUNDERS:

Back in '89, when Dennis Swanson was running ABC Sports, I was in his hotel room in Seattle for the Final Four, and he asked me if I would leave ESPN and host college football on ABC. In one of the scariest moments since I've been in this business, I said, "That sounds great. Have you talked to Steve Bornstein about this?" And Dennis just went off. He had been reclining on his bed and he jumped off and started screaming, "This is not the effing Steve Bornstein network. I'll do what I want to do." He just went crazy. As it turned out, Steve had his way and said, "No, John, you're not going to do it," and so I didn't.

BRENT MUSBURGER:

I actually ran into people from ABC Sports who would put down the productions at ESPN and say they weren't up to the gold standard that had been started by Roone Arledge. Most of the time, the folks at ABC would not go out of their way at all to help the ESPN crews that would come in. I'd been at meetings with producers from both entities getting ready to do golf tournaments, and it was clear that the ESPN guys were on their own and would have to round up their own interviews and make their own way. I made sure that I didn't take any kind of a side and that I would get along with everybody over at ESPN. That was premeditated on my part because anybody who has any understanding of business knew what was coming.

FRED GAUDELLI:

We were going to have a huge college football game on ESPN, and Chuck Howard [ABC producer] called Terry Lingner and said, "Hey, we'd like to do a live shot out of your truck," and Terry said, "Yeah, I'll be happy to do it for you, but you've got to promote our game." And Chuck just started in on him: "Who the fuck do you think you are? You fucking cable network, you don't fucking tell me what to do!" So Terry goes, "Well, if you don't want the shot, that's fine, but that's what it's going to take to get it." I'll never forget that. They ended up having to do it to get the shot.

DON OHLMEYER:

Once ESPN made it into the nineties, there was no reason for there to be an ABC Sports.

The only thing that was in the way was the union, and it took ABC a certain amount of time to shed those contracts.

STEVE BORNSTEIN:

We tried to kill ABC Sports early on, but we couldn't. There were a lot of union issues. What we didn't want was to in any way get ESPN contaminated and have any kind of union in there.

MIKE PEARL, *Executive Producer:*

It's a definite advantage to be in a union-free shop. I had a show once where we had just one more edit to go, and the tape operator wouldn't finish the edit because as soon as the second hand hit midnight, he was due an hour break, and sure enough, he left and went off to play cards with somebody. By the time he came back and set up, it was quarter to two in the morning, to do five minutes of work.

STEVE BORNSTEIN:

By 1997 it was game, set, match. For every dollar I'm taking in, sixty-five cents of it is coming from a subscription fee; thirty-five is coming from advertising, and the shmoe next door to me is getting everything from advertising. It's over. That doesn't mean it's a quick death; it doesn't mean that the other place doesn't survive. But the name of the game to me is make as much money as you can for as long as you can, and we had a better model.

GEOFF MASON:

In '98, it was decided we were going to do the World Cup together, which was going to air on ESPN *and* ABC. It made no sense for us to ship a production team from ABC to Paris and to send another production team from ESPN there as well. As long as we weren't on U.S. soil, we could combine forces because the union issues wouldn't come to bear. So they put me in charge of building a team composed of the best that we could find from both ABC Sports and ESPN. I handpicked a group of people that I knew would get along, and we were laughing the whole time. It was great. It worked. And that was the first time both organizations looked at each other and said, "This is the way to do it."

But when we got off the plane from France, it wasn't like, "Okay, we're together now." Not by a long shot.

Indeed, the battle between ABC Sports and ESPN would continue to escalate, with increased levels of frustration and resentment; unfortunately, it would be years before a solution (albeit a controversial and difficult one) could be forged. Meanwhile, life continued for ESPNers in Bristol and elsewhere.

BRETT HABER:

In '97, I was at the end of my three-year contract, and I think if you had to summarize it in a nutshell, I was a dumb-ass. I got there when I was twenty-four turning twenty-five—and I think my ability on the air just always outstripped my ability to get along in the workplace. I think I had a chip on my shoulder, and that manifested itself in handling myself poorly with some coworkers, and I ended up paying the price for it. It was entirely my doing. My thing had nothing to do with any of that misconduct, sexual or whatever; I'm sure anyone would tell you that, including my bosses. I had a propensity for being a hothead and for not treating my coworkers with the respect they deserved. And there were a couple of incidents that I paid the price for. One in particular was when I got into an argument with one of our staff photographers at the US Open and used some foul language with him. I got suspended over the phone, told not to come in for three or four days. Beyond that, I don't think there were any super-flagrant, egregious things. I never got into a fight with anybody, a physical fight. I just was an asshole.

I'd be lying to you if I said that I had no regrets about it and hadn't wondered how things would have turned out if I was better equipped to handle myself in that workplace, but I walked out of there with the most advanced degree in sports television that anybody could have.

There was probably a year after I left that I couldn't even watch it [ESPN]. If I had it to do over, I do wish I could go back and apologize to everybody.

BONNIE BERNSTEIN:
There weren't a ton of women at ESPN during that time, and my boss, Jim Cohen, told me he wanted to have a discussion with me about how I presented myself as a woman. He wanted me to realize that if I wasn't careful, perceptions about me could

change. I really appreciated that, because in my naïveté, that was never on the radar. I was just going about doing my job, be-bopping around, working on establishing a level of trust with athletes and coaches. ESPN was my first network job. I needed to realize I wasn't working in local TV anymore; I was operating on a national platform. People were trying to get a sense of my credibility. I remember my hair was cut short at the time, and I wore boxy suits because I wanted to make sure people focused more on the information I was gathering and disseminating than on what I was wearing.

I had several really uncomfortable moments with athletes, including one where an athlete literally said to me, "Sure, I'll do this one-on-one interview with you, but I want you to meet me in my apartment downtown afterward." I was out-of-my-mind pissed off. I called Bristol and told my producer, "That's it, I'm done, I'm out." My poor producer had to talk me off the ledge. But I was much younger then—I would say twenty-seven—and I really think that time and perspective have provided me with a lot of insights so I could gain more longevity in the business. I don't have to deal with too much now, because quite frankly, I'm forty and could be half these kids' mother. But on the occasions when I do come up against it, I'm prepared. I deal with it all through humor, because it's like when a shark senses fear, they win. If an athlete knows that they're backing you into a corner, and you respond in a fashion that shows them that you can't handle yourself, they win — whether you cave to their request or not. So if a player or coach ever hits on me, I'm like, "Honey, you don't want to go there; you can't handle it." I just make a joke about it. Then it doesn't make them feel uncomfortable that they're being rejected. By handling it that way, I've found that maybe I get a little smidgen of extra respect, because I don't try to diminish them, and I don't make what could have plausibly been a real awkward moment even more so by the way I responded.

MITCH ALBOM:

Skip Bayless and I were hired to do a version of *Sports Reporters* on ESPN's prime Monday football program, along with Joe Theismann, Phil Simms, and Mike Tirico. So I had to be in Bristol on Mondays. The next morning, I'd wake up and go see Morrie [Schwartz], and that's how it ended up being *Tuesdays with Morrie.* It was such a contrast because on Monday night I'd be talking all this football stuff, arguing over whether John Elway still has it, and then boom, the next day I'm sitting with Morrie, who is dying and it's all about the meaning of life and terminal illness. I thought, "Wow, this is a lot of life rolled into twenty-four hours."

I didn't decide to do the book until I found out that Morrie didn't have the money for his medical bills. The whole reason I wrote the book was to pay his medical bills. Sometimes I would go down to New York after seeing him, to try to find a publisher to publish the book; we got turned down everywhere. It was "No, no, you're a sportswriter; this is about death, it's boring, nobody wants it." It was only two weeks before he died that we actually finally solidified the deal with Doubleday.

They printed twenty thousand copies when I wrote it, and I gave Morrie all the money and just said, "Pay off your bills." It was a labor of love. They printed twenty thousand more copies the following August. Now, worldwide, it has sold sixteen or seventeen million copies.

HOWARD KATZ:

The Clinton White House approached us about doing a show on race relations in the United States and offered the president to be the host and moderator of a panel discussion. We did a live town hall meeting in April of 1998, and it was great television. Two days later, we had an ESPN group meeting in New York, and I walked into the board meeting and Roone stood up and gave me a hug. He said, "I've never been so proud to be associated with ESPN as I was last night, to see the president of the United States hosting a show on ESPN on a really important and relevant topic. I really can't tell you how proud I am." Well, for me, that was absolutely as good as it got.

BOB LEY:

The entire national press corps was in the back of the hall because they wanted their shot at him about Monica Lewinsky, which had bubbled up several months earlier. I wasn't allowed to ask him anything about the intern issue, because there were ground rules surrounding his appearance. Trust me, I was not about to take that opportunity.

SUZY KOLBER:

My contract was coming up, and pretty much every assignment they had given me I had done pretty well, *SportsCenter, Extreme Games,* or whatever. [Fox Sports president] David Hill called me, and my agent, Kenny Linder, really wanted me to go to Fox; the money was unbelievable. ESPN, I think, had a right to match anything, and I think it was John Walsh who called me and said, "We're not going to match the number you're saying right now, but go out and see what you can find." I said, "John, the number's going to get bigger." And it sure did. I still didn't want to go, and they didn't want me to leave. But it's like one of those things that sometimes you just have to do. I was pacing around my house. I was so stressed, but I went, and it changed my pay scale for the rest of my career. It was the launch of what was going to be the competitor — the whole regional sports network out there. And I was the first person hired for that.

Steve Bornstein FedExed me a letter that said, "The door's always open. Come back any time."

My first meeting after being hired at Fox was with [vice president] Robert Banagan, and on my way to it, I got caught up in L.A. traffic, which I was experiencing for the first time. Back then, I didn't have a cell phone in the car to let him know that I was running late. When I got there, I was flustered and he was irate that I was late. And he started fighting! He started telling me how they have writers, and I said, "Well, I've never had a writer. I write my own stuff." And he stood up and put his face in my face and literally yelled. It was unbelievable. That's how the whole thing started.

My assignments at the time were split between Fox Sports Net and the Fox network. I went to David Hill and said, "I'm so torn up about this," and he picked up the phone, got me off that network, and rolled my whole contract over to just the Fox side. I remember at our big NFL seminar, Pam Oliver and I, who were always friends, sat together, and it was almost like the executives were pointing at us like they expected a catfight. Maybe it's unfair now to say all of this without more specific examples, because I can't remember them, but I just know that it didn't feel right.

As I neared the end of my Fox contract, I bumped into folks from ESPN, and we started discussing my return; then those talks became serious. But ESPN wasn't offering everything I wanted. I believe I called

Steve [Bornstein] and said, "This thing seems to be falling apart again." He said, "Well, everyone knows you want out of there," meaning he didn't think I had a lot of leverage, but I replied that I could make it [Fox] work if I had to, and the lifestyle at Fox was pretty good. That's when ESPN sweetened their offer and the deal got done.

You are always more valuable to them when you leave; that's the great thing about leaving. I really wanted the NFL, so when I came back to ESPN, part of the deal was that I would do an NFL show. That's how I got it, and that show helped to really get me my credibility.

BONNIE BERNSTEIN:

CBS had been on sort of a football hiatus and then they got the AFC back from NBC and needed to hire more talent. They had reached out to me to inquire about my contract situation, so I went to my boss, Howard Katz, and I said, "CBS is interested," and he was like, "Well, we're planning on picking up your option." So my agent went back to Sean McManus, who then was the boss at CBS, and Sean called Howard personally and said, "Look, we know you want to keep Bonnie, but we can provide her with an opportunity here that you can't, because ESPN has Sunday night and that was it. So would you consider letting her go?" Howard called me and said, "I care about you personally and professionally, and if you think this is an opportunity that you want to pursue, I don't want to stand in your way. Just know that the door will always be open."

That meant so much to me. So I thought about it, and actually sought the advice of Robin Roberts and Bob Costas, both of whom I respect tremendously, and they gave me some great advice. I didn't want to leave. Why leave a job that I love for another job? And of course, there's always that fear of the unknown. But I thought, this is an opportunity to work at the network, and these opportunities don't come along very often, and so I was going to take it. Then at the eleventh hour, [producer] Mo Davenport called me and he said, "Okay, if you want to stay, we can offer you sidelines for *Sunday Night Football*." I was like, "Awgh!" It was brutal, 'cause that made it so hard, but I had made up my mind. It turned out ESPN wanted something in return, so they negotiated with CBS to let ESPN stay on the field for an extra period of time prior to kickoff for NFL games. So I guess I'm the first sideline reporter ever to be traded for a time slot to be named later.

KEITH OLBERMANN:

I had a story in '97 that we worked all damn day on, that Mario Lemieux, who had been treated for Hodgkin's successfully and was exhausted, was going to take at least a year off. They [Pittsburgh Penguins] had already made a personnel move to obtain a player to at least fill his spot on the roster. I stumbled onto this story by a guy who was a source of mine who knew people around Mario and had this sort of secondhand, so we were bidding all day for a second source. We finally got the player they had traded for to replace Lemieux in the lineup. I had this blockbuster lead story that was essentially of my own work, and whatever we had on beforehand—I presume it was a Sunday night baseball game—I was thinking, "Get this over with. Come on. We got a big story. Let's do it before the AP gets it." It was moments like that that were particularly thrilling. You knew you were coming on with something that almost nobody else had, literally, and certainly none of the civilians watching had any idea was the case. If you could pause long enough after saying, "Mario Lemieux will retire for at least one season and possibly more from the Pittsburgh Penguins, ESPN has learned tonight," you could almost hear the wind being sucked out of Bristol, Connecticut, by everybody gasping, especially in Pittsburgh. To drop a bombshell like that on people was a privilege and a great thrill.

JIMMY ROBERTS:

After the '97 Masters, the Golf Channel, CNN, and a couple others were all in this room that the Masters allowed us to set up in to do interviews with the winner. When Tiger came in, he said no to the others but did the interview with me. I had a very good relationship with him at the time, but I'm sure a lot of it had to do with the fact that he loved ESPN. He was a big fan.

It was the "get." As a journalist, you know how great it feels when you get something that nobody else can get.

HOWIE SCHWAB:

I was actually with Charley Steiner for the Holyfield-Tyson ear-bite fight. What I loved about Charley was he always had fun, but that night was wild. We were in the press area, watching the fight on big screens, and I didn't realize what had happened at first and then I saw the replay of the bite, and we were like, "Did he really do that?" Then I started laughing because I had Holyfield in round three. I had ten bucks at 25-to-1, so the next day I had to cash my ticket before I flew out. There was a riot at the hotel and there was absolute insanity, but fortunately I was able to cash it.

CHARLEY STEINER:

A year before that fight, I had gone to Howard Katz's office and said, "I can't do this anymore. I'm tired of making excuses for Mike Tyson and trying to defend a sport that is going to shit." I had been ESPN's boxing guy since '88, and he asked me to give it just one more year. So I did the fight, and when it was over said something to the effect that "Evander

Holyfield and a portion of his right ear were rushed to the hospital tonight... in separate cars." Those were my parting words to boxing. I got back from Vegas that Monday, saw Howard, and he said, "Say no more. You're done with boxing." I told him I always wanted to do baseball, and that was that.

BRIAN KENNY, *Anchor:*

I told the guys that I was an amateur fighter who trained at D'Amato's Gym, alongside Mike Tyson, and was fighting myself in all these boxing clubs. So I said, "You should use me this way." Charley Steiner had just stepped away from boxing, so I was like, "I'm your guy."

They said, "Hey, can you do some auditions?" So I auditioned with Teddy Atlas and Max Kellerman, the first two guys that got the jobs for *Friday Night Fights*. Afterward, they were stunned. They were like, "Wow, you really know your stuff. Have you done this before?" And I was thinking, "That's what I've been trying to tell you people!"

MAX KELLERMAN, *Boxing Analyst:*

Basically, my first year at ESPN, I partied with my friends. "Look at me, I'm on ESPN." I was on only once a week as their in-studio analyst for the new *Friday Night Fights* series, so I had a lot of time to hang out and just have a ball.

There had never been anything like the *Friday*

Night Fights studio show; it brought *SportsCenter* production quality to boxing highlights and analysis. At the time I remember telling a columnist that it felt like that *Cheers* episode when Norm got the job as a beer taster.

I remember running into Mike Tyson for the first time at a fight in Vegas. He approached me and said, "You shouldn't talk about my personal life on the air." I said, "Mike, it's nothing personal; my job is to comment on the news. When you make news outside the ring and I'm asked about it point-blank, I have to comment. I always try to be fair." He said that he'd watched me when I was a kid on Public Access in New York when he was living on Second Avenue, and that he had no real beef with me, but that he just wanted his personal life left alone.

And then after about a year and a half of just doing *Friday Night Fights,* I thought, "Okay, I'm twenty-six years old, it's probably time to get serious." To be totally honest, I didn't find much of the boxing on ESPN to be particularly compelling. I was more interested in what was going on with the Yankees, the Giants, and the Knicks. So I left the Tuesday Night series the following year.

GARY MILLER:
I always hated mascots, and it seemed like they were always around because of all the commercials we were doing. I almost got in a fistfight with Herbie

the Husker [the University of Nebraska mascot]. We were sitting in the background because the mascots are always hanging out, doing handstands or just walking around, and we were in the cafeteria getting ready to do a commercial. Herbie was sitting across from me, and I just start ripping into him. Mascots are unbelievable because they won't speak under any condition, no matter what I would say to them. Like one time I told Billy the Marlin, "God, I'd give anything for a harpoon right now," but he would only shake his head. So with Herbie the Husker, I said, "I wish I had a combine I could drive in here." And he literally got very upset but wouldn't say anything. A female anchor had to intervene and tell him to settle down. The more upset he got, the more I just kept razzing him; he's such a ridiculous mascot anyway. One *SportsCenter* commercial that I really wish I had done was when Charley [Steiner] got to punch the Syracuse Orange. That would have been great.

KEITH OLBERMANN:

When interleague play was proposed by Bud Selig, *USA Today* people called and asked me, having heard on the air that I disagreed with the concept, to write an op-ed for them for *Baseball Weekly*. And they said it would be on a page opposite somebody who was for it. I said, "Okay, fine." So I just stated my case and sent it in to them, and when I opened the newspaper later in the week, to my horror, I was the con, the pro was Bud Selig, and it was a speech to the owners announcing it that had simply been transcribed. So there was the official statement of the commissioner of baseball, and speaking against the proposal was me.

One day, I guess every month or so, they bring in somebody who will be coming in for business meetings and have them meet with the staff, or you'd be invited to have lunch in the cafeteria, whatever, two hundred people at a time, or something like that. And one day it was the commissioner, and I didn't go—I had something to do in the midday—so I didn't come in to work until the regular time. And on my desk was a handwritten note that said, "Dear Keith: I stopped by in hopes of defending myself. Sorry to find you out. We'll have to pick up this conversation later. Bud Selig." I just thought, "This really gives me an idea of just exactly where we stand in this industry." It's not like he came to Bristol, believe me, to leave that note, but I know that he was going nowhere near my desk and yet came over to make sure I got the message that a battle had been joined.

Yet somehow, it was easier for Olbermann to deal with the commissioner of baseball than several members of the management. It's fair to say that things were reaching a boiling point.

JOHN WALSH:

The Olbermann and Patrick *SportsCenter* was aimed at the highest level of intellectuals who loved sports, but I don't think it was as appealing to the average-IQ sports fan. I don't think he had that much broad appeal. Some people hated to see Keith go, but at a certain point no matter who it is, if they really don't want to be there and they're at cross-purposes with the people who are running the company, it's inevitable.

RICH EISEN:

When I got there, I was obviously very much influenced by Keith's style, and everything I did, I tried to make a joke. All my on-cameras, I had a smile on my face. Every highlight had to have something funny about it. So I walked by Keith one day in the hallway, and he just goes to me, "Nope, not yet," and kept walking. About three days later, I walked past him again and he goes, "Nope, not yet," and walks on again. So I finally asked him, "Keith, you keep telling me 'not yet,' but what do you mean?" He goes, "You're not even close to doing this show the way you should be doing it or can do it." I'm like, "Tell me, fill me up with whatever you want to fill me up with," and I think the fact that I had the same agent as him led him to do that. So one day I get an interoffice envelope in my box, and I open it up, and it's a cover letter from Keith basically saying, "I got this letter from a fan." It was a three-page letter to Keith essentially saying, "Who is this new guy on *SportsCenter*? Why has he hijacked my program? He's treating it like it's a comedy store. If he's going to be on this much, fix him." And Keith's cover letter said, "Don't take this personally, but he essentially has a point."

And he also said that my home-run call—everybody at ESPN has to have one—was so bad that people were mocking me for it. I was absolutely crestfallen. So I went to Keith and said, "All right, man, I don't know how to respond to this." He basically said, "Listen, just do one highlight without a joke. Just one. Then try to do one segment without a joke. Then two segments. Then do an entire show where you go home at night and say, 'That was the most boring show I've ever done.' And do that for an entire week." He essentially gave me the long-standing concept of less is more, that if I was going to do something really outrageous in the [second segment], then I shouldn't do anything until I bring it back in the [fifth segment]. Hands down the best advice I've ever been given.

KENNY MAYNE:
I think Keith has a warm side; it's sometimes hidden under a vest. You just can't see it. Keith is something of a tortured genius. He was rough on the help at ESPN, but he was always good to me. We lost twin

sons—Crayton and Connor—back in 1996. Crayton died at birth, and Connor died after six months. And in their memory, Keith made a real nice donation to the Ronald McDonald House up there. He also worked for me both Christmas and New Year's that year while it was all going on. My wife and I will never forget those things.

STEVE LEVY:

When I first got to ESPN, I wasn't being myself on the air. I was trying to be either Dan or Keith, and that was the trap that a lot of new anchors fell into. The height of *SportsCenter* was with those two; they were the signature figures. I don't think that'll be different seventy-five years from now.

RECE DAVIS:

The first couple of days that I'm here, someone introduces me to Keith, and he kind of looks down his nose at me and says, "Run! Get out! There's still time to save your career!"—and turns and walks away. But he was great to me. Early on, I got an opportunity to do a Saturday night *SportsCenter,* and when I got home, at 3:30 Sunday morning, my message light was on. I figure it's my mom, she probably stayed up and watched it. I check; it's Keith. And I'd had *zero* relationship with him up to that point. He said, "This is K.O. I assume this is what you want to do, and I plan to go in to management on Monday

and tell them you should be doing more of these" —
click. That meant the world to me because at that
time you're filling in, you don't know how long you're
going to get to do it, and I've never forgotten it.

When people from local markets would call
me and ask, "What do I need to do to improve?" I
would tell them, "Don't try to be Keith; he's a genius.
He's the artist you can't copy. If you want to watch
delivery, tone, and mannerisms, watch Dan. He's a
textbook."

KARL RAVECH:

I've never seen anybody do *SportsCenter* as well as
Olbermann. Nobody. It hasn't even been close.

LINDA COHN:

Keith got into trouble a lot. Athletes couldn't stand
him. Among us broadcasting people, we thought he
was a genius because he was so quick-witted and
smart, but he would make fun of athletes, and those
athletes would be like, "You never played; you don't
know what we go through."

DAN PATRICK:

I remember when Olbermann said to me, "Do you
how much this job is worth?" And I said no. He said,
"It's worth a million fucking dollars." And I said,
"Really?" I was making less than $200,000. He goes
"Yes," and I said, "Wow, I didn't know that." We were

doing 175 *SportsCenters* a year, and I thought, "We're doing *sports,* for God's sake." But Keith looked at it as a businessman, saying, "Do you know what they're making off of this?" I was a terrible businessman, but I was a damn good employee. I didn't look at the monetary aspect of it, but I appreciated Keith doing it.

KEITH OLBERMANN:

Early in 1997, I produced a really long memo to Howard Katz about the pay disparities. I showed him my math, based on the reported profits of the *Today* show and the salaries of its key figures that suggested that a fair ratio was to pay your talent a total figure of about 10 percent of their show's profits. By this methodology, working off numbers I had gotten from a sales guy in the NYC office, I calculated that the correct salaries for Dan and me were about $2,750,000 a year. I actually calculated a nonrounded number; I just don't remember it now. The next time I saw Howard, he looked at me like I was Medusa. And a year and a half later, Fox offered me a contract for something like $2,813,000 a year.

Up to that point, the top salary paid to anybody doing *SportsCenter* had been whatever I was getting, which I think topped out around $310,000 a year.

JACK EDWARDS:

The number-one thing that surprised me about ESPN was how little team spirit there was for a place that said that its business was sports. If I said, "I think you're wrong" to someone who was higher in the organizational chart than I was, what I would get back was "You're not a team player." And on more than one occasion I responded, "When's the last time *you* wore a jockstrap?" Because there are a lot of people in the administration at ESPN who throw around phrases like "be a team player" and they've never really been part of a team. A team is where you have your teammate's back regardless of what happens; you defend them and you sort out any dirty laundry quietly and privately behind closed doors.

There was almost none of that at ESPN. When people would do a great job, nobody from management would pat them on the back. There was not one person who would even say, "Hey, that was a great line," or "That was a terrific way you guys did that story," or say to the producer, "I really like the way you laid out the show." There was no encouragement, because the atmosphere was one of stick the knife in his back, climb the corporate ladder, get as big a domain as you can, dominate it, and then punish your alleged teammates and retain the biggest fiefdom that you possibly can. It was a very, very negative place to work. Don't believe the mascot promos. Life is not like that at *SportsCenter*. It is not a place where guys give each other high-fives after scoring a touchdown. It's just not that way, at least it wasn't when I left.

The prevailing idea was that the network was much more important than individuals, and that prevented the star system from starting there. In many ways, Chris Berman is their greatest nightmare, because he is a fabulously talented, extraordinarily hardworking, obsessed, dedicated, funny man who relates directly one-on-one to everyone who's ever watched him on television. They have done everything in their power to prevent anybody from getting that kind of power again. Their greatest corporate nightmare is to need someone more than that person needs ESPN.

HERB GRANATH:

I was enraged by Olbermann. Guys like that just piss me off, you know, because there's no loyalty. It's just me, me, me. Of course you have to take care of yourself, but at the same time, there's a way to do it and a way not to do it. He chose the way not to do it, in my estimation. And yet he was very popular, so Steve didn't want to immediately cut his head off. But eventually, the guy dug himself a deep hole. There was no choice but to get rid of him.

BILL WOLFF:

He didn't get along with the management? He *lived* for that. That's who Keith is. Keith and authority don't get along—ever. Well, let's say this: they don't get along for extended periods of time. There are going to be times when Keith battles authority, but he can also be one of the most loyal employees. Do not take a shot at Keith's guys; he will protect them, always. He is a total team player, actually. But he bucked authority in Bristol. There's no question; he made it hard for them. He was their best guy and he was hard to manage—I mean *hard!* Keith is a dark guy. If you take everything Keith says at face value, you will find your reason for living diminished.

KEITH OLBERMANN:

Everybody assumes there was a constant state of war there. There were wars, but not continuous. I didn't go along with that cockamamy ESPN2 idea or split my days off to keep doing radio because I was a bad employee. In that place, my team player skills were no lower than B-minus.

Puckishly titled The Big Show—*the wry nickname they gave* SportsCenter *when memorably co-anchoring it—Keith Olbermann and Dan Patrick's dual memoir was an attempt to put between covers the kind of crowd-pleasing tomfoolery they did during their years on the air together. It was subtitled "A Tribute to SportsCenter," and the authors vowed to donate a portion of the proceeds to the family of Tom Mees.*

ESPN protocol requires on-air talent to get management's permission before appearing on other networks, and though Olbermann knew the rule, he didn't bother to ask anybody before joining former ESPN comrade Craig Kilborn on Comedy Central's Daily Show *to promote the book. Olbermann's acknowledgment of the rule consisted of asking Kilborn's audience to "keep it a secret" that he'd been there.*

Olbermann further irked ESPN officials at the end of the show when, asked by Kilborn to name "the most godforsaken place" in the eastern United States, Olbermann blurted out "Bristol, Connecticut." For these offenses, ESPN's John Walsh suspended Olbermann for two weeks—with pay—even though Walsh claimed that of course he would have given Olbermann permission if only he'd asked in advance.

BOB LEY:

Olbermann was finally given a couple of weeks off when his behavior had just become intolerable. And don't think it didn't bother a lot of people; this was a *paid* two weeks off. The message being sent? "For misbehaving, he gets another two weeks off with pay to think about whether he wants to stay here or take a better offer." And he took the better offer [from Fox].

HOWARD KATZ:

Keith is as talented as anybody I've ever worked with. He is a brilliant writer, but he was a terribly unhappy person while he was up in Bristol. First of all, he was single. He didn't drive. He was living in

Southington, Connecticut. What kind of social life can you possibly have? He was not a happy camper up there, and it showed. People just didn't want to work with him anymore; he was an incredibly negative force in the workplace. He was tearing the newsroom apart. Keith had to fight management on every single point. As brilliant as he was, he was a terribly destructive force.

I had done everything I thought possible to try to build a personal relationship with Keith. I wanted him to trust me, and I thought I had a decent relationship with Keith, but Keith lashed out at management and at me. The things that Keith said publicly about John Walsh and Steve Anderson were indefensible and inexcusable. So I finally came to the conclusion that despite his brilliance and talent, we would be better off without Keith. I didn't fire Keith; I just chose not to renew his contract. He was causing so much damage, it got to the point where nobody wanted to be around him. It was ugly. That was a very difficult decision for me to make, and when I ultimately made it, Keith did not respond to it well—although I'm sure it didn't come as a surprise.

BOB LEY:

I saw Walsh in the hallway and I said, "Our long national nightmare is over, huh?" Apparently Dan said the same thing to him independently.

We felt not so much relief when Keith left as

unrestrained fucking joy. People were thrilled. And it may not be fair to him, because I don't know what his issues are. Whatever they are, they are. There was a fair amount of "Why did it take so long?" Some of what happened with him back then is romanticized, but there are still people there who remember how people were treated, spoken to, referred to, and no amount of subsequent gentle behavior is going to erase that. I honestly hope he's happy. He wasn't happy here.

JOHN WALSH:

We got four and a half great years from Keith, and then it was time for him to leave. Guys like that, it's their nature; it doesn't matter where they are, they hate the corporate mentality, they're at odds with management all the time. One thing we knew from the beginning: *SportsCenter* was a show that was great when it had fantastic talent. We were much more worried about Chris Berman leaving in the early days, because there weren't that many personalities. One thing most people don't know: in a ratings sense, the eleven o'clock *SportsCenter*'s highest-rated year, in the history of the show, was when Dan Patrick and Bob Ley were hosting—*not* Dan Patrick and Keith Olbermann.

STEVE BORNSTEIN:

Dan and Keith were magic. I recognized how big they were, and I also knew that theirs was a one-in-a-hundred pairing. They've never been able to replicate that. We tried.

RECE DAVIS:

Keith was tough on everybody. There was a rumor a few years ago that maybe he would come back, and one of our coordinating producers said, "I think it would be a good idea but with one caveat. If we hire Olbermann back, he first has to stand in the reception area and everybody who wants to, gets to come up and punch him in the stomach."

JUDY FEARING:

Steve Bornstein had taken us to off-sites when Fox was going to come out with their all-sports, twenty-four-hours-a-day programming. Everyone was asking, "What are we going to do?" because this was the first serious attack on ESPN, plus Fox has the resources. And then one day, John [Walsh] came in and said, "We don't have to worry about Fox." And we asked, "Why?" and he said, "They're hiring Keith. That will be their demise. They'll have internal fighting and internal bickering. They'll never be able to develop the culture that they want."

DAVID HILL:

I went off to run the network, and before I knew it, Keith had been hired. I said, "I love Keith's stuff. I think he's a genius. I think that he has a way of presenting sports which is totally unique. But he was so tarred by the ESPN brush that, by putting him on camera, we had totally destroyed any chance for Fox to create its own persona." We were ESPN5 by hiring Keith Olbermann. Now, the executives that did that, none of them are here anymore. Our ratings dropped because, in my opinion, people said, "You know, this is the same as ESPN, it's not *Fox Live,* it's not different. It's like ESPN. So, you know, I'll go back to watching ESPN, I won't watch this new show." Keith came in here and, to be honest, we hadn't budgeted enough for the news, and I think Keith got a little frustrated.

GARY MILLER:
Billy Fucking Fairweather from Boston. He was a real party boy. That was originally our bond, and eventually our demise. By the time October of '97 rolled around, if there was a party going on and a lot of drinking, he was part of it. I remember going into the men's room before leaving the American League party and he's next to me at the other urinal, and says, "I'm going to kill you with alcohol tonight." I said, "Uhhh...that's nice."

We were at Papa John's Basement, I think, a popular place that we had been going to for years whenever we went to Cleveland. So I'm upstairs and eventually everyone leaves, and I'm pretty hammered and I'm one of the only people left up in this back room. And I have to take a leak really bad, so I walk out and see the line is all the way across the bar and up the stairs to go to the men's room. I say, "No, I'm never going to make it through that." So I go back, and there was really nobody that I could see upstairs, so I found an empty bottle in the corner and I'm peeing into this bottle, and I finish doing that, and I didn't really turn around, and these guys grab me and say, "You're under arrest." And I said, "Why? What for?" "You just peed out that window onto an off-duty cop." And I said, "I didn't pee out of any window." And so they grab me and wrestle me down the stairs, and there were people who recognized me and were laughing and saying stuff to me. They eventually charged me with aggravated resisting arrest, aggravated disorderly conduct, and public indecency.

So I get down to the station, and it's like two in the morning. I'm standing there in the bright lights, still in handcuffs, and five cops are just standing there laughing at me. And they're saying, "Oh, what's ESPN going to think of this?" They're just having a good time. Then they empty my pockets and book me. And because I drank a lot back then, to prevent hangovers I had aspirin and Rolaids. So now it's six in the morning, and I still haven't gotten out. I'm trying to get Billy to come down and bail me out, and then I'm hearing from the news desk that they're reporting the thing on AP, including that I had on me "an instrument used for drugs" and "suspected drug residue," in quotations. So I'm just losing it, going crazy. I got help finding a lawyer, but it was Yom Kippur, so here I am, calling this lawyer on the Saturday of Yom Kippur. Reaching him was almost impossible, but I finally did, and they got me out that afternoon. Billy came to get me. And I'm going, "What in the world is all this drug talk?" That was in *USA Today,* my hometown paper, and every other paper in the country. I'm going, "Oh, my God." I'm absolutely humiliated, and scared to death. The so-called "instrument used for drugs" was a toothpick, one of those white, plastic dental picks that you carry around like a permanent toothpick. The "drug residue" turned out to be dust from the Rolaids and aspirin.

I was basically locked in my hotel for the next two days until I was going to be arraignment on that Monday. So I talked to the lawyer and actually we had a pretty good defense ready. I really did have this urination problem from all the drinking days where I had some very famous public urinations, because when I had to go, I had to go. So I had that diagnosed. And I had a bruise I had diagnosed at the Cleveland clinic from the cops' being aggressive when they arrested me. I agreed with the lawyer when he said, "Let's just get rid of this thing. If you try it, it's going to cost you a ton of money. The cops will get their side out, and they're adamant that you pissed on them. We've got one witness that says you didn't, but they've got one witness that says you did." I just decided that's enough when I saw in the paper: Gary Miller, forty, and what I was arrested for. I just said, "This is not what I want for the first line of my obituary. This is not what I worked my whole career to be known as." And I swear to this day, I did not piss out any window. It was a total setup by these cops for whatever reason. I talked to Brian Anderson, who pitched for the Indians, and he said, "Oh, yeah, they did that once to a friend of mine who was visiting town. They just kind of set people up."

We made a deal to plead no contest and contribute some money to the Ronald McDonald House, and it just sort of went away.

KARL RAVECH:

Early in the afternoon of November 3, 1998, I was playing a pickup basketball game with a bunch of guys from ESPN when I began to experience pain in my chest. I thought it was indigestion or a stomach-ache, but once the pain was accompanied by a tingling in my forearm, I was smart enough to realize that it could be more than that. I sat down for a while to see if the pain would subside, and when it didn't, I asked [ESPN news anchor] Bill Pidto to drive me to the hospital where my wife, Diane, was employed in the planning and marketing department. My hope was that once I was checked out, the doctors would allow me to get a ride home with her. I blacked out for a few seconds on the ride to the hospital and told

Bill, "I think we should hurry." In the emergency room, the doctor told me that I was having a heart attack and I remember thinking to myself, "At least I'm in the right place." Never once did I understand the severity of the situation and always believed I would be fine. A couple of days later, I was released with virtually undetectable muscle damage. I came to understand that my poor eating habits (at the time, my weight was 173), lack of regular exercise, heredity (my grandfather suffered three heart attacks), and my elevated level of homocysteine and slightly elevated levels of cholesterol all contributed to the attack.

I believe anyone who correlates the stress of my job with my heart attack would be clinically inaccurate. One month after suffering the heart attack I was running every day and I even flew—my choice—to Australia to cover the President's Cup.

CHARLEY STEINER:
In '98, John [Walsh] was working us to the bone. We had meetings in the morning, we had meetings to schedule meetings, and we had what they called postmortem meetings after shows. I used to call those the PMS. And we were just running ragged, working ten to twelve hours a day every day. Howard [Katz] wanted to know why people wanted off *SportsCenter*, and we told him, all these meetings are killing us. Keith, Robin, and I were kind of the spokesmen for talent. Of our little group, Keith was the real anar-

chist, I was a moderate anarchist, and Robin, of course, was Switzerland. Then Howard, John, and Norby Williamson ran a meeting where we had a discussion of why people were wearing out. John was a big proponent of meetings, and we said, "An editorial meeting every day, terrific, but we don't need to have a 10:30 a.m. meeting for a show that goes on the air at six or seven o'clock that night. And if we did, that's why they have squawk boxes." But, no, we had to *be there*. He felt the whole group had to be there so there's not going to be any caste system. We said, "Well, that's why people want off the show. You're killing us." And I remember Howard telling John, "You got a problem here. Fix it."

For ESPN, a full season of the NFL remained an elusive holy grail. As of 1987, the most ESPN could get was a split season, and if the network really wanted to reach a higher level—to become the "Worldwide Leader" and not just use the term as a slogan—only a full NFL season would do.

Two big, stubborn roadblocks remained. First, Ted Turner: in the early eighties, when college football first became available, Turner outbid ESPN and walked off with the rights to the first-round package that ESPN had basically created. Later, when ESPN had seemingly wrapped up a big pro-basketball deal, Turner waved more money in the NBA's face and ESPN again experienced the agony of you know what. It reached a point where many in the cable community felt that neither ESPN nor any other contender would ever be able to outbid Turner for anything.

The second major obstacle was dollars: Bornstein knew the price for a full season would be so high that he would have to get Michael Eisner to approve any deal that would satisfy the league. Bornstein quickly got to work on a presentation tape designed to excite Eisner and the Disney board about the prospect of Monday Night Football, *and it came complete with gung-ho quotes from NFL stars: "It's always better on Monday night."—Drew Bledsoe; "*Monday Night Football— *how can you not be excited by it?"—Warren Sapp; "We have everybody's undivided attention."—Shannon Sharpe. The words were supplemented with sensational pictures of NFL action and clips from a Monday-night clash between Dallas and Philadelphia that the Cowboys won in a thriller, 21–20. The tape conveyed not only the wild ride of the game itself but also the tumult behind the scenes, with the director frantically calling for shots from all the cameras as the clock ticked down the final moments.*

The presentation video combined the spectacle of Ben-Hur *with the nail-biting tension of a Hitchcock thriller. If this didn't bring Eisner and the board around, Bornstein must have thought, nothing could. But Eisner was less interested in what happened with professional football players and more focused on what was going on with cable operators.*

STEVE BORNSTEIN:

As soon as Disney acquired CapCities/ABC, I wrote a pretty detailed memorandum to Michael Eisner at his request, telling him what he had just bought with ESPN. It was one of my best memos ever, nine pages, and I identified for him all our assets, and also took the opportunity to let him know where I thought ESPN could grow and prosper in the future, with a particular heads-up on the renegotiations for the NFL rights deal which was coming soon. I believed that deal was critical to our future and needed him to get on board as soon as possible.

MICHAEL EISNER:

Steve Bornstein stressed to me the importance to ESPN of getting a full season of NFL. When we made the deal to acquire CapCites/ABC, we immediately gave ourselves a two-to-three-hundred-million-dollar loss on *Monday Night Football*. Not surprisingly, there was a general feeling that *Monday Night Football* couldn't be renewed because it was too expensive and would cause the network to lose more money, probably another two-to-three-hundred-million-dollar loss per year. The financial analysts would kill me. The press would kill me. And they did, somewhat. But then there was ESPN. If we agreed to *Monday Night Football* at a loss to ABC, we could acquire *Sunday Night Football* for ESPN and build that company for the future.

STEVE BORNSTEIN:

I had been competing with Ted Turner for high-profile sports rights since early 1980, and he could always outbid me whenever he wanted to, and often did. He had just basically sold his company to Time Warner, and he was the major shareholder. Turner had the right of first negotiation for their half of the season and they had the opportunity to extend their package. If we were going to get a full season, I had to outbid him, which wasn't going to be easy with a guy with that kind of authority. Time Warner was a big company if not the biggest media company in the world. We would have to pay significantly more than what he was willing to do.

I will forever be indebted to the movie *Waterworld*, which was Kevin Costner's Time Warner movie that went grossly over budget and tanked. I don't know if it came out a week before or a month before the negotiations, but it was very much in their consciousness. When Turner's boys came in, they had those losses in their minds and were very disciplined. That was all I needed to know. Now I had to get Eisner to come up with the money.

MICHAEL EISNER:

I was wandering around, looking at ESPN, when I met this young salesman, George Bodenheimer, who knew all about the cable operator deals and also had gone to the same college I went to, Denison, except that he went about eight hundred decades later. I said to George, "Explain to me what you think you can do if we get a full season." He said, "I think if we can get the other games away from Turner, I can get a 20 percent increase in rates." I said, "That's okay, but I don't know if that really does it. *Can you get 20 percent every year?*" He said, "I'll get back to you on that."

George calls me back and says, "Yes, they will give us a 20 percent increase compounded every year." I can't remember if it was a six- or seven-year deal, but I did a little arithmetic and called him back. I said, "No way, George; this is impossible. Nobody can give you 20 percent compounded every year for that long. Do you know what that means for them at the end of the contract with ESPN?" So I told him to go back and check again. "I need you to go back and ask again, but don't ask in such a way as to alarm them. Just do it casually over lunch, and say, 'Now, let's write this down, it's 20 percent on top of this, and the same for the next year, and so on.' Just play with it. Make sure they understand. And you can't go to just one cable company; I want to make sure this is across the board." Well, he must have gone everywhere, I don't know, but he came back again and said, "The answer is still yes."

GEORGE BODENHEIMER:

I remember those conversations. I would say, "Yes, we can keep it going." I don't know if *amazed* is the right word—perhaps *ecstatic*—but he was way beyond pleasantly surprised. For a couple years in a row, he would say to me, "Tell me again how you were able to negotiate these contracts." He asked me that question repeatedly. "Tell me how you did this," "Tell me again how you did this."

MICHAEL EISNER:

What George Bodenheimer did then is the most important thing done in broadcasting since Bill Paley stole all of NBC's stars. It *made* the CapCities/ABC deal. The CBS purchase would have been cheaper, but it didn't have this.

I couldn't say publicly that we did the deal because cable had agreed to this 20 percent compounded increase every year, because I couldn't afford to have them know about it. Eventually, of course, they knew about it, but not till about the third year.

VIC GANZI, *CEO, Hearst Corporation*:

Do the math. A 20 percent compounded increase for the cable fees doubles in about three and a half years, so if the number is one in the first year, it's two just three and a half years later, and it's all the way up to four three and a half years after that! So if I remember correctly, we were around forty cents at the beginning and the numbers just compounded up dramatically. All of a sudden you're at $3.20.

STEVE BORNSTEIN:

Look, I don't have the nicest things to say about Michael Eisner, but I do respect him. He was smart enough to buy ABC over CBS because of the cable asset of ESPN, but it wasn't the trigger for Disney to buy CapCities. That's a bridge too far.

That 20 percent compounded interest is the most important thing that ever happened to ESPN financially and still probably the most significant contributor to ESPN's success today, and how deep its moat is around it. And it was certainly the reason Eisner had the balls to green-light an $8.8 billion acquisition of NFL football for the Walt Disney Company.

Bodenheimer was instrumental in making those contracts flexible; he was the one that sold it through. It was his idea. I just don't think anybody ever anticipated we would be able to get the full season, or that we would have the audacity to go for the full 20 percent. The fact that you have the ability to go up to 20 percent doesn't mean you have to do all of it, but that's where Michael came in big time. I give him credit. He had no qualms about stepping on the accelerator. He took the maximum amount. I figured we were going to do it for five years, but he ended up doing it for the full seven years of the deal.

BRIAN ROBERTS, *CEO, Comcast:*

Michael Eisner knew that the NFL was unlike any other programming, and he used it to impose the most dramatic rate increases ever on cable customers. ESPN raised their rates more than 20 percent for seven straight years. We just didn't see that coming.

STEVE BORNSTEIN:

The cable industry knew about the 20 percent because it was in their contracts. Come on, no one has ever accused John Malone of not knowing what's in his contracts, or Brian Roberts. These are people that are as intelligent as Mr. Eisner.

STEVE BURKE, *ESPN Board Member:*

In 1998, when ABC and ESPN bid on the NFL, I was peripherally there and saw all the numbers, and what happened was, I think Steve Bornstein and Bob Iger had just come back from doing the new deal, and Tom Murphy's jaw dropped, his face turned all white, and he said, "I'm not going to be around making these calls, but this will go down as one of the top five worst deals of all time."

STEVE BORNSTEIN:

This deal was about billions and billions in revenue and asset value, and the fact is that every other business that Eisner was running, including his animation business and his television network, was going in the crapper. This was the only thing that was making money. I don't think Tom Murphy or Dan Burke would've allowed me to do that. They would've not seen the risk as worth it.

STEVE BURKE:

I was there when Michael [Eisner] called and they patched in Warren Buffett. Warren was great. Within five seconds he said, "It looks like with the NFL on ESPN you just built the biggest moat around the biggest castle in the world."

That NFL deal really made ESPN.

As if the cable surcharges weren't enough, Disney shareholders could thank Eisner for adding one more layer of protection onto the deal. As a 20 percent owner in ESPN, Hearst was expected to pay for 20 percent of deals, but for a deal this big, Eisner got Hearst to adjust the allocation between ABC and ESPN so that the network paid less and ESPN paid more. That meant Hearst would have to contribute more than 20 percent.

From the moment he arrived at ESPN in 1980, Steve Bornstein proved himself one of the most competitive and aggressive executives in television. It's doubtful that anyone else could have or would have been as determined and resourceful in pushing his new boss to acquire a full season of NFL games as Bornstein was with Michael Eisner. But to succeed, Bornstein's plan needed a foundation built on contacts and contracts with cable operators — fortunately, a subculture with which George Bodenheimer had been masterfully familiar for fifteen years. And yet, even if Bornstein and Bodenheimer had gotten their act together without a single hitch, they needed Michael Eisner to get it past the Disney board. The involvement of all three men was necessary to pull off the landmark NFL deal. If one had been missing, it very likely would not have happened.

ESPN's acquisition of a full season of NFL games in 1998 — Step Number Eight in ESPN's rise to world dominance.

CHRIS BERMAN:

When we got the full season, I called a few people to talk about whether I should go into the booth. I asked each of them, "Should I do this?" I even called Ohlmeyer on my own, and talked to him awhile about it. I remember Steve Sabol, in the classic jargon of football, told me, "That would be like taking Jim Brown and making him a flanker. You'd be a great flanker, but why would you do it? You're already either the star running back or the quarterback." I really appreciated that.

FRED GAUDELLI:

When ESPN acquired the rights to the full season, Bornstein brought in Steve Anderson [then executive producer of ABC Sports] and a bunch of us from ABC and ESPN who were involved in *Monday Night Football* on the remote side and the studio side. He said, "I want to co-mingle these two brands. You guys figure out how far we should go." So we had a series of meetings and everybody in the room, everybody, was in agreement that *Monday Night Football* was a very special brand, so ABC should keep Hank Williams, the crashing helmets, and the theme songs. If ESPN wanted to have the same graphic or promo look for Sunday night, that would be okay, but we should keep all those iconic *Monday Night Football* elements tied to Mondays and ABC.

Then we met with Bornstein and told him what we had come up with, and he says, "You know what? All you guys are fucked up. I want Hank Williams on *Sunday Night Football,* crashing helmets on *Sunday Night Football, Monday Night Football* theme music on *Sunday Night Football.* I want these two fucking shows to look the same!" So that's what happened, and that was a big mistake. Yes, you had to think of a way to make *Sunday Night Football* on ESPN more of an event, but not at the expense of *Monday Night Football.*

In 1993, ESPN ventured into the magazine world with something called Total Sports, *published in conjunction with Hearst. Teaming with Hearst made sense — Hearst was a minority partner and had been a major name in American publishing for decades — but* Total Sports *appeared only sporadically, if not erratically, and never developed a faithful following. And as a monthly feature magazine, marginal by nature, it couldn't lay a glove on* Sports Illustrated, *the undisputed champion.*

MICHAEL MacCAMBRIDGE, *Author*:

John Walsh was this kind of mythic figure in the sports journalism field. If Mark Mulvoy at *Sports Illustrated* was Ahab, Walsh was the white whale. Mulvoy was just obsessed with whatever ESPN was doing. A lot of the writers at *Sports Illustrated* couldn't understand that and asked, "Why are we so worried about ESPN?" but to Mulvoy's credit, he saw that the paradigm was changing and the primacy that *Sports Illustrated* had enjoyed in the media world was being usurped by ESPN. And the reason was not because ESPN was a cable network with *x* number of viewers; the reason was Walsh had invested *SportsCenter* with a journalistic authority that had not existed before he got there, and that did not exist anywhere else where people did sports reporting on TV. Mulvoy was scared and, in retrospect, he was right to be.

Gary Hoenig, who had shepherded the joint effort with Hearst, knew it wouldn't survive but also didn't want to give up. He had pluck. The arrival of Disney on the ESPN scene, meanwhile, brought new characters into the continuing saga, prominent among them John Skipper, who as senior vice president of Disney Publishing group had overseen all books and magazines published by Disney in the U.S. Prior to his years at Disney, Skipper had logged stints with other magazines—as president and publishing director of Spin, *publisher of* Us, *and far most notably,* Rolling Stone.

When he answered the call to take a look at the Hearst-ESPN effort, Skipper wasn't particularly impressed. But soon enough, he and John Walsh were conspiring to trash Total Sports *in its totality and develop an entirely new ESPN magazine, one that aimed a lot higher than* Total Sports *ever had. Bornstein hated the idea of throwing everything out and starting over—a lot of effort and money had already been sunk into the magazine—but Skipper and Walsh were able to wear him down and wheedle sufficient exploratory funding to see what could be done.*

STEVE BORNSTEIN:

To me, the reason for the magazine was that it would go into a space that we couldn't get into with TV or radio, whether that was a bathroom or a train.

GARY HOENIG, *Editorial Director:*

We had done a mock-up for Bennack in 1994, but the project was declared dead by Hearst that summer. Mr. Walsh, however, refused to take no for an answer, though Steve was less than enthusiastic, and so my crew scurried around doing test magazines while I tried to convince various ESPN and CapCities execs to come along for the ride. Then Disney bought Cap-Cities, Mr. Skipper met Mr. Walsh, and they decide to junk the Hearst project, which was admittedly more than a little rough around the edges, and fire the bunch of us. We convinced them to do otherwise, a decision I'm sure they've had occasion to regret, and most of that crew joined on in 1997 to work on a new launch.

JOHN SKIPPER, *Executive Vice President for Content:*

How are you going to take on *Sports Illustrated* with a monthly magazine, a magazine that was so timid in its association with ESPN that they called it *Total Sports*? You have the best brand name in sports, and you call it *Total Sports*. So we recommended to Steve something he hated at the time: shut it down and start over. And that's what we did, and that's when I moved to ESPN.

FRANK BENNACK:

Not only were we consulted, we did the internal development of the prototype, then handed that back to them and they made decisions which were quite different in many respects from what our people internally saw ought to be the outcome. Certainly it was not a biweekly; I can assure you of that. We were afraid of weeklies because of the huge cost and particularly going head-to-head against *Sports Illustrated*, but we saw it as a monthly.

DICK GLOVER:

I assumed Skipper would be some Disney wonk who was attending a meeting they made him take, but in walked the biggest sports fan next to me that I'd ever met, and this was a meeting he was greatly looking forward to. Little did I know at that point in time that Skipper's dream was to run an ESPN magazine. He told me, "I know publishing, I know magazines, and I know this is a great idea." So Skipper and I put some things together, and then John Walsh was the third part, but it was 100 percent Skipper's idea: the magazine was to be oversize and biweekly. So I wrote a big memo as to exactly what it was going to be and why we should do it, and, in the interim, Time Warner launched CNN SI Network. That just made it more compelling that they shouldn't have a place to attack us from print. *We* should be attacking *them*.

JANN WENNER:

When John Walsh was here, he got along great with Hunter Thompson, but as a leader of people, he was a disaster. He was blowing this place apart more than harmonizing and building it up. There's no way you can call him hip, or of that culture, either. He's a very square, rigorous guy, kind of like a Jesuit trainee. Everybody liked him, and yet he just didn't fit. He couldn't get any traction to work with anybody, because nobody really wanted to work with him. He just didn't fit in, that's all. He was here for about six months or so, maybe a little longer.

Skipper was here much longer. He worked at *Rolling Stone* for three years. In his time, Skipper was very much a part of the *Rolling Stone* culture and milieu. He had a lot of friends. In those days it was quite the socially intertwined organization, and people had major parts of their social life totally interconnected with the place, you know, free-flowing cocaine, young people intensely involved in their work. And John fit right in with everybody. He was beloved in the editorial department. He was beloved in the circ [circulation] department. We all knew each other, and I enjoyed him tremendously. He was fun to be with, he would sometimes smoke pot with me, and he's got that wry sense of humor, and that devotion to music. In every way that John Walsh was an outsider and got rejected, you know, because he's just completely square, John Skipper was an insider, a fun young boy, and I liked that aspect of him. He wound up growing up on the job, from circulation flunky to publisher of *Us.* I eventually fired him, but to this day, I view John Skipper as part of *Rolling Stone.* At one or two points I even asked him to come back.

JOHN PAPANEK, *Editor:*
The first words out of Steve Bornstein's mouth were "Are you ready to fuck *Sports Illustrated*?" — knowing that I had worked there. I said, "Yeah." But

then we got into the argument of weekly versus biweekly. They had already agreed to go biweekly, but Steve was still under the assumption that after we got going, we would roll up to weekly. I told him, "Before this magazine ever goes weekly, it'll go daily, because if you try to be timely on a weekly basis, you will fail miserably. If you're on a biweekly basis, you don't have to be timely. You're only looking ahead; you're never looking back.

I think that I served ESPN's purpose. It went in their favor that they got a certain kind of attention when I was announced. *SI* was already a little nervous about them doing a magazine, and I think they got more nervous when I signed up. They also anticipated, correctly, that some other folks from their camp would join me; that bothered them more than a bit.

GARY HOENIG:

Steve was pretty bitter about the biweekly thing. He was angry. It was Skipper's idea. I don't know that he necessarily did it to be like *Rolling Stone,* but when I heard it, I thought it was perfect. It breaks you out of the news cycle, because the idea is that what already happened is no longer for magazines.

JOHN SKIPPER:

I'm shocked it wasn't more transparent to people who reviewed it when it came out: It's *Rolling Stone* crossed with *Sports Illustrated.* It's a biweekly magazine, oversize, printed in the same plant as *Rolling Stone,* started by two people, John [Walsh] and I, who grew up reading *Sports Illustrated* and had been at *Rolling Stone.* But the *SI* audience was getting older, and we felt there was a publishing flaw to it, which was they were still trying to do news in a weekly format when you didn't need news weeklies anymore. ESPN was the company that ruined that. Everything we wanted to do was a clear delineation with that's them and that's old, and that's last generation, and that's the thing that happened yesterday, and we're today and we're looking forward and we're young and hip. Publicly we were of the damn-with-faint-praise school. I had a patter I used every time I got interviewed: I love *Sports Illustrated.* I grew up with it. I'm forty-two, it's my magazine, I grew up with it, it's beautiful, it's great. Gee, in the days when you needed to get your news, it was great. So it's past tense, things have changed.

Jann [Wenner] has always been quite complimentary of ESPN. He has never been anything but generous with counsel, including his praise of the magazine. I think he once told me that the type was too small, and I think I told him he was not the target demo. But I've never heard a peep from him that "Gee, you took something." I think if anything, Jann was proud.

JANN WENNER:

I'm not an ESPN magazine reader. Every time I pick it up, I can't read it. To me, it's badly designed. I mean, it made its name with its cool design, and it's youthful and zippy and has big graphics, but I just find it impossible to read. I don't find it satisfying; I throw it away.

JOHN SKIPPER:

We were asking for over $100 million. We had wanted it to be under one hundred, but the strategic planning guys kept taking it up. They were trying to get the price tag higher and higher so Michael would kill it. We had several knockdown, drag-out fights where they said to us, "You need more money." They hired three New York publishing consultants, three experts, and all three looked at the plan and said, "Generally, good plan, we like it," but one of them said, "I don't think you're going to get those ad CPMs [costs per thousand], I think it's a little aggressive." Another said, "Your editorial budget's not high enough, everything else is pretty much okay." And one of them said, "Your production costs aren't high enough." So we just kept going up and up and up.

Then again, maybe it wasn't all the analysis, presentations, conference calls, and pleading that convinced Eisner to go ahead with the magazine.

MICHAEL EISNER:

Ted Turner started a sports channel, CNN Sports, which really pissed me off. And as only Ted Turner could, he's saying to me, "I'm going to bury you, ESPN is shit, I know cable, you guys don't know cable!" And I said—taking a note from [former chairman of MCA Universal] Lew Wasserman—"Don't get angry, get even." I knew our strategic planning division didn't want to go into the magazine business—after all, we were selling off our magazines that we owned—but I walked into Disney the next day and said, "We are going to kick Time Warner's ass. We are going to bury *Sports Illustrated*. And I'm going to call Ted Turner and tell him." I called him that afternoon and said, "You're going to do CNN Sports? Well, we're going to bury your flagship. *Sports Illustrated* is old, and it is boring. Ted, you've got six hours to get out of town!" And we never stepped back. I could've cared less about the economics.

I will say, the combination of John Skipper, John Walsh, Steve Bornstein, and George Bodenheimer gave me the ability to compete with this very arrogant, terrific guy who actually invented cable, Ted Turner. And I thought doing the magazine would make us cool in the magazine world and make Time Warner uncool in the magazine world. While the magazine turned out not to be a giant economic driver, it's been very good for the brand. I believe in brands.

JOHN WALSH:
We had a big meeting in New York, and the first thing Eisner said was, "Let's make one thing clear

here: the magazine is going to be called *ESPN*. If anybody here disagrees with that, they can leave right now." And that's the only demand he ever made. Because of the pride/arrogance of all magazine editors, they wouldn't settle for *ESPN*, it had to be *ESPN: The Magazine*—which prompted Gregg Easterbrook to say we lived on "Earth, the Planet."

NEIL FINE, *Executive Editor:*
The tone really came from Gary Hoenig, who had this whole sports bar idea; he wanted the magazine to sound like guys hanging out and watching a game and having a beer. I think he hired me because I had never worked at a mainstream magazine before. My previous job was at *Diabetes Self-Management* [magazine], so to be honest, he saved me from a life of medical publishing. I had none of the stuff in my head about how sportswriting was supposed to sound. But I'm a big sports fan, so when I started writing and editing stuff, it just came out naturally.

GARY BELSKY, *Editor in Chief:*
The philosophy was clear when I got here: half the people being hired had conventional sports journalism backgrounds and the other half didn't.

FRANK DeFORD, *Columnist:*
They made a real big push for me at *ESPN: The Magazine* when they first started up. It came at a time

when my contract at *Newsweek* was running out, and there had been personnel changes at *Sports Illustrated,* and so they wanted me back. So I was in the enviable position of having three magazines fighting over me. I was like a free agent on the market. It was wonderful. I can't remember all the money details, but it wasn't that different between the three magazines. That wasn't the determining factor. It was art rather than substance which was the issue. I just felt that the ESPN audience was probably not best for me. I was a man in my late fifties, and the ESPN audience was much younger, so I just felt it was bad casting, to use a theatrical word. It was a bad part for me. And I think I made the right decision.

DAVE EGGERS, *Author:*

Gary Hoenig reached out to me after seeing a little cult magazine I used to publish called *Might* magazine out here in San Francisco. ESPN had just gotten the go-ahead to incubate their magazine and called a few of us that night, just to try to bring in young magazine editor people. I'm a medium sports fan. I always know generally what's going on, and I read the sports page every day, and I went to a Big Ten college and went to all the games there. I know generally enough about every sport, but I've never been a rabid, watching-tons-of-games-on-TV sort of a guy. I know enough to get by, and I think that they liked the fact that I wasn't so inside the machine. I think they wanted an outsider's perspective to bring the magazine maybe a slightly more casual audience and a different flavor.

I had just moved to New York to work at *Esquire,* and I had sort of a loosely defined role there, so I could take on some freelance stuff as well. So I went to meet with them, and they were working out of what seemed like a storage closet at the time. I remember getting off the elevator and their office was kind of an elevator lobby next to brooms and cleaning supplies. This was during the very early stages and I worked with Jeff Fohl, another one of our editors at *Might,* who also came in, and we sort of hashed out ideas for what the magazine could do and what hadn't been done before with sports magazines, and in particular the front section.

We wrote probably a hundred different ideas, and a lot of them ended up in there—like the "Betting Line" and "The Answer Guys"—probably at least a dozen or more things that came and went at different times. But "The Answer Guys" was my thing for a couple years, where I would just take some seemingly obvious thing—you know, why a checkerboard design is on a soccer ball—and try to trace it back to the origins of that shape. And the same thing with like a backboard for basketball; that's such a bizarre shape that we don't really examine it that much, and it could've been ten other shapes.

GARY BELSKY:

Papanek came in over Hoenig, who had been number one. So he should have, by any rights, wanted to get rid of him. He should have thought, "Hoenig can only be a cancer." But he didn't. Likewise, Hoenig should have responded to being passed over by saying, "I'm going to get the hell out of here." But he didn't. I think both of them had enough experiences in their careers, good and bad, that made them open to seeing what might happen. Their attitudes set the tone for the whole place.

NEIL FINE:

Of course that didn't shelter us from "the drive-bys."

GARY BELSKY:

That term was invented by one of the editors in the early days to describe John Walsh's visits to our offices.

NEIL FINE:

Walsh lived near Bristol, and he was never down here in New York much before the launch. But once we launched, he was here *a lot*.

GARY BELSKY:

When I came to the magazine, I didn't know who John Walsh was. He was just this polite albino man who looked like Santa Claus, but it was clear that he was to be respected and feared, not from a punishment point of view, but because he was looking at every single thing we were doing — and he cared. For the first year really, he was here all the time.

NEIL FINE:

When we were closing our first issue, Walsh had me cornered, literally against a wall in a corner! Not threatening me, just pressing a point intensely. I had never had that sort of give-and-take with an editor before, or with any superior. I was arguing about something I felt really strongly about, and in the end I think I probably got to do some version of what I wanted. It turns out Walsh just likes the dialectic of it all. He likes having the conversation, but once it's over, it's over.

Sundays, when we would close an issue, Walsh would just show up at four o'clock and start telling us all the things we shouldn't have done or that we should change. I was working on the front of the book — stuff that was supposed to be clever or humorous — and he'd stop by my desk, holding page proofs, and say, "This isn't funny." And walk away.

JOHN PAPANEK:

John Walsh is very moralistic. It's not that he's afraid of insulting people, I just don't think he likes it. And apart from ESPN's business relationships with the leagues and their bosses, he was always very, very, very vigilant of how someone was portrayed. We had this feature called "Chump Cards," and we would pick for each issue someone to be Chump. It might be the president of the American League or Bud Selig. One time, Walsh took a shoe and banged it on the table and said, "There will be no Chumps! That's the end of the argument!"

I have a personal private collection of Chump Cards that never got published because Walsh banned them from the premises.

GARY BELSKY:
Early in the magazine's history, in a snarky news-commentary section we had called the "Big 10," we were taking friendly shots at Bob Costas. We weren't saying anything really bad, just that he was a stuffed shirt or something. We like Bob. He gave us one of our best young editors, a woman who handles college basketball and the NHL for us, and she was instrumental in convincing a lot of athletes to agree to take off their clothes for our first "Body" issue. She's very talented, and she was recommended to us by Bob. So we love Bob Costas, we really do. But at the beginning of the magazine, we were poking fun at him. Then John Walsh came down and gave us all these reasons why we shouldn't poke fun at him: he's this, he's that, he's a legend, all of which was true. But that's also why you sometimes make fun of public people,

because they're legends, *because* they're a little bit puffed up. It turned out the company was also talking to Bob at that point about doing something for us. And that was the real reason John wanted us to stop poking fun at him. If John had simply said that, we would have been like, "Okay, we'll lay off. That makes sense. We get it. It's business." Had John just told us that, it would have been fine. But instead we spent two weeks going back and forth with him explaining to us, journalistically, why it didn't work to make fun of a legend in a section where we made fun of everybody. And we're like, *"Of course it makes sense!"*

NEIL FINE:

Skipper would tell us what he liked and what he didn't like, but after the fact. Walsh didn't want to wait until the magazine came out. I mean, I love the guy, but he had opinions that he couldn't wait to express. And he was right just enough of the time that you had to listen to him.

GARY BELSKY:

That was probably the most annoying thing about Walsh back then: he was right just enough of the time that you needed to pay attention.

JOHN WALSH:

I spent four days out of every two weeks at the magazine. I wanted to read every single word of every issue. On Sundays, I would get in at noon, and wouldn't leave till midnight. I had three goals in mind: first, to make sure the magazine was integrated properly into ESPN; second, to ensure that standards of excellence were part of the magazine; and third, to give people autonomy. I bowed to those guys' wishes a lot.

GARY BELSKY:

When I got here I was told they had a "no asshole policy" in terms of hiring. And for the most part it worked. Even when people got mad, nobody took it personally. It was impressive. But we had hired lots of comedy writers, people we knew were way funnier than us, and still we'd get notes or a drive-by from Walsh saying, "This isn't funny." It got so frustrating that Neil and I adopted this trope that we would revert to. We'd say, "You mean, this isn't funny...*to me*." We were thinking, "You hired us to be funny. We think we're pretty funny, people seem to laugh at us, but more importantly, we know the people we hired are funny, professionally funny, and they're producing this content. Trust us, it's funny. Leave us alone."

But eventually we realized that we weren't always getting the right message. Meaning, Papanek or Walsh would send something back and say it's not funny, but what they were really saying was, "It's not worth this joke to piss this person off." And they were probably right. We were never held back from serious journalism or commentary, but a joke better be funny enough to weather a call from the commissioner of this or that league. And what we found was, some commissioners—David Stern, for example—had big senses of humor. We'd do a visual joke and get a call from the NBA saying, "Can you give us [an original print] of the page, 'cause we want to have it framed?" But other commissioners, whose names shall not be mentioned, would be pissed off. So we started to realize that our bosses were responding to us because a series of phone calls could result if a silly joke pissed off somebody important.

NEIL FINE:

Walsh was arguing from both a business perspective and a moral aesthetic. He doesn't want you taking a cheap shot. He doesn't want you to be mean. He's not wrong about that, although it is the easiest way to be funny sometimes.

GARY BELSKY:

You can be really funny, and even cutting, without being mean. That's one of the things that Walsh was basically saying: don't be mean. Hoenig was the same way. He hated fat jokes, for example; he thought they were cheap and nasty. There are always people who will make fun of other people's physical presence—not just fat jokes but however somebody looked. But Hoenig didn't let us. He was like, "You can make fun of Matt Millen for how bad a job he did as the general manager of the Lions, but don't make fun of how Matt Millen looks or what he wears, because that's just mean."

DONNELL ALEXANDER, *Writer*:

They had a crew of people that were sort of looking for different voices, and my sense was that those people didn't get to make as much of a new path as they had wanted to. They didn't really get the magazine that they had set out to develop.

I wasn't happy with it. I had some problems with racial policies. I don't really want to put it all in one incident, but in particular I remember being really upset when they put Ricky Williams on the cover with the dress. It seemed like a very unfair thing to do to a young athlete, and that was the beginning of a very difficult road for Ricky Williams. I know journalism is also a business, but I didn't really respect the business of ESPN at a certain point.

I had sex in the office. I did drugs in the office. People knew I was mischievous. Just so it's on the record, I wasn't like some big drug addict at the office. People drank a lot at ESPN; I probably drank more then. But I'm just saying it was possible to be a bad boy then. Maybe because I wasn't in Bristol. I misbehaved with a lot of people on staff. It was live and loose back then.

JOHN WALSH:

The magazine was way overrated for its importance. We figured *SI* in its heyday was making $150 million, and we figured we could come in and make $50 to $70 million a year, but I don't think we ever made $30 million in the decade that we did it.

When Michael Jordan reigned as the world's biggest athletic superstar, no detail about him seemed too small for ESPN to report. The network might as well have turned itself into a 24/7 Michael Jordan Reality Show for all the attention lavished upon him—and the public's apparent appetite for even more. A gigantic far-flung army of sports journalists was in constant competition for Jordan's time, so access became key—and virtual currency. Here, ESPN lucked out, big-time. The network had, on staff, two people Jordan liked and to whom he granted special access: Andrea Kremer and Dan Patrick.

ANDREA KREMER:

I don't know why Michael Jordan always liked me as much as he did; certainly I was always very straight with him. I covered his games and sat down with him each year. One time I did my yearly Jordan thing and instead of just a sit-down, I had an idea which wasn't done a whole lot back then. I called it "Jordan on Jordan," where I sat with him and we watched video of him playing. And he told me that he'd never done it before, that he doesn't even watch coaching films. It was fascinating for me to watch him watch himself. And I told him, "Here's what I want you to do, almost a stream of consciousness. I want you to just tell me what's going on in your mind throughout everything that you're seeing." And there was the great amazing shot against the Lakers where he goes up with his right hand and switches midair, and I had him take me through plays like that, or six three-pointers in the first half against Portland in the Finals. I've always strongly believed that when you get these athletes out of their automatic pilot, you get them to think a little bit differently, and then you got 'em in your hand.

DAN PATRICK:

Michael came in after they won the title in Utah, and I got to witness the crowning moment of a career. He came in without shoes on, because he would always give his shoes to the Bulls' art director, his shirttail was out, he was soaked with champagne, had a cigar in his mouth, and had the basketball with him. He was a completed man; he just looked like that was everything that needed to be there for Michael Jordan, and had a smile that would take up the entire front row of an NBA game. I worked hard to get that access, so I didn't feel like I was getting something I didn't deserve. I did my homework and made sure that I was respectful when I needed to be respectful. I didn't ask too often. I tried to be fair to him. I appreciated Michael Jordan. I didn't view him as Michael or Air Jordan. He'd be Mike, and that's the way I always treated him. But I wasn't going to bow down to him, and I think he was so competitive that he loved a little bit of that "let me see what you're going to say and what I'm going to say back to you." When he got up, I said, "I still think I could score on you." And he turned around and goes, "What?!" I said, "I'd like to play you one time." He said, "You think you could fuckin' score on me? Stand up. Stand up. How are you going to guard me?" I put my arm out against his backside, and he said, "A lot of motherfuckin' teams in the NBA have tried that shit," and I saw that look for just a second, and then he smiled as he walked out the door.

BONNIE BERNSTEIN:
Michael was really great with me. For my first basketball assignment, they called me and said, "Hey, go get a one-on-one with Michael Jordan." So I was like, "Okay!" At this point, I don't know Michael Jordan from a hole in the wall. So I walk up to Mike, extend my hand, and say, "Mike, hey, I'm Bonnie Bernstein, I'm the new kid on the block, we need a one-on-one with you, we're set up over there, you know, come over whenever you want." And he looked at me like, "Who *is* this?!" But sure enough, he came over and did it. He sat down with me for, like, fifteen minutes.

Little did I know that in the course of my three-year tenure in Chicago, I would only get one other one-on-one with him.

But at the next year's training camp, in 1996, I was passing him in the hallway, and I was like, "Hey, what's up?" And he said, "Hey, I've been watching you in the off-season, you do a really good job." And, you know, my parents love me, and they think I do a good job, and friends have always been complimentary, but there have been three people in the course of my near twenty-year career now who have given me compliments that I've taken to heart and will always remember, and Michael's one of them. I just so appreciated that he actually took a random moment out of his day to share his feedback with me. Bill Parcells was another, when he was coaching the Jets. It was one of the first times I interacted with him, and I had mentioned I grew up in New Jersey, and he said, "Jersey girl, you do a nice job. I can tell you study." I grew up a Giants fan, so that was obviously a really big deal to me. And the third important one was Bob Costas, someone I grew up admiring. It was my first year on the Bulls beat, the '95–'96 playoffs, Bob was doing a game for NBC and I was standing by the scorer's table. Bob's young son was with him. And Bob walked up to me, out of the blue, extended his hand, and said, "Bonnie? Bob Costas. This is my son, Keith Costas. I really enjoy your work." I was twenty-five years old, I'd just started at ESPN in September of '95 and hadn't really been there long enough to establish myself yet, and I was so flabbergasted that Bob Costas even knew my name, I was literally shaking. I went into the bathroom, looked at myself in the mirror, and tears welled up in my eyes. And I thought, "Bob Costas knows who I am, and he thinks I'm good. Maybe I actually do have what it takes to make it." It was, unquestionably, one of the greatest moments of my career.

ANDREA KREMER:

I can't specifically remember why we chose to do an interview with Cris Carter rather than some other player, but I can tell you it's not like we said, "Let's do Cris Carter and his history of drug abuse." It was one of those things which everybody knew about but nobody talked about because he never talked about it. He never came out and acknowledged his past. Everybody knew that he had a lot of issues in Philadelphia and was let go. Everybody remembers Cris—all he ever did was catch touchdowns, and letting him go was the biggest mistake Buddy Ryan ever made—but there was never any in-depth introspection on what it was all about.

When you've done gazillions of interviews, you more often than not have an idea what somebody's going to say. But when you go into an interview and someone starts talking about something that you weren't expecting, to me that's one of the most riveting things professionally that you can go through. That's when you really get to be interviewer/therapist. We started off broadly and, once it was clear that he wanted to talk about this, then we started getting into a lot of the specifics. He had been through counseling and therapy, and as we later discussed, my interview was going to be another step for him, to be able to speak publicly for the first time about his drug and alcohol abuse. Then he gave me permission to speak for background to this woman who was basically his therapist, and I spoke to Melanie, his wife, to get her perspective. It turned out to be pretty significant, because he'd never come out like this.

I was in my office on Monday—the story ran the day before—my phone rang, and it was Cris. I swear my heart was beating so fast, because several things were flying through my head. Did he like it? Did he not like it? Is he sorry he did it? Is he angry? In our screwed-up business, a lot of times you're much too reliant on other people's opinions. Cris told me that he and Melanie watched it and it was strange because he said, "Even though you're watching a story about yourself, it's like you're watching somebody else." And he also said, and this was amazing to me, that "we picked the right time, and the right person to do it."

Predicting a career in communications for Mark Shapiro wouldn't have been hard even when he was a smart-alecky tyke running through the corridors of power at

Time Inc. His divorced mother, Judith, worked there, and though young Mark lived with Dad, his regular visits to Mom in Manhattan invariably found him hanging out at Time's corporate headquarters and rubbing elbows with Time managing editor Walter Isaacson and other luminaries. He even got to sit in on story meetings, layout meetings, cover meetings — all kinds of meetings, few of which would have interested a "normal" kid. When he boldly told legendary Sports Illustrated editor Ray Cave that he thought the magazine had too many ads, he was invited in for an hour-long chat instead of being tossed out on his ear.

Definitely a go-getter from the get-go, Shapiro knew even in high school that he yearned for a career in sports broadcasting; in fact, he started and hosted a cable-access sports show while still a student. Not wanting to wait for a mere formality like graduating from college (though he did — in 1992), he applied for an internship at NBC while still a sophomore at the University of Iowa. Only three internships were available and only one of those full-time, but Shapiro brushed aside six hundred other applicants and walked away with it. To make ends meet, he had to take a part-time job selling the New York Times over the telephone at night.

When the internship was over and Shapiro returned to school full-time, NBC kept him on as a weekend production assistant. On weekends he commuted to Notre Dame football games and, for his first major traveling event, got to go to Wimbledon (which would make a *huge impression on him) and, later, the Barcelona Olympics in 1992, and a Super Bowl or two—all this before leaving college. His first job after graduating was with NBC Sports—a job that gave him the chance to work with producer David Michaels, brother of sportscaster Al Michaels.*

Michaels soon moved Shapiro to Los Angeles, where, six months after Shapiro's arrival, he got a call from ESPN2 about a new sports talk show it was starting with the incendiary Jim Rome as host. The salary was $20,000 a year, not the stuff with which dreams are paid for. Plus, Shapiro was told, the job was temporary, and ESPN could guarantee him nothing beyond six months.

Meanwhile, Shapiro was still in demand at NBC, where he had worked his way up to associate producer at double the salary ESPN was offering—though there was no certainty that if he stayed at NBC he would be working in sports. In a way, he had too many opportunities staring him in his youthful face. Confused, he asked his father what he should do, and Dad came through with a pithy and potent five-word response:

"The future is in cable."

This made a much bigger impression on Mark Shapiro than the middle-aged man uttering "one word: plastics" did for Dustin Hoffman in The Graduate. *Shapiro even took a pay cut from $40,000 to $20,000 to join ESPN. Mark Shapiro, who celebrated his ninth birthday the year ESPN went on the air, figured his future was in cable too.*

MARK SHAPIRO:

John Walsh knew I had a real passion for sports history, so I got a call from him. He told me, "We're going to start this project, Looking Back Through 100 Years of Sports. We're going to do ancillary things, magazine supplements, a book, all these hours of programming, radio—you name it. Twenty-five million dollars is the budget for this project. You'd be the number-two guy. I said, "What do you mean 'number two'?!" He said, "You're twenty-six years old, we're not going to give you the project 100 Years of Sports." I told my wife—we were engaged at the time—"I'm not going to take it unless I get the number-one job."

STEVE BORNSTEIN:

I basically wet-nursed Mark. We gave him the shot on *SportsCentury* much to John Walsh's objection. I had to pull rank over John, who didn't think Mark was experienced enough or had the right temperament to handle a job of this size. I'd like to say we saw a real genius there, but we didn't; we did see a guy that had the right amount of energy. Part of the ESPN culture is to give people maybe younger and inexperienced an opportunity to succeed in a more responsible position.

MARK SHAPIRO:

I got into the room for the interview, and they start with, "For money or ego, we got a lot of important people wanting this thing. People like Rick Kaplan, Av Westin, Steve Friedman, and so on. Tell us about you." So aside from just trying to sell myself, I went into a whole speech which might have sounded like I was arrogant but was said with total sincerity. I started bringing up historic examples of young people—whether it was Alexander the Great or Mozart—who had done great things at an early age. I wanted them to get beyond the whole age thing, and I wanted to show them how much I loved history. I said, "If I'm the right guy, I'm the right guy." They could have said to themselves, "Who the fuck does this guy think he is?" but they didn't. I totally sold it.

BILL CREASY:

He wasn't a finger-snapping Hollywood schmuck. He was very impressive. He had great energy and an obvious desire for this job.

It finally got down to, "John, we're going to hire this fucker, and you and I are going to control him or it's going to be our ass."

MARK SHAPIRO:

A few weeks later they offered me the number-one job at $100,000 a year.

The person who really deserves the credit for the project was George Bodenheimer. Just before we got started in late '97, Steve [Bornstein] got cold feet. The production budget was $25 million, and at that point we only had GM as a presenting sponsor. If we were unable to secure new sponsors at a premium to what they typically paid for this genre of programming, the company was looking at a big loss. A meeting was held at the Stamford Country Club with George, six senior executives, and Bill Creasy. Steve had delegated the decision to George. He opened the discussion by asking the group, "Tell me why I should tell Steve we should do this." Everyone was stone silent. This was my first window into the fact that Steve intimidated everyone. No one wanted to be responsible for being wrong if this project was a loser. Creasy finally got the ball rolling, the decision was bantered around for a good hour, and then George said, "We can't afford *not* to do this. When it comes to sports, we have to make ourselves the destination for this kind of prestigious programming."

PAT SMITH, *Consultant*:

I came up with the title *SportsCentury*. We were sitting in a meeting, Creasy, Shapiro, John Kosner, and I think John Walsh was there. And we were talking about what to name the program. I was doodling on a pad and I was thinking *SportsCenter* and I just added a *U-R-Y* and took out the *E* at the end, and thought it had some patriotism in there. I wasn't going to say anything, but Kosner was looking at it over my shoulder, and said, "Hey, what about this?"

A couple of weeks later, somebody announced that Sales really liked it, and so that's what we called it, *SportsCentury*.

BUD MORGAN, *Writer*:

Mark really wanted to be out from under the pressure of having to satisfy John Walsh on a daily basis. That's why we did the show in Westport and not in Bristol. He wanted to be his own man, and John Walsh, whatever his talents—and they're considerable—is a very controlling individual in my opinion. He's also very Machiavellian. So you have to watch yourself.

MARK SHAPIRO:

One of the most controversial decisions I made with the project was my intent to shoot all original interviews with a custom, stylized look developed by Peter Franchella, an award-winning director of photography. I held firm to this decision, although my peers in Bristol were very disturbed by it. They didn't get it. They thought I was being foolish, and thumbing my nose at the collection of interviews in the Bristol library. But I wasn't. I wanted one consistent, slick, warm, intimate feel to permeate the series. I wanted a mood, and since the profiles were going to be overdosed with testimonials as the common and primary element, they were the pivotal pieces to establish that mood. Of course, contextual elements such as sound bites, films, commercials, TV appearances, newsreels, press conferences, or local television interviews were going to be used, but no sit-down interviews that ESPN had already churned out through the factory. Even if an athlete or observer had passed away and the only sit-down interview had been done by ESPN and was lying in a warehouse somewhere, my direction to my producers was to watch it for research purposes, but it was not to be used. I simply wasn't going to have a potpourri of different looks and ugly sit-down interviews messing with the tone. Walsh couldn't believe I wouldn't use snippets of a ten-hour sit-down interview the company had done with the late Arthur Ashe. I told him that the viewer would see plenty of Ashe speaking on camera by the way of contextual elements, but not an on-camera interview. I also promised him that he'd thank me for it in the years to come, as we'd be building the best collection of interviews of any news organization anywhere, a great intangible benefit to ESPN that you could never put a price on.

I couldn't guarantee that all of the firsthand participants, the athletes themselves, were going to agree to be interviewed for the project. You had to figure that recluses like Bill Russell, Johnny Unitas, and Sandy Koufax, athletes that never did interviews, especially without some kind of compensation, were not going to share their time. So our strategy was founded on getting firsthand witnesses — writers and observers that were there and had reported on the story—to sit down and retell the stories. The athletes also weren't always so candid or colorful. They might have a bias or remember the game from just their point of view with a certain slant. On the other hand, the writers were often personable, full of detail, and more objective. And there were so many of them.

Probably my favorite parts of the project were those actual testimonial interviews. Walsh and I clashed about me doing the interviews. He wanted me in the office, but I said no way. First off, interviewing was my passion. Secondly, you were literally sitting there hearing the stories firsthand from legendary writers. They were there. They could talk about Jesse Owens like he was a member of the family, given the amount of time they spent with these athletes on the road. I must have done over one hundred interviews myself, covering twenty to thirty topics with each writer. I did the last interview ever with both Jim Murray from the *Los Angeles Times* and Shirley Povich of the *Washington Post*. I had Shirley in the chair for almost four hours. He actually passed out and fell out of the chair two hours in—the lights were hot, and he was in his nineties—but I made him keep going.

PETER BONVENTRE, *Consultant:*

Walsh called me about the time they were starting *SportsCentury* and told me that this young kid, Mark Shapiro, was going to be calling me to do an interview, and would I be nice and help him out. Mainly he wanted to talk about Muhammad Ali because I had followed Ali and done a lot of writing on him. I was in Manila and had a lot of good stories. So I invited Mark over and said, "I'll give you an hour and that's really all I can do." He says, "Fine! No problem!" He sits down in our conference room, and he asks me about Ali. I tell him Ali stories, and then he says, "Did you ever do Pete Rose?" "Yes." "And John McEnroe?" "Yes." And he keeps going on. Then I said, "We've got to cut this short, I've been here an hour and a half," but he said, "No, no, I've got a few more questions." Two hours, three hours, went by. He kept me in that conference room for *four hours* asking me about every athlete, coach, or manager I ever covered. Finally I said, "Now that's it. No more! It's over." So he said, "Gee, this has been so great, can I buy you a drink?" I said absolutely, so we go across the street and it turned out I knew his mother, Judith, because she used to work at *Time* magazine. As we're leaving, he says to me, "I want you to know, I will never forget you for what you've done for me today." And I'm thinking, this little *pisher,* what is he ever going to do for me? Well, he eventually was very generous with me and we became very good friends.

GARY MILLER:

He's kind of a maniac. He had a reputation. He had worked with the guys I worked with at *Up Close,* so they were well aware of him. I didn't know him until he became the bigwig in Bristol. I had met him at Todd Fritz's. Todd was actually our booker at *Up Close* and the greatest booker in the history of television. Anyway, he got married and I went to his wedding and that's where I first met Mark Shapiro. I had heard plenty of stories about him. Like Myers would be asking somebody a question or whatever, on the air, and Shapiro would be producing those shows, and as soon as Myers asked the coach or whoever a question, Mark would be in his ear screaming, *"What the fuck kind of question was that?"* and I'm sitting there imagining how in the world you could possibly do a show with all that going on.

BUD MORGAN:

I'll tell you when I knew *SportsCentury* was going to be a success. We had not gone on the air yet, and there was a show that had been freelanced out on Secretariat, the racehorse. It was one of the fifty, and it was kind of controversial because a lot of people took the attitude "What is a four-legged animal doing on this list?" And it came back late, and it was a mess. If I remember correctly, it came in on a Tuesday, and it had to air on a Friday. So Shapiro said he wanted me and an associate producer to assemble every single bite that had the word Secretariat in it. We used this retrieval system, and got it all done by about three in the morning. The next day Shapiro looked at the material twice and then from memory redid the show from top to bottom. From that moment on, I knew we were in good hands and that it would be a success. And it was.

BOB COSTAS, *Sportscaster*:

They sat me down on three different occasions and asked me about a variety of issues and people, and those interviews became part of these shows. *SportsCentury* was magnificent. Not only was it a great bit of work done by ESPN, but I mean it when I say I think it's one of the best pieces of *television* of the last decade.

The crew chosen by ESPN for its SportsCentury *panel to name the top hundred athletes of the twentieth century included ABC News and Sports president Roone Arledge, Berkeley sociology professor Harry Edwards, columnist and bestselling author Sally Jenkins, and deep thinker David Halberstam, along with ESPNers such as Berman, Patrick, and Kornheiser.*

Michael Jordan wound up being number one, with Babe Ruth, Muhammad Ali, Jim Brown, and Wayne Gretzky rounding out the top five. Baseball landed twenty-three names in the honored one hundred; of the remainder, twenty came from football, twelve from track and field, eleven from basketball, and the rest miscellaneous. Naturally there had to be some controversy.

BOB COSTAS:

They never really spelled out the criteria, so each person had their own. I took it as a combination of excellence in the primary sport but also all-around ability if that could be measured. Then if there was a further tiebreaker, I factored in what was their sport's significance in their time. Did they have a greater standing in their time that goes beyond just pure performance and pure statistics?

I had Babe Ruth as my number one, but I think the list they came up with was a good one; everybody more or less deserved to be there, with the exception of Secretariat. I thought that was silly. Plus, if I'm not mistaken, Secretariat was either one ahead or one behind Mickey Mantle, and that personally infuriated me. My boyhood idol cannot trail a horse.

TONY KORNHEISER:

My top three were Babe Ruth, Muhammad Ali, and Michael Jordan. I can't conceive of how Ruth didn't finish number one. He had the greatest impact of anybody on a sport by far. I was willing to place Ali so high because of the way he dominated sports for so many years, but what was frustrating was that I was specifically advised not to vote for people on the basis of cultural importance, and I believed Jackie Robinson was the most important sports figure of the century. Michael Jordan didn't have as many championships as Bill Russell and didn't score as many points as Wilt Chamberlain, and really didn't do anything to advance his sport, so maybe in retrospect I upgraded him a bit too much because the way he performed was so spectacular, and because of television I got to see highlights. They may have overpersuaded a lot of us.

The flaw in the results is that the age of the voters on the panel and their personal experience determined to a large degree how they voted. For example, Dick Schaap was a contemporary of Jim Brown, so he knew that Brown was maybe the best athlete of all. I was just a kid when Brown was playing. Did Jim Thorpe get the praise he deserved? Probably not, because there weren't enough people old enough to really remember him. In the end, there were many people named in the top fifty whose careers were contemporaneous with many of the voters.

CHARLEY STEINER:

Jordan was never number one for me. I think picking him as number one was a generational decision, not a historical one. Babe Ruth deserved it more. My biggest complaint was that I've never believed golf is a sport. It's more of a skill, in the same fashion as archery. And we used to have these wonderful debates back in *SportsCentury* about it. I think a sport involves either cardiovascular abilities or defense, one or the other, but generally both. Golf has neither.

GEORGE F. WILL, *Columnist*:

Jackie Robinson was on my list because he may be the best athlete America ever produced: baseball and track star, football record holder, and he picked up a tennis racket one day and won a tournament. There's never been anyone like him.

MARK SHAPIRO:

The project came in right on budget and was very profitable. It also garnered an Emmy and the company's first Peabody Award.

STEVE BORNSTEIN:

It was a tremendous success. Mark passed with flying colors. After *SportsCentury,* we put him into programming, because I believe it's an incredibly important department.

MICHAEL MacCAMBRIDGE:

I think it's a good indicator of the scope of what ESPN was about at the end of the nineties that in addition to this hundred-part series, this huge countdown, all these insert features between shows, and these little two- and three-minute *SportsCentury* moments, they said, "Let's also do a big coffee-table book, and not just any coffee-table book, let's do a coffee-table book with the best designer in the business, get all these heavyweight writers like Roy

Blount Jr., Joyce Carol Oates, and Wilfred Sheed to contribute, and have David Halberstam write the introduction."

 So John [Walsh] brought me in to edit that, and I was really worried because after our initial conversations, I didn't hear anything from Halberstam for three months and the book was closing. I called John and said, "You've got to put a call in," and John's like, "Yeah, yeah, don't worry, you'll have it." I think it was a day or two before the drop-dead date, we had some pages saved, and he was going to write a three-thousand-word essay. Finally he called me back and said, "Okay, I'll fax it to you in the morning." So the next morning I'm at my fax machine and the pages start spitting out. My first concern was, would it be long enough? Then I see single-spaced pages come out; after five or six pages, I'm like, okay, it's going to be long enough. But the pages keep coming. They keep coming and coming and coming, and it wound up being, I think, seventy-eight pages in all. It was supposed to be a three-thousand-word essay, and it was, I think, forty thousand words. It was kind of like the old saying "If I owe you a thousand dollars, I've got a problem; if I owe you a hundred thousand dollars, *you've* got a problem." Well, if I have to cut Halberstam by a thousand words, he's got a problem; but if I have to cut him by thirty-seven thousand words, *I've* got a problem. I called up John and he's very blasé: "Didn't I tell you he'd come through?" And I said,

"Yeah, John, he came through. He sent us forty thousand words. What the fuck am I going to do?" And John just laughed, and he said, "My friend, you are the editor. You're going to tell David Halberstam 'Thank you' and then you are going to do some editing."

The draft was sprawling, with all these loose connections. There were all these long paragraphs that began with *If,* and then there'd be, like, a hundred words, and then there would be *then,* and there would be another hundred words. It was, like, sort of the first draft of *Fear and Loathing* if Halberstam wrote it about sports rather than Vegas. It was just intimidating to get through it all, but in the midst there, in the nugget of that, was a really good essay. It was just frightening to have to boil it all down. It was terrifying. David, bless him, was just "Oh sure, you just edit it any way you want." I had to come back and say, "I had to take out four-fifths of your essay, do you want to read it?" He said, "No, I'm sure it's going to be fine." I think I insisted that at some point he take a look at the final draft, and he had a few notations, but it turned out okay.

At the end of it all, we produced a terrific coffee-table book that wound up on the bestseller list. They had a big party when the book came out. Spike Lee was there and a lot of others, and it occurred to me that what I had spent the last year and half working on — this immensely expensive book, this immensely lavishly produced book—was just a drop in the bucket of all the other stuff in the ESPN empire.

The legacy of SportsCentury, *and the precedent it set for excellence in documentary filmmaking, would carry forth into the next century of ESPN. It proved conclusively that ESPN was more than* SportsCenter, *games, and news coverage. For the network, it was like a Super Bowl victory or a World Series championship—a trophy that can never be taken away.*

ESPN's documentary series, SportsCentury—*Step Number Nine in ESPN's rise to world dominance.*

RICK SUTCLIFFE, *Baseball Analyst:*

My first year working with ESPN full-time they had me doing *Baseball Tonight.* I was sitting there playing cards with my grandpa, and he said, "How's that broadcast thing?" I said, "Well, it's going fine. The biggest problem, Grandpa, you know, is I don't like wearing ties. And I still haven't learned how to tie a tie right. I may have to borrow your red clip-on." He always wore it to weddings and funerals, and I said it jokingly. But a month later, Grandpa gives me, as a present, a red clip-on tie. I started to laugh, but I looked at him, and he wasn't laughing. He goes, "I think it's the color all those guys are wearing. I hope it works for you, I hope you like it." I get it home and tell my wife and daughter, and they go, "You've got to wear it; you know he's going to be watching."

Since this is my first year, I'm nervous to begin with, and here I am, getting ready in the ESPN bathroom to put my tie on, and I got ties in my hand. I'm five minutes from going on national frickin' television, and instead of thinking about what I'm supposed to talk about, I'm trying to figure out what tie I'm going to wear. So finally I go, "You know what? My grandpa, he's always been there for me. He got me into baseball when my parents were divorced. I moved in with him when I was eleven. For everything he's done, I would rather get fired and disappoint ESPN than disappoint my grandpa." So I put on the clip-on tie.

So I go walking in, they were at a commercial break, and I have to walk right in front of the desk with Dan Patrick and Kenny Mayne. I had known Dan for a while and he goes, "Hey, Sut, how you doing?" I shake his hand, and he says, "Is that a clip-on tie you got on?" I said, "Dan, you touch it, I'll kill you. My grandpa gave this to me, I have to wear it." And all of sudden they go, "Ten seconds, boys...nine, eight, seven..." So I get over to my desk, and sure enough, Grandpa's at home watching. Before the next commercial break, Dan says, "And we'll be right back with *Baseball Tonight*, Karl Ravech, Rick Sutcliffe, and Grandpa's tie."

JED DRAKE:

In 1998, we got into business with Sportvision, a technology start-up with venture-capital funding.

Some of the principals had worked for News Corp., so they knew TV, and they approached us with the concept of a 1st and Ten Line, which would appear on the screen during our coverage of football games. As soon as we heard it, Howard Katz and I knew this was something of great interest. Now, whenever there's a new technological development, we always try to negotiate a position of exclusivity; we don't want our competitors to have what we've developed, and we like as much distinction as possible for our brand. We made a big preseason announcement that we had something really cool coming along but didn't provide any details. Then we showed it to Commissioner Tagliabue to give him a heads-up, and we were very pleased when he liked what he saw. Make no mistake: this was a big deal for us.

When we launched it, I remember telling myself, "Okay, there's no turning back now." At first, it didn't work as well as it should have—it moved around and jittered a lot—but we stuck with it and continued to make improvements with Sportvision. We were hearing that the other networks thought it was a stupid gimmick, but then Sportvision came to us and asked, "Would you be willing to release your exclusivity so that Fox could use the 1st and Ten system on the Super Bowl?" We had a lot of internal discussions here and ultimately came to the conclusion that we were not willing to release our exclusivity. Then I found out that Fox was claiming they had come up with the idea in the first place. I wound up telling a reporter for the *Miami Herald* that I wanted to congratulate David Hill. I said, "He can add the yard-marker device to his long list of accomplishments, including color TV, instant replay, and the handheld camera. Like my father once said, there's a big difference between saying you had an idea and actually making it happen." Fox had no further comment, and we won an Emmy for 1st and Ten. We were incredibly proud.

MICHAEL EISNER:

When we bought Infoseek [in 1998], it was the number-two search engine, behind Yahoo. Google was in its infancy then. The Internet was a big priority for us, and Steve Bornstein was the biggest star CEO in the Walt Disney Company, so I made him run this Internet company. He didn't want to do it, and he knew nothing about it. That wasn't good for them and it wasn't good for him. It also took him out of ESPN.

STEVE BORNSTEIN:

I turned down the ABC job twice. I thought Michael was making a big mistake, because the big driver of the business was ESPN, and those kind of things don't manage themselves. Then Eisner deployed Tom Murphy, the chairman of CapCities, probably the greatest media company ever, saying to me, "Steve, your chairman has asked you to do something that's important to him. You cannot say no. You really don't have a choice here." And so I took the job and moved to the West Coast.

Faced with a vacancy at the top of the organizational chart as ESPN was in 1998, most companies would immediately summon a big headhunting firm and cast a wide net for intriguing executive talent. Not ESPN. Bristol breeds its own. Not since Chet Simmons's arrival in 1979 had an outsider ever snatched the presidency, and that was before the network had even made it onto the air. This partly had to do with the hermetic nature of the ESPN culture, and with being headquartered not in just another New York skyscraper but spread horizontally over a one-of-a-kind campus. It would've taken most new arrivals a year merely to figure out who was who, what was what, and how things that needed doing could be done.

It was hardly a shock, then, that no outsider was seriously considered. David Zucker, ESPN's key man overseas, had expressed interest, while many ESPNers assumed that Howard Katz, Steve Bornstein's number-two man in Bristol, would be the chosen one, particularly given his vast background in production. But there was another candidate, a quieter one, if you will, whose name didn't spring to a lot of minds in terms of programming or production but who nevertheless had qualities that made him ideal.

George W. Bodenheimer had spent many of his ESPN years on the road, hammering out agreements with tough-minded cable operators, and he knew the business side of the ESPN equation as well as anyone. His knowledge and expertise proved critical to such major developments as the launch of ESPN2 and the veritably monumental football negotiations of 1998. In addition, much to his credit and despite all those years of travel, Bodenheimer was well known to many at the company. Beginning with his mail-room days, he had forged strong relationships with coworkers and was resolute about maintaining them. He also made sure to stay current on what was happening all over campus, demonstrating a knack for keeping in the know and keeping his name alive.

One more factor in Bodenheimer's favor: Bornstein loved springing surprises.

STEVE BORNSTEIN:

Picking George as my successor was my call. I could have picked any number of people. I don't think anybody would have really questioned me on any of them. I gave serious consideration to Howard Katz. He was really the only other executive that I thought was able to do the job, but I thought George had the bigger balls. That obviously impacted my relationship with Howard.

HERB GRANATH:

When Bornstein was going west, Tom Murphy said to me, "Who are you going to replace him with?" and I said, "George Bodenheimer, he's the executive vice president," and he said, "Who?" I said, "Tom, you've met him a number of times. He's just a quiet guy. He's the kind of guy I want to work with; if I give him a job, I won't have to worry, because I know it will be done." I felt George had a great deal of heart, and he was accepted by the crew because he started at the very bottom and came up through the ranks. He never threw his weight around, just quietly went around and got things done.

GEORGE BODENHEIMER:

When I became executive vice president of Sales and Marketing in 1996, it was the first time I thought, "Gee, maybe I could become president of the company." I had a good understanding of our content, having been at the company from the beginning, and I had a lot of contacts on the programming and production side. We had done *SportsCentury,* and I was heavily involved because we were selling it. Steve and I had established a great relationship both professionally and personally over the years. It wasn't like there was a big meeting where he said something like, "Gee, I think you have potential," and I said something like, "Gee, I think I can fulfill the job." I don't recall any of those big "here's what could be" discussions. It just felt kind of natural at the time.

ROSA GATTI:

We had a management meeting at a restaurant in Greenwich, and during the cocktail reception, Steve called me over and said, "I want you to get a press release ready that will say George Bodenheimer is going to become the next president." Well, I was stunned. At that point, George's name was not bandied about.

When each person became president, I would sit and talk with them about their philosophy of public relations and how they wanted to handle the announcement. I had learned to be proactive, not to assume anything, so while preparing George's release, I said, "It would be really refreshing to put in the press release that you started in the mail room." And he thought about it, and maybe the next day we went with it. And that was the headline: "From Mail Room to President."

I became concerned those first months because here's a fellow that grew up in the company but was not known on Wall Street, and how would this reflect on him? What about his credibility? At the time, all the press was, "Okay, who is this guy?" And I'm also dealing with investor relations with Disney, and "Who is this George Bodenheimer?" People did not know who he was because he was understated. And I second-guessed myself for several months.

It turned out fine. The analysts really developed a quick respect for him. People saw who he was, how engaging he was, and how down-to-earth. My interest was making him look good, in making the company look good. They came to find out he was about the roots of the company, about never forgetting where we came from, and he doesn't seek the glory. It's always about the team. That's George.

HOWARD KATZ:

I was really supportive of George getting the job. I thought he was the right choice. At one point, Steve had asked me if I wanted to be considered as a candidate for that job, and I was sort of flattered that he asked, but at the time I felt that I really didn't have any background in the revenue side of the business. I knew programming and production, but I didn't know the affiliate or advertising side at all, and I thought that would be a huge drawback. So I just thought George was better suited than I was for the job.

Many believed that Katz took the top job over at ABC Sports, where he had labored and learned under Roone Arledge, as a way of dealing with the disappointment of not succeeding Bornstein. But to Katz, it seemed like a dream position—a step up in many ways. Maybe he should have remembered the wise old adage "When the Lord wants to punish you, He answers your prayers."

STEVE BORNSTEIN:

It was a nice solution for me, because I needed a grown-up to run that business, and Howard was very good at that. And it got him out of a circumstance of working for George, which I don't think his ego was comfortable with. I felt that ESPN suffered because of it, because Howard was a damn good production executive.

HOWARD KATZ:

There are people who have said to me over the years, "God, it's too bad, I wish you had never left. I wish you had stayed. A lot of things would've been different. I know you, Howard, you wouldn't have allowed this to happen, you wouldn't have allowed that to happen." And I'm flattered when people say that to me. I just want to set the record straight that I didn't leave because I didn't get that top job. I think that was a coincidence of timing. The notion that I was upset that George got it and I left as a result couldn't be further from the truth.

In hindsight, maybe I should've stayed at ESPN. Years and years later, I say to myself it was probably a bad career move not telling Steve I was interested in that job at ESPN. Maybe I could've done it and maybe I sold myself short. Maybe I would have found out for myself if I was a capable leader.

STEVE BORNSTEIN:

When Howard took the job, he thought there was still an ABC Sports. I think he was a little naive, but it's hard to take a person of that age who has toiled that long in the business of sports television and not have him romanticize about it. It was a legacy that was unparalleled. There were three sports divisions and the greatest ever was ABC. They made a lot of money in those days and had a hell of a lot of fun, and you're being able to be the president of that division? That's pretty compelling.

HOWARD KATZ:

I started my career at ABC Sports. It had been the gold standard for so many years in sports television that I thought Disney could have two effective sports brands: ABC Sports on network and ESPN on cable. When I had the opportunity to go back there and try and rebuild it, it was something I couldn't say no to. But I was foolish enough to think I'd actually have the chance to try and do that. I did some things I was really proud of at ABC Sports, but eventually it became really clear that they were going to shut it down. They just didn't need ABC Sports anymore, and it went beyond union issues. It was at the Super Bowl in San Diego that I realized it was the end when I couldn't look ABC Sports staffers in the eye and tell them their futures were best served staying at ABC Sports.

JOHN SKIPPER:

With Steve, it was Darwinian: I'm going to put my guys against each other and the stronger ones are going to survive. When you went to a Steve staff meeting, you were a little on edge, you were tense, and you had to prepare because you knew at some point you might get tested. And if you didn't know what you needed to do, you'd get killed. With George, the meetings were calm, collaborative. He would not put up with anybody going after somebody else. Steve is testing you and he jumps on the mistakes. George trusts you from the get-go; he's trying to understand it all. It's a different approach.

When it came to the ESPYs, the network's attempt at a sports Academy Awards show, it seemed nothing would ever equal Jim Valvano's moving speech in 1993 for unforgettable emotional impact. In ensuing years, the ESPYs struggled to find an identity and to be accepted as a legitimate recognition of athletic excellence. Making that difficult was the fact that recognition of athletic excellence was already rife in American society; in addition, an ESPY on the mantel didn't really translate into tangible benefits. When you won an Oscar or a Grammy, good things often happened to your career. When you won an ESPY, little if anything changed about your life; there were no real benefits. Just a moderately handsome doorstop or paperweight.

The ESPYs were also hampered by problems with the voting. Originally, winners were selected by actual players; there was even an ESPY official who made the rounds of the leagues armed with ballots to help ensure greater player participation. Unfortunately, response was still paltry, and a switch was made to having a blue-ribbon panel determine winners. Not surprisingly, it became an ESPN-dominated blue-ribbon panel, which created still another set of issues. Finally came the matter of hosts, with results being uneven at best. Dennis Miller wryly handled the first two ESPY specials, followed in 1995 by actor John Goodman, in 1996 by comic actor Tony Danza, in 1997 by "redneck" stand-up comedian Jeff Foxworthy, in 1998 by Saturday Night Live's *Norm MacDonald—who proved a tad too irreverent for ESPN executives—and in 1999 by versatile actor Samuel L. Jackson, whom the producers loved. The first seven shows were all staged in New York, though they didn't necessarily air "live from New York"; producers liked the safety cushion they got from taping the program and airing it, edited, later.*

One of the key turning points for the ESPYs occurred in 2000, when the setting was moved to Las Vegas and players of the decade were featured. Many prominent athletes showed up; the show's popularity grew, and sports stars who'd snubbed it in the early years got out their tuxedos and turned out in greater numbers as the new century dawned. The award itself may still have meant next to nothing, but the TV special was becoming a bona fide annual event.

DAVID STEINBERG:

Money was a big issue with ESPN. That was the toughest part. They always wanted everything for nothing. One year the guy who was running the ESPYs for ESPN called me on the phone and said they were moving the show to Radio City Music Hall, and said, "I already got the budget approved." And I said, "But I haven't even given you a budget." He said, "It's just the same budget," and I said, "You can't do the show at Radio City for the same budget you did it elsewhere. What are you going to do with the set?" He said, "We'll use the same set." I said, "Do you know the size of the stage we just did the show on compared with the size of Radio City?"

They had this big meeting in Hartford. God, there must have been a hundred people from every department at ESPN, and the director, Bruce Gowers, showed them a mock-up of the set to scale and put it down on a Radio City stage so they could see it was the silliest thing in the world. But you know what? They held to their dollars. We had to just do a crappy set. But that was ESPN.

NORM MacDONALD, *ESPY Host:*

I wound up doing the ESPYs right after I got fired from *Saturday Night Live.* When I did *SNL* "Weekend Update," nobody really noticed much, but when I got fired, people had to make it a story in the press and pretend that they liked me so they could say that Don Ohlmeyer, who fired me, was a bad guy. So the timing for the ESPYs kind of worked.

Charles Woodson had won the Heisman Trophy

that year for best whatever the fuck it was, best college player? So I said, "Well, you know, that's one they never take away from you, unless you kill your wife and a waiter" — because they were talking about taking O.J.'s away from him. The audience was laughing like crazy, but I did hear later some people were offended. I mean, come on. Although I guess it was their night to shine and they didn't want a double homicide brought up. I can understand that. At the time, though, I was blissfully unaware that anyone had taken offense at anything in my monologue. I certainly wouldn't have wanted to go through the show with a bunch of giant guys waiting to beat me up.

PEYTON MANNING, *NFL Quarterback:*

I remember the first ESPY I won, it was back in 1998, for College Player of the Year. I had my little brother Cooper with me, and it was in New York at the time. I guess I'd been to New York a couple times but it was kind of the first time having a chance to meet some of these other famous professional athletes, and of course some of the movie actors and entertainers. That's still exciting today for me, but certainly as a twenty-two-year-old, it was really great.

They put us up in a hotel and just told us what time the event was the next day. Back then, the planning was very word-of-mouth. Cooper and I went down to the lobby, and we saw Dan Patrick, who said to us, "Hootie and the Blowfish are playing tonight, if you guys want to come, there'll be some other ESPN guys and athletes there." So we went there, and wound up seeing Chris Berman get up onstage and sing with Hootie and the Blowfish. There was more fun the next night, we met a bunch of people, but nothing like seeing Berman up there.

NORM MacDONALD:

The audience at the ESPYs was about 5 percent athletes and 95 percent New Yorkers, and the athletes get all the good seats. I was making these sports jokes, which were going over really well with the New York guys, but what I didn't know is behind me they were showing pictures of athletes' faces, and they were angry, because they weren't used to people joking around about them. It turns out they don't care for that. It's like you're in fucking high school or some shit, and there's some big jock. Now, do you think that guy wants some fucker making jokes about him? No, and his natural instinct would just be to beat the shit out of you.

Tiger liked me, though, and Tiger's, like, my favorite. He was there and up for an award, and I made him laugh because I said, "Who's going to beat Tiger? This is the most retarded ESPYs ever." And they cut to him laughing, 'cause he knew I was telling him how good he was. It's one of the shows where the fuckin' winners are already known, so only one guy's there from the category, but you have to pretend anyway. It's always like "Achievement of the Year!" And then it's the fuckin' team that won the World Series, you know?

But the funniest thing I ever saw at the ESPYs wasn't the year I hosted, but was when Bill Murray was giving out the Comeback Player of the Year award, and it was between Monica Seles, who had been stabbed, and Michael Jordan because he had come back from baseball. So fuckin' Bill Murray was just hysterical, because as he's giving the award to Michael, he says, "Michael, I know you came back and everything from baseball, and you had to get back to conditioning—but the girl was *stabbed!*" It was really funny. Michael was, like, a little mad. He looked like "I want this one too."

SAMUEL L. JACKSON, *ESPY Host:*

I'm not sure how or why they asked me to host, but I probably met somebody at a golf tournament somewhere, because I had just started playing around '99 and that's the first time I hosted. I'd seen the show, because I watch ESPN a lot. But the show's kind of straitlaced, athletes in tuxedos making speeches, it's almost like a dinner without the food. And I guess they were trying to spice the show up and make it something different. I'm pretty outspoken and I don't mind making fun of myself or other people—including athletes. But I have a healthy respect for what they do in terms of the amount of work it takes to get to be so good at it.

The pay was pretty good, and, oh yeah, I had a great time. I got to meet some athletes who I didn't know that I would have an opportunity to talk to and laugh with, and some of them are really interesting people. Despite all the things that they can do that I couldn't do, they still marveled at what I did. They have an inordinate amount of downtime, so they know a lot about my movies because they watch them, so we have interesting conversations about me watching them and them watching me, so it's kind of a mutual admiration society. But then I met some athletes who said, "You know, I want to be an actor when I finish" — they thought they could "do the acting thing." I thought, "Hmm, okay, man, just play ball."

MAURA MANDT:

The year 2000 was amazing. We had Michael Jordan, Wayne Gretzky, Tiger Woods, Lance Armstrong, Derek Jeter, Marion Jones, Mario Lemieux, Mark McGwire, and a bunch of other big names. I went up to Jordan in the front row right before the show was going to start and asked him if he needed anything, and he said, "Yes, a wet towel." I was a bit taken aback, but I had to race around to get one in time.

CHRIS LaPLACA:

Michael Jordan and Wayne Gretzky both said they would do some press immediately afterward—which for me was amazing. So they come offstage and the first thing they do is go the wrong way and disappear into the shadows of backstage. I'm thinking, this is bad, we're never going to get them back. We all had to wear tuxedos that night, and there's a guy on my team named Rob Tobias chasing them in his tuxedo. Next thing I see is the two of them emerging from the shadows and they're walking back toward me. Inside the pressroom, Chris Berman was talking, so now I've got to entertain Michael Jordan and Wayne Gretzky before they bolt and blow this off. So I engaged them in conversation. I don't remember what I said, but Berman was still talking and eventually Gretzky looked into the room, looked at Michael, looked at me, and said, "They don't want to talk to me; they're really here to see Michael. I think I'll just go." I said, "Please, no, wait. Really they do. Chris will be done in a second." But Berman and the press kept going.

So now I'm starting to panic because Gretzky is really getting anxious and to have both Jordan and Gretzky go out there together was going to be a really nice moment for us. So we talk a little bit more, and then Wayne says again, "Really, no, really, they just want Mike, they don't want me. I'm going to go." I guess out of desperation, I turned to him and said, "Hey, Wayne, you're the only guy in the building who's named The Great One. I think they'll want to talk to you." Jordan started to laugh, and Wayne calmed down. Berman finished soon thereafter and the two guys walked out together. So we got that one done.

By the late 1990s, ESPN reached more than 75 million American homes, and was the most widely distributed cable network in the United States. ESPN2 now had 50 million U.S. subscribers, and internationally, ESPN reached over 150 million homes in over 160 countries, in twenty languages.

But it was once again time for some big new thing to emerge. And obligingly enough, one arrived—with a roar.

ESPN's first live college football game was Louisiana's Independence Bowl in December 1982. Two years later, ESPN began televising regular season games, and in 1987, the network debuted College GameDay, *a weekly analysis of college football games. Tim Brando would be the first host, with former coach Lee Corso and TV gadfly Beano Cook as his co-anchors. It was Bill Creasy's baby, his idea, and probably no one else could have convinced Steve Bornstein to pony up the dough to launch it. Certainly nobody but Creasy could have secured the necessary money when, in 1993, he'd said, in effect, "Let's take this show on the road." From then on, each show (airing frequently at first, but not yet weekly) was shot live on a campus where a big college game would be played later that day, even if the game wasn't shown on ESPN.*

What started as a small following on the campuses began to grow. By the end of the decade, the GameDay *screen was now regularly filled with hordes of students waving banners, hoisting placards, and displaying painted faces in orgies of youthful bravado. Hosts Lee Corso, Chris Fowler, and Kirk Herbstreit made for an unbeatable trio, utterly at ease in their respective roles, each among the best at what he did.*

Herbstreit was especially impressive for having made the transition from player to performer. The former Ohio State star's analysis and delivery were accomplished, as if he'd been doing it for years; his telegenic looks didn't hurt, either. Corso, despite being old enough to be the students' grandfather, evinced an effortless affinity for relating to them. And Fowler showed himself to be a great student of the game, always prepared, verbally agile, and not at all interested in making the show about himself.

The show became a demonstration of what fandom is, of easy interaction between ESPN's pros and the mobs of supportive students, and of how narrow a gap separated ESPN from its audience—probably the narrowest of any big-time commercial network, ever.

BILL CREASY:

We had it in the studio, but I kept saying, "Take it out on the road." But in those early years, that would have been just too much money. I did believe from day one, though, that it would be a huge hit inside the college dorms. College dorms and bars may not be rated by Nielsen, so I have always believed that our audience was much bigger.

LEE CORSO:

This show is about the passion we have for college game days, and it's about the passion of the crowds. They tried it with the NFL, they couldn't get it. They tried it with basketball, they couldn't get it. They can't get nothing. The passion of college football is what makes *College GameDay* great.

BEANO COOK:

I was at *College GameDay* for the first four years, until my mother got ill. College football had never seen anything like it. The NFL had their great pre-game shows, but nothing before had ever promoted college football like *GameDay*.

When Miami and Notre Dame played each other and they were both undefeated, I predicted Notre Dame would win. Tim Brando said he would sing the Notre Dame victory march on the air if I was right, and sure enough, they won and he did.

CHRIS FOWLER:

We took it on the road for our first regular season game in '93, late in the season. It was this Notre Dame–Florida State mega showdown—one versus two in South Bend in November. Notre Dame's larger than life, and we didn't really know what we were doing, but Creasy and others took a big leap of faith. We had been wanting to do it for a while, and we finally got the game that justified it. Technically the show was probably raw and somewhat inept, but we knew we had something. And it just took one show to figure out "this is what we've got to be doing. We've got to get this thing out of the studio, onto campuses." The next year we did about five or six, and the next year we did more.

Back in the early days, we didn't feel like the West Coast was ever respected. We had a hell of a hard time getting a show out of the eastern and central time zones and bringing it to the West Coast. But we didn't think people would show up that early in the morning at places that were not considered traditional hotbeds.

KIRK HERBSTREIT, *College Football Analyst:*

In '95 I did a number of games with Dewayne Staats and Todd Christensen and I kept asking Moe [Davenport] if there was going to be a game where I could do color, because I really wanted to do that. Sure enough, there was an opening late in the year, Wisconsin versus Minnesota, and I called the game with Gary Thorne. I was just blown away by having this chance. I'd never even called a high school game, and here I am calling a game in a sold-out Metrodome. And I fell in love with it. Once the season ended, I got another call from Moe, saying that Craig James had left and he went to CBS. He said, "We'd love for you to come in and audition for the spot on *College GameDay*." And I remember his quote very well. He said, "You're not going to get the job, but it'd be really good for you at this stage of your career to just go through the experience of being up on the set with Lee and Chris, and this will give you a little experience with an audience." So here I am, three years out of college, fresh into the business, and this was my kind of ten-year dream goal. Lo and behold, they flew me in, and I'm sitting next to Chris and Lee and the music starts up, and I was just, "Somebody pinch me. I cannot believe I'm sitting next to Corso right now." We did a fake segment, and then went through another segment and that was it. I thought it went okay, but I didn't have any expectations. A few months went by, and I got a call from my agent who said, "They want to hire you for *College GameDay*." It was incredible.

CHRIS FOWLER:

The crowds in '99 were kind of a turning point for *College GameDay*. That's when we realized that it was more than just popping a set down where tailgating was going on, and that it had become a real campus happening. The campuses were taking great pride in using the show as a vehicle to showcase their game-day spirit, what they felt about their program. They were there to show the world that there's no place better on a Saturday, no place has more spirit and passion about their team than Virginia Tech or Nebraska or places like Kansas State. They began to see it as a benchmark for their program: "We made it when *GameDay* was here."

The passions about college football are different than almost every other sport. Unless you're talking about the Red Sox and Yankees, or a few other isolated rivalries in other sports, I would submit that the passions run deeper, people take it much more personally.

As the crowds grew, the disparity between what you see on camera and what's happened before the show increased, particularly the confiscation of signs. A lot of the stuff is completely inappropriate. We started to have sign police out there. Don't get me wrong, I believe in the First Amendment, but some of the stuff is both tasteless and profane.

LEE CORSO:

In 1999, I ended up picking the correct winner in twelve straight games with my head, twelve straight games. It put a lot of pressure on me. Then I had sixteen straight. That will never happen again, I promise you. Can you believe I had sixteen straight games that I could have bet on?

CHRIS FOWLER:

I'm opening doors back up here that have been closed for a long time. It was 1998. In the weeks leading up to the Heisman announcement, when we talked about it on *GameDay,* I would just point out that if you read the tea leaves, it was not going to be a slam dunk for Peyton Manning, which you were hearing a lot of ahead of time. People assumed Peyton Manning had the Heisman won. All I said was that this wasn't a done deal. I wasn't trying to hype Charles Woodson or the show for that matter. The show was going to rate what it rated. I was just doing my job. But there were people at Tennessee who were frustrated and took it very personally. ESPN didn't have the SEC games at that point, didn't have as much of a relationship with the conference as we do now. We were seen as "the Big Ten Conference" by some people in that part of the world, and we were perceived to have an agenda.

I hosted the Heisman show and did the presentation. So I go on the air and introduce the winner, Charles Woodson. I'm the one there when he gets handed the trophy, and I'm on the scene when Peyton Manning and his family are deeply disappointed.

Immediately, the story wasn't that Charles Woodson won the Heisman; the story was that Peyton Manning *didn't* win it. And I was the guy that was seen giving it to Woodson. I got a lot of negative feedback. The phone was ringing off the hook that night. Then I got a lot of letters, and a lot of other hateful stuff directed at me personally. I was across a chain-link fence at the Orange Bowl from Tennessee fans a month later, and it was really, really edgy; very difficult and uncomfortable. And it stayed that way for a while. We didn't go back to Knoxville with *GameDay* for a few years, and when we did, we paid attention to security.

By the way, I had voted for Peyton Manning to win the Heisman Trophy.

By 1998, ESPN had four domestic networks following the purchase of the Classic Sports Network and ESPN News, plus twenty-one international networks, and had launched two brand extensions, ESPN: The Magazine *and ESPN Zone restaurants. The result? ESPN and The Disney Channel together increased Disney's revenues by $427 million, primarily because of subscriber growth at ESPN and increases in ad revenues, thanks to the 1998 soccer World Cup.*

With the increase in size came the inevitable rise of comings and goings in the workforce. The "one big happy family" image had certainly become obsolete.

LEE ANN DALY, *Senior Vice President of Marketing:*

About a month before my official start date, Judy Fearing asked me to cover a commercial shoot so I could get an advance look at what they were up to with their ad campaigns. So I went up to Columbia University, where they were shooting the first round of the Bristol University campaign. Bristol University was this sort of fictional institution of higher learning that was populated by "Professor Berman" and all the different guys from *Countdown,* basically. And it was a campaign for professional football, not for college football. So it had a bit of a flaw in it in terms of just pure logic, but it was funny and the writing from that first year of the campaign was great. I was introduced to [Berman], and my title was mentioned. He was like, "Oh, goddammit, do we need another vice president?" And I just said, "Nice to meet you, too, Mr. Berman." I didn't ask to have that title. I interviewed for the job and was offered it, so there was really no need to be a jerk. But that kind of stuck with me. I noticed that Chris Berman was rarely happy. He was always very difficult to please. After the fact, when something was good, you would sometimes get credit from him, and he would say, "Hey, that was pretty good." But it didn't matter what had happened the last time, because every time was like the first time in terms of having to prove yourself. I learned that you have to be able to just say, "Whatever."

When I got there, I found it remarkable and unlike any shoot I'd ever been on—and I'd been on plenty of them because I came from advertising—in the waiting areas there were Ping-Pong tables and video games and a pool table, and there were all these PAs—female PAs—playing Donkey Kong and pool and stuff. I was really surprised to see all this and was sort of like, "Why are all these nubile cuties wandering around?" I quickly gathered that it was to keep the guys from wandering off the set.

BILL FAIRWEATHER:

With *SportsCenter,* you could say, "The show is heavy, so drop the Clippers highlights," and you get off on time. With *NFL Primetime,* you didn't have that luxury. There had to be a highlight of every single game regardless of how short and how long and regardless if you have a triple-overtime game that was a late four o'clock start. So there were a lot of things that were tricky about producing that show. Anyway, here I was, my first show, all organized and feeling on track to have a good show. But about a half hour before we go on air, Chris starts getting really worked up. "I don't have notes for this. Where's the highlight for that? I haven't seen this yet." And what could have been an easy day all of a sudden started really getting frenetic. And now we're getting closer to airtime and there's more "I haven't seen this highlight and where's the shot sheet for this?" and Chris is really getting worked up. And, of course, I'm trying to get everything done, at the same time thinking, now I'm about to screw up the greatest show on the network.

And it's everything we can do to get him on the set, and every ten seconds he's asking me another question. I'm trying to get answers for him, and now we hit the open and I'm like, there's no way this thing is going to fly. But the light goes on, and Chris says, "Hello, everybody, welcome to *NFL Primetime*." And the show went fine.

I realized at that point in time that it was almost Chris's own internal way of getting himself prepared, getting himself fired up, getting his adrenaline flowing where it needed to be to deliver this piece of work to the audience. And, sure enough, the next week the same thing happened again and I was thinking, "You're not going to get me this time 'cause I know that this is just the way you do it."

JACK EDWARDS:
I did my last *SportsCenter* in July of 1999 with Bob Ley, who is not only a pioneer but also a survivor. And because he had that seniority, he was able to say a line and not get reprimanded for it. After I'd said my little fifteen-second good-bye, Bob Ley said, as we were dipping to black, "And another one escapes underneath the fence."

TONY BRUNO:

Al Gore came on with us in '99 at the first BCS championship game in Arizona. Tennessee had won, so he wanted to come on our radio show. I introduced him by saying, "Ladies and gentlemen, the next president of the United States of America, Vice President Al Gore." And he says, "Well, I don't know about that, but thank you for mentioning it." Oh, he was great—not as good as Clinton, but he handled a couple of curveballs that I threw at him and talked fantasy football.

By then, they had finally taken me off weekends, and I was doing the morning show with Mike Golic. They hired Mike, who was doing radio in Phoenix, and Mike wanted to come out to work with me. So before there was Mike Greenberg—Mike and Mike—there was Tony Bruno and Mike Golic. That was the morning drive show. When we launched, we were just on in Chicago, and they were really slow to bring us out as a national radio show. They weren't sure that people would take a syndicated morning show, so Mike and I did that for a year and then they changed management people. The new guy was very Disney-ized.

STEVE ANDERSON:

Tony was much better at night reacting to games. Once we put him on in the morning with Mike Golic, Tony and I had strong disagreements on taste issues. Tony felt strongly that the audience wanted "guy talk," and he wanted to go places that I didn't think were good for the show or for ESPN. Tony didn't want to change, so I felt it was important that we go in another direction. Tony was taken off the show, and within a few months, we made the move to pair Mike Greenberg with Mike Golic. It was a move that turned out very well for the two Mikes, the show, and ESPN Radio.

TONY BRUNO:

People think that I left ESPN on bad terms, but I really didn't. Steve Anderson was the guy that pretty much led to my resigning from ESPN. He just kept micromanaging the show to the point where I resigned. I couldn't do what he wanted me to do. I did the shows that they loved for eight years, and then all of a sudden, because Anderson didn't like the fact that I was having too much fun—which, oh, by the way, was what I had done my whole life—I finally said, "Hey Steve, you know what, I can't do this anymore." So I resigned. I started at ESPN making $35,000 a year and went to making half a million dollars when I left. Even Keith Olbermann wasn't making that much. Chris Berman and I were two of the highest-paid guys at ESPN. So in 1999, I walked away from a half-a-million-dollar-a-year contract— not to take another job, just because I couldn't do what they wanted me to do.

MIKE GREENBERG, *Anchor:*

I think *SportsCenter* is the Rolls-Royce of sports news broadcasting; it's number one and nothing is number two. So that is why I came, to do *SportsCenter.* I wanted to be like Keith Olbermann and Dan Patrick. That's what an entire generation of young sports broadcasters wanted to be. Golic was doing the show before me with someone else first, and when that person left, they spent a long time trying to figure out who to put in the spot. I happened to come in by accident. They just asked me to come in and fill in for a couple of days because they knew I had done radio in Chicago and they needed someone while they figured out what to do. After one show, they immediately liked our chemistry and offered me the gig. I did literally one show, and then they offered me the job. I had just started doing *SportsCenter,* so when they asked me, I said, "You gotta be crazy." We eventually reached an agreement where I would do both. I would have never done the radio show if an agreement wasn't in place for me to also do *SportsCenter.*

TONY HAWK:

Having my 900 [a 2.5 aerial revolution on a skateboard ramp] be a highlight on *SportsCenter* was the first time there was any sort of crossover between regular ESPN and ESPN2 for our sports, where there was any sort of recognition on that level. I had *a lot* of people around that time say, "Oh, I saw you on *SportsCenter,*" and that just didn't happen back then.

The 900 had been this quest of mine for nearly ten years of my life. It wasn't something that I thought would transcend skating itself or my career, it was just something I wanted to do. But to have done it in such a venue and in front of an audience like ESPN's just changed everything for me.

ESPN and NASCAR grew up together and helped each other grow, so it was hard to imagine their sibling-like friendship ever coming to an end. But it came to one, all right, on December 15, 1999, when a coalition made up of Fox Sports, Fox's ballsy FX network, NBC, and TNT agreed to pay $2.4 billion to NASCAR for a new six-year package, one that included the Winston/Nextel Cup Series and the Busch Series races. ESPN retained the rights only to the Craftsman Truck Series through 2002 under a separate pact.

When the announcement hit Bristol, one executive said the campus was "like a morgue." Many felt spurned and bitter. ESPN had aired NASCAR when no one else wanted it; now that NASCAR had grown big and popular, ESPN was being ungratefully dumped. The truth was closer to the proverbial "offer they couldn't refuse": ESPN was simply outbid. In refusing to budge, ESPN avoided a deal that was certain to lose money on its own — but was also certain to earn big ratings.

In television, hits serve as tentpoles that raise up the programs around them. In losing the highly rated NAS-CAR races, ESPN also suffered ratings damage to programming that used to follow them — even the mighty SportsCenter. ESPN had nothing comparably popular to replace NASCAR, at least not at first, and the company became mired in an overall ratings downturn that would eventually force new president George Bodenheimer to shake things up.

PAUL BROOKS:

We asked all the potential TV partners for a presentation on how they would approach the future, not only economically, but also from a marketing point of view and what their coverage would be like, all directed to taking our sport to the next level. ESPN really didn't process the request. Others had a bigger vision and bigger commitment to what the future could be. I think there was a lot happening in the overall ESPN/ABC world that directed focus away from this. I think the timing was difficult for them.

The day before the decision, George Bodenheimer called [NASCAR CEO] Bill France and asked if they could meet for lunch, one-on-one. Clearly, our antennas were up, and I ended up going to that lunch with Bill and George. We needed a lot if we were going to grow as a sport, and something seemed to be holding them back at the very end. It was a good lunch, but we could all tell it was not going to go the right way. It was a huge disappointment. ESPN had truly become a big part of our sport.

JERRY PUNCH, *Racing Analyst:*

There's no way that I ever anticipated NASCAR would walk away from ESPN. Bill France had understood and appreciated what ESPN had done for his sport. It was a symbiotic relationship; we were holding hands and grew up together. When we started putting live qualifying trials on ESPN2, people were just hammering their local cable affiliates saying, "We've got to have ESPN2!" and that was because of us. The problem was, Mr. France had gotten ill, and the negotiations were now in the hands of people who did not share the same respect and loyalty to ESPN. These people who were negotiating for NASCAR had been given a small percentage that was going to be theirs, their cut for whatever they'd negotiate. So they cleverly planted rumors in newspapers and large national publications about the value of the sport. In my opinion, I think there was a lot of backroom politics. And I still believe that had Mr. France been actively involved, and had he not been ill, ESPN would not have lost.

I know ESPN was prepared to pay a lot of money to stay a part of this, and when it all came down, I was shocked, I was flabbergasted, I was disappointed. I felt betrayed, and I told people at the top level of

NASCAR, "This shouldn't happen this way. It absolutely shouldn't happen. We're a family. And suddenly we're going to show up at the family reunion and we're not invited?" The new partners, Fox and NBC, primarily Fox, didn't even want ESPN to have a presence. They wouldn't even let us in the racetrack.

But from a pure business standpoint, taking away the emotion, the money that NBC and Fox spent was a great deal for NASCAR. There was no doubt Fox and NBC were going to lose big-time. Which they did. They lost a lot of money.

When they got NASCAR, both Fox and NBC called right away, the day it was announced, and offered very good opportunities. But the way I was raised in North Carolina by my father and my grandfather was that when you shook somebody's hand, that was the guy you bought it from. And I shook ESPN's hand and said, "I'm going to be here for five years." So what happened was it gave me a chance to move into the broadcast booth, where I did college football for ABC, and sometimes subbed for Brent Musburger. And I got a chance to play-by-play college basketball, which I love. It was always "When we get NASCAR back, you're going to have a major role, because you're the only person on our whole team that's staying." So that was basically the whole NASCAR department at ESPN: me.

RICH FEINBERG:

My hardest day at the company was the day we lost NASCAR. It was like your heart had been ripped out. You felt like you gave so much of yourself—not just professionally, but because it was such a passion. There was a huge connection between the growth of NASCAR and the growth of ESPN. We traveled a very parallel path, and I think that's part of the reason why there was so much surprise that we were separating.

We lost it in '99, so we had to do all of 2000 as a lame-duck team. Our last race was in Atlanta that year, and George Bodenheimer came down. He asked me that Sunday morning before the race, "Rich, could you gather everybody in the tent? We've been doing this for twenty-something years, and after today we're not doing it anymore, for at least six years, so I'd like to thank them on behalf of the company." That morning was a very, very rainy morning—cold and dreary, the weather a perfect complement to the sadness that many of us felt. And I'm an emotional person. George said, "I'd like you to introduce me because not everybody knows my name, especially the engineers." So we're all in the tent, and the breakfast ends, and somebody yells for quiet. Now I have to get up and introduce George. I had asked George if I could take a moment to thank everybody, and I remember that I broke down. I cried in front of the entire staff, I could barely say the words "George Bodenheimer" and thank him.

FRED GAUDELLI:

Right around the time ESPN lost NASCAR — this is like 1999 — ESPN's got *Sunday Night Football,* and inside the booth are Mike Patrick, Paul Maguire, and Joe Theismann. We're doing a Bears–Lions game at Detroit. The Lions block a Bears field goal and we go to commercial. So I cue up the replay and I see this linebacker, Stephen Boyd, basically run into a defensive lineman, smash into his back, and blow him through the hole to block the kick. I mean really hammer him through the hole. I immediately go back in my mind to 1991 at Redskins Park. We were getting ready to do a Redskins game, and the week before, the Redskins blocked three field goals, and I watched it on tape, just to see how they block kicks, in case it came up in my game. So I'm watching the tape and, unbelievable coincidence, in walks the special teams coach of the Redskins, Wayne Sevier. So I say, "Hey, can I ask you a question? It's really interesting what you do here on these kicks, where you take a guy and basically blow him into another guy and force him through." He's like, "Oh, yeah, we call that double-fudge."

And I'm like, "Why?" And he goes, "You know, like fudge-packer, you know, like two gay guys, a fudge-packer?" So I start laughing, and Joe Theismann came in at that point and I asked him, "You know what they call this?" He goes, "Oh, yeah, they call that double-fudge," and I'm like, "I think that's pretty funny." So now I see this same play eight years later in the Bears–Lions game, and I throw it up on a monitor and go, "Joe, check this out. It's like 'double-fudge,' remember?" He starts laughing and says, "Oh, yeah, yeah, I remember that." So I said, "Okay guys, when we come out of the break, let's just show them how they blocked the kick here and then we'll go right to the kickoff." And Joe says, "No problem."

So I count them out of the break, and Mike Patrick goes, "Okay, it's ah, 7–3 Chicago. Joe, how'd they block that kick?" Joe goes, "Mike, this is what they call the old 'fudge-packer.'" All of a sudden, Patrick and Maguire gasp, and my director asks me, "What the fuck did he just say?" And I say in his ear, "Joe, what are you doing!" So he goes on to draw the play, and Maguire and Patrick cannot stop laughing. They're like uncontrollable, and Patrick says, "Joe, just stay over there, I need a lot of room to work." So now throughout the whole game, every time we go to commercial, we just can't let it go, man, we're just like, "Joe, what were you thinking about?!" Our next game was going to be in San Francisco, and my director was Marc Payton, and he said, "Hey, Joe, we just got a call here from San Francisco. They're going to be throwing a parade in your honor next week." So this thing went on through the whole game, and in the local Chicago market they picked up on it. There's a sports talk show, and whenever Joe appears on it, they start out by playing, "This is what they call the old 'fudge-packer.'"

JOHN ANDERSON:

A guy from my hometown newspaper in Green Bay called me after I had been here for a short while and asked me what it was like to be in a place with ninety million homes. I told him, "It's odd, I never once think about this, because when you sit in the studio, you're just sitting at a desk in front of one camera with one guy behind it. And that's been the same whether I was in college, or working at local stations in Tulsa and Phoenix." I then told him I worried much more about what Bob Ley, Chris Berman, and Dan Patrick were thinking when they saw me.

STEVE BERTHIAUME, *Anchor:*

I got to ESPN in December of '99 and had pretty much been doing the 10:00 p.m. to midnight shift at ESPN News and always thought to myself, "I'm just going to try to stay out of trouble, do a good job, and hope it works out." They would send out e-mails when the anchor schedules were put out, and I remember the first time that, bang, there they were: two or three *SportsCenters* next to my name. I just stared at the schedule and thought, "Wow! That's pretty fucking cool. I'm going to be on *SportsCenter*."

I looked around the newsroom, gave myself thirty seconds of celebration, then put my head back down and went back to work.

JIMMY ROBERTS:

By 2000, I'd been at ESPN for twelve years, and Dick Ebersol began courting me very aggressively. My wife and I had two children, and at ESPN, I not only had to travel a lot, but travel on very little notice. That's just the nature of the beast; that's the way ESPN works. Dick was very persuasive; he offered me the opportunity to do the feature segment during the Olympics in prime time every night. It was going to be my own. Dick said, "I want you to cover golf during the year, and I want you to come and work for me at the Olympics, where you'll have this spot. You'll come and tell a story for me every night — that's what I want you to do." I couldn't have ever asked for a better dream.

It was very difficult telling everyone at ESPN that I was going to leave. I tried to explain to them that I wasn't leaving because of something ESPN wasn't; I was leaving because I needed to do something for myself and my family. To this day, some of my best friends are still with ESPN.

JEREMY SCHAAP, *Reporter*:

In 2000, I was in Madison, Wisconsin, doing a story about their walk-on program for football, and all hell was breaking loose in Bloomington. Bob Knight had put his hand on this kid named Kent Harvey who had walked into Assembly Hall and said to him, "Hey, what's up, Knight?" and Knight told him not to call him Knight, to address him with more respect, not an unreasonable request. Now Knight calls a press conference in Bloomington, and I'm the closest reporter because I'm in Madison.

I get a phone call telling me I need to get to Bloomington immediately. So we get travel on the phone and they say I will have to fly out of Madison to Detroit and then from Detroit to Indianapolis, then drive an hour to Bloomington. There are no commercial flights into Bloomington; there's no way I will be able to make it in time for the press conference. So then they say, "What about a private plane?" and they have to call the office of Bob Iger—at the time he was the ABC president—because he had to approve the use of private jets. They told me they would get the approval and to just head out to the airport. By the time I got to the Madison airport, which was only ten minutes away, they literally had this jet fueling up and ready to go. Iger's office had said yes. So I'm thinking, "All right, this is pretty cool. I'm flying a private jet to Bloomington for a press conference." It took only forty-eight minutes, and next thing I know, I'm at the press conference, where Knight said he didn't do anything wrong. But nothing else happens. Nobody fires him. There's no

744 Those Guys Have All the Fun

statement from the school or anything. So the next day, I take a bus from Bloomington to Indianapolis, fly Northwest from Indianapolis to Detroit, Detroit back to Madison—it takes me six hours to do what I'd done in forty-eight minutes the day before—for the Wisconsin–Minnesota game. And then the next day, all of a sudden, they fire Knight. So now I have to go back to Bloomington to cover whatever there will be to cover, and I get a call from David Brofsky, who was in charge of all the bureaus and reporters, and he says, "I think you might be interviewing Bob Knight tomorrow. Live. [Former Notre Dame basketball coach] Digger Phelps has gotten him to agree to do an interview with ESPN, and he's been given a choice of three different reporters, you, Bob Ley, and Dan Patrick, and I think he's leaning toward you." I knew immediately this would be the hardest thing I'd ever done, and the most scrutinized.

The interview was unusual—unusual because it was live in prime time, and unusual because it's the only situation I've ever been in where the interview itself became an event. There were velvet ropes and police tape, and there were satellite trucks from every news entity in the country. I felt like I was going into a heavyweight match, which I guess I was. And I hadn't seen Bob since the press conference in Assembly Hall a few days earlier. I spent all day avoiding him. Digger called me several times to say, "Bob wants you to go to the house, Bob feels he needs to talk to you before we do this tonight." I said no, because sometimes the worst thing to do is to have a conversation just before you conduct a serious interview with the interviewee. I didn't want to give him the chance to tell me his side of the story before the interview. So I literally did everything I could do to avoid seeing him until we were together in the room and about to do the interview. Meanwhile, me and several of my bosses were having meetings about what kinds of questions I should ask and what has to be on the list. This is a big deal; there's a lot of attention focused on it.

So I'm in the room where we will do the interview and I'm nervous as hell and I know what's at stake here. And Bob walks in a few minutes before we go on live, and I've got a clipboard or notepad or something—and I turn around and, suddenly, what happened to my notepad? He's grabbed it off my chair and starts looking at the questions. I say, "Bob, what are you doing?" And he's not himself. No hello, nothing. Just straight for my notes. But he doesn't even really look at it before giving it back. He says, "We're going to talk about this zero tolerance thing [regarding Knight's treatment of players], right?" "Yes, of course we're going to talk about the zero tolerance." I thought that was strange. Of course, that's what we were going to talk about. That's why he got fired, for violating it. And he's fiery. He's worked up. I mean he's usually near the boiling point, and he is at a steady boil now. And there's kind of this weird dynamic in the room because there are all these people around and the cameras and a backdrop, like a stage, and Digger is sitting in a chair off to Bob's side. And then there are people behind me, but I don't know who they are other than the camera operators, and I only found out later that it's Bob's wife, Karen; Bob Hammel, his longtime friend and a local sportswriter in Bloomington with whom he'd collaborate on his memoir; and Isiah Thomas, who had been estranged from Knight for many years, but now he's in Indiana with the Pacers and suddenly he's back in the Knight camp.

Finally, we're in the chairs and Bob Ley throws it to me and things start. We do two long segments with one commercial break. Things started okay. I asked him a very innocuous opening question, something to the effect of, Did you ever imagine that it would come to this, getting fired? And he starts talking about his mentors and players he's coached, et cetera, and he's rambling, and they're screaming into my ear, "Cut him off! Cut him off!" But you can't cut him off on the first answer. Norby Williamson is in the truck with David Brofsky, and they were talking in my ear. I don't remember what happened exactly in the first segment, but Bob was frustrated that I wasn't allowing him to filibuster, that I was actually trying to keep the interview on track—there was a lot to get to in a limited amount of time—and when

we went to break, he started taking off his microphone and getting up out of the chair, and they start
screaming in my ear, "Where's he going? Is he done?!"
They think the interview's over. But he wasn't that
angry, he was just going to the bathroom, I think.

Norby and David were wondering if he would get
back in the chair. He comes back in time, and he gets
back into the chair. The commercial break ends, and
we start again, and then somehow he gets to the point
where he's talking about Patrick, his son, his assistant
coach, and he says something to the effect of, Let's
talk about the real victim here. "You know the real
victim here is Pat. He hasn't done anything wrong." I
said, "Wait a second, Bob. Would Pat be a victim if
you had adhered to the zero tolerance policy?" And
that's when he turned, that moment. In the first segment, we had the argument about whether I was cutting him off. That was why he was contentious in the
first segment. And I was cutting him off because he
was filibustering. But my question about Pat, which
was fair, set him off. And that's when he turned, and
he paused, and he gave me the evil grin and said,
"You got a long way to go to be as good as your father;
you better keep that in mind." Nine years later, I still
remember that line. I said, "I appreciate that," and we
continued.

We had one more argument during the interview.
I asked him something like, Do you recognize the
elements of tragedy in this story, an icon going out in

this fashion? And he says, "This isn't a tragedy. You don't know what a tragedy is. A tragedy is my wife's friend has cancer"—trying to make me look stupid for calling this a tragedy. He knew exactly what I meant—tragedy in a dramatic sense, a fallen idol. And that's okay. That's how he is.

And so the interview ended. The guys in the truck were very happy with it. I'm emotionally drained, and I'm still sitting in the chair. Bob bolts out of his chair, walks right up to me. I put out my hand. He refuses to shake it and says, "You've got a lot to learn, you've got a lot to learn," and he walks out. Those were the last words he ever spoke to me. The whole time I felt this weird sensation about what was going on behind me, but I was told that his wife, Karen, was crying throughout the interview. I assume she saw what was going on and felt bad that Bob had squandered an opportunity here to really explain himself and instead had displayed a side of himself that was unappealing. He was in a way interviewing for his next job but showed no capacity for self-examination or awareness. He wasn't willing to concede anything.

It never occurred to me that it would be the firestorm that it was in terms of the coverage. It turned out to be the biggest thing I've ever done. At ESPN everybody called me to say "good job," including George Bodenheimer. It was on the front page of all the newspapers. The interview itself, not what Knight said, was the subject of much of the coverage the next day. On the back page of the *New York Post*, there was a head-line: "ESPN's Schaap Stands Up to Bully Knight."

The best thing to come out of the interview for me was the parting shot my father delivered.

MIKE LUPICA, *Columnist:*

Dick Schaap and Bob Knight had been extremely close. Knight always had a core group of media guys, but they were constantly shifting because you got kicked out of the club the second you wrote some-thing he didn't like. I used to get along fine with him until he started calling me up and yelling at me, because I'd feel like, you can't do that to me when I'm having dinner. And Knight had gone after Jeremy at the end of their interview. So on our *Sports Reporters* show, Dick did an amazing parting shot. Dick just lit into him. We always rehearse before the taping, so I knew it was coming, and I just sat back and listened to Dick deliver this wonderful, forty-five-second, basically newspaper column where he took Knight to the woodshed. I was thinking, "Wow." It was a tight-rope for him to walk because he was talking about his kid, but it was just awesome. That to me was Dick Schaap at his best. He went after Bob Knight that day and hit him right between the eyes.

JEREMY SCHAAP:

When Knight started doing college basketball on ESPN, they called me up to get my reaction after he had started on the air, and I just said, "He has a long way to go before he's as good as Digger Phelps." And I mean that 100 percent.

BOB KNIGHT:

They gave me three people to choose from who would do that interview, and I picked Schaap because of his dad. I didn't even know the kid. I had Digger tell Schaap that there was a question that I'd like for him to ask, and he refused to ask it. He told Digger, "I can't do that. I can't ask something that he wants asked." I didn't enjoy the interview at all. I thought the guy was a chickenshit little cocksucker. Forget that guy. I have no interest in talking about that. Jesus Christ, enough of this bullshit.

6

The Garden of Forking Paths: 2001–2004

"What an excellent horse do they lose,
for want of address and boldness to manage him."
—*Alexander the Great*

Over the years, certain prescribed guidelines had been developed by ESPN management for a death in the sports world, foremost among them: "We don't have to be first." It was a rule born of chagrin and regret: on July 3, 1993, in an effort to beat the competition, ESPN Radio rushed onto the air with the sad news that Hall of Famer Don Drysdale had died. The only major problem with the reporting was that Drysdale's wife, former basketball star Ann Meyers—who happened to work as an analyst at ESPN—hadn't been told. She heard it over the radio with everybody else.

Thus ended the ESPN practice of making mad dashes to broadcast the latest fatality before the competition did.

The second covenant on reporting deaths was that there was never to be any humor attached to these accounts without approval from executives at the highest levels of management—which basically translated as "Never, ever."

In the late nineties, ESPN insiders took notice of the aging population of sports superstars from the second half of the century, and realized that many legends or near-legends were approaching their golden years and beyond. So, beginning in 2000, and under Vince Doria's supervision, many obituaries and biographical packages were assembled in advance, just as major newspapers had routinely done for a long time. Material was gathered and stored so that, when the bell tolled for large-looming iconic figures like Muhammad Ali, George Steinbrenner, or John Wooden, there'd be less frantic scurrying to produce a proper tribute.

There was at least one large, obvious flaw in this approach: it didn't take into account sudden, shocking tragedies—like the one that occurred on February 18, 2001.

DAN PATRICK:

I saw the accident and thought it didn't seem like much, but then there was no movement and all I kept saying was, "Get out of the car, get out of the car." A little while later, I was in the back corner of the newsroom, and one of the producers came out and said,

"He's dead, he's dead." And you just stop yourself and you go, "It can't be. Dale Earnhardt doesn't die."

JERRY PUNCH:

Dale and I were very close friends. When Dale didn't get out of the car, I knew it was not good, because if there'd been any way at all, he would have been up there in the victory lane to congratulate Michael and Dale Junior. So I waited a few minutes, and I had them page the trauma surgeon who'd worked with me in Florida. He called me back within thirty seconds and said, "I thought you'd be calling." I said, "Do I want to know?" He said, "You don't. It's really, really bad." Just as he said that, the door opens and a producer said, "We're ready for you to go on *SportsCenter* and talk about the race." So I'm sitting in the studio pretty much believing that Dale Earnhardt may have been critically injured or worse.

But then, while we were on the air, they made the announcement that he was gone, and it was the most difficult day of my professional career. I was on live national television and one of my friends I grew up with, and had so many private conversations with, was dead.

DAN PATRICK:

There were about thirty-five people in the news-room, and it's always noisy with people yelling to one another and phones ringing. At that moment, though, I don't think anybody said a word. It was almost as if the newsroom was giving Dale Senior a moment of silence.

JERRY PUNCH:

When I got home, to me, it was like when Elvis died. NBC, *Nightline, Good Morning America,* and HBO were coming to my house and setting up satellite dishes. Some people couldn't understand why thousands and thousands of people were dropping everything they were doing, calling in sick at work, and getting in their cars and driving cross-country so they could be at Dale Earnhardt's home to sit there on their knees with flowers and cry. I wanted people to realize he was the great American success story — the kid who grew up with next to nothing, whose dad died of a heart attack, and who was left alone to do it on his own. He had only a seventh-grade education, but he was one of the smartest men I ever knew. And he refused to believe that he could not be successful. He was special. He was more than just a race-car driver. He was hope to millions of people.

STAN VERRETT, *Anchor*:

I had worked in Norfolk, Virginia, for six years before I came to ESPN, and that's NASCAR country, so I actually had experience covering Dale Earnhardt's career. When he died, it really affected me, but because I'm an African American, no one really expected that. We had to do a half-hour special on ESPNews, and I said, "Don't worry about it, I got it." And a lot of people looked at me like, "Who's this black guy who knows all the stuff about Dale Earnhardt? He's taking over the show. He's writing all the stuff!" One of the lines I wrote in the script actually wound up in a song about Dale Earnhardt. The line was "There's a saying in NASCAR that the worst thing that another driver could see is the three car in your rearview mirror. Sunday we found out that there was something worse."

NEIL EVERETT, *Anchor:*

One of the first stories I ever did at ESPNews was when Dale Earnhardt hit the wall, and I had to talk to a lot of people about what his death meant to them. At that moment, I reminded myself that no one was turning on the television to find out what I knew about Dale Earnhardt; they were watching to find out what the guy I was interviewing knew about Dale Earnhardt.

For more than twenty years, William N. Creasy Jr. was, simply put, one of the most influential personalities in the history of ESPN. He found and hired Steve Bornstein, conceived College GameDay, *and was involved in more decisions than anyone would imagine, especially since he stayed in the shadows much of the time.*

When Bornstein was promoted and transplanted to Burbank, George Bodenheimer kept Creasy on as a consultant and made him part of his kitchen cabinet. A less secure chief executive might well have worried that Creasy would run back to Bornstein with inside information, given their close friendship. But Bodenheimer trusted Creasy, and, perhaps equally important, although Bodenheimer felt he was on terra firma with issues regarding affiliates, marketing, and ad sales, he knew he could benefit from advice on programming matters, which were now in his bailiwick—and stirring up a mess of trouble.

ARTIE BULGRIN, *Senior Vice President of Research:*

The network's yearly coverage rating—the percentage of subscribing homes that watch the network in an average minute—peaked at a 0.87 rating in 1990 [488,00 homes], but we were experiencing some softness in the years leading into 2001: a 0.78 in 1998, 0.74 in 1999, and a 0.69 in 2000, which was the lowest that number had ever been up to that time. We had some good reasons to explain these declines: at about this time, digital cable was just launching, and DirecTV and EchoStar were really starting to proliferate. This was the onset of the five-hundred-channel universe.

But as we analyzed the Nielsen data further, we found a disturbing trend leading into 2001: not only were fewer households tuning in to ESPN, they were also spending less time watching. This was a concern in that some of our content was becoming less "engaging" to the audience, forcing them to tune out. For example, in fourth-quarter 1999, the average "viewing" household spent twenty-two hours and forty-five minutes watching ESPN, and by fourth-quarter 2000, that declined to just over twenty hours. This was a disturbing trend and a programming issue that needed to be fixed. George Bodenheimer was adamant about us finding a solution and wouldn't accept excuses or theories. In retrospect, this represented a turning point for ESPN.

BILL CREASY:

John Walsh and I have considerable respect for each other, but John had it in his mind that after Mark did *SportsCentury* and [ESPN] Classic, he was moving too fast for his own good. My position was, he couldn't move fast enough. When you came to ESPN, you went through steps, and that's what John was thinking when he said the famous line to Mark we all remember: "You gotta go do the B-game, you're going to produce Boise State playing somebody." Mark said, "What are you talking about? I don't do that shit." I think that irritated John a bit; he's been in any number of jobs, jumped all over the place, but he was old-school. He said, "You gotta do this for two or three years and then you can move up the ladder." I was not about to stand for Mark being assigned to some fucking Boise State game somewhere out there. I said, "You can't do this. It's ludicrous. This kid has just done the most successful series outside of the guy who does the Olympic shows." And beyond what he did with *SportsCentury* was all that he had done with Classic. Yes, he drove people hard, but he made people better. I told John and George, "This is a guy who is going to come in, take charge, and stir the pot up good."

MARK SHAPIRO:

After wrapping my second anniversary as GM for the Classic network, George took me for a walk in Central Park. He said that he wanted to put me in charge of programming for all of the ESPN networks. This meant not just the program-schedule decisions, but spearheading every program, and property negotiation with every league. The company was under a bit of pressure, actually. Don't get me wrong: thanks to some brilliant carriage agreements with significant annual rate increases, ESPN as a business was in no danger. Still, we'd lost NASCAR to Fox and NBC, and ratings had been plummeting. George wanted to ratchet things up and see if he couldn't spark some new thinking and new ideas about our overall programming decisions and philosophy. I remember he said to me, "I don't know much about ratings. All I know is they're down and I'm tired of reading about it. Fix it."

So at thirty-two years of age, I was put in charge of all programming on ESPN, ESPN2, and ESPN Classic—with one clear and defined mission: drive ratings.

Michael Eisner phoned to congratulate me on the job and he underscored my mission in a way only he could. He told me, "You have one job to do and that is increase ratings. When I ran ABC at a young age, I found my ratings weapon in *Happy Days;* that series ignited our success. Find your *Happy Days.*"

STEVE BORNSTEIN:

Shapiro's a unique talent. He is every bit as good, arrogant, and aggressive as his reputation. I had to hit him upside the head with a two-by-four a couple times, but that's what he responds to.

Mark Shapiro's appointment and ascent would fuel one of the most dramatic transformations in the culture of ESPN. Apart perhaps from the moment when the blustery and supremely confident Steve Bornstein was promoted and the softer-spoken, unassuming George Bodenheimer took over from him, no contrast in attitudes and behavior had been as striking.

Suddenly, perhaps because of Shapiro's age or his almost frighteningly high energy level, the company was divided: some younger employees were thrilled at the new vigor Shapiro brought, while others resented one of their peers making such a swift rise to the top. After all, he had jumped over his two older bosses. Among older workers, some were, as one executive put it, "absolutely terrified" by the force of Shapiro's personality and his ambitious agenda; others thought a shakeup was over-due. And for some, the tremendous contrast between Shapiro and his predecessors was simply disorienting.

VINCE DORIA:

Did it take people by surprise? Did people have angst about it? Yes and yes. It was something that had never really quite transpired here before. I remember John Walsh saying to me and other people, "We need to do some big things here this year to show George, or otherwise we're all going to be reporting to Mark Shapiro," and John said it in a way like, "And the world is going to end."

DAN PATRICK:

Many people were freaked out to see how much Shapiro, in the words of one producer, "made Walsh his bitch." It was like one moment Walsh is there on top of things and then the next, Mark is talking down to John in front of everyone in meetings. John got put in the corner and Steve Anderson got kicked to the curb.

JOHN WALSH:

I was his boss for the first ten years. Then he was my boss.

MARK SHAPIRO:

I knew how to put John in a box, if you will, because John's like a Unabomber: he's got a lot of ideas, but some of them end up messing things up. You have to manage John. He'd walk into a production meeting and he would go over his ideas and people were thinking, "Do we have to listen to him?" His power had been greatly diminished, and people began to put him aside. He just wore people out.

TOM JACKSON:

I wish you could have seen our hierarchy walking around when Mark was in charge. You talk about guys under the gun constantly; it was crazy, it was crazy. I'm just telling you, it was just crazy.

CHRIS BERMAN:

SportsCentury wasn't done in Bristol. Shapiro had a lot of autonomy for a very big project, which was, for the most part, very well done. But I didn't see the rise coming. I was too busy working. All of a sudden, he's broken about eight tackles and we didn't realize it would result in a touchdown, a crippling touchdown.

LEE ANN DALY:

There should have been more of a real search for people to put around Mark before he got put into such a high-level position. Mark was the kind of person who just wanted to bark in everybody's face, to make them go away so he could do what he wanted to do. He was very much like, "I know what's best and everybody just needs to shut up and go away." He wanted to tell everybody how it was going to be and that you just needed to accept it. That was, I think, very destructive. And it was not something that I wanted to be around.

CHRIS BERMAN:

Look, the good part about Mark was that he made decisions. There's a lot to be said for that. And just because we're a kinder, gentler people doesn't mean every now and then you don't need somebody to shake it up a little. That's why Mark, in theory, was okay. The unfortunate part about Mark is that—he might tell you this himself—he should treat people a little better.

We would meet quite a bit. I was pretty secure in where I was and what I was doing. I had been there at that point for over twenty years, from the beginning, and I wasn't about to leave because this guy was there. I have the public. I walk down the street and it's like, "Thanks for twenty years!" Eventually, you could see that he was a power guy, and power guys and I don't match up very well, whoever you are. Shapiro's affection for me was not the same as Steve Bornstein's or most everyone else's there, let's put it that way, because, remember, Mark was smarter than the rest of us. Remember that.

LEE ANN DALY:

I was at the ESPYs in Las Vegas and Mark came up to me and asked, "Where's your press agent?" And I said, "I don't have one," and he said, "What the fuck are you talking about?" He couldn't believe I didn't have a press agent of my own.

MIKE SOLTYS:

On the very positive side of things, Mark really elevated the PR function and its importance in this company, and it's lasted after he left. His understanding of how the media can be a tool to really help your company build was something that our department knew but the company didn't embrace in the eighties the way it did with Mark leading the charge. So his enthusiasm for playing the PR game was wonderful, but he needed more of a filter on certain things.

MARK SHAPIRO:

Communication was so big for me. I think people really appreciated it, because I would get up and I'd say in brutal honesty, "Here's where we're going, here's the vision." You could disagree, but you knew where you stood as a worker and you knew where we were going as a company. I met one-on-one with all my direct reports; I called them biweekly meetings. So if you reported to me, we'd have a day where we would sit down for an hour and a half to two hours. Just the two of us. I have an agenda; you have an agenda.

I would also have a senior staff meeting every single week, eighteen or nineteen people, all the heads of the divisions. The meeting would generally go from eight in the morning until about one. There was no eating, and no individual bathroom breaks. My belief was if you go to the bathroom when I'm talking, you'll miss something, and then somewhere we'll get a break in the chain—something like, "We never talked about that," then, "Yes, we did," then, "Oh, it must have been when you went to the bathroom." So when we break, we all break—period. "You don't leave the room" was my rule. We would do bathroom breaks as a group. Even when George called, I wouldn't go out and be interrupted. And no speakerphone. If you're not there in person, you're not there. I'm not doing that. With a speakerphone, the guy on the other end is usually working on something else anyway.

I wanted it to be "Disagree all you want in here, but when we walk out, we are one voice. End of story." I didn't want any negative energy; Bristol had suffered from that all the time. It had been a very, very political quagmire. I was crazy about stopping that, and God help you if I find out you're out there back-talking, being two-faced, or whispering. I'm telling you these people got on board. They marched big-time. The key was not being so tough that I suppressed what they really thought. That's the balance. I wanted them to have a voice.

RICK BARRY, *Vice President of Production and Administration:*

You really had to know your stuff for those meetings; you had to be buttoned up. What really irked me was there were no pee breaks. *No pee breaks!* When I was thirty-four, I could hold it, but at fifty, that prostate was getting a little big.

We had just gotten these PDAs that were coming out then, and I'd keep mine in the bathroom at night, and at two in the morning, if I had to take a whiz, I'd walk in and the light was blinking, and it would be a midnight message from Mark. So I would reply back, thinking he wouldn't see it at two o'clock in the morning. But then I'd be shaken when the message would come back right away. I don't know when he slept!

BOB COSTAS:

I have a good personal relationship with Mark that dates back to *SportsCentury.* We became friendly because they interviewed me for a lot of the installments of that. When he brought up the idea of my coming over to ESPN, I heard them out. They had planned to use me on some of their big events and then also to create a Larry King of Sports–type show that would air every night for an hour with sports as its general topic but not necessarily limited to sports. The concept certainly made sense, but I have a long-standing relationship with NBC and at that time I was able to combine it with HBO, and that just made more sense. It seemed a better fit for me to stay where I was.

On September 11, 2001, the sports world stopped dead, paralyzed by nightmarish national tragedy. Baseball postponed its complete schedule. The NFL rescheduled its September 16–17 games for January. And the PGA postponed the Ryder Cup for an entire year.

In the wake of the attacks, ESPN, for the first time in its history, preempted its own programming and replaced it with ABC's straight news coverage. When the sports world resumed its life, so did ESPN, focusing on scheduled events and on the meaning and significance that athletic competition held for a deeply troubled country.

MARK SHAPIRO:
George and I had been to the Monday night game on September 10. The next morning, we were in the airport, boarding a plane for the flight home. Suddenly they took us and all the other passengers off, and the flight was canceled. Something had happened. We go into the United lounge, and at first just

thought some idiot had crashed into the building. But when the second plane hit, all hell broke loose. George and I got stuck in Denver for three to four days. We went to the Gap, downtown, to buy clothes; George had almost nothing with him. This was my Munich, if you will. I don't mean to sound insensitive, but I would have conference calls from George's room around the clock. I made the decision to put the ABC network on ESPN's air.

Historically, ESPN had been too conservative when it came to breaking news — there was always some excuse as to why a studio couldn't be fired up, or why we couldn't break into regularly scheduled programming. I didn't want any of that to happen now. After all, no other network would be looking at this from a sports perspective. This was our corner, and I wanted to be live on-air for as many hours as production could literally fill. So production was leading the way and scripting our coverage. Now, as head of programming, I was clearly crossing the line into Steve Anderson and John Walsh's world, and I was doing it two thousand miles away from Denver. I recognized that I had to be diplomatic. At the same time, however, I wasn't going to let anyone tell me there wasn't enough news for us to report, or that we didn't have enough correspondents or assets ready to go.

My team and I had multiple daily conference calls with production — discussing, debating, and contemplating just how much we could cover. Games were getting canceled right and left, so we had a choice of either airing archival classics or going live with news reports. I'm proud to say we wound up carrying more live hours of coverage with each passing day. Since George and I were both holed up in his Denver hotel room, he got to witness firsthand how a combined programming and production operation would work under my leadership. Don't get me wrong, George was very involved, and to his credit, provided great leadership. He was incredibly dynamic during that time and had a strong sense of what to do, but I do believe the entire episode definitely played a motivating role in his ultimate decision to combine the programming and production groups and put me in charge.

There really aren't a lot of stars at ESPN. Stuart Scott's a star; I made him a bigger one. Dan Patrick's a star; I tried to make him a bigger star there. Berman's a star, but he's maxed out. There's no more that he can do. He can't do play-by-play. But Bob Ley was a star with regard to journalism. So when 9/11 happened, that was the thing that really sealed Bob's getting in the chair.

BOB LEY:
The day of the attacks, without a pressing need to go on the air immediately, there was a pretty robust debate about whether we should be doing anything,

whether we should be on the air instead of just airing ABC. It was pretty passionate. Nobody was right, and nobody was wrong. Some people were saying, "We have no role to play; it's as far from sports as it can be; this is as irrelevant to us as anything you can imagine." And yet others were saying, "Yeah, but all of this is going to impact the world of sports, in some way, shape, or form." I think by about two o'clock the idea was "All right, let's go on and do a show at six. And then we'll play the news." I was certainly in the camp of "This is horrible, this is irrelevant to sports, this has nothing to do with us, but there's a necessity to put down a historical record for this network of just whatever tangential elements exist in service of sports. We're going to get lost otherwise." And so we did the show. It was not an easy show to do, obviously.

STEVE ANDERSON:

George called me that Tuesday morning and I remember him saying, "So, Steve, how's the security at ESPN, how secure are we at ESPN?" And I don't mean to make light of it, but I said, "George, you've been here as long as I have. We don't *have* any security." And we didn't, really. In those days, you could literally drive on campus, walk on campus, and walk into the buildings. I think we realized then that if terrorists wanted to communicate to the whole country, they could do it from this facility. We weren't prepared, at that point, to stop them. We were here in this sleepy little town feeling safe and secure. But 9/11 changed all of that. Gates went up, and it changed the way we thought about who we are and what we are regarding security.

JEREMY SCHAAP:

My father probably had been hosting *The Sports Reporters* for ten years before he ever set foot in Bristol, and that really amused him. He had no firsthand knowledge of Bristol, so he wound up being an important part of ESPN while being completely removed from the day-to-day life of the network. What was clear was how much it meant to him that ESPN valued him as much as it did. In television, elder statesmen are often shoved out the door. I don't think that was ever going to happen to my father at ESPN. The network gave him the respect he deserved, and he rewarded them with brilliant work.

He would steer the conversations, offer perspective and wit, and drive home the most salient points in the discussions. He also liked to counterpunch and play off the panelists, and his "parting shots" were a responsibility he took very seriously. He'd take shots, but not cheap shots. I remember one about Patrick Ewing. My father read a small item in *Newsday* that Ewing, who at the time was out for the season with an injury, had refused to sign autographs for a group of children suffering from terminal illnesses. Ewing had told the kids he didn't sign on game days — even though he was in a suit and wasn't playing the rest of the season. My father was appalled. He had no patience for that kind of nonsense, and he really dressed down Ewing.

JOE VALERIO, *Producer*, The Sports Reporters:

The last *Sports Reporters* show that Dick [Schaap] did was the Sunday after 9/11. It was September sixteenth. Of all the shows we've ever done, it's without question the one I am most proud of. All the NFL games had been canceled and Mark Shapiro had told me he wanted us to do a full hour on Sunday morning. I told all the guys that I really wanted the "parting shot" to be what it's like to be an American citizen. Dick was very resistant to doing something like that. He didn't like to show a personal side of himself, and he always thought that journalists should keep their private opinions and lives to themselves. But he wound up delivering a very eloquently written commentary, which included recollections of when President Kennedy had died. All of us were very pleased.

Dick went into the hospital for his hip operation the following Thursday, and what happened was terribly unfortunate. The problem was, he developed an infection and a fever that Saturday and the hospital was understaffed. Very few doctors were around because so many of them were at memorials for people who had died on 9/11. He didn't get the care that he should have gotten. I called up Norby Williamson and told him, "I think we're going to have some real problems. Dick isn't going to be coming back for quite a while." I was thinking in terms of maybe by the spring, so we thought about who could replace Dick for the interim period. We tossed around some names and he came back to me and said, "What do you think about John Saunders?"

When I called John up, he was very hesitant and skeptical. He came in when Dick was in the hospital and did a great job, but he thought the guys working on the show were very, very egotistical. I think he mistook their commitment to the show for egotism. Meanwhile, I was going to the hospital to see Dick on Sundays, but for a long stretch he was in an induced coma. I guess the last time I was in his room was the week before he died. It was very sad. After we went to Dick's memorial service in early January, John was very reluctant to continue with the show. He said, "Why would I want to replace such an iconic figure?" I said, "John, don't look at it that way. The show is going to stay on the air. We're going to continue to do the best job we can."

JOHN SAUNDERS:
Originally they approached me just to fill in for a week or two, and I'm not sure why, other than the fact that maybe because I live in New York it wouldn't cost them a hotel room or a car service to get me down here. I thought Dick Schaap was not just the

greatest writer and host but also a gracious, gentle human being. I didn't know him well, but every time I saw him, every time I had an interaction with him, he treated me so well that it was an honor, and so I felt it would be an honor to fill in for him. After I did the show, I went home and said to my wife, "I don't know if I can do this again. I'm not sure I'm the guy that can handle those personalities." But as I continued to do the show week after week, and got to know the personalities a little better, I realized the show was in some ways tailor-made for my personality, because it allowed the other guys to be who they were. When it comes to television, my philosophy has always been that I don't get upset at people, I don't have a big ego about it, and I'm not in it for the celebrity.

JEREMY SCHAAP:

When my father died, I certainly had no expectation that anyone would want me to try to replace him as host, and as far as I know, no one did. It would have been a bad decision. At thirty-two, I was still trying to build my own identity, and in many ways it would have been a challenge, especially emotionally. Beyond that, I thought John Saunders was a terrific choice.

ARTIE BULGRIN:

In 2001, my research team analyzed everything we were putting on air using Nielsen data. Essentially we gave our network a complete physical to find out where the vital signs were strong, where they were weak, and why. We called these analyses X-Rays, and they were eye-opening. We discovered that during a good chunk of the day, we had content that was just filler programming and not very appealing. Much of it was re-aired anthology stuff, repeated events, or syndicated sports programming. The X-Rays revealed that this just wasn't sticky content—you could see the audience turnover in the analysis. We categorized this as "other" programming, while most of our "premium" content was represented by live events, *SportsCenter,* or other live news and information studio programming. This "other" content filled up time periods mostly during the day and disrupted the flow of the audience into more highly rated material. The research team knew now that we needed a clearer, more systematic approach to programming the network.

MARK SHAPIRO:
When I was twenty-five, I had tried to sell Walsh some ideas for shows. The first was a *Nightline* for sports, and I wanted the General [Bob Ley] to do it. I mean, come on, Bob doesn't even look like a guy who would be on TV, and that's what I loved about him. He wants to tell a story. He wants to break news. But Walsh didn't respond. Then I spent months calling up Nielsen and working up a ratings analysis for the show and sent it to Walsh. He didn't respond. Then I gave Walsh *Pardon the Interruption* and he rejected it.

So I stopped giving him shows. I said to myself, "You know what? I'm just going to wait." Well, the *Nightline* of sports became the daily *Outside the Lines,* which I put on, and *PTI* became *PTI.*

JIM COHEN, *Vice President of News:*

Mark called me into his office and said, "I want you to start a new show. I want two guys yelling at each other, and I'm thinking Kornheiser should be one of them." I asked him about a budget and he said, "There isn't one," so I said, "I've done a lot of things, in charge of a news operation, in charge of a documentary operation, and I can manage people, but I've never launched a show that has no staff, no budget, no studios, no talent, and the rest of ESPN probably isn't on board." He looked at me and said, "Figure it out."

TONY KORNHEISER:

I had the same feeling that all sportswriters had, which was utter contempt for television, utter contempt for anybody involved in television sports, because they weren't newspaper writers. They were hairdos who just got in the way in the locker room — other than Cosell, that is. I mean, why would you want to be on air? The first guy who turned me around on that was Dick Schaap, because I knew Dick's background. He had been a great writer for a long time, and then he showed up on local Channel 4 in New York City. If Dick Schaap did it, then it was okay to do. I couldn't look down my nose on TV in quite the same way. And then you began to hear about the money that was involved.

But I looked in the mirror. I couldn't get on television. I wasn't pretty enough to get on television. I had no chance of getting on television. Howard Cosell is famously quoted as saying this of me—and he was my friend—"Doesn't Tony Kornheiser know he's unsightly?" Can you imagine that? Howard said that—talk about the pot calling the kettle black.

You know how I found out about *PTI*? It started in October of 2001, and in May or so of that year, Wilbon called me and said, "So you signed up?" I said, "For what?" He said, "The ESPN show." I said, "What ESPN show?" and he said, "You and I, we're going to do an ESPN show." I said, "Really?"

MICHAEL WILBON, *Columnist:*

CNN called me to do something in 1987, when I was seven years into my work at the *Washington Post*. They wanted me to be a guest on some show, but I had never cared about being on TV. I never saw it as a viable thing. Mine was a print-obsessed life. I didn't trust TV.

TONY KORNHEISER:

There's an old story about the guy who goes to Wimbledon for the first time and he looks at the grass courts and he says, "Oh, my God, these are beautiful.

How did they get so green?" And his friend answers, "Well, you start with five thousand years of rain." You can't just put people in a booth together and say, "Have chemistry." It doesn't work that way. What Wilbon and I have is five thousand years of rain. It started in 1980. We didn't go on the air until 2001. We never thought about going on the air. We were friends, we had adjoining offices, we yelled at each other. When *PTI* went on the air, and it was on the TV sets in the sports department at the *Washington Post,* people didn't even look up. They'd heard us argue so many times, they simply assumed we were in the building. After a while they looked up because we weren't cursing—that would be the only difference on television. If *PTI* had been on HBO, nobody would've ever looked up because the show's open would always be the same: "Pardon the interruption, I'm Mike Wilbon...blah blah blah, I'm Tony Kornheiser, how the fuck are you?"

CHRISTINE BRENNAN, *Reporter:*

I'd be on my phone at my desk at the *Post,* and Kornheiser and Wilbon would be screaming and arguing, and I'd say, "Excuse me," and I'd put my hand over the phone and say to them, "Hey, guys, can you take it somewhere else?" Well, they took it somewhere else, all right.

MICHAEL WILBON:

Tony and I both said we wouldn't do the show if we had to do it in Bristol. I had interacted with enough people at ESPN to know there's a certain reverence that Tony and I do *not* buy into. We didn't grow up at ESPN, we grew up as cynics, and cynical is not the mood "on campus."

Erik Rydholm had grown up in Chicago, and got his television experience bouncing from one midwestern TV newsroom to another in the early 1990s. Then the Internet began to bubble and, with friends Tom and David Gardner, Rydholm founded the Motley Fool, a stock-tip service that was originally affiliated with AOL and, when it became a success, migrated to a website of its own.

Having been enormously impressed with how smart Rydholm was during six months he spent working in the Chicago bureau, Jim Cohen mounted an aggressive campaign to land him as producer of PTI. But Rydholm didn't want to work for a big company. All righty, then: Cohen took care of that by telling him to start his own, which wound up helping ESPN, because at the time, Disney had imposed an employee head-count freeze. Cohen and Rydholm worked out an agreement whereby Rydholm would hire and pay employees and all ESPN had to do was provide offices and technical facilities. Cohen even took care of Rydholm's disinterest in techni-

cal production, promising him that he would be responsible only for editorial matters.

So it was that Erik Rydholm rode into Washington, D.C., and in the process changed the direction of his life and that of quite a few others — principally Tony Kornheiser and Michael Wilbon. The unusual arrangement proved to be one of ESPN's most important hires of the decade, bringing a big brain and relatively small ego — rare in a single individual — into the ESPN fold.

ERIK RYDHOLM, *Executive Producer:*

Cohen asked me if I read Kornheiser and Wilbon, and I said yes, then he told me, "The idea is to have a daily show with daily takes on the news. Do you think that's a good idea?" I said yes again, and then wrote him eighteen pages as to why. I thought if they actually talked about today's issues, ratings would go up, because there was no other place for people to watch sports television in that time slot. Then Jim asked me if I wanted to produce the show, and I said no.

I didn't want to be a television producer again — but I really wanted to be involved with those two guys. One older, one younger; one black, one white; one Jewish, one gentile. And they were so well educated, and had such an interest in, and perspective on, a world beyond sports. They also had the only relationship I'd ever seen in which two people who clearly loved each other could scream at each other but neither took it personally.

The first time I met Tony, Wilbon and I walked into a restaurant where Tony was having breakfast, wearing sunglasses indoors and eating his eggs. I sat down and was very nervous because this is Tony Kornheiser. He's incredibly gruff, and Mike was doing a little bit of a sales thing on me, but I was thinking, "Wow, this is not an easygoing guy. I've never dealt with a guy like this." The conversation was a little awkward. And then, just spilling out all the different thoughts I had on things, I said, "I don't think that this show should be afraid of tackling any of the hard issues in sports, any of the soft issues in sports, or even tackling Britney Spears." Tony stopped eating, looked up, and said, "Then I think you're the right person for this job." I thought, "Wow, that was freaking easy, all I had to do was drop Britney Spears's name."

JIM COHEN:

Tony was very skeptical, but I remember at one point he said, "If I do this show, can I wear a dress?" And I said, "Absolutely." That changed his mood; that changed everything.

TONY KORNHEISER:

My head was spinning. I had no idea what was going on, and then suddenly they said, "We're going to give you a 'three' contract. The first two years are guaranteed. The third year is at our option; here's the numbers." I said to Wilbon, "This is great. We're going to go down in flames in two to three weeks and we're going to get two years' worth of money. Fantastic!" I knew the show had no chance, zero chance. Look at us. Who is going to tune in and look at us? Wilbon said just the opposite. He thought it would be a hit right away.

ERIK RYDHOLM:

We brought Tony by the office a day later and we had about five or six people in their chairs and he looked around. He was amazed by the fact that he might have a dressing room with his own shower, his own bathroom. He couldn't believe it, because, you know, he and Michael came out of newspapers. He said, "If I decide to do this show, I believe it will last fewer than three months, but I have several other jobs so I'll be just fine." And then he left. Everyone else looked around and said, "Shit! *I* don't have any other jobs!"

Cohen's orders were to make it look totally unlike anything else on TV, and also make it "the best show on television." Well, thanks, that'll be easy, right? To make it look different, I scanned all the cable channels, and found that most shows were saying to the viewer, "Invest two minutes and get interested in what we're talking about." Two minutes is an enormous ask—in fact, it's arrogant. I wasn't going to sit there and say, "Whatever we're talking about you should be interested in because we're talking about it." Coming out of the Internet, I felt like we had a higher responsibility toward the viewer's investment of time. To convince the customer to come into our conversation, we put a rundown on the screen of what we were talking about—in case people weren't interested in that subject, they might be interested in what was coming next.

Matthew Kelliher, *PTT*'s coordinating producer, is the one who came up with the clock on each of the topics. I had sort of devised this idea of maybe a thirty-minute clock that counts down to *SportsCenter*, and he said, "Why don't we just put it on every topic?" What was key to me about the clock was that, in television, a minute and a half is a long freaking time. If you put on a minute-and-a-half piece and you start watching—if you're not interested in the first ten or fifteen seconds, you're going to bail, because it feels like a long time, even if intellectually a minute and a half is not a long time at all. So by putting the clock up there, what we essentially did was appeal to the rational part of your brain over the emotional part—that is, if you've checked out on this conversation and it doesn't interest you at all, you know it's going to be over in 1:15, 1:14, 1:13, so you can make the decision, "I will hang out for 1:13 until they change topics." Whereas when you're watching a piece on television and there isn't that cue, you have no idea. You get bored and you move on to something else that interests you more.

Prior to launch, as we were figuring all this stuff out, I took a trip to Bristol. I went out to dinner with some colleagues, and Trey Wingo was there. He said, "I have a question for you. You have two old guys sitting around the table talking about sports. That is the antithesis of everything all of our market research tells us that people are interested in. They want music, they want faster video, they want exciting plays, and the last thing they seem to want is ESPN Classic–type stuff with two old guys talking to each other. Why do you think that this is going to work?" And my response was "Because no one showed me that research before I decided to take the job."

Before our first show, I told Tony, "Mark Shapiro wants the first show to be an hour long." And Tony says, "No fucking way, he's out of his fucking mind!" I said, "Jim Cohen doesn't think he can tell him no," and Tony goes, "Fuck that, *I'll* tell him no. Give me his number." So he goes into the other room, picks up the phone, and says, "We're not doing an hour! We're doing half an hour on the first show! If we do an hour, you're like Michael Cimino making fucking *Heaven's Gate*!" And then there was a pause. Tony goes, "Uh-huh, ha ha ha. Okay." He hangs up the phone and he goes, "It's a half hour. The first show's half an hour." And I was like, "Tony's going to be very valuable here," because nobody says no to Shapiro.

However you feel about Mark Shapiro, he really knows television. He really knows what works and what doesn't. We did our first show, and I felt like it was a mess. Shapiro got on a conference call the morning after. He had a ton of feedback and all of it was totally on the mark, down to minute details like "Don't run any natural sound on your video." And it wasn't like, "You might want to try," it was "Don't do this, do this. Don't do that, do that." Then, at the end he said, "I thought it was a good start, I really do. Congratulations."

MICHAEL WILBON:

Sometime in 2001 or 2002, when the show was fairly new, I went into the locker room of an NBA team and they told me they had actually changed their practice time so they could watch the show. I was like, "Get out of here, this is total bullshit," but it was true. Mike Krzyzewski told us that he wanted to come on the show as a guest because his kids watched and it would earn him some cool points, and even Shaq had some great things to say about it. Then I was in Chicago back when Barack Obama was deciding whether to run for the Senate, and I was in his office and Barack was like, "You guys are onto something here."

ERIK RYDHOLM:

Everyone knew *PTI* was a success. It had been doing ratings that were well beyond what *Up Close,* the previous show, had been getting. Mark and Jim

[Cohen] had come to us and said they wanted to create a sister show, a companion show, called *Around the Horn*, and Matt Kelliher and I sat down and tried to sketch out some ideas. One of the things that had come up in our minds was that there were more and more of these shows with talking heads, but no one was holding them accountable. Just because they're sitting in this chair, what makes them so great? Why don't we have a show where we pass judgment on those who pass judgment?

There was resistance to my idea of who the talent would be on the show, not in terms of the panelists but in terms of the moderator. I wanted an old newspaper editor, a guy who could say your argument's bullshit because of this or that. And they wanted Max Kellerman. Now, I really, really like Max Kellerman. Whenever he came on to talk about boxing on *SportsCenter,* he lit up the screen. He was young and had great opinions. But I also thought he was a shooting guard and not a point guard. He would be the guy you'd pass the ball to for a shot, and to put him in a moderator's chair where he was going to judge other people's arguments, which he had no real background in—he hadn't been a sportswriter, he hadn't worked in a newspaper sports department, didn't know much about a variety of sports—wasn't right. So I loved Max, just not in this role. When they decided that's the direction they wanted to go, Matt and I talked about it and I said, "If we can't get everything that we want to get on this show to make it our show, I don't want to do it. I feel like I'm going to be fighting battles that are going to detract from *PTI.*" So we pulled out.

MAX KELLERMAN:

Mark Shapiro came up with the broad idea for the show: "We want a different sportswriter in each different time zone," and Jim Cohen named me the host and Bill Wolff the coordinating producer. Just a couple months before, I had told my manager that I was quitting talking about boxing and that I wanted to be an actor. I had taken Meisner technique for two years, and by this time I was twenty-seven. I met with Michael Price, my manager, and he told me, "You're not going to quit your job and become an actor. This is what I think you need to do if we want to work together: I think we need to cross you over from boxing into sports talk." Within two weeks, I was auditioning for *Around the Horn,* and within four to six weeks, I was named the new host.

BILL WOLFF:

Jim Cohen called me and said they wanted to spin off *Pardon the Interruption* and do a show with this asshole big-mouth know-it-all, Max Kellerman. You ever hear of him? Actually, I call him an asshole and a big mouth right to his face. And he eats it up. That's who he is. And for the record, Max Kellerman is the best guy I met in all of sports television, and the most loyal. I'd take a bullet for him. People who don't like his bravado are just insecure.

So Max was going to be the host and they were going to surround him with some bastards. Cohen asked me what I thought, and I said, "It sounds miserable, lonely, and terrible. I'll do it." So I rejoined ESPN to produce *Around the Horn*.

MAX KELLERMAN:

I believe I invented the mute button, which I wanted to call the mooch button, but we all made contributions. On *PTI* they have Stat Boy to clean them up at the end, and I thought, "Okay, we should have a Stat Boy equivalent," and I started thinking of *Mork and Mindy*, like when at the end of every episode Mork would talk to Orson, so I figured that the equivalent on our show could be a disembodied voice who I wanted to call Orson. But again, Jim Cohen, who's very sensible, said, "No one's going to get the reference; let's call it the Disembodied Voice."

Bill Wolff's idea was that the set should look like a cross between a video game and a game show. We're sending up the genre. The sports talk shows take the genre so seriously. It's not that we don't take sports seriously—we're all very passionate about it—but at the moment that you've gotten carried away, that you're in the throes of your passion, you have to catch yourself and make fun of yourself, because the fact is, it's a trivial subject. The emotions are real; it's just that the consequences aren't.

The idea of *Around the Horn* was that no one ever wins a sports argument. So we're going to score it. We're going to keep track of who's winning and who's losing. It's wink-wink, you know; we're joking, and very loudly, with everyone arguing. When I see shows where they're calmly discussing sports—when is it ever like that in life? No one ever calmly discusses it; we're passionate about it.

We were sending up *Sports Reporters* too, with more cutting-edge analysis and a much bigger sense of humor about ourselves—more like a genuine sports bar argument. *Sports Reporters* was not for a generation who grew up on *Sesame Street*. That was where we felt there was a major departure. We got criticized in the media critics' circle about it being this crazy show and it's not sophisticated and dah dah dah. They were missing the point. It wasn't for them. You know, who's watching TV at five in the afternoon? College kids, frats, and young adults; it was for them.

BILL WOLFF:

Very few things in my career have ever been more poorly received than *Around the Horn*. The sports media just destroyed us, destroyed us. After all, we had music, we had Woody Paige acting like a clown, and we had Jay Mariotti, whom every other sportswriter hates. And yet not only did Shapiro like it, the audience liked it. You know why? Because it was funny. It was satirizing sports talk. I mean, the host has a mute button! There's a winner! People said the scoring system didn't make any sense, but it wasn't supposed to make any sense. We were just making fun of the idea that anyone could ever win a sports argument. No one has ever won a sports argument in the history of sports arguments—*ever*. The Cardinals are better than the Cubs. The Cubs are better than the Cardinals. Let's have at it. I mean, we talk forever. It's like waiting for Godot. It'll never happen. No one will ever win a sports argument. But every day on *Around the Horn,* somebody has to win.

When Max left and got a big fat deal from Fox Sports Net—which is a double misnomer; it's not sports and it's not a net—I wanted to become the host. I had designed this show; I deserved that show. It was my thing. But Shapiro wouldn't even think about it. I wasn't really that close to Shapiro. He was a big blustery guy who would cut your balls off and he was really known to be a very tough character.

It's not that he was physically big; I could bust his face open. I mean, I'm not scared of him physically. But he was the kind of guy who was ruthless, a tough guy who would do what had to be done and not have a lot of sentiment about it. And I'm not that sort of person. So I was a little bit intimated by him, and I never approached him directly. And when I didn't get the host job, I had hard feelings. I had very hard feelings. So when Fox Sports asked me if I would come be Max Kellerman's EP [executive producer] on their show, I said, "Yes, for a 50 percent raise," and they gave it to me! So I left again.

ERIK RYDHOLM:

The turbulence wasn't because the show wasn't doing well, it was precisely because the show *was* doing well. Max's contract came up, and he wanted a lot of money. Little Tony Reali guested a couple times when Max didn't show up for work because of contract negotiations, and then Max decided he didn't want to do the show anymore. Max took along the producer, the director, and, eventually, the executive producer. Jim came to me and said, "Will you take it over?" We made a few slight changes and then went from there.

TIM COWLISHAW, *Columnist:*

In my mind, at the beginning, Woody [Paige] didn't fit into the show. It turns out I was dead wrong. Woody was the key to the show. Once I embraced that fact and figured out how to play off it, I had a lot of fun. The show got much better once it changed hosts. I like Max a lot, but the show was about him; with Reali, who does such a good job, the show became about us.

TONY REALI, *Host:*

My start on *Around the Horn* was probably the low point of television history. I went to work that morning thinking I was just going to be helping out on research for *PTI* as usual, but Max had a sty in his eye, so they knocked on the door and said, "We need you to host *Around the Horn*." I'm twenty-four years old, and this isn't just talking, it's "Ten seconds to break; look at camera 5 right now; get to the commercial," things like that. I had no clothes to wear so I used Max's, and before I went on, I went into the bathroom and said a Hail Mary. I remember not being able to focus on the camera, looking all around. It was not good. Then I did it another time when Max was sick. Bill [Wolff] was always very complimentary afterward, but I really didn't know what anybody thought of how I did.

Then Super Bowl night, the Patriots and Panthers are playing and it's about ten-thirty. I get a call from Bill, who tells me Max is in negotiations to continue on, but they aren't going well. Then he tells me, "Max is not going to be doing *Around the Horn* tomorrow. We need you to fill in. You're the only one nearby and we can't call someone up late on a Sunday night and expect them to be good tomorrow. You've done it twice before; just do it tomorrow." But this was not just a Monday in February, it was a day after the Super Bowl, a great Super Bowl, with a winning drive in the last four minutes, and the Justin Timberlake–Janet Jackson fiasco with the wardrobe malfunction from halftime. The show did stories on the boob for months!

Max wound up not coming in for the rest of the week. I ran out of ties on Wednesday and had to go shopping. Max never came back. I was hearing that ESPN was going to bring people in for tryouts, but for whatever reason — I never asked the reason and I don't even know the reason — they never did. I did four months' worth of shows on a daily contract — which I was happy to have because it was an on-air contract for hosting, which was more than I was making as a researcher for *PTI*. I signed my first contract a year and three months after Max left.

BOB RYAN, *Reporter:*

I'm a ham, an unvarnished ham. You have to be to survive and flourish on *Around the Horn*. Clearly, it's performance art. It's hard to say no because first and foremost, I'm an impoverished writer looking for outside income. But *PTI* is simply the most fun you can have on television. There's only two of you, not four or five, and there's something about the way it's put together by that incredible staff. If you're an egomaniac, it's the show for you.

For every PTI *or* Around the Horn, *there had to be a miss — or two or three.* Beg Borrow & Deal, *for one,* was a thinly disguised imitation of the CBS hit Amazing Race. *Two four-contestant teams had to bluff and finagle their way across state lines using their wits but no chits; no cash, checks, or credit cards. They also had to complete "sports-related tasks" en route. Originally titled* Beg, Borrow, and B.S., *the reality game lasted two seasons of seven episodes each (Rich Eisen hosted the first season, Summer Sanders the second) and managed to earn barrel-bottom ratings from its premiere in September of 2002 right through to its feeble finale in August of 2003.*

Mohr Sports *was, according to executive producer (and former cast member of* Saturday Night Live*) Jay Mohr, a cross between* The Chris Rock Show *and* SportsCenter. *Guests over the course of the talk show's run included Alec Baldwin, Bill Maher, Snoop Dogg, Jimmy Kimmel, and Wesley Snipes. The series premiered on ESPN on April 2, 2002, and, after being tried out in nine different time slots and failing in all of them, closed down for good on August 20 of the same year. "It was a bit of a train wreck from the beginning,"* Mohr conceded.

Unscripted, *hosted by former* Rolling Stone *writer Chris Connelly, featured big-time sports stars in "real-time" interviews — without edits or postproduction tinkering — talking intimately and casually about their private and public lives. Although it fell short of completing a full year on the air (premiering October 22, 2001, and ending June 25, 2002), the show, with its novel approach to a tired format, was ambitious enough to make an impression on viewers. Guests ranged from Barry Bonds to Hulk Hogan to Sammy Sosa.*

Although it was no failure, another ESPN original was scheduled to run only one night: Pete Rose on Trial. The ramblin', gamblin' guy himself did not appear, but such baseball stars as Steve Garvey and Jim Palmer (witnesses for the prosecution) and Hank Aaron and Bill Lee (for the defense) did, taking part in make-believe courtroom proceedings that ESPN televised in July of 2003. A jury of twelve, after listening for two hours to defense attorney Johnnie Cochran (of the infamous O. J. Simpson criminal trial) and prosecutor Alan Dershowitz, was supposed to decide two questions: whether Rose deserved a place in the Baseball Hall of Fame and whether Rose did in fact bet on ball games, even though by this time everybody knew he had.

In a quixotic combination of verdicts, eight jurors said Rose did belong in the Hall of Fame and yet eleven of the same twelve ruled that yes, he'd gambled on games. It didn't make much sense, but many viewers found the "trial" entertaining and provocative, with Jeffrey Toobin providing expert legal analysis.

CHARLEY STEINER:
    After the 2001 baseball season, I was offered wonderful opportunities with the Giants and the Yankees doing play-by-play on a full-time basis. My father in New York was in ill health and that was the overrid-

ing issue. He spent the last few years of his life having the chance to listen to the kid who used to scream his bloody head off in the basement actually doing it for a living.

I had been at ESPN for fourteen years. I didn't know if I had enough in me to make a last stand, and I really didn't want to be doing *SportsCenter* much anymore. I'd done about 2,500 of them — from godawful in the beginning to reasonably decent at the end. Bob Ley and I were the antithesis of glitz and glamour. In our own little way, I suppose, we were kind of like a Woodward and Bernstein. Bob was a Catholic guy; I was a Jewish guy. He was a straight Republican, and I was off there on the left somewhere. But together we had a pretty good ride. And we were grown-ups. To Shapiro's credit, *SportsCentury* was terrific stuff, but he was a guy who had answers to everything and very few questions. How do you fight that? I simply chose not to. I was worn out by then — by then and by them.

DAN PATRICK:

You have to remember that Mark Shapiro had told me that I was over the hill, that I was making too much, and that I wouldn't get a job anywhere else. I'll admit it, part of me believed what Shapiro was saying, but at the same time, he motivated me because I was thinking, "Fuck you, you're not going to get me." So I agreed to a schedule that I think was the worst in ESPN history. I'd come in in the morning and get ready for the radio show and have an early *SportsCenter* meeting, then I would be on the radio from one to four. After that, I would go back to my office, where I had a sleeping bag, and take a nap for an hour until five, then begin writing the eleven o'clock *SportsCenter*. I left the building after midnight. When I look back on my career, doing that schedule was my biggest regret. It meant that I didn't see my kids Monday through Friday, and that was awful. But it all comes back to what people say about the place—they don't care about talent. Couldn't care less. "We don't need you, fuck you, we've got NFL games."

Mark Shapiro had dramatic, eventful relationships with virtually all the league commissioners and with the ruling chieftains of most other sports. But his association with NBA commissioner David Stern was the most "it's complicated" of them all. Stern, very protective of his product and progeny, may well have expected Shapiro to look up to him for guidance or wisdom. Good luck with that, David.

MARK SHAPIRO:

I always knew the NBA would be a game changer for ESPN. I was a big fan of the game, and one only had to look at the success Turner had with the league to know what it could do for us. We had more men and younger men [in our audience], so I figured if it was good for them it would be even better for us. The NBA deal provided us with tonnage—forty to fifty games—plus playoffs, and, most important, it would enhance our credibility. Taking it off NBC would also be a major coup. Once again, we relied on the 360-degree approach in order to convince the league that we were the place to be in the post-Jordan era, when they needed exposure in the worst way: the finals on ABC, games on ESPN2, vintage games for ESPN Classic, footage across our other platforms, and a monster marketing campaign.

The league had a lot of options, as both NBC and Turner wanted to stay in the game. But we stole it from NBC. They simply couldn't compete with the dual revenue stream we had, which gave us the ability to pay more. I'd like to think that our multiplatform strategy also had something to do with it. It was the right time for the league to make such a move to cable. And it did bring us happy days on the ratings front. It was a big game changer.

ADAM SILVER, *NBA Deputy Commissioner:*

It was Mark who crafted the strategy of co-partnering with Turner, because historically we had a network partner and we had a cable partner—NBC and Turner. And the belief in the industry was that ESPN's opportunity was to replace Turner, because we were going to stay with NBC—we had such a longtime and strong personal relationship with Dick Ebersol, and we had so much success in those NBC years. I even remember Mark calling me over a weekend to discuss sharing the package with Turner, which is something we hadn't previously considered possible. We said we were willing to do that if Disney bought the network package for ABC as well. He deserves credit for that because I think it was very creative on his part. It wasn't the way people in the industry thought it would go. And I think most of the observers out there thought we would stay with NBC. Mark's willingness to co-partner with Turner opened the door for the relationship that we ended up having. So I give him a lot of credit on the business side.

MARK SHAPIRO:

David Stern was by far the best and most intimidating negotiator I'd ever faced. No one stands up to David, and to have me standing up to him, not just once, but multiple times over the course of the relationship, especially given that "who the hell is this kid versus me" thing of his, never went well. I tried to be respectful, but I wasn't afraid to push back. David would just scream and yell. Scream and yell. He'd even scream and yell at George; he didn't care. We got off on the wrong foot over the WNBA. He wanted the WNBA on the air. I told him the WNBA stinks, it doesn't rate, and I didn't want it. No one watches it. Men don't watch it. Women don't watch it! My goal was to get it off the air. It wasn't a diversity thing because I think diversity of programming is very important, which is why we amped up the number of women's college basketball hours because at least there's a demand and an audience for that. The WNBA didn't have either. I told that to Stern, and he hated me for it. I wanted it off altogether, but he went above me to George—and, I think, Iger—and won. It was one of the few times George ever overruled me. At least I got it put on ESPN2, where it couldn't hurt us.

DAVID STERN, *NBA Commissioner:*

I can say this for the record: Mark Shapiro was strong-willed and quite opinionated, and we had some differing views with respect to the presentation of our brand. In the name of diplomacy, we had some very open and frank dialogues with Mark, and, yes, sometimes that led to me talking with George.

ADAM SILVER:

A lot of what people say about there being a difficult relationship between David and Mark was not about business dealings. And it wasn't about editorial. I hope even Mark would acknowledge it was not over content per se. It wasn't "How dare you report that such and such player got fined or suspended," or that attendance is down or whatever else. We always recognized that they were in the news business and they had an independent obligation to report the news as they saw it.

MIKE TIRICO:

David Stern has had as much of an impact on the way his sport is presented as any commissioner. I certainly think commissioner Tagliabue had, and Goodell now has, a huge impact on how football appears on TV, but I think the NBA has done more of the steering of the ship over time. David's impact on how games are broadcast over the last couple of decades is one of the reasons the NBA is so television-friendly.

MARK SHAPIRO:

We paid around $400 million a year for six years when we first acquired the NBA. It was crazy, but Stern is as good as it gets. Even after the WNBA situation had been resolved, he never liked me. You might think it was because he saw me as wet behind the ears, but in reality it was because I pushed back— pushed back on using Brad Nessler as our first play-by-play announcer over Marv Albert in order to establish our own identity (I was wrong), pushed back on scheduling, pushed back on Stephen A. Smith when Stern didn't want us to put him on, and pushed back when he tried to disadvantage ESPN against Turner, or treat us like the ugly stepsister to

ABC. He'd always make his position widely known, even calling Iger frequently when he wasn't getting his way. To his credit, he never forced his opinions on us. Instead, he just held a grudge against me.

DAVID STERN:

We are a league, but we are an active brand manager as well. We have learned a great deal through our relationships with CBS, NBC, Turner, and ESPN. In the case of Disney, I've been doing business with Bob Iger for probably thirty years, so I know he's protective over his brand as well. We've had to walk through a diplomatic thicket at times in the past. That manifests itself in terms of ESPN's choice of talent, the way they promote our league, their production values, and, of course, their content. In the case of talent, we have a right to ask, "What does your research show about this person?"

I don't think it's a secret that we had hoped arrangements would be made for Marv Albert to work at ESPN, but Mark was very open and honest and told us he had somebody who he thought was better—Brad Nessler. And we said, "Okay, if you think so, fine."

ADAM SILVER:

And we were being told by others in their organization who knew the league that they disagreed with that choice.

MARK SHAPIRO:

In that very first season, Iger would often take phone calls from Stern complaining about what we weren't doing right. After working with the same partner, NBC, for so many years, there were bound to be difficult growing pains with a new network, but Stern didn't have any patience for it.

ADAM SILVER:

Bob [Iger] is married to our former longtime colleague and cohost of *Inside Stuff,* Willow Bay, so there's a special place in our hearts for Bob. We've heard all the stories about the extent of David's calls to Bob or Michael and they're all overstated. Did he ever call Eisner? Yes, but it was probably twice. Has he called Iger out of frustration? Absolutely.

And we feel very close to George too. George is very protective of his guys. Whether they're wrong or wrong, he stands behind them. That wasn't an accident. I didn't say right and wrong, I said whether they're wrong or wrong, George stands up to protect them. And we respect that.

DAVID STERN:

In terms of when I talk to Burbank, Bob Iger is one of the best managers in the history of media. He's incredibly busy. So you go to the well only very sporadically.

MIKE TIRICO:

They gave us a tape and said, "Here's how we want the games." It was a tape of a 1970s Knicks game—I kid you not—where they put the camera and you followed the players—it was tight. It wasn't these wide shots where you show the whole court. It was "You're dribbling up and you're covering." And "You don't need to go that wide." I mean, how do you react? That's what we do. Why do they think they know better? Second of all, it's wrong. "Do you see that? We can teach you, you know." It's just humiliating. I mean, it's patronizing. They wanted to significantly bring in the wide shot and, even more than that, to go tight when guys dribble off the ball. You can't go, "You're out of your mind." You have to be like, "Oh, that's interesting. Let us look at that." And you don't get anywhere by trying to challenge him. You just have to know when to pick your spot. Otherwise you'd be fighting with him all the time.

MARK SHAPIRO:

We as a network weren't used to a league being so involved in production matters. By contract, they couldn't tell us what to do, but they certainly carried a heavy stick and they knew what they wanted from a production and marketing perspective. Bottom line is that Stern usually got his way. He'd scream and scream and we'd cave. It was exhausting. One day, he was yelling at George, and I actually witnessed George hang up on him. He said, "I can't take this," and he slammed down the phone. I couldn't believe it. *George* actually hung up on someone!

TIM LEGLER, *Basketball Analyst:*

I've never had anybody at ESPN directly say to me, "The league would like this, the league would like that." Obviously I'm not naive. I know those conversations take place and eventually, in some way, shape, or form, it is passed on to us in a meeting or a memo or a show preparation or, maybe without us even knowing it, the on-air changes of focus in the direction of where we want to go with something. I know that some of that is dictated by the league. I understand that's how it works.

For me, the hardest thing about the transition from player to commentator was just getting used to the idea that you weren't part of the action anymore, that you were just *talking about* the action. I just missed playing so much. I retired prematurely—it really wasn't on my terms. I had a severe knee injury in 1996 and I played three more years and never really got back to the level I was at when I got hurt. I retired at thirty-two years old—and I felt like I still had four or five years left, but I just couldn't do it physically anymore. So to then be commenting on it, talking about it, and analyzing it, when I couldn't be out there playing—to me that was the most difficult part.

I've heard guys say that they found it difficult to be forthright and honest about guys that are playing when you might have just been playing against them last season. I never had a problem with that. If I couldn't say what I wanted to say, be what I wanted to be, and just really break down basketball the way that I wanted to, then I didn't really want to do the job. That's what I think they liked about me initially—I could be honest and, when I opened my mouth, they felt like I had something to say rather than like I was just a guy who didn't want to upset any of the players.

RECE DAVIS:

I have worked on NBA projects here before and I think the biggest difference with doing college games is that you're a little more careful when you critique a college player's performance because you don't want to stray too far into that area. You have to remember he may be on scholarship, he may be high-profile, he may get a lot of attention, and he may generate revenue, but he's still not a pro. He's still in school. With the pros, everything is fair.

In July of 2002, ESPN management temporarily banished Kornheiser from his own radio show and sentenced him to a one-week suspension without pay from PTI. *He had been hired as a Peck's Bad Boy of broadcasting, but apparently played the role too well for his bosses at*

ESPN. What did Kornheiser say to provoke the front office? Among other things, he complained bitterly on his radio show about ESPN executives having fired two of his favorite producers, and shared his thoughts on Eric Schoenfeld, who was general manager in the radio division and with whom he had crossed swords over content on the Internet. ESPN had been making the show available on its dot-com arm: when the radio show took a break for its affiliates, the dot-com feed would continue. Kornheiser used those occasions to season his remarks with profanity, arguing that the FCC didn't police the Internet and, therefore, anything went. But Schoenfeld said to forget about the FCC, telling him that ESPN has its own standards. Kornheiser predictably disagreed and told his listeners that they should petition the company by e-mail and letter for Schoenfeld to be fired. Some listeners even got hold of Schoenfeld's home address and he received some unwanted mail there.

Although known to be chronically insecure, Kornheiser probably counted on support and protection from John Walsh, his buddy of more than thirty years. But if Kornheiser expected Walsh to intercede, he'd be cruelly disappointed.

JOHN WALSH:

We had been at the Tampa Super Bowl, and Steve Anderson and I went to the hotel lobby to sit down with Tony. Steve, in no unequivocal way, said, "You're not going to trash ESPN talent, you're not allowed to do it. They're your colleagues." He was very clear. And we went back and Tony continued to do what Tony did, and Steve made a judgment to suspend him.

Where I screwed up in the relationship piece of it—and Tony was right—was we called Tony up to Bristol to have the meeting, to tell him about it, and Tony had occasion to be with me and I was kind of nervous about it and I didn't tell him what was coming. And he had a right to be upset about that. He didn't have a right to be upset about what was happening because he was clearly in violation of what was mentioned to him, but he was right in the sense that my relationship went back so far with him that, if anything significant happened, I should have said, "Hey, Tony, you're going to go into this meeting. It's not going to be fun for you. And, you know, you're in violation of what you were told in Tampa and there's going to be some consequences." I should have said that to him, in retrospect.

But it was not agonizing in the sense that I knew what was right. I knew Tony was wrong. I have no problem with that part of it, none whatsoever. When Steve Anderson made a judgment like that, he was dead right, he was dead right.

STEVE ANDERSON:
He was talking about people in our workplace, including the guy who was running radio and some

poor kid who worked there as well. He was blasting our promotions.

It was a no-brainer; he had crossed the line—way over the line.

TONY KORNHEISER:

I was sitting by the pool at the Otesaga Hotel in Cooperstown, New York, on vacation, and I got a phone call from my agent, and he said, "We gotta go to Bristol." I asked him, "Why do we have to go to Bristol? I'm on vacation." He said, "We gotta go to Bristol. They want to see us in Bristol." "Well, what's this about?" "I don't know, but they really want to see us."

I knew they were angry at me. I made a mistake and I insulted a product. But not only did I immediately say, "This is a mistake," I said, "What can I do to correct this?" There were two, I guess. I made fun of Toyota, which I didn't think was so terrible, but there was some guy who took out an ad and I basically said he was a charlatan, and I made my apologies on that. And I was wrong about that, and then I cursed on the *In-ter-net,* okay? I never cursed on the air. I never came close to that line on the air. I *never* did that.

Now, somebody may have felt that I was trying to become a Howard Stern, but I wasn't. I was just different than the others, and I was an outsider, and I didn't do it there, so there was antagonism toward me. When I had a national show and they said, "You better have someone from San Diego today," and I'd go, "What the fuck..." it was that. Now they don't care if they ever talk to athletes. They just want to talk to sportswriters. Everything I did then and got in trouble for, they now do. Everything.

I always wanted to make the radio show more about me, which worked for me in Washington. I always wanted to make it more about me than about ESPN, and I did. I'm guilty of that. I'm guilty of understanding what radio is. It's the most personal medium there is. TV is not, radio is. I'm guilty of knowing that and I tried to do that. And when they went to hire me for radio, I said to John Walsh, "You don't want me. You don't want me; I'm not going to do the show you want."

"Oh yeah, yeah, yeah, we want the show you do." "No, you don't." "No, we do."

Well, of course they didn't. I started doing the show, and they didn't want the show that I did in Washington for four or five years before they hired me. I had some sense that they were angry at me because I had said some negative things about a coworker and a sponsor, and I had a real terrible conflict with my boss at the time, who is no longer at the company—an imbecile and a spiteful little asshole who shouldn't be in charge of anything, including a washroom. He would yell at me right in the middle of my radio show. You don't do that to talent in the middle of the show. Are you crazy? You pay me a lot of money; presumably you think I'm pretty good. And he would always micromanage me and was a dick. And so we had an e-mail jihad at some point to just make fun of him, and he started screaming about how he was violated and he felt raped and I said, "Fuck you. Shut the fuck up." And then he went and researched all the bad things that I had done and gave Steve Anderson a bill of particulars—like curse on the Internet. Who gives a shit? I didn't curse on the air. Insult a sponsor, you know, show lack of respect, all of the things that Howard Stern and Don Imus have been doing for years, which made them giants— and everybody thought I had the best radio show that they had up there. I forget who was in the room, but I know Anderson and Walsh were there. Anderson gave me a letter that basically said I was suspended and the worst employee in the history of ESPN—the most troublesome. And this is after Olbermann! It also said if I did anything else wrong again, I would be fired with cause. When Shapiro heard about it, I said, "Do you want to see the letter? You're welcome to see it." He said, "Get the fuck out of here—you have it with you?" I told him I had made twenty copies and carried it with me all the time in my briefcase, and that I read it if I ever start feeling a little too high.

I was so hurt by Walsh. I felt he had stabbed me in the back. He fuckin' hung me out to dry. When Anderson was talking to me, I was looking at Walsh and he didn't say anything. I was really furious and hurt. I didn't talk to him for about a year. Steve Anderson used to send me Christmas cards afterward, and I would mark them "return to sender." It hurt me so much because I love his father, Dave Anderson, and grew up with him at the *New York Times*. How could Steve Anderson be such a dope when his father is such a great man? But the hurt from Walsh was the most. I was suspended because of a personality conflict with Eric—that's ultimately what it was about—who went in the archives and dug up a bill of particulars of things that I had done wrong, which Steve Anderson then signed off on. It was a terrible week, what a terrible week. I left ESPN Radio because of that. I left a million dollars on the table. I could not get out soon enough. I hated it. And when they hired Bruce Gilbert, whom I loved and could have worked for easily, the bridges had all been burned, the water was all disgusting. I got hosed. I got totally hosed.

Just so you know, all the press was on my side, so that was good. And Mark Shapiro saved me, returned all the money from my suspension, and said, "I'll be your rabbi and this will never happen again."

MARK SHAPIRO:
Wimbledon was my very first rights-fee deal, in 2003. George and I did it with [IMG chairman and sports agent] Mark McCormack. We were the last ones to meet with McCormack before he died. He

did all his deals on a paper napkin: when he died, there was no record of anything we had agreed to, so I almost lost the deal. IMG sent in Bill Sinrich to clean it all up. We met at the Ritz-Carlton in Laguna Beach during Super Bowl week. We spent over two hours in the lobby lounge. It was a bit contentious, given that I was adamant that they stick to the terms agreed upon by McCormack, but because Bill had no record of the terms, it turned into a heated negotiation.

The All England Club wanted more money than what they were getting at HBO, which was an outrageously rich deal, but I knew HBO's desire for the property had waned and they simply couldn't match the multiplatform, 360 degrees of programming and marketing that we had developed for this acquisition. I wanted Wimbledon badly because it was a Tiffany product that would enhance the image of ESPN yet simultaneously be an innings eater — two weeks, lots of hours, particularly in the morning. Bill and I cut a five-year deal at six million per year. What I'll remember most about closing that deal was that after Bill and I finished our slugfest, he got up to leave and the back of his shirt was completely drenched, from the collar on down. It was as if he just got out of a pool. I felt such a sense of satisfaction and victory.

ROSS GREENBURG, *President, HBO Sports:*

There was pre–Mark Shapiro ESPN and post–Mark Shapiro ESPN, and in between it was sometimes very odd. I really have a lot of respect for Mark; he was a shoot-from-the-hip, creative programmer. But he developed a certain mean-spirited kind of competitiveness that was a little irksome. I'll give you an example: if we did a high-profile piece on *Real Sports,* he would tell his troops, "Hey, go see if you can get that interview so we can sabotage HBO and put the guy on our *Sunday Conversation* before their Tuesday broadcast." And they would do silly things like if we were doing a documentary, they would somehow try to put something on similar to ours two days before. I think it always irritated Mark that HBO Sports had a dominant position in areas like movies and documentaries, areas where he felt ESPN should have been the leader.

He was a bulldog negotiator, and in talking to league people, you would hear stories about how he was very demanding—"take it or leave it at the table," that kind of thing. He got off on that. Oh, he loves confrontation.

MERRIL HOGE, *Football Analyst:*

When I was diagnosed with cancer in 2003, I called Mark Shapiro. He was the first guy I called. I told him of my situation and that I still planned on doing the draft and that's really the only obligation I had contractually during my chemotherapy time. And he's like, "Listen, we're behind you 100 percent. You do whatever you want to do. If you want to do it, you're doing the draft. If you feel like you can't, you don't have to do the draft, and I don't want you to worry a second about work." He was really supportive and that was very meaningful to me and my family.

THEA ANDREWS, *Anchor:*

I always had a lot of faith in everything about Mark, especially as a leader. I believed he was a visionary, and what he was trying to do was incredibly smart and innovative. He's one of those people you want to follow into battle. You don't ask questions, you just go. That's what leadership is, I guess; I just believed in him.

I'm sure there are people who disagree with me, but there are two things no one can disagree with: first, he's one of the most charismatic people on the planet, and second, he's an unbelievable television producer. I remember the first time I saw him break down a piece of television and explain what was good and what was bad about it. That's when I said, this guy knows exactly how to make good TV and if I can just follow him, I will be in good hands.

You may never know where the next great idea is going to come from, but you have to put yourself in a position to be open to it.

MARK SHAPIRO:

I had four thousand people reporting to me, and would say at town-hall meetings that anyone could get fifteen minutes with me one-on-one. Anyone. I did admit it might take six months to get on my schedule, but no one was ever declined. I wanted everyone to bring their ideas forward, regardless of their position. So a guy named Fred Christenson, a midlevel director in our Programming department, asked for some time. He comes into my office and tells me if I double the hours we were devoting to poker, and gave him some money for a new camera that had been developed, he was convinced poker would really take off. Now, at the time, we were broadcasting eight hours a week of poker and not really paying much attention to it. I talked with David Berson, and we both decided we didn't want to do anything more at that time. A couple months later, Fred was back again, asking for the same things. He was usually a mild-mannered guy, but he was so passionate about poker's potential that I just had to say yes. It was for ESPN2 and I had plenty of space over there, so I figured, why not give the guy a chance?

FRED CHRISTENSON, *Director of Programming:*

My sell was that we needed to put money into production. Quality was historically bad on all poker produced on any level, but in order to justify increased production costs we needed a multiyear rights deal from the Binions, who were the rights holders at the time. I went to Becky Binion and her husband, Jack, and hammered out a five-year rights deal in which we paid next to nothing in rights fees, so all the money could go into production. From then on, we produced poker like it was a big event.

MARK SHAPIRO:

Then I hired Norman Chad because I knew him and knew he was a big-time gambler who would be perfect for us as an analyst. We added Norman, we added the hours, and we put in this whole new camera. And the thing took off immediately!

NORMAN CHAD, *Analyst:*

A confluence of events led to this poker boom. The Travel Channel started a new thing called the World Poker Tour at the same time that ESPN started the World Series of Poker. And then people started playing poker on the Internet. You couldn't play poker on the Internet ten or fifteen years ago. That alone sustains poker on television, to tell you the truth — the Internet. And then that first year there was this unlikely story about a Tennessee accountant named Chris Moneymaker — his name sounded like it was made up — who turned a forty-dollar investment into a $2.5 million first prize; that gave the poker thing legs at the beginning.

They'd always done World Series of Poker as a one-hour telecast each year, and then in 2003 they decided to produce more telecasts from the contract, and they went from seven hours that first year to twenty-four hours pretty quickly. The unusual thing they found is that, unlike their other properties—basketball, football, baseball, tennis—they could re-air poker in perpetuity, at odd hours and with zero production costs, and it would get a decent enough tiny number for the advertising dollars still to flow in.

Poker would wind up being shown more than anything else on ESPN. Nothing else is close—except *SportsCenter*. ESPN networks show between 1,500 and 2,000 hours of poker a year. One of the ESPN networks shows thirty hours every week of the year. They keep re-airing them and it takes up more time on ESPN than any other quote-unquote sport. It's not a sport, it's a game.

MARK SHAPIRO:

Get this: other than Sunday night NFL and Saturday college football, poker wound up being our highest-rated series. It tied Sunday night baseball! It also wound up being an incredibly valuable lead-in to *Playmakers*.

There were a hundred good reasons to do Playmakers, *ESPN's ambitious scripted series about the personal lives*

of (fictitious) pro football players, but there was one reason not to—and that one reason outweighed the hundred others. The strange case of this celebrated and
castigated dramatic show vividly illustrates where reach
and grasp differ at ESPN, and how the network's tan-
gled alliances can affect—and restrict—what goes on
the air.

The brainchild of writer-producer John Eisendrath,
Playmakers had the potential to take ESPN not just
down a "road less traveled" but, in fact, down a road
never traveled, at least for the all-sports-always network.
The show was not escapist fantasy, but instead verged on
docudrama. The private and public lives of the Cougars, the fictional Playmakers team, had striking similarities to the lives of real football players—and not by
coincidence, either.

By presenting the stories as fiction, the writers were
free to address real-life issues without using real-life
names (and getting real-life sued), and the drama was
absolutely overflowing with authentic problems representative of those going on in the league at the time. The
second episode, titled "Piss Man," included a scene in
which a drug-abusing player injects someone else's
"clean" urine into his bladder as a way of beating a drug
test. Substance abuse, such a touchy issue among NFL
teams, was dealt with in many of the eleven Playmakers
episodes that aired during its one-and-only season.

Spousal abuse was another of the social issues treated
in scripts for the show. In one of the early episodes, a

shooting occurred outside a nightclub where African American players liked to party, and, in a later installment, one of the husky Cougars is forced to admit he's gay when "outed" by an angry boyfriend in front of the other players.

Now, why on earth would the NFL have a problem with any of that?

MARK SHAPIRO:

I told the world I wanted to go big on original programming. Big and scripted. That was the new twist. George asked me what the strategy was, and I said, "We need more women viewers, we need more casual viewers. We need viewers who are going to sit with us because they want to be engrossed in a story, especially women who are forced to watch us because of their sons. Eighty percent of our audience are hard x's and o's. If we can even get a little more casual, it would be great for our future." And then I said, "Here's the best thing: they're going to write about us in the Life section of *USA Today*." He said, "What do you mean? ESPN would never be in the Life section; we're never mentioned there, just in the sports pages." I told him, "We can start getting in the Life section," and sure enough, the first thing we did, the Bobby Knight movie, winds up on the front page of the Life section with a big picture and story about us breaking into scripted drama. And George was like, "Holy cow, this is great."

JOHN EISENDRATH, *Writer*:

In the beginning, none of us felt like it would be this big controversy, that the NFL wouldn't like it, or that people would think it was besmirching the image of the NFL, and we were shocked at the reaction it got. I thought, "Doesn't anybody read the newspapers?" It was crazy. Mark told me he didn't feel that any show about sports on ESPN, or that had sports as a backdrop on ESPN, could succeed if the audience felt like it was bullshit, like we were soft-pedaling it. It was like, "Of course this stuff goes on in the NFL. What else would one write about?"

ANDREA KREMER:

There had been a bunch of players busted for pot, so we were doing a story on marijuana use in the NFL and drug testing. I managed to find out that Shawn King, who had played for the Panthers and the Colts, had failed a drug test. So I'm on the phone with the guy, and I'll never forget, my producer was there too, and while I am listening, my hand is over the phone and I'm like mouthing, "Oh, my God. Oh, my God." It turns out that when his test came back, it said he was pregnant. He had used substitute urine from a female friend who happened to be pregnant. I guess he hadn't realized that would show up. I was so excited to find someone who had failed a test and was willing to talk, and then he agreed to talk to me on camera. We went to see him and he told the whole story. You always worry if they're going to be as forthright on camera as they've been on the phone with you. But my point of telling the story is that I remember getting off the phone and being so excited because I love telling stories that nobody else has. On the other side, I took it way too seriously when I didn't get stuff. I would take it personally and I'd really let it bother me. And that's a bad thing.

MARK SHAPIRO:

I don't know how I sold *Playmakers,* to be honest with you. I went to George and I said we need to make sure the NFL understands this is fictional, it's a soap opera, but that we were going to be like *Law & Order,* with stories right from the headlines. Goodell was in the meeting and they were okay with it when I told them about it, but they didn't have a script. They did make it very clear there was to be no NFL attachment at all, no trademarks, no logos, no helmets.

I was very hands-on with it and it just busted out. I would send Bob Iger sealed scripts for *Playmakers,* and he would give me great notes. Eisner went to a Wall Street analyst conference and somebody said, "You got a thirty-three- or thirty-four-year-old guy there launching a show that is irritating one of your biggest clients," and Eisner's line was "I'll take a hundred Mark Shapiros if I can find them. I want risk takers. I want communicators. I want bold thinkers. I want decision makers." It was a great response.

We did have one funny screwup. I remember it was a Saturday morning and I was taking my family to Newport for the day and I got a call from George. His voice was shaking. He told me he needed to see every episode, and I said, "I know you do, and I will give them to you." He asked me, "Do you have us protected here? Because you know I trust you with everything," and I told him yes, but I could tell he was concerned. It turns out some PA had sent a rough draft of an episode to me and to George at the same time, and then he says to me, "Hold on, I have to close the door." Then he whispers to me that he had just read the script, and some guy was getting a blow job in it. I laughed and said, "George, you won't see that on the screen." It was clear, though, that he was very concerned from then on.

JOHN WALSH:

Mark liked introducing new programs. *Playmakers* was his baby and it was a big hit for a season, and would still probably be on the air if not for the fact that it pissed off the NFL.

JOHN EISENDRATH:

Once the show was on, I think the NFL probably felt it couldn't totally ignore it, which I'm sure would have been their preferred course of action, but this was clearly not going to go away. It got the double whammy too, because television critics were writing about it, and so were sportswriters. It was getting twice the amount of notoriety that a show might otherwise get. I'm very certain that about two-thirds of the way through the season, under pressure from the NFL, Gatorade dropped their sponsorship.

MICHAEL EISNER:

During the weekend, NFL team owners watch their own games, but every owner in football watches *Monday Night Football.* They're all home. So on a Monday night they actually put up a promotion for *Playmakers,* and what do they put in the promotion? Everything you would not want an owner to see: drinking, driving while drinking, homosexuality, drugs, steroids, all of this crammed into a thirty-second promo. As soon as I saw it on the air, I called George at home and I said, "George, are you guys insane?! What are you doing? It's like throwing meat to a starving dog!"

PAUL TAGLIABUE, *NFL Commissioner:*

Over the summer I started to see promos on ESPN for *Playmakers.* I didn't know anything about it. I think I learned later that there were some discussions with ESPN about using the uniforms or NFL colors and marks and logos, but I didn't know anything about the program until I started to see those promos. And I thought they were very negative, that they traded in racial stereotypes that were very unfair to

NFL players and, for that matter, to African Americans generally. So I asked someone in our broadcasting group to get me a tape of one or more of the actual episodes because I didn't want to draw any conclusions just based on the promos. But when I looked at a couple of the episodes, they confirmed my worst fears—the way the players were cast was demeaning to African Americans and really the worst of racial stereotypes about black athletes and young black males generally.

I decided just to call Eisner directly. I didn't see any reason to talk to anybody at ESPN because the way I viewed it, it was the kind of issue that he would be interested in just in terms of how the Walt Disney Company viewed itself and how he viewed ESPN. I called him and told him I thought the programming was a terrible disservice to athletes and to society. He said, "Well, you know, I understand what you're saying, but there've been things that are not exactly positive published about, or presented on television about NFL players before, such as Pete Gent's book *North Dallas Forty.*"

I said, "*North Dallas Forty,* are you kidding me? It's got nothing to do with this issue. The author of *North Dallas Forty* did not have a contractual relationship with the NFL. He was an independent author, a former player, who was not under an obligation to present NFL football, NFL players, NFL teams in a way that makes it a valuable, credible, respected product. You have that obligation, and I think what you're doing here is directly undercutting that. People want to watch sports when they can respect the athletes. This program leads them to have a view of the athletes that leads them to disrespect the athletes." I said, "Expectations as to how professional athletes conduct themselves are much higher today than they were twenty-five years ago. We at the NFL have tried to do a lot to raise those expectations of the players and demonstrate to the public that these athletes are responsible individuals, and that they do manage their lives—not just on the field but off the field—in mature ways. And what you're presenting is so one-sided, it directly undercuts all of that, and that's a big issue for us." I then told Eisner, "It's ridiculous, I don't see why you're doing it, and I don't think you should be running it." He defended it. The principal point he made was that you can't expect every show to be great and upbeat. There's a reality out there and some people are negative. I said, "Yeah, some people are negative—but some people are positive. Your show is completely negative. And it's stereotypical."

CHRIS BERMAN:

I'm a simple guy. I don't watch TV. I don't go on the Internet. So I never watched *Playmakers,* but I knew if the league was pissed, I probably should be pissed.

STEVE BORNSTEIN:

Was *Playmakers* a good show? It was excellent. It was terrific, but I don't believe it was the right direction for ESPN, and I would not have green-lighted it because of the relationship with the NFL, our most important customer. My wife loved *Playmakers;* the only time she's ever watched ESPN in her life was when *Playmakers* was on. And my argument is, I really don't need my wife to watch ESPN. She's welcome to, but I want her to like what *we* put on there, not what she's looking for.

BOB IGER:

Playmakers was an aggressive—and effective— programming play for ESPN at the time. It was a critical and ratings success. It was a risk and it did everything you'd want it to do, except one thing: it upset a valued partner, in this case the NFL. At the end of the day, ESPN decided on its own to end the show after one year. And they were very honest as to why—they came to the conclusion that they were not in the business of alienating important business partners.

STEVE BORNSTEIN:

The NFL didn't hate *Playmakers,* they were very embarrassed by it. They didn't believe it represented their sport well, and so they were basically confused as to why a partner that's important to them would embarrass them that way. It was nothing more than that. We frankly knew that all it was going to take was a phone call from Paul [Tagliabue] to Michael Eisner and *Playmakers* would go away.

GEORGE BODENHEIMER:

The league reaction wasn't good. They were very upset with it. And at the end of the day I made a decision not to continue to produce something that was that upsetting to one of our major partners. It wasn't good business.

MARK SHAPIRO:

It was very controversial, but no one was calling me to complain. They weren't even calling George. They were calling Iger and Eisner, saying, "What are you doing?" And they were not fucking around. Given how many shows had already aired, I thought we had already stomached all the pain, but in the end, the league started to insinuate that our NFL deal was going to be at risk if we kept putting this in their face. I understood. I didn't even fight it.

It was the first time in history that a show was canceled for being too good.

JOHN EISENDRATH:

The thing that I really admire about Mark was that when he called me to tell me the show was being canceled, he didn't say, "Look, John, you know we don't have room on the schedule next year for it, we need to put on the Iditarod." He just said, "Look, it just was too controversial, and we got squeezed." He was honest about it.

It's awful having a show that is one of the few to be censored off the air. Shows die because they're unpopular, but taking a popular show off the air? I don't know if you could find any others. You certainly can't find five others that have ever been taken off the air because some group told the company that owned the network, "We don't want that show on your air."

I would have thought that, for the billion dollars they were giving the NFL, ESPN could say to them, "Thank you, we will give you the billion dollars, now shut the fuck up." And the whole idea that the NFL was ever going to go anywhere else — come on, really? ESPN has the ability to pay more than everybody else; that's why they have *Monday Night Football*. So really, the NFL was going to shut out ABC and ESPN as a punitive measure? I mean, honestly! Who really had the power in that relationship? But no, lawyers and doctors can get written about, cops can get written about, even the president of the United States gets written about. Powerful people get fictionalized on television all the time, and that's just the way it is. But for some inexplicable reason, sports leagues can't accept that that is also going to happen to them. Crazy.

Here's the deal: I think that the NFL, like Major League Baseball and the NBA, is a monopoly. A monopoly is by definition a bully. They can bully anybody they want, any way they want. That's the power that they've been given. Maybe that's why there are very few things to which we grant monopoly status in this country.

GARY BETTMAN:

After they did *Playmakers* and the NFL threw a fit, I was having lunch with Shapiro, and he said to me, "If you're going to have a work stoppage next year, how about if we do the equivalent of *Playmakers* for hockey? It'll be good exposure for the game." I looked at him and said, "Are you kidding me? Do you think we're that dumb?"

Of the many irate voices raised in perpetual outrage on America's talk-radio stations, few were as powerful or controversial in the 1990s and in the new millennium as Rush Limbaugh, the opinionated conservative heard in 650 markets worldwide. Hoping to capitalize on Limbaugh's popularity—even though it meant a complete about-face from ESPN's usual avoidance of political content—John Walsh signed Limbaugh in 2003 for a coveted slot on Sunday NFL Countdown *after pursuing him for more than a year.*

It was a bold, adventurous idea, and it only took three weeks for it to collapse completely.

With considerable promotional fanfare, and after much debate about whether Limbaugh was an appropriate choice, the talk star who sometimes called his followers dittoheads made his NFL Countdown *debut on September 7, 2003. On September 28, during a discussion of Eagles quarterback Donovan McNabb, Limbaugh said, "I think what we've had here is a little social concern in the NFL. The media has been very desirous that a black quarterback do well.... There is a little hope invested in McNabb, and he got a lot of credit for the performance of this team that he didn't deserve. The defense carried this team."*

Oddly or not, backlash was not immediate. None of the other Countdown *members said anything that day, but that Tuesday, reacting to Limbaugh's comments, McNabb himself said, "It's sad that you've got to go to skin color. I thought we were through with that whole deal." Following the comments, Democratic presidential candidates Wesley Clark, Howard Dean, and Al Sharpton all urged ESPN to fire Limbaugh. Similarly, the National Association of Black Journalists demanded that ESPN cut Limbaugh loose.*

RUSH LIMBAUGH, *Radio Personality:*

The first time I'd been approached about coming to ESPN, we couldn't figure out what to do. I was talking with John Walsh, and he told me they had this idea that they'd put me in the studio show as a fifth person, not on the main panel but off to the side at my own desk. I would be ostensibly the voice of the fan in the studio, and during the discussion segments throughout the two-hour show, if there was any time I wanted to interrupt and disagree or offer another point to what the professionals were saying, then I would hit a buzzer and on the screen there would be a red flag being thrown, like I was a referee throwing in, and I would then enter the discussion.

I had also tried out for ABC's *Monday Night Football* the year Dennis Miller got it. I auditioned with Al Michaels. Don Ohlmeyer was back producing and I went out to L.A. with a tape of a Buffalo Bills–Tennessee Titans playoff game. I didn't get the gig because Don said, "You've got a radio show. I got production meetings all day on Monday. I just don't think you have the time to do it." I think he was also a little afraid of the reaction if I'd gotten that job. That was okay by me. Don and Al have since become two of my closest friends.

Once I got on the show, I dealt mostly with John Walsh and Norby Williamson, who said to me after a couple weeks, "We need to punch things up. You don't need to be afraid here. We don't expect you to be an x's and o's football guy." So I got the impression that they were a little bored.

Before the McNabb game, we had a production meeting where we'd go through every segment of the show, and that particular show there were two segments on the Eagles and McNabb. Both segments were devoted to "What's wrong?" The Eagles record was one and three, or two and two, and I remember Chris Berman in the production meeting saying, "What the hell's wrong with McNabb?" He also said, "I called Andy Reid and even he doesn't know." So nobody could figure it out, but I'm taking notes and I'm hearing what these guys are going to say on the show the next day.

My job was if I felt like jumping in, to jump in, and my opinion at this point in the season was that the defense of the Eagles was being shortchanged; much of the credit that the Eagles were getting was not going properly to the defense because there was almost a groupie-like approach to McNabb. When I listened to people talk about McNabb on all the networks, I had a sense they were pulling for him in an affirmative-action kind of way. I'm a political guy and I'm sensitive to those kinds of things. There was never an admonition given to me to keep politics out of this, because there was never any assumption that there would be politics in it, and I didn't really consider the comment I made to be political. So I made the comment, and if you go back and look at the tape, there was some spirited disagreement, but Steve Young piled on and said, "Actually, I think there's something to this." I'm paraphrasing, but he started talking about how McNabb is not doing a good job managing a game. Tommy Jackson said, "Well, Rush, somebody's thrown those touchdowns."

And I said, "Well, I'm not saying he's not a good quarterback, you guys. I just think maybe you're looking at the wrong place here in trying to figure out what's wrong with the Eagles. Don't you think maybe he's a little bit overrated?" And at the end of the whole segment that caused all the controversy, if you listen to it all the way through, you'll hear Michael Irvin say, "Rush is right." Those are the last words. There were no other comments about that for the rest of the show.

When the show was over we always went to the room with all the TVs to watch all the games, and nobody was upset. Nobody in management. Nobody on the show. Nobody even said a word. The show was in the can. It was done. Everybody thought it was a good show. When they did a postmortem, my comment didn't even come up.

And on the Monday following that, during the ESPN pregame show for *Monday Night Football,* it didn't come up. Tuesday morning is when the firestorm happened. McNabb made his comments and every columnist in the Philadelphia print media wrote about it. When the Philadelphia media shitstorm hit on Tuesday morning, Mark Shapiro called me and said, "This is great. Can you imagine the numbers we're going to have Sunday?" And I said, "Well, we'll see." But the point is he was pleased. Nobody was pissed, nobody was expressing anger to me as of Tuesday morning.

Look, I understand everybody's reaction. My comment was a little too nuanced for a football pregame show. It was a little bit too honest. I believe in a color-blind society.

MARK SHAPIRO:

I was in Saint Thomas on vacation and did not see the show that Sunday, and I didn't hear anything at all about it on Monday. Chris LaPlaca called me Tuesday morning and told me Rush had made some insensitive comments about McNabb, which reeked of racial overtones. My very first response was "What did everyone else on the set say?" When Chris told me no one realized what he said, that really set me off. I asked him, "Why didn't they say anything?" I was furious. This was our Al Campanis moment and we had blown it! Ted Koppel had listened to Al when he said that African Americans weren't as qualified as white people were for baseball management jobs, and Ted responded right away, opening up the floodgates for a national dialogue. We were supposed to be journalists! It's our job to challenge! The guys on the air should have interrupted him, they should have questioned his position: they didn't, so they took a black eye.

CHRIS BERMAN:

You finish a two-hour show and you go on to the next thing. There wasn't a meeting of five or six of us where we said, "Oh, my God, what the hell did we just do?" or "We have a bombshell on our hands." That never happened. I don't think we immediately grasped the seriousness of the situation.

TOM JACKSON:

Look, I had understood what Rush was before he was hired. When we met him in New York earlier in the year, I remember at that time thinking, "My goodness, we have Rush Limbaugh on our show: I know some of his rhetoric that he uses on his radio show, but I was told he was going to represent the passionate fan and that his political views would never come into play on our show." Now, there was a sense even as you were hearing it that you would have to be very naive to believe that, but I think we all, in an effort to get along and keep our jobs, said, "Okay." But there was never any departure from his political views. The first essay he did was all about the Rooney Rule and whether it was something that was fraudulent or not.

When Rush said what he did, my reply to him in short was "Well, someone won those games that put them in championship games." I understood that he had said something that was certainly—no pun intended—"off-color," but I did not realize how serious it was until the following night, when the guy who headed up our NFL programming, Bob Rauscher, came to me and said, "When you think about what Rush said yesterday, how did it affect you?" I said, "Well, certainly you could tell it was offensive." Then Bob said, "We're getting a lot of calls from people who want copies of the transcript of what he said." And at that moment, I realized really the magnitude of what we were dealing with. That was the moment that it struck me.

RUSH LIMBAUGH:

[Eagles owner] Jeff Lurie then came out and said that ESPN is institutionally racist: "They have Limbaugh and they're running this *Playmakers* series and we've got to do something about it." He accused me of being a racist and saying racial things about McNabb, which I hadn't done. You have to remember at the time that ESPN was also running *Playmakers* and it was about a black running back who they portrayed as getting coked up before games and basically being a reprobate.

In an interview with USA Today's *Rudy Martzke, Shapiro made it clear that he believed what Limbaugh said was "not a politically motivated comment. This is a sports and media argument." He went on to say, "We brought Rush in for no-holds-barred opinion. Early on, he has delivered."*

TOM JACKSON:

The following day, all hell was breaking loose. When I heard that Mark publicly gave Rush that vote of confidence, that was the thing that sent me over the edge. They — "they" being ESPN hierarchy — had come out and said Rush had given them what they wanted; they knew he was going to be controversial. I was very angry: I probably said a few things to Mark and the others that I shouldn't have said, although, as I look back on it, I certainly don't mind that I said them. I know one of the things that I said was that they had made a huge mistake in putting him on the air with us. I said, "You put this guy twenty feet from us to do what he did and now we all have to answer for it."

I was watching Donovan McNabb being left to wiggle in the wind, having basically to defend himself against something that had little to do with him. So I talked it over with my wife, Jennifer, and my agent, Lou Oppenheim, and said I didn't think I could work at ESPN anymore if Rush Limbaugh was going to be there. Lou told me, basically, "Don't tell anybody else," and I remember he set up a conference call between myself, Steve Anderson, and Mark Shapiro.

MARK SHAPIRO:
Steve Anderson told me Tom was a mess and was thinking the company was letting him hang out to dry. He was receiving a lot of calls and letters accusing him of being an Uncle Tom, and he wanted us to take him off the hook. So I flew to Cincinnati to have

dinner with him. While I did so to offer him support, I couldn't excuse the fact of what he hadn't done. What could I say—that none of our analysts thought that it was insensitive and that's why they didn't say anything? Why didn't they say anything?!

JOHN SAUNDERS:

The person I felt the worst for through the whole thing was Tom Jackson, because he was in a live TV show and he has a colleague on the air say something so reprehensible, but he also has somebody in his ear who may have been talking at the same time Rush was saying those words. Even if he wasn't, when you do shows like that, if you're going to be good at your job, you've got 70 percent of your brain listening to them and 30 percent of your brain preparing for what you are going to say next.

TOM JACKSON:

Mark asked, "What do you think we should do?" And I remember telling him rather strongly, "I don't know what the hell you should do. I'm waiting for my company to do the right thing." I had told Lou, "I want to see if ESPN will be comfortable with the show coming on on Sunday with me not there and with Rush Limbaugh on that set." But because Lou had said to me, "Whatever you do, do not tell them you quit," those words never really came out of my mouth. I think they had understood from different places that I actually made calls to at least one other network trying to find out if there might be interest in me if I wasn't working for ESPN anymore.

I will say this: the couple of words I had on the phone with Mark that day—I knew he had never heard anyone talk to him like that. It's amazing the things you say when your job at that moment has no value to you. So it was a pretty tension-filled couple of days. You don't know what it's like to answer the phone and hear, "Hello, this is Bill Cosby." And I go, "Is this *Bill Cosby* Bill Cosby?" He didn't mention race, he just said, "I know the way things can be when these situations come up, and I just wanted to call and offer my support." And I was like, "Wow." All it indicated to me was how big this thing had gotten.

RUSH LIMBAUGH:

Then Wednesday, during my show, I get an e-mail from Shapiro saying, "We're losing Tommy"—meaning Tommy Jackson. "He's saying it's either you or him. Will you call him?" So I said, "Sure." So after my show ended at three o'clock I called Jackson, but I got voice mail. I then had to fly to Philadelphia for a speech, and Shapiro calls me and says, "Tommy is out there saying young black kids are coming up to him saying, 'Does this mean I can't play quarterback in the NFL anymore?'" Al Sharpton and Jesse Jackson also got in gear and said I should be fired, that there was no place for this kind of thing inside the

National Football League, and I wouldn't be surprised if someone had gotten hold of Tom Jackson and said, "Tom, you sat there and didn't do anything? Didn't say anything? A buh buh buh buh..." Pressuring him because of his race. So who knows? I could see where it was going. Tom Jackson at that time had been there sixteen or seventeen years. This was my fifth week.

Shapiro called me and I talked to him Wednesday night from my hotel room in Philadelphia. That's when I'd also made the decision that I was going to get professional help for my addiction to pain pills; it all happened in the same week. And with those two decisions, I was destined not to be on that ESPN show. Shapiro was probably going to ask me to quit if I didn't mention it first, and I made the decision then to just resign because the last thing I wanted to be was a distraction.

MARK SHAPIRO:

It was pretty clean. He got on the phone with me and said, "Do you want me to walk away?" and I immediately told Bob [Iger] and George. They said, "Take it." So I called him back and said, "Yes," and within twenty-four hours he was out the door.

GEORGE BODENHEIMER:

I okayed the hiring of Rush Limbaugh and I was involved in the decision to end the association. I spoke with Rush after his comments, and he said, "Welcome to my world. You guys have been great. You gave me an opportunity. I love ESPN. Let's agree to part friends. But you don't need this." So I remember him being extremely gracious about the whole situation, and I've seen him subsequently and it's been the same.

I was in Bristol the following weekend to talk to our people. The thing that bothered me the most with all of that was not the criticism the company took or the various media folks who give their opinions. That comes with the territory. What bothered me was that it hurt our employees, and to me, there's really nothing that's worth that.

RUSH LIMBAUGH:

After the whole thing blew up, it was Thursday and I was in my New York apartment and Chris Berman called and said, "Are you okay?" And I said, "Yeah." He said, "I'm sorry this happened. I just want to make sure you're okay." And then I tune in to watch the show on Sunday and they took turns dumping on me. Berman apologized for failing to be a good traffic cop: he said he should have realized what had happened at the moment, and then they all said I had violated a promise never to bring politics into it. It was clear they were saving their own asses. It was clear the pressure from way high up was dictating how this was going to be handled on ESPN. I should also tell you that the guy I was closest to throughout those five weeks was Michael Irvin. I had more fun conversations with him than with any of the other guys on the group. I remain close to him today.

Now, I don't want to mention any names because I don't want to cause any more stink, but the following March, I played in a golf tournament and there were two guys from ESPN—they're both still at ESPN—and they told me that after the Philadelphia stuff started on Tuesday they were under orders not to defend me, and if my name came up I was to be criticized and blamed for violating a promise not to bring politics into the show.

Jim Nance said to me after the McNabb situation, "Rush, you have to know they were gunning for you. They resented you being in their world and they were waiting for you to step in it to make a big deal out of it." And who knows? He may be right.

TOM JACKSON:
I got a call probably around midnight on either Wednesday or Thursday from Mark, and he said Rush had resigned his position from ESPN.

The statement I read on Sunday, I wrote late, late on Thursday night. During that entire week, I can't remember sleeping much at all. But at some point I got on my computer and wrote that statement. It was so volatile. There was still a bit of anger in me, so when I wrote it, I didn't pull any punches about what I thought was going on in terms of the race issues that were being addressed, and what had gone on behind the scenes in terms of Rush. I do think that in retrospect, it would not have gone over well with everyone. We spent much of that day kind of picking through this word for word, and it was adjusted by numerous people who got involved. What you saw on Sunday was a slightly diluted version of what I had written Thursday night. The one thing that I made them put in, which someone requested we take out, was that those of us on the show were in no way responsible for Rush being on our show. And what I was told during the meeting was "Everybody knows that, so there's no need to say that." My response was "If everybody knows, what difference does it make that we put it in?" And then everybody knows what I did on TV: I gave our statement and I think there was a tremendous sense of relief after that, that it was over.

Jackson's statement began with "It was not our decision to have Rush Limbaugh on this show," apparently speaking for his colleagues as well as himself in criticizing the hire. "Rush was brought here to talk football, and he broke that trust," Jackson charged. "The fact that Donovan McNabb's skin color was brought up at all was wrong—especially in the context of the brotherhood that we feel we have on this show." Reaction to

Limbaugh's remarks was not immediate, Jackson said, because their "depth and insensitive nature...weren't fully felt until it seemed too late to reply." That Limbaugh was known in advance "for the divisive nature of his rhetoric" should have disqualified him from ever appearing, Jackson implied, ending his statement with "Rush Limbaugh was not a fit for NFL Countdown."

JOHN SAUNDERS:

To ESPN's credit, they allowed Tom to come on and say his thoughts, but I think it would have also been helpful if they would have just picked up the phone and said, "John Saunders, Robin Roberts, Stuart Scott, what do you think about this story? What do you think about how we're reporting this story?" When Charles Barkley made his comment about hating white people and we made a huge deal of that, huge deal, even demonized him at the time, I called up somebody who was on the assignment desk and said, "Are you people aware that Charles's wife is white?" And they were like, "What?!" I said, "I guarantee you Charles, in making a statement like that, is only talking about how he feels in certain situations. He's not saying he hates white people as a whole; you need to do your homework and examine it." There have been several instances like that over the years that have bothered me.

ED DURSO, *Executive Vice President of Administration:*

I do think the Limbaugh episode was ultimately of some benefit to us. It raised our awareness and sensitivity to issues of race in sports and how we handled them. It made clear that we needed to have a deeper understanding and broader perspective. I think it showed up in our later coverage of issues like Imus and Michael Vick. I believe we did a better job of reporting and offering perspective from the African American community coming off the Limbaugh episode.

TOM JACKSON:

We received a letter—it was just kind of crazy—that there was going to be a session of sensitivity training for people who were on air so that we wouldn't have the kind of blunder that had occurred with Rush on TV. And it said to see your department head: they would have scheduling for them, and it would be a session that would be rather lengthy, five or six hours. My department head was Bob Rauscher, and Bob got in touch with me and I immediately told him—and I remember this verbatim—I said, "You do know I'm not going to do that." Bob said, "Why?" and I said, "I'm not going to sensitivity training because I haven't done anything to have to attend sensitivity training." Then I said, "I'll go if Mark goes."

We finished up at eight-thirty at night. And you know the only person who wasn't in attendance— Mark Shapiro.

MARK SHAPIRO:

I only have one thing that bothered me about the incident, and that was that I was misquoted. I would never excuse what Rush did, but with Rush we knew what we were getting. We knew this guy had very distinct and sharp opinions. We made a deal with him to come on and talk football, and when he went outside those boundaries, he had to go. Rush Limbaugh's going to draw some ratings, there's no question, but maybe we were guilty of thinking he could leave everything else at the door and just do sports. That was the risk we took. That's the whole point of taking risks. Some things were hits, some things not. What if Rush had stayed within the rules—would the ratings have gone up? They sure as hell seemed like they were going that way, and he was offering good perspective. Did he bring insight to the table, was he doing his homework each week, making phone calls to get information from the players and coaches? He was doing all that, and if he hadn't screwed up, he would still absolutely be on the air.

Limbaugh wasn't the only ESPN employee to offer potentially offensive commentary. Over on ESPN.com, writer Gregg Easterbrook found himself in deep water for something he wrote that had nothing to do with his specialty, professional football.

GREGG EASTERBROOK, *Columnist:*

I was writing about football for *Slate* in 2000 and they asked me to do it again in 2001, and I said okay. The day after, John Walsh, who I had never met, called me out of the blue and said, "This is exactly where we want ESPN.com to go. We've got to get smarter. We want to be involved in things that are witty and sort of off-the-wall and intelligent, so will you do it for us?" I said, "I can't, I just agreed to do it for *Slate* for another year, but at the end of the year, then we can talk." So I did it for *Slate* for another year and then got hired for ESPN.com.

I saw the movie *Kill Bill*. I intensely despised it. And what especially upset me is I'd played some very peripheral role in the company that had produced it, since it was a Miramax movie, which means it's a Disney movie. [Disney had purchased Miramax in 1993.] And I'm a moralist on this, and I really didn't argue about whether moralism is correct or not, but I hate movies that glorify violence. I despise the fact that people make them. And I'm not talking about serious movies that show the violent aspects of history, like the movie *The Pianist,* for example. If you've seen it, you know it is a horrifically violent movie, but it needs to be because it's about the Holocaust. So I wrote an extremely negative review of *Kill Bill* for the

New Republic website and I had a sentence in there saying, "Jeez, the guy who runs this company, Michael Eisner, is Jewish and — of all people, to approve a product that glorifies violence — shouldn't a Jewish person be exceptionally sensitive to the glorification of violence?" And that pretty much got me fired twenty-four hours later.

Now, I was puzzled because the *New York Times* ran a news-section article about my blog post as if it should have been a speech to the United Nations General Assembly. But it was the *New York Times* article that called this to everybody's attention.

Now, I will also say, I apologize for what I wrote. If you go back and look up exactly what I said, within the context, it's a defensible point, but I did a terrible job of writing it.

On October 20, 2003, Mark Shapiro and his deputy, Jim Cohen, launched yet another new show, but this one was from New York. They were convinced that sports fans — i.e., ESPN viewers — were also deeply interested in the news, politics, and pop culture of the day, and that shared belief served as the foundation for Cold Pizza, *ESPN's answer to the* Today *show and* Good Morning America. *The hope was that the series would satisfy all of a typical viewer's informational needs and serve as a one-stop-shopping experience for two hours live each day (with the live two hours then repeated on tape, for a four-hour total); theoretically, there'd be no need for viewers to go wandering off among nonsports channels in search of nonsports information. That was, anyway, the theory.*

Cohosts over the show's four-year run included Dana Jacobson, Jay Crawford, Jeremy Schaap, Linda Cohn, Tom Rinaldi, Ahmad Rashad, and others, with Skip Bayless and Woody Paige handling a segment called 1st and Ten, Victoria's Secret models reading weather reports, and such notable guest contributors as Peter Bonventre, a sports buff who was also an editor at Entertainment Weekly. *Celebrities as diverse as Senator John McCain and bling-bedecked Dennis Rodman stopped by to be interviewed.*

ESPN, along with at least several high-paid consultants, tried a slew of adjustments in an attempt to save Cold Pizza, *but the high costs stemming from the New York location and tepid response from viewers would eventually kill it.*

While ESPN was busily trying to invent new forms of sports journalism, it had already been hard at work trying to reinvent a staple of sports coverage. The Great American Sideline Reporter—job and species—had been hanging around football fields since 1974, at least according to Jim Lampley, who claims to have been the first in history, working the outer limits during college football games televised by ABC Sports. Lampley was "discovered" during a talent search by ABC, whose executives thought handsome or pretty young-looking personalities would help lure larger numbers of youthful viewers to ABC's coverage.

Then the traditionally male sideline-reporter role morphed through the years into a traditionally female role, which then created its own set of problems, including people being accused of getting jobs just because of their looks and, perhaps inevitably, extracurricular activities. Whether it was weightless palaver about baking cookies for athletes, or having affairs with coaches and dating players, there doesn't seem to have been a season in recent memory during which people weren't talking. If a female reporter got an interview with a key player or coach, rumor would be that she was likely sleeping with the subject.

But no sideline reporter had ever encountered what ESPN's Suzy Kolber did on December 20, 2003, when she did what was supposed to be a quick interview with New York Jets legend Joe Namath.

JAY ROTHMAN, *Senior Coordinating Producer:*

This is the God's honest fucking truth, I promise you: Namath was my idol growing up. I had white Riddells. The whole deal. So we were doing this Jets game, and they were celebrating their forty-fifth year, and they asked us if we wanted anybody on the sidelines. So I looked at the list, saw Namath's name, and told them I would love Namath right before halftime. I'm thinking this could be a really fun thing. So now the game's going on and it's freezing. I mean, it's so fucking December nighttime cold at the Meadowlands that the wind is whipping and I could tell from a report that Suzy did earlier in the game that her jaws were, like, locked shut. It was so cold it was hard to talk. So we get a phone call from the Jets in mid-first quarter that Namath's on his way down, and I'm saying, "No, no, no. It's too early. We haven't even developed the game." I have a little speaker that Suzy could use to communicate with me during the game and she's like, "Hey, Namath is down here. Do you want him?" And I said, "No, I don't want him. Not now. I told them right before halftime." Now I'm getting communication from her that Namath's hovering. "He's kind of hovering all over me. Can we just do it and be done with it?" So I decide "What the fuck, let's just do this interview."

Now I have Mike Patrick throw it down to Suzy. Now, I swear to you. I don't know if you've had one of these surreal moments, you know, in your life like it's a bad dream that you have no control over. I swear to God, that's what it felt like. She starts interviewing him and he starts talking and I'm sitting to the right of my director, my partner in crime for many, many years, Chip Dean, and I'm leaning in watching, and I said, "Did he have a fucking stroke? Or is he cold?" And then Suzy throws back. At the same time, Mike Patrick says on his callback to me, "Jay, do I throw back?" You know, in other words to follow up the second question. And I said, "Fuck it, yeah. Go back for one more." So he throws back and then as Mike throws back, and she starts asking the question, Joe

Theismann hits his talkback button and says to me, "He's fucking drunk!" But it was too late.

SUZY KOLBER:

The only thing that I felt was odd at the start was that we never had a chance to really chat before we went on air because he kept walking away. At one point, I even said to the PR guys, "Is everything okay?" and they said, "Yeah." When Jay said he was ready for him, I grabbed him and was holding his arm because he wouldn't stand still. I asked the first question, and his speech was very slow and deliberate. I was wondering if it was because it was really cold. Something didn't seem right, but nobody in the truck was saying anything: nobody said, "Stop, there's something's wrong with Joe," and Jay said to keep going. The second question was about the Jets struggling, and Namath just looked at me and said, "I want to kiss you. I couldn't care less about the team struggling."

At the time, I thought, "He's embarrassing himself." People in the crowd were cheering for him; Jay is this huge fan of his, and I'm thinking, "How do I get him out of this?" I just handled it sort of like I was at a bar and getting hit on by somebody I really didn't want to get hit on by; it's late, and I'm trying to excuse myself. All I remember saying was, "Thanks for the compliment," before throwing it back. As soon as we were off, I just rolled my eyes and thought it was over forever.

JAY ROTHMAN:

As soon as he started with the whole "Can I kiss you?" thing I just went, "Ohh, fuck." It was just one of those huge disasters. I just died. I got a deathly feeling inside. It was just brutal. And unfortunately, in life, you can't get that moment back. Everybody felt sorry for Suzy—oh, my God, he put her on the spot. Suzy could give a shit, really; she just rolled with it.

By the way, at halftime, when Namath was introduced, he fell on his face at midfield. That's how stinking drunk he was. Of course, we were never going to show that.

SUZY KOLBER:

After the game, we were all sitting on the bus in the stadium parking lot, and it's almost two in the morning, and Chip always has the games on DVD, so when he got on the bus, everybody started chanting, "Put on Joe." They fired up the DVD in the bus, and I got to see it for the first time, and we were rolling out of our seats. They played it a couple times because we were laughing so hard, and I remember thinking, "I'd do it all again" because everybody had such a great laugh that night.

At about five in the morning, there was a knock on my hotel door and it was Jay. He said, "You're not going to believe this, but it's everywhere," and I said,

"Oh, shit." When we got to the game that night, everyone was talking about it. Even the officials came up to me. Shannon Sharpe was still playing, and we had some guys miked, and we heard him saying to Rod Smith, "Did you see Joe and Suzy last night?" Kenny Mayne left me a message saying it was the funniest thing he'd ever seen, but the best was my mom. Her message was "It's good to see Joe still has good taste in women."

Every single news outlet in the country wanted to talk to me and I refused. There were lots of press requests, but I said I wasn't going to talk to anyone.

JAY ROTHMAN:
That Sunday, the phones are ringing off the hook in our truck. *Sports Illustrated,* the *New York Times,* AP, the whole thing. And I'm thinking, "Son of a bitch." They wanted to know what happened, they wanted interviews with Suzy, they want the whole nine yards. So I said to Jed [Drake], "You've got to do me a favor. I've got to produce this fucking game. You need to field all calls here," which he did. So now I do the officials meeting before the game and then my little tradition is I lap the field and walk inside the stadium just to feel the buzz before I have to go into my little tin can and produce the hell out of the game. So I'm lapping the field, and, sure as shit, who do I

stumble upon? My high school classmate [White House press secretary] Ari Fleischer. He gives me a big hug, and I said, "Come with me." I shared with him the disaster that transpired the night before, which he was well aware of, and I walk him in the truck and introduce him to Jed. I said, "Jed, I want you to meet somebody that can help you out with these phone calls you've been getting all day. Jed, meet Ari Fleischer."

SUZY KOLBER:

Then it became: Oh, God, Joe wants to apologize. So he called me and the first five seconds were on the record—he said he was sorry and I said I accepted. Then we talked for forty-five minutes. He said it was the most humiliating moment of his life and that he was sorry for my family. I told him what my mother said, and he really appreciated that. I told him I was fine, and that there would be a silver lining. He was so mortified that day, and I wanted him to know that I thought something good would come out of this. And it did. He didn't drink after that. He got his daughters back. It changed his whole life.

JAY ROTHMAN:

What I felt bad about and still feel bad about to this day is I know Suzy very well. She works her ass off. She's credible as could be, but at every fucking airport that she travels into it's "Can I kiss you?" There's even a website now.

ESPN's first attempt at reality television, Beg, Borrow, and Deal, had lasted only two seasons before being canceled in 2003, but ESPN gamely bounced back on February 22, 2004, with a second reality attempt—Dream Job, a contest designed to find a new anchor for the very iconic SportsCenter. This time, Stuart Scott was the host doling out the fabulous prizes, the most fabulous being a one-year contract with the network—and a new car! The winner then had to play a trivia quiz to determine his or her salary, all under the supervision of four celebrity judges: Tony Kornheiser, Kit Hoover, NFL linebacker Lavar Arrington, and ESPN vice president of talent Al Jaffe. It may sound silly, but the show garnered a walloping 1.3 rating—unheard of at ESPN for a nonsporting event.

MARK SHAPIRO:
As soon as I heard the pitch for *Dream Job* from Carol Silver, a junior exec, I instantly thought we should create a series in which Al Jaffe's daily talent-evaluation process was on full display. If we could discover a new, young, raw news anchor that could be chosen by the fans and get a full-time gig on ESPNews, I was convinced it would be a hit and at the same time give our viewers an appreciation for the *SportsCenter*

machine. Convincing the *SportsCenter* newsroom that we weren't devaluing their everyday existence was another story altogether. It was a tough sell.

AL JAFFE:

Dream Job gave me a real appreciation for what talent does, because all of a sudden I was on camera. I learned about what talent has to go through, including some of the things that we in management take for granted. I think the show also taught America just how hard it is to be a sports anchor. I don't think people realized before that a lot of highlights are just a shot sheet; there's no real script. Some of our guys are so good, it just comes out as a seamless narrative, like they've written every word and changed it ten times, when in reality, it's all just off-the-cuff. But a lot of those young contestants on the show were really talented.

STUART SCOTT:

I sucked when I was their age. There's no way I could have done as well as a lot of them did. I wouldn't have made it. Initially, we had some backlash from anchors in the building who had spent a lot of time paying their dues and thought it was wrong that someone could just come along, win the contest, and sit in an anchor chair. But as the show went on, that criticism died down. Besides, there's lots of different ways to pay dues.

MARK SHAPIRO:

When the ratings came out, the series was delivering the same numbers as *SportsCenter* itself! Jaffe became a quasi cult figure, and the newsroom folks stopped taking themselves so seriously and got behind the series. *Dream Job* was a big hit and Jaffe ended up making me think about Howie Schwab.

HOWIE SCHWAB:

Mark Shapiro called me into his office one day and said, "We're starting a new show, a trivia show." I said, "Great, I worked on *2 Minute Drill,* can I work on it?" And he said, "No, it's called *Stump the Schwab,* and you're going to be *on* it." I said, "Are you fucking serious?"

My total record was 64–16. Only twice was I really pissed off when I lost. Once, the question was "Maori tribesmen destroyed what trophy?" I guessed World Cup, and it was America's Cup. The second time was this kid who really pissed me off. He was just a bad, nasty kid. As soon as the show started, he was mouthing off—"I'm gonna beat him"—and I just stared at him. Then, at the end, he beat me on stupidity. I don't think he psyched me out; I just missed a couple questions. I remember saying to myself, "I can't believe I'm going to lose to this fucking asshole!"

Chuck Pagano had been a bearded, long-haired, "freakin' radical hippie" and disc jockey in the early seventies and, for three months, a roadie for Steely Dan, the memory of which became, he recalls, "just one big blur." Then he got serious.

Progressing through a long series of job titles, Pagano was eventually named ESPN's executive vice president of technology, engineering, and operations—a kind of mad scientist in residence. All the work he'd done over the years could have been considered a prologue to the creation of ESPN's Digital Center, one of the most sophisticated TV production facilities in the world. It opened for business on June 7, 2004, when it broadcast the first high-definition SportsCenter.

The digital center would occupy 120,000 square feet on the Bristol campus and house three high-definition television studios of 9,000, 5,000, and 3,000 square feet. Its existence would mean that ESPN viewers could see 3,500 hours of original HD studio programming per year, as well as HD telecasts from Major League Baseball, the NHL, the NFL, and the NBA. And thirteen hours of HD SportsCenters each day, besides.

Pagano, who got a bachelor of science degree in electrical engineering from the University of Hartford in 1984, quickly became known around ESPN not only for his talent but for his ability to get along with virtually everybody. Giant but nimble, he covers a lot of ground each day walking briskly through the campus, so affable and hard to provoke that he became known as the unofficial "mayor of ESPN." He did not shrink from that title; he welcomed it.

CHUCK PAGANO:

Mark Shapiro had a very charismatic style to his leadership. I'm sure there were other parts in the organization that didn't get along with him, but I sort of enjoyed his clarity. The key was gaining his respect. If you did that, he would basically let you do your job and do it well.

I remember in my very first meeting with him, he goes, "I just want you to know one thing. I yell at people, so get used to it." I said, "Okay, but in the openness of this conversation, I should warn you about one thing about me, Mark." And he goes, "What's that?" I said, "If you yell at me, I will respond accordingly and aggressively; it's as simple as that. I don't accept anybody yelling at me. So be forewarned, I don't accept that behavior. You yell at me, you better run for the door." He came back to me later and goes, "Thank you. I was waiting for someone to stand up to me."

When we launched *SportsCenter* from the new digital center, you couldn't tell at home, but the control room that handled *SportsCenter* basically imploded that night. It was as close to a thermonuclear disruption as anything I'd experienced in my life. We were trying to do too much and we just overloaded every system. And luckily—I'm being sarcastic here—Shapiro was there with a significant number of his guests for the launch, so that made it even more intriguing. He was a little agitated, but to his credit, he got my message, which was "Get the fuck out of the control room, we gotta fix this." And he did. He left right away and that was really appreciated. I really just wanted him to let us do our job; we could worry about the shrapnel later.

BILL LAMB:

Yup, forty-five minutes into the first *SportsCenter* that we did in high-def, all of the servers failed. They had all of the content, and all of the highlights, on them, and one by one, they went down—just a catastrophic cascade of failure. Once the director noticed, he started running videotaped versions of the pieces that had been made, so there was an absolutely instantaneous, seamless transition; the audience saw no evidence whatsoever of any problems.

But there were probably forty people outside the control room, including the press, and they were all staring at what was going on, and you had the director's PL, which is the director's private line, intercommed and amplified on a PA system in the hallway, so it was all incredibly evident. When I heard the director say, "Okay, we're going to videotape," I thought my life was over right there. That was the nice-to-know-you-Bill moment. When they came out, I thought, "Well, I'm dead." Instead, they said, "Eh! Figure it out later." I've been here half my adult life, and it was reinforcement and incredible testimony to the character that this place is all about, even under tough circumstances. We went right downstairs and had champagne to celebrate the first show we had done out of that control room. There were no grudges, and no anger. It was just like, "Okay—we lost this game; we'll win the next one." Phenomenal!

The digital center proved to be our crowning moment. That was the point at which ESPN leapfrogged over all our competition by about five years. And once we got on that track and got good at doing that, we've been in the lead position ever since.

She may have a musical and alliterative name, but there's very little about Maura Mandt that friends or colleagues would call frivolous. Executive producer of ESPN's ESPY Awards since 2002, Mandt quickly became known as one of the toughest and most influential women, and one of the most tireless workers of either gender, ever to work at the sports network. Coworkers would have been justified comparing her to hard-driving Diana Christensen, the fire-breathing programmer played by Faye Dunaway in Paddy Chayefsky's Network.

Many were in awe of Mandt's ability to bend executives to her will when need be—with John Walsh seeming especially susceptible. Mandt clearly respected Walsh but also managed to get her way nearly every time: apart from Walsh's best friend, Steve Anderson, and comrade-in-arms John Skipper, there may not have been anyone else with that success rate.

When Mandt was promoted to executive producer of the show, she set about giving the production new energy and increased star power. Rubbing elbows with big-time Hollywood luminaries—increasingly attracted to the ESPYs as its reputation improved—Mandt incurred jealousy from fellow ESPN producers who coveted her big budgets and the glamorous company she kept. But headquartered in New York, focused on Los Angeles, and linked to sports celebrities around the globe, Mandt had no time for games. At least, not with her coworkers.

MAURA MANDT:

In 2002, the first year I was executive producer of the show, there were some changes that had happened with the voting. Mark Shapiro wanted only fans to decide on all the winners. This was the year that Tom Brady had won his first Super Bowl, and a couple days before the show it looked like no one would be able to catch Brady in the category of Best Breakthrough [Athlete], but the Patriots were probably not going to have enough votes for Best Team. Now, George had told Mark that we needed to get [Patriots owner] Robert Kraft on stage somehow, but since the Patriots weren't likely to win, I didn't really know how we were going to do that. Then when we were at a rundown meeting, Mark says, "When Tom Brady wins, Robert Kraft is going to go up and accept the award." And my reaction immediately was, that is a horrible idea. It wasn't like Brady wasn't going to be there; he was already confirmed. So I suggested that we have Kraft present the award, but Mark just wouldn't listen to me at all. I tried for two days to convince him to have Kraft present rather than accept an award Brady had won, and he just kept saying emphatically, "Robert Kraft will accept this award, Maura; make it happen!" The day before the show, I was panicking and was literally in tears thinking, "It's going to kill me if this is the way it's going to be with Mark."

Since this was my first year, Mark had asked Fred Gaudelli to be there, I guess to make sure that I didn't mess up. So Freddie comes in and I'm walking him through the show and he says, "Why is Kraft accepting for Tom Brady?" I told him the story and asked him if he would try to change Shapiro's mind. Freddie didn't think it would make a difference since I had already tried, but in the last meeting before the show, Freddie tells Mark, "I think it's really weird to have Kraft accept. Why don't you have him present the award to Brady?" and Mark looks at Freddie and without much pause says, "I think that's a great idea."

After the meeting Freddie just turned to me and said, "I can't explain why that just happened," and I said, "I can: I don't have a set of balls; you do."

PEYTON MANNING:

A couple years back, my brother Eli went to the ESPYs because he was up for a college award. He brought some friends with him, and one of them was just a huge, huge movie buff. And we're sitting there talking to Vince Vaughn about the movie *Rudy,* and about Vince's character, who changed a play and threw a halfback pass so they could score a touchdown and kick off, all so Rudy could get to play in that game on defense. It wasn't a prominent role in the movie, but this friend of Eli's, the movie buff, was asking Vince Vaughn if he actually threw that pass or did he have to call in a stunt double to do it. And Vince tells us that they shot the scene at a Notre Dame game—I think it was at halftime—and the director said to him, "Look, we've got two shots at this, that's it, we've got to get it." And Vince Vaughn was like, "I can do it, I can do it, I can do it." So he goes out there in the huddle and all of a sudden the director says, "Vaughn can't do it, I can't risk it, get in the double." Vince said he had to come out and make like the walk of shame out of the huddle so the double could come in and the pass wouldn't fail. As Vince was telling that story, we were all laughing, and to see the smile on his friend's face made me feel really good. That's what the ESPYs are all about.

DWYANE WADE, *Professional Basketball Player:*

I'm one of the guys who watches the WNBA. I'd been a big fan of Diana Taurasi, even at UConn. So I'm at the ESPYs and see her in the back, and I'm excited, you know? I've been watching her since she was in college. I waited to go up to her, and then she comes up to me and says, "I'm a big fan of yours." And I was like, "Wow!" In my rookie year, when I went to the ESPYs, Ray Lewis came up to me before I could come up to him and told me, "I love the way you play, I love the way you carry yourself." That really surprised me. I was just like, "Man, this is Ray Lewis!" There are a lot of moments like that at the ESPYs.

In 2004, for the first time, ESPN's SportsCenter *went on the road—all the way to Kuwait, where two thousand members of the First Armored Division were waiting to see them. Rigging a spare hangar with bleachers for seven hundred service members, ESPN personalities and crew televised two entire shows before a live audience—the 1:00 a.m. and 2:00 a.m. editions of* SportsCenter—*from September 11 through September 17, with special segments taped in Kuwait for other editions. When not doing live shows or taping features, the ESPN crowd hung out with the troops, playing football and other games and seeing how long it took for an ice-cream cone to melt in the 120-degree heat of the desert. Answer: not long.*

STEVE LEVY:

The best thing I've ever done at ESPN — and no matter how long I stay here, nothing will ever be able to top the experience — was when we went to Kuwait. *SportsCenter* was taken on the road to Camp Arifjan in Kuwait, and we brought a crew with us — thirty people, I would say. Camp Arifjan was the place where all the troops went before and after they headed into real combat. They had to stop there for orientation, and then they stopped again on their way home to get oriented back into the real world. The on-air guys were myself, Kenny Mayne, Stuart Scott, Sean Salisbury, and Lisa Salters. It was our chance to bond with the troops — just the highlight of my career and one of the top five highlights of my life, that's all. We did the show live from the camp, on the U.S. military base. This was going to be our thing, our helping of the troops, our Bob Hope moment. As we tend to be politically correct, we were saying, "We're not choosing sides in everything that's going on. We are merely going over to support and give our uniformed personnel a taste of home. Bring them a taste of apple pie while they're working in the conditions they're working in." I remember landing in the airport in Kuwait and we had armed bodyguards and armed escorts with us all the time, and there were armed people standing outside our hotel on the Persian Gulf. We traveled in coach buses during the night because of the time difference, based on when our show was airing in the East. It was still 1:00 a.m. there, but it was early morning in Kuwait, and we had to have the curtains drawn; they did not want people seeing who was on the bus. From time to time, they would stop and get out and check for explosives hidden in the road. This was the real deal. This was pretty scary stuff.

The first day we got to the base, it was the middle of the night there, and the troops were lined up waiting for us. It looked like two hundred soldiers in uniform. We thought they were there for us, but they were just waiting to be let inside because we had the big screens and the monitors on the wall, and they were able to watch *Monday Night Football*. And that was something that I would never forget. We set up temporary stands like you would at a football game or a basketball game so they could watch the show. They had nonalcoholic beer and popcorn and were cheering on their favorite team, and it made everybody working at ESPN feel really good that we were able to give them a chance to be regular, as if they were back home watching *Monday Night Football* with their buddies.

NORBY WILLIAMSON:
This was 2004, in Kuwait, right on the border of Iraq. They had scares and missiles; it wasn't like

hanging out with whatever, but I felt good enough that we weren't going to put people in danger.

Every *SportsCenter* that we did for a week had an audience. It was fantastic. You thought you were doing something good going over there. When you were over there, you *knew* you were doing something good. I mean it was off the charts. We probably played to four hundred a show, maybe more. There was no truck we could roll in there, so we had to basically ship boxes of control-room pieces from Europe and then assemble them there. It was like the first time we'd really done that; we didn't know if it was going to work. The satellite was the real test: could we really get the signal out of there and back here and ultimately into people's homes? We had trouble because we're in the Middle East and the pitch was too low: we had to get the dish on top of the barracks to get a better shot at the satellite. Then a dust storm came in. We eventually got up, got it, and we were on TV. It was amazing.

STUART SCOTT:

Before the first show, they introduced us, and the applause we got from the troops was thunderous. I mean, we get cheered places sometimes, but I had never experienced anything like this. And I remember thinking, "This should be reversed. It should be us cheering for them." I've never experienced anything else like it in my professional career.

STEVE LEVY:

It was 120 degrees, sandy and dusty, and we had the hot television lights besides, but the executives made us wear suits and ties. I tend to perspire, and after the first day I was just drenched. And so the next day I come back, and the troops—the servicemen and servicewomen—had built a huge air-conditioning vent positioned right between my legs, under the desk so nobody could see it, blowing very cold air right to that critical area. Of course, in the military, everything is "Operation Something," so they called this "Operation Cool Nuts."

NORBY WILLIAMSON:

It was the most humbling thing ever. It was like we were giving the soldiers a ticket home. It's still one of the top five experiences of my life.

Less than a decade after the Walt Disney Company bought Capital Cities/ABC (for only $19 billion) and became ESPN's owner, it looked as though the sports network might be getting new corporate parents yet again. Comcast, the nation's biggest cable operator, made a surprise $54 million bid for Disney in 2004. Some analysts said the most attractive part of the deal for Comcast was that it included the acquisition of ESPN, which would make Comcast both buyer and seller when it came to sports programming. It would *also, presumably, bring an end to Comcast's complaints about the high cost of ESPN's prodigious output.*

Michael Eisner was under fire from Roy Disney and others for, among other things, losing distribution rights to products from the highly praised and highly valued Pixar company, creators of Toy Story. *Stanley Gold, a Disney board member, said he hoped the board would handle the deal with the best interests of Disney share-holders — "and not the best interest of Michael Eis-ner" — in mind. If the Disney board voted to accept the proposition, the combined enterprise would become the world's biggest media company, unseating Time War-ner. But the board rejected Comcast's offer, and the deal fell through.*

STEVE BURKE:

The majority of the value when we bid for Disney was ESPN. Our model actually put no value on the ABC network; ESPN, we felt, was almost priceless. We were told by members of the Disney board that they would look positively if we made an offer for the company. When we bid, their board quickly rallied around Michael and we knew we were dead.

BRIAN ROBERTS, *Comcast CEO:*

When we looked at Disney, we saw a treasure trove of assets — Disney Channel, Disney animation, Dis-ney movies, the ABC and Disney brands — and, of course, ESPN. As a cable company, we were well aware of what ESPN was doing and what it could be worth. We felt there was a real underappreciation of all the Disney assets at that moment in time, particularly ESPN.

BOB LEY:

This is a very proud place, and in 2004, we had *ESPN25*. It was hardly restrained. We closed the highway, there were flyovers at night, helicopter shots, spotlights, we even had turn-back-the-clock *SportsCenter*. I mean, we turned it loose. But for me, the best part of the celebration was when I took a bottle of Cristal and sat with Tom Reilly, the original producer—who's still here—George [Bodenheimer], and Boomer. There we were, drinking $200 champagne out of Styrofoam cups till two thirty in the morning, telling stories.

It might have been just another minor basketball skirmish if not for a nasty fan, a sprint into the stands, and some controversial commentary. As huge a jolt as it was to the NBA, the tremor also shook the Richter scale at ESPN, where in the days and nights after the melee, fractious reaction threatened the concept of editorial independence and exacerbated racial tensions.

Less than forty-six seconds remained on the clock at the regular-season matchup between the Pistons and the Pacers in Detroit's Palace of Auburn Hills on Friday, November 19, 2004. Detroit's Ben Wallace took the ball in the low post, spun around, and, as he went for the basket, was fouled by Indiana's Ron Artest. Wallace immediately came back at Artest and gave him a shove that sent Artest pedaling backward all the way to the three-point line.

Shoving and shouting ensued, and soon the fray became more of a brawl, except that Artest simply stretched out his 6 feet and 7 inches on the scorers' table, and lay on his back with his hands clasped behind his head, as if resting in a hammock. Apart from the fact that it was hard to get Ben Wallace back to his bench, that might have been that.

But then, from out of the stands, a reckless spectator threw a cup of Diet Coke at Artest and hit him upside the head. Bad idea, bad behavior, and from that point on, bad night at the Palace. The fight resumed, with one unusual embellishment: Artest, followed by fellow Pacers Stephen Jackson and Jermaine O'Neill, leaped into the stands, heading for the cup-hurling fan. Eventually, anyone within fist-swinging distance became embroiled.

From their vantage point back at the Bristol studio, ESPN commentators John Saunders, Stephen A. Smith, Tim Legler, and Greg Anthony watched in stark dismay, if not disgust. They were to varying degrees indignant and outraged. But at whom?

GREG ANTHONY, *Basketball Analyst:*

The brawl at the Palace really left an indelible mark on my mind. We were in studio the night that it occurred, and the fallout from that, moving forward, sucked, and always will. That was probably one of the most powerful moments, I'd say, for me working in television. There was shock in how it all transpired and how it escalated. It wasn't something that anybody was prepared to see happen. In a lot of ways, it was like walking down the street and you see somebody getting mugged or someone pulling a gun on you. You may think in your mind you know how you'll handle that stuff, but you don't really know until that moment of truth. This was not a skit, with everything laid out in advance. It was going on right then. You don't have a lot of time to collect your thoughts. You gotta basically talk about what you just saw, and what you felt.

STEPHEN A. SMITH, *Columnist:*

When Ron ran up in the stands, my initial reaction on the air was somebody must have thrown something at him. In a moment like that, let me tell you, your emotions take over, and I think that was the case with all of us—John Saunders, Greg Anthony, and myself. When we went to commercial, I got a call from Joe Dumars, who told me, "You can't say that. There is never an excuse for a player to do that." Then Rob Parker, the great columnist for the *Detroit News,* called me and was screaming the same thing at me. When we came back on air, I said that I was glad Joe had called, because he put the whole thing in perspective. Nobody affiliated with the NBA should ever do what Ron had just done. The next morning, Mark Shapiro woke me up with a phone call and he was really upset by what the others had said, and the excuses they made for Ron. I told Mark, "We all messed up. We all made mistakes last night."

JOHN SAUNDERS:

I'm gonna first say that while it's one of the most controversial things that happened in my career, I still stand by everything I said. I'm not sure that I had the right to take that forum, which belongs basically to ESPN, and use it on my own, but I still stand by what I said.

What happened was the fight starts at the Palace, and I'm jumping up and all of us—Greg Anthony, Tim Legler, and Stephen A. Smith, we're all, "Oh, my God, do you believe this?!" And all of a sudden I'm looking at Ron Artest lying down on the table and I say, "Oh, Ron Artest, for once, is taking the high road." And then I see the drink come flying over. Now I'm losing my mind. And I'm losing my mind for a couple of reasons. One, because as an African American—African Canadian—I truly believe that had a white player been lying on the bench there, I don't believe that cup would have been thrown. Number two, as Ron Artest then goes into the stands, I could empathize because as a black hockey player, I took a lot of crap playing hockey from players on the ice and people in the stands. And on at least one occasion, I went into the stands. I was playing in a game and the guy hit me with a stick and cut me over the top of my eye, and I was going into the locker room to get stitched up, and as I was going in, somebody from the stands used the *N* word and I went into the stands after him. I hit him and got thrown out of the game.

So I could empathize. Now, as it gets more and more out of control, I'm getting more and more worked up. What I'm seeing, what David Stern at home is seeing, is his product deteriorating. Now the scene goes to the floor, fans on the floor, okay, so now we've crossed both areas. Not only have the players gone into the stands, the fans have come onto the floor, they have come into the player's workplace, as far as I'm concerned. Now, to me, if you're dumb enough to come onto the floor, with these 6-feet-8, 6-feet-11, 270-pound guys, then you deserve what you get. That's what I'm thinking. But again, emotions are building. Now the last thing we see as the players are leaving are fans pouring beer and soda and popcorn onto the Indiana players as they're leaving. And right then, they go to me, "You're on!" and I hear, "Let's go back to John Saunders." And my blood is boiling. The first thing that comes out of my mouth is "The Detroit Pistons fans are a bunch of punks and sissies." Then I said, "Ron Artest had every right to go into the stands. If he were walking in Times

Square right now, outside of our building right here, and someone were to throw a drink at him, any one of us I think would all respond in the same way, we would go after the person." I was really caught up. The other guys on the panel—I'm not sure shared my views 100 percent, but they adopted them, and they kind of emotionally got caught up in it as well. Our producer, Mike McQuade, was in my ear, but he wasn't leading me in any way, and he wasn't dissuading me from giving my opinion. He was trying to say, "Be strong, make sure you cover this as you see it." I think if you talk to Mike today, he would say that in hindsight, he would have probably had us give both sides, as opposed to just reacting to our opinions about it, and say, "Yes, a player should never go into the stands." If I added that one sentence, there would have been no controversy over it.

MIKE McQUADE:

I was producing that night. Brr. Chaos really. Not only from the league's standpoint, but from our standpoint. The brawl happens, and the next thing you know, we're on the air. And as soon as we started, John was very, very offended by what the fans had done. I was as culpable as everyone else. I got caught up too.

Was it chaotic? Sure. But that's what the producer's there for. The producer is supposed to cut through the chaos and be able to be the voice of reason and get guys back on track. But I didn't do that. I allowed them to continue down one path. It's okay to have an opinion, but if you're not going to balance that opinion—especially on a sensitive topic like this one—it doesn't become just an opinion anymore, it becomes "the network stance."

I had a two-hour ride home after doing the show in New York, and it was tough. That's when it hit me: we did not do ourselves proud today.

JOHN SAUNDERS:

So the next day is Saturday, and I'm in the studio at ABC, doing college football. The phone rings, and it's Mark Shapiro. I'm thinking, "Oh, he probably wants to congratulate me for what a nice job I did covering the fight last night." So I get on the phone and he goes, "John, what were you thinking?! You can't say that! You can't take on the fans! You can't support the players for going into the stands!" And we had a very spirited discussion about it. I said the same thing: "Mark, if someone were to come up and throw a cup on you, you trying to tell me you would just walk away? You know you would go after the person. Anybody would." And I said, "The other thing, Mark, is that you don't understand what it's like to be an athlete in the arena and have your adrenaline peaked to a certain level just to play the game, and now it's peaked even higher by what's going on, because a fight breaks out, and now somebody throws something at you, and you're not reacting rationally but it's understandable why you're not reacting rationally. The other thing you don't understand is what it's like to be black and to be in that situation. You feel immediately disrespected. It's not just that somebody threw a cup of water on you. The immediate thought as it happened is, they threw it on me because I'm black." And so we had the conversation, and he totally disagreed with me. I don't know this for a fact, but I have heard through a third party that David Stern had asked for me to be fired. Again, I don't know that for a fact.

DAVID STERN:

I have never asked that someone at ESPN be removed or suspended for any opinion expressed about the NBA. It is complete fabrication if anyone suggests otherwise.

JOHN SAUNDERS:

They did have a meeting: Mark Shapiro, John Walsh, Steve Anderson, Norby Williamson, and, I believe, Vince Doria. They were all white faces in the room. I pointed that out: "You're trying to tell me I need to adjust and promise y'all I will never do this again, but there's not one of you in here who can understand where I was coming from." And sometimes that happens with content as well.

JIM GRAY:

The night Ron Artest went into the stands, I was courtside. Mark didn't like the way the studio folks had responded on the air. He thought it was harsh to call fans punks and he thought it was so wrong to basically be siding with the player. He called me up after the game and said, "You're the only one that made us proud last night; you were the only one that held the objectivity from a journalistic standpoint. You were the only one that was asking the players, participants, fans, and the police all the right questions, and it was a great moment for you." And he added, "I gotta get the rest of us on board." I'm not trying to be critical of the people I was on the air with, Mike Breen and Bill Walton. I think they handled it very well, but the studio wasn't on the course he wanted to chart. And you know, it turned out to be a whole big megillah because obviously David Stern didn't like it either. And David Stern didn't like the fact that in any way, shape, or form, whether the fans were responsible or not, they could be blamed. Going into the stands was a cardinal sin.

The next day, they had me do some reporting from L.A. and I eventually got the first interview with Artest some time later. But Artest got me on the phone that night and I reported it on *SportsCenter*. He said he was just acting in self-defense, it was just a reaction. Then the next day he told me Ben Wallace had called to apologize to him. Wallace denies that to this day.

JOHN SAUNDERS:

I was hosting *College GameDay* one time and Todd Boseman, the coach at Cal at the time, reached around and took a punch or a swing at a fan during a game, and the producer in my ear said, "This just came over the wire, we gotta do this story, Todd Boseman threw a punch." And I said, "Does it say in the wire story why he threw a punch?" And he said, "No." Then I asked, "Does it say in the wire story what the fan behind the bench said to Boseman?" and the producer said, "No, it doesn't," and I said, "Then I'm not going to do the story. Because I guarantee you that the fan used the *N* word. That's the only thing I can think of that would cause a black coach to turn around and take a swing at a fan." The producer was trying to be adamant: "You gotta do this." I said, "Unless you're going to come down here, pull me out of the chair, sit in the chair yourself, and do the story, those words are not coming out of my mouth." About an hour later, the wire came over again, and it turned out that was exactly the case. The fan had called him a nigger, and that's what had turned him, and so then I went with the story.

JASON WHITLOCK, *Writer:*

Race at ESPN is a complicated issue. I give ESPN credit for hiring a lot of minorities, but I do think that under Mark Shapiro there was a certain type of minority that they loved to promote — the more animated, stereotypical, hip-hop, or whatever. I went to a meeting on the campus at Bristol with Mark Shapiro and Vince Doria, and afterward, Vince Doria told me in private — and these aren't his exact words — that it was a great time to be like Stuart Scott and Stephen A. Smith, and the message seemed to be "You need to hip-hop-up your delivery on ESPN. It needs to be more rapperish" — or whatever. Those aren't his exact words, but I almost think he said "stereotypically black."

I do think they had an image that they thought worked for black people on their air, and they wanted everybody to be more like Stuart Scott and Stephen A. Smith, and that's just not the shtick I wanted to do on television. Again, I give them credit for giving blacks a lot of opportunities, but I think they bought into a certain style of being black as what they thought would work. At one time at ESPN.com you had Ralph Wiley as one of your top columnists, and Bill Simmons. Ralph Wiley is one of the best journalists among black journalists and a mentor-friend of mine. He had a lot of leverage and was very well-respected and he was difficult to deal with because you couldn't tell him anything. But when Ralph Wiley passed away, they said, "We're not going to have any more guys like this," and it's why they started promoting a guy like Scoop Jackson, who had been writing for

Slam magazine and had been kind of a hip-hop sportswriter, and they installed him as the replacement for Ralph Wiley. Some of us didn't think he took it all that seriously. His positions were easy to dismiss because you didn't have to take him all that seriously.

This is why I think ESPN struggles: it's almost like—I've got to be careful—but it's almost like you've got to be cartoonish to be black and have success at ESPN. Wilbon flies in the face of that because he's very professional and very talented and has to be respected, but for the most part, I felt like with everybody else, they were looking for a cartoon character. I think that's changed a little bit of late. Still, ESPN's not a place that's going to have a very serious discussion of the race issue led by any minorities for the most part. Maybe they think the issue of race is too dangerous; I don't know why. I felt that in order for me to reach my full potential as a columnist on the Internet, I needed to get away from there because they just didn't "get" me, or maybe they just didn't want any part of me.

STUART SCOTT:
I've heard and read things, you know, people who say, "Stuart tries to be black, but he's not really black, he's blah blah," or "He's as vanilla as so-and-so," or "He's trying to be too black." Can I really be concerned with what other people think about me who

don't know me? What I've done on television is try to work hard, try to be factually correct, try and write creatively and compellingly. I want to be myself, and anyone who says, "Oh well, he's a hip-hop anchor," well, that's what I grew up on. I grew up on mostly hip-hop and show tunes. I grew up on *West Side Story, The Wiz, Godspell,* but also Public Enemy.

I didn't pay a lot of attention to ESPN before I got here. I knew who Chris Berman was, I knew who Dan Patrick was, but I didn't watch them regularly. I looked up to John Saunders because he was an African American, actually an African Canadian. Tom Jackson is one of my favorite people ever. I recognize that I was one of the first African Americans of prominence here. One of them—not *the* first, but one of them. Mike Tirico was here. If I can open eyes and if someone feels like I can open doors, good, because it was done for me.

I think that, more than most people, as an African American you have to make sure that you can carry yourself wherever you go and keep it real. What I do on television is part of who I am. I'm not trying to be anyone else. I've always been of the mind-set "Be who you are; just do the job and work hard."

I've read two blogs in my life. I'm not a big Internet guy. I was talking to a colleague of mine who works here and he said, "Man, I get on the Internet, I see all this stuff written about me and I'm firing off e-mails..." And I'm like, "Why? Why are you firing off e-mails?" I'm not trying to be cool; I just think that if there are people who say I'm trying to do this, and I'm trying to do that, they can believe it if they want.

For twenty-one years, ESPN and the NHL had played nicely together. That is, they happily entered into one agreement after another. In time, though, relations grew less chummy, in part because the Walt Disney Company, both as a rights holder and as owner of the Anaheim Ducks hockey team, was extremely frustrated that the league wasn't doing enough to bolster lackluster TV ratings.

Hoping to get those numbers up, Michael Eisner had gone so far as to meet with NHL ownership and present them with ten ideas on how to lure more viewers. (Among them: have players on the bench remove their helmets, so fans on TV could more clearly see their faces, thus making it easier for stars to be developed.) The owners refused to implement any of Eisner's ideas, however, and that, coupled with the sizable losses ABC had incurred with its NHL deal, caused the Disney chief to throw up his hands in exasperation.

BILL CLEMENT:

We always tried ways, so many different conversations, meetings; we wanted to improve the sport and it was really difficult. We wanted to do so many things that the NHL just said nope, nope, nope,

nope, nope to. Access, interviews, cameras here, there. I prayed for linkage during the lockout. In other words, I wanted salaries to be linked to revenue. Because I knew if they were, then the players and the teams would have incentive to help us grow the sport. We felt like a network at ESPN trying to grow a sport without any cooperation from the different constituents within the sport.

ESPN wasn't entirely without blame for the NHL's tensions. The network had totally screwed the NHL by booting its games off the mother ship and relegating them to ESPN2. In essence, the network had thrown the NHL under the proverbial bus to make room for the ESPN Original Entertainment lineup, which was so important to Shapiro and the network, and once the NHL was installed on ESPN2, ratings indicated that only friends and relatives were watching.

To make matters still worse for the NHL, ESPN was attempting to close a new and very costly deal with Major League Baseball, and Eisner, Iger, and Bodenheimer had agreed that they would not splurge on both hockey and baseball. Shapiro was directed to meet with NHL commissioner Gary Bettman and tell him the ugly truth: ESPN only had $30 million for the deal. Bettman was incredulous. Couldn't ESPN take some money away from its deals with other leagues? Wasn't there any way to come up with more cash? Shapiro's response was *a brutally honest "take it or leave it": if Bettman said no to the $30 million, there would be no deal at all; this was not a negotiation. Bettman felt insulted by the puny offer and, in a huff, bade all the ESPN networks good-bye. He and hockey wound up limping over to Outdoor Life Network, the sports network owned by cable giant Comcast.*

It wasn't long, however, before some team owners were complaining to the commissioner that he should have taken the ESPN deal, insulting or not.

GARY BETTMAN:

I always like to stay with my partners. I'm a relationship kind of guy. I try to be low-maintenance. I try to make clear what I think we need. So we've never looked to move for the sake of moving. That was the five-year, $600 million deal that we, the NHL, made with ABC/ESPN. And if you go back and you check, the response to some press report said I wasn't wearing a mask and I didn't have a gun, because they had stepped up big-time.

There's always been a connection between ESPN and hockey. If you were working in Bristol, you went to see the Hartford Whalers play — that was their professional team. The earliest hockey programming at a professional level was the Whalers, and ESPN2 was built on the NHL and all the tonnage we gave them. But when the NBA moved to ESPN, my immediate reaction was that I knew the NHL was going to have a problem with the next negotiation because I had reason to believe that when they were doing the NBA deal, they budgeted what they could pay them based on the fact that they thought they could drive a tougher bargain with us. This is a small world that we live in; I knew what was coming.

I believed that if they weren't paying us a fair rate, paying us what we were worth relative to other sports and everything else, then they'd never have an incentive to grow our games. We wouldn't get the type of priority treatment that we need—first of all coming back from the work stoppage and secondly that I thought we were entitled to as one of the four major sports.

We'd been partners all those years; they'd built ESPN2 into this behemoth on our back for virtually no cost for our programming. We had just come through one of the most difficult and extraordinary times that a sports league had ever been through, and their answer, instead of embracing us and trying to make it right, was "We're going to take another pound of flesh." Unlike when Dick Ebersol came to the board meeting during the work stoppage and said, "We know you guys have business to take care of. Do what you have to do and we'll be there when you get done."

BILL CLEMENT:

Well, ESPN had NHL rights in 1985 all the way to 2004 with the exception of three years. There were three or four years when SportsChannel America had it, but when ESPN lost it in '04, it was a bad day for all of us who are hockey lovers. There's a certain loyalty that borderlines addiction to the sport of hockey. Just ask fans. It's a connective kind of sport. There were a lot of people who had a lot of emotion invested and time, effort, everything else. But more than that emotion invested is their attachment to their sport.

It bothered all of the hockey people, including producers and people at ESPN, that hockey was always one of the last items to make air on *Sports-Center*. And it bothered people within the industry that the stepchild status, that redheaded stepchild thing, was always confirmed based on the pecking order that hockey fell into on *SportsCenter,* which is way down on the rundown. But *SportsCenter* is an autonomous entity at ESPN that has to cater to its viewers. And there were enough hockey people to warrant putting great hockey highlights at the top of the show, which is a constant reminder of where hockey was in the pecking order of things.

We bitched and complained all we could. Everybody did. But nothing changed. Basically, you had frustration and pride manifesting themselves—our pride in our sport and our frustration at other people not loving it as much as we did.

GARY BETTMAN:

In that environment, if you're being trashed publicly, and they're not paying you what they had agreed the asking price was, why stay? People say, "It's ESPN; you had to be on ESPN." You know what? I was also the first commissioner to shut down a sports league for an entire year. We weren't going to be treated the way we were being treated. And I believed that if they got us too cheap, they would never treat us the way we needed to be treated.

Putting aside what Mark was saying publicly, I didn't put as much stock into it because I knew what he was doing. If we had agreed to a date for a meeting, I knew when I would read in the newspapers some negative comment. I viewed it a little bit differently, in the context of how we were being treated. And that's when I said, "I will not do a package with you, even if I have nowhere else to go, at less than the option price." I then took a drive down to Philadelphia and met my new best friends, Comcast. Brian Roberts and Steve Burke, who had recently gone there, decided that they wanted to make us their team number-one most important program on OLN, soon to be Versus. They paid us more money than even the option price that we had with ESPN, they had promised us treatment, but we understood that they needed to increase their distribution. So I decided it was time to break out and do something new and different. I believed that we could come back from the work stoppage undamaged—and, interestingly enough, we had record attendance that first year back after a year off, and record revenues. No business in the history of business, any industry, has ever done that, having been shut down for an entire year, okay? Never been done. And I didn't want my broadcast partner, my TV partner, to bring us down, and that's what ESPN, I felt, was going to do. I think they had a right to match, and when we came in with numbers even higher than the option price, they decided not to match. And George told me in a late-night conversation that they were disappointed, but they weren't going to match.

BARRY MELROSE, *Hockey Analyst:*

Shapiro and Bettman came to hate each other. And Gary is a lawyer and a tough negotiator, and I think he felt that ESPN was trying to take advantage of the NHL and lowball them with the price.

LINDA COHN:

I wasn't in the room during the negotiations, but it just sounds like two egos going at it and no one looking at the big picture. There were mistakes on both sides. I was angry and so were the people who were passionate about hockey.

STEVE LEVY:

I can tell you from inside the building, people love the hockey and the day we lost the rights it was like people had lost their dog. I don't know if I would say people were openly sobbing, but people were moved. There was a lot of emotion in the building. It seems like hockey grips the building in a different way from the other sports, and it's not just the on-air people and the producers. It's the camera people and the audio guys. Everybody behind the scenes seems to be a big hockey fan, and I think it really hurt the morale in the building when we lost the sport.

FRED GAUDELLI:

What they did to the National Hockey League was insane. From the time that I got to ESPN to the time that I left, our philosophy was that we wanted to be known as people who you want to be in business with; we wanted to be good partners, and have good relationships with the leagues. We didn't want to thump our chests at them, and we didn't want to thump our chests at the media. As a result, ESPN for a long time had a reputation for being really good guys who do good work.

When Mark came in, he brought an arrogance. His regime or style, however you want to put it, was basically the turning point for ESPN going from the good guy to the arrogant guy. I don't care what they tell you, ESPN is not well liked at 280 Park [NFL headquarters], they are not well liked at the NBA, and they are not well liked at Major League Baseball. So you saw it in their relationships with partners, and you saw it on the air with the way they overpromoted the stupidest things, like the Bobby Knight movie. And that's what Mark brought into the company.

I think it speaks to what George really wanted delegated. He didn't feel like he was qualified to really weigh in on production decisions. Now, obviously these decisions that were being made were having an effect far beyond what was on television. When you go from having great relationships with leagues to having tenuous relationships with leagues, that affects your business. They began to have a hard time, because none of the leagues was looking to do any favors for ESPN.

STEVE LEVY:

ESPN wanted hockey but we wanted it at a certain price, and the ratings dictated where the price should be. The people at Versus offered essentially more than twice what we did, and the NHL, and I believe this is shortsighted, took the money. And the league has made this mistake before over the years with that SportsChannel America. They got to make a few extra bucks, but nobody could see the games.

It's not as bad, but it's somewhat similar. I'm constantly being told by players and the players' association and the NHL that the guys are frustrated. Can't get the games. Don't know what channel it's on. Can't get it in the hotel when they're on the road. They can't watch their own sport. And in essence that's driven a lot of people probably to ESPN because they can at least get the highlights and analysis. I think we've actually stepped up our hockey coverage since we haven't had the sport. We've cut down on a lot of remotes here at ESPN due to financial constraints, yet we were still on the road for the Stanley Cup Final for all seven games. Had a three-man crew for that last critical game seven. So I think we've done as good a job as we can, but, but I don't believe we did anything wrong as a company, as a network. I thought we made a fair offer. Nobody promotes the game the way we do. I wouldn't swear by the financial figures, but I think it meant, by going to Versus, an extra one million dollars per team. So it was a $30 million difference, or something close to that.

And I think that's shortsighted for the lack of promotion and the lack of visibility for the sport. Every time I see any of the execs, I think everybody would like to have hockey back. We always joke, "ey, we'll take the NBC deal where we don't have to ı rights fee and if there is a profit, we'll be happy 't it with you." But I don't believe we were 'hat.

GARY BETTMAN:

Once they have you, there's no incentive to grow you because it costs them more money. Mark played tough with us because he could. I think they were trying to send a message, but they overplayed their hand because they drove me to the point of creating a new partnership.

BARRY MELROSE:

If you look at the time of the year when hockey is at its best, there's a lull here at ESPN. It's sort of before baseball gets going, before football gets going, before the NBA playoffs really get going, it's sort of our own little niche there. And you can like hockey, hate hockey, whatever, but if you watch the NHL playoffs, you love the sport. There's nothing like playoff hockey in the NHL.

BILL CLEMENT:

Most fans prefer to watch a fight than a good play. You want to create a buzz in the arena, drop the gloves. It's that morbid sense of curiosity that everyone has. I would have put the fights on too had I been making the editorial decision at *SportsCenter*. It does not capture what the essence of the sport is. But if I want people to watch my show, I'd put the fights on too. The truth is, the fighting is a huge exception to everything else that happens. It's very often the mos memorable event of the game. It certainly creates a huge void in the appreciation of the sport, but it is what it is.

BARRY MELROSE:

The thing I've learned at ESPN is, even though we've got a lot of guys who love hockey here, the important thing is ratings. You have to have ratings. I always say the ratings are going up in the NHL on Versus and on NBC with the outdoor game and stuff, and that the best thing for the NHL is to get back on ESPN. And now ESPN is saying, "You know, jeez, maybe it's time to look at the NHL again and get back into it." So there's hope.

BILL CLEMENT:

I left ESPN because hockey left ESPN. No more hockey there. It became apparent immediately that there weren't any slots left. Barry's there because he was the face of hockey in the studio and they still want to have some hockey presence because it's a national sport. I was the lead game analyst, so because there were no more games, there were no more jobs for a game analyst. Understood it completely.

7

Reconciling the Dream: 2005–2008

"We have to distrust each other. It's our only
defense against betrayal."
— *Tennessee Williams*

*In 2005, ESPN was monarch of all it surveyed, master
of its domain, a top dog earning top dollar, and deserving of other clichés too predictable to mention. Financially the network was all but stamping out Franklins in
its Bristol basement, thanks in part to the enduring
genius of its dual-stream revenue — advertising revenues plus cable subscriber fees. It was a little like selling
cake and getting paid to eat it too.*

*Despite losing hockey the previous year, ESPN was
now gleefully obsessed with its professional football, baseball, and basketball coverage. In addition,* College
GameDay *had developed into a certifiable phenomenon, drawing bigger crowds than ever before and becoming arguably the best sports show on television;* ESPN:
The Magazine *was winning awards and new readers;
hungry fans were crowding into ESPN Zone restaurants;*

the breadth and depth of ESPN's online offerings had made them a must-see for the rest of the industry; and the opening of a new $100 million–plus digital center made the company's Bristol headquarters one of the wonders of the media world. While other networks were still planning a switch to high-definition, ESPN was already there.

But a rather large cloud was threatening to block the sun. A new round of negotiations for rights to broadcast the most popular, most expensive, and most desirable properties in all of sports television—National Football League games—was looming on the horizon. The NFL was offering up its entire inventory: Sunday afternoons, Sunday nights, and Monday night football. ESPN had been paying handsomely for rights to Sunday night games since 1987, but Monday night was glittering conspicuously against the black velvet because for the first time since its inception in 1970, it looked like ABC might drop the ball—even throw it away.

Monday Night Football *had not only aired exclusively on ABC throughout its existence but seemed inextricably part of the network. Nevertheless, embattled Disney chief Michael Eisner reportedly no longer wanted* Monday Night Football *on the Disney-owned ABC television network. It was, like so much about television, a dollars-and-cents issue: the golden goose had been laying leaden eggs to the tune of at least $150 million in losses annually for the past several years. Falling ratings combined with rising costs is no formula for success in* *television, and in the face of grim figures, Eisner in effect said, "To hell with prestige and tradition; we're losing money!"*

There were even rumors that one year, at the prestigious Allen & Company media summits in Sun Valley, Idaho, Eisner had offered the Monday night package to Les Moonves at CBS one year, and to Bob Wright at NBC the next—not that Eisner necessarily had the rights to do it without the NFL's approval. In addition, the burgeoning success of ABC Entertainment's Desperate Housewives *and* Grey's Anatomy *on Sunday night suggested that Eisner would not want to disturb such rarities as prime-time scripted hits.*

Virtually every department at ESPN geared up for the bargaining. In all likelihood, this would be the most expensive deal anyone in Bristol had ever imagined. Sean Bratches, executive vice president of Sales and Marketing, held innumerable discussions with his team about a new football package, seen as the perfect vehicle for landing new A-list commercial clients and further strengthening bonds with those already signed. And Mark Shapiro, whose empire now included responsibility for ABC Sports, was actively developing plans for Monday night games, including a possible SportsCenter *at halftime, or maybe even an episode of* Pardon the Interruption. *Everyone was optimistic. The excitement level was off the charts.*

And then pop! *went the balloon, or at least the "ssss" of a slow leak. The NFL announced that its chief negotiator would be none other than former ESPN president (and briefly ABC president) Steve Bornstein, who in his new job as the NFL's executive vice president of media would be making all critical TV decisions for the team owners. That meant Bornstein would be the driving force behind which properties and packages went where, and he was hardly considered a disinterested party.*

In Bristol, some thought having Bornstein across the table would be the ultimate home-court advantage. After all, Bornstein had helped build the place, had handpicked George Bodenheimer as his successor, had mentored Mark Shapiro, and could claim many other friends at the network. But others at ESPN were far less sanguine. Bornstein was anything but the sentimental sort, and the four years that had passed since he was bounced from his executive post at ABC had done little if anything to mute his anger and resentment toward Michael Eisner and Bob Iger, the men who had forced him out.

For many, it looked as though Bornstein finally had at his disposal the perfect vehicle for revenge. The question at hand: Would his desire to strike back at Iger and Eisner trump whatever affection and loyalty he still felt for his dear old alma mater, ESPN?

BILL CREASY:

Iger had won. It was Iger versus Steve, and Eisner picked Iger. Steve was smart enough to know that he would be accused of running a hard deal against ESPN because of his history with Eisner and Iger. The other side of that coin was that he would go out of his way to make a deal so that he wouldn't be accused of that sort of heavy bullshit. He was in a tough position.

BOB IGER:

It is not unusual for negotiations of this magnitude to become difficult, and it is common for a certain level of frustration to arise at different stages. No one is totally immune from the ebb and flow of deals that big. That said, business never becomes personal for me. The NFL deal was always just business. It may have been personal for others, but I can assure you, it never became that way for me. As the steward of a multibillion-dollar company, allowing personal emotions to enter the equation would be a huge mistake.

STEVE BORNSTEIN:

Have you ever had a colonoscopy? Negotiation is similar to that. I have been involved in five different contracts for television rights from the NFL. The first four, I was on the ESPN side of the table, and then the fifth one, I was on the NFL side. The first one that we did at $53 million was an incredibly expensive deal for ESPN at that time, as was the second at $108 million. The third, $135 million, represented a more modest increase—still a big chunk for us. But the fourth deal, the one that I did at $600 million a year, was a career maker or breaker for me personally. It worked out, but each one was a very, very pricey deal. Each one took your breath away.

GEORGE BODENHEIMER:

To me, NFL negotiations at this level are purely business. There are billions of dollars flowing. I grew up negotiating in the company—not for programming but for carriage and license fees, so I can tell you that while some of those negotiations can be tension-filled, they can also be fun, and you can derive a tremendous amount of satisfaction from them. I personally enjoy them. I would say they are exhilarating.

CHRISTINE DRIESSEN:

The way we work is fairly collegial at ESPN. We have what I would call a strategic team that looks at any acquisition from a rights standpoint, and we sit and meet as a team. So we have George, most importantly. Mark was there. We'd have somebody from Production. My team would be represented. Ad Sales would be represented. And we would then analyze what the product was worth, and what it meant for us. We have a pretty good barometer on what we can afford. We even have a piece of paper detailing when we will walk away.

MARK SHAPIRO:

Chris doesn't negotiate at all. I would never bring her into a negotiating room with me on any deal. Do the background stuff; get me prepared to do what I need to do; work with me, help me; let's run a P&L; let's think about this; what are we missing? I mean, on the crap work for NFL negotiations her team does a really good job. But you've got to keep her out of the negotiating room.

CHRISTINE DRIESSEN:

The large important programming deals that were done under Mark when he was head of programming were driven by George Bodenheimer. Sometimes people lose sight of that because Mark was very vocal about his contributions and very visible. George is visible when he needs to be, but he isn't concerned with getting credit for himself; he'd rather give credit to the team. George made the final call. Under George's leadership, the big change here is that he has a negotiating style of being very honest and straightforward. When George says something, he has credibility.

At the end of the day, a lot of people talk passionately about the emotions driving these kinds of decisions, but a lot of that is overblown.

HOWARD KATZ:

The people who worked for Mark swore by him; the people he negotiated with swore *at* him. Watching him and Steve Bornstein negotiating with each other, the teacher and the student, you could sell tickets. Mark was brilliant and had incredible command of a room; he had an incredible ability to motivate people who worked for him, but he also had an incredible ability to piss people off. He may not have appreciated the sensitivity of the relationship between certain rights holders and ESPN, because he was a ruthless negotiator.

GEORGE BODENHEIMER:

ABC was losing $150 million or more a year on *Monday Night Football,* and the clock had just run out on ABC's interest in continuing to do that. They were ready to move into a profitable, entertainment-based schedule. At the same time, you had a burgeoning ESPN always looking for more, always looking to improve itself, all of a sudden having an opportunity to step up to *Monday Night Football.* That's an opportunity that we gladly embraced. Everybody in the United States knows when *Monday Night Football* is on. It's the preeminent sport property. Having been at ESPN since 1981, you tell me I've got an opportunity to program *Monday Night Football* on ESPN, you better believe we're going to take advantage of that opportunity.

There were never any serious discussions, however, to acquire two packages, both Sunday and Monday.

MARK SHAPIRO:

I wanted both. I wanted to keep Sunday night on ESPN and Monday night on ABC as long as the price was reasonable, say $1.5 billion a year. I thought we could have gotten it at one point, but Iger passed. What can I do? What you need to realize is, no matter how big one thinks I might have been in that job, when it came to *Monday Night Football* or the NFL in general, and spending that kind of money, I had input, George had input, and our voices were heard, but we couldn't make the decision. Michael Eisner and Bob Iger were running the ship.

But were Eisner and Iger really "running the ship"? Was anyone truly in a position to lead and make timely decisions for Disney during such critical negotiations? With Eisner clearly on his way out, Bob Iger felt the time had come at last for him to take control of Disney and save the day. His executive dexterity had been on display throughout his career but was never as evident as when he navigated the tightrope he had been walking under Eisner. Somehow, he had managed to serve under an increasingly controversial Eisner without being linked to him. Even though Iger was enormously successful and markedly handsome, and had an admirable track record, people who might have been expected to hate him didn't. There was something about the guy that disarmed skeptics and made people like him.

Many assumed Iger had the inside track and would effortlessly get Eisner's job, but others, including at least one member of the Disney board, believed that the company needed a totally fresh start. They wanted to make a clean break from everything Eisner. Either way, Iger was never one to suffer from hubris, and he had received no assurances that the job was to be his. Indeed, eBay's Meg Whitman had already been mentioned as a possible candidate.

Arguably the last thing that Iger wanted at this precarious moment was for Disney to throw billions of dollars at an NFL package that had lost the company tens of millions in the past, so for the second half of 2004 and the first few months of 2005, Iger decided the best course of action was to sit tight and do nothing with the NFL.

Critical to Iger's wait-it-out strategy was his belief that he wouldn't have to worry about competition from NBC, which had walked away from the NFL in 1998. NBC was slogging through tough economic times, and NBC Sports chairman Dick Ebersol hadn't voiced any interest in returning to the NFL.

Steve Bornstein had figured out from the start of negotiations that, as he put it, Disney was in "disarray," that Eisner didn't have the clout anymore to make such a huge decision, and that Iger would be hard-pressed to make a move. Sensing Iger's reluctance to act, Bornstein decided to box him in.

Bornstein spent over a year romancing NBC's Dick Ebersol; together the two developed a new Sunday night concept of a prime-time game, including a highlight show before, and "flex" scheduling, which would give Ebersol the opportunity to pick his choice of game during the critical second half of the season. The strategy was clear: If Bornstein could convince Fox and CBS to renew Sunday afternoons, and get NBC to step up for Sunday nights, that would leave Disney with only Monday Night Football *— and no bargaining position whatever.*

Bornstein was ready with his first big message to Iger. When George Bodenheimer was inducted into the Broadcasting Hall of Fame in the fall of 2004, Bornstein took the opportunity to tell Iger that CBS and Fox had already renewed their deals for Sunday afternoons. Iger instantly understood what this meant: the number of remaining bidders had been drastically reduced. The second big message Bornstein sent was that Disney shouldn't consider its position unassailable, and what better way to convey that than a very public lunch with NBC — the same NBC that Iger was convinced wouldn't get back into football?

DICK EBERSOL:

We had a very famous lunch with the NFL at 21. It was Paul Tagliabue, Roger Goodell, and Steve Bornstein from their side, and they invited me, Jeff Zucker [President, NBC Universal], and Randy

Falco. I said, we've got a private dining room, why not have it here? But I should have seen it coming, because we opened up the *New York Post* the next day, and there it was on Page Six.

They asked us if we would take over the Monday night schedule, because Eisner was desperate to get out of it, and we told them—as we had about a year and a half before—that the answer was no. We had done our due diligence and said, "Guys, we could never afford to pay you as much as they're paying you, because the losses are so extraordinary and our losses would be so much bigger because we would be cutting into our late-night show on Monday night by doing it." But we also said, "If you're ever interested in Sunday night, we'd love to do Sunday night. We would take that over from ESPN, and we'd want the highlight package, so we'd have the game and fill four hours of prime time."

STEVE BORNSTEIN:
Bob's position was tenuous, and it was difficult for them to act. This was going to be a very big deal—a big transaction. Other than when Disney bought CapCities, this was the largest deal Michael Eisner ever did. It was getting very pricey, so that's not for the faint of heart. If you're insecure as to what the board is thinking and whether the board is going to support you, there would be some hesitation there.

RANDY FALCO, *President, NBC Universal Television Network Group:*

I'll be perfectly honest: my first choice in all of this was to try to get a Thursday night package for our USA Network. The reason I thought that was so important for us is there are really only a handful of cable networks that have the rights to nationally televised sports. I wanted to take advantage of that if I could and separate USA Network from the competition. Obviously at the time Steve was trying to get a package for the NFL Network on Thursday night, so that probably wasn't his first choice, but they were very good about listening to the prospect of us coming up with something for Thursday night on USA.

SEAN McMANUS:

Our main priority was keeping the Sunday afternoon package because I think that's the most important window. I think we and Fox have the best packages—the highest rated by far, much bigger than Sunday night. That was our first priority.

One of the reasons we got as much money to spend from Leslie [Moonves] and, at the time, Mel [Karmazin] as we did originally back in '98 was because Leslie believed the NFL could help him launch a lot of successful prime-time programs out of NFL football—and he did with *CSI, King of Queens,*

NCIS, and many more. As far as I know, NBC hasn't launched one successful show out of NFL football. So you can make the argument that the premium we paid to get football was worth it. I think Leslie would agree that one of the major reasons CBS was so successful in prime time was because of the hundreds of millions of dollars we've gotten in free promotional times with our NFL games.

With that in mind, we did look at Sunday night and had a plan. One concept was to start the Sunday night game at 8:45 or nine o'clock. The Monday night game used to start at nine o'clock. Our plan was to basically get off the air at, like, 7:15, which we do now, do *60 Minutes* as a full hour, and then come on with the football pregame show. And the football pregame show would be collapsible, so even if the first game went into overtime, we could still do a full *60 Minutes* and not be late for the second game. Also part of our plan—which I thought was really valuable—was asking for complete flexibility in moving any of our games on a two-week notice to the prime-time window. It would have been the ultimate flex scheduling. And they would have been all our games anyway, so it wouldn't be like the lobbying we have now with the NFL when NBC wants one of our games.

We were asked to come in and do a deal for Sunday afternoon early before we needed to, and we got a deal done pretty quickly. Fox got a deal done pretty quickly too. We didn't pay a large increase. We're very happy with our package, and I think it was a good deal for both CBS and the NFL.

DAVID HILL:

Here it is in a nutshell: We make our money by selling ads on television shows, so we already make money on Monday nights. By putting football in on Sunday afternoons, we can sell ads and make some money. On Sunday nights we make money, on Monday nights we make money, so we never wanted Monday night. Sunday afternoon is just fine for us. As soon as you displace prime-time programming with NFL football, you lose a revenue stream.

RANDY FALCO:

I always looked at those kinds of acquisitions in three ways: Does it have marquee value? Certainly Sunday night did. Does it have strategic value? That would be if it would help us in prime time, and maybe give us time to rebuild the rest of our prime-time schedule and keep us relevant. And the third piece was the economic value. Now, here it seemed to me that if we were going to invest that kind of money, even though the NFL was a sure thing ratings-wise, maybe it would have been wiser for us to take the money and invest it in regular programming that we could build a franchise with—you know, along the lines of *Law & Order* or *CSI*. Remember we had just purchased Universal Studios. My only issue personally with the Sunday night package was the economics of it.

DICK EBERSOL:

Pat Bowlen [owner of the Denver Broncos] was the first person to say to me, "There still may be a chance for Sunday night. Steve Bornstein and I really have come around, and we believe Sunday night with you guys has more of an opportunity for us to maintain our rating. You should call Paul." So I called Tagliabue and I talked to him for an hour, and he basically said the same thing. Then he said, "We can't do anything until we get ESPN to move." This was the end of January.

The league agreed to extend the deadline to April 15. So now it's the very beginning of March, and I'm living in our house in Colorado, and one Sunday morning, the second Sunday in March, I called Pat at work — I just knew he'd be at work — and I said, "I can take *Sunday Night Football*," and he asked me about a number. I told him I thought it could be done for about $600 million, and then he said, "All right, but I want you to put this to a vote of your coworkers. I want to make sure they're all in this thing. I don't want to find out later that you and Jeff were the only hot passionate guys and the others were forced to do something." So I went around to everybody and we were all on board for $600 million. And then we just waited.

AL MICHAELS:

I did find out a day or two before the whole thing came down that NBC was the other player, and I called Bob [Iger], and he said, "That can't be. They're out of it." I said, "Bob, I can't tell you how I know, but I know it's NBC. I'm 99 percent certain." He said, "But that doesn't make any sense."

Friday, April 14, 2005, proved to be a major day in the histories of ESPN, the National Football League, and the National Broadcasting Company. Breakfast was served on the fifteenth floor of the NFL's headquarters in Manhattan. Iger, Bodenheimer, and Shapiro arrived and were met by Bornstein, NFL commissioner Paul Tagliabue, his deputy Roger Goodell, New England Patriots owner Robert Kraft, and Pat Bowlen, owner of the Denver Broncos.

Iger told the NFL guys that he had an offer for Monday night, but they didn't want to hear about it, at least not then. "We're not going to accept offers for Monday night," Bowlen announced. "You want to be in prime-time football, you have to be on Sunday *night." Iger said he didn't want to do it that way, and proceeded to make a $1.5 billion offer: $1 billion for Sunday night football on ESPN, and $500 million for Monday night football on ABC. So much for ABC dumping* Monday Night Football.

Bowlen exploded; Kraft was frustrated. They couldn't

believe Iger was now making a bid that Bowlen had practically begged him to make more than six months earlier. The NFL gang was so miffed, they left the room.

ROBERT KRAFT, *Owner, New England Patriots:*
I never used the word "insulting" about their offer. I don't think anyone can use that word when you're talking about $1.5 billion. What I did feel was that their offer didn't reflect fair value for both nights, and we were pleased that the market proved that belief to be right.

While Iger agonized, NFL chief operating officer Roger Goodell called Dick Ebersol and asked how quickly he could get over there. Ebersol was at 280 Park Avenue in twenty minutes and was spirited up by a back elevator. The NFL negotiating team asked Ebersol if he was still willing to pay $600 million for Sunday night. Ebersol said yes, and the NFL guys said, "Congratulations, you have a new football night."

Minutes later, Commissioner Tagliabue told Iger and Bodenheimer that Sunday night was no longer an option. The 21 lunch notwithstanding, Iger had been told by at least one knowledgeable insider that NBC was in the bidding and had simply refused to believe it. Now he knew it was true, whether it made sense or not. Sunday night was gone; only Monday night remained. And Iger knew what Bornstein had known for close to two decades: he just couldn't let ESPN go without football because it would brutally harm the brand, and more important, between 30 and 35 percent of its affiliate fees were from football. ESPN had to have football.

There would be no more ABC Monday Night Football. *With almost no bargaining position, a situation aggravated by the fact that Bornstein knew from eons of experience how much ESPN could afford to spend, Disney had to bid up to $1.1 billion a year for eight years to place* Monday Night Football *on ESPN's roster. But there would be none of the flex scheduling that NBC received and, most shocking, no playoff games.*

DICK EBERSOL:

There's no question that if ABC-ESPN had made the deal within two weeks of the time the other networks did, they would have held on to both packages, and I'd be shocked if they couldn't have held on to it for, like, a million-four for both. And that Sunday night package had one wild-card Saturday. But the point was, they ended up paying a billion-one, losing Sunday night, and not having any playoff games.

STEVE BORNSTEIN:

They lost *Monday Night Football* after a thirty-six-year run on the network. You don't lose your number-one series after nearly four decades and not feel some disappointment. That was really part of the problem of being last. They weren't able to set the table. They were only able to react to what was left.

DON OHLMEYER:

Steve could not have pushed any harder for ESPN to make the deal back in October. In a way, it cost them [Disney] a couple hundred million dollars by not listening to Steve—or, to put it another way, Steve made a couple hundred million dollars more for the league when they didn't listen.

BILL CREASY:

I've heard there is criticism up in Bristol that the price ended up so high because of Mark. It is my 100 percent opinion that if Iger and George were not in the room, if the league and ESPN just put Steve and Mark in a room and said, "Don't come out until you make a deal," you would have never heard the price that they eventually agreed to. Mark and Steve would have hacked out a deal. I think Mark was frustrated. He knew he could make a deal but they never listened to him. From the league's point of view, ESPN messed around too much.

BOB IGER:

I was feeling good that we had secured an eight-year deal for sports television's most venerable franchise when the other TV packages went for six years. I also felt good that we had clearly strengthened one of Disney's core brands, ESPN, and had created a new opportunity for ABC on Monday nights. And ultimately ABC created a franchise, *Dancing with the Stars,* that has given Disney a strong, enviable position with both men and women on Monday nights.

STEVE BORNSTEIN:

I don't want to sound smug. I was pleased with the end result of these negotiations. Essentially, the NFL got paid more money for less product. We created a new package, and we got another hour of prime-time television because NBC was going to program the seven-to-eight-o'clock block promoting our sport. By 2006, the first year of this new deal, our ratings were up double digits on every platform.

ESPN should be thrilled with the football package, and I think most people there are. They're making big money. It's the premier sports network and they have the premier sports product—they have the crown jewel in sports marketing called *Monday Night Football.* There is nothing better than that.

Some say they pay more than other partners and the other partners have playoff games. That's a specious argument. Who's extracted the most value out of their association with the NFL? ESPN, ESPN, ESPN. So anybody at ESPN who is disappointed or angry is not really being intelligent.

AL MICHAELS:

Was ESPN going to do okay? Absolutely. Their template because of sub fees doesn't allow them to fail. But they could have had Sunday night and Monday night and blown NBC out the door. Instead, NBC winds up with the number-one package. It was a major blown opportunity.

DAVID HILL:

Disney paid the big bucks on Monday night so they could jack up their cable prices; that's all it is. Sunday afternoon is great for us because we didn't sell advertising there and we do now. It's very simple.

SEAN McMANUS:

We thought the break-even number was $425 million, and NBC paid $600 million. You can ask them if they're making or losing money on it, but I know what the economics are, and I know how many more playoff games we have and what our ratings are, and I know that we generate probably 30 percent more rating points each year. So while we looked at it and thought it would make sense for us to go right from Sunday afternoon football to Sunday night football, we just couldn't get to the level that NBC eventually did.

I believe Disney could have swept in and kept NBC out of the marketplace, but I'm not sure they ever really appreciated—at least to the degree that NBC did—the value of the prime-time network package. They just decided that ESPN was strategically more important to them than the ABC television network—which was no surprise.

MICHAEL EISNER:

By 2004, we had *Lost, Desperate Housewives, Grey's Anatomy*, and they had all done very well, but you can't give up football; it's The American Pastime, and it would be bad from a PR point of view. So by putting the big franchise, Monday night, on ESPN, we no longer had to have it Monday nights on ABC. It was a fantastic decision worth maybe a billion dollars to the company. So now you had Sunday night on NBC, which is a big loss for them, and Monday night on ESPN.

ESPN goes from a Ping-Pong network and a surfing network, and whatever else they were doing there in the beginning, to the key sports franchise.

STEVE BORNSTEIN:

Running these broadcast networks without a male delivery system, which is what *Monday Night Football* is, is really hard to do. ABC may be better positioned given the cross-promotional opportunities that they have within ESPN, but they'll want back in as well. Every time any of the big four networks has ever lost the football package, they've come back in.

GEORGE BODENHEIMER:

Would we like to pay less? Would we like to have a few more benefits than we had? Sure, as in any negotiation. The good news is, those negotiations continue to come around every few years. And we're not going anywhere.

Lost in the palaver about Monday night versus Sunday night, and in the widespread astonishment at the $1.1 billion price tag, was the fact that NBC had also acquired the highlight show that preceded each Sunday night game. And that meant an abrupt bye-bye to NFL Primetime, *the long-running ESPN institution hosted by Chris Berman.*

CHRIS BERMAN:

It was a fuckup of the tenth magnitude. I knew somehow ESPN would maintain their NFL package, which was what we did, but what I didn't understand was that *Primetime* was at risk. NBC came in through the bathroom window, to quote Joe Cocker or the Beatles. I didn't think that the world was going to change, that we—ABC-ESPN—would lose one of the two. I didn't know that. How could I know? Nobody knew.

MARK SHAPIRO:

All Berman cared about was *NFL Primetime.* We said, "Chris, we got *Monday Night Football*! Chris, we got eight years! Chris, we got Spanish language!" All he cared about was that *Primetime* would go away. That was his showcase. That was his baby. He called Tagliabue. He called Bowlen, trying to save it. Couldn't do it.

CHRIS BERMAN:

If you put my professional tombstone up, the first sentence would be: "He did *NFL Primetime*." First one.

TOM JACKSON:

I cannot remember the exact moment we found out we had lost *Primetime,* but I knew we were late in the negotiations. It was the loss of something that was very special to Chris. I know that he was disappointed, as I was. There couldn't have been anyone at our company who didn't know how important it was. In fact, I can't imagine there was anybody, including the NFL hierarchy, that was happy about that program disappearing—maybe with the exception of NBC. It certainly was one of those moments where everybody knew that they were losing something; you walk away with one of those feelings like "How could it happen? How could you let this happen?"

CHRIS BERMAN:

That show made football famous. I would always hear, "You guys made me a football fan. Now I can watch a whole game" or "We watch *NFL Primetime* together as a family."

In the early nineties, Don Shula told me he watched *NFL Primetime*. I said, "I know you're a football fan, Coach, but do you use it professionally because you have game film?" He said, "Yeah, I do." He told me, "We're playing the NFC East this year for the first time in four years, and starting about four weeks out, I'll pay a little closer attention to the Giants highlights that I haven't seen in four years on tape, and I might just make a couple of notes from your show when we get a little closer." I said, "Whoa, now you're just blowing me away."

It was the highest-rated studio show in the history of cable television by the way—sports or otherwise. And what I liked about it most was it was just football. There were no pretenses. It was not "Let's be stars." There was no script. Tommy and I would just finish each other's lines. It was great. And the beauty of that show was there was very little time for management to tell you how to do it, because nothing happened until 1:01 on Sunday. We'd spend six days formatting the pregame show but six hours doing the night show.

We'd spend all week figuring out why New England was going to clobber so-and-so and then they wouldn't, and it's like "Oh, what the hell happened there?" Then we get to talk about it. And I loved that. I was feeding off the energy of our building, of our job, and the fact that we were all football fans. Look, I still love the game, and I still really enjoy the people who run it. It's just that now, in getting to the post, if you will, getting the horse in the frickin' gate so we can run the race, is certainly a lot more challenging than it used to be.

STEPHANIE DRULEY, *Coordinating Producer:*

It is disappointing that we can't do those long high-lights, because that's really where Boomer was at his best. When he's voicing highlights, they feel big and important and exciting. Nobody does it better than he did with that show. And whatever you try to do, you can't really re-create that immediacy, because it was right after a game. But we romanticize *Primetime* because it's been gone for a couple of years. You have to wonder today, with all the different ways you can get your highlights, would it have been as popular now?

Triumph was the title Jeremy Schaap gave his book about Jesse Owens's historic performance at the 1936 Berlin Olympics, when Germany had been taken over by Adolf Hitler and his Nazi party. But Schaap would score an impressive triumph of his own in 2005, two years before the book was published.

He'd already won a total of four Sports Emmys for his work and was arguably the best on-air reporter at ESPN, but nothing compared to his confrontation in Iceland with quixotic chess champion Bobby Fischer. Perhaps it was because the American expatriate, whose reaction to the terrorist attacks of September 11, 2001, was to say, "I want to see the U.S. wiped out," had been thought of as insane; perhaps it was Fischer calling Jeremy's late father, the legendary Dick Schaap, a "Jewish snake."

Whatever it was, the stage was set for a poignant confrontation.

JEREMY SCHAAP:

Ever since I became a reporter at ESPN, I wanted to do a Bobby Fischer story because of the family connection. When Bobby was twelve years old and he was the U.S. national champion, he and my father developed a close relationship. My father was a writer at *Newsweek,* and he was covering chess among other things. Bobby didn't really have a male figure in his life. He was raised by his mother, sisters, and grandmother. My father became kind of a surrogate father. He'd take him to ball games and play tennis with him. They became very close. When Bobby was moving up the ranks internationally in the sixties, my father kept very close tabs on him, often writing about him in magazines. When Bobby would come back from having defeated some grand master somewhere, the first person he'd see waiting for him at Kennedy or Idlewild would be my father, and that would often be the only TV interview he'd do. And when he came back after winning the world championship, my father was the MC of Bobby Fischer Day at Seton Hall. My dad even threw a party for him. And then Bobby disappeared.

Nobody could find him. I mean literally no one in the West interviewed him in twenty-five years, maybe more than that. He was a white whale for a lot of reporters. Then, in 2004, he surfaces in Japan, where he gets arrested on a passport violation. His U.S. passport had expired, and they put him in jail. So now at least we know where he is. And a producer I worked with a lot named Jon Fish told me there were rumblings that he was going to be released. Then we hear that the Japanese are letting him go and that Iceland is going to grant him citizenship. We also found out a private plane is going to take him all the way to Iceland from Japan. He's going to be in the air for sixteen hours.

Some of ESPN's loftiest qualities came together in that moment and in the buildup to it, turning the encounter into a stunning piece of personal and yet professional journalism. ESPN also showed itself, perhaps contrary to its reputation, willing to spend whatever was necessary to chase down a big story, even if superficially it seemed to have little to do with sports.

JEREMY SCHAAP:

I knew I had to get to Iceland. This might be our only chance to get the guy, 'cause he's going to step off that plane and then probably go back into seclusion. So I'm looking at the flights. There's one flight a day from the United States to Iceland and it was at

7:30 in the evening. It's now 3:30 in the afternoon. So I call Glenn Jacobs, who at the time was coordinating producer and number two in the feature story unit, and explain the situation. I said, "You gotta make a decision right now. I need a crew, and you gotta get us on a plane tonight." I knew it was going to be an expensive proposition. And he just said, "Go." I threw some clothes into a bag and ran for the airport. We landed at two in the morning in Iceland.

When Bobby arrived at the airport, he looked very scary. He was hustled off right away. I did get a chance to say my name, but he didn't stop, he didn't even blink. I spent the entire night thinking he must have forgotten my father. The next day was bizarre at every level. I was shocked he decided to hold a press conference — he hadn't done one since 1992 — and he did it at the same hotel where he stayed during the '72 match with Spassky. There were only two American news organizations, the rest were Russian, English, Icelandic, and a couple other places. The room was packed. I was expecting a typical press conference and was hoping I'd get in some questions. It never occurred to me for a second that that thing would deteriorate into a one-on-one confrontation. None of my questions mentioned my father. I was trying to ask questions that any American media would be asking, like why he thought the attacks on 9/11 were the chickens coming home to roost for the United States. I asked him why he went into seclusion. He had never before put himself in a position to be asked, and I was thinking about all the ground I had to cover. But I was getting no help from the rest of the media. They wanted to know if he was going to learn the Icelandic language. There was a question: Would he plan to go whale watching? And there were a number of specific questions from the Russians about chess. I was literally standing there thinking, these people are crazier than Fischer.

Then he started ranting about the Jews and the U.S. and George Bush and said he wanted to come back to me. He looked over at me and said, "Your father was Jewish, wasn't he?" I said, "Yes, as are you." If I had to do it over again, I wouldn't have said that to him, but it was very emotional, I was in the middle of this island in the Atlantic Ocean, and I was feeling disoriented.

Then, we're having this strange, bizarre, intense back-and-forth. He's saying the most horrible things to me while explaining to the entire room the relationship he had with my father. There were moments of lucidity throughout and almost sweetness in the way he would phrase things. It seemed sometimes like he was actually really hurt that my father, as he saw it, had turned on him. There was obviously some unresolved history between them. But then he called my father "a typical Jewish snake," I remember those exact words. It was the last straw. I decided I couldn't stand there anymore. I didn't give a shit about his answers anymore. He was telling everyone that my father had written that he didn't have a sane bone in his body and asked me if I read it. I told him I wasn't sure if I had but added, "You've done nothing here to disprove anything he said." Then I walked out. The room was silent. He didn't say a word for a good twenty seconds.

I was shaken and called Vince Doria to tell him what happened. He wanted the tape and we had to go through seventy different paths to get it fed back to the U.S. They ran the piece and then a couple weeks later, I did a bigger piece which ran on *World News Tonight,* and that piece made an even bigger impact.

On June 23, 2005, in an announcement that did noth-ing to alleviate stress levels, ABC Sports employees were summoned to an important meeting in the thirteenth-floor conference room at ABC corporate headquarters in New York. Word of the meeting heightened anxiety, already rampant, among the ABC Sports staff about the rapidly encroaching dominance of ESPN, moving like lava from a volcano over their work and, they feared, their futures.

Fortunately, George Bodenheimer was there to calm them, reassure them, and promote cooperation—even though, as he knew, the message flew in the face of history.

MICHAEL EISNER:

We had decided that we were going to get rid of ABC Sports, and ESPN would be on ABC. ESPN was "The Brand!"

MARK MANDEL, *VP of Media Relations:*

All of us from ABC Sports knew that we would have to adapt to new business realities once ESPN took over. Like many of my colleagues at ABC, we believed our brand was valuable and could have thrived under ESPN. But we soon came to recognize that merging the two under the ESPN brand was the right business decision, even if that was difficult for us personally. So we were on board and eager to contribute to ESPN, and I along with others expressed this to George.

We were told at the beginning that we would be welcomed onto the ESPN team and that the process to combine the two entities would be an "integration." On June 23, George came to the ABC Sports offices to make it official. The entire ABC sports staff was assembled in the thirteenth-floor conference room. I was traveling but listened in on the conference call. George's point that day was, this was going to be a great thing for everybody in the room because it would create more opportunities, and the combined company would make us all even stronger.

I wasn't in the room, so I couldn't smell anything, but what I heard was sheer mendacity. This was not an integration; this was a hostile takeover.

Immediately after returning to his office from that meeting, at least one longtime ABC executive was issued his walking papers. That very day. Within months, many others learned their fates, and the process of eliminating ABCers continued methodically. In 2005, there were approximately seventy-five to ninety full-time people working at ABC. By 2008, there were about forty who survived to work at ESPN. By 2010, there were about ten. And any of us who were "lucky" enough to have employment at ESPN had to accept diminished roles. You would have thought at least a few people from ABC would get top jobs within ESPN — it's the law of averages that some people at ABC would have been better than their counterparts at ESPN. Every single ABC Sports employee had their responsibilities diminished. We either lost our jobs or had to accept lesser roles. I was even told by an ESPN senior vice president that the people of ESPN didn't believe that the people of ABC Sports worked very hard. Perhaps it was inevitable that the big Bristol bureaucracy would clash with the small, efficient ABC Sports team that produced a lot of the most memorable sports television during the last forty years.

BRENT MUSBURGER:

Bornstein came over and became the head of ABC, and then Bodenheimer did. They tried to run it as different shops, but you knew that eventually the accountants would take a look at the books and say, "Why do we need to pay two guys when we can pay one guy and get the same job done?" And management at Disney was absolutely right; there was no question about it. ESPN had experienced a lot of resentment about the way they had been treated for so many years. There was definitely a feeling on the part of ABC Sports that "we are the big guy and we will tell ESPN what to do." So, believe me, those guys really enjoyed it when they finally took over all of ABC. There's no question about that.

MARK MANDEL:

Three years after we were "integrated" and supposedly full-fledged ESPN employees, all of the thirty-seven remaining former ABC employees who were now working for ESPN received an ominous e-mail informing us to report to one of two conference rooms the next morning for a very important meeting. It turned out that twenty-five were assigned to a conference room in which they were told they would have to move to Bristol or lose their jobs. The other twelve of us, who were also rounded up in a conference room, were told that we were safe for now and we could remain in New York. It was clear that all thirty-seven of us were different from our fellow ESPN employees. After all, there were many ESPN employees who worked in New York who were not corralled into conference rooms and had to fear for their jobs that morning. Only ex-ABCers were subjected to this pain and suffering. It was clear to those of us who were rounded up only to be told we would keep our jobs in New York: we could be rounded up again, anytime.

ESPN often claims great reverence for the history of ABC Sports but obviously had a collective bias against the ABC Sports employees.

On December 26, 2005, the Patriots and the Jets would collide for the 555th NFL game to air on ABC. It would be the end of a long-standing tradition — the last NFL game on ABC.

DON OHLMEYER:

To me, the legacy of Roone lives on in what ESPN does. But there was no reason anymore for the existence of ABC Sports.

Nearly everyone at ESPN and across the TV sports world assumed that the new Monday Night Football would look just like the old, except it would be on a different network. That would mean the stellar duo of John Madden and Al Michaels would continue to man the booth, backed by popular producer Fred Gaudelli, who joined ESPN in the early eighties and was generally regarded as its top producer, and director Drew Esocoff, Gaudelli's partner and one of the most highly respected directors in the business.

They obviously hadn't been talking with Mark Shapiro.

AL MICHAELS:

In October of '05, in our lame-duck *Monday Night* year on ABC, Bodenheimer comes to Indianapolis for a game. I'm walking out onto the field with him before the game, and I am hearing from unimpeachable sources that the *Monday Night* schedule beginning in '06 will look a lot like the *Sunday Night* schedule had looked in previous years, and that *Sunday Night* is going to get the *Monday Night* schedule. This meant the league wanted to make *Sunday Night* the primary night.

I knew the guys who were making out the schedules, and I knew Bornstein had an ax to grind, and Howard Katz, who was now at the NFL, had also been let go by Disney. So I'm walking out onto the field and I said, "George, I'm nervous about the schedule next year." He said, "Why?" I said, "Because I'm hearing the schedule is going to be far inferior to the way it's been." He said, "Oh, no, Mark said we're going to get the *Monday Night* schedule." And I looked at him and I said, "I tell you what, here's the litmus test, George. In all of the years I've been on *Monday Night Football,* save maybe one or two, the defending Super Bowl champion has been on the schedule three times, which was the maximum number of appearances that they could have (this was of course pre-flex). So the litmus test is going to be next year, to make sure they're on three times. Here's what I'm hearing. They will not be on three times, they will not even be on twice, we're going to get 'em once." He said, "No, Mark said we're going to get the *Monday Night* schedule."

George had always been straight with me, so I think he got bamboozled, because here's how the schedule turned out: in 2006, the first year of ESPN football on Monday nights, the Super Bowl champion Steelers did not appear three times, they didn't appear two times, they appeared just once—week three on the road at Jacksonville.

HOWARD KATZ:

We had the deal, and were getting ready to negotiate the long-form agreement. We sat there with a bunch of lawyers and said tactically, how should we approach this meeting since the fundamental issue was them [ESPN] understanding what they bought? And we started the meeting by saying to Mark, you understand what you bought now, right? It's the Sunday night cable package moved to Monday night. Mark said, "I know."

SANDY MONTAG, *Agent, IMG:*

So Madden is at *Monday Night Football* and has a great run there with Al Michaels. He loved working with Al. For him, as a coach, having Howard Cosell broadcast your game was the best. When John became a broadcaster, he probably didn't say it at the time, but in his heart, his career would not have been complete if he'd never gone to *Monday Night Football*. So he was thrilled. So then the world changes and NBC gets back in, and *Monday Night Football* goes to ESPN. And we're thinking, "Well, same company." Really we're thinking he'd just move over to ESPN and do *Monday Night* there.

I'm on vacation at Hilton Head in April, and I get a call from George Bodenheimer and Mark Shapiro. In addition to representing John Madden, I also represented Joe Theismann at the time, along with Fred Gaudelli and Drew Esocoff. They said to me, "Well, we have a decision to make. Which team do we pick for *Monday Night Football*? Do we take Mike Patrick, Joe Theismann, [Jay] Rothman, and [Chip] Dean, or do we take Al, John, Fred, and Drew?" And with all due respect to my friend Joe Theismann, I thought they were joking. Mark being one of my best friends, I just thought they were pulling my leg. Because look, Al and John? They're legendary. Then I quickly realized, these guys aren't joking. They really think that they have a decision to make.

So my next call was to John. In his mind he was somewhat surprised they hadn't already re-signed him, because at the time you knew that *Monday Night Football* would stay on ABC or go to ESPN. But they hadn't done that. So John asked me, "Did you talk to George?" "Yeah, I talked to George." "So, what's the timing here?" For a second there I thought maybe I shouldn't tell him, because maybe these guys will go to sleep, wake up, and say, "What were we thinking?! Forget about what we said yesterday." But I told him what I knew. I said, "I've got to tell ya, John, they told me they have a decision to make." And John says right away, "Well, that's the end of them."

You don't do that with John Madden. It's over. Done. When you stumble at the line with John Madden — when you show an ounce of weakness — the game is over.

JOHN MADDEN, *Announcer:*

George called me when I was in my truck driving with my son after a lunch. He told me ESPN had got *Monday Night Football,* and that I should hold tight, because they weren't sure what they were going to do about the booth. He said, "I'll get back to you." That's a call I remember.

It definitely shocked me. First, because when you look at the growth of pro football, there are three or four things that jump out at you: One was the

Giants–Baltimore Colts game, the second was the AFL–NFL merger, and the third was *Monday Night Football* bumping it up to another level. To me, ABC was such a big part of NFL football. It was the only game on that day, and there wouldn't be another game until the next Sunday. It was just something that ABC started and I thought it would always be there.

Then I found out the schedules were going to be reversed, that Monday night would be Sunday night and Sunday night would be Monday night, and that's when I decided I wasn't going to be stuck with the old Sunday night football schedule. Dick Ebersol called me and said, "I'll be out there tomorrow."

FRED GAUDELLI:
John was fuckin' pissed. It was the first time I ever heard him like that, man. He called me and said, "I got a call today from Bodenheimer, and he said they didn't know what they were going to do with their talent and production teams. He said they felt like they had two great teams." And he paused, and I said, "Yeah, and what do you think?" And he goes, "Forget them." Now, when George placed that call telling John he had two great production teams and didn't know what he was going to do, guess who was sitting in John's office? Dick Ebersol.

They actually said, "We have two great production teams, now what are we going to do?" That's like tomfoolery! That's like, you gotta be kidding me, man. You're talking about the greatest television analyst who ever lived, and may ever live, and you can't decide what you want to do?! I remember I got a call the day it was going down from George saying, "Hey, look, we're losing *Monday Night Football;* I just want you to know you always have a job at ESPN. I can't tell you what that job is going to be, but we're not going to let you go. You're going to be fine." He said, "I can't say that for everyone on your show, but you and Drew [my director] are going to be fine." Okay, great. So a month later I get another call from George and this time he says, "Hey, Fred, Mark and I are meeting with Al Michaels today, and we're going to tell him that you're not producing *Monday Night Football* after this year." I said, "All right." He then said, "Mark Shapiro will be in contact with you."

AL MICHAELS:
They'd given Mark the deed to the ranch in terms of production and he'd already determined that Jay Rothman and Chip Dean would be producing and directing *MNF.* George always felt uncomfortable dealing with anything that we would term the creative side. It was as if, if it had to do with content, with editorial, with production, he just acquiesced to Shapiro. "Capitulated" would be a better word. I always thought he should have given himself more credit.

MARK SHAPIRO:

This is a defining moment. ESPN, the biggest brand in sports unarguably, succeeds in getting the biggest property in sports. George walks into my office with one of those toy semi trucks with *Monday Night Football* on it and gives me a hug. So I have to think, "Who are we going to give this to?" To Jay, who's been toiling for, like, thirteen years as our guy, or are we going to go with Freddie, who was working over at ABC. When Freddie went over to ABC Sports, things changed. Fred was not an ESPN guy anymore. Fred became one of "them," the guys who frowned on the cable guys.

Sandy Montag called me and said, "You're making the wrong decision. Gaudelli is better than Rothman." And I know that was the general consensus, but I said, "Look, I think Jay's better. Al Michaels controls his guys. Jay tells it like it is. He would beat the shit out of Theismann. But even if their talents are even, maybe Freddie's a little better, maybe Jay's a little better, it's pretty much even. Okay? I'm going to go with the guy who's loyal."

FRED GAUDELLI:

Mark Shapiro called me and said, "I want to meet with you," and I said, "All right, fine." He made me come to a restaurant near his house at, like, seven in the morning on July 4, and he walks in and says,

"Look, you can have any job you want in this company other than *Monday Night Football*. Is there anything you really like?" But before I can answer, he asks, "How about management? Would you do management? Would you come in and would you run all of college sports?" I told him, "I'm not interested in management." Then he says, "How about if you come in and be the executive producer of NASCAR?" I said, "I have no affinity for that sport, and I don't want to acquire one." So he's, like, "All right, just give me one. Just tell me what it is." I said, "You know Mark, I don't really know, there's not a lot left. Maybe the NBA Finals would intrigue me, yes, how about the NBA Finals?" He said, "Argh, you can't have that job either." So I said, "Why not?" He said, "You know we got to be loyal to Eddie." Eddie is Ed Feibischoff, who had come from NBC a year and a half earlier.

I just looked at him. "Well, hold on, man, I spent twenty years at ESPN. I did every major show in the remote production department that ESPN had. So you're telling me that a guy who's been here less than three years—and you can't even put us in the same league as producers—and you're going to apply loyalty to him and not to me?" He said, "I'm sorry, I hired him." That's when I was just, like, "This is ridiculous." So then he started throwing out other jobs that I don't want to mention because these are jobs that my friends currently have. And I was, like, "Those guys are my friends. I can't just come in and take their job." And he's, like, "Oh, they won't mind. We'll just give them something else to do." I said, "No, no, no, they *will* mind." Then I said, "Maybe we should just table this conversation for now and have it again." Where I left it for me was, ESPN is going to be my last resort. I'm going to pursue every other job that I can possibly get, just knowing that ESPN is the fall-back, but I don't want to go back to ESPN because I don't want to work for this guy.

AL MICHAELS:

I don't want to say "stunned," but I was very disap-pointed when *Monday Night* was no longer going to be on ABC. At that point, there was never a question in my mind that if I wanted to remain on *Monday Night,* I'd be the guy.

It was upsetting when I was told by George that Jay Rothman was going to be the producer and not Fred Gaudelli because of "a loyalty factor." That's when I said to George, "I don't understand this. What do you mean by loyalty? Fred has been with the com-pany longer than Jay, and he went from *Sunday Night* to *Monday Night* at the behest of the company. Clearly that meant that Fred was the best man, because *Mon-day Night* is the crown jewel package." So I never understood what that "loyalty factor" was. I read that to mean that loyalty only extended to the ESPN brand, and when Fred went to ABC he was no longer an ESPN guy—even though they asked him to make the move and ESPN and ABC were both under the same umbrella.

I felt for Freddie. Fred Gaudelli had been their best guy, and they wouldn't have elevated him to *Monday Night Football* if they thought somebody else was better. And, by the way, nobody is. Freddie is the best producer I have ever worked with.

HOWARD KATZ:

Freddie Gaudelli is the best football producer on the planet. I respect a lot of other people's work, I just think Freddie's the best. So I was sort of surprised that Mark made the decision that he did. In Mark's mind, I think he was trying to be loyal to his guys. Well, you know, Freddie had been one of his guys too, so to that extent Freddie certainly got caught in the crossfire.

FRED GAUDELLI:

There is no loyalty in business; we all know that. But for me it was just the up-close and personal example that it really doesn't exist, it really doesn't. When I sat there and thought, "Okay, why is he choosing Jay over me?" and I'm just kind of making a checklist — you know, experience and all these different things — I mean, I don't want to make this about me and Jay, but there was no comparison. This was, like, crazy! John, Al, myself, and Drew had all done this for quite a while, and certainly Al and John had achieved a mega-status in their roles, and I'd been doing mine for a long time. Even Mark had said publicly more than a few times that I had set the standard for football production. He was quoted on that from the producers' standpoint in various places. So I knew what it was about.

I was not jumping onto the Kool-Aid wagon. Mark Shapiro ran a dictatorship, and ESPN still suffers from it today.

NORBY WILLIAMSON:

There were people here who haven't been around that long, and they thought of Freddie as an ABC guy. No, that's wrong. He's part of the fabric of this place. He helped build this place. That was a tough one, a really tough one. And that's what happens sometimes. We have a spoil of riches. We have a lot of talented people. That was a high-profile decision with two high-profile unbelievably talented people. There are a lot of people here vying for positions who are unbelievably talented. That's the thing about this place.

SANDY MONTAG:

I called Dick Ebersol. John had hosted *Saturday Night Live* when Dick was there, and they had known each other since then. I also called Sean McManus, who's been a good friend of mine. I told them, "I really don't want to put you in a three-man booth, but if it were a three-man booth at CBS with Nance and Simms, that one might work." John loved Phil Simms. I basically felt I could have done a deal with either place, to be honest with you.

Dick Ebersol can be as charming as anyone in our business. You don't want to say that John Madden fell in love, but the passion that Dick has for production and the passion that John has, it's almost like two light bulbs went off and they'd invented something. So then I get a call from Al Michaels. During the season. That would be fall '04. And he says, "You know what? I want to stay with John. I want to get out of my contract, and I think you're the only person who can get me out of it because of your relationships." I said, "Really? Okay." So first I thought, "Well, I have to see if Dick wants Al Michaels. He may not." I have a whole diary I kept during that time. My wife said, "Sandy, you're having these calls every day, which are mind-boggling. Write everything down." So Dick and I talked, and because we can trust each other, he says, "Are you serious?" And I said, "If I can get him out, and I don't know how, but if I *can* get him out, would you take Al Michaels?" And he said, "Well, I have Collinsworth, but how can I not take Al Michaels?"

At some point in late spring, Mark came back and said, "Well, we're not 100 percent sure with our decision. We may want to keep John." At that point I said, "The ship sailed."

But I still had a Fred Gaudelli problem because he was out of a job. Now during this time, Dick and I became very, very close. We had a lot in common, we spent a lot of time together, and I became a confidant of his in a lot of different areas. So at some point I said, "I want you to do me a favor, and after that, if you don't like it, I'll drop it. I want to go to *Monday Night Football* with you, and I want you to see Fred Gaudelli in action." So Dick and I fly to a game in Baltimore in fall '04. Very quietly I get us credentials. Not a lot of fanfare. Freddie knew we were coming. I said, "After the game starts, at some point, just so you know, I'm going to come into the truck with Dick. We're going to stand in the back. Pay no attention." So we do that—and Dick has been in more trucks than anyone in our business—and within ten minutes he turns to me and goes, "This is like watching the frickin' ballet." Meaning how they work together. If you ever see a sport production truck that's in sync, it's this truck. That just the way it is. So he says, "Tell Fred to meet us in the suite after." We go back to the Harbor Court Hotel to Dick's suite, and Dick tells Fred, "Congratulations. You're the new producer of *Sunday Night Football* next season."

FRED GAUDELLI:

Dick came to a Monday night game in December, and he sat in the truck and watched me produce for the first half. At half time, he said to me, "Hey, I'll talk to you later." Then my agent, Sandy, called me after the game and said I should go up to his room after the game. Dick offered me the job and I accepted it. Then he goes, "And let's go downstairs and talk to your play-by-play man." So we go downstairs to the bar, and the whole crew is there. I pretty much tell them I'm going to NBC, and then Dick cozies up to Al and proceeds to have, like, an hour conversation. So now John's going, Drew's going, I'm going, and now I think Al starts to really question what he's going to do, because his entire team is moving over to NBC without him.

SANDY MONTAG:

Clearly Mark was making the decisions then. Mark had as much power at ESPN as any number two there, ever. Even now. That's just Mark Shapiro. He made every major and minor production and talent decision.

AL MICHAELS:

Within twenty-four hours of NBC getting Sunday nights, I knew Dick Ebersol had already told John how much he wanted him to come to *Sunday Night* and pretty much be the centerpiece of the package. It also became very clear to me that Ebersol wanted me to come to NBC as well, if there was a deal to be made, and he said just that in a conference call in June when they announced that John Madden was joining NBC.

As it turned out, we couldn't come to an agreement. I was willing to take less money to go to NBC, but the gap between what I was making at ABC and what NBC was offering then was just too wide. So I agreed to sign with ESPN for Monday night.

When it became obvious that Gaudelli and Esocoff were going to NBC, there were a lot of sleepless nights, for me. I had met with Jay Rothman—he'd flown out here a couple of times—but John had made it clear he wanted me to be his partner at NBC, and when Esocoff and then Gaudelli joined him, they wanted it as well. I had no faith in what would be the new *Monday Night* schedule, but more importantly, I was without John, Freddie, and Drew. I knew in my heart that at that point in my life and my career, to start over with a completely different group of colleagues was not something I was going to be comfortable with, so at that point, my lawyer, Sam Fisher, and I asked ESPN for permission to negotiate with NBC.

SANDY MONTAG:

I went to George and asked, "Will you let Al Michaels out of his contract?" Al had one year left, and George said, "I don't know," because at that time it was going to be Michaels and Theismann in their booth. At the Super Bowl in '04, I remember being with George and going to the booth after the game and having an awkward moment with George and

Al. George wanted to hear it from Al directly. "Do you want out of your contract?" and Al said yes. Bob Iger had a good relationship with Al and said, "Okay, George, go ahead."

From what I understand, the precursor to Mickey Mouse is a character called Oswald the Lucky Rabbit. It was an initial drawing, which was before Mickey Mouse, which the Disney family knew about. For some reason, it went to Universal Studios, and no one knew this, but NBC Universal owned the rights. George says to me at the time, "I'm going to give you a list of six things that we want. If Dick agrees to all six, we will let Al out of his contract." The first thing he says is, "We want the rights to Oswald the Lucky Rabbit." I go, "I can't believe George Bodenheimer is making a joke at a time like this." I'm up in my office and I googled "Oswald the Lucky Rabbit." A mouse — a rabbit-y mouse — comes up, and I go, "Holy shit. Universal owns this character?" And the grandkids to Walt Disney knew that for years and wanted the rights back. Bob Iger knows this and says, essentially, "I'm going to deliver this back to the Disney family." So that's number one. I'm, like, "Unbelievable." And then there's a list of, like, five other things, like insular rights on something, some web thing, some US Open promo, whatever.

So then I call Dick, and he says, "So you have the list?" "Yup." So I said, "First one, they want the rights to *Oswald the Lucky Rabbit*."

Now Dick Ebersol in his infinite wisdom knows *Oswald the Lucky Rabbit*. So he called Ron Myer, head of Universal Studios. "What are you doing with this rabbit? Anything?" "No problem with the rabbit." Then we worked the trade out.

AL MICHAELS:

I looked around and realized that I was one of the last guys standing from an ABC Sports operation that had basically been told to move on. There was a scarlet letter put on anyone who had been at ABC, with Freddie being Exhibit A.

To their credit, ESPN understood how unhappy I was and allowed me to go back again and see if an agreement could be reached with NBC. This time it worked. I wound up asking to get out of my contract with ESPN to sign for less money with NBC, even though I knew it was probably going to cost me the NBA—which it did. No matter. That decision was one of the best of my entire career.

JED DRAKE:

Freddie left here to do *Monday Night Football*, and Jay had been here doing *Sunday Night Football*. So Jay was on staff and deserving of the position and was given it. It's that simple.

Freddie is a great football producer. And by that I mean that he produces the game very, very well. Where we like to take our productions is to not just limit it to the game, but to bring in, when appropriate—and that's the key thing, that's the art of producing, *when appropriate*—other elements that may be germane to that game, that telecast, ultimately, to the viewers. We might think that the story needs a discussion point—whereas Freddie is going to stick to the game, the game, and nothing but the game. Which is okay. That's fine. It's a different presentation. And you can absolutely be certain that that view is the view of Al Michaels and then John Madden, and Freddie and Drew. Tony Kornheiser was the biggest personification of the very difference in philosophy that I just suggested.

FRED GAUDELLI:

At the end of the day, if I'd gotten the Monday night job, we would have been in constant conflict. Because in my opinion—having done football for twenty years—that's not the way you set up an NFL telecast. To call it a platform for something larger is just wrong. That's looking at it from the wrong perspective. You just paid all this money for this product. You can do things around it and use it to make your network better, as Dick has done with Sunday night. But you don't stop producing around the game. That just shows your inexperience and lets people know you don't know what you're doing.

Think about if ESPN goes the other way, okay? If it's Al and John and Drew and me on *Monday Night*

Football. Number one, they'd probably get better games because the league's going to want to give Madden better games, and they don't have to go through three years of fighting off the critics about all the shit in the booth. That show has been in total flux from the beginning because they didn't make the easy decision, and they made a bunch of wrong ones. The announcers—Tirico, Jaworski, Kornheiser are terrible; they're terrible. They're nowhere near Nantz and Simms, or fuckin' Aikman, let alone Michaels and Madden.

TONY KORNHEISER:

Fred Gaudelli has gone out of his way to say mean things about me. We met once in our life for ten seconds in Tampa or Orlando before the whole thing started. He is quoted saying that I'm a "rinky-dink bullshit guy," and that I've ruined the telecast. He got a better job. Why's he attacking me? I'm fine with Jay. I have problems with Jay because Jay is sort of like a Dalmatian in the firehouse, when the bell rings, it doesn't matter what's said, it's going to be this particular way, but we talk, and I love him.

FRED GAUDELLI:

We had this great synergy amongst the four of us. Each of us knew what the other was thinking, when they were thinking, and what the other required. It just made for enjoyable and productive work. And that meant that we could function at a really high level. I remember when John joined the show, people said to me, "Oh, my God, you're going to get Al and John, it's going to be a nightmare." Nightmare? It was the easiest time I ever had. I had the two best guys who had ever done it, and all they cared about was getting it right.

DICK EBERSOL:
Freddie was the producer from '01 to '05 for the last years ABC had Monday nights, and Drew was the director. They were both available to me for reasons I will never understand. Those two guys were born at ESPN, rose all the way through the ranks, then they were told, in front of the entire industry, that they didn't get the job producing this billion-point-one property because the other guys were the loyal guys who had stayed with ESPN. But you fucking made the decision to take them from ESPN to ABC!

Now, I thank you immensely, I'm the luckiest guy in the world. Freddie and Drew are the two best hires I've ever had in my sporting life as a producer and director—their skills and their temperament and their ability to teach young people are unparalleled. Freddie told me Mark said, "These guys who stay here are really the loyal ones." What kind of system develops that kind of fucked-up logic? Mark, by the way, made the decision and left two months later. He wouldn't have been able to control Freddie and Drew.

MARK SHAPIRO:

When I first took the reins of programming and production, I saw two divisions that were lacking leadership. They lacked risk takers and decisive decision-making. Communication was weak, and in such a big place, that led to morale issues. We worked very hard to change dialogue and feedback—in both directions.

Employees needed to not just understand my vision, I also wanted them to fully appreciate their role inside of the journey to reach that vision. Toward that end, I felt it was my duty to inspire, push, and reward. But I was also committed to listening to them, and being open to their ideas. I took great pride in holding town meetings so I could listen directly to as many of them as possible, and I spent a lot of time on the road going to events and meeting crews to make sure everybody felt a part of it all, and they had a personal connection with me. This was the culture I felt I had to create in order to move this massive organization forward.

DAVID BERSON:

We were in the middle of a big run of programming acquisitions and knew we had to pass on some.

We played close attention to where these properties would go. NFL rights ultimately went to NFL Network, PGA Tour to the Golf Channel, NHL to Versus, MLB's second cable package to Turner, just to name a few. It played out very well for us, as they were scattered across several networks. And in the interim we acquired or re-upped NASCAR, World Cup, NBA, Big Ten, SEC, US Open [golf and tennis], BCS, and others.

GEORGE McNEILLY, *Senior Director of Communications:*

There was an incredible amount of excitement when we announced NASCAR would be returning. The sport and the network had truly missed one another, and we were prepared to devote unprecedented amounts of people and technology to the effort. NASCAR was great to us as well, offering access to the drivers and crews that was second to none. A lot of people have talked about how NASCAR and ESPN grew up together, but they had been away from each other for the previous six years, and during that time, ESPN had become more determined than ever to cover not just events but news from the sports world. And that went for rights holders too. After the deal was announced, I vividly remember telling NASCAR's longtime head of corporate communications, Jim Hunter, that he should be careful what he wishes for, because the network would not play favorites with the league in terms of news gathering. And that's exactly what happened. ESPN covered all parts of the NASCAR world, from attendance drops to suspensions and civil suits. No other sports network was as comprehensive.

CARL EDWARDS:

When they first said they were going to have an in-car reporter, they asked, would I be interested in doing that, and I thought, man, that's a great idea. If a fan likes to watch, I love when they talk to drivers in the car, and so ESPN said, "Hey, we're going to take this idea to a new level and have an official in-car, in-race reporter. And so I was on board for that along with Dale [Jr.] There was definitely some nervousness over the idea, but I wound up having a good time doing it, and Rusty [Wallace] and some of the on-air guys did as well.

FRED GAUDELLI:

ESPN had always been a place where you could have productive discourse. That's what made the place—that people were free to disagree, free to argue, and free to make your point, but at the end of the day, whoever was in charge when they made the decision, everybody got on board. That was just the way it was. That was not the way Mark Shapiro operated.

Mark Shapiro left ESPN in October 2005 and went to work for Washington Redskins owner Daniel Snyder and his Six Flags amusement parks. His salary jump was one of the broadest on record: he'd been making $425,000 at ESPN ("What a joke," he recalls) and Snyder gave him a base salary of $4 million plus benefits. Oh, there was also a signing bonus: $10 million.

Those who'd regarded Shapiro as a ruthless boss would have this bit of reality to consider: no fewer than sixteen ESPN employees would follow him to Six Flags.

AL MICHAELS:

There was a running gag among the *Monday Night Football* crew that there should have been bumper stickers made saying, "Honk if you haven't been told by Shapiro that he's getting ten million dollars from Snyder."

MARK SHAPIRO:

When I look back on my final year, it's with a great sense of satisfaction and accomplishment. I had surrounded myself with an extraordinary team, and we secured ESPN's position in the marketplace, with the sports fan, and in the industry for years to come. I was so proud. I had worked relentlessly and sacrificed an unbelievable amount of time with my family to accomplish all this.

And then an odd thing happened: some people wanted to just stamp me with the original entertainment label, like that was the headline of my legacy. In a way, I could see how this might have happened, since the shows my regime created, like *PTI, Around the Horn, Rome Is Burning, OTL Daily*, were such huge hits for the network.

But to characterize it as just entertainment was so wrong. It was the combination of all that incredible development plus the right stick-and-ball properties that gave ESPN brand dominance in the sports world. No one can rewrite that history, and all they have to do is look at what we did. We moved the biggest game in sports, *Monday Night Football*, to ESPN. We extended our Major League Baseball contract for another seven years, and we brought NASCAR back to ESPN. Add to that, three of the four tennis grand slams, the Belmont and Breeders Cup. We gave birth to the poker craze with the *World Series of Poker*, and we capitalized on the television reality craze with the hit series *Dream Job*. And *Mike & Mike* exploded on the radio. The greatest digital facility in the world opened on our campus, and we launched both HD channels and ESPN Deportes. ESPN2 had serious traction; ESPN Classic was now in over seventy million homes. We had also invested in our journalistic enterprise and had the deepest, most authoritative reporting organization in sports. We were honored with the company's first two Peabody Awards. And perhaps most importantly, I had to look back at my mandate upon being hired—improve ratings—and in my final two years, they were on fire: eight straight quarters of growth.

So when the offer came in from Dan Snyder, I believed ESPN was now going to be in the driver's seat with or without me. I looked out at the next three years and really viewed them as maintenance years. Surely ESPN would grow, but not at the speed I had been accustomed to driving. Disney would be more conservative with ESPN, digest the enormous profitability, while they invested in other areas and looked to cut costs. This was the right window for me.

I felt I had accomplished all that I had been charged to do. I was in search of a new challenge. Something more entrepreneurial. Another platform to turn around, fix, and grow.

Look, did we make some mistakes? Of course, who doesn't? Do I have any regrets? Absolutely not.

Once Shapiro decided to leave for his next challenge and its $10 million signing bonus, he began a series of talks with Bodenheimer about succession plans for ESPN. Shapiro's choice was Tony Petitti, then the number-two man at CBS Sports under Sean McManus. Shapiro believed Petitti's prior history at ABC would mitigate any outsider status working against him, and that a breath of "outside air" might actually do the company good. Bodenheimer gave Shapiro the okay to make a play for Petitti, but McManus got wind of it and hur-

riedly notified CBS boss Les Moonves, who made a counteroffer that Petitti couldn't refuse. It marked the second time that CBS had to defend its borders against big-game hunters: Shapiro's first choice for the Monday Night Football *booth had been Jim Nance, but CBS had Nance's two great loves — the Masters and the NCAA basketball tournament. He was going nowhere.*

With Petitti out of the running, Shapiro was "forced to look inward," and suggested to Bodenheimer that John Skipper be given the title of editor in chief, with Jed Drake and Norby Williamson reporting to him. The title fit Skipper's publishing background, Shapiro thought, but it made Bodenheimer uncomfortable; it didn't sound like television to him. Norby, meanwhile, made his attempt to oversee production, but Bodenheimer nixed that idea. With no clear heirs apparent, ESPN's organizational chart was suddenly in treacherous flux.

JOHN SKIPPER:

When Mark Shapiro resigned, I called George within hours and asked if I could speak with him about the job. I think it was on a Friday morning. George said sure — in fact, he said, why don't we go out for a little boat ride tomorrow and discuss? Now, George is not a fancy guy. He has a boat, but it is just a little fishing boat.

So Saturday comes and I am more than a little

nervous. First off, I am not a fisherman or a boat guy despite being a Skipper. We meet, head out into the Long Island Sound, and aren't out of the harbor before I say, "George, I want you to consider me for Mark's job." He expressed surprise, and maybe what he meant was it was surprising to hear a guy who had not a lick of experience in television ask for a job producing and programming television.

He asked me what my thoughts were about the job and may have been surprised again to see me pull out a wad of yellow legal pages with my prepared thoughts about what I would do. I had spent the night before on the phone with John Walsh coming up with all of it. I had had significant differences of opinion about the direction we were headed with our programming, so it was not a chore to come up with a plan.

When we returned to the dock, George, who is a close-to-the-vest guy, gave me no clue as to whether he liked it or not but simply suggested that he would think about it.

I do suspect that at some point he turned to John Walsh and asked, "What do you think? Can he really do this?" Of course, John was invested in saying yes. And remember, John and I had been partners already in launching the magazine and in running ESPN.com.

However it happened, it is a great job and a fun job. And I think it has mostly worked out.

GEORGE BODENHEIMER:

I felt like I had an executive in John Skipper with great untapped potential. I thought that with John's creativity and business acumen he could quickly learn what he needed to prosper in that position. And I feel like ESPN has the culture where you can plug somebody into a spot who may not on a piece of paper have all the experience that you might call for from central casting if you were asking for a head of all content. But he has—we had—still do today—a tremendous executive team underneath that position.

When rights to the 2010 World Cup became available and preliminary discussions began between ESPN and FIFA, global soccer's governing body, observers saw nothing like the Mark Shapiro whose triumphant rampages of determination had landed rights to the NBA, Wimbledon, and other big events. Seemingly apathetic (for him), Shapiro clearly wasn't of like mind when it came to soccer.

With ESPN holding back from the bidding war, it wasn't surprising that Gary Zenkel, Dick Ebersol's number two at NBC Sports, was able to secure a handshake deal for the rights, reflecting the lack of enthusiasm by other networks. But then something happened: Chuck Blazer, the only U.S. citizen ever to serve on the FIFA executive committee, went into a tirade, denouncing the NBC deal to the board and claiming it could mean the death of soccer in the United States.

For every person who thought Blazer sincerely believed that NBC lacked sufficient commitment to the sport, several others saw a different explanation. At that time, Shapiro was "suspected" of having accepted an offer for a new executive position from sports magnate Daniel Snyder, and rumors flew that the soccer-loving Skipper might soon be moving into Shapiro's old office. Indeed, at that very moment, Skipper was making the World Cup one of the central items in his pitch to Bodenheimer for the top job.

Despite the fact that FIFA's finance committee had approved the deal—which traditionally led to semi-automatic acceptance from the full board—the board suddenly balked and voted to table the NBC deal. NBC's delegation was not even present for the board vote because FIFA executive Jerome Valke had told them not to bother, that approval was mere formality. Naturally, the NBC troop was more than aghast at the board's about-face. But again they were cautioned not to worry; the deal would be theirs after a two-month delay.

Within forty-eight hours of getting his new job as executive vice president for content—and with Bodenheimer's blessing—Skipper was on a plane to Switzerland, accompanied by programming executive Leah LaPlaca and house attorney Eric Kemmler. Their mission: a full-tilt campaign to nab the 2010 World Cup rights for ESPN.

Skipper and his fellow executives were aware of the extensive talks between NBC and FIFA and knew the two sides might even have worked out an agreement, but Skipper was undaunted, determined to snatch the tournament away. Fortunately for him, FIFA members knew of Skipper's love for soccer and were gratified to have him on board. And a fight for the U.S. rights would only drive the price up.

Meanwhile, Ebersol, Zenkel, and the whole NBC network were waiting for word from the board, not knowing that for six of those eight weeks of delay, some board members were quietly meeting with Skipper.

Skipper pulled out all the stops and offered $100 million from ESPN and another $345 million from Telemundo's prosperous chief competitor, Univision. Promises made to FIFA included televising every game in high-definition, whether on ESPN or ABC, with many games also streamed live on the Internet. In addition, twenty-five matches would air on ESPN's new poke-in-the-eye 3-D channel, even though few Americans were technologically equipped to watch them that way.

It didn't seem to matter that NBC had offered the same distribution arrangements as ESPN, or that the network went as high as $325 million with Telemundo. FIFA never asked NBC to match ESPN's offer. NBC had made its bid thinking this was a one-on-one situation.

The FIFA board was elated and delighted with the ESPN proposal. Now all that remained was to break the bad news to NBC: ESPN had won the rights to the 19th World Cup games in 2010. "You've lost," said a FIFA functionary in a call to NBC Sports. But NBC wanted to know, "Where did ESPN come from?" and to register a hardly surprising gripe: "You told us we had it. We were just waiting for the board to meet again."

Naturally, it was great news for John Skipper—but with the rights came a new array of pressures and stresses. Would he learn, after all the wrangling and scheming, that ESPN was overreaching, that it really didn't have the resources for such a colossal project? Skipper knew that the network's reputation would be on the line with this most immense of all its undertakings so far—and so would his.

JOHN SKIPPER:

I fell in love with soccer back around 2001–2002 when, as a fairly small assignment, I had some responsibilities relative to [ESPN-owned] Soccernet in the U.K., and I took half a dozen trips to the U.K., started going to games with the guys who run Soccernet, and fell in love with the game. Then I started spending a lot of time watching it, including watching the World Cup in 2002, and loved the spectacle of it.

I got this position in 2005 literally the week that the rights for the World Cup were sort of tipping away from us. We had never bought the rights of the World Cup; we had sublicensed them from SUM [Soccer United Marketing], which is the marketing arm of Major League Soccer. NBC and Telemundo had decided that they wanted to buy the World Cup, made a bid, which was sort of approved by the board or not approved by the board. NBC and Telemundo were not interested in Major League Soccer, and they had cut out Univision, which had been the broadcaster for Spanish-language rights in the U.S. They had also gone around Comcast. So there were a number of constituencies that were not pleased that there was a potential deal which was between FIFA, NBC, and Telemundo. I got the job and asked George—even before I got the job—for permission. "I realize we could all be wrong, and it's been a long time coming, but I'm gonna be the latest guy to tell you, George, that soccer is actually going to happen in this country. It's a world sport. The demography of this country is changing. The rest of the world can't be wrong. And it's gonna come. And it's gonna come down from World Cup to our national team to our domestic team."

At the time, I did not understand how important international soccer could be in that equation. So it's actually turned out to be World Cup, international soccer, European Cup, Champions League, Barclays Premier League, national team, and Major League Soccer—all those things.

I'll tell you it was $108 million. I mean, I told Don [Garber, Major League Soccer's Commissioner], "Look, I'm committed to doing something with the MLS,

I understand if I'm going to do this overall soccer plan, it will include your league." And Don trusted me that I would do something with him. He said, "I'm going to lend you a certain amount of support"—which wasn't going to be official, since Don didn't have a vote, but he certainly made it clear that he wanted soccer to be a growing sport in the United States. Here they had an alternative that would support the national team, would support the domestic league. I didn't have the international piece at all in line at that point.

Skipper may have been playing offense when it came to soccer, but he needed to be on the defensive when it came to the network's NFL talent. Having surgically removed John Madden from the ABC/ESPN ranks, Dick Ebersol turned to the next item on his wish list: a top-notch sideline reporter for NBC's upcoming Sunday night NFL games. His first choice happened also to be at ESPN— Andrea Kremer, commonly regarded in Bristol as one of the best reporters at the network, if also high on the high-strung list.

Ebersol put in a call to Kremer's agent, Sandy Montag, and asked him to make it happen. Montag, never out of the loop, knew that Mark Shapiro was making plans to leave ESPN, and what better time to ask Shapiro for a gentlemanly farewell favor—let Montag talk to Ebersol outside the exclusive negotiating window.

Shapiro even told Bodenheimer that he was going to let Ebersol talk to him.

Shapiro had said yes, basing his decision not just on his regard for Montag, but also on his respect and fondness for Kremer. He figured out NBC would be offering Kremer assignments that ESPN would never be able to match, including work at the next Olympics, something at which Shapiro knew she would excel. Montag delivered the good news to Ebersol, and Kremer agreed to go to NBC for the next six years at $400,000 a year, a contract worth $2.4 million, which seemed like a bonanza at the time. All was well with the world.

Or seemed to be—until John Skipper took over from Shapiro. By the time Skipper finished securing the rights to the upcoming World Cup competition for ESPN, he was more than merely peeved to learn that Kremer, whom he considered one of his resident superstars, was all set to leave for NBC. Skipper turned to John Walsh, then making a dramatic return from the equivalent of a banishment to Siberia during the Shapiro years and enjoying new status as a minister (without portfolio) in the Skipper regime.

Both were appalled at the thought of losing Kremer and launched an intense campaign to keep her. Skipper flew to Los Angeles and began wooing her—with compliments (on her first-rate NFL reportage); with the lure of glamorous gigs (major roles on Sunday's NFL Countdown, Monday Night Football, *Super Bowl coverage,* *plus hosting duties on a new weekly magazine show); and, oh yeah, with money. And more money. As much as $700,000 per year.*

However tempting and however generous the offer, Montag advised Kremer to turn it down. For one thing—one very important thing—he did not want to betray or alienate Ebersol, the man who'd just signed Montag's star client, John Madden, to a fabulous deal of his own.

ANDREA KREMER:

I did not leave ESPN for more money. That's almost comical—ESPN ended up offering me a lot more money than NBC—and the reasons that I chose to go to NBC were threefold. First, I'd never worked full-time in remote production. I had the opportunity to work on the top-rated show on the network, to do a prime-time broadcast with Al Michaels and John Madden, and to work first and foremost with Dick Ebersol, who to my mind is the top sports producer in the business. To work with him is something I always wanted. That's all number one. Number two, I'd never worked an Olympics before. And, finally, I had the opportunity to work with [HBO's] *Real Sports,* which enabled me to tell stories, and that's what I built my career on. So after seventeen years in one place, I would get to do something new. You have to understand, I was very content at ESPN. I was not looking to leave. I never solicited anything.

MARK SHAPIRO:

Some people get away, you lose 'em, okay. But some people you can't lose. And there's very few of those at ESPN. I would never have let Andrea get away. She is the best reporter, the best correspondent, we had. Andrea would have never left if I had stayed; not in a million years would I have ever let her get away. She never would have wanted to leave. But this was just before I left there myself. So she calls me as a friend: "I need your advice. ESPN blah, blah, blah. NBC this and that." She said, "The money's going to be more at NBC, but I think I can push this." Sandy called me, you know, "What do you think?" I said, "She's a huge asset. If they lose her, that's their fault. But you're asking me now outside of ESPN — I'm not wearing my ESPN hat now — what I think she should do." Andrea really trusted me. That's why they were calling me. And I said, "Not even a contest."

When she went to NBC, she told me, "I have you to thank." It's the only time I know that anybody over at ESPN got mad at me about anything I did, because I really stayed away. I was told that a lot of people said my fingerprints were on it, and what a jerk I was to let her move out of there. But she was asking me as a friend, and I felt like I couldn't lie to her. "You're going to get to work the Olympics and do *Sunday Night Football*. And your work load will be 20 percent what it was at ESPN. And they're going to pay you just as much, if not more? Get out of there!" And she went.

"What is it about you?" David Letterman asked Keith Olbermann on a 2007 Late Show *broadcast. "You seem to burn bridges wherever you leave." To which Olbermann replied, "I don't burn bridges, I burn rivers. If you burn a bridge, you can possibly build a new bridge, but if there's no river anymore, that's a lot of trouble."*

Back in Bristol, Mike Soltys, vice president for communications, remarked, "Keith Olbermann doesn't burn bridges; he napalms them."

Olbermann did come back to the wonderful world of ESPN, but ESPN executives were damned if they'd embrace him without caveats and qualifiers. Bloggers reported, and Olbermann confirmed to Letterman, that although Olbermann did return to the empire in 2005 via ESPN Radio, cohosting an hour-long segment of the Dan Patrick Show *with his old* SportsCenter *cohort, ESPN issued a warning that under no circumstances was Olbermann permitted to set foot on the Bristol campus. They didn't say security guards would shoot him on sight but came just short of that.*

For Olbermann, being banned from Bristol was probably not a devastating blow. He was never fond of the facility or the town in the first place. Besides, Pat-

rick's radio show originated at ABC studios in New York City—and even ESPN muckety-mucks were powerless to ban him from there.

KEITH OLBERMANN:

Dan first managed to talk a few in management into having me contribute once a week to the radio show. He'd wanted us to do radio together since 1992 and used to negotiate with Walsh in hopes of getting us our own show and then lessen the *SportsCenter* schedule—even though I didn't want to do it.

Late in '05, I guess, we went from once a week to an hour a day, and of course I loved it. We were much, much better on the radio than on TV, though it's tougher to be psychic on TV. In any event, there was talk at this time, I guess from Shapiro, of moving the 6:00 p.m. *SportsCenter* to New York, possibly to the ESPN Zone restaurant, and of moving the 2:00 a.m. to L.A. Dan's pitch was to bring me back to co-anchor with him, and Shapiro seemed warm to it. This is in the pre–Special Comment era, and I had no idea where things would be going at MSNBC, and I thought, "What a great solution." Just like the Sundays-only idea in '97—they'd never have to deal with me in person, nor I with them, and it was so much fun to work with Dan again.

Then Shapiro left and Bodenheimer was still pissed at something I'd said about him when they'd hired that overmatched ex-Fox reporter to work the sidelines (namely that he should've been led away in handcuffs), and the idea died.

"Reality TV" has been called one of the most egregious misnomers in television history — it's TV, all right, but is it reality? — and yet, when it became the rage, especially on cable channels, early in the twenty-first century, ESPN decided it had to get in there and snare a piece of the action. But whose reality would it be? Came the answer: Barry Bonds, the elusive and outspoken slugger who was expected to break both Babe Ruth's and Hank Aaron's career home-run records in the summer of 2006.

What better time to follow Bonds around with cameras and strap a microphone pack to his back? Whatever Bonds was seen doing in the show, it was bound to seem at least interesting, maybe fascinating, to the fans at home. There was one little problem, however: Barry and his representatives wanted the subject of steroid use avoided, which was a pretty big request considering it had been all over the papers, as well as on TV and radio, for months. Steroids were, in fact, considered potentially responsible for Bonds's hitting seventy-three home runs in 2001 and bulking up in 2003.

Steroid use in baseball proved to be the show's proverbial elephant in the room — or eight-hundred-pound gorilla, if you like — and it was going to be awfully hard to shoot around it. The series premiered on April 4, 2006, and by June, relations between the producers

(Mike Tollin and Brian Robbins) and Bonds's agents and lawyers—and Bonds—were so bad that the final show was yanked from the schedule and never aired.

But then, relations weren't the only things that were bad. So were the ratings. ESPN wasn't exactly risking a huge public outcry when it canceled the series and called it a day.

JOHN SKIPPER:

There are people who've been up there for twenty-eight years who still think, "It's the little company that can, we're up here in Bristol, middle of nowhere, we're the underdog." It's the classic mentality that created the place. The most typical experience I've had, and John along with me in this, was the Barry Bonds thing, where we contracted with a filmmaker named Mike Tollin to do a reality series in which he would follow Barry Bonds around.

MIKE TOLLIN, *Producer:*

I wasn't close with Barry, but it was a nice relationship and we knew each other a little bit.

Barry's injured, but he comes back the last month and hits like eight homers to get within like eight of Babe Ruth's record. He gets to 706 or 708. And it's like, wow, Barry was hurt but Barry's still got it, and next year's going to be amazing; all the eyes of the sporting world are going to be on Barry. And so Rachael [Vizcarra, Bond's PR person] called me out of the blue and asked to have lunch and sat down and said, "We want to know if you'd be interested in doing for Barry what you did for Hank." That's where it started. What does that mean? "Do a documentary which shows the other dimensions of Barry Bonds and introduces a Barry Bonds to the world that nobody ever sees because all anybody thinks of is this Barry Bonds, this surly, arrogant, aloof home-run hitter, steroids abuser. Right?" So I said, "I'm thinking, Barry Bonds is not Hank Aaron. So that's a tall order. But I'm interested because I'm a filmmaker, I'm a sports lover. I'm really a documentarian at heart. And what could be a greater challenge?" People for the next year would come up to me and say, "What *were* you thinking?" That's what I was thinking. I'm thinking this is a really interesting challenge and I don't know what's there.

But the first thing we do is that Barry and I sit down to discuss what his expectations would be and what sort of—the level to which I'd have free rein, and what kinds of control—I mean, yes. The point I was trying to make was that I'm intrigued but I'm skeptical, and it's all going to depend on the dynamic between Barry and me. So it wasn't really necessary to discuss it with Rachael. It was important to discuss it with Barry. Right? He's the one that's either giving me the keys to the kingdom or not.

If you're a celebrity and you're shy, it's perceived as arrogance, aloofness, or superiority. But what I found was a guy who was almost desperate to come out of the shell and reintroduce himself to the world, which is what, as a filmmaker, you would hope. The discussion didn't really take place on a pragmatic level, like, "Do we do this?" or "What limitations would be imposed?" or "What are the expectations?" It was really Barry telling his story. It's almost like he was auditioning for me.

So I'm thinking, with Barry, there are a lot of surprises, and there are going to be a lot of discoveries for an audience to make, and so I'm intrigued. At which point I started talking to ESPN.

A documentary, first of all, is one film. You have the opportunity to collect material, spend the time necessary to massage it, nurture it, and shape it, and the ability to reflect and really live with the material and essentially write the script in the edit room — to tell a story that will stand on its own. A reality series, by definition, or by convention at this point, is following reality as it unfolds and spitting it out immediately.

But I'm sort of passionate about telling this story and, as we were getting closer and as Barry was proving to be very agreeable every step of the way, I got excited about the challenge as a filmmaker. And now ESPN's putting a whole other kind of deal on the table, a seven-figure deal for multiple episodes. It's pretty lucrative, and I start lining up all the things that I would need.

There was reluctance everywhere, and incredulity, like, "What are you doing?" and "Are you sure you want to do this?" and "Are you *crazy?*"

But it was going pretty well in spring training, and I really was getting the access. An excerpted *Game of Shadows* came out. And everything kind of changed.

PEDRO GOMEZ, *Reporter:*

If you remember Barry Bonds's first day of spring training, he tended to have a press conference — kind of a "state of the Bonds," so to speak, and this was the infamous day when he walked in and called every reporter a liar. "All y'all are lying." He walked by, and I'm sitting there on the aisle, and I'd covered Bonds in the past because I'd been a baseball beat writer and I worked in the Bay Area, so he definitely knew who I was, but we didn't have any big interaction at that point. I'm sitting on the edge right there, and he walks by and looks down at me and says, "You still lying, Gomez?" And he keeps walking up to the dais where he was going to sit at the table. That was the very first thing he said to me that spring. At that point he had no idea that I was going to be there every day.

And then the next morning, I approached him and said, "By the way, ESPN has given me this assignment where I am basically going to be here every day chronicling you." And he just said, "Okay, dude, whatever," and walked away. That was the season he was on the D.L. — the disabled list. If you remember, he had those three surgeries during spring training. The first one was simply to clean out some cartilage; he was supposed to be back within three to four weeks, but then he rushed himself. He tried to get back within two, and he ended up worsening his knee and had to have another surgery. And then his knee had gotten infected, so he had to have a third surgery before the end of spring training. And he was on the D.L. until either late August or early September. He didn't play until that time. It was one of those things where he might play in two weeks or he might play next week. So it was always this little—I don't want to say "cat and mouse," but there's always this expectation that he'd come off the list. Bristol said to stay with him every day. And it was a difficult season. I remember saying to Bristol, "Are you sure you want to do this? He's still on the D.L." Bristol said, "Yes, we still want to be there."

There were times when it was contentious. There were times when it was actually fairly good, but that's really the way Bonds is with a lot of people. His mood swings were legendary. Late in the season, when he had only been activated about a week, the Giants were at Dodger Stadium, and I asked him something in the postgame, and he looked at me and said "Pedro, dude. You've got issues." I had to really, really bite my tongue, because it was one of those things where you know how it is with a reporter, you don't want to become the story. So I didn't say anything back. I just said, "Okay, yeah, whatever." But I remember thinking to myself, "I have issues? Me? I have issues?! Have you ever looked in the mirror?"

JOHN SKIPPER:
It was widely reported that Barry Bonds had creative approval — not true. Widely reputed that Barry Bonds was getting paid — also not true.

JOHN WALSH:
Some of that stuff in that show was really, really good. Mike got him to take cameras into a warehouse in San Francisco and took him on a tour of the warehouse where Bonds has videotapes of every home run he's hit from like 380 on, and he has a storehouse of the socks he wore for each home run, the uniform he wore — they're all different. He has a whole warehouse of memorabilia. He took us on a tour of it. It was great.

If you really got to know him, you could see what he wanted to reveal, and the insecurity he had over it. I think that show had a shot to do something very special that no one else would do.

Anybody who knew Mike knew nobody was going to tell Mike what to show. Mike was a real diplomat, he knew how to figure things out, and in fact, the show wound up being killed because Bonds said, "You're going to have to do this," and Mike said, "I'm not doing it." And that's why the whole thing ended.

GEORGE SOLOMON, *Ombudsman:*

Barry Bonds had his own reality show when he was in the midst of the steroid controversy. And I criticized that a lot. That was awful. They did about six, and I had big problems with that; it would be the same thing if NBC in the last six months of the Bush administration did a reality show with Cheney. You know, you just wouldn't do it. They have an entertainment division, it was done by that group. They palmed it off on them. They've got a million subsidiaries, they can do whatever they want.

JOHN SKIPPER:

We endured a fair amount of criticism about: What are we doing in bed with this guy whom we also have to cover? If that came up at CBS and CBS was doing a reality series about Barry Bonds, nobody would say, "Gee, you can't do a reality series about Barry Bonds because CBS News covers Barry Bonds." They have it compartmentalized, so it's okay. Well, we sort of think we have it compartmentalized. We have our news group—they do the news. We have an ESPN development group—they did the Barry Bonds series. But that isn't accepted. People look at ESPN as kind of a totality. It's "You guys have these fun-loving anchors—are they journalists or are they entertainers? You've got games, you're in bed with your partners, with the leagues, but yet you're covering them as well."

To me, and I'm not a journalist by trade, the company is remarkably conscientious about separating those ventures. I've asked Vince Doria, who runs our news, "Vince, have you ever been told to pull off of something and not go after the NFL because we will damage our relationship?" His answer is no. Now more subtle is the pressure of "Should I do that because we're in partnership and it will cause trouble?"

JASON WHITLOCK:

On *The Sports Reporters,* Mike Lupica and Joe Valerio had a problem with my perspective on the steroid issue. They had pretty much decided that they were going to beat up Barry Bonds and kind of portray him as the most evil person in sports because of his steroid use, and I came at it differently because I felt like all these guys were using steroids. We'd have arguments before the show, and I would kind of express that perspective, and this was before it became clear that steroid use was rampant throughout all of baseball and really throughout all of sports.

Joe Valerio and these guys would try to send a message to me that they didn't like the way I addressed it, so they'd keep me off the show for a month or two—they just wouldn't ask me to come on. And it would just so happen that every time I would come back on, something would happen in the news related to steroids; the last time I think it happened, it was the guy who won the Tour de France after Lance Armstrong, I can't think of his name. And I'll never forget it, Lupica says to me on the air, "You know what? Then maybe you need to be on the *Entertainment Tonight Sports Reporters.*" It was basically a threat—he told me on the air that "we're booting your ass off the show." I said something like, "Hey, Mike, do you know what the 'E' in ESPN stands for? It stands for Entertainment. We're already on that show"—which was basically my point.

Those guys were pissed at me after the show— Lupica and Joe Valerio—the exchange was pretty heated. It was great television. So the next day, I called Jim Cohen, who was in charge of *The Sports Reporters,* and just said, "Man, these guys are pissed at me." He said, "Look, I saw it, it was great television. I don't understand why they were pissed." And then I think I did an interview with that blog *The Big Lead,* and they asked questions about my work at ESPN and I took potshots at Lupica and then at Scoop Jackson, who was writing for ESPN.com. And I did it knowing it was going to piss Lupica off, but, you know, I didn't care.

Jim Cohen called me the next day and said, "Hey, man, you can't be on our TV shows anymore." And I said, "Fine, no problem." I think ESPN's original thing was "Okay, we're going to suspend him from our TV shows and that'll show him and shut him up." But I was, like, fine, no problem, and I wrote a column for a dot-com the next day saying, "ESPN called and fired me because of X, Y, and Z." I'd had it with Lupica, I'd just had it with the whole deal, so I didn't care what they did—and that was that.

JOHN WALSH:

David Stern said at one time, "Would you have liked to have a camera in the bunker with Hitler, yes or no?" It's an interesting analogy. You'd have access to stories. I think we mishandled that internally, because internally there was such a brouhaha over it and the press got it and it was, like, "This is journalism, this is journalism." Probably the most famous modern-day interview of a president, which is now made into a Broadway play and looks like an award-winning movie, was a paid interview. That doesn't justify it or make it right, but that happened. I spent one evening with Barry Bonds. And I think that Barry Bonds is an interesting character who would love to tell his story but he's got to be made comfortable telling it. And given all the factors coming into play for this particular show, that wasn't going to happen—because there was this knee-jerk need for us to ask him every other minute, "Have you taken steroids?" Do I think that there's a great story there? Absolutely. I don't know if we would have had it, but in the time I spent with him and watching him talk about himself, talk about his life, I think there was a chance that we might have gotten a real interesting look at him.

Booths were originally meant to be heard from, rarely seen, in televised sports — until ABC invented Monday Night Football *in 1970. Suddenly the booth had a new identity, a new role, and such a high profile that it sometimes upstaged the football game going on far below.*

The practice of inviting occasional non-football guests into the booth began in the ABC era. Not all the guests were lightweights from showbiz. One fateful night, both John Lennon and a pre-presidential Ronald Reagan were slated to appear. Before the game, when it was time to decide who would interview whom, Frank Gifford remembers Howard Cosell telling him, "I'll take the Beatle and you take the governor."

If ABC was chided for occasionally turning the Monday Night Football *booth into a watering hole for the glitzerati and an opportunity to promote the network's shows, as part of its renovation ESPN cranked up the celebrity machine even more. It could get awfully crowded in there.*

The New ESPN Booth of 2006 looked as much like a parallel TV talk show as a mere adjunct to football. When it increased the frequency of gratuitous celebrity appearances, ESPN risked appalling purists and die-hard sports fans.

Monday Night Football *had become a sports event that transcended sports. Was that good? ESPN's invited guests tended to be mostly TV "stars," and ABC sent its whole lineup. Eva Longoria stopped by that season to plug* Desperate Housewives, *Patrick Dempsey stopped by to plug* Grey's Anatomy, *and Matthew Fox stopped by to plug* Lost.

Others who made appearances: "actress" and Internet sex-tape star Paris Hilton; producer-director Spike Lee; actors Ashton Kutcher, Jim Belushi, and Ben Stiller; rap star Ludacris; actor and ESPY awards host Samuel L. Jackson; and Arnold Schwarzenegger, former bodybuilder and movie star and, at the time, governor of California.

One unexpected arrival in the booth, though very much part of the sports world, was Tony Kornheiser. Kornheiser was tetchy and opinionated enough to inspire comparisons with the great man Howard Cosell himself, though Kornheiser did not irritate fans to such an extreme that they threw mock bricks at TV screens. Nor, for the record, did Kornheiser wear neckties embroidered with the names of his grandchildren as the softhearted Cosell did.

Joining the Monday Night Football *party in 2006, Kornheiser wrote and delivered a series of "essays" dealing with such sports topics as Brett Favre and the "demise of the Oakland Raiders," and such non-sports topics as the inadequacy of rescue operations following Hurricane Katrina. Some viewers loved him, some didn't. But then, not everybody was crazy about ESPN's glitzed-up booth, either.*

MIKE TIRICO:

I think every one of us who does football play-by-play dreams of a couple of things: of doing the Super Bowl, and then of being involved in some network's lead broadcast team. Al had done *Monday Night Football* for, what, twenty years at that point? Once it was announced that we had the rights and Al was going to be coming over and staying with *Monday Night* and coming to our place to do it, there wasn't much thought about it beyond that. It's certainly one of those unbelievable career jobs that you don't think will ever be on your radar. So even when we acquired it, knowing Al was there kept it from being "Oh boy, how disappointing." It was "Oh, that's great for us that Al will be working at ESPN, because he's associated with it as much as anyone. He's as associated with it as Cosell and Gifford were over the years."

When I heard that he was leaving, I was pretty intrigued. I was doing college football for ESPN and our Thursday and Saturday package of games. I had a lot of exposure to the NFL doing the *Monday Night* pregame show that we did for about a decade. I thought that with all the moving parts, there was a possibility it might happen. I thought that my work as our lead golf announcer and the big football assignments I had been given—whether Thursday night games, or big bowl games, or significant games with ABC and Bowl Championship Series—plus my NFL experience would make me a good candidate. But by no means did I think it was a no-brainer. Hopeful? Absolutely. But thinking it was really going to happen? Nope, not realistically, to be quite frank.

TONY KORNHEISER:

I had never watched *Monday Night Football*. It was on too late. I went to sleep. I never saw one complete game in twenty years.

Walsh called up and said, "Skipper and I are coming down." I hadn't known Skipper well. I hadn't met him very often, a few times here and there. "What do you want?" "We want to talk to you." "What do you want to talk to me about?" "We just want to talk to you." "Okay." I hung up, and I said to my wife, "This is going to be bad." She said, "Why?" I said, "They could offer me *Monday Night Football*." So they came down and told me they wanted me to do *Monday Night Football*. And my exact response was "Get the fuck out of here. No, seriously, get the fuck out of here. Why me? Why are you doing this? *Why are you ruining my life?*"

They said, "Why are we ruining your life?" and I said, "Because I have to take it. I love my life now. I got radio. I got *PTI*. I'm happy. I just bought a house in Delaware, you know? Everything is great, and I'm going to have to do this because no one can refuse this." Then I said, "I'm not qualified for it. I don't know anything about football. I don't particularly like football. I'm terrified of airplanes. I don't know how to do this—and I cannot say no to you. Get out and die!"

Here's what I thought: "I'm going to fail."

I had to do it because Cosell had done it, and I thought, "Why should only jocks do this? Where is it written in the Constitution that because a guy played football, he has the automatic right to sit in that booth? Goddammit, I want this for people like me." And I don't want to sound selfless here, but that's part of the thinking—because if I do well or well enough, then maybe the next person doesn't have to be a jock. How hard is football? If I've spent thirty-five years as a sportswriter, you think I don't know you get six for a touchdown? You think I don't know that? You think I don't know you get three for a field goal? C'mon, c'mon. And I can actually speak English okay, so that would be a difference between me and the guy who spent his whole life playing football. Now, not all of them are like that, but it's that thinking that says, "We have divine right of booth." No, you don't. No, you don't.

MIKE TIRICO:

Monday Night Football is one of the unique things in our business because it's lasted so long. I mean, stuff doesn't last forty years in sports, in television, and especially in sports television — and at that point it was thirty-six. So the whole uniqueness of it made it one of those "wow" moments of my life. I remember being in the house and taking the phone call. I think my delay in saying yes came out of shock, to be honest with you. It certainly was a surprise.

I knew that Kornheiser was in the mix right away, and I assumed that Joe was staying. When it got to my radar, I was pretty much under the assumption it was going to be myself, Joe, and Tony. I was not in the pre-Tony discussion, and candidly, I think part of the equation was, I think, Tony would certainly be different, less like calling a pure game and more of the elements of a studio show, because Tony is topic driven and issue driven. Because of that, my experience of hosting studio shows for many years *and* doing play-by-play made the natural triangle work with Joe and Tony. At least in concept it was going to work.

JOE THEISMANN:
The first telecast we did, he sat there sweating, and I kept telling him, "Don't worry. You'll be great." Tony was as nervous a puppy as you're going to absolutely find. When he first sat down in front of that camera, I sort of chuckled. Amy is the girl that takes care of him, and God bless her. You know, Tony would need his bottles of water. He'd have to have his little pretzel before. He'd have his washcloth that he

brought to pat himself down with. He was a little finicky. It was fun to watch. We all have our little idiosyncrasies. I'd watch Tony, the way he'd prepare. The things he would try and inject into the football game. The whole telecast was set up really to try and include Tony in it, because he really wasn't a football guy. We'd bring guests in, and Tony would ask the questions. They're all friends of mine, so I'd end up in conversation with them, so it was really funny. I wasn't supposed to ask them a question but here I am in dialogue with them.

TONY KORNHEISER:

When we started, we never got panned. We got praised beyond words, beyond words! It was like we came down from the mountain with the Ten Commandments. It was great, so I knew that had to end. I knew that I was going to be in for something much rougher than that. And I was afraid of failure.

JAY ROTHMAN:

God bless Mark Shapiro. I love him to death. He was on a mission, and he got what he wanted, man. When we first got *Monday Night Football,* he was shrewd but there was also this whole enthusiasm going around that "We're going to do it bigger and better than ever. We're going to blow it out. We're going to have a great opening. It's going to be star-studded. It's going to be a celebration. It's going to be a bigger-than-the-game kind of thing." And we all bought into this stuff.

One part of that was we were going to have booth guests every show. Huge stars every week. That obviously didn't pan out, but there were a couple that were pretty good. And you know a funny thing? Truthfully, the reaction that these stupid things got. If you talk about actual TV time, by the time these people actually sat in the booth was like nothing out of a three-hour telecast, and yet from the negative reaction and criticism and feedback that we got, you'd think that we were, you know, violating something. It was outrageous the feedback we got. I think the playbook we were running with was not aligned with what our fans wanted.

JOE THEISMANN:

ESPN hired Rush Limbaugh. ABC hired Dennis Miller. So you have to understand that ESPN to a degree catches itself in the middle of sports and entertainment. It knows that it does sports better than anybody in the world, but it keeps wanting to sort of reach over into this world of entertainment and see if it can combine both in certain areas, which is part of the progressive nature of ESPN. But when it comes to football, I think that the game is something that the football fan wants to see. So in an effort trying to increase the demographic, they add certain entities, certain individuals. And in doing so, it doesn't work.

And they always wind up going back to a football booth. What everybody at ESPN has tried to do—and ABC—is try to recapture the Howard Cosell, Don Meredith, Frank Gifford booth. And you can't do that. I think you have to allow people to create their own identities. And that's really what Paul [Maguire], Mike, and I did. We're as different as night and day to those three guys, but the fun part was we were able to make our own connection to the fans.

RON JAWORSKI, *Football Analyst:*

I'll be blatantly honest with you. When guys like Christian Slater and some of these other booth guests came by, I would have to ask my wife who they were and what they did. I'm pretty much a television guy. I wish I could say I was this worldly guy that understood all the movies and things like that, but I'm not. I was a football guy. And I would have to ask my wife and kids, "Hey, what movies did this guy do?" Quite honestly, it was a distraction for me. I knew it was a direction that ESPN wanted—the entertainment part. But it was very difficult to maintain flow and to stay focused when you'd go eight or ten minutes and pretty much not break down the game.

MIKE TIRICO:

We had Russell Crowe and Christian Slater in the booth. When those guys are in the booth, you're trying to broadcast a football game and trying to get these guys involved in it. With Sylvester Stallone it was easy. With Charles Barkley it was easy, because he was talking about football and the game right in front of you. But when you get somebody who is a superstar and a *huge* attraction but they can't add one drop to what's going on in front of you, those are the times of frustration. Slater was frustrating. So was Russell Crowe. We had gone down to meet him in his suite before the game and were just kind of talking to him, and I remember walking back from the hotel going, "What the hell are we going to do with this guy?"

JOE THEISMANN:

They wanted to recreate *PTI*. But this is what executives don't understand sometimes: the dynamic of a booth. On *PTI*, Tony and Mike can spend a minute and thirty seconds in conversation on a subject. In a booth you have about an eight- to ten-second sound bite, and Tony really needed time to set things up. Every one of his opens was telepromted. It had to be because that's what Tony was used to. Tony came from a different element of television than the live booth.

I loved working with Tony. And I really felt like toward the end of the year we had started to develop, I guess, what management was looking for—not that management ever told me or anyone else what they wanted.

TONY KORNHEISER:

Joe's always the quarterback. I had terrible reservations about working with Joe because I could picture me literally kneeling at his feet, taking quotes at his locker after a game, because I covered him, I wrote columns, I had to get quotes. I didn't think that was a good posture for two people working together as equals.

But Joe could not have been more welcoming to me. Joe said, "This is going to be great. I really like your work. I've loved your work for a long time and this is going to be great." But—and these are the parts that I'm reluctant to say—Joe would say things like, "You just stick with me, I'll lead us, everything will be fine." Joe's the quarterback. Joe had to be the quarterback. Joe didn't even respond to me in the booth. So I had *two* guys not responding to me.

JOE THEISMANN:

On March 23, 2007, I was called to New York for a meeting with the executives, and what they basically did was explain to me that they wanted to make some changes. And you see, here's the thing: Jaws, Ronnie, and Tony had done some stuff—Jaws had done some stuff on *PTI* with Tony, and I think they liked the chemistry and interaction. So what they did was—this is only pure hypothetical on my part— they liked the looks of it, and I'm only assuming that that's the way it went because Jaws wound up taking my spot in the booth. So at that meeting they explained that they wanted to take the show in a different direction, and this is a direct quote: They noticed that when the telecast came back to me, I talked about *football*.

I had been *asked* to talk about football. This is what Jay wanted me to do, focus on football. You basically follow orders, and when they ask you to take a certain approach, you just do the best you can. And that's what I tried to do. The thing I said to Norby and Skipper was "Look, you already made your mind up. You don't want me, so I'm not going to sit here and beg for my job." But I did say to them, "The only thing that I would've liked was, if you didn't like my work, I would've at least appreciated the opportunity for you to say to me, 'Joe, we would like you to do this.'" I think if you don't like something that someone is doing, if you want to keep them, you give them a chance to modify. It was never pointed out to me that I had to do something different. In fact, they were extremely complimentary of my work when I got into the meeting. They said they thought it was one of the best years I had. That's when I knew that something was coming. That's when you sort of stick your jaw out and wait for the right hook.

Jay had no idea that I was fired. I called Jay and told him. Normal management, if there is such a thing, sits down with the people in charge of an entity that they put them in charge of and talks about changes that they want to make. The only thing that bothers me about the whole situation is that I only would have liked Norby and Skipper to sit down and honestly look me in the eye and tell me the truth, and the truth was: "Hey, Joe, look. We've taken over from Mark Shapiro. We're changing the booth and we're going to bring in our guys." That's all you had to say, just be honest with me. But then again, you're talking about television, and it doesn't work that way.

You get hurt, but you understand the nature of the business. We're only leasing space in time anyway. I look at it this way: our time here on this earth is limited. The amount of energy that you want to spend being bitter or upset you could be spending doing positive things in your life and enjoying life. What's done is done.

Don't kid yourself and think it didn't hurt. I mean, it hurt as deep as anything. I did learn a great lesson, and that was simply this: don't ever do things in life and don't ever work in life for the satisfaction of someone else.

TONY KORNHEISER:

I called Joe. I didn't really know what to say. I can't honestly say I was terribly surprised, because I saw what happened with Boomer Esiason. I think this happens a lot; it's just a business I don't understand.

Was I surprised it was him and not me? Yeah, a little bit. He had a longer contract and he'd been doing this for a long time and he was the expert. Theismann and Jaworski and Aikman—when you sit in that booth, it's incredible. They don't need replay. They can see it, they can see it all. I can't even see it *with* the replay. So I just assumed if there was going to be a change, somebody was going to say, "Well, Tony, we need to make a change," because what was I bringing that was so special? I seemed to be the person that was polarizing.

MIKE TIRICO:

I was just told, same thing as with Tony. I don't exactly wield a huge amount of power here. I'm on the *told* end, not the *input* end, with this stuff.

I was disappointed that Joe left, just because Joe had been a friend. When I first started doing the NFL in '93 at ESPN, it was with Joe in the studio. And over fifteen years you just get to know people and get to like people, and I always liked Joe. I think for whatever reason, whether it was the critics, writers, or people talking about us not doing something, or us being a part of the pop culture portion of the show, that created a negative feel about what we were doing and then created a feeling that something needed to change. That's probably where things led to a change.

I thought Joe tried to adjust and change when we all got it going the first year. What Joe did in those games was a lot different from what Joe had done earlier. I'm sure in some ways it was frustrating to him, but I don't necessarily think that was the problem, to be honest with you.

JIMMY KIMMEL, *Comedian:*

I got banned from *Monday Night Football.* Here's what happened: I was on in Seattle, and the truth is, no one up there seemed to like Joe Theismann. Everywhere I went, every ESPN person I ran into said, "Hey, you going to do jokes about Joe? You going to fuck with Joe? You've got to say something to Joe." So it made me wonder, "What's going on?" I didn't know Joe Theismann, I didn't know anything about him, but it certainly didn't seem like there was harmony in the booth. So when I was in the booth, I did a few jokes to Joe. I asked him how his leg was. He was a little bit annoyed. He said, "That was twenty-five years ago." I said, "I know, I haven't seen you since then." It was pretty light.

But then the second time I was on the show the next year, again I got people, like, "Oh, you've got to say something about Joe" — even though he was no longer in the booth. There's a lot of whispering about me saying something about Joe. And I did say something about Joe because it seemed like the elephant in the room to me, the fact that Joe wasn't there and nothing had ever been said about that. And to be honest, I enjoy making people uncomfortable, especially on live television, where there's nothing they can cut out. So I said something to the effect of, "Do you think Joe Theismann's watching right now? He probably has steam coming out of his ears." The truth of the matter is, the guys in the booth were laughing, but you don't see the video, you only hear the voices, so the guys in the booth are covering their mouths and cracking up, nervously laughing but you can't hear any laughter on television. And afterward, everybody seemed very happy with the appearance. They gave me T-shirts, thanked me, they walked me out to my car, various people said, "Oh, that was hilarious," and the next morning I read, I think in the *New York Times,* that Rothman said I was "classless." He called me later and apologized, and then said I was welcome on *Monday Night Football* anytime—although I have not yet been invited. I guess if I just happen to drop by the booth, I'll be welcomed in.

I think what happened was, these sports reporters are ridiculous. You get a guy like [*New York Post* columnist] Phil Mushnick, for instance; you would think the guy was a cardinal or something, he is so puritanical, and he takes shots at everybody for everything; if he sees somebody spitting, he lambasts them about what a terrible example it is for American kids. The truth of the matter is, the guy writes for the *New*

York Post, which — really, they've got to be kidding. Somebody gets their head chopped off and they've got a pun on the front page of the newspaper.

When somebody does something that's way over the line, like Michael Vick, for instance, these sportscasters go nuts. They go out of their way to get up on their high horses and really let the guy have it. And I think the reason they do that is it's a smoke screen because of all the other terrible things that these players do all year round that people don't find out about, all these lousy things that go on. It's like if they trumpet the big ones, nobody will notice that no one ever says anything about the little ones.

There's a lot of hypocrisy. When there's blood in the water, they will all feast, but no one will ever say anything about the little things. People like to make big stands over nonissues. You watch football and everybody's got their pink shoes on, and it's breast cancer this and breast cancer that — certainly this is a worthwhile charity, but it's PR. You've got a lot of guys on the field who are flat-out criminals, and they're wearing breast cancer scarves, so it makes it all okay.

It's so obvious to me. I guess because they have the final word and there really aren't too many voices that can point that out. Even your sports talk radio hosts who make their living giving their opinions, most of them work for one of the major sports providers —

ESPN or some network that relies on a team to fill their programming time, so everyone is handcuffed and no one says anything about this stuff.

I think that really in the heat of the moment, Rothman said something about me that he wished he wouldn't have. He's an okay guy, there's just this standard in sportscasting that is so far beyond the standards of any other area of broadcasting. I really can't explain it; it's very strange.

RON JAWORSKI:

I've always had a great advantage: I live twenty minutes away from NFL Films. I'm sitting in my office right now, looking at the Super Bowl tape. And it's an advantage that really no one else has. And I can sit here thirty to forty hours a week and just look at football. And being at NFL Films, there are always coaches, players, coming through. And we sit and talk and look at tapes. So as a guy that probably hasn't thrown a pass in nineteen years, I stay close to the game basically by studying the game. Fortunately I was doing preseason games, so I had the in-booth experience—obviously not the profile of *Monday Night Football,* but I was doing preseason games for the Philadelphia Eagles, the Tampa Bay Buccaneers, the New Orleans Saints. I was doing five and six preseason games a year. I did the Senior Bowl back in '96–'97. I was doing some college football. So I was working in the booth. I wasn't a complete novice. I was aware of the dynamics.

Monday Night Football is an extravaganza with some of the most talented people in the television business that you could ever meet. I realized at those early meetings that I had a lot to learn — the camera positions, the replays, the angles that we have, the Skycam, all those things. I never had a problem with the football side, but on the technical side, because of the amount of resources and equipment and technology that ESPN throws into the game, I had a lot to learn in that regard.

MIKE TIRICO:

I'd had a lot of experience in a three-man booth, plus I had studio experience; *PTI* is a studio show, and that's where Tony thrives. Tony had done some radio hosting and things like that, so Tony's skill set for what he could bring to the game, the vision of what he was going to bring to the game, I think they felt that my pure experience would make them work and would give them the best chance to succeed. So that's where I think I ended up as the person that they pointed to regarding that. I hope it doesn't come off as conceited. I think the work I had done as a football play-by-play guy in college for most of those eight, nine years before that — on those merits I deserved the opportunity as well. I had not done it at the NFL level, but I had hosted NFL studio shows for over a decade. I heard there was a lot of effort to make Tony understand the rhythm of the booth and that it was very difficult in the first year. We tried to rewrite the way football on television had been broadcast. I think a lot of it gets pointed to Tony, but there was also the philosophical decision to be more than just broadcasting the football games, that it would be stepping out a little bit for pop culture, incorporating some of that within *Monday Night*. The difficulty came when we tried to rewrite the way football on television had been broadcast. We were the only broadcast that was trying to do that, so there was uniqueness to that. Take that and combine it with someone who had never worked a football game before, and you had some pretty significant hurdles, no doubt about it.

TONY KORNHEISER:

They may have had Cosell on their minds, but I'm not Howard, I don't have that intellect. I don't have that bombast, and unlike Howard, I never worked in that setting before. Howard was so brilliant. I used to watch Howard do his radio show. There's no clock on the wall, and Howard gets to three minutes and fifty seconds [*snaps fingers*]—ends the story, that's a wrap, it's done, you can go home, and you go, "Oh, my God." The only other person I've ever seen do that is Costas. It's Costas and Howard—Howard one and Costas two. Nobody else can do that, clocks in their heads *all* the time, know how to end it, how to stretch it, how to make it work. I was awestruck by that. But it's hard for me because there's a game going on and you're supposed to talk to the game. I mean, I used to like to hear Howard say, "I had breakfast with Liza the other day and Liza..." But they apparently didn't want that from me. I'd hope they'd want that, but they didn't want that from me.

JOE THEISMANN:

Tony's tough on everybody. Tony's a cynic. Tony doesn't like anybody. Come on, let's be honest. As a matter of fact, I worked hard to get Tony to go to production meetings. Tony didn't want to go to production meetings, and he'll tell you that. Tony's very honest about that whole thing. I loved working with Tony. It was going to be a lot of fun. I really feel like I could have helped him a little bit more possibly, given the opportunity. But Tony did not want to meet with coaches, and the reason he didn't want to meet with coaches or players is that he was afraid he would like them. And if he liked them, he couldn't be critical of them. And it would take away what Tony is famous for. That's criticism. Everybody's got a shtick, okay? Tony's is liking nothing.

TONY KORNHEISER:

In my life as a sportswriter, I never believed that athletes didn't read the papers when they said they didn't read the papers. I believed they read them and they just said they didn't. The first criticism I read of me was in my own newspaper by Paul Farhi, a duplicitous backstabbing snake and weasel who I would happily back over with a bus, okay? After I read that, I said, "You know what, I'm done. I'm not reading anything else." When my son would read something and say, "You know what, this guy hates you," I would say, "Michael, don't tell me that. If you want to read it, read it. Don't tell me anything good and don't tell me anything bad." My picture popped up on AOL, and my wife would say, "They think you're the worst guy," and I said, "Please, I don't want to know."

I listened to my good friend Mitch Albom, who was in that trouble in Detroit where he quoted a couple of guys and said that they were at a game and they didn't actually get to the game, and I defended Mitch for this because he's my dear friend and because I believe in his position. I said, "Do you read what's written?" And he goes, "No, because I don't want to have to change any friends." I don't google myself, and I didn't read things specific to *Monday Night Football*. I had a sense that there was a lot of criticism. I told people, "You can gather all this stuff and put it in a box and I'll read it at the end of the season." But I never read a word.

MIKE TIRICO:
Tony is brilliant. I enjoy watching Tony work. I enjoyed working with Tony, I really did. I learned a

lot. Tony has been incredibly successful in places where you come to hear Tony's opinion on something, like his column or *PTI*. You come for Tony's opinion. To me, you come to a football game for the football game. The football game is surrounded by a bevy of wide-ranging opinions in the pregame shows, the postgame shows, the talk shows during the week. People come to the game for the game itself. So it's trying to take what Tony does best—strong, interesting, intelligent, and timely opinions on people in the game—and make that work within the body of the game.

That was the challenge, and I'm going to tell you, it pisses me off that people will look at those three years and say, "Well, it wasn't that good." Or they'll say, "Oh, Christian Slater was on." If you took all the non-football people who were on—although anybody who worked on the show will tell you I was not a huge fan of it—at most 2 percent of our three years of Tony or two years of having "celebrities" in the booth, 2 percent of our broadcast was that. The other 98 percent was football or football content. So I think people have done an incredible disservice of overdramatizing the impact that had on the broadcast.

The problem working in the booth was that you're trying to cover the game, and then you're trying to get Tony's opinion on the stuff that's going on. We were the only football show that was nominated for an Emmy three years in a row. So I still stand on that merit; the show was not the be-all and end-all, trust me, but the shows we did were pretty good football shows.

The challenge day to day, hour to hour, play to play, was that a play happens on the field, right in front of us, and we're so used to watching TV — "Here's a play, here's a replay, here's what happened" — but Tony couldn't *add* to what just happened. He could add to the person and give it some definite context, but the viewer has become conditioned to hear someone say what happened.

The brilliant success of Madden over the years was that he turned a lot of viewers into wannabe defensive coordinators. Nobody could draw up a chalkboard and do all this stuff and squeeze x's and o's inside the twenty seconds between a play until Madden. I think that's just become the way that job is measured. So having a non-football guy in one of those traditional seats was just hard for people to get used to.

I absolutely love the fact that for eighteen years I've worked for a place that is willing to try something different. We see people do the same TV over and over, and it gets very stale. Who would've been ridiculous enough to put *SportsCenter* on live in the morning? Who would've been silly enough to put two columnists on TV carrying on their in-the-hallway conversations? Who would've been silly enough to do all these different shows we've done over the years? Well, guess what? More ideas we've had as a company work. And this was an attempt to say, you know what, football is done the same way by everybody, can we add something? Can we make it broader and better? Because at the end of the day, we're a business. The bottom line of our business is to attract more viewers. How do you attract more viewers? Maybe you grow the audience by expanding the audience. Or maybe people would've come to look forward to that segment as the years went on—who knows? I think we realized that it wasn't the best road to go down.

JOHN SKIPPER:

John Walsh wanted to extend journalism to everything we do, including event production. I mean, John—and this is not without controversy—still believes that within the event broadcast we should be doing journalism. We should be covering stories. I believe Jed Drake is the original guy who used the visual image of concentric circles to talk to the announcers. It's not my favorite conceptual way to talk about it. It is fairly simplistic. There are a series of concentric circles and the game itself lies at the center of the circles. The circles outside are the things that aren't actually happening in the action but which are closest to the action. You're watching a game and it's the first circle. The second circle is, let's say, the star quarterback and his football life. The third circle is his personal life. The fourth circle, larger trends. It's meant to show the game is the most important thing, and the more intense the game is, the less you go outside. But if you get to a game that's 40–0 in the third quarter, you get further outside. And there is a place — I don't know which circle it is; it's not quite as well constructed as Dante's inferno, but it's almost as painful. There is one circle where you get outside the sport itself and that is where you begin to get into great controversy, where you bring a guest into the *Monday Night Football* booth where Tony is talking about the election. John [Walsh] loves to tweak convention and to tweak the gods, and there's where you offend the sports guys, right?

MIKE TIRICO:

One of the places where I know Tony expressed to me that he felt uncomfortable, and I certainly understand it, was "Can you look at me and talk to me more during the game and engage me in conversation back and forth on things?" That's really hard when you got ninety guys on the football field and you're trying to identify who made the tackle, what's the gain, what's the down and distance, what's the game situation, what's the time-outs, challenge a play — the things that are the play-by-play person's number-one priority. And to me, whether it was accurate or not, and varying people have their opinions on it, I maintained that the most important thing for me to do was "Who's got the ball? What's the down? What's the distance? What's the game situation?" All that above and beyond engaging Tony in conversation.

JOHN SKIPPER:

We wanted to put Kornheiser in the booth. We thought, with it moving over to ESPN, how cool would it be if we could re-create a little of the Howard Cosell magic? And I think we succeeded. We said, "Gee, we want the production to be really big. We don't want there to be any sense as it moved from ABC to ESPN that the stature of it, the sort of number of cameras and elements, had declined a little. We don't want it to feel like it's lessened."

Let me give credit to my bosses who let us experiment. We said this was what we wanted to do. We want to try something. By the way, I think it was a pretty interesting contemplation. Tony is so good. He's so smart. Anybody who knows him at least understands what we hoped we would get on the air. To me the ideal booth would make every fan think that being the fourth guy sitting next to those three guys on the sofa is the best place to watch a football game. It's fun. It's insightful. It's just relaxed. I said, "Please make it feel like you guys are having fun, you love the game, you're cracking wise a little bit, you're sharing a little bit of information, and the best place in the world to be would be in the next seat." I shouldn't say we don't want people to take it seriously; we do. But personally, as a sports fan, I love sports. I do get emotionally involved, but I never lose the perspective that you're just watching a game.

The fans actually ultimately understand whether there's something going on that's fun, that's interesting. I'm not sure that Meredith and Cosell and Gifford loved each other, but you had something electric going on, and we didn't get that either.

I don't think Howard Cosell cared if anybody wanted him there or not. And Tony ultimately is a sensitive human being and cared about whether somebody wanted him there.

TONY KORNHEISER:

Our season ends, no playoffs. We're paying *double!* And no flex and the worst schedule humanly possible. If you get steady diets of Jacksonville and Carolina and Tennessee even when they've got a 10–0 record, you're not getting the big cities. There's no compelling reason to watch the game. We had Jacksonville at Houston. Jacksonville at Houston? I did an essay on how nobody's going to watch this game.

NBC gets flex and NBC can live on the NFC East; you know, Dallas every week, and you'll be fine. It's unbelievable, but it says that ESPN is cable and it's second-rate, it's the minors. Look, look—Mike Tirico, Tony Kornheiser, Ron Jaworski—that is not Al Michaels, John Madden. That is not Joe Buck and Troy Aikman in peoples' minds. That's not. It's just not.

Jaws is my friend now, which I never thought would be possible for any kind of jock and me. He is my friend, and I dearly love him. I've looked for the devil in Ron Jaworski for two years — there is no devil in Ron Jaworski. He was drafted into the pros in two sports. He was a Super Bowl quarterback, a multiple Pro Bowl quarterback; there is nothing that he does or says that would indicate to you he was anything other than a *guy*, just a guy. We play golf together. Our kids play golf together. He's patient with everyone. He's made a ton of money in a ton of different things by being a nice fella, by never having any airs. There's no air of superiority. There's an air of superiority with Theismann, but he can't help it.

RON JAWORSKI:

I had worked with Tony on radio shows and *PTI* and things like that, so we got a good relationship. And it was interesting because — and I don't know this to be fact, but the undercurrent was that Joe and Tony just didn't get along. But Tony and I forged a great relationship and a friendship, and our families did. I enjoyed every second with Tony.

I think people turn on *Monday Night Football* for *Monday Night Football*. Does that make sense? They want to watch a football game. I think everyone, at least at ABC and then at ESPN, was about football/entertainment, and that was always the hard juggling act, because I was pretty much a football guy and Tony had a different perspective on the game. I think the way he verbalized it was 100 percent correct. He saw the game from the outside in; I saw the game from the inside out. I was in the locker room; he was outside the locker room. But I thought it made for good commentary; it lent a positive aspect because we saw the game differently. Mike always had a difficult job because the first couple years we were still using booth guests and things like that, and it did make it a little more difficult because he never really developed a flow for the game. So in regards to Mike, I think it put him in a tough position.

SUZY KOLBER:

When I was originally offered the sidelines job for *Sunday Night Football,* I was a reporter on *Sunday Countdown,* and really enjoyed what I was doing. So I wanted assurances that it wasn't a typical injury-report role, that it was going to have more substance to it. The official job offer came from Steve Anderson, but Jay is who I talked with about what the role would be. And, at the time, we discussed me defining the role, because he had worked with Lynn Swann on ABC, and Lynn almost acted as another analyst out on the field. And he knew my background—that I did so many different things: I was an anchor and I was a reporter and I was a good storyteller. So he wanted to be able to utilize all of that. And we talked about redefining the role in a sense that I would be another voice—three guys upstairs and I was the fourth voice of the broadcast.

What I really enjoyed about it was that on *Monday Night Football* there was a separate producer in the truck for the sideline, but Jay wanted to talk to all of us. So I had direct communication with him and was just considered another voice in the broadcast. I was integrated much more than any other sideline reporter. I did highlight packages and told stories, and I did significantly more than what other sideline reporters were doing.

When we made the switch to Monday night, Michele Tafoya and I both felt comfortable because Freddie also used her a lot on the broadcast. I was probably used a little bit more, but we were used in similar ways. And what made that transition easier for the two of us suddenly being put together on Monday night was that right before that switch, we did the Super Bowl together. I thought we were both used really well in that game.

So it became Michele and I plus the three guys in the booth. Jay is producing. And there's clearly too many voices. And it's a lot of pressure on Jay because he feels obligated to use everybody, but the broadcast is too crowded. So right in the middle of the season, right in the middle of the day, the entire philosophy changed. We were in Philadelphia, and Jed Drake delivered the news that they're changing their philosophy and how we're now going to be used. He said, "We'll be strictly interested in observations that you might see but not really any sort of depth to the storytelling." And I remember it's like being hit by a truck. All right, could you have told us before we prepared for the game? The game is in four hours. I was pretty angry at the sudden shift. There was no warning.

MICHELE TAFOYA, *Reporter:*

Three guys in the booth, two people on the field. I certainly understood that, and I was very much okay with the notion that all I would be doing on the sideline was observations and breaking news. Nothing prepared. Nothing like that. But then it came down to we're told not even to do observations. I remember covering Brett Favre with the Jets last season, and having covered Brett for so many years—watching the difference in his sideline demeanor, learning this new offense—versus the guy he was in Green Bay. I did a report on that. I thought it was very appropriate. It was an observation I was able to make standing right next to him on the sidelines, and I was told days later that we can't even do that anymore. We're not going to do that. That's not the philosophy, you know? Basically, if someone major breaks a leg, that's now what you're covering. So that, in a nutshell—if you can call that a nutshell—is the rather dramatic shift that the role has taken.

Suzy and I are trying to make the most of our roles now, but I'd be lying if I said I wasn't frustrated with the lack of opportunities to have an impact on the telecast. It's tough when you've worked as hard as Suzy and I have, developing relationships with players and coaches and trainers and coordinators, where you feel you have something really relevant to add to what's happening on the field, and you're seeing it right there, close up, not through the lenses of a camera but right there with your own eyes. And you know the context of it because you've been down there the entire game observing the body languages. You've been hearing people talk. You've been watching interactions. You've been seeing it all right there, close up. I think to say that none of that is worthwhile is a shame, but unfortunately it's just what I have to live with right now.

I remember watching John Teerlinck of the Indianapolis Colts just jawing into his offensive line. It was fierce. It was a long chewing-out. It was getting to the point where a couple players were clearly displeased with what they were hearing. It was quite visual. We had plenty of time to get a camera over there and show this to the audience as well, with some explanation—but that did not make air.

You know, we asked for other opportunities after *Monday Night Football*. We've asked to be involved in some of those things. I think what ends up happening in Bristol is that people who work for ESPN but don't live there and aren't at the compound every day get forgotten about to a certain extent. If I was really ready to pound my fist and say, "I want to do this story. There's a story I really want to do. I feel really strongly about this," and I chased and chased it, I'm sure they'd consider it and think about letting me do it. The diminished role on *Monday Night Football* is one reason they did come to me and ask me if I wanted to call play-by-play on college football. So that was one particular opening, but again, my desire to do that was not there.

HEATHER COX, *Reporter:*
The hardest part, I think, about reporting is you only get two, three, four questions at the most, so I really have to figure out what is the most important story line and what I want to hit home. If we could sit down for twenty minutes, I'd love to ask fifteen questions. But we just never have the opportunity to do that, and to develop a real in-depth, Barbara Walters–type interview. It just doesn't happen in the format that we're given.

ERIN ANDREWS, *Reporter:*
When I was younger, I would always come home on Monday night, and I would always love to watch *Monday Night Football*. I would always love to see what the sideline reporter was doing that night. I would sit there and critique them when I was younger, and it made me really, really want to be a part of it.

When I was at Florida I used to camp out for *College GameDay*. I always would try to get my picture with Kirk [Herbstreit] and Chris [Fowler] and Lee [Corso], and there's a couple of times where my camera didn't work and Kirk would come back and take another photo and Chris would too, and I just remembered how nice they were to stand and how great they were and how appreciative toward their fans. And I always try to remember that, because I think at the same time, when people are screaming your name and "We love you. We love you," I just think to myself, "I'm the biggest dork. I sit on my couch and I'm watching *NFL Live* right now. I'm just a dork." I guess I just don't take it too seriously. I never have.

As the years started to pass, I started developing great relationships with a lot of coaches and a lot of athletes, and to be honest with you, they don't give me inside information, and they don't allow me to just call them up and ask them questions or help because of the way I look. They've got more things to do than worry about that. Within the last couple years, I've started to take pride in the fact that I can "up" Mac Brown. I can call Urban Meyer. I can call Pete Carroll and just say, "Hey, can you help me out with this? I'm working on a game and I need some stuff for this." These guys, you know, they see pretty girls every day. They don't care. They don't have time for it. They know how hard I work. And another thing that's helped me: I have great talent around me—Chris Fowler, Craig James, Kirk Herbstreit—and I think that these coaches see that I have a good relationship with them, and they trust me. "Well, gosh. If Herbie trusts Erin, and Chris Fowler does too, then she's going to be great with me on the sidelines."

LISA SALTERS, *Reporter:*

I watch the NFL and I watch how we've basically gotten rid of the sideline reporters — two of the best sideline reporters that are out there, we've just gotten ridden of them for *Monday Night Football.* I don't understand how that happened. But it happened. And in college football as well, they've really trimmed down. Not all of the games have sideline reporters anymore. Thankfully the game that I do, the prime-time game with Brent and Kirk, we still do; otherwise, I would be not doing it anymore either.

I think it's kind of unfair to kind of lump all sideline reporters in together when, to me, on any network there are some who are better than others. So I don't want to be judged — I don't want my work to be judged by the work of somebody else who I might think isn't as good. Or I wouldn't think that Michele Tafoya or Suzy Kolber would be judged by somebody else on another network who I would think, like — well, of course you would say the sideline reporter isn't that good, because that person is doing it. But if you had Michele or Suzy doing it, it would be a lot — you would get a lot more value out of it.

MICHELE TAFOYA:

I don't feel that the playing field is completely level. I can only speak from the roles that I handle, which are primarily reporting, and that's one aspect of it. I think that women are predominantly looked at as reporters. I think we have our share of anchors and so forth, but we're predominantly reporters. We're always thought of as quote-unquote "sideline reporters." "Female sideline reporters." I hear those terms an awful lot. So just by virtue of that, I don't think the playing field is particularly level. However, I have never, ever, ever used my gender or my sex as any kind of excuse. I never had a chip about it. When I started in this business back in 1993, I told myself as I marched off to Charlotte, North Carolina, to work in sports talk radio that I was going to be a reporter. Not a "female reporter." Just a reporter. Diane Sawyer. Barbara Walters. Women that are being allowed to age gracefully in their roles, for lack of a better term. I don't see that happening in sports. I don't see a sixty-year-old woman being able to continue on covering sports, because I just don't think that idea goes over well with viewers and therefore with management. Now is that unacceptable? I don't know. It is what it is, but it underscores just one more time that the playing field ain't level, and you can have one guy doing sports who is bald and maybe twenty pounds overweight. If you had a woman who was deemed less attractive, she might not get those same roles that the more attractive women get. That makes it an unlevel playing field.

Hosting the 14th Annual ESPY Awards in 2006, Lance Armstrong looked out at the audience in Hollywood's Kodak Theatre and said he was surprised to see Brokeback Mountain *costar Jake Gyllenhaal sitting in the front row—having assumed from the movie that the actor "likes it in the rear." Armstrong told other arguably tasteless jokes that night, but this one got the most attention—and the attention was certainly not in the form of lavish praise or even "ha ha, good one"(although the joke did get loud laughs from the audience that night—including from Gyllenhaal).*

Most of the comments provoked by the joke had to do with disbelief that it wasn't edited out of the tape before broadcast, since when given the chance to edit out questionable material, ESPN usually reaches for the scissors. Critics pointed out that ESPN's own SportsCenter anchors would have been in big trouble if they'd told the same joke on that program, even one of the editions airing at a later hour than the ESPYs did. John Walsh had made practically a crusade out of keeping humor at the awards show positive and—to use his favorite adjective in this context—"celebratory."

"When you're trying to attract the best, most contemporary, and most talented people from the entertainment community, they have an expectation of being

attached to a show that takes risks," Walsh said in response to criticism, but his would not be the last word.

LANCE ARMSTRONG, *ESPY Host:*

Well, I was honored that ESPN would be willing to take a risk on an athlete hosting the show. It was a bit weird to be taking jabs at some people in sport, but I think most appreciated that it was all in good fun. I was extremely nervous. It is easy to participate in a live sporting event because most of the time you don't see the cameras or you are so focused on the race. But when that curtain went up, it was real. And you are feet away from your peers in sports.

You do the rehearsals and it seems funny, but you never know until you start going live and have to face that audience.

JOHN WALSH:

The sports guy in late night is Jimmy Kimmel. He did the ESPYs one year, and we hated him. He did a terrible job. He's a nice guy, a big sports fan. So we hired him, and I said, "Jimmy, you understand, this is not late-night television, it's not a nightclub. It's a celebration of sports. We're here in prime time to celebrate sports. It's not raunchy." Then we told him the monologue is four minutes. So he writes a monologue and delivers it—eight minutes and thirty seconds. We cut out all the bad stuff, the stuff that was *not* celebratory, and he was *so* pissed off.

JIMMY KIMMEL:

I had a lot of material. I knew some of the stuff was going to be cut out, I just didn't know how much. I understood some of it, but some of it made absolutely no sense to me. Like you can't make fun of soccer. Everything was so political. I didn't realize cuts were made until I watched the broadcast. I was at Huey Lewis's house in Montana, fly-fishing, and we said, "Hey, let's watch this." And we did.

It was a lesson for me, I think. The lesson was that I should have expected that to happen in the first place, and they had wanted me to sign a five-year deal to host every year.

The fact of the matter is, they can't afford to make jokes at the expense of the characters in their world. And they're not used to that sort of thing. They're just not willing to take that risk. They claim they cut the stuff for time, but eh. "David Beckham comes to L.A. this month. I have to say I have never seen my gardener so excited." Maybe that one seemed racist, I don't know.

The truth of the matter is, ESPN is great. It's just when you make the mistake like I did of thinking you can do something edgy on that network, and you can't. You just can't. It's McDonald's.

DANICA PATRICK, *Race Car Driver:*

The ESPYs are just the coolest party that I get to go to all year. I'm kind of girly—I like to get made-up and walk the red carpet and look like a girl for the night. It's nice to show everyone that I'm a girl. Not many people really see that because most of my photos and interviews are done without any makeup or without anything done to my hair except maybe a ponytail. And it's always flattering to hear what people say.

I also get to meet a lot of people who I wouldn't normally meet. I particularly enjoyed meeting Will Ferrell. That was pretty cool. I was presenting with Luke Wilson and we were talking when Will came over. He had just done a little skit onstage and he said, "Oh, my gosh, my two favorite people!" and I thought, "Wow, this is so cool." I was so flattered he remembered me.

DWYANE WADE:

When I first started going, Jamie Foxx was the host, and he was hilarious. I loved the skits. When LeBron hosted, I thought he did a good job. He was funny and entertaining, and he really showed another side of him that was kind of cool. And it looked good for a basketball player to be doing that.

I'm a big fan of the game, but I'm also a student of the game. You have to do your homework. So I watch

SportsCenter, ESPN News, and go on ESPN.com all the time. You just gotta do your homework.

SHAUN WHITE, *Professional Skateboarder and Snowboarder:*

I was standing at the ESPYs and some famous football player came up to me and he was, like, "There's no way in the world I could do what you do." And I just looked at him and said, "Well, there's no way I could go tackle someone." There's just a common respect at the ESPYs between all the athletes that you don't get anywhere else.

But for me, ESPN is obviously also about the X Games. Before our sport really took off anywhere, back before I even started, X Games were our Olympics. ESPN had Travis Pastrana jumping his motorcycle into the water in San Francisco. I remember I wasn't even allowed to compete, I was so young — but it was my goal to end up getting in the event. And by the time I was old enough and all that, it really started to take off, so it was kind of our platform to get noticed. The X Games have grown from the little backyard event that it was to a full-fledged marketed thing. And now it's a cultural thing too, because everyone is used to seeing football and basketball, but our sport has grown dramatically all across the world, so it's become something where they need us. You know what I mean? We're the new thing, and they're open to us. I gave them input all the time, and always made sure I was around to help with any course design or any feedback, like if the course wasn't working, because it's a very rider-driven thing. It's been a great relationship, and we've certainly helped each other out.

STEVE YOUNG, *Football Analyst:*

Oh, there've been some classic fumbles, that's for sure. Tom Jackson loves this one: I had written down a quote from a player that he'd told me, that I felt like I needed to say on the air verbatim, and so at some point in my comments, I looked down at my piece of paper to read it—but my handwriting is very, very small. It was so small, I couldn't read it. I was trying to read the quote and Tom had to say on the air, "You can't read your own writing," and I had to admit it. I said, "Yes, you're right, I can't read my own writing."

There are times when I go on the air and my wife will text me, "You forgot to shave half your mustache" or "You look awful; comb your hair." Because at ESPN, they just talk sports, they don't look at you before you go on. I was actually on-set at the game and my hair was flying up in the air, and it goes back to Chris in Bristol, and Chris says, "Steve, that was electrifying."

COLIN COWHERD:

If this were a small business and I owned it, I'd just have to be accountable for me. But as it is, I have to be accountable for advertisers and the affiliates and the company, and as I've grown in stature at the company, that's a bigger shield to carry. I'm always okay taking the heat. It doesn't bother me. But I always worry about my kids, or the company, or my bosses, or the brand. That's where it gets uncomfortable. I'm never uncomfortable reading about me because I know me better than anybody else knows me, and I know I'm a good guy. I get along with my ex-wife. I get along with every woman I've dated. I don't have any enemies. My best friends have been my friends for years. I have an incredible group of friends. So I'm never worried about the criticism of me. What I'm worried about is that other people suffer because they're associated with me — my kids, my friends, my company, my advertisers. So when I'm being broadly attacked, I tend to, like most people, build a fence around those who are close. I get closer to my kids, probably. I spend more time with the people I trust. I think any time you're a politician or a media person, if you're going through a horrible personal tragedy, you just draw closer to the safest and most loving people. I think you have to come to terms with it. The one thing that I shake my head at is people who criticize yet can't be criticized. I always laugh at these people. Keith Olbermann's brilliant but he's so thin-skinned, and yet he criticizes for a living, sharply and often with daggers. You can't do that for a living and then not take a punch. I'm always shocked at the talented people who criticize and then are seemingly outraged at any salvo directed at them. I know the way I speak is going to generate hate mail and criticism, and I'm ready for it. I accept it.

That "end zone" thing was really just nothing. That was more Internet babble. I read something that somebody sent to me anonymously. I'd never seen it before. I just said, "This is funny," and then we read it on the air. We didn't know who it was. And then we got a bunch of people e-mailing us and killing us for it, and after a while I e-mailed back to somebody and said, "Come on, dude. Get over it. We get it. We made a mistake." And then I wanted to apologize, and the company said, hey, they wanted to review the situation. ESPN's an aircraft carrier, not a sailboat. Our turning radius is pretty slow; when controversy happens, it takes twenty-four or thirty-six hours to get everybody huddled, listen to the tape, see what they think. So I would have apologized immediately but management said, "Stay away from it for twenty-four hours, then we'll address it." And I did. But that was nothing. Now with the Sean Taylor thing, my superior, Mo Davenport, an African American, listened to it and had no problem with it. A lot of it was turned into a racial issue. "Insensitive." And I would say it again. Sean Taylor came out of the University of Miami with a reputation. I really leaned on African American journalists — Stephen A. Smith, Michael Wilbon — who were critical of him. This is a guy who had an SUV riddled with bullets several years earlier. His best friend told him, "Stay out of Miami." If you listen to my commentary and go to the Internet, it was warranted, it was reasonable, and yes, it could have been wrong. But I'm not in the business of reviewing everything before I talk about it. I'm in talk radio. A story breaks, I need an opinion. I'm not ESPN News.

I came out later and said, "Here are the facts. Here is the truth." I never really apologized. I came on the air and said, "Many of you were offended. You were offended by my tone or tenor. I understand it. That's my Colin tenor. Some people love it. Some people hate it. But I'm not going to apologize for my tone. Go back and look at exactly what I said." One of the comments that bothered people—people said, "He turned his life around." And I came out and said, "Hey, a lot of times you clean the carpet, but you don't get all the stains out." And people are, like, "What does that mean?" Well, just because you turn your life around doesn't mean everybody else is going to accept your apology. I mean, Sean had made a lot of enemies in his life apparently.

There's been a coarsening of the country. I'm not blaming conservative radio, but I think there's just been a coarsening of the airwaves over the last fifteen years. Much more partisan. Much more anger. And in sports, because the athletes have separated themselves from the common guy, it costs significantly

more to go to games, so fans feel more of an ownership. "I'm paying for this, so I'll damn well say what I
please." There's clearly a feeling of ownership of the
player because you're paying his salary and because
there's a distance now between the athlete and the
media and the athlete and the fans. There's a resentment that's built up, and that caustic sort of resentment bares itself on the radio on a daily basis. It's
funny; many people have labeled me "controversial."
I find myself to be so overwhelmingly reasonable. I
often go on the air and I say, "People, settle down.
We're overreacting here. Michael Vick? We're overreacting." But the ratings are in overreacting. So I listen
to a lot of radio and some of the stuff that comes out
of political radio talkers' mouths is just wrong. It's
just absurd. It's clearly stirring the masses — often the
less-educated masses who react emotionally to everything. So some of it can be blamed on the media.
Some of it can be blamed on the ticket prices and the
separation of fan from player. And some of it is just
the coarsening of the country. We have more media.
People see more now. People get numb to stuff. And I
think as civilizations age, you see this all over. You
just see a coarsening because we see more, we get used
to more, we get numb to harsher action and harsher
dialogue.

I do believe that I bear some responsibility — all of
us do — to know that our words can create actions.
And there have been times where I've tried to cool

volatile situations. There are other times where I've probably riled people up. But I know that when you get a very emotional racial situation or social situation, my psychology is "We're going to be okay. Let's settle down. Let's stop overreacting." The most educated people I've ever met in my life not only have a high IQ, they have a high EQ, an "emotional quotient." People who overreact tend almost always to be wrong. The truth is always gray, not black and white. The truth is almost always in the middle and emotions need to be tempered.

People are happy at ESPN. People smile. A lot of people wanted to work in sports, and they are working in sports. And they have a good health plan, a nice company, a beautiful campus, a good cafeteria, and I find people enjoy ESPN. Now there are the downfalls of corporate America. The ills of corporate. But by and large, I've never worked at a happier place. And that goes a long way in quality of life. I don't know what the pay is at ESPN compared to other media companies, but the happy quotient is way above average. And I've worked for several good media companies that didn't have this general sense of contentment.

I'm not some shill. It's a big corporation. As I said earlier, it's an aircraft carrier, not a sailboat. The turning radius is slow and gradual, and sometimes you have to wait for stuff, and you're, like, "Can't we cut through the red tape?" But that's just corporate America. It's different than a law firm with eight guys or gals. So that is just innate in a company of our size.

JALEN ROSE, *Basketball Analyst:*

The funny thing about athletes and even entertainers is that they all say the same two things: first, they don't care what the media says about them — they never watch or read anything about themselves and it doesn't matter or motivate them at all; and second, it's not about the money. Well, they're lying on both.

VENUS WILLIAMS, *Tennis Player:*

I don't listen to a lot of what's said about me, especially if I'm playing. I find it never helps to evaluate someone else's opinion of you. So when I watch my matches, I usually watch with the sound off. When I do listen, I hardly ever agree with anything they say, to be honest with you. I sometimes think, "Don't they know the game at all?" There are very few commentators who I actually agree with. But then I've never done a commentating job. You probably have to find some way to keep the conversation going, so you might end up saying anything.

Not even ESPN can win them all. Of ESPN's misfires, there is probably no better example than the great

Mobile Phone Runaround of 2006, a case of ESPN trying to branch out in a forest where it was a complete stranger—and so quickly that it promptly got lost. It sounded good: a mobile phone that supplied not only the basics of a telephone but also, for the sports fan, nearly instant access to scores (five whole seconds before they'd appear on a TV screen!), breaking sports news, columnists, and other assorted jock poop. A specially designed phone seemed a handsome creation in black with red buttons. It had a retro aura, but if anything, viewers of ESPN are accustomed to high-tech glitz— bold graphics, futuristic displays.

But design was only a small factor in the phone's failure—and it definitely did fail. When 240,000 customers are projected for a service, and only 10,000 show up, that's not success. Disney also had a troubled mobile phone division, and in fiscal year 2006, the combined loss from the Disney and ESPN phones was $135 million.

The story goes that ESPN president George Bodenheimer attended the first Disney board meeting in Orlando, Florida, just after the company had bought Pixar, the innovative animation factory, and spotted Apple CEO Steve Jobs in a hallway. It seemed like a good time to introduce himself. "I am George Bodenheimer," he said to Jobs. "I run ESPN." Jobs just looked at him and said nothing other than "Your phone is the dumbest fucking idea I have ever heard," then turned and walked away.

STEVE BORNSTEIN:

The phone was a stupid idea. I told that to George and to Skipper. It was a big bet that was bound to fail also thought it was off-brand, because I get very angry at my cell phone when it doesn't work. When the phone doesn't work—which is every fucking day—I don't want to be angry at ESPN. I'd rather get angry at Verizon. That's what I mean by off-brand. I didn't want to have to call ESPN and say, "From my house to my office, it's six point six miles, can you just make it so I can make a fucking phone call on my way to work?"

JOHN SKIPPER:

Going into the mobile phone business, there were a few fathers, despite it being a failure, and I was one of them. But there were a number of other people. The strategic planning guys at Disney had identified that going into the mobile phone business might be a good idea. Remember you had a model in Europe and Asia where these things had been big business, and we have the philosophy at ESPN that we are not going to allow ourselves to be flanked by a platform, the way lots of companies have been.

SALIL MEHTA, *Executive Vice President of ESPN Enterprises:*

I was working at Disney's Corporate Strategic Planning group and we developed the first business plans for the branded Disney cell phone and ESPN cell phone. We made the first feasibility assessments, then started advocating the concept to a handful of ESPN executives. Yes, there were concerns: for example, would subscriber frustration at an ESPN phone's call quality boomerang to become resentment for ESPN? But for the most part, ESPN executives, especially John Skipper, aggressively supported the concept, using the mission of ESPN — "to serve sports fans" — as a key rationale. "If fans were going to get their sports on cell phones, ESPN has to be there," he would argue. It evoked a long line of successful new-product introductions at ESPN. Skipper himself argued several years prior that if fans were reading about sports in a magazine, ESPN had to be there. Others had argued that if fans were going to try to get scores on the Internet, ESPN had to be there.

JOHN SKIPPER:

Sports Illustrated was a magazine; they ended up getting flanked by cable television and Internet, any number of things. We decided we were never going to get flanked by anything. Where fans get sports news and information, we're going to be there.

We completely miscalculated two things — primarily, in my opinion, with two major outside factors. We had made the calculation that approximately 5 percent of people change carriers in any given month. Gee, well, when you make it possible to take your phone number, that percentage is going to 6, 7, and 8, right? But what happened is, all the phone companies did massive retention efforts—Verizon, T-Mobile, and Sprint, who was our partner but also a competitor. Everybody went, "No way we're letting people move," so they did lots and lots of plans—"Stay with Us," Verizon Family Plan, they did all these things to keep people, so it actually went from 5 to, like, 3. Our pool to get customers from is only the people who are switching, and that pool went down.

By the way, this all happened under me. I was in charge of the mobile phone. It was Skipper's Debacle. It was the company's. We've moved on, and we've done well, and by the way, under George, yes, it was livable, there didn't have to be a scapegoat. A lot of companies might have made me a scapegoat, right? "He fucked up, he's out of here." Not here.

SALIL MEHTA:

The decision to approve the project went all the way to Michael Eisner, and to tell the truth, this was actually one of the easier projects to get funded in my experience at Disney. The combination of the enormous passion that ESPN brought out in its fans, along with the unique ability for an ESPN phone to give you one-click access to the world of ESPN convinced Disney's senior team that an ESPN service was close to a slam dunk.

We could not have been more confident in our

eventual success. But almost immediately after it went on sale, the phone ran into problems: (1) We underestimated the stickiness of the big carrier networks and their newly introduced "free in-plan calling" offers; (2) the ESPN bulky handset was no match for the slender appeal of the Motorola RAZR; (3) the first price was far too high; (4) we were only available at Best Buy; (5) in truth, consumers simply did not pick phone service for even the best possible content experience. We began cutting the price and flooding the ESPN airwaves with our marketing message, but to no avail. Within six months of the launch, it became clear that we were not going to make it. The phone experience really did show the limits of ESPN. Market research backed up our intuition that if the mobile phone's screen could really showcase ESPN, consumers would sign up. But in reality, mobile phone service is an extremely complicated selection decision for consumers, and not even the best content experience, nor the best marketing from ESPN, could really impact that.

That said, we surmised that the ESPN content experience would be extremely attractive to the big carriers. We were able to establish an auction between AT&T, Sprint, and Verizon, and reached an innovative agreement to license the Mobile ESPN application to Verizon. The deal was lucrative enough to help offset most of the losses incurred by the experience. But far more importantly, the experience gave

ESPN a critical edge that it still enjoys today in mobile. There are strong competitors to ESPN.com online, but there is no one close to ESPN's position in mobile. And as mobile only increases in importance, the Mobile ESPN experience will in the long run prove critical to ESPN's ability to continue its dominance on all platforms.

JOHN KOSNER, *Senior Vice President of Digital Media:*

I think it was the right intention, but I think it was a business miscalculation, meaning that we tried to get into a business that was different than what we specialize at. We got into a business built around hardware. We got into a business where the purchase intent is determined by a lot of factors other than what we really do great. So, if you take a look at our success in mobile today, where we have like 65 percent market share on the mobile web for sports, a lot of that was born of the work that went into Mobile ESPN. Some of the work on the product side was quite good. I think overall they took a look at what they thought the idea was and what they thought the business plan was and they decided that they could make it work. Again, this is a company that largely has been very successful at everything that it has tried. I've been at other companies where that's been up and down, and so sometimes when you've been involved in some big failures, it gives you hesitation the next time. But this is a company that has always succeeded, and I think that is part of what led into it.

GEORGE BODENHEIMER:

I love it when people want to talk to me about how the phone was a flaw or a mistake or a black mark on my record. I don't look at it as anything like that. It was a tremendous learning opportunity in a portion of the sports media business that's going to be huge. If you're not doing things to learn and try to get out in front, then you're truly going to diminish your company. We tried, but we were on the wrong business plan; we made a quick correction and shifted gears and now we have the largest sports mobile website that exists. So we're off to the races. There's absolutely margin for error here. Any time something like that happens, I think it's good for the employees and good for all of us. ESPN isn't bulletproof, and the day we start thinking we are will be a bad day.

BOB IGER:

Companies that don't take risks don't grow. We are going to keep trying new things to improve the fan experience, and ESPN's move to local websites and a 3-D network are just the latest iterations of entrepreneurial thinking that's smart, and calculated, even if the future isn't crystal clear.

*By 2008, bloggers, online columnists, and instant ana-
lyzers were beginning to dominate the newly digitalized
world of sports, and ESPN increasingly found itself a
target: "Turner was better on basketball"; "Watch*
Monday Night Football *with the sound turned down";
"Joe Morgan sucked on* Sunday Night Baseball"; "*The
network blew it with NASCAR," and so on, and on.*

*But for Mark Gross, Norby Williamson's right-hand
man and one of the highest regarded executives at ESPN,
none of those things mattered, because Gross was in
charge of a show unique to the network—a show prized
as if it were the Golden Fleece and the Hope Diamond
put together. Above all the whining and bellyaching,
one could almost hear Gross and his fellow executives
saying, "Thank you, Lord, for* College GameDay." *And
the Lord said, "You're welcome."*

GameDay *wasn't just "the show that had everything"; it was the show that defined what "everything"
about college football was. That included the best analysis, the best predictions, and the best inside information,
all served up amid the excitement and spectacle of a
great American celebration.*

*One big plus was the equivalent of perfect casting in
a drama or sitcom: Kirk Herbstreit had graduated from
quarterback at Ohio State to highly credible football
analyst on* GameDay; *Lee Corso, surviving member of
the original 1987 starting lineup, would go to great
lengths, yet somehow never too great, to get a laugh; host*

Chris Fowler captained the ship and kept it steadily on course; and cohost Erin Andrews had great contacts among the coaching ranks and great popularity among the college crowd, having replaced the old Farrah Fawcett poster as reigning campus sex symbol. Who needed a poster when you could see and hear the living goddess in person holding forth with effortless expertise?

CHRIS FOWLER:

Virginia Tech obviously has had a close relationship with the college football unit and with *GameDay* since the late nineties. Very few other campuses are as close-knit, had the sense of unity, had the sense of pride that came from being somewhat isolated geographically, a little bit of an outsider, a latecomer to the landscape. So when you go there, you sense that, if your antenna is up at all, there's something different about this place.

When the shootings happened, I didn't like the national media coverage; I thought it was missing the point. I think that people who had parachuted in, descending upon Blacksburg, had no understanding of what they were doing. I don't think it was being represented in a way that was all that informed.

Now, I'm an outsider, I'm not a Hokie. But I felt like I was qualified to write an essay expressing what I saw on the TV screen over those few days. And it wasn't intended to be a healing thing for Virginia Tech. I would never presume to speak for them. I was just trying to explain to people that this isn't just another campus, so when something like this happens here, it has a little bit of a different poignancy than even something that awful would have somewhere else.

I never had any kind of response to anything I've written like that. I mean, the comments that were made after the piece was posted, the way that it was getting virally spread around the community of the alums and students, and the responses that I got were unbelievable. It shook me up. My wife and I would sit there and read notes on it. I wasn't trying to provide them medicine for their grief. But they really appreciated that perspective from an outsider. I still get comments.

GameDay going there was not a big part of the event. Being that together for the first time, in that big a number as a community after they'd been away all summer, *that* was the event, the pregame ceremony, the team running out, how [Virginia Tech football coach Frank] Beamer and the team chose to draw inspiration, and what it meant to have the football team on the field for those students — *that* was the thing. I was very proud of the collective effort and the sensibility that prevailed.

LEE CORSO:

I can describe *College GameDay* for you like this: in the studio, it's like an actor who's doing a TV show with a canned audience. There's no audience, no feedback, no nothing. And then there's the actor that goes on Broadway. He immediately gets a rush because he's playing to an audience. That's exactly the way it feels. And you know that actors will tell you they have to do Broadway every once in a while just to stay sharp.

It's the most gratifying thing to be done at ESPN. Because you get instant reaction to the performance and that's great stuff. College football is our vehicle, but we're in the entertainment business. And once you lose that, you're never going to make it.

KIRK HERBSTREIT:

My dad played at Ohio State. He was a captain there. So before I even went to Ohio State, I was probably more of an Ohio State fan than I was while I was *at* Ohio State as a player, and since leaving. Now, I'm not going to hide the fact or pretend that when the camera's off I am not an Ohio State fan and that my four boys aren't dressed every Saturday in their scarlet-and-gray jerseys and are at home with my wife singing the fight song when they wake up to breakfast. I mean, that's just the way I am and that's the way I always will be and that's the way my kids will be. But with that being said, I still feel that I would challenge anybody to look at me in the fifteen years that I've been on air to ever see if—without somebody on set kind of needling me about Ohio State, you wouldn't know where

I went to school. And that's my goal: just to tell it like I see it, and if it's good, it's good, and if it's bad, it's bad, and nothing personal. For me, for whatever reason, it's not difficult to analyze teams and, if they happen to be Ohio State or Tennessee or Texas, it's just what you do. And away we go.

Parting was much more sorrowful than sweet when Dan Patrick announced, in the summer of 2007, that he was leaving ESPN after eighteen years with the company. Fans were heartbroken; Patrick had been not just popular but deeply popular—a "voice of witty sanity," as Richard Sandomir put it in the New York Times. *Patrick was one of the ESPN greats, and he personified the kind of integrity that can't be faked.*

Patrick had played just about every role available at ESPN on nearly every possible show, but of course his greatest success had come as co-anchor with Keith Olbermann on SportsCenter. *But Patrick's versatility had become something of a curse. ESPN worked him to a frazzle, and in announcing his retirement from the network, Patrick said that "management knew I was tired and needed to recharge my battery" while denying there was any "animosity" between him and his ESPN bosses. Inside observers were skeptical. Patrick conceded he'd just been "going through the motions" in his last couple of years at the network.*

Executives balked when Patrick wanted to talk on his ESPN Radio show about where he might go next

and issued a terse, hard-nosed statement: "ESPN con-
tractually bans all employees from making specific
announcement of their futures on the airwaves." Later,
executives would grumble about, and threaten, any
ESPN personalities who wanted to appear as Patrick's
guests at his new venues.

A devoted family man and clever wordsmith, Patrick
could write even better than he talked, contributing
popular features and columns to ESPN: The Magazine
and later serving as senior writer for Sports Illustrated.
He was one of a kind, yet so productive and prolific that
there often seemed to be three or four of him working at
the same time.

DAN PATRICK:

All I wanted to do was simplify my schedule so I
could be at home with my kids—that was it. It was
nothing. It wasn't money. I don't care what anybody
will tell you. It was so simple that the quality of life
was all that I was asking for, and they refused to do it.
All I'd asked George to do is help me stay there, and
he didn't, and it was disheartening that I only heard
from him after I left, and then he called to say, as if
he was reading from a piece of paper, "Dan Patrick,
we really appreciate you being here," and after that I
was, "Yeah, okay, great. Thank you, George."

No matter what anybody says there, that was what
it came down to—"give me quality of life," and

Norby wouldn't do it. I obviously got knocked back—it took the wind out of me. So I blame myself because I could have said to Shapiro, "Fuck you," but I didn't, because this is where I'm supposed to work, so it was "Thank you, sir, may I have another?"

I'm not a victim, and I don't want to come across as "Oh, woe is me." I thought it could have been run in a more civil way, like grown-ups, but everything was precedent setting, and that's a shame, because I didn't want it to end like that. I just felt bad that that's the way it ended. And it didn't have to. That's why I told you, if I was taken advantage of or manipulated or whatever, I did it to myself—big deal. Big boy. All I wanted was a little respect in the final days there; if we could have done something, I would have been a lifer.

Television is, of course, awash in awards. ESPN not only doles them out but has shelves full of those it has won. Among the most meaningful were the first two that the network ever received from a group called Military Reporters and Editors (MRE), which, in 2007, gave top prizes to "An Un-American Tragedy," a four-part series that appeared on ESPN.com, and Tillman's Final Mission, *a half-hour documentary hosted by Bob Ley; the film also won a prize from the Deadline Club of New York and was nominated for an Emmy. Tillman was Pat Tillman, a seeming hero who led what appeared to be an idealized all-American life: playing pro football for the Arizona Cardinals, then quitting to enlist in the U.S. Army Rangers. On April 22, 2004, in Afghanistan, three bullets brought that all-American life to an end.*

A simple story of heroism and courage? To investigative reporter Mike Fish, who already had an array of awards under his belt, something seemed wrong. Many months of work resulted in the revelatory online series and documentary in 2006. Fish's work was heaped with praise — perhaps most poignantly from one of those Internet websites that seem always to be negative: "We bloggers bash ESPN a lot, and often with good reason, but they sometimes do phenomenal journalism at the Worldwide Leader, and this is one instance of that."

MIKE FISH, *Investigative Reporter:*

Imagine this whole image of Pat Tillman, the great American who joins the Army and whatnot: his death was shocking. I think a lot of people were just really taken aback by it. And I personally was, because I'd followed his career, knew who he was, and he was someone, from a distance, I thought very highly of. And his death obviously jarred me and jarred a lot of other people. I think the stories that followed are what triggered my investigation. The people at ESPN encouraged me to pursue it. None of it seemed to make sense. It didn't add up. The idea that he's supposedly shot by the enemy, tried to charge up this hill—it sounded too much like a drama or a movie, if you will. Too scripted.

And then the fact that it was sometime after that that it was revealed that he wasn't shot by the enemy, that indeed he may have been shot by friendly fire. Then a lot of things started to come out. There were a lot of holes in the image that the government was putting out, that he was this great war hero, and it turns out that he was also in adjudication with Noam Chomsky, who was antiwar, and all sorts of things were starting to leak out. And at that point, probably a half dozen people at ESPN had a very strong interest in this particular story and encouraged me. Soon I was battling the military and the Washington establishment, plus trying to gain the confidence of Tillman's family. And the other thing is the effort back in Bristol of putting that package together, like the graphics and the way it was designed—all those kinds of things which I'm totally clueless on and were magnificent.

A lot of people were really moved by it. It's probably the thing I've written that has moved the most people that really had a passion and really had a lot of concern about it and really enjoyed it. There was also a faction that was just adamant, that thought that "Hey, you signed up for the military. Pat Tillman's no different than, you know, Joe Jones from Hoboken or Saginaw, Michigan. And why are we playing up this professional football player?" Then there were other people who thought it was, you know, uh, we were denigrating the war effort or being critical of the administration, stuff like that. It went both ways.

Ultimately—I'm not saying it necessarily resulted in, but I think that the story itself kind of fueled, the Congressional hearings that followed. And at the end of the day... Well, let others judge, but I think what we did really stood out.

Perhaps in an attempt to expunge all the tales of ESPN's allegedly having been a wild wellspring of sexual misconduct in its youth, the network got very tough with employees who faced such charges in its adulthood. Two of the saddest cases reflected the new severity: Harold Reynolds in 2006 and Sean Salisbury two years later. They seem linked by circumstance; it was even said that when Reynolds was confronted with allegations, he complained that others, including, by name, Sean, were getting away with worse.

Salisbury would merely suffer the indignity of not having his contract renewed. But Reynolds was outright fired by a tribunal that included Norby Williamson, Marcia Keegan, and Steve Anderson. Whatever the similarities, there also seems to be a wide disparity between the two offenses. Reynolds supposedly gave an overly enthusiastic "hug" (some called it a "grab") to a twenty-one-year-old intern while dining ever so elegantly at an Outback Steakhouse. Salisbury's principal misdeed was decidedly more colorful; he took a cell-phone photo of his "junk"—his genitalia—and showed it to coworkers while gamboling at a bar.

Reynolds, a baseball analyst, was an eleven-year veteran of ESPN, and Salisbury had logged twelve years as an NFL analyst for the network. It would be years before Salisbury owned up to precisely what he'd done, but always he maintained that while it was "stupid," "dumb," and "sophomoric," it was not a firing offense. In the hypersensitive new climate, however, and whether or not the exhibition of the photograph had met with approval or revulsion, Salisbury's fate was sealed.

His reaction was to go ballistic, threatening even to sue Deadspin, the web mag that had never been successfully sued even though it ran inside scuttlebutt all the time. Reynolds went less public with his anger, even though his firing occurred just four months after he signed a six-year, $5 million contract.

Lest the punishments seem unduly harsh, both men suffered from damaged reputations—from previous complaints that had been biding time in their files. Reynolds probably had the thicker file, and yet he was also a particularly well liked guy around the office—and elsewhere. A former pro ballplayer, he volunteered time to Little League kids and became "the Pied Piper" of the sport, according to a colleague who also accurately summed up the case: "Sad, it was sad, but it is what it is."

SEAN SALISBURY:

The incident didn't happen on campus, it was at a bar. It was just a stupid couple-of-minutes incident. It was not like somebody went into the bathroom. It was just a thing that college kids do. I'm not pooh-poohing it. It was dumb. I take full 100 percent responsibility. But I also know that I wouldn't sell out the other couple guys that are superstars that could have got in trouble. I wouldn't do it. I would never give up a name. You don't sell people out, and if I'd sold them out it would have caused them embarrassment for their careers. I wouldn't have done it, and I still won't to this day, and nobody will ever know who it is. I will never ever let anybody inside on that, ever. Because it's friends of mine, and they're popular, and I would never ever get anybody in trouble. So we'll leave it at that.

MIKE SOLTYS:

In Harold's case, you've got a twenty-, twenty-one-year-old college student who's in your employ, who wide-eyed trusts him, goes right along, and then he grabs her. And it all was work related. In Sean's case, he's doing crazy things at local bars. And ultimately he didn't get renewed.

SEAN SALISBURY:

When you're having a few drinks with buddies, and you do something stupid, you've got to sometimes suffer the ramifications that come with it. And you ask if it was off campus, you ask if it was a private cell phone, you ask if it wasn't walking around showing thirty people, but if it offends one person, then you've done wrong, and ESPN's right. I was raised to make good decisions, and sometimes I make stupid decisions, and it's amazing how a very short few minutes or few seconds of time can have a lasting effect on your career and life. And that incident for me did. I'm trying to forgive myself.

Believe me, I have probably done worse in my life than what I did with that cell phone in a bar one night, honestly. We've all gotten behind the wheel of a car when we've had probably three beers instead of one, saying, "I shouldn't be doing this." We've all done that, and that's far more tragic than me doing what I did. But it's really helped me rehab my life— my social life and the rest of it, and how I appreciate it more. I'll never ever take for granted what I did, and I'll always pat ESPN on the back for what they did for me, and there's still some major hurt that I have inside. Since then I've gone to anger management because I was hurt inside, and it was the same time my dad was dying, so I'm to blame for allowing something to creep in; I allowed them to have that decision to make.

I worked for two more years, I didn't get fired. Then on March 2 or 3 of 2008, I had a meeting, and we sat there and talked, and they said because they had just signed Cris Carter and I had been there twelve years, they said, "You know what? We're not going to renew your contract." I really didn't think they were going to anyway. I mean, I knew they loved me, and had the incident in 2006 not happened, I believe I'd still be there. I know I would be.

But I also understood the position they felt that they were in. I was up for another raise and it would have been a lot of money, and they felt it was time to move on, and I said, "Okay." You know, what are you going to say? It's not like they looked at me and said, "You're fired because of the incident two years ago." I shook hands with Steve Anderson and Norby Williamson and we talked for a few minutes, they wished me luck, and I was out the door, and that was it. It was pretty much that simple.

MATT SANDULLI:
Harold Reynolds was the first and only Major League Baseball player ever to introduce himself to me, which I kid him about to this day. He was a Mariner and I was in Detroit doing a feature on Dave Fleming, the left-hander for Seattle who pitched at Georgia. I was standing outside of their dugout, and Harold comes up. It's three o'clock in the afternoon when he walks up, looks at me, and goes, "Hey, I'm Harold Reynolds." I'm, like, "Hey, I'm Matt Sandulli from ESPN." "So what are you doing?" "I'm doing a feature on Dave Fleming, dah, dah, dah, dah." Just

out of the blue he decided to come say hello to me. I don't know what he was doing or whatever. I kidded him about that when he came to work for us. But from a professional standpoint, one thing I would say about Harold, when he first got here, he really didn't have much to say—he was, like, oh boy, enthusiasm, great personality, good guy, not sure he's going to do well because he doesn't have much to say. And he really worked at it and got himself to talk. He does a good job. I loved working with him on the college games because when he was analyzing the game, he did it from a coaching perspective. He was teaching; the whole game, he was teaching. It was the perfect forum for him.

I was on vacation when it happened, so it was July, and I got an e-mail. I'm, like, "Okay." As a group we were told that Harold was no longer with the company.

DANA JACOBSON, *Anchor:*
In one of the end zones there's a mural called *Word of Life,* but nicknamed Touchdown Jesus, and this is part of Notre Dame football. I'm a Michigan grad, and I bet on Michigan–Notre Dame games. So in 2008, when I spoke at this roast for Mike Greenberg and Mike Golic [of ESPN's *Mike & Mike in the Morning*], I was obviously going to rip Notre Dame and make fun of Notre Dame football. Drunk, in the state I was in—not funny, cursing around the

reference to Touchdown Jesus—not funny. I think it was a combination of the amount of cursing that I did, of continually going back to Notre Dame, of referencing Touchdown Jesus, it was probably just the combination. There's a great picture on the Internet; I drank vodka from the bottle. I think I said something like "it's my liquid courage."

It was probably the most embarrassing night that I've ever had. Some of my bosses were there, and then the next morning having to send out e-mails right away and apologize—that is *so* not like me. I've been at a million events before and never been drunk and a million events after. It was just a bad night.

Deadspin broke the story when I had already been suspended. A week had gone by, and I was suspended for the following week for inappropriate behavior, one week's suspension without pay. I had already sent a bunch of "I'm sorry's" especially to Greenie and Golic; it was their night, and I felt that I had embarrassed them from just being drunk and making a fool of myself, being inappropriate and being that drunk on a stage with a microphone.

My biggest thing that I have stood firm on is I just don't like the fact that people think I "cursed Jesus." That I was drunk? Fine. That I was inappropriate? Yeah. That I was at a level of out of control that I shouldn't have been at a work-sponsored roast? You bet. I made a fool of myself. I embarrassed myself, I embarrassed the company. But I did not curse Jesus!

I was scared for my job, even. I didn't get in trouble ever in my life, except once in sixth grade, I think, on the playground. So I was scared; was I going to have a job? What was going to happen? I was suspended before the *Deadspin* article came out. I was suspended on Friday, the *Deadspin* article came out on Sunday. It was a week. A week's suspension without pay. I accepted that as my punishment. I knew when one of my supervisors came down after the show on Friday that clearly I was going to be suspended. There was no other reason that he was down there. Then we needed to go to building five, which was Human Resources. I was, like, "Okay, I'm getting suspended," and the worst thing, in some ways, was I missed the Winter X Games from it, and I do stuff there and I left them in a lurch. So even worse that I had already embarrassed myself and let people down, I then let them down as well. Calling my parents that weekend to tell them was one of the worst phone calls I've ever had to make, knowing that it was in an Atlantic City paper, knowing that my dad goes into work and googles.

I got some nasty mail; there were a lot of phone calls. It was not a bright, shining spot of my career. The following Monday, when I came back to work, I did an apology on the air that I wrote—a lot of people think it was written for me; it wasn't, I wrote it. I mean, it makes me laugh, I'm a writer for television, it's what I do, I write my stuff; why would somebody else apologize for something I did? Golic and Greenie were great actually. I called them Sunday right after it happened and I was very emotional, crying on both their voice mails. When I came in on Monday and saw both of them, they both just gave me a big hug.

RECE DAVIS:

We've all had our moments. I remember we were once doing a series where Jay Bilas had gone all-access with different basketball programs throughout the country, and he had done something with Sherri Coale and the Oklahoma women's basketball program. I don't use a prompter unless I'm doing *SportsCenter,* so what came out on the air was, "Jay Bilas takes you inside the Oklahoma women." As soon as the tape rolled, my head immediately hit the desk. Bilas was across the room cackling and just killing me.

DANYELLE SARGENT, *Reporter:*

It was an after-midnight show, it was me and Robert Flores, and it was literally about 1:30, two o'clock in the morning. We were just waiting for one game to be over so we could finish our show. And the ESPN board went out on *SportsCenter.* So they, like, tossed it over to us and we had no idea what we were doing. They were, like, we're coming over to you. And so we vamped for, like, ten, fifteen seconds, and they had cut to a tape segment we had already done because they had nothing—technical crew had nothing ready to go because we weren't even supposed to be on. So they cut to a taped segment of Robert and me saying, "What the f—was that?" It was not really my personality, though. I don't get wound up with this kind of stuff. My audio person never cut my mic, so I blasted the United States.

Right after they told me about it, I was, like, oh, my god, I'm, like, am I gonna get fired? And then the next morning, I called the guy who was in charge of ESPN news at the time. He was, like, yeah, come in and talk to me. And they weren't making a big deal about it. They were, like, yeah, you shouldn't have done that. Anyone who works in TV knows it's something that everybody does. It's no excuse.

BONNIE BERNSTEIN:
I have an insatiable need to learn and an equally insatiable desire to share—and to provide global perspective. And I think global perspective can be really effective if you can share analogies outside of sports. So I was on *Mike & Mike,* and we were talking about high school basketball players, and I thought about the *New York Times* article before I shared it, and I said to myself, "As long as you attribute it, before you share, while you're sharing, after you share, people will understand that this is not some opinion that you concocted on your own, it was information you gleaned from a first-person article in one of the most

reputable newspapers in the world." That's the way I thought about it. And so I prefaced it by saying, "This is an article in the *New York Times*. It was a female Palestinian suicide bomber who couldn't understand why she couldn't fight for the nobility of her country the way her brother and father did." And then I brought it back to young basketball players who are told not to worry about the classroom and just focus on basketball.

The analogy was 100 percent applicable. What I failed to understand was sports talk radio is simply not the forum for sharing those types of intricate analogies, because people will take a very small snippet of that and attach it to your thought processes. It's wrong, if you listen to it — which many of the people who wrote about it probably didn't — but that's the way the world spins. My intentions were nothing but pure: to try to spin it to where I'm comparing high school kids to Palestinian suicide bombers is ludicrous and offensive, especially if you know anything about my background and how my circle of friends is nothing short of a veritable melting pot.

So I wanted to put an apology out there to try to set the record straight, and the interesting thing is, the president of, like, the Palestinian Journalists' Association wrote me the sweetest e-mail. We wound up getting a wonderful e-mail exchange going — so much so that he wrote an article that ended up in the

Huffington Post, commending me for reaching out and trying to rectify the situation. And while for that brief news cycle it was really disheartening, I actually felt good about it on the other side because I'd made a new friend. I thought that we were able to come to an adult understanding about it, and you know, ultimately those things live through a news cycle and we move on. Nobody's perfect. And it was a great lesson learned for me, and I felt like I was a smarter and better person for having gone through it.

LOU HOLTZ, *College Football Analyst:*

Forty-seven years ago my wife bought me a pipe, and I started smoking at age twenty-six. Now she wants me to give it up. I said to her, "I don't abuse you verbally or physically. I don't gamble. I don't drink, and I don't run around. Which one of those vices do you want me to take up? I'm going to have a vice, and if you want me to run around, I'll put the pipe down and never pick it up again." She said, "The pipe is fine."

It's amazing how many people recognize me on TV as "Dr. Lou" and don't have a clue that I'm in the Hall of Fame as a coach or had the second most wins at Notre Dame. I never thought people would recognize me for being on TV. I'm surprised by how many people not only watch ESPN but live and die with ESPN.

What I said about Hitler was taken out of context. I talked about leadership, and leadership on a losing football team. People said, "They need leadership," and I said, "I disagree, they have leadership. Every organization has leadership." And I said, "A good leader leads a people forward. Hitler was a good leader, for a bad cause. Just because you have people follow you and you're a leader doesn't mean it's necessarily positive. They got leadership on that football team, but obviously it's not the right type of leadership, because they're losing." Jimmy Jones was a good leader but nine hundred people died for a bad cause. All I was trying to say is that not all leadership is good. Maybe I didn't express it as well as I should have. If Jimmy Jones wasn't a leader, he wouldn't have been able to talk nine hundred people into drinking the poisoned Kool-Aid. Every football team has leadership, and it doesn't necessarily mean it's good leadership. Leadership means people follow you. If you're leading for a good cause, that's great. But if people are following you for a bad cause, that's bad. That's the only point I was trying to make.

RECE DAVIS:

I knew exactly what Lou Holtz meant. Lou served in the military and is to some degree a student of military history, and I think from that generation I've heard that analogy used before, that because of the message and the way people followed him, Hitler exhibited qualities of leadership, but they were leading in the wrong direction. That's all he meant—that when you're a leader, you have to make sure that you're leading to the right place. But in our culture now, that's one of the taboo words, that's one of the taboo analogies. It was why I immediately tried to extricate him from it on the air and say—I think if I remember correctly, what I said was, "What you mean was, Hitler was a bad leader. He led them to the wrong place." And I tried to mitigate it as much as I could, because I sensed what the reaction would be, even though I knew exactly what he meant. I knew he wasn't comparing Rich Rodriguez to Adolf Hitler; that was obvious if you listen to what he said.

LOU HOLTZ:

I had to apologize, and I really didn't want to, because my intentions were good. I think the point I made was very valid, very solid, and it was a different angle than the way people look at it. I did tell ESPN I didn't want to apologize, as a matter of fact. I didn't think I should. But for the benefit of ESPN, I did. They had it written up there. I would have rather put it in my own words, but I read what they put up there, and it was the right thing to do for ESPN. I felt that what I was trying to say was a very solid point that people don't always look at in that way. I think what I said was true and accurate.

RECE DAVIS:

You want Lou to be himself. That's the magic of Lou Holtz. It's not that he's trained at the Connecticut School of Broadcasting. The magic of Lou Holtz is that he is a master communicator because of his personality. I remember he once was trying to make a point right off the top of the show that you have a winner and a loser, but what he said was, "Every week, 50 percent of the teams lose and 50 percent win." What he meant was somebody has to win, and I just sort of looked at him then looked at the camera and said, "I promise we'll try to get more insightful as we go along."

GERRY MATALON, *Senior Coordinating Producer:*

I often say, talent are the same as us and different from us, and we need to recognize when they're the same and when they're different. To me, they're the same when they're sitting in a cafeteria talking about a family situation or something they have to fix in the house. But it's totally different when we go to do our jobs, because when I have a bad day, what happens? I get a bad phone call, a bad e-mail, have a bad meeting, or possibly a change of assignment. Those guys have a bad day and they get all four that I got, plus it shows up in newspapers and on the Internet. And it's there forever.

STUART SCOTT:

I can't be that concerned with how I'm perceived. I care about how my mother and father think about me and how my friends and how my loved ones think about me. I care about how my ex-wife thinks about me; she and I are still good friends and we do a good job raising our kids. It matters to me. But it doesn't matter to me what people who are writing a blog on the Internet think. I can't think about that.

Being a father. That's it. That's the answer. That's my answer. I'm convinced of that. I remember there was a day — my oldest daughter, who is fourteen now, but when she was about two or three, there was a show called *Gullah Gullah Island,* a Disney show, that was her favorite TV show. I was doing the late-night *SportsCenter* that aired all morning long. So there was one morning and I'd done the show the night before, and I got up and I said, "Taylor, do you want to watch Daddy on TV?" And she said — and it's not just what she said but how she said it — "No, I want to watch *Gullah Gullah Island.*" And I remembered thinking that day, if it's not a big deal to her, and she was my life, then it can't be that big of a deal.

JIM ROME:

Of course, I don't want a bunch of lunatics calling up and ranting and raving irresponsibly and recklessly.

If they take offense at something I say, and they want to challenge me or go up against me, great. That's fine. I'd say the same thing about a guest. Most people would never ever call a radio show. Who can afford to stay on hold for an hour or ninety minutes or two hours to call a radio show? Our research indicates that, like, 1 or 2 percent of the audience would ever call in. You need to program to the 98 percent that would never call and not cater just to the 2 percent that does. You gotta know your room. There's a wide sampling of the audience that would never call the show, so don't assume that everybody who calls in is everybody who's listening and that it's one and the same, because it's not.

CHRIS BERMAN:

I've been treated unfairly by the TV sports critics. They say I'm a clown. It's an act. When they use the word "act," it's like *"aaact."* "Act" would be playing a character who you're clearly not, by definition in Webster's. To act is to take on the characteristics of someone else. "We don't like Berman's style." Fine. "Don't like Berman's act" is, *"What act?!"* What is that? What would that be? Or that he's a clown. You mean I don't come prepared? Stop. Stop. The most hurtful thing they write is that I'm just out there making events be about me. God, no. I'm just excited to be part of it. So maybe it's a little over the top for some people. But some people aren't excited enough.

I think, "God, I wish he would show a little bit of excitement. Doesn't he like being at this football game?" The company really hasn't had my back on that front. They never felt it was important enough.

STUART SCOTT:

I had cancer last year. I had appendicular cancer, which is very, very, very rare, like extremely rare. I had appendicitis. It didn't rupture. It was inflamed, it got taken out—I was in Pittsburgh for the Monday night game. It was malignant.

So three or four days later I had surgery to remove, like, anything close. I got a big scar. They took apart my colon, anything. I did six months' chemotherapy. Now, after they finished the surgery, they didn't find any more cancer, but they said to do chemo anyway. Every six months I have to have a CT scan. Now, I've been clean. I worry, what if this comes back and I've got to live every day? So juxtapose that up against what somebody says.

As late as 2000, Bill Simmons was still thinking seriously about quitting the sports business and getting into real estate, imagining he'd never make it as a writer.

Many years earlier, little William J. Simmons III had first been turned on to sports journalism when he read David Halberstam's 1981 bestseller The Breaks of the Game, *an account of the author's travels with the Portland Trail Blazers during their 1979–80 season.*

Halberstam reflected on what he'd learned about the NBA, pro sports, and life in general while traveling with the team. Simmons "plowed through" the book in one weekend and kept rereading it over months, and years, to come.

After earning a BA in Political Science from Holy Cross College in 1992 and a masters in print journalism from Boston University in 1994, Simmons went looking for work. Hired to report on high school sports for the Boston Herald, he found himself mainly going on "food runs" for the "real" writers on the staff. A subsequent gig at the Boston Phoenix left him so discouraged and broke that he quit the paper to work as a bartender.

Then, in 2001, he gathered his resolve and what money he had and launched his own website, Boston SportsGuy.com—while holding on to the bartending job just in case.

BILL SIMMONS, *Columnist:*

My first goal was to play pro sports. My dad had season tickets for the Celtics, and he took me to games. I just assumed I was going to play for them. But my backup plan was writing a sports column. I was always writing as a kid, I was always reading the best sportswriters, and I had every sports book from the last forty years. I had a popular column in college, and this was the early nineties, the toughest point probably to break into newspapers because everybody had the same idea: "I'll go to college, I'll write, and then I'll work for a newspaper." I worked at the *Boston Herald* for three years, covering high school sports and writing features, but it became pretty clear to me that nobody ahead of me was leaving. It was like being on an NBA team where you don't get to start until you're forty-five years old.

So I just kind of gave up, and in 1996 I decided to leave. I didn't know what I was going to do. I started bartending, but I felt like something was missing. So I started a website that you could only get with an AOL account. It was with this website called Digital City Boston. At the time, the thinking was it was going to be an electronic newspaper.

I was killing myself, and making $50 a week, but in two years, I built my audience to two thousand diehards, which sounds low now, except that there weren't a lot of people online at the time. By 2001, I was up to, like, fifteen or sixteen thousand readers, and that's when ESPN came calling. It's funny; the reason they came calling was because in February of 2001 I was doing these running diaries, where I'd watch something on TV and just write down my thoughts as it happened. Now it's called the live blog, but at the time I'd write everything down and hone it and keep the best jokes and then that's what I'd post. And I did this scathing diary of the 2001 ESPYs, I just killed it. I went after everybody. It was a terrible show. They had Joe Theismann doing comedy, and it was like everything people hate about ESPN. It was perfect for me; I made fun of everything. Well, somebody at ESPN read it, and it started getting passed around to the higher-ups and it landed with John Walsh, who started following me. Then he went back and read all my columns.

JAY LOVINGER, *Editor:*

When I got to ESPN and started working on the Internet, I realized two powerful things about being an editor on the Web: it got rid of the tyranny of time, and it got rid of the tyranny of space. You could run stuff as long as you wanted, and you realized that when you weren't spending a huge amount of time trying to fit text into some kind of arbitrary hole, you had twice as much time to do meaningful work. Not only could you close stuff and have it be published immediately, but even after you closed it, you could then go back and change things if somebody pointed out an error, or if you had something to add or remove. So for me it was really kind of liberating and even fun to edit on the Internet.

Walsh found Bill when he was doing his sportsguy thing in Boston and recommended him for our Page 2 [columns and commentary], and Simmons did some stuff for us that was really good. The first piece he ever did, "Roger Clemens, the Antichrist," was a great piece. He started doing stuff for us on an irregular basis, and we were futzing around; we wanted to hire him, but ESPN kind of see themselves as being able to hire whomever they want, so they never want to seem in too much of a hurry unless it's a competitive thing.

I was speaking to Bill after he'd been doing freelance stuff here for about a year and he told me he was thinking about taking a job the next week at the *Boston Herald*. So I called Walsh up and I said, "John, you've got to do something right now or we're going to lose this guy, and that's really going to be a mistake." So Walsh said something like "We're working on it," and I said, "No, you can't 'work on it.' Call him right now and make him an offer or it's going to be too late." So he did, and the rest was history.

Bill's obviously good for the company, it's just that he's an incredibly pain-in-the-ass guy to work with. You don't really edit him. He turns in his thing, you suggest stuff, he writes "Stet all changes" on the copy, you fight with him over things, he goes to Walsh or Skipper to complain, and you say to yourself, "I don't need this grief." His goal is to get you to the point where it's such a pain in the neck that you just put the stuff through—unless there's something that you're going to get sued over.

I also edited Olbermann, at *Sports Illustrated*. He was a pain in the ass and a whining little baby, but ultimately he was more professional than Simmons. If you edited Keith, he'd whine and scream as if you had betrayed him in some way, but then he'd read the thing, and if the editing was actually helpful, he'd respond—unlike Bill, who would just say no. Bill's thing is "I know what I'm doing, so that's it." You know: "Don't touch anything." It was more satisfying editing Olbermann.

JIMMY KIMMEL:

Simmons is a guy I really like. ESPN.com was my homepage for a long time. I'm not the kind of person who posts things, and I'd never heard of Bill, I'd just happened upon him myself, but he wrote some things that really rang true with me—even some non-sports things. The thing that really made me take notice is that he wrote about the movie *Fast Break,* which was one of my favorite movies as a kid. I couldn't believe that anyone else had even *seen* it. But Bill gave a detailed analysis of the film. Then a few months later, he wrote something nice about my appearance on a Shaquille O'Neal roast, and I sent him an e-mail thanking him. We started corresponding, and when I got a talk show, I hired him to be one of the writers. He's a character. He likes analyzing the show more than writing for it. He's great to work with, a very funny guy who came up with a lot of good ideas, and I miss having him here.

JOHN SKIPPER:

When I went to run ESPN.com, I am not sure I had ever been on the site. I didn't know the first thing about the Internet; I was not an early adopter of technology. In fact, I believed in not being overly involved in the agony and the ecstasy of the early adopters— "Oh, we're the leaders of a new movement!" It's almost evangelical.

John and I didn't have that. We're not leading a movement; we're coming over there to create great content. So we hire Hunter Thompson and David Halberstam and Ralph Wiley and Bill Simmons; we like to read. By the way, you look at the Internet from 2001 to 2003—we brought in feature writers and design and photography; we *magazine'd* ESPN. com. The piece we did miss early on, we missed the big piece on technology. Technology is *part* of the content.

RICK REILLY, *Columnist*:

In 1997, Skipper came to me and said, "Look, we're starting a new magazine, and we want you to write for it." And so a guy named John Papanek, who used to be at *SI,* and I met a bunch, and I was, like, "Why would I leave *SI* for this?" and it was going to be a big, broad, cheap-looking magazine, and they were going to have columns by the announcers, and I just thought it sounded awful. And he says, "No, it's going to be great! It's going to be like *Inside Sports.*"

So I thought about it and said no. Five years later, when I had my contract renewed, they came to me again, and I got closer but still felt like the magazine wasn't anywhere nearly as good as *SI.* But because

Skipper had given me this attention in 1997, I went to *SI* and said, "Look, they're offering me this great job!" And my boss, a guy named Bill Colson, said, "Well, what do you want?" And I said, "I want to write the back-page column every week," because they'd never had anybody write it every week, and I just felt like it needed one guy. And they said okay. And so I really loved doing that. And it worked out great, and then in 2002, they said, "Will you come this time?" And I said no — but I got a little raise out of it. Then in 2007, Skipper sees me at the NBA All-Star Game, and he said, "This time I'm not going to take no for an answer. Whatever they offer you, I am going to offer more." It's like you put your finger in your ear to make sure, did he just say that? I was ready to try something new. I'd been at *SI* for twenty-two years, I loved it, I think it's the best magazine in the country, it's got the most loyal readership — but I just had done it. And I wanted to shake up my life. And he said, "Think of it as a Chinese menu: take three from column A, two from column B, and five from column C," and so he let me just totally carve out what I wanted to do. And what I wanted to do is do an interview show on TV, I wanted to learn how to write on the Internet, I wanted to see if I could bring my kind of writing to TV, I wanted to still do televised essays like I did for NBC for a while on golf and tennis — and he said, "You got it!" And Skipper just wouldn't take no for an answer. Every time *SI* would offer something else, he would go 50 percent higher. And I'm, like, "Wow, it sounds fun, it sounds like a change of pace, and I really like him; he's one of my favorite guys." And so I jumped at it.

I can almost tell a guy coming up to me in an airport or restaurant, depending on his age, what he's going to say to me. If he's over forty or forty-five, he's going to say, "Why did you leave *Sports Illustrated*? Oh, my God, that was the first thing we'd read. I'd call my son and we'd talk about it or call my dad and we'd talk about it." And they'd say, "Why'd you give up writing?" And I'm, like, "I haven't given up writing. I do the exact same kind of column every week on ESPN.com and in *ESPN: The Magazine,* and they always go, "You do?" And then if it's a young guy, he'll come up and say something like, "I read you on ESPN.com all the time. Where were you before this?" It's like two totally separate worlds.

JAY LOVINGER:

Reilly was the king of *Sports Illustrated* and now he's not even a factor—but he makes a huge amount of money. He's probably the highest-paid person ever, a writer for a normal publication. Bill Simmons might be the closest one. If Bill was making less than Oprah Winfrey, it wouldn't be close enough. Only "Bill World" will ever satisfy Bill. He's really made it big, though, hasn't he? I wonder sometimes what's going on out there in America.

By the way, Reilly was a total pro when I worked with him. Hardworking total pro. I don't know if that's still the case. I think that kind of money can really spoil you.

RICK REILLY:

Bill Simmons writes so many words. I kid him, you can only get five thousand words on Kevin Garnett for this week. But he breaks it up in kind of a brilliant way so that people can skim and look for stuff that they want to read. I still like well-chosen words. I think it's harder to be short. It's, you know, the old line, "I'm sorry this piece is so long, I didn't have time to make it short." He's obviously a brilliant writer. I think he needs a Greyhound bus full of editors. He doesn't want any words cut. But that's because he grew up with no fences. I grew up with an eight-hundred-word fence: that's how long a column was. He has no predetermined length of what a column is, because in the cyber world he can go until it's done.

I hadn't read him much till I got there. I hadn't met him. He said something on the radio, on Boston radio or something, like "What do you think about working with Rick Reilly?" And he said something like "He needs me." Ha ha, which is kind of funny. And then someone from the *New York Times* asked me, "What do you think of Simmons's writing?" and I pretended the phone wasn't working and didn't answer. So he kind of had to apologize to me for that, and I had to apologize to him for that. And now we get along fine. I just think we are two completely different types of writers. He loves the games, he loves the score, he loves the trades, and who's going to win and how many points the guy had—I'm just writing about people. All I really love is the stories about "people who happen to play sports," and I just find that sports has some really great human stories. So I think it's a pretty good mix. He loves the games and I love the people who play them.

JEMELE HILL, *Columnist:*

When you get to ESPN, people assume you're more seasoned than you actually are, but it changes your life. Before I got to ESPN.com, I was used to writing columns and getting maybe twenty e-mails; at ESPN, I was getting five hundred or a thousand. I wrote a column once about Kobe being better than Michael Jordan and got 2,200 e-mails!

Sometimes it's a little jarring. I was used to being part of the background, not part of the story. But ESPN intentionally and unintentionally created the celebrity sports journalist. People were all of a sudden recognizing me, writing about me, and it was difficult. I also had to get used to the difference between print and television. TV is about how things look and sound, but mostly about how things look. I was a pretty secure person until I started doing TV. Once you start doing it, especially if you're a woman, you become superaware of your weight, your hair, and how you physically appeal to viewers. I think viewers value my opinions, but I understand that you have to be a little bit of eye candy too. I mean you're going to tantalize the viewer. I guess an analogy would be, you're constantly lifting your skirt up. Being on TV taught me a different way of looking at things, not only on the screen but about journalism and what I did on the print side.

One would have thought the worldwide leader in sports would be thrilled to land an interview with potential Free World–wide leader Barack Obama. Suddenly and mysteriously, however, ESPN canceled Bill Simmons's scheduled podcast with Obama, then the front-runner among Democratic presidential contenders, in April of 2008. Stuart Scott's planned sit-down with Obama was also killed.

Network executives may have had sensible reasons for pulling the plug, but if they did, they weren't sharing. Instead, public relations vice president Josh Krulewitz was trotted out to say tersely, "Fans don't expect political coverage on our outlets." They don't? Critics were quick to counter that in Election Year 2004, George W. Bush and John Kerry were each interviewed twice for ESPN by Jim Gray. Bush was even the subject of a special four-part series. And Simmons was not likely to have asked Obama "political" questions anyway, since the candidate was known as a major sports fan.

One blogger derided the cancellation as a "stupid move from the worldwide follower," while another jeeringly called ESPN officials "nervous Nellies." Still another speculated there was fear in Bristol that the event "would embarrass the rest of ESPN's coverage by actually being relevant to the world." A popular blog had one word for the decision: "Insanity."

Even The Atlantic, *stately old periodical though it be, had harsh words on its website, suggesting sarcastically that since "a Simmons-Obama podcast would have been widely listened to and gotten a lot of attention," then "naturally, ESPN decided the right thing to do was kill the idea and cancel the podcast." The Obama campaign, meanwhile, decided to high-road it, with spokesman Tommy Vietor saying simply, "Senator Obama would be happy to appear on ESPN at any time."*

BILL SIMMONS:

When they wouldn't let me have Obama on my podcast, they had this whole edict in place that none of their talent was allowed to editorialize about the election. I'm handing in an NFL-picks column the day before Sarah Palin gives a speech in front of fifty-five million people or whatever, and I'm not allowed to reference it in my column. So at some point—as I made the case passionately and repeatedly—are we not reflecting what real life is like? Everybody I know is talking about Sarah Palin's speech and I'm not even allowed to breathe a mention of that in my column? What kind of alternate universe are we trying to create here? If they want to do this right, then designate your six, seven people who can talk about whatever they want and make it seem like a little bit better reflection of what real life is like.

Skipper has been my boss, and really, anything I've wanted to — other than interview Obama for the podcast — I've been able to do. They've never stood in my way, they've always tried to make things happen, and they're always asking how to figure out how to do what I do under some of the constraints that we have, which I feel I've kind of figured out for the most part. So then the Obama thing happened. Just 'cause I felt like the guy was gonna be president and I wanted to tell my kids fifty years from now that I interviewed this guy before he was gonna be president. And I really had a hard time dealing with that.

CHRIS BERMAN:

Everybody thought it was cool. Several people changed their vote because they said McCain was nicer to me than Obama was.

BOB LEY:

I interviewed John McCain during the campaign, and they had to drive him away from me, his handlers, to keep him on schedule, at a raceway in New

Hampshire, because he wanted to talk about the Ohio State–USC game the night before, this and that. Same thing when I interviewed Bush at the White House, for our twenty-fifth-anniversary project. He shows up early, which he had a wont to do when he was in office, so he sat for twenty and he stood around for another twenty-five to shoot the breeze with us on sports. He was supposed to go out and introduce Jack Danforth as the new UN ambassador, but they kept that waiting for a few minutes. This was the second Bush. First Bush I interviewed a couple times as well. Politicians are fans. They're part of the numbers that people may scoff at, but there's that cultural affinity.

In fact, I interviewed Bush 43 at the White House on the same day that Saddam Hussein made his first appearance in court. So I had a chance to ask Bush about that.

It's quite something to go knee to knee with the president and he starts telling the story of 9/11 again. Throwing the first pitch out. Like tears in his eyes telling it. But it didn't even occur to me, because I had Dan Bartlett right over there, saying, "None of this stuff's airing today, right?" and I didn't respond to that. Imagine if I had jumped in with a question as to Saddam. It would have poisoned the relationship. I mean there are ground rules you have to respect. We're granted an interview under certain parameters.

John Walsh was determined to round up really good writers for ESPN, and sometimes he found them even when he wasn't looking. Like when he paid a visit to the journalism school at the University of Missouri, his alma mater, to pick up an alumni award. He was intercepted at the airport by a student who said he was Walsh's driver, even though Walsh had specifically requested that there be no car and driver waiting. He wanted to take the bus and thereby relive school days of yore—or so he said.

But the self-appointed driver, Wright Thompson, wouldn't take "go away" for an answer, and for the next few days, he drove Walsh all over the city. Although he grew up in the same southern town—Clarksdale, Mississippi—as playwright Tennessee Williams, Thompson's favorite among fellow southern writers was William Faulkner. He was also influenced by such bad boys of American literature as Ernest Hemingway and Norman Mailer.

He and Walsh had plenty to talk about.

Thompson went on to graduate from Missouri and find work at a southern newspaper or two. Then one day Walsh got a call from his former driver: "I'm ready to come to ESPN, if you'll have me," Thompson told him. Walsh offered Thompson a job, and in 2006 Thompson was named senior writer for ESPN.com.

Described by colleagues as relentless, in a constant state of educating himself, being a "literary lion," and maintaining a stubbornly positive outlook on life,

Thompson will call people who work at the company to ask them what they want to read about — and take it from there.

Thompson has written many a memorable story over the course of his career, including, in 2007, the profile of a young Georgia man, a promising high school athlete and homecoming king, who was sentenced to ten years in prison for receiving oral sex from a high school girl two years younger than he was. Thompson's persistent reporting and poignant prose got the young man sprung from the slammer after serving only thirty-two months of his sentence.

"It just reminds you," Thompson told an admiring interviewer, "that these things that we write can have power and can do something good in the world." With Liz Merrill, Howard Bryant, Jeff MacGregor, and Wayne Drehs, Thompson is part of an auspiciously talented bench for ESPN.com and produces what has been called not only some of the best sportswriting in the country, but some of the best writing, period.

WRIGHT THOMPSON, *Writer:*

About a year and a half before the 2008 Olympics, my editors and I came up with a story we thought was important. The idea was to drive across China, on back roads, into the small places, into the places that weren't getting a lot of attention outside of the cities. We wanted to see what people really felt about these Olympics.

I wrote a long pitch to John Papanek, who was then the editor of ESPN.com, and made my case. The top editors, I think, were worried about what we could do in China, what we could do efficiently, what we could do affordably. And I basically said, if this were the 1930s and we were prepping for the Berlin games, I would hope we would go write a story about what was happening in Germany. I think when a sporting event coincides with a force that is changing our world, it's our job to cover that.

The trip itself was nuts. The road was Highway 108, and the driver spoke no English and drove like a maniac. His name was Singing Songs and he roared around these thin mountain switchbacks. We were in a green Jeep Grand Cherokee that we really beat the hell out of. In my small act of cultural exchange, I introduced Singing Songs to Mötley Crüe and Bruce Springsteen.

ROB KING:

Wright's got a bunch of talent. I didn't have anything to do with bringing Wright here, but one of the first things I did when I got here was make sure that he had a contract that laid out for him a huge commitment to making sure that he gets to cover the kinds of stories he wants to cover for some time. He just asks the kinds of questions and talks to the kinds of people that make the experience for the reader deeper and richer. I am far from the only person at ESPN who understands how important he is as a storyteller, and that's one of the reasons why he found himself on *E:60.*

Rob King had held many jobs during his twenty-two years in print journalism — even editorial cartoonist and graphic artist — before arriving at ESPN in 2004. In those next few years, his responsibilities ranged from golf coverage, including the Masters and the US Open, to Outside the Lines. *But the biggest job, and one of the most strategically important at ESPN, came in August 2007, when King was named editor in chief of ESPN. com, the empire's Internet voice.*

King's extremely varied background in both print and television had to serve him well in dot-com, since, as he's said himself, "The Internet is a space where all those things tend to coexist." ESPN's website claims eighteen million unique visits monthly and draws upon talent from the entire ESPN spectrum. King reports to John Kosner, general manager of digital media.

Though he hasn't tried his hand at on-camera work, King cuts a striking figure on the campus. The fact that he's African American has helped inspire him to promote the employee diversity in which ESPN was once considered deficient. King's father, Colbert I. King, is a Pulitzer Prize–winning (2003, Commentary) columnist for the Washington Post. *Rob says, however, that his father actually went into journalism after Rob did.*

Twitterers who follow King know that many of his tweets relate to his kids—example: "Picasso said it took his whole life to learn to draw like a child. Amen."

RICK REILLY:

I think the moment I realized the power of the Internet was when I wrote this column about Virginia football and they had this new rule that you couldn't bring signs into the game—no signs.

Al Groh, the coach there, had had a bunch of bad years, and I was, like, "Are you kidding? What they're trying to do is censor the students, because the students were unhappy with Al Groh." I said, "That can't happen at Virginia! This is Thomas Jefferson's school! He practically invented freedom of speech." I said, "Students of Virginia, you can't take this: riot, protest, have a sit-in at the president's office, wear white T-shirts that say this is not a sign, hold up white pieces of poster board with nothing on it. You cannot let this happen at Virginia of all places, because if they start taking away your freedom of speech in the stadium, they're going to take it away with the law next, and then pretty soon they're going to take it away with the student elections after that." Well, it was just my usual ranting and stuff. But these kids at Virginia read the column and started forwarding it around to each other and decided that they *would* protest the rules at the next game. And with two minutes to go in each quarter, seven thousand kids stood up with blank pieces of paper all over the stadium. And it did make a big splash down in Virginia, and it got the athletic director all upset and thinking, so he reversed the rule. He went back to, "Okay, you can bring your stupid signs in," and the next year, Al Groh was fired. My point is, that would never have happened at *SI*. At *SI* people used to say, "Oh, I clipped it out and I've got it hanging behind my desk" or "Oh, you know, we buried it with Grandma" or "I Xeroxed it and faxed it to twenty of my friends." Well, you take twenty people to read it at *SI*: you can get two thousand at ESPN.com! And so I just think it opened my eyes to what can happen there.

JEMELE HILL:

It was the Celtics–Lakers finals in 2008. With me being from Detroit, I decided I would write a Celtics column, since they were on the verge of winning the series. Growing up in Detroit, I hated the Celtics because they had such an intense rivalry with my Pistons. But I noticed a strange thing. A lot of people from Detroit were actually rooting for the Celtics because Paul Pierce, Kevin Garnett, and Ray Allen are all likable and popular guys. So I wanted to write about how, even after all these years, it was still difficult to see them win. I also wanted to get on Detroit fans in a good-natured way for forgetting that we're Detroiters; it's ingrained in us to hate the Celtics, whether we like their players or not.

So I write the column, file it, and because it was a weekend, a Saturday, the editing chain wasn't the same as it might be on a regular workday. I'm not sure exactly who edited the column; even now I don't know and have never bothered to find out, because that wasn't important to me. I just know it was read by more than one person.

Sometime late Saturday night I ran into one of our NBA editors in the media hospitality room, and he says, "Oh, we had a little bit of a problem with your column, but it got fixed." I asked, "What was the problem?" He said, "I took something out." He was kind of vague about it, but it didn't seem like a big issue. I figured if it was a big deal, someone would have reached out to me already.

The next day was Sunday and I was leaving for Bristol before Game Five because I was appearing on *First Take* on Monday morning. I'm in the security line at LAX and all of a sudden, my cell phone starts blowing up. I'm getting call after call from the 860 area code, which is Bristol's. The first person I talked to was one of my editors, Kevin Jackson, and he's like, "Where are you?" I told him, and then he said, "We got a major problem."

He then explains that the Celtics column hit like a total shitstorm. He was, like, "Have you been online today? Have you seen any of this?" I was, like, "No, literally I got up to catch my flight, and that was it." I hadn't seen anything. I had no clue Boston fans were outraged.

The irony is, the column wasn't really supposed to be a dig at Boston fans but at Detroit fans who were rooting for Boston. I was calling them traitors. In the column, I named a bunch of these crazy, silly, stupid analogies, as a supposed comparison to how crazy it was for Detroiters to root for the Celtics. And one of the analogies was if a Detroit fan cheers for the Celtics that's as bad as somebody rooting for Hitler. Stupidest thing I've ever written. I look at it now and can't believe I actually put that in a column.

Anyway, Kevin Jackson told me the column posted with that Hitler line in it. He didn't edit it but saw it online and went in the system and wiped it out. It was only up for an hour and an half, but in that short time, everything just went *poof.* Everything went crazy. The *Boston Herald* picked up the story, a Boston TV station picked up the story. It was all over the blogosphere. It then went national. Kevin told me, "I know what you were trying to say, but at this point we're in containment mode. Go ahead and board your flight. We'll talk more about this when you land."

When I got off the plane, the first person I called was my manager. As I'm talking to him, Rob King, the editor in chief of ESPN.com, called and told me, "You're not going on the air today. I think you need to come to my office." I was petrified. I'm thinking, "Oh, my God. Am I about to lose my job?!" You see your career just flashing before your eyes. Nobody at ESPN said I was going to be fired, and on the plane ride to Bristol I was trying to reassure myself, thinking, "Okay, I can get out of this situation. It'll die down. Today's game will go on and nobody will care because they want to watch Game Five." That changed once I got to Bristol. I met with Rob, and while he comforted me, I didn't leave feeling good about my job security.

I flew back home to Orlando. My manager called me with updates every time he talked to a higher-up. He told me, "Everyone knows you didn't do it intentionally, but people are thinking you should have known better. But I'm containing things. Everything's okay." Once again, I thought it would die down, but it just seemed to pick up more speed. A *Boston Herald* columnist essentially called me an idiot, and they had another news story quoting Rob, who said, essentially, ESPN was taking the matter seriously. Sometime after that, Rob called me and told me I was suspended for a week — no writing, no TV. I understood he had to suspend me because I put him in a tough spot. I'm not angry about it. It was my fault. I got what I deserved.

Once I was officially suspended, I stayed away from the Internet for about a week. I was embarrassed and humiliated. I was deeply concerned about my professional reputation. I didn't want my colleagues or friends in the business—many who are Jewish—to think less of me or believe I was an insensitive jerk.

Then the same day I was suspended, I started getting these phone calls at my house—people calling and hanging up, one after another. I didn't understand it. It seemed bizarre. Why are people calling just to hang up? Then one of my friends sent me an e-mail telling me that a Boston radio station gave out my phone number on air and posted it along with my home address on their website.

That was the only time I was really pissed off. Then someone at ESPN told me that same radio station, just before Game Five, had a poster up outside of the Celtics arena that said "Fire Jemele Hill" and they were handing out fliers expressing the same sentiment. That was kind of strangely cool, but giving out my address and my number jeopardized my safety.

During my suspension, I was put on military silence with the media. People think I didn't talk because I didn't want to face it. I wanted to face it. I wanted to do interviews, but ESPN didn't think that was best. They wanted it to die down and thought if I started responding to media requests, that would keep it alive in the news cycle. I just thought people needed to hear from me. I wrote my own apology statement. No one at ESPN did it for me. I wrote it on the plane from LA and gave it to an ESPN PR person on Monday when I got to Bristol, but they didn't release it until Tuesday. So then some people assumed I wasn't sorry or contrite, and I only wrote it because I was told to. None of that was true. Thankfully, I got the opportunity to do an apology column once I came off suspension. I just hope that showed people what was really in my character.

I'm never going to forget what happened. Besides, I couldn't if I wanted to since my name and "Hitler" is the first thing that comes up when you put my name in the Google search engine. Not that career mark I'd hoped for.

8

Parade of Horribles: 2009 and Beyond

"Son, I don't relish shooting a mosquito with an elephant gun, so why don't you just shuffle along?"
—*J. J. Hunsecker*

The year 2009 promised to be huge for ESPN, and John Skipper couldn't wait. As wallet-ready "2009–2010 Company Priorities" cards were doled out to employees (who were expected to tote them around in purses and billfolds for instant consultation), three items listed under the EMERGE STRONGER category were meant to seize their attention: First, "Support, develop and empower our people in this challenging environment"; second, "World Cup 2010 in South Africa"; and third, "Accelerate and accentuate the emerging businesses of ESPN mobile, ESPN360.com and ESPNU," all ambitious ventures if hardly household terms.

For Skipper, the second item on the list was much more than a business priority—he was, as the Blues

Brothers would have put it, on a "mission from God."
The World Cup was going to be the centerpiece of his
new administration—a World Series, a Super Bowl,
and a Final Four rolled into one. Pulling it off would
require resources, logistics, and elaborate planning on
an enormous new scale, but Skipper was proudly confi-
dent. The on- and off-the-air misstatements and rueful
remarks of the past were receding ever deeper into his-
tory, clearing the way for a fruitful future. January went
smoothly. But in February, Scott Van Pelt, one of the
brighter and more thoughtful anchors in Bristol, one
day decided to do his radio show—as Lyndon Johnson
used to say—"with the bark off," and went after Major
League Baseball commissioner Bud Selig.

"I must admit that my first reaction when I heard
that Bud Selig got paid more than eighteen million bucks
in 2007 was to choke on my vomit," Van Pelt declared.
"I think I puked in my mouth a little bit. The man came
on this show, and he could not have been any nicer, and
he said that he listened to the show—which makes it a
little awkward to have to say this. Let's hope that the
commissioner is listening to something else today. But
when you think of Bud Selig, what do you think of?
What is the picture you have in your mind? I'm pretty
sure 'pimp' and 'Bud Selig' were used in the same sen-
tence for the first time just moments ago. But I see a guy
who looks like a computer programmer or a substitute
teacher or a government worker in some form of a brown
suit or tweed sports jacket. It just seems like a ton of

money for a man who isn't actually dripping charisma and who many point the finger at for being responsible for baseball's hypersteroidal past. Or, if not responsible, then at least complicit for just looking the other way."

Van Pelt's reward for this candor was a suspension, along with strict orders to make a public apology.

GARY HOENIG:

The reason baseball does so well is because it's an amazing fucking sport. Its resilience is incredible. People love the game of baseball. I love the game of baseball. No matter what you do to that game, people still love it. It's even survived Bud Selig in denial while the players grew biceps the size of watermelons. But criticizing Bud? We can't say five words about him. He's got the thinnest skin in sports.

SCOTT VAN PELT, *Anchor:*

I thought it was important that I speak with Mr. Selig, who it turned out was listening to the segment and clearly did not understand my attempt at satire. I apologized—not the "if I offended you in any way" kind of apology, but because I felt the man deserved more respect than to have been described the way I did. It was a completely surreal experience to attempt to explain to Bud Selig that using the word "pimp" in the slang of the moment is actually a compliment. But I couldn't expect him to understand, "Commish, it's what the kids say."

The best part of what turned into a twenty-minute conversation was that we got to talk about the end of the '82 season. Baltimore trailed Milwaukee by three with four to play, so they had to win every game for the division. I was at the doubleheader on Friday night that the O's swept, and Bud told me he was there too. I told him had I seen him that night, I would have said far worse to him and would have meant it. We laughed about that. So out of a situation that was far from ideal, an odd thing happened: I got to know Bud Selig a little and vice versa. Far from the worst thing ever.

If George Bodenheimer, John Skipper, and his chief lieutenant, Norby Williamson, thought that would be the last time an ESPNer would be in trouble in 2009, they were kidding themselves. Skipper was not known as a screamer or as a guy who got wildly frustrated or alarmed, but in the next twelve months, his mild temperament would be severely tested. After he finished with Van Pelt, the carpeting outside his and Williamson's offices would be worn down by Stephen A. Smith, Tony Kornheiser, Vince Doria, Erin Andrews, Steve Phillips, Bill Simmons, and Hannah Storm, along with an encore appearance by Kornheiser—just to name a few. It is quite possible that in the history of broadcast journalism, there hasn't ever been quite such an eventful twelve months at one network as those. Each episode was important in its own way, and came with its own atten-

dant issues. Each posed a threat to the precious culture of ESPN that was so slavishly prized by President Bodenheimer.

Fortunately, a brief stop in Washington provided relief.

ANDY KATZ:

As soon as they announced Senator Obama had won the presidency on election night, I immediately began to plot out when I should begin to make arrangements for him to fill out the [NCAA Basketball Tournament] bracket with me. He had made the commitment to me if he won, and he was going to keep his word—it was just a matter of locking in on a date. The key was to keep this secret, even to everyone at ESPN except those that had to know.

When we arrived at the White House on Tuesday, the guards at the gate were immediately in tune to what we were doing. The detail asked us to predict who the president would select. When we were in the Map Room, Secret Service or White House staffers would come by asking about their respective teams, especially teams in the D.C. area like Maryland and Georgetown. When the president entered the room, he immediately disarmed everyone when he said, "Hey, Andy, how are you?"

While going through the bracket, the president was at ease with his picks and loved the give-and-take on various selections. He certainly wasn't afraid to throw a few barbs back my way. The White House honored the exclusive and didn't let the president's picks out until after our Baracketology piece ran the following Wednesday at noon on *SportsCenter*. The exclusivity meant that every news outlet had to credit us. The piece went viral. From NBC News with Brian Williams to of course ABC News to CNN to *Inside Edition* to overseas newspapers—the bracket and ESPN were credited. CBS had to reference it throughout the tournament. Obama picked North Carolina, and the bracket received even more exposure because of his selection. When Obama was abroad he was asked if he could do a soccer bracket, and when Carolina went to the White House in May of '09, Obama referenced his bracket again, and said that his bracket had rallied after a difficult first round. The president of the United States had never filled out an NCAA Tournament bracket in public before, and on television, and the authenticity of the event was clearly celebrated.

This wasn't Watergate; this wasn't the Pentagon Papers. This was a bracket. Yet it became one of the most recognizable media feature events from Obama's first year. The original bracket, with Obama's signature, now hangs in the ESPN Café.

BARACK OBAMA:
Coach K wasn't too pleased with my pick of UNC a couple years ago, but it was all in good fun. Of

course, I have to point out that I got it right. Coach K had the last laugh, though. He won it the next year. And I think he enjoyed coming to the White House and reminding me not to make the same mistake again.

I have watched ESPN and *SportsCenter* for as long as I can remember. I watched it in a lot of hotel rooms as we traveled the country. On the road during the campaign, we used to turn on ESPN to get a break from the speculation and the chatter that was all over the cable news channels. Things are a little busier these days. I have a few more things to worry about. But just like millions of Americans, I still like to decompress after a long day by catching up on scores and highlights on *SportsCenter*. One of the great things about watching sports is that it offers a break from the stress of the workday. I know a lot of Americans use sports to unwind, and I'm no different.

The guys over at ESPN seem to be doing just fine without me. But if I were president of the network for a day, I might find some time to devote to working together and moving beyond the same old debates year after year—by finally creating a college football playoff system.

When Alex Rodriguez decided in February of 2009 that he would discuss his long-denied steroid problem in an exclusive interview with ESPN's Peter Gammons, there was much backroom maneuvering in Bristol. Despite

Gammons's tenure, ability, and professional stature, ESPN executives wanted him to sit down with über– interview coach John Sawatsky for a refresher course.

Sawatsky had come to Bristol initially as a consultant after John Walsh read an article about him—"The Question Man"—in the American Journalism Review. *But Mark Shapiro wanted him full-time—on staff—and brought him on-campus. Born in Winkler, Manitoba, Canada, in 1948, Sawatsky worked as an investigative journalist in the eighties (blowing the lid off, among others, the "misdeeds" of Canadian Mount- ies) but grew increasingly fascinated by the art and sci- ence of interviewing. He developed a three-day seminar that dispensed such imparted wisdom as "Questions are precise instruments" and tactics to avoid asking anything that could be answered with a yes or no.*

After his arrival in Bristol, anchors, reporters, and producers were encouraged, or required, to take Sawatsky's exhaustive three-day workshop. Many found it helpful, despite complaints that it went on too long. Some of those who participated changed their interview- ing style as a result; many would even arrange to meet up with Sawatsky prior to embarking on a big assign- ment. Others, however—usually big stars and big names—balked at attending the seminars at all or went grudgingly.

JOHN SAWATSKY, *Senior Director of Talent Development:*

We've had some real successes here. Of course there were some complete misses as well. I was deeply involved with the A-Rod interview. When we got the interview, Vince Doria, my boss, put me on the case to get some questions going. I talked with a few others and came up with a comprehensive question list. Now, the problem here sometimes is when you get a big personality like Peter Gammons, who is a Hall of Famer, they don't want the help. He basically put the question list aside and went on his own, but he didn't even ask the most basic questions. Consequently, A-Rod had to do a press conference later on to fill in all the missing links, all the blanks for questions that Peter didn't ask.

After Rodriguez admitted taking steroids, some people felt that Gammons should have pressed him harder for more information about when, how much, and why; Gammons had let Rodriguez off "easy," it was charged. Gammons wasn't going to be bothered by critics or comments from the blogosphere, however. He approached the case from a different vantage point.

PETER GAMMONS:

I was working out at a gym in Boston, and got a call from a guy I knew who had been helping Alex with the SI.com story that he had flunked the drug test. He said, "Would you be interested in coming down to Miami? I think that Alex is going to have to tell his side here." So I got a hold of Vince and Jay Levy and they said, "Yeah, go ahead." I got the first plane I could get down to Miami. What was funny was that Alex originally was going to do it at seven or eight o'clock at night, but he was not prepared. So we sat and talked, and he told me some story that was convoluted. So even though I had prepared a long list of questions, I came back the next day, prepared for this to be something of a dodgeball interview. I don't remember exactly the first question I asked, but it was about the revelation that he had flunked the drug test in 2003. He immediately took off on it, and it really stunned me. I still ended up asking him a lot of the things I had prepared for, but it got to be a little bit of a freelance interview.

Alex was extremely emotional. I don't believe I've ever interviewed anyone who was that emotional. It was as if he had pulled up that veil that he had covered himself with all his professional life. He was extremely tense and nervous. I mean, he was sweating. I thought at one point he was going to hyperventilate. And it was difficult to keep the interview on track. I asked several questions twice, and I knew that I really felt that if I kept going and badgering him, the whole thing was going to break down. I was afraid his head was going to explode. I don't think he or anyone else is capable of faking that kind of emotion. I just tried to get through and ask all the questions I thought had to be asked, repeating as many of them as I thought I had to. Keeping it on track was the most difficult thing about the whole interview.

Frank Deford said to me, "I really understand how difficult that was, because Alex Rodriguez has always believed that he's playing the role of Alex Rodriguez in a movie about Alex Rodriguez." And I thought that was absolutely right. Alex always liked to be perceived as close to perfect. And yet, because I found him so frail in that interview, so human and so contrary to the Hollywood image that he puts across, I'm really far more fond of Alex than I ever was before.

The dynamics were extraordinary. He later told me that after our interview, he just went right to bed and slept for like fourteen hours because he was so exhausted from it. It was extremely exhausting for me as well.

JOHN SAWATSKY:

Here's the irony: Peter Gammons is a professional journalist. He's been one all his career. And that's where I get the most resistance. Nobody ever comes out and says they're not going to do it the way you've discussed; they just go and do it the way they wanted. You don't get that from ex-athletes, they are highly coachable. This is what always astounds me so much. But it actually shouldn't because they've been coached all their life and one of the reasons they've excelled in their profession is they know how to take instruction.

Gammons and I didn't have anything to do with each other for the last couple years he was here. He didn't even respond to my e-mails. He thought he was above this. And that's why he's in this position where he can't improve — because he doesn't realize that he has weaknesses. Except now, maybe, because the reaction to that interview in the journalistic community was so strong, he has to realize now that he blew it.

Peter Gammons would announce that same year that he would leave ESPN for the Major League Baseball Network. For John Walsh, who had proudly brought Gammons to ESPN twenty years earlier, it was a moment of genuine frustration. Walsh had thought there were ways to keep Gammons, who basically didn't want to work less, just do more of that work from his home rather than the studio or the road. As simple as a solution sounds, no deal could be hammered out — and off went Gammons to a new and serious competitor for ESPN.

PETER GAMMONS:

The MLB network is entirely baseball. Everything I'll do now is basically centered on baseball. Bob [Costas] is tremendous to work with, and I'm back with a lot of friends of mine, like Harold Reynolds,

Sean Casey, and Barry Larkin. This will also allow me more time to work on book projects, which I really need. There isn't a lot of time to get that done at ESPN—which is understandable. It's a twenty-four-hour news cycle.

ESPN's brilliantly moved to being basically an NFL College Sports network. It's really well done; they're going to control all the college sports. It's a great business plan. But baseball hasn't worked entirely for them.

DAVID BERSON:

From day one, the MLB Network was seen as a greater threat to us than the NFL Network. Baseball has a long season, with games every night, and they've got a smart programming approach—live highlights and analysis all night every night—which we viewed as a viable long-term alternative to *Baseball Tonight* and fan habits of turning to ESPN as the sole source of expansive nightly highlights.

We used to have a lot of baseball on our air—way more than any other network. By 2004, we have five games a week, plus the division series. But we decided to cut back a bit and save some money for NASCAR, which added a lot more hours and got us a different audience and different advertisers. We kept the marquee baseball windows of Sunday, Monday, and Wednesday nights, but we gave up our rights to the division series, which was a tough loss.

TIM KURKJIAN, *Baseball Reporter:*

I've never been at a place like ESPN. What interests me so much about it is there's an expert here on everything. There's a guy in our research department here named Mark Simon who could tell you who made the last out of every World Series back into the 1930s. I'm serious. If you ask him who made the last out of the 1936 World Series, he can tell you. We have another guy named Jeff Bennett who can tell you what every baseball card looks like from 1979 to 1985. I challenged him one day and said, "All right. Robin Yount, 1982." And he said, without hesitation, "Well, he's got two cards, one he's looking like this at the third base coach and the second one, he's running out of the batter's box." And then he sent me those pictures just to make sure that I knew that he wasn't trying to fool me. And he was exactly right. And we have Judson Burch, who knows the number of every umpire in the Major Leagues. I didn't even know they had numbers, but they have them on their shoulders. The other night, he walked into the room where Buck Showalter and I were watching a whole bunch of baseball games, and I said, "Jud, who's working third base in Texas tonight?" and he went, "Adrian Johnson." There were fifteen games on TV that night, and sure enough, he knew who was working third base. He's also a huge Phillies fan, the biggest in the world. We played a game with him where somebody gave him a random date. "Okay,

May the third, 2003. What happened to the Phillies that day?" And he goes, "They played the Cardinals and beat 'em seven to three. St. Louis got two in the first, Philly got three in the bottom of the first . . ." and—get this—"Charlie Relaford worked the plate."

BUCK SHOWALTER, *Baseball Analyst:*

Live TV is tough. There's no "do-over." There's jargon in the dugout that you really can't use on the air. One of the first shows I did, I was still using the baseball jargon, and they were talking about umpires. What did I think that pitch was? And I said "Obviously, it's right down the cock." And it was! That pitch was right down the cock—but you know, I didn't mean anatomically; that's just what we say in the dugout. And I've learned through the years that how you would describe something in the locker room is not how you would describe something on the air. That one didn't go over too good.

JOHN KRUK, *Baseball Analyst:*

I'll make a comment about "a player shouldn't be in this position, he should be in that position," and if the player thinks I'm taking a personal shot at him, he's wrong. I don't have personal vendettas. There are players I watch and I wouldn't want that guy on my team, but you still don't rip him just for that. I'm going to give my opinions; if players get mad, they get mad. I don't really care.

OREL HERSHISER:

The biggest challenge for me as a broadcaster is dissecting the seven things I see that I could talk about and getting it down to one, then knowing I'm going to do that one subject the best I can. Because you have to do what the whole crew can do; you can't just do what you see. But I will tell you, the six others will still haunt me. As far as talking about guys I knew as fellow players, you cross over from the light side to the dark side. You're on the dark side once you're in the media, and you have to be careful. When I was a player, I always remembered to speak about a teammate in the media like he was standing right next to me. What I would say about them had to be something I would say if the guy and I were standing face-to-face. Now if I have to be really harsh, I will start it out with, "If you ask So-and-So, he would tell you he needed to get to this ball," because I know the standards these guys hold themselves to. I know they're going to fail sometimes, because I failed too. But it's our job to point out those moments even though it's impossible for them to be perfect.

BUSTER OLNEY, *Reporter:*

I usually get up at 4:00 or 4:30 depending on what other responsibilities I have during the course of the day. I go newspaper by newspaper across the country, collect the links. Most of the time I write the lead of my column in the morning. Sometimes you sort of play off whatever the news story of the day is. If there's some trade thing developing, you know, maybe something that's been reported on the night before, you sort of just rip off a lot of things that happen in the morning paper, collect all that, and put it out by 7:30. Then I start my day. I go up to Bristol, have *Mike and Mike* at 6:25 and 6:42, then do *SportsCenter* at 9:00, 10:00, 11:00, and noon. Then there's more reporting and planning the show. *Baseball Tonight* will be on from 7:00 to 8:00.

NOMAR GARCIAPARRA, *Baseball Analyst:*

I was contemplating retirement when they asked me to come out and audition. They said, "We really liked you. What do you think?" I had gotten to the point where my body wasn't able to do what I wanted it to do, even in the off-season, so we started talking, and it worked out.

They ask you if you're going to be critical; you can be critical of the play but not the individual, especially when you know the guys. You can talk about the play because you played, and it might make sense because it came from you. But in this game we're used to people being critical of us all the time. Some people have a tendency to make it about the person as compared to the play, and you have to be aware of that.

Stephen A. Smith had blown into Bristol about as subtly as a Michael Bay disaster movie. As a columnist at the

Philadelphia Inquirer, the outspoken Smith had proven himself a natural and controversial attention-getter, which is what Mark Shapiro's gut had told him when he hired Smith in an effort to boost ratings. What many thought Shapiro may have failed to consider was that while controversy can attract and titillate viewers, it can also scare them and potential sponsors away and rub other high-ranking executives the wrong way. NBA commissioner David Stern had already been wrongly rubbed; he was no fan of Smith's style being more prominent than the NBA brand, and neither were varyingly important persons on the Bristol campus who thought "Stephen A" had too much to say about athletes, coaches — and himself.

As Smith's contract came up for renewal, John Skipper had to weigh the benefits of keeping him versus letting him go. Smith was highly paid — at one point making even more than the company's other rising star, Bill Simmons — and while he knew that his number-one fan Mark Shapiro was now gone, Smith nonetheless assumed he would be begged to remain on-air at ESPN or have plenty of options elsewhere.

ROB KING:

It's my first day on the job as the deputy sports editor of the *Philadelphia Inquirer.* I'm out getting lunch at the food truck, and I hear somebody walk up behind me. "Robert King! Stephen A. Smith! Do you know that I am the lowest-paid NBA writer for a major franchise in a major city?" And that's how I met him.

JOHN SAUNDERS:

Stephen A. Smith and I became pretty close; we still are. When they first wanted to put him on *Sports Reporters,* there was some pushback from people who didn't want him on the show. They didn't think he would be right for it. But to his credit, he came on, and after being on two or three times, he understood that the show wasn't about him, and I thought he got very good. To the credit of the other people on the show—the Mitch Alboms, the Bob Ryans, the Mike Lupicas—I believe they accepted him and that over time he could have been a great contributor.

What worked against Stephen A. Smith was that ESPN wanted him to be bombastic and loud. He gave them what they wanted, but then they punished him for it. And you know who almost predicted it? Mike Lupica. Mike and I were talking one day, and he said, "John, the one thing with Stephen A. Smith is, they are creating this individual now, but what happens when they don't want that individual?" And that's exactly what happened. Shapiro whipped him up, leaves, then Skipper and Norby say, "We don't want that, good-bye." Now, that's unfortunately one of the things in this business that applies not just to Stephen A. Smith but to anybody. If Norby and Skipper were to leave, somebody could come in, sit down one Sunday, watch *Sports Reporters,* and go, "Oh man, I hate John Saunders, he's terrible, I don't want him on"—and I'm gone. If you hit .300 in the Major Leagues, you're going to have a place to play every year, a place on the team. That's not necessarily the case in this business. The other thing with Stephen A. is that he has strong opinions, not just on the air but off the air, and sometimes that does not work very well in this business. And if you have enough run-ins with enough different people, it can cost you, and that happened to Stephen A. too. He's a smart guy, a talented guy, and a good writer—very knowledgeable with great opinions. I still feel bad about it.

ROB KING:

Mark Shapiro was absolutely instrumental to Stephen's being omnipresent, and like most cases, when one person feels strongly about somebody, that doesn't necessarily mean that everybody else feels exactly the same way. Do I believe that there were people who supported Stephen's rise in the company mainly because it was important to Mark? Absolutely. But I also am close enough to Stephen to know that he shares some measure of responsibility for how it all came down.

DAVID STERN:

With Stephen A. we simply wanted clarification. We thought he had two different personalities—the

Stephen A. on CNN, and the Stephen A. from his column. I call Stephen A. a friend—he is smart and articulate—and all I said to him was "There's somebody who is trying to program you in a way that is not you." I told him I thought that was a mistake, that he should be directed and produced differently, because in our opinion, he was caught between those two different types.

MIKE TIRICO:

Stephen A. was certainly not afraid to give his opinion. I think it was not just what he was saying but how he said it. He said it at a volume that was pretty loud. He was strong and confident and challenging of people if they didn't agree with him. I always think that method only works if that's the way you are. You have to be really comfortable to be that boisterous or that outgoing or strong-minded on the air. I think if you try to act like that and it's not really what you believe, it shows over time. It's really hard to be something you're not on the air. After time, if you're only an act, it ends up wearing you down, or it ends up showing that it's only an act.

I think Stephen was pretty strong in his convictions, but it probably didn't please a ton of people that he covered them the way he did. Still, I admire him for it. If you have the courage to say some of the things he said on the air, good for you. I take my hat off to you.

STEPHEN A. SMITH:

It was a job I never wanted to leave. But I didn't want to be limited, either. I didn't have aspirations to just do the NBA; I didn't have aspirations to just do radio. I also wanted to host *SportsCenter;* I wanted that experience. And more importantly, I wanted the freedom to go on other networks to talk about issues that you would never talk about on ESPN. The police aimed fifty bullets in Sean Bell's direction just five minutes from where I grew up, and CNN wants to talk to me. I want to talk about that. Barack Obama runs for president and the African American vote and community suddenly become pivotal issues, and MSNBC wants to talk to me about that. I want to go on. If Fox News wants to talk to me about the problem with education within the African American community or the fact that the unemployment rate has now escalated to above 15 percent, that's what I want to talk about. But that's not what ESPN wanted me to do.

This is where I'm being totally open: fear has to drive you if you are a sportswriter in this day and time. ESPN has contracts with everybody; it is a partnership. Now, at no time did they ask me to compromise myself or my journalistic ethics or principles, but that doesn't mean that as a human being I don't see the specter of Commissioner Stern hovering over me, or Roger Goodell hovering over me, or Bud Selig hovering over me. And if you want to be in that position and your foundation is journalism, breaking news stories, telling it like it is, being willing to reveal stuff that most people wouldn't reveal, and you work for a company where there are contracts with these people, it does scare you that one day you'll wake up and everything that you've accomplished will be gone at the snap of a finger. It scares the hell out of you! What you need to do at that point is diversify your portfolio so at least you're working for the next forty years or so. I'm forty-one years old. I'm not about to retire within the next couple of decades. I want to know that I can work, and I don't want to be where somebody can snap their fingers and all the work that I've put in over the past sixteen years is gone just like that.

On April 3, 2009, John Skipper let me know that ESPN was not renewing my contract. It's their right to do that, but it doesn't take Einstein to see what happened. All you have to do is just look. It was very, very obvious.

What people need to remember is I was a general columnist for the magazine, I was a columnist for ESPN.com, I was a radio host for ESPN Radio, I was a television host for *Quite Frankly* on ESPN2, and I was the NBA analyst for ESPN. And then, by one person's wand, it was gone. Because everything was under their umbrella, I was out of five jobs! Not many people are talented enough to have five jobs—but I did.

JOHN SKIPPER:

I like Stephen, and he did many good things for ESPN. He rapidly became a signature voice for us, and we did pile on the work. He had a daily television show, *Quite Frankly;* a daily radio show; he continued to write a column for the *Philadelphia Inquirer;* and he was one of our regulars on *NBA Studio.* And with each of these assignments came more money. We cancelled *Quite Frankly,* and we wanted Stephen to leave the paper. We did want him to concentrate on fewer things, and with that came less money. We made him an offer, and he chose to pursue other options.

ROB KING:

Stephen blazed a meteoric path here to the point where he had his own show based in New York. He was bringing different voices to our air and working on several platforms, including having quite a following on radio. From my perspective, that was a pretty tall order, and he started spreading himself fairly thin. Personally, I never had a day where I couldn't get Stephen on the phone, never had a problem with getting him to do things for me. But I think there were some other folks who didn't have the same experience. I would hear he missed some meetings and would be checking e-mails in the middle of a meeting, and generally didn't seem engaged. Now, is that fair to Stephen or just the result of him being over-whelmed by so many endeavors? But it didn't meet his vision of what a substantial role is. Stephen has very clear ideas about what he wants and what he expects.

GEORGE SOLOMON:

I mentored Stephen A. Smith for a few years. I never hired him, but I used to give him advice when he was coming up. Then one day I looked at *Sports Illustrated* and there was five thousand words on him! With a big picture! And you know why? Because they gave him a TV show. Stephen A. screamed a lot, but Stephen A. had his own following. And I liked him. But then they took away his show, and his world fell apart. Very often their worlds fall apart fast. You see these anchors and then they're just replaced. ESPN doesn't tell you why; they just disappear. In newspa-pers, there's often a final column. In TV, they just disappear. Like the Mafia! I used to tell Vince and Norby, "If someone's been replaced, why don't you say it?" They just said, "We just don't do that."

STEPHEN A. SMITH:

I have no animosity. This is an industry that is about big-boy rules. You cannot get caught up in people, and they have an obligation to do what they feel is best. If they didn't feel that I was best, I have to respect their decision. I don't agree with that—they knew that—especially as it pertains to the NBA. Because I'm not going to lie, I feel I'm the best. I truly believe that: when it comes to covering the NBA, I feel I'm the best. But if they don't feel that way, what am I supposed to do? If they feel I'm too controversial, what am I supposed to do? There's nothing I can do.

KEITH CLINKSCALES, *Senior Vice President, Content Development:*

I do not believe Stuart Scott was the first African American on ESPN, but he certainly was influential because on *SportsCenter,* early on, he used hip-hop vernacular; he said things on the air that I knew when I heard them that the white producers who had approved it didn't know what he was talking about. So it was like our own little codified thing. It was almost like, "If he's cool enough to say that on the air, and no one's stopping him, then this network is cool enough to watch."

I don't want to commit hyperbole here, but Stuart's delivery on *SportsCenter*—his willingness to stick with it despite getting complaints, and the producers letting him stick with it—is one of the great cultural moments that African American culture has ever had. It made us relevant in sports.

Sports journalism's record on hiring minorities is abysmal, and network television's record is abysmal. If you look at some of the greatest sports media institutions we have before you even get to ESPN, they didn't hire a lot of people of color, especially black men. And black women.

GARY BELSKY:

When we did the first body issue of the magazine, the reason we were so concerned about how we portrayed African American men with their shirts off was because early in the magazine's history we received a lot of criticism, unfounded, that we seemed to always take off black men's shirts but not white guys' shirts. Of course, it was mostly photographers on sets who were making these choices. They were just out there on the shoots deciding how to photograph an athlete; it wasn't any kind of conspiratorial plan. But we've always been sensitive to, or aware of, that criticism — which we should be, by the way, because fundamentally there's a reality that has to have us thinking about how we represent women versus men, thinking about how we represent men and women of different ethnicities. We have to think about these things because our readers will be thinking about them once we put an image out there.

KEITH CLINKSCALES:

Let's make no mistake — the urban audience is African American, Latino, and those men spend an awful lot of time watching ESPN. ESPN is the number-one station in the country for black men twenty-five to fifty-four. Not BET. Not TV One. It's ESPN. And ESPN is number two among black men eighteen to twenty-four. ESPN never leaves the top three for ratings with black men. So for the demo, it makes business sense that you have more ways to talk and things like that.

I run a show-development lab, working with black filmmakers, Latino filmmakers, and we've been able to bring folks in that might not ordinarily get a chance to swing at the plate because they don't have the journalistic pedigree, they don't have the sports pedigree. We already know that very few African Americans have a sports pedigree that would be worthy of an ESPN, because history has not hired us. If you go to the nation's newspapers, of all sports editors, less than 1 percent are black people. And then the same type of figure is there for news editors, when you look at all the nation's news channels and local television. So if you don't have sports editors, and you don't have news editors, you're not going to have the kind of people that the ESPNs of the world and the CNNs of the world want to hire and then elevate.

Then there was the grand Tony Kornheiser experiment. John Skipper and John Walsh had rolled the dice on their biggest crap table — Monday Night Football, with its $1.1 billion per season price tag — when they bet on Kornheiser to be the third man in the booth. By 2009, Kornheiser had been on for three seasons, *and while it is true that there had been improvements with each, there were also fundamental problems that remained—chief among them, Tirico and Kornheiser... and Berman and Kornheiser.*

Yes, there was absolutely no chemistry between Berman and Kornheiser, and yes, Kornheiser would repeatedly tell colleagues and friends that Berman had never even addressed him by his first name. It's not like the two hated each other. Oh wait, they did.

TONY KORNHEISER:

The whole time I was on *Monday Night,* Berman never mentioned my name. He loathes me, in part because of stuff I used to write about him. Berman and I have an antagonism that goes back many, many years, long before I ever got to ESPN. Once in Minnesota, the big grand poo-bah stood there and lectured me, screaming at me about how great he was, how significant he was, how he built the network, and how I ought to be more grateful. That was when he accused me of writing the blog about him and that leather thing. He said, "I know how it got on the Internet." I asked him, "What the hell are you talking about?"

CHRIS BERMAN:

In the mid-nineties, somebody said I was in a bar and used a pickup line on a woman wearing leather and she left with me. I really didn't know what they were talking about. But a colleague of mine, Mr. Kornheiser, chose to run with it, and the Internet chose to run with it for years. I don't even know what "it" is, but it's a very dangerous thing, especially when a colleague piles on and gives credence to it.

I can't believe it still has legs. Legs of what? We're all learning what the Internet can do. A lot of good, a lot not so good. Guess I was at the head of the boat, the first one in our place to be run through the Internet mill. But we just had to let it go. No choice but to move on from there.

TONY KORNHEISER:
Walsh had wanted me to mend fences with him, and I remember going to Walsh and saying, "Well, I tried. I just got screamed at."

Still, Berman was in the studio and Kornheiser was on the road. Tirico and Kornheiser, on the other hand, were locked in a booth together, inches apart, every week, performing for an audience in the millions. There was no way to hide the clash. Each approached the assignment in a totally different way. Tirico would spend hours studying players, games, strategies, teams, and league history. Kornheiser didn't have the patience for any of that. He believed—and this made sense to his supporters—that you didn't want two guys like that in the booth (actually three, since Ron "Jaws" Jaworski was as knowledge-hungry as Tirico). No, Kornheiser believed in doing what he did best — making off-the-cuff sardonic references to both sport and the culture at large that made viewers laugh.

That was Kornheiser's idea of the division of labor, but it wasn't Tirico's, and no amount of prodding from Skipper, Walsh, Williamson, or producer Jay Rothman — who became Henry Kissinger–like, shuttling between the parties and imploring them to work better together — could solve it. Some on campus had lost patience for all the booth drama and were upset at both Kornheiser and Tirico for making it tough on everyone. A few key individuals even brought race into the mix. "Tirico played it smart," one ESPNer surmised. "He knew there could never be an all-white booth, and he had calculated that they were never going to replace him with either Stuart [Scott] or Stan [Verett]. So in his mind, he really didn't have to listen when they pleaded with him to be better with Tony."

Truth is, it wasn't Tirico's fault; it wasn't Kornheiser's fault. Those who blamed Rothman for not being able to control the talent were being unfair. He tried repeatedly, but he had been dealt a bad deck. Management just got it wrong. It simply wasn't the right fit. The boys in the booth couldn't or wouldn't change their ways to mesh with each other.

MIKE TIRICO:

Tony is brilliant. I enjoyed watching Tony work. I enjoyed working with Tony, I really did. Tony has been incredibly successful in places where you come to hear Tony's opinion on something, and that was obviously his column, which made him, and the radio show—national and local, which were terrific—and *Pardon the Interruption.* You came to all those for Tony's opinion. But to me, you come to a football game for the football game. The football game is surrounded by a bevy of wide-ranging opinions in the pregame shows, the postgame shows, and the talk shows during the week. People come to the game for the game itself. So we were trying to make what Tony does best—strong opinions—work within the body of the game; that was the challenge. The problem for me working in the booth was you're trying to cover the game and you're trying to get Tony's opinion too. A play happens on the field, right in front of us, and here's a replay. Tony couldn't add to what just happened. He could add to the person and give it some definite context there, but the viewer has become conditioned—at least from where I sit—to "tell me why that happened."

It pisses me off that people will look at those three years and throw a blanket over them and say, "Well, they weren't very good." We were the only football show that was nominated for an Emmy three years in a row, by our peers. So I still stand on that merit that the show was not the be-all, end-all, trust me, but the shows we did were pretty good football shows. I'll take some of the games that we did, Buffalo-Dallas, the return game in New Orleans, the Patriots playing Baltimore, where they're trying to get the undefeated season and Don Shula is in the booth during that game. I'll put those broadcasts up with anybody's broadcast of anything. They were damn good. And Tony was a huge part of that.

JOHN SKIPPER:

Anybody who knows Tony at least understands what we hoped we would get on the air. I told those guys that for me, the ideal booth would make every fan think that being the fourth guy sitting next to those three guys on the sofa is the best place to watch a football game. It's fun. It's insightful. It's relaxed. I said, "Please make it feel like you guys are having fun, you love the game, you're cracking wise a little bit, and you're listening to each other." The fans ultimately understand whether there's something going on that's fun, and that doesn't mean you have to love each other. I'm not sure that Meredith and Cosell and Gifford loved each other, but with them you had something electric going on, and we didn't get that either. We just couldn't quite get the chemistry right.

TONY KORNHEISER:

The schedule was terrible. I looked at it and began to shake. It was a nightmare. Two games in Washington, one game in Boston that you could drive to in eight to nine hours, one game, I think, in Cleveland.

Everything else separated by at least eleven hundred miles. I have a contract that says I can fly private planes and I did it four or five times in '08, but nobody offered to give me the Disney jet, and even if they offered to give me the Disney jet, my fear *is* being in a jet. My fear is being separated from the ground. I hate flying. I don't like bridges. I don't like being on boats. I have all the attendant phobias that go with this—the classic hallmark, textbook phobias. And I couldn't drive to those games without missing a lot of *PTI.* It was untenable. It was not going to work. It came to the point where they delayed and delayed and delayed talking to me and I delayed and delayed and delayed talking to them, and then we talked.

I had never ever heard a discouraging word about my part in the performance—never from Skipper, Walsh, or Norby. So, if they had been planning a change, I was utterly oblivious to it.

Look, Mike Tirico's charming. He's witty. He's clever. He's an amiable dinner companion. But if you injected him with truth serum and asked him if I was ever his first choice to be in the booth with him, he would say no. Mike once said to me, "I'm stuck, Tony. I really don't know what to ask you. You didn't coach. You didn't play. I don't really know what to go with." I think he saw in me someone who was essentially plowing the same ground that he would have plowed—looking from the outside in, being somewhat literate, being somewhat jocular, and taking it out wider. So it was really: if *I'm* there, what is *he* going to talk about?

We had a lot of philosophical disagreements, especially about the extent to which it was an entertainment show. When they had guests in the booth, many of them stunk beyond words. But I was for conceptual guests in the booth. I was for *Monday Night Football* as I remembered it as a child with Cosell and Meredith and Gifford, but Mike really just wanted to be the play-by-play guy on *Monday Night Football*.

Early on together I said, "Mike, you know what really works well on *PTI* is when Mike and I talk over each other—" and he cut me off right there and says, "That's a nice little studio show, but *Monday Night Football* is very important, so don't ever interrupt me when I'm talking." You think that works with a guy sitting one foot to your left for three hours a night?

I had watched Mike Tirico on air for years, and this guy was poured into a tuxedo, he was so smooth. I watched what he did in golf. He took unlikable Nick Faldo and Paul Azinger and he made them into Desi and Lucy. He's got a great ability to bring out the best in people when he wants to. And the same goes for me. I had done that with Wilbon, so it wasn't crazy for me to keep thinking that it would happen between me and Tirico. But for two years he didn't even look at me.

Finally I said, "What do you want from me? Why

don't you even call me by my name?" He told me,
"I'm so disappointed in you because you don't prepare. You're just not prepared. You're not professional." I said, "I don't prepare like you prepare.
It doesn't mean I'm not prepared. I'm not here to
know the names and the colleges of these people.
That's not my job." So it went on and on and on and
on. I felt as if we were competing against each other
rather than working with each other, and I kept on
waiting for him to treat me like he had treated so
many others in the past who he had worked with.
Look, I know that Mike Tirico is smart and funny
and as quick if not quicker than I am. I admire him
and respect him, but it killed me that he had none of
that for me. After many conversations, I came to
believe that he has little respect for sportswriters and
remembers all the sportswriters who wrote bad shit
about him. He loves it when sportswriters get something wrong. And I felt he put me in that group,
because I'm part of them. It wasn't that I was right
and he was wrong. We just couldn't agree. I had lots
of conversations with Rothman and Walsh and some
even with Norby, and I'll admit I would get upset. I
said, "He's killing me, and it keeps happening." They
would say, "We've talked to him, and it's going to get
better," but it never did. He was doing it deliberately;
anybody with eyes could see it. He just wouldn't
engage with me.

Look, am I happy now? Absolutely. In *PTI*, I've got the best show in America. I'm thrilled. But I thought I could have been better on *Monday Night Football*. I did the best that I could, given everything we were working with. But the happiest guy in America today is Mike Tirico, because I'm not in that booth and he's got a coach, so he doesn't have to worry about anything else.

BILL SIMMONS:

Announcing is like wrestling; if you're not going to sell the other guy or guys in the ring, they are going to look like they suck. Tirico's always been nice to me, and I think he's a talented guy, but I thought how he acted was unforgivable, and I continue to feel bad for Tony. He never wanted to work with Tony. He had made a decision that he wasn't going to sell him at all and that he was going to undermine him as subtly as he could. So ultimately, ESPN was going to have to choose between them.

I had watched all of those Kornheiser games thinking, "If I was in that spot, and the expectation was that I was supposed to entertain, and I had this guy with me who was subtly undermining me, changing the subject on me and greeting my jokes with dead silence, I would eventually strangle this person on live TV." Kornheiser is a better person than I am, apparently.

RON JAWORSKI:

Usually around April, Tony and I would begin talking for the next season and play some golf. It was funny; when the schedule came out, I called Tony and said, "Oh great, man, we're going to be in San Francisco; we can play Olympic. We got San Diego; we can play Torrey Pines." I'm naming all these golf courses we would be getting a chance to play at, but I could sense his anxiety. So he says, "Ah, ah, I don't know if I can do this again." Well, obviously Tony's always kind of whining a little bit in a fun way, but I really sensed he had some reservations about doing *Monday Night Football* again.

Then a couple days before my golf tournament in Atlantic City, which he was coming to, he said he's not going to do *Monday Night Football* again, that it was kind of his choice and ESPN's choice to move in a different direction. I really don't know whether it was Tony's choice or that [Jon] Gruden became available—I'm not sure how that dynamic worked out—but clearly Tony was looking to leave maybe six weeks before the actual announcement.

Historians will debate which came first, Jon Gruden losing his job coaching for the Tampa Bay Buccaneers or Tony Kornheiser—Mr. Fear of Flying—looking at the new season schedule and realizing he couldn't do it all by bus. But even if all the Monday Night Football *games had been scheduled to take place in a twenty-five-mile radius, Tony's time was up once Gruden became available. They had all tried—some harder than others—to make it work, but this dog just wouldn't hunt.*

In Kornheiser's announcement, he said, "My fear of planes is legendary and sadly true. When I looked at the upcoming schedule, it was the perfect storm that would've frequently moved me from the bus to the air." Chris Berman and his "Boomer" buds reportedly celebrated with a chorus of "Ding dong, the witch is dead," and competitors at other networks began the countdown for when Gruden would get his next coaching job.

BILL SIMMONS:

Tirico doesn't sell Tony for three fucking years, then has the gall to say nice things about him after Tony leaves? Come on. What kills me is that Tony got the rap for blowing this when nobody on the planet can succeed in TV if their play-by-play guy isn't selling them. Period. Five minutes into their first regular-season Monday night game, Tirico had already laughed at more Gruden jokes than he did for three years of Kornheiser. I never thought he wanted Tony in the booth, and that became obvious during the 2009 season, as he turned into Mr. Gregarious and sold Gruden and Jaworski the way a play-by-play guy is supposed to sell his partners. He failed Kornheiser.

Sports Business Journal ran a whole long story about

how our ratings are up since Tony left and we're back to the basics and all that shit. It was all designed to make Kornheiser look bad, and to trumpet how they went in a different direction and "How great are we?" Meanwhile, the reason their ratings went up is that they had two awesome matchups, including the Favre-returns-against-the-Packers game. Of course your ratings are going to go up. We've also had a number of other good games. But that's the only reason the ratings went up. Nobody on the planet watches a sports game for the fucking announcers. And that's the thing we have never understood. Mike Tirico could leave tomorrow and we could replace him with Mike Greenberg or one of forty other guys, and the rating would not budge .00001. Nobody watches for Mike Tirico. Zero. No one. And then you have Jaws and Gruden: "This guy's great. Great throw. What a play. It's a great call. Good timeout." They don't say anything negative.

You know, it is interesting that the really passionate people who don't like authority also seem to be the people who have had problems at ESPN in the past. I've heard about the struggles that Olbermann had with the company and now that I know Kornheiser, knowing some of the shit that he's dealt with, it does seem like we're all certain types. Olbermann's much crazier than I am. But we're all kind of like the same mold — very impassioned almost to a fault, and we just can't believe ESPN works this way, and why can't it work better, and it's just like we're a bad match for a company like that, and I think that's why a lot of those people have left. Kornheiser left and then came back for *PTI* but really only because of [producer] Erik Rydholm. If it was anybody else I don't think he would have lasted.

FRED GAUDELLI:

Everybody knew that *Monday Night* broadcast was bad except for Skipper and Walsh, and I mean *everybody*. Walsh loves Kornheiser. Now, everyone knows how much I respect Walsh, but he has no feel for this part of the business — none. Then you think back and remember that Shapiro could have had Al and John, which would have truly brought *Monday Night Football* to ESPN.

Has anyone missed Kornheiser? Hardly. Now they got Gruden, and he's good, but here's what's happened because of Gruden: he made Jaws superfluous. They don't need Jaws. But the problem is, what are you going to do now? You can't get rid of Jaws, and Gruden's going to be coaching somewhere soon.

JON GRUDEN, *Football Analyst:*

The biggest surprise is how much I enjoy it. My first preseason, we got on the bus in Pittsburgh. We did the Steelers-Cardinals game, and we drove up to watch the Giants in training camp — about an eight-hour bus ride to Albany to watch the Giants practice.

Then we did the Giants-Carolina game. We had eight or nine days when we were together and really got to know each other, Ron and Mike and I, and Jay and Chip and Jeff Leonardo, our bus driver. It was kind of like our training camp, and I really felt comfortable with the guys I was with and hopefully they became more comfortable with me. It was all football all the time, and it was the start of some really special relationships.

Going back to Lambeau Field in Green Bay and to the 49ers game in San Francisco, places where my coaching career started, those were two of my favorite trips. During the San Francisco trip, I went back to Ruby Hill, where I lived when I coached the Raiders. And of course in Green Bay, I had a chance to hang out with Mike McCarthy, who I worked with at Pittsburgh. I got a chance to go to Brett Favre's Steakhouse—that wasn't there when I was coaching. And I got a picture of me next to Mike Holmgren Street.

We did something in every town. When I was in Dallas I had a chance to sneak a lunch in with Randy White. I took the guys to Splitsville. I'm a part owner of a bowling alley. It's probably not doing very well, but I took the guys up there and we rolled balls down the alley. We went to the Cleveland Cavaliers game when we were in Cleveland, my first time seeing LeBron James play. I got to go to the Rock and Roll Hall of Fame. I even got to go curling! You know, every town we went to, Saturday night was kind of our night to be together. I got to go over to Archie Manning's house and meet Archie and Olivia Manning in New Orleans, right there in their house where Peyton and Eli Manning played catch in the backyard. That was pretty cool.

Another fun thing about being part of *Monday Night Football* was hearing from friends and people I hadn't spoken with in years. I got a letter not long ago from my fifth-grade schoolteacher back in Bloomington, Indiana, Mrs. Williams, who said she was a big fan of *Monday Night Football*. That blew my mind.

FRED GAUDELLI:

This was not from Jerry Jones but came from someone in the league office about the first game at Texas Stadium—I can't give this person up—but he said, "The difference between doing this game on NBC and ESPN is, NBC will make it all about the Cowboys and the National Football League; ESPN will make it all about ESPN." That was recognized everywhere. They think, "Let's make it all about ourselves."

It was understandably big news when, on July 17, 2009, a civil suit was filed in Nevada District Court accusing star quarterback of the Pittsburgh Steelers Ben Roethlisberger of sexual assault—the same Ben Roethlisberger who had been featured in one of ESPN's SportsCenter *commercials and been given a prime seat at the ESPY Awards.*

Another story soon grew out of the civil suit, however. The Roethlisberger story was news virtually every-where—except on ESPN. For two and a half days, ESPN failed to report on the Roethlisberger charges any-where in its empire—with the exception of its local Pittsburgh TV station. In response to criticism, network representatives claimed that ESPN was not reporting the story because no criminal suit had been filed.

That explanation hardly satisfied those critical of the network. "Since when," asked John Gonzalez in the Philadelphia Inquirer, *"has an athlete's silence or lack of cooperation prevented ESPN from covering a story?" He cited ESPN's coverage of civil suits against Adam Jones, Roberto Alomar, and Shannon Brown. Gonzalez also quoted an unnamed ESPN source who said, "People were going insane. Fox News was doing the story; the AP had it. And they wouldn't even let us mention it."*

Bryan Burwell of the St. Louis Post-Dispatch *wrote, "Every other major sports news operation has reported that the lawsuit has been filed, [but] the biggest sports news organization in the country . . . has been mysteri-ously silent."*

Gradually, the attacks on ESPN became harsher and more severe, some pointing out a potential conflict of interest. Mike Florio of Pro Football Talk *on* NBC-Sports.com *wrote that ESPN's inaction "makes us won-*

der whether there's a complete firewall between the business functions of ESPN and its journalistic activities." Mike Francesa of WFAN said, "The bottom line is that ESPN is extremely protective of athletes, especially the ones that do commercials with them.... When they are in bed with athletes, they just protect them. We know that. That's nothing new."

And veteran sports reporter Frank Deford wrote, "ESPN's refusal to report the story gave rise to criticism that it was not only protecting Roethlisberger's reputation but... also shielding its TV partner, the NFL. It had taken a seemingly inviolate position that accusations in a civil suit could be false, yet incendiary enough to damage Roethlisberger's reputation."

In an instance of perfect timing, the whole thing blew up just after ESPN had named Don Ohlmeyer as its new ombudsman. In his first column on ESPN.com, Ohlmeyer wrote, "Even if ESPN judged that it should not report the Roethlisberger suit, not acknowledging a sports story that's blanketing the airways requires an explanation to your viewers, listeners and readers. And in today's world they are owed that explanation right away — to do otherwise is just plain irresponsible. It forces your audience to ask why the story was omitted. It forces them to manufacture a motive. And it ultimately forces them to question your credibility."

After two days, John Skipper told Vince Doria the story was too big to ignore any longer, and the network got on the case. What ESPN finally did was less the issue, *however, than how long it had taken them to do it. In the ESPN newsroom, spirits were down.*

VINCE DORIA:

When Ben Roethlisberger was accused — in a civil lawsuit — of sexual assault, we did not initially report it. This was consistent with our policy on these types of stories. Accusations of sexual misconduct are damaging, of course, and regardless of the outcome of those allegations, they often continue to be part of an individual's reputation. There are a number of factors to consider in making the decision to report a story like this. Does the individual have any history of this nature? Roethlisberger did not. Have the police investigated the charge? In this case, the police were never contacted. Is the accusation coming in the middle of a season, the playoffs, etc., that might cause the attention to impact on-field performance? In this case, it was the off-season. Has the accused individual, at his own initiative, addressed the charges publicly? Initially, Roethlisberger did not.

Based on those factors, we did not report the story when it broke, fully understanding that at some point, some of the factors would likely change, which would prompt us to then report the story. And we did assign a reporter to look into the story. There were, of course, assertions in the media that we were protecting Roethlisberger, a prominent NFL quarterback, because we didn't want to lose access to him in the future. Or because we are an NFL rights holder, and in that role, a business partner of the league. Or because Roethlisberger had recently appeared at the ESPYs. None of these things were factors in the decision. Two days after the story broke, an internal decision was made to report the story. And while I didn't agree with doing it when we did it, I agreed to comply with that decision. As it turned out, roughly twelve hours later, Roethlisberger held a press conference to address the accusations, an act that would have been the trigger for us to report the story.

PETER BONVENTRE:

Put this on the record: if Mark Shapiro had been there, that thing would have been covered right away. Unless he had a fucking concussion, Mark would have been all over it, and I don't think he ever would have said, "This is a civil action; we don't cover civil actions." What does that mean, "We don't cover civil actions"? And then another thing happens with the guy and makes you look really, really stupid. You can't do that. The guy's got a problem, and they just don't want to deal with it. It's nuts.

VINCE DORIA:

While increased media attention was always a factor in our decision of when to report, we have, in the wake of the Roethlisberger story, been more attentive to that coverage, and probably reported on issues like this more quickly. Our justification is that when a certain amount of media attention builds, our intent to avoid damaging a reputation becomes moot. I'm not in love with that justification, but it is a practical one in the current landscape. As to the difficulty in making these calls, we are in a unique position, one that probably differs from any other news organization. On one hand, we are in business with virtually every league, conference, and association, essentially the largest rights holder in sports broadcasting. On the other hand, we have the largest and, I would like to think, the most aggressive news-gathering operation in the area of sports information.

It makes for hard calls, on often critical stories, that may make our business partners unhappy. Yet we do it on a daily basis. And while it creates a challenge that, as noted, is somewhat unique, in many ways it constitutes the real fun in the job. And I don't say that to suggest there is any joy in reporting bad news. But there is real satisfaction that comes from reporting that makes it clear that we are strongly independent as a news organization and not influenced by our business relationships. While I understand that some people might view that assertion with a certain amount of skepticism, I think we have a lengthy track record of tough stories.

GARY BELSKY:

We've never been told not to do a story because we're partners with a league. Not once. Our bosses really only ask us two things: First, be right. Second, give them warning if we think there could be flack. I probably send a couple of dozen "heads-up" e-mails a year, but even that's left up to us; it's us deciding to send word of a story up the ranks just so that they can be prepared for it. So when we published a big NAS-CAR story about a driver with a drug problem, a guy who raced while on heroin, we let our bosses know. I think we even sent the edited article to John Skipper, just so he could understand the scope. It was a pretty crazy piece. But the only thing I got was an e-mail from John Wildhack, who handles a lot of our high-level league interactions, saying, "Good story." Maybe he warned his contacts that something was coming; maybe he just appreciated the heads-up. I don't know.

In the time I've been running *The Magazine* I've never been asked to hold back. Honestly, sometimes I think, "What the hell are they doing, letting us do this?" I was a business writer before I came here, and from a business perspective a lot of the serious journalism we do doesn't make sense. This is a television company. Our principal business is entertainment, and our partnerships with leagues, even though we're paying them, are complex and fragile. Our bosses don't really need to let us do the type of journalism we do here, because the stories can lead to headaches for them, and as a magazine we're not going to make that much of a difference to ESPN's bottom line. But I think they recognize that good journalism enhances the brand.

In addition to the magazine and the newsroom itself, ESPN's journalistic mission takes many forms — among them Outside the Lines, E:60, *and the Enterprise Unit, which serves as a cross-platform group devoted to long-form reporting and investigative journalism. With a steady output of stories, many investigative, each division has worked to disprove what they consider a common misperception: that ESPN's coziness with rights holders — the leagues — can compromise and even cripple its journalism, and that the real business of the network is sucking up to commissioners and league officials.*

Even though examples like the Roethlisberger incident have intruded from time to time, plenty of evidence exists in the form of well-reported stories that have validated the independence of the news teams (often coordinated with work by ESPN.com). Despite huge and lucrative deals with the NCAA, for instance, the Enterprise Unit produced a multipart series about ways that commercialism has crept, or plunged, into college sports. Among the examples cited were Florida State football's suspiciously malleable academic standards, a lawsuit involving the NCAA and the issue of who

*owns player likenesses used in video games, and even
ESPN's own role, along with other TV networks, in the
phenomenon.*

    *As part of the buildup to its World Cup coverage, the
network dove into the prickly issue of human trafficking
in South Africa, even questioning whether FIFA and
the South African government were taking enough steps
to thwart this form of twenty-first-century slavery.
Undercover work in the brothels of Johannesburg and
Cape Town was an important facet of the reporting.*

    *In the something-to-anger-every-league department,
ESPN offered a disconcerting piece on stadium food —
and what may be "lurking" inside it. Reporters exam-
ined health-and-safety violations facing every NBA,
NFL, and MLB team in 107 facilities throughout the
U.S. and Canada. Also on the health front, Enterprise
continued its years-long investigation into concussions
suffered by players in the NFL, interviewing the doctor
assigned to oversee the ongoing problem and discussing
the league's reluctance to confront it openly.*

    *At ESPN.com, in addition to stories that originated
in other units, high-impact pieces on modern times
included a July 2010 examination of a dilemma facing
MLB as its annual All-Star Game approached: whether
to play that game in Arizona, as scheduled, despite the
state's infamous, Draconian, and, some said, outright
racist immigration legislation. In October of the same
year, ESPN.com carried a very strong opinion piece by
Howard Bryant on the matrix of crises and controversies*

facing the NFL, with Bryant assailing football as a "death sport" that will have to change radically in the decade ahead to ensure its own survival.

For its part, OTL took a look at the strange phenomenon of sex addiction in an Ides-of-March piece that aired a month after Tiger Woods's televised statement about the charges of incredible promiscuity lodged against him. Winston Bennett, basketball coach at Mid-Continent University in Mayfield, Kentucky, watched with heightened interest, subsequently going public with what he said was his own sexual addiction problem, a compulsion that led to relations with "hundreds" of women each year, flouting his twenty-year marriage to wife Peggy.

JOHN SKIPPER:

People look at ESPN as kind of a totality and so it is, "You guys have these fun-loving anchors—are they journalists or are they entertainers? You got games. You're in bed with your partner, with the leagues, yet you're covering them as well."

To me, and I'm not a journalist by trade, the company is remarkably conscientious about separating those ventures. You'll have trouble finding any of our news guys who will say I've pulled them off stories, because the answer is I never have. Now, more subtle, is the pressure of "Should I do that?"—because we're in partnership with that organization and it will cause trouble.

I supervise the people who acquire the rights from the NFL and manage relationships with the NFL. I also supervise the people who manage the news of reporting on the NFL. I manage it all by keeping them completely separate. The people who I'm in business with don't like that. But Roger Goodell understands we're a news-gathering organization. We're going to report on the league. We're going to call him for comment but we're not going to tell him what the story is. We won't let him approve questions. I think we follow all the rules over here.

RUSH LIMBAUGH:

The McNabb controversy affected how ESPN covered my bid to buy the Rams. Somehow my name was the only name that got leaked as a member of the Dave Checketts group. There were supposedly two other groups, but the names of people in those groups didn't get leaked. The only people that knew who the bidders were and the members of the groups were the Rams; Goldman Sachs, who were brokering it; and, of course, the NFL.

The first reaction that Kornheiser and Wilbon had on *Pardon the Interruption* was all positive. I remember, because I got an e-mail from Checketts about it; he was all excited. Kornheiser had said, "Do you think Rush should get in there after the game and hug those big sweaty black guys all taped up?" And Wilbon said, "Oh, yeah! Oh, yeah!" But the next day, everyone had done a total 180, and all these phony quotes that I had never said got circulated.

SKIP BAYLESS, *Columnist:*

From the bottom of my heart the most shocking thing to me about being at this network is that no one has ever told me, "You can't say that"—after I said it—or told me I can't say something before I say it. Ever. Not one time. I'm honored by that and I'm proud of it. I'm not a clichéd speaker; I just give it to you from the bottom of my journalist's soul. Not once has anyone ever said no. And that's despite the fact that I feel like the token controversial guy. I'm obsessive-compulsive. I'm fanatical. I live this job. I watch everything at night, I read everything and I call all the people that I know in every sport, every night. I'm not half-cocked. I'm not unplugged. I'm not knee-jerk. I don't care what anybody else thinks of me, and I never have. Andre Iguodala nicknamed me "the diabolical hater." I always kid back, "Nope, I'm the diabolical truth teller."

In the summer of 2009, it was discovered that a crazed and overzealous "fan" had stalked Erin Andrews and videotaped her as she brushed her hair and put on makeup while naked in what she thought was the privacy of her hotel room. Reversing the peephole in the door (ironically installed there for a guest's security) and using a cell phone as a camera, Michael David Barrett secretly taped Andrews three different times, and some of the footage popped up on the Internet before being discovered and removed.

Actually, it wasn't as simple as that. There is more than a hint of dispute as to how that process developed and who was responsible for what. Andrews was understandably distressed when the story broke on a Thursday night and immediately went to ESPN, asking them to get the offending site to take down the video. David Pahl, general counsel of ESPN, wrote to the site and used the following language: "It has come to my attention that you have posted on your site pictures of a young, blonde woman" and then gave the link. He said the pictures constituted "a trespass/assault on the rights of the woman involved." Most importantly, at no point did he mention the name Erin Andrews, and it is fair to say, as one ESPN executive noted, that "there was still disbelief and doubt as to who it was."

Approximately twenty-four hours later, Andrews hired an attorney, who then issued a statement: "While alone in the privacy of her hotel room, Erin Andrews was surreptitiously videotaped without her knowledge or consent." It took blogs about a nanosecond to connect the statement with the video images.

Andrews, chosen by Playboy magazine as America's "sexiest sportscaster" in 2007 and 2008, was understandably mortified. She even worried aloud that the incident might end her career. The scandal spiraled off into other unseemly indignities. The Walt Disney

Company and Rupert Murdoch's Fox empire, never exactly chummy, got into a wrangle when Murdoch's New York Post ran still photos of the naked Andrews made from frames of the stalker's video. ESPN charged the Post with going "beyond the boundaries of common decency in the interest of sensationalism" and broke off all ties with the newspaper. The Post shot back via its popular Page Six feature, ridiculing "the Mickey Mouse sports network" for its huffy and supposedly hypocritical reaction.

To Andrews's annoyance and perhaps bafflement, the story took yet another peculiar turn when Christine Brennan, ESPN analyst and columnist for USA Today, seemed to blame Andrews in part for what happened. In a radio appearance and a Twitter tweet, Brennan said Andrews should "rely on her talent and brains" instead of "playing to the frat house." She said part of Andrews's "shtick" was "being a little bit out there" and suggested she was thus "encouraging the complete nut case to drill a hole in your room."

STEVE ANDREWS, *Erin's Father:*

When she called me that night, she was in hysterics. Erin was frantic. I sort of went into reporter mode, you know: Who, what, where, when, how, why? The more unglued she became, the more I tried to remain low key. At the time I thought, "It's on the Internet, we can't change that right now," so protecting her safety was the priority. We didn't know what or who was involved in this. It was terribly frightening, and it was devastating to see my daughter being humiliated this way.

I suggested she call ESPN to let them know what was going on, and ask them to help get the thing off the Web.

Erin and I, along with her two point attorneys, met with two FBI agents and Wes Hsu, an assistant U.S. attorney that July day in Los Angeles. It was Mr. Hsu who politely and almost apologetically said, "I know you are a victim of a crime, we're just not sure it is a federal crime and that we have jurisdiction." My comment to them was, "It may not be a federal crime, but I know she is a victim and I don't want to be back here in a few months sitting at this table listening to you all explain to me why she is dead."

When I think about the enormity of what she's been through, I tear up and begin to cry.

ERIN ANDREWS:

My dad is amazing. He is my best friend, and he's in the business, so I can talk to him a lot about my frustrations or my accomplishments or just things I have questions about. I have always had that kind of relationship with him. It's the reason why I'm in the industry. I would sit and watch the Boston Celtics and the Red Sox with him all the time. He is truly my best friend. I talk to him four to five times a day. If it wasn't for him I don't how I would have been able to get through any of it.

My family and I were living under a rock during that whole thing, but we knew exactly what people were saying—who was saying what and who wasn't saying anything. I'll be honest with you; Christine's comments hurt me so bad. It disappointed me beyond belief. I got put in a position where I was basically exposed to anyone and everyone. You have to keep in mind, my life got turned upside down, ripped apart by something I didn't even see coming. We didn't even know where this person was. We didn't know anything about him, and then all of a sudden, everything just blew up. I have paparazzi on my front doorstep. I've got people saying I did this to myself. I mean, it's like, what is happening? It was a nightmare. Every day and every night, every entertainment show was covering it. I don't think people realized how damaging and humiliating it was for me, what it was doing to me and my family. They had no idea.

CHRISTINE BRENNAN:

The first words I said in a radio interview about what happened to Erin were that it was "gross" and "despicable," and I then went on to say several times that Erin never deserved what happened to her. It's unfortunate that those comments were almost completely ignored.

When I used the phrase about not playing to the frat house, it was not meant to be pointed specifically at Erin, and I clarified that the next day in a *USA Today* story. It's a comment I have used hundreds of times in speeches and conversation in an effort to mentor younger women on how to live their lives in the field of sports journalism.

If you're a woman and you're in this business, you hear some things that you never would have imagined. When I first started covering the Washington Redskins in 1985, I happened to give a quick hug to a local sportscaster as we said hello at practice one day. A couple of days later, he came up to me and said that some of the players were now asking him if he and I were dating. Another time, a player told me that because I had come by his locker to interview him a few times in the same week, his teammates were wondering if we were dating. Both of these things really surprised me, so I learned early in my career that women in the sports media are judged in a very different way than men, and I think it's important to talk about that. I spend a lot of time encouraging women to find careers in the sports media, but I also think it's smart to discuss the things we need to be careful about in a predominantly male world.

MICHELLE BEADLE, *Anchor:*

I felt bad for her. She looked fabulous but it was such a violation. I mean, I've had moments in my apartment in New York when the blinds were up for one brief second and you think, "Ugh!" but that's nothing compared to what happened to her. Nothing.

I think things might have been handled differently, but she seems to be moving on. Sometimes these things turn out better for people.

ERIN ANDREWS:

Through my whole ordeal, Norby and I developed a pretty—gosh, I don't want to say "intense"—but it was a lot different relationship than anybody would ever have with their boss. I was calling him when he was on vacation with his kids and he was stepping away to take my calls. I was so thankful. He basically told me that whatever I wanted to do, they would respect. To this day it's still awful and hurtful and that was one of the reasons why we developed a relationship—because he was understanding.

I didn't want to talk about it. I wanted to move on and just go back to work, but there were reasons why I decided to talk. I've been put in this position and I can't hide from it, and it is now my responsibility to help out other victims. I have been made the face of this; I can either walk away like a coward or I can deal with it and help other women. I got tons of letters from women that said, "Please, you have a face. You have ESPN supporting you with a lawyer, and please fight this." And I knew I couldn't walk away.

CHRIS FOWLER:

Erin's a close friend. I respect her professionally and like her a lot personally. So I didn't react as a member of the media, or even react as a colleague, as much as I did a close friend. It was horrible. She was the victim of a crime for which there is not a hell of a lot of precedent. And it's not a crime that you can fully understand unless you've been a victim of the same type of thing. She did nothing wrong.

ERIN ANDREWS:

I'll be very honest: I got calls from coaches people wouldn't even imagine. The guys called me and just said, "You can't leave." They didn't know if I was ever going to come back. Nobody really knew. I had coaches say to me, "You better come back because if you don't, our sport will miss you so much. You make up our sport." And I don't think coaches would say that because of the way I look. That was a really gratifying moment for me, just seeing all the support, and the reason why they were calling was because they respected my work.

Urban [Meyer] and Mac Brown were incredibly supportive. They were checking in weekly, always looking out for me. I think two phone calls floored me. One was an incredible message from John Cali-pari, and he just said, "I've got a daughter and I'm very sorry. Do not let this person win. You have to come back. If you don't come back, college basketball will just be miserable without you. You are so good for our sport." The other person—I haven't even worked on one of his games—was Les Miles. He reached out to me, and I remember I was doing laun-dry at my house and I was kind of tearing up because he said, "You know, I have a daughter, and if we don't have you on the sidelines, what's the point?" And then all of a sudden he went into football coach–speak and I literally was ready to tackle a wall. I understood why guys get so jacked up before games. It was awesome.

CHRIS FOWLER:

Erin showed a ton of strength, and she's grown in ways that she didn't expect. She has so much to be proud of about how she has handled this. To face a room full of college kids, predominantly male, after this shows a ton of guts. To walk into a room of coaches after this stuff has been in the *New York Post* is incredibly tough. A bunch of us, including the close corps of people from Thursday nights, were deter-mined to try to do everything we could to help her through it, particularly since college football was her first foray back into things after the incident. We were all very protective, more so than we were before. And it's very dispiriting to hear some of the callous reactions that some people had.

RACHEL NICHOLS, *Reporter:*

There are times when you're traveling and you realize that you're vulnerable because there are people who recognize you, and you hope the prosecution of this guy has been enough of an example to anybody else who had this idea, that if you want to copycat this, guess how many years in jail you're going to have!

Once you walk into a hotel lobby, you're seen. You can register under a fake name if you want, but if you're Stuart Scott, Chris Berman, and others, I'm sure you get recognized everywhere you go. I'm sure Erin gets recognized wherever she goes. But for me, it's hit or miss. I went to a restaurant in Manhattan, and the fashionista girl behind the desk didn't know who I was, but the guy in the parking lot did. He's got ESPN on for twelve hours during his shift. So the minute I walk out of the restaurant, the guy is like, "Oh, my God, Oh, my God." Hotels are the same way. The kids at the front desk, checking you in, they know exactly who you are. So it's not as if I can register under a fake name. What's that going to do? It's scary at times. You have to just forge ahead. Is that something that's going to stop me from doing what I want to do? Absolutely not. There's a greater goal.

RECE DAVIS:

There's a real infatuation with her among the college fans, I think, because she's an attractive woman and—oh, guess what?—she knows sports. So I think because of that it has created this dream scenario for them, and they want to be close to her, touch her, get pictures with her, and tell their buddy that she said, "Hi."

You see people go over the top a little bit in ways that you think would make her uncomfortable, but she has a way of keeping a distance without leaving them feeling like she was rude. And I think it's just natural for her.

CINDY BRUNSON, *Anchor:*

Erin is a big Gator alum, and we hung out with her for a while tailgating, and I have to say, I was afraid for her. These twenty-two-year-old, twenty-five-year-old men are pawing at her and grabbing at her, and every time she turns around some guy with a cell phone is taking a picture. And some other guy is putting his arm around her. I get the attention and everything, that's one thing, but I was physically frightened for her.

STEVE BERTHIAUME:

She's got to be used to it by now, but it made us uncomfortable. It just isn't safe. Forget about annoying; this is *dangerous*.

RECE DAVIS:

She's a very gregarious and outgoing girl. She's very talkative and nice, and she's friendly with people, but she understands the distance she needs to keep and does a good job of it. It's really not easy. Especially people who will sometimes have a little liquid courage and—maybe "mob mentality" is too strong a term to use—but when there are ten frat guys together, and one of them is a little braver than the next, it's just tough.

Amidst the various suspensions and firings, one little-noticed arrival in Bristol, although lacking the dazzle of some others, would prove to be the gift that kept on giving for the network. That was the hiring of Michelle Beadle as a new on-air personality.

Growing up, Beadle had never imagined being on air for ESPN. She was so insecure about her looks, she wouldn't even wear shorts. Beadle attended the University of Texas at San Antonio and wound up taking off three years between her junior and senior years, much to the dismay of her parents. She waited tables and traveled around the country. When she got back home, her father told her, "Do something. I don't care what it is, just do something," so she interned for the San Antonio Spurs. They shoved her in front of the camera one day and, though the first attempt was (according to her) "hideous," the camera man told Beadle, "Just ignore the camera." She did, and things were immediately better. She never looked back.

Beadle bounced among many jobs and several networks before hearing about auditions for the new SportsNation *program on ESPN2.* SportsNation *was going to be a daily afternoon sports show that heavily solicited viewer contributions, ideas, and opinions, the concept being to bridge the gap between viewers and viewed. The last of 142 people to audition, Beadle balked when asked to compose a list of improvements she'd make to the show. Considering the assignment a joke, Beadle said later that she simply dashed off "a sarcastic list of ten stupid things"—doing such an amusing job of it that ESPN executives felt she'd be perfect.*

Beadle turned out to be the ideal cohost (opposite the especially quirky Colin Cowherd, a man who seemed never to have an unspoken thought): smart but ingenuous, pretty but not distractingly sexual. "Beadlemania" was born and helped make SportsNation *not just a success but also a draw for ESPN's youngest and most heavily male audience—a sponsor's dream.*

Disarmingly unaffected and self-effacing, Beadle prefers to "come off as intelligent and witty and myself" rather than be regarded as a babe. She takes her new fame and status in stride—perhaps because she doesn't quite believe it's actually happening.

MICHELLE BEADLE:

I met with the guys who came up with the show—Jamie Horowitz, Kevin Wilde, and David Jacoby. I didn't know it was a meeting for a specific show; I just thought it was another of those meetings my agent had been dragging me to and which would never amount to anything. But it wasn't even a meeting; it was literally us sitting around a table telling inappropriate stories. And then I came in and auditioned. I was the last one, due to scheduling issues.

They knew they wanted Colin; he was already part of the deal. I'd heard nightmares about him—misogynist, jerk, he's this, he's that—so I came in with my wall up a little bit, but it was the most fun audition I'd ever had.

COLIN COWHERD:

They had me be part of the interviews with seven or eight women. I told the producers, "I just need someone who can throw a punch and take a punch, because the stuff I'm vomiting on the air can be offensive, and she can't be stunned. She's got to pitch it right back. She has to have good core strength—be able to take a blow and dish one right back." That's all I cared about. I just wanted good TV.

MICHELLE BEADLE:

Probably six months after I arrived, I was leaving a concert in Jersey, and from behind me I hear, "I really love you on *SportsNation*!" and it was a twenty-one-year-old girl, and I just said, "Well, thank you." It was a little weird. I said to my mom later, "I totally got recognized."

I think my parents are still a little bit shocked that this is what I do. I went to my dad's birthday party and all his friends wanted to do was talk about Oklahoma State.

COLIN COWHERD:

Michelle's really bright, and she has talent and confidence. It's kind of an "it" quality, and she's got it. But she's also vulnerable, and that makes her work hard.

Insecurity's a great motivator. I'm insecure; that's why I work so hard. I think anybody that goes on camera for a living or behind a microphone, if you go deep into their psyche, they either want to be noticed or want to be liked. I don't have all the answers. I'm not Freud here. But I think a lot of us in this business are vulnerable. That's probably the same for actors and performers. Actually, I've never considered myself a journalist. I just consider myself a performer.

My mom used to say to me all the time, "You like being liked." And yes, I think that probably comes from insecurity, because of the way I grew up, sort of isolated in the middle of rural Washington State. But I learned to be very self-reliant, and because of that, I think I tend to be defiant. I had to fight my way through a lot of divorces in my family. My mom and dad have been divorced a combination of eight times.

MICHELLE BEADLE:

Colin's forty-five and I'm thirty-four. We're definitely different-thinking regarding the way men and women are in relationships. He's just old-fashioned. It cracks me up because there are times when it feels like he's sixty-five years old. If I go out and come home at 2:00 a.m., his reaction is ridiculous, so I've learned what I can and cannot say around him. And his pop-culture knowledge is embarrassing at times. He references shows that haven't been on the air in, like, fifteen years—it's always *Seinfeld*. I'm like, "There are other shows that have been on the air since then, you know." He's such a bizarre, eclectic dude.

As ESPN approached its thirtieth anniversary, powerful paradoxes were at work. The American economy—in fact, the global economy—was continuing to suffer, and yet the company was coming off the best year in its history, a record year for growth and profits. The dichotomy was resolved with an all-systems-go order on aggressive acquisitions and technological development, but significant restrictions regarding staffing.

Bodenheimer announced a hiring freeze for what was left of 2009 and all of 2010 and put the kibosh on merit-pay increases for any employee who'd reached the level of senior director or higher; funds available in the "merit pool" for those ranking below senior director were reduced. Bodenheimer also suggested streamlining, downsizing, and belt-tightening for the entire organization.

At the same time, however, Bodenheimer said work would continue on an extravagant new Los Angeles production facility for the network; on Building 13 and a new child-care facility, both in Bristol; on the launch of Employee Research Groups; and on continued "smart investments in our future, both in the U.S. and internationally."

CHRISTINE DRIESSEN:

We continue to play the "little engine that could" card with all our employees and the business community we work in. Despite people knowing we're very successful, I think what we have tried to drill down in our organization is that when we spend money, we're going to spend money on the product that goes on the air to serve the fans. We are not Hollywood. We are not the broadcast networks. We have a different culture here about how we spend money. I'd rather have us spend a dollar on great production, great cameras, and great technology than a private dining room for the executives. You're not going to have cars and limos. Al Jaffe is on the front line talking with the agents and talent and he tells them, "It's a different world here. There are no stars." We're all part of this incredible organization that has great pride and quality, but no one's that important at the end of the day. George gets so much credit for this. He has taken us back to a more humble organization. We're extremely lean. We're known that way in the Walt Disney Company. And we pride ourselves on that.

GEORGE BODENHEIMER:

It's a pretty darn good buy, the bundle of product you receive for about forty dollars a month. You get in excess of a hundred channels, each with twenty-four-hour entertainment. If you buy a cup of coffee for four bucks and add a sandwich, you get to ten bucks, then drive across the George Washington Bridge, where the toll is eight bucks—these are everyday things that you don't even think twice about. Like if you take the family to a game or go to the movies, you're going to spend far in excess of what is asked for cable television. I believe cable is perhaps the greatest bargain in history.

We're very careful about what we acquire and what we spend. We have never felt that we can own everything; we don't have a desire to do that. We're focused on adding world-class properties to our offerings, and in the last several years we've acquired the Masters,

US Open tennis, the SEC, British Open golf, Big Ten, the Rose Bowl, the BCS, the ACC, and Barclays Premier League. We're focused on putting out the best possible sports product we can, but that does not, and will not, mean that ESPN acquires product that doesn't strengthen our position with sports fans.

DAVID HILL:

Perhaps the most interesting thing of all is that for the most part, I think ESPN rates something like a 0.7. So that means that 99.3 percent of Americans — somewhere around 299 million people — don't give a rat's ass about ESPN. Yet somehow, ESPN has convinced cable operators that the people will rise up with torches and pitchforks and storm the castle if they ever take it off the air. And that's how ESPN has convinced cable owners to pay them a lot of money every month. And that's how they're able to be so unbelievably profitable. God bless them.

JOHN SAUNDERS:

Bob Ley and Chris Berman have been here for thirty years; I've been here around twenty-three years, so I was third in the pecking order. For the thirtieth-anniversary show, it would have been very easy for them to just use Bob and Chris, but Norby put me on the show, and when I went to thank him, he told me that Chris Berman had been the one who said, "You know, John should be on this show too." For Chris to do that, and for Norby to agree to it, was great. I've never saved tapes—there are people in this business who save every tape or DVD of every show they've ever done—but I did with this one. It was probably the moment that made me feel proudest of my accomplishments here at ESPN.

Nothing in the ESPN rulebook specifically forbade office romances (indeed, there had been almost a dozen marriages between ESPN employees), and no one had ever been dismissed because of an affair with a colleague. That didn't mean there weren't confrontations. After one male producer had basically created a totally different life for himself on the road, with a woman in every city, someone on the staff decided to fly his wife out to surprise him for his birthday, knowing that his private life would be discovered. Another time, someone on the production crew made audiotapes of amorous conversations between a married producer and a reporter.

    There have actually been at least eight marriages between coworkers in which both parties remained at the network. But relationships among equals are different than affairs between on-air talent and young production assistants. Baseball analyst Steve Phillips had one such relationship in 2009, and it erupted into a horrendous mess for the network and for all actual and potential lovers within its sphere. Cynics and critics feasted on facts and rumors, with the latter perhaps deemed the more delectable; the tabloids gorged as if invited to a free all-you-can-eat luau. One website suggested the network change its slogan to "worldwide leader in sex." The decision to pull Phillips off the air immediately was a desperate attempt to make it all go away.

Outside of its own digital operations, ESPN's attempts to thrive within the larger world of the Internet made for one long period of adjustment. At first, they tried ignoring the chat rooms, comments sections, and blossoming blogosphere, but eventually they figured out that, unlike much of the sports world, the Web wasn't going to adapt to ESPN—the network would have to adapt to the Web. For ESPN, the biggest fly in the ointment was a relentless ESPN-obsessed blog called Deadspin.

Thinking the worst course of action when dealing with Deadspinners would be to stonewall, obfuscate, or erect barricades to hide behind—that would only provoke them—ESPN management decided to deal as directly and openly as possible with the bloggers, granting the same degree of access given to the established mainstream press. They even went so far as to invite Deadspin to thirtieth-anniversary activities. But if they thought cozying up, in the late summer of 2009, was going to earn them brownie points, they couldn't have been more naive or mistaken. Just a couple weeks after the late summer 2009 festivities, A. J. Daulerio, Deadspin's editor and one of the most prominent bloggers covering sports in general (and ESPN in particular), called the network after receiving a tip that Phillips was involved in a "Harold Reynolds type of situation" and was going to be fired. Public relations VP Josh Krulewitz told Daulerio, "You would be wrong if you ran that story," so Daulerio sat on the item. Fast-forward several weeks to a big fat headline on the front page of the New York Post about Phillips's affair with the twenty-two-year-old and the news that he was taking a leave of absence because of it.

Daulerio went ballistic. He felt like a sap who had been lied to by the company, and so he decided to adopt a scorched-earth policy, emptying out his files for what he blatantly termed "sordid rumors we've received over the years about various ESPN employees" and posting many of them on the site. "Chances are," Daulerio wrote, "at this point, there's some truth to them."

JOHN SKIPPER:

I became aware of the Steve Phillips situation from Norby Williamson. We took Steve off the air that day as we investigated, and it became clear we could not return him to the air. He would not have credibility and we would not have credibility with our employees relative to the environment we were trying to create. Miss Hundley made inconsistent statements and acted inappropriately, so we decided she had forfeited her privilege to work here. Simple as that.

JOHN LACK:

ESPN suspending Steve Phillips as a commentator because he's a married man having an affair with an employee is like going to Harlem and saying we're going to arrest all black men who cross the street.

For ESPN, this was more significant than losing a base-ball analyst. It was anything but insignificant, especially for one prominent couple. David Berson, thirty-seven-year-old vice president of programming, had been with ESPN since 1994 and was listed among Business Week's *"100 most influential people in sports"; Katie Lacey, forty-four, was the company's senior vice president of marketing and had been on the job since late 2005. Both had excellent reputations on- and off-campus when the married Berson and the single Lacey began an affair in 2007.*

In a bit of business seemingly unrelated to her love life, Lacey prepared a performance review for her executive assistant (inherited from a predecessor) at the end of '07. She and the assistant had realized that their arrangement wasn't working and that efforts should be made to reassign the young woman or have her return to school. It all seemed civilized enough. But what Lacey didn't know was that her assistant had been busily helping herself to her boss's e-mails and printing them out since Lacey's third month on the job. One month after the performance review, the very angry assistant fired off an incriminating letter about her boss to the New York State Department of Human Services (Lacey's main office was in New York) and iced that cake with a letter to ESPN management detailing Lacey's relationship with Berson.

What may have sounded like libidinous innuendo to the assistant was in most cases just innocent chitchat. Still, there were enough personal exchanges in the e-mails to make it obvious that Lacey and Berson were involved.

By the time management confronted Lacey and Berson with questions, the two had actually broken off the affair; they admitted it had happened and declared their intention to remain friends. Fine, said management, telling them to keep two directives in mind: first, if the relationship should rekindle in the future, they needed to disclose it to management; and second, they should take care not to use company e-mail for personal missives. When, sure enough, Lacey and a now separated Berson found themselves drawn together romantically six months later, they kept the guidelines in mind and dutifully divulged to management that they were at it again. Management's reaction was revealing: executives told the pair to go public with the relationship right away so there would be less gossip than if it became public down the line.

It's important to note at this point that even though management clearly had proof of an affair, including the couple's confession, neither Berson nor Lacey was reprimanded in any way. Indeed, on October 29, 2009, the New York Post *updated the story. Lacey's and Berson's respective bosses, Sean Bratches and John Skipper, issued a joint statement: "Katie Lacey and David Berson are employees in good standing and valued colleagues. Any issues raised...were addressed, and we consider the matter closed."*

Consequently, neither Berson nor Lacey had reason to believe that a revived relationship would negatively affect their thriving careers at ESPN.

The night before the Phillips scandal broke, Berson and Lacey found themselves sitting at the same table, though not next to each other, at a cable-awards dinner. ESPN's head of human resources was overheard playfully chiding them for not sitting together and even said—jokingly or not—that he hoped somewhere down the road they'd name their first child after him.

And then, blooey.

Deadspin *editors, furious with ESPN's PR department for having denied the Phillips affair to them, played up the Lacey-Berson story with a vengeance. Rumors flew wildly, among them allegations that Lacey and Berson had been suspended the year before because of their relationship and that both had falsified travel expense reports and used corporate funds for personal encounters. None of the charges were true, but it didn't seem to matter.*

On a cold November 20th, Lacey and Berson were summoned into their bosses' offices, where they were told that their contracts would not be renewed and that their ESPN careers were over, immediately. They were to vacate their offices that day and not return to the campus.

What had happened? Why were Lacey and Berson shown the door when management was already on the record as supporting their relationship? Besides, many in the company knew that others had engaged in similar activities. It looked as though honesty was now the worst policy.

No answer made sense. Berson and Lacey wound up being collateral damage, serving as requisite sacrificial lambs. Throughout the company, employees who had engaged in similar activities — and worse — held their breath and awaited additional firings and suspensions. It was no longer possible to be too paranoid.

But those additional firings and suspensions? They never came. The most a senior executive would say was that examples from the past were just that: history. No other punishments were deemed necessary. Somehow Berson and Lacey slipped in under the wire — and were left hanging from it.

STEVE BERTHIAUME:

This place is its people — the people in your show units, the people at your pod, the people that you connect with or, in my case, marry. My wife is Cindy Brunson; she's an anchor here. It's sort of a company secret. We met here; she started about three months before I did. We always try to make it a nonissue. We never ever go to ESPN and say, "Hey, we need special treatment, we need special attention, we need this situation, we need that consideration." We don't *ever* do that.

It's never come up, to their credit, from their end or our end. They're very funny about having us not anchor shows together. I don't know what they think would happen — is she going to hit me in the head with a frying pan or something? That's not going to happen. We're not going to become Regis and Joy Philbin.

JOHN SKIPPER:
As I took the job in October 2005, it was certainly my intention to diversify our group and to provide an environment without harassment. It was an overall priority for our company. It has certainly been the case that the behavior of a few individuals has muddied this effort, and so we made a decision to have less tolerance for such behavior. If they were paying attention, employees should have had a clear understanding of what constituted inappropriate behavior between them. We took a number of steps to ensure that they paid attention.

I have never knowingly placed anybody in charge of any production after being told, "Do you know you're putting them in charge of somebody they have now or in the past had a relationship with?" We may

have had situations come up, but I've never knowingly said, "Gee, you're now in charge of X, are you
aware you're creating a conflict there?"

The hardest thing about this is the fact that from
the very top of our company, there's a sincere dedication and insistence that everyone here behave appro-
priately—and the vast majority of our employees
come to work every day, work very hard, and we don't
hear anything about them except that they're doing a
great job. We have learned we must expect coverage
and scrutiny. We are ESPN. We have close to a thousand people who we put on-air. Many of them are
quite prominent—former players, former coaches.
No one else comes close to having that many people
on-air.

ED DURSO:

We'll address anything that's inappropriate. It can
come up in any number of ways under the general
heading of workplace behavior, language, demeanor,
approach. Certainly there are conflicts of interest,
inappropriate behavior when dealing with vendors or
whatever you have—others cheating, putting false
stuff on your bank account. So we're dealing with an
array of potential problems and issues. All [our policies are] calculated in a way to run our business honestly, fairly, openly, as best we can. We're trying to do
something of value.

There are no sacred cows in our organization. We

are not going to provide somebody higher up or lower down with anything different in terms of meting out discipline because of their position. There's no one so important to our company that we would pull punches on that.

JOHN SKIPPER:

As someone whose memos have been leaked, and whose words said at meetings have appeared on the Internet, I can tell you that we have learned that we have to be careful about what we say. However, we have also chosen not to let it cripple us. We continue to be candid with our employees, to share a lot of information, because we believe that the greater good is still to do that. Is it disappointing when things get leaked? Yes, it is. It's not nearly as debilitating day-to-day as I think it feels when at the senior level of the company we're trying to figure out what to do. Last year we had a 96 percent retention rate. We do internal surveys on a regular basis to ask our employees how they feel, and they overwhelmingly feel excellent about working here. If I took all the resumes we got in the past two or three years from people who want to come here, it would fill up this office. Did we not have more than ten thousand applications last year for about sixty internships? So it is still regarded as an outstanding place to work by the people outside.

Internally, this is a little bit of an inside-the-Belt-way problem that we care about because we care about the reputation of our company. It matters for our business; it matters to us; it matters to our employees, who are proud of the company. So that's what's disappointing—we're all proud of our company and what we do, and to have this blemish on it is disappointing, although that's all it is, a superficial blemish. It does not, I believe, affect what we do from day to day. It matters, in the same way you'd go to a dermatologist if you had something sitting on your cheek and were trying to get it off. But it doesn't prevent me from driving or jogging or going out to dinner, as long as I wear a Band-Aid.

RECE DAVIS:

We have to serve the fan—but the best way you can serve the fan is by being a pro, by being honest, and by being fair. And if you start falling into reading *Deadspin*, *Awful Announcing*, Ohio State blog, Alabama blog, and Texas blog, and every time they don't like something you see, you try to either explain it the next time you come on-air or you change it or you get upset about it, you probably aren't doing your job as effectively as you ought to be.

BOB LEY:

I check in from time to time with the sports blogs—*Deadspin*, *Awful Announcing*, or *The Big Lead*—but it's like shopping in a discount store. I say that with respect; there's some good stuff, but you've got to find what's interesting beyond the prurient stuff and the stuff that's rumor-based. They're devilishly well written. When Will Leach was writing for *Deadspin*, you'd read stuff that was wet-your-pants funny.

I've told my kids and my wife, "Do not google me. You will not come away happy." I know they've done it anyway. It's the shit out there that's written about you that is quasi-satiric, venal, vindictive, whatever, that you don't want your family to see. So I tell people around the office, "Don't google yourself. It will not end well."

MATTHEW BERRY, *Football Analyst:*

I come from the Howard Stern school of broadcasting. I am a huge, huge Howard Stern fan. I think there are a lot of important lessons, regardless of whether you like his content or not, that you can learn from how he conducts his business and how he works as a broadcaster. One thing I think Howard is brilliant at is, he is 100 percent honest. He says, "Here's the guy who hates me, here's the guys who love me." That's what I would love to do, but obviously I am not always able to do that. The ESPN brand is bigger than any individual brand. In Howard's world, Howard's the biggest brand, but in this particular case, ESPN's brand is much, much bigger than mine or anyone else's. So, unfortunately, I can't always be as honest as I want to be.

Prior to coming to ESPN, I would respond to a lot of criticism, and I would say, "Here's right and here's wrong." That's one of the things I'm known for, printing hate mail and making fun of it. Sometimes I'll just say, "Hey, you caught me, I can't predict the future." What are you going to do? I'm a human being and there are times when it gets tough, where you're like, Wow, that person has really gotten personal. But you get more and more used to it. There used to be a time when I responded to every single e-mail, positive or negative, and now there are just too many. I literally get thousands a day. There are not enough hours in the day, unfortunately. So "detachment" is a good word.

"Appropriate measures" in the matter of Bill Simmons and his testy tweets on Twitter were taken in November 2009. ESPN Radio had been in business with Boston's WEEI just one month when a nasty wound was reopened. Simmons still lived in Boston then and was known as The Boston Sports Guy. He had never been a fan of the station's afternoon sports show, nor pretended to be, and its hosts attacked him in response. One can only imagine, then, Simmons's reaction to learning that ESPN had made WEEI a part of the network's ever-expanding family, because that meant Simmons could appear only on that station when he did Boston radio.

On a book tour, Simmons visited WEEI's morning show to hype the tome, and all went well—until just before the book signing that night, when the station's afternoon crew took a few more verbal swings at him. It was disconcerting: one part of the ESPN family publicly attacking another, who was arguably one of the network's biggest names. Simmons felt no compunction about coming back at them in response. "WEEI's Big Show was apparently ripping me today," Simmons tweeted tendentiously. "Good to get feedback from two washed-up athletes and a sixty-year-old fat guy with no neck." There was more: "Hey, WEEI, you were wrong. I did a Boston interview today—with your competition. Rather give them ratings over deceitful scumbags like you."

ESPN Radio executives never punished, suspended, or otherwise penalized anyone at the station—even though the old playground defense, "They started it," would certainly seem applicable. Simmons, however, didn't escape unscathed. Even though he had merely been responding in kind to broadsides fired at him, his Twittered taunts were too much for ESPN vice president Rob King. Simmons would be slapped with a two-week suspension, King announced—softening the blow somewhat by permitting Simmons to tweet his little heart out about his book and the tour.

BILL SIMMONS:

So Berman's doing Applebee's, and Tom Jackson is using his Twitter to promote GMC. Check out Tom Jackson's Twitter—fifty posts, and fifteen are about GMC or something. Oh, that's acceptable? But "deceitful scumbags" is a way *not* to represent ESPN?

To be honest, I knew the "deceitful scumbag" posting would cause a splash, and I did it intentionally. That's the same reason I went on the rival radio show. My attitude was, You guys aren't handling this. You have let this fester and it's become a real issue in Boston with these guys killing me for two weeks. I have a thick skin, and I'm totally used to getting killed by people, but this is our alleged partner, and they have on their website that I'm the fraud of the week, and you guys have done nothing. I escalated things intentionally to make them look at it and have meetings about it and fucking waste their day. That made me happy. I'm glad they had two days of meetings about how to handle it, because they should have had those meetings two weeks before.

I met with Norby, who I'd never met before and who I can't decide if I liked or not. He clearly was trying to intimidate me in the meeting, but I was in a really good mood, and my book had just come out. And in person, I'm not intimidatable, and I'm actually like a really happy, gregarious guy. It's just very hard for people to rattle me. And even when they try, it's just not going to work. So I think Norby envisioned this as some sort of showdown where he told me, "This is how ESPN works and you're not playing the game." It's like a bad sports movie. And I'm just sitting there with a big smile on my face, like, Oh, it's great that we finally met, and within five minutes I disarmed him, but he still had to go into the whole "People here don't think you're a team player, you think the rules don't apply to you." And I said, "I'm actually kind of feeling like maybe they shouldn't to some degree. Maybe I should be able to get away with more in my column. I've been your best guy on the website for nine years. I should have a little more leeway. I'd get that leeway anywhere else."

We ended up in a decent place and he told me that he thought they were afraid. The perception was that I was in the Walsh/Skipper camp on this stuff and that everybody was afraid to crack down on me because I was Walsh's boy. I don't know. I was like, Honestly, who cares? You guys make two billion a year; why do you let it bother you? Why is this even an issue?

CHRIS BERMAN:
I don't know Bill Simmons. I wouldn't know him if he sat here right next to me. I'm not knocking him, because I know he's important to the company, but that's some other limb of the tree that I don't touch.

BILL SIMMONS:
I don't know if the company is designed for people like me, but we'll figure something out. It'd be a whole lot easier for me if I didn't love Skipper and Walsh. If that dynamic was removed, it would be cut-

and-dried, and I would leave. When my book got to number one, I can honestly say that other than my dad, I don't think anyone was happier for me than those two guys. So that's the stuff, like, I think about when I ask myself, Is there ever going to be a point when I'm going to leave? because I also have to ask, Am I ever going to work for somebody that cares about me this much?

Walsh e-mailed me pretty early on. First of all, this is terrible because I love Walsh, but I kept the book away from him as long as I could. And he kept asking to see it and I'd say, "It's not ready yet. It's not ready yet." And then I handed it in and then I e-mailed him and said, "All right, the book's ready." But they had already started the process so he couldn't do anything to it. I know he's Catholic and he was very concerned about the F-bomb and stuff like that. And he did talk me into taking out some of the F-bombs and a couple other small things. I had a nice Chris Berman joke, which—God forbid *he's* ever discussed. But I had a lot of other stuff in there. I made fun of Skip Bayless and Stephen A. Smith and Nancy Lieberman and all the announcers and all that. It's all in good fun. It's really hard to write a definitive book about basketball without mentioning ESPN, since we've been involved with the NBA for thirty years. Not busting the balls of some of our people—like I was doing with CBS and TNT—would have been unfair.

MALCOLM GLADWELL, *Author:*

I've been reading Simmons for years, and then he mentioned me once, so I e-mailed him to thank him. He suggested we do a podcast together, but I don't even own an iPod. I've never listened to a podcast in my life. I didn't want to do something that I had no familiarity with, and I don't think I'm as good speaking spontaneously as I am when I can think about things and then write, so I just thought it played to my strengths better to do the column. And it was so much fun, because I rarely get the chance to write about sports even though I'm a massive sports fan. Bill is the perfect foil. He's an infinite source of funny things, cool observations, and he's indefatigable too; he could write forever. So you could bounce things off him forever. It was an incredibly fun writing exercise.

The attention-to-work ratio for those columns I did with Bill was astonishing. I can't tell you the number of people who have come up to me and said, "I love that thing you did with Simmons." I've never since done a public appearance where some portion of the audience didn't mention those columns. It's absolutely astonishing feedback. I honestly don't believe anyone has a following like Bill Simmons has. He has attracted this insanely loyal fan base. It's not just that he has a zillion readers, because there are lots of writers with a zillion readers; it's that they are so unbelievably involved and engaged and dialed in to what he's doing.

BILL SIMMONS:

I need to figure out a way that I can operate in my own sphere and not deal with Bristol as much. Nothing against Bristol, but I do worry that it becomes a little cultish after a while. You go there and there's ESPN everywhere. At the cafeteria, there's Mike and Mike getting a sandwich and there's Matthew Berry and, hey, there's Mark Schlereth. It's really hard to think out of the box when you're trapped in that box the whole time. I think that's one of the reasons *PTI* succeeds—it's in Washington, it's out of the box, they leave it alone. I am not afraid to leave. If it happens, I will kill myself trying to haunt them somewhere else.

ADAM SCHEFTER, *Reporter*:

I'll tell you a true story that speaks to how different a day and age we're living in right now. I remember back in Denver, where Trevor Price was a Pro Bowl defensive lineman, and he didn't show up for training camp that year. There was a team meeting at 7:00, and I got to work at 8:00 and he still wasn't there. I made some calls, worked the story, and filed it with the *Denver Post*. It appeared on people's doorsteps the next morning at 6:00 a.m. Then it was on sports talk radio throughout that day. So there was a twelve-hour lag time before it became public.

This summer, I was driving, and Roddy White didn't show up for a 6:30 meeting with the Atlanta Falcons. He was a holdout. And literally at 6:31, I got a message about it; at 6:32 it was on Twitter, and at 6:35 it was on our website. You get the idea.

So you have to be very careful about everything. You're always at the mercy of where you're getting your information from, so you have to try to get the best information from the best possible people and confirm it as many times as you can, but even then, you never know. You just try to do the best you can to get your facts right, and when you don't, you apologize to the people. It's one of the most uncomfortable parts of my profession, because I don't like to make anybody mad.

Sometimes you fly into patches of tumultuous turbulence with no warning whatsoever. On an otherwise normal day in February 2010, Tony Kornheiser, one of the most popular personalities ever to emerge from ESPN—and one of the most controversial—thought he was being the playfully outspoken scoundrel that his audience expected when he took time on his radio show to offer an impromptu and unsolicited commentary on the outfit that SportsCenter *co-anchor Hannah Storm had chosen to wear that day.*

"Hannah Storm is in a horrifying, horrifying outfit today," he began.

"She's got on red go-go boots and a Catholic-school plaid skirt way too short for somebody in her forties — or maybe early fifties by now . . . She's got on her typically very, very tight shirt. She looks like she has sausage-casing wrapping around her upper body . . . I know she's very good, and I'm not supposed to be critical of ESPN people, so I won't . . . but Hannah Storm, come on, now! Stop! What are you doing? . . . She's what I would call a Holden Caulfield fantasy at this point."

Kornheiser's brief career as a fashion critic would bounce back and smack him right in the face — and with a severity he couldn't have expected. He didn't just stick his foot in a hornet's nest; he somehow managed to get his entire body in there. Hannah Storm just happened to be one of Norby Williamson's favorites, and John Skipper had been through a veritable Southeast Asian ground war with Kornheiser since his promotion over Monday Night Football. *But it was ESPN president George Bodenheimer who scored the highest on this Richter scale. Bodenheimer was a big Storm fan as well, but more importantly, the principle behind Ronald Reagan's eleventh commandment — "Thou shalt not speak negatively about another Republican" — was the same for Bodenheimer and ESPN. Bodenheimer's favorite indoor sport is discussing "the culture" at ESPN, and the notion of one employee speaking ill of another got him about as mad as he had been in a long time.*

It was left to Skipper to hand down a punishment that included a two-week unpaid suspension from PTI. Given that Kornheiser earn between $900,000 and $1 million annually, the suspension cost him almost $40,000. More painful perhaps was being banned from the airwaves, for Kornheiser is a guy who loves, and lives, to talk.

Those who felt that the penalty was as inappropriate as the original remarks theorized that ESPN was making a scapegoat of Kornheiser as transparent recompense for the network's dreadful record on sexual harassment. Kornheiser spent fifteen minutes on the phone, it was subsequently reported, apologizing to Storm.

TONY KORNHEISER:

I understand that I was suspended for saying bad things about a colleague. I was not suspended for saying, "Fuck Jesus," okay, like somebody else was suspended for; I was not suspended for some drunken episode; I was not suspended for taking a picture of my dick and sending that around to employees; and I was not suspended for sexual harassment. I was suspended for saying something about a coworker that I shouldn't have said, and I apologized.

DIGGER PHELPS, *College Basketball Analyst:*

Tony's the worst dresser in America, okay? If Goodwill has a sale, he may buy something; that's Kornheiser's wardrobe, and you can quote me.

HANNAH STORM:

I'm a pretty busy person. I have my three kids, my work at ESPN, a production company, and I also run a foundation where I raise money to help children with debilitating and disfiguring birthmarks. I grew up with a birthmark on my face — I look like I have a black eye when I don't have makeup on — and so appearance is something that I can put in a pretty healthy perspective. I definitely have very solid philosophical and personal feelings about appearance and how important it is, but not in terms of some shallow, crazy ratings game. I dress the way I do because that's how I like to dress and that's my personality. I'm not doing it to court attention. My whole thing is just being myself and being confident in that. That's something I was forced to grow into because of the way I looked growing up. I couldn't be self-conscious about my looks and I couldn't be afraid.

Nobody was aware of what had happened until it became a really big firestorm. It started off small — I started getting some phone calls, "Hey, how are things doing?" and, "How are you holding up?" and, "Is there anything we can do for you, are you okay?" And then it just blew up.

The episode also unleashed a lot of voices out there on the Internet. I received really nasty e-mails, really hateful stuff about my clothes. Even voice mails. Once, I had a tabloid reporter and photographer come to my home. It was horrendous to open up the *New York Post* and see yourself there in a cartoon and be dragged down into this hateful realm. That was really sad.

I don't think there's anything anyone can say that can really disparage anything about my work, my work ethic, my knowledge, or anything that I say or do professionally. So to have a discussion away from how good I am at what I do, to what I'm actually wearing and how old I am, was painful. But it passed.

You're looking at a company that was trying to do the right thing, trying not to have the situation happen again. I'm a woman in a completely nontraditional female field, and I'm old enough to have been one of the trailblazers in this field. It's funny because I thought by now we would have moved beyond sexism and ageism. I thought, "Aren't we past all this?" And I guess maybe with some people we're never going to be. I've never let that kind of thing discourage me before, and it certainly won't now.

JOSH ELLIOTT, *Anchor:*

If you ask Hannah, she'll tell you that there might be a handful of people who've ever discussed her wardrobe choices with her consistently, and I am number one on that list. The wardrobe choice in question—she'd worn something similar to it about a month or two prior, and when I'd seen it, I said, "Hannah, never wear that again."

From day one, her wardrobe felt like the only thing anybody wanted to talk about. I would get messages during the shows, "What was she wearing?" And I would get calls after the shows, "What was she thinking?" Hannah is a grown woman and can make her own choices. That said, I don't think Tony was trying to be hurtful, but the issue I always had with it wasn't so much what he said with regard to her wardrobe as it was the references to her age. I think especially for a woman in our business, when you start referring to their age in a snarky way, you are in the process of writing a professional obituary. That was poor form. That to me is far more hands-off than comments about her wardrobe. That was unfair. I feel like that really hurt her.

CINDY BRUNSON:

I have these shorts that are really fantastic. When I first saw them on *Fashion Week* several years ago, I just fell in love. What a great option: it's not a skirt, it's not a dress, it's not pants, but it's still sporty yet dressy enough to work in sports television. So I have like six or seven pairs now and loved wearing them. Then about a month ago, there was a chain of phone calls and e-mails from people here, then somebody from the talent office pulled me in and said, "You can no longer wear them." To which I said, "Well, why is this a problem now? I've worn them for three years." And I really wasn't given a good reason.

STEVE BERTHIAUME:

First it was the red leather jacket we got on our honeymoon. That was a biggie. We had bought this unbelievable jacket in Florence. It was pretty Hollywood.

CINDY BRUNSON:

It has a custom red zipper up the front, it's fantastic, and Dan Patrick, on his radio show at the time, said he could not tune away from ESPN News because I was on overnight at the time and it was re-airing. He said, "Every time Cindy Brunson pops up I just lose all train of thought. You *have* to see this leather jacket." So I'm getting ready for work and I'm cursing Dan because I just know it's going to be a problem, and sure enough, as soon as I hit the door, Rob King, who at the time was in charge of news, told me to never wear that jacket again.

BILL SIMMONS:

The week I did my book, I didn't have a podcast because I was promoting it the whole time, and somebody's driving home and listening to my podcast with Seth Meyers thinking that it was a podcast I had done this week or that week. But it was a podcast I had really done in July, four months before. In that podcast we were talking about soccer and I was talking about how they call exhibition games "friendlies" in soccer, and I had made some sort of joke like, "Note to soccer: if you want people to think you're a little less gay, don't call exhibition games 'friendlies.'" And we joked about it and moved on. So this guy or this girl—I don't know if it was a male or female—hears this and flips out and sends an e-mail to Norby that I gay-bashed on the podcast. Everyone flips out, and they're listening to my last podcast that's up, which is from the Friday before my book came out and is with my buddy Jacko.

So they listen to that whole thing and the "gay" remark is not in there. They listen to the one before and it's not in that one either. They listen to, like, three weeks of podcasts and can't find the thing, and the guy's like, "I swear I heard it. It's with Seth Meyers." So finally they realize that it was a replay of a podcast that ran in July—a podcast that had been listened to two hundred thousand times, by the way. And nobody had said a peep, and all my editors heard it, and everybody had signed off and that was it. So now they don't know if they should suspend me for a week. And it's like, "Oh, shit. That came out four and a half months ago." Finally, I get an e-mail from Rob [King], like, "Did you say something about soccer being a little too gay in the Seth Meyers podcast?" And I replied, "From the summer? I don't remember. I don't remember what I said a week ago." And that was the last I heard of it. Then I come to find out that this is one of the reasons why they've cracked down on the content of my podcast even though I have a disclaimer—because of this soccer/gay thing that not one person had complained about. Zero. Could Jon Stewart say that on *The Daily Show*? Yes. Could *South Park* make that joke? Yes. Could Jimmy Kimmel make that joke on his late-night show? Yes. But they start cracking down. So I ask Super Dave Osborne. He finishes the podcast I do with him. He tells this joke about—it's a little off-color. They take it out. Little do they know he told the same joke on Conan O'Brien four days before, and it stayed in. So I'm like, "Now you're telling me I don't have as much leeway as an 11:30 late-night show on NBC? I have less leeway than that for a podcast with a fucking disclaimer on it?"

They've reached a point now where they have code words, and if you hit the code word, it just comes out. And it's podcast or dot-com or whatever. Gay? Out. Jew? Out. Hitler? Out. If Matt Berry wants to talk about his "five hottest Jews in the draft"? Out. No discussion, just out. And that's the way it is now. It's like the new version of George Carlin's "seven dirty words." I worry about ESPN becoming too conservative. Although here's the part I don't get: how do you explain my book? It's a book released by ESPN that has dick jokes and porn jokes in it. It has jokes about how I smoked too much pot in 1995. I compare Shaq to Peter North. Hell, I probably pushed the line too hard. Why was that not a problem for anyone at

ESPN? Sometimes I wonder if they're willing to look the other way unless it ends up in the *Sports Business Journal*—if it gets in there, they know George is going to see it. I'm convinced that as long as nobody lands in there, it's fine.

DICK EBERSOL:

ESPN basically has to have one of their talent talk about Hitler or put a picture of their dick on a phone—which is what that Salisbury guy did— before they'll do anything about any of these various crazies, because they don't have to. Nobody can touch them.

For all the jokes by late-night comics about America's alleged indifference to soccer—including hoots at the importation by the L.A. Galaxy of international soccer superstar and sex symbol David Beckham for $250 million—soccer's popularity was growing. It should hardly have been surprising that ESPN was involved.

Now that it had ponied up a fortune for the rights to the 2010 World Cup games from South Africa, ESPN had to prove itself equal to the task. One of the beneficial side effects of its victory was that after years of people saying that ESPN's coverage did not equal, in quality or class, that of the traditional broadcast networks, parity had been established at last: ESPN was as good as the big boys, maybe better—and, actually, even bigger. Audience levels for the first three games played by the U.S. were up 68 percent compared with the 2006 games. An average 11.1 million viewers caught the English and Spanish-language broadcasts for each of the three U.S. Group C matchups, up from 6.6 million viewers in 2006.

U.S. interest did not even appear to rely entirely on American success at the game, much less dominance of it, as had always been the case with regular-season games on ESPN. History may have repeated itself when, in 2010, Ghana beat the United States 2–1 in extra time, eliminating the Americans from the World Cup on a Saturday, but the weekend match was the most-watched men's game in FIFA World Cup history in the United States. For more than two hours on a Saturday afternoon, an average 14.9 million viewers tuned in to ABC, 13 percent more than for the highly anticipated U.S.–U.K. World Cup game on June 12, which ended in a 1–1 draw. Combined with viewers from Spanish TV network Univision, the number exceeded 19 million. One million people tried ESPN's new Mobile TV during the World Cup tournament—more mobile visitors than the next four contenders combined.

An executive at Nielsen Media Research declared that the 2010 ratings "demonstrated the remarkable increase of interest in U.S. soccer over the last four years." Although "more people than ever chose to watch live streaming video of the games from their computers and mobile devices," he said, "TV viewing climbed even higher." And TV comics shifted their joking about soccer, or at least the World Cup, away from the sport's *alleged unpopularity to such topics as the dread vuvuz-elas, long cheap horns blown en masse at pivotal moments by hundreds of soccer fans from other countries. (They made such a racket that ESPN, responding to viewer complaints, took measures to lower their volume on the TV sound track.) Philosophically speaking, though, the seemingly plaintive wail of the vuvuzela was sweet music to ESPN, to ABC, and to all those pushing for greater acceptance of soccer in the U.S.—and, naturally, to John Skipper.*

Of course, there was always room for the dissenting view in the land of three hundred million opinions. "I don't get it," grumped sports vet Beano Smith when confronted with World Cup fever. He was "convinced" that "so many people from Europe came to America because they did not like soccer and wanted to watch football and basketball" instead.

MATT SANDULLI:

It's like you never leave this place. No matter where you go, ESPN is there. You can see the brand; you can touch the brand. When I went to South Africa before the World Cup for a meeting at a hotel with a host broadcaster, I was in the lobby and there was a magazine with George Bodenheimer on the cover. It was bizarre. There's great pride when you think you have something to do with what this amazing thing has become. And there's always going to be protectiveness over it, and loyalty to it.

IAN DARKE, *Soccer Commentator:*

It was quite a big decision to go with English commentators who were not American on a major American network. But as it was explained to me, I think they'd had some criticism in the past and they wanted, in their words, the "authentic voices of the sport as used in the English Premier League," and didn't want to open themselves up to that kind of criticism again. So I was asked if I would do it, and I was very happy to say yes.

My feeling doing the U.S.A. games was that I would call them basically from a neutral standpoint, and I think it would be the same if I'd been covering England in England or France in France, wherever. You're aware that most of the people watching you are wanting the U.S.A. to win and they're rooting for the U.S.A. whether they're watching at home or in bars or whatever, and it's an ongoing drama. You're not setting out to do a biased commentary or anything like that, you call the game accurately, I think I said at some point. John Harkes got it into his head that the officials were set against the U.S.A. because a couple of bad calls had gone against them, and I think I said in the commentary, there's no big campaign here.

LANDON DONOVAN, *Soccer Player:*

The way they promoted the World Cup in general, specifically the way they promoted our team, made this World Cup the most fun to be a part of for all of us, because it meant that so many more people back home were paying attention. ESPN has the ability to market and push things just because of their resources, but the passion and the creativity really struck me. And it starts with John Skipper, who is a very, very big fan of soccer. He's a big fan of our team. He wanted to make this a really big deal, and it wouldn't have happened without him. We're very grateful to have him. One of my favorite moments for the entire World Cup was walking off the field after the England game and looking up and seeing a man literally jumping up and down like he was a young kid with excitement. And I looked and it was Skipper. I just remember seeing him and smiling and making eye contact and just feeling so proud that a company of that stature was willing to go the extra mile. And some of the things they did were just so cool for us and just so memorable.

After we advanced against Algeria, we were very aware that they were continuing to push and push and push and support us. It was such a nice feeling to know that we were finally going to have the type of audience that we've always wanted to have. The most beautiful thing for me to watch was the YouTube videos and all the different reactions, you're watching people that are in some cases not very wealthy, casual fans. In some cases hardcore fans, in some cases very affluent, wealthy CEOs of companies, high-level executives. You're watching them all have the exact same organic, real reaction. These are people who see sports every day, in some ways they're desensitized to these moments, but what I gathered from all of it was there was such a real, genuine joyous eruption in that moment, and that for me makes it awesome.

IAN DARKE:

I suppose if you just heard that bit of commentary now it sounds kind of incongruous and maybe a bit frantic and biased. But I believe all commentary moments are of their moment. It was almost the last kick of the game so it was just this amazing outpouring of emotion, really. I was aware that my audience was sitting and watching that and were exploding with joy. You hope you say something that captures the moment. I don't know if it did, but I hope it did.

LANDON DONOVAN:

I guess at the end of the day, people, no matter what is going on in their life, can appreciate a genuine moment like that. And they want to be a part of that, it makes them feel good, no matter how conflicted we might be, no matter what is going on financially in our world, spiritually in our world, with our families—everybody likes a moment like that because it's so real. It's so genuine. I try to picture what would have been had ESPN not promoted it the same way. And if two million people were watching versus eight million or ten or fifteen million. Or if we didn't have the Internet the way we do now and nobody saw these videos online, how it would have been perceived. And thankfully we had someone like ESPN in our corner to make this all possible.

IAN DARKE:

I got the feeling that it was a breakthrough moment for the game of soccer in the United States. Because people who had watched it for years and said, "Well, this is all dull. Nothing happens. There are no goals, it goes on for ninety minutes," maybe now have got the idea that you can sit and watch, and it comes to a boil, and it can produce a moment like that, and that the great joy is *because* of the rarity of the goals. I'd like to think that now that a generation of kids in America have played the game, they're getting it, and I just got the feeling that a penny dropped, as we say in the U.K., at that moment with a lot of the audience, and that this is quite a big thing.

JOHN SKIPPER:

One of the biggest surprises in South Africa was that our ability to succeed had almost nothing to do with legacy and almost everything to do with enterprise and energy. I'll give you a really funny example: We had the best hosts' set and the best location up on a hill. I went the year before, and Geoff Mason, Jed Drake, and Tim Scanlon walked me up to the top of a hill and said, "What do you think about this place for where we'll do all our studio work from?"

And I'm like, "Wow, this is great, we're right here, we're overlooking the stadium, it's the closest set to the broadcast center so we'll have the least distance to cover," as you go back and forth a lot. "How do we claim this ground?" And the answer from Geoff Mason was "If we go ask now, we'll get it, 'cause we're the first ones here." There was none of that "You guys have to be in the back because you haven't been here before" stuff.

This was something grander for us. Everybody else in the world was there. It was most like the Olympics, of course, but it was just immense. The other thing that struck me was, as a company, our level of ambition was probably higher than anybody else's there. We did more cultural programming than anybody, like when we talked with Edgar Peterson about the student riots and Soweto, and the apartheid museum.

I've been asked this a lot: "Was the World Cup an audition for ESPN to carry the Olympics?" I mean it completely sincerely when I say, "This is not an audition. We are fine with this in and of itself." However, the fact that we brought all those people to South Africa—not the easiest of locations to move things in and out of in terms of infrastructure and technology—was proof that we can do a big international event. I'll be quite surprised if some powers that be don't notice that.

As John Skipper and the company basked in the global glow of the World Cup triumph, another little piece of programming was being put together. Hastily dubbed "The Decision," it would, incredibly enough, soon over-whelm the $100 million investment in the soccer epic and carry through to the ESPYs in Hollywood the fol-lowing week and well beyond.

Although the two periods are commonly considered opposites, some facets of the old three-network era have been held over for the age of the 500-channel universe. One of the most common: forced to choose between rat-ings success and critical praise, media executives will not—surprisingly—pick being a big fat hit every time.

In the aftermath of "The Decision," the ESPN spe-cial on which LeBron James announced in an exclusive interview that he was moving from the Cleveland Cav-aliers to the Miami Heat, ESPN officials may have felt as if they were dodging brickbats and rotten tomatoes hurled by an angry mob. Seldom had an ESPN pro-gram produced such unanimity of response: everybody hated it. Or said they did. It's worth noting that if there were fewer questions in advance of the announcement, and James had made a different Decision—if he'd said that he, and his "talents," were staying in dear old Cleveland, and then he'd brought out Dwyane Wade and Chris Bosh as his new Cavalier teammates—the reaction probably would have been less harsh, and the furor much less ferocious.

Some columnists who normally never wrote about ESPN or its programming were so angered by the prime-time hour that they departed from their own precedent and reviewed the show. One conspicuous example: Maureen Dowd, the distinguished yet entertaining op-ed columnist for the New York Times, who stepped down from a fairly lofty perch to write not only about television but about cable television—and sports television as well.

Apparently the interview with LeBron had qualified as a genuine cultural event, something to be analyzed for its significance as well as pummeled for its shameless commercialism. Dowd referred to the interview as "a special—and specially obnoxious—show," which amounted to "twenty-eight minutes of contrived suspense" that she compared to "The Bachelor, [but] without the rose for the winner." James's move from Cleveland to what Dowd called "My-Am-Me" might be good for him, she speculated, but she lamented the fact that James "seems to have no idea of the public relations damage he has inflicted upon himself."

There was more, not only from Dowd but about her. Other bloggers and columnists took to their keyboards to opine about Dowd's opinions. In a variation on "six degrees of separation," other columnists joined the fray. For all that, ESPN officials still had plenty of consola-

tion, courtesy of Nielsen Media Research. It seems "The Decision" had been a decisive hit for the network, registering a very unusual 7.3 rating for ESPN and attracting an audience estimated at just under 10 million homes.

With results like that, slings and arrows from critics and op-ed columnists really didn't cause much damage or serious injury. The ancient line about "crying all the way to the bank" was apt once more.

JIM GRAY:

I don't care what anybody else's version was or is, I never once spoke to ESPN about doing an interview with LeBron James. Here is exactly what happened: Maverick Carter [CEO of LeBron James's marketing company] was sitting with [agent] Ari Emanuel next to the Lakers bench at Game Two of the NBA Finals between the Celtics and the Lakers. I went to that game with my wife as a guest of the commissioner. During halftime, I walked down to say hello. I've known Maverick for a long time; I had done an interview with LeBron when he was in high school; I was there when he was drafted; and I did the broadcast of LeBron's first game as a pro. So I have a long history with him.

I asked, "Maverick, how's this free agency process going?" Now, this was before it could actually start, and he said, "Good, there'll be a lot going on, a lot of interest," so we chitchatted, and then I said, "I'd like to have the first interview with LeBron when he decides what he's doing." He said, "Okay, we'll think about that, sounds pretty good." But by the end of this conversation, I said, "Better yet, Maverick, why don't we do this: Why don't we go buy an hour of network time, you produce the show, you own the show, I get to do the interview, and you have LeBron make the announcement of where he's going to go." Before I got the last three words out of my mouth, Ari said, "That's a brilliant idea. That's unbelievable. Maverick, you ought to do that!" Then Maverick looked at Ari and said, "Okay. You want to handle it?" Ari said, "Yeah, that's great, let's do this." Maverick then said, "You know what, we can raise a bunch of money for charity, so that no one will think LeBron is going to profit from this." Then Maverick told me to stay in touch with him, and Ari, and that was that.

As the process went on, I would text Maverick to ask, "What's going on?" and he'd say, "We're doing this, we're doing that, Ari's working on it, stay in touch." I would say, "Need help?" "No, not yet." What was happening was that Ari and Maverick were trying to *buy* an hour on a network. They came back to me and asked, "Do you mind if we do this on ABC and ESPN? They really should have first choice because they're the network that carries a lot of LeBron's games, and the finals." I said, "I don't have a problem with that, but you have to check with them to see if they have a problem with me." ABC was going to do it and then I heard that [ABC Entertainment President] Steve McPherson had talked to Skipper, and Ari had talked to [Keith] Clinkscales, who said, "We'll donate the time."

ESPN assigned a man named Bob Rauscher who has been there a long time to produce the program. Three or four days before the show I called Bob, just so I would know what the format was, and he told me what would go on in the first segment, what would go on in the second segment, and that they would get to me fifteen or twenty minutes into the program. "Fifteen to twenty minutes into the program?!" At this point, I called my friend Eddie Fabershaw to help me out as a friend and consultant on the project. He was not authorized, and wasn't paid a penny. He had been through a lot of wars with me at NBC and ESPN, and he's a wonderful guy. I needed someone to collaborate with, since I wasn't hearing anything from ESPN. So I tell Bob what I want to do: ten or twelve questions before we get to the big one because I think it's important to establish who knows, when he let them know, how tough this was, and who had influence. I even gave him an idea of almost all the questions. And Rauscher said, "We agree. Absolutely. Go ahead." I said, "But you have to leave me room to follow up in case he says something unexpected. I need to be able to listen." Rauscher said, "No problem. We got it."

That night, I was with LeBron two or three hours before the show because we taped a segment for the charity. I could see that he was happy; his fiancée was with him along with his guys, he was laughing and enjoying himself, and yet it wasn't a pull-out-the-champagne kind of thing. I didn't want to ask him anything because I didn't want to risk something slipping out, but I did ask Leon Rose, "Have the teams been informed?" And he says, "They will be when you go on the air. We're going to let them know." So that was really the only question that I knew the answer to. I didn't want to know the answers to any others. I wanted it to be real.

All of the questions I asked were very legitimate questions, and for anybody to say otherwise, we're just going to disagree. Okay, I did ask about the nails. That was a throwaway line that I probably shouldn't have done, but he was a nail biter and it was meant as a joke. But all the people I was working on this project with knew all that was coming. Not only did they know it, they wanted it and agreed with it. Okay? So it's convenient for them to say, after the fact, "We would have preferred that we got to it earlier, but ultimately it's in the interviewer's hands." Well, they were in cooperation with the interviewer. So to throw me under the bus and say, like, "Our hands are off this. We didn't pay him. He's not a part of it. We wouldn't have had anything to do." Come on!

JOHN SKIPPER:

On balance, the way we did it had some upsides and some downsides. Steve McPherson called me and said Ari had talked to him about a time buy on ABC, but said, "They really should be talking to you. This thing doesn't really fit onto our schedule." You know why we said yes? The first date they gave us was the fourteenth, and we wanted to do it as a lead-in to the ESPYs. Then they called and said, "It won't hold till then. We'd like to do it on the eighth." I said "Okay, we'll do it," even though I knew we were losing the lead-in. I thought it was worth it for relationship purposes with Ari, Maverick, and LeBron. I also thought we'd do a good number, and it would position us at the epicenter of sports decisions. We did negotiate what I thought was a reasonable way to go, which was "We'll do an hour special, but you guys will be responsible for the Jim Gray segment, we'll take some level of distance from that."

We worried about allowing LeBron to manage the process, but Ari said that Jim Gray had brought him the idea and he wasn't going to cut Jim Gray loose. And we ultimately agreed with that, because this was big enough news.

Look, I did the deal, this is a fault of mine. I was responsible for putting it together and then I turned it over and let those other guys execute it. Whether it's a fault of not being enough of a hands-on manager for all things, at least the rationalization I made in my mind is "I've got a lot going on."

George was in the loop and approved of the general concept. He had a good level of understanding of the issues.

JIM GRAY:

We never had one conversation about money. I never asked for a dollar, never negotiated for a dollar, never took a dollar. I believe ESPN was asked to pay me, and they said, "Jim's coming as part of the package; we're not paying him." I was told two days before the interview that I was booked with ESPN travel. I have the e-mails. ESPN did pay my expenses.

After the show, I never heard one negative word from ESPN. Not one. I had a meeting with John Skipper, and he told me we got the highest rating in the history of the network other than the NFL. Only two other shows beat us: the USC–Ohio State football game, and Mark McGwire's sixty-first home run. So my interview was the highest-rated studio show in the history of their network.

I worked for this. I created this. I came up with the concept. Maverick Carter and Ari Emanuel are two of the most stand-up, honorable, loyal people I've been engaged with in television, in all my thirty-five years. When ESPN wanted to replace me and throw me under the bus, they stood firm and said, "No, Jim

Gray is with us, he gave us the idea, he is tied to this, and we're not going to change."

I had the first interview with Kobe after the sexual allegations. I had the first interview with Mike Tyson after the ear biting—it won an Emmy—and I had the first interview with him after he got out of prison; it got tremendous critical acclaim. I had Ron Artest after he went into the stands. I'm the only guy who Barry Bonds sat down and talked to after he broke Hank Aaron's record and after he broke Babe Ruth's record. I did the first interview that Tiger Woods gave when he was eight years old: "When I grow up, I'm going to win all the majors and beat all the pros." It was turned into a very famous and memorable commercial. Okay? There isn't a track record like this in sports, so all of these guys who were dismissive and say, "Why him? He's this, he's that, he's a sideline reporter," they have no idea. They're all jealous. Jealousy is a horrible thing.

GEORGE BODENHEIMER:

This was a pretty unique moment in time, with a rare set of circumstances. It was not, as some suggested, a model for any future efforts, and we were pretty clear about that in our public statements. Consistently trying new things has helped to define our culture—and our success—over the years. Being first, and then learning and evolving, is also one of our hallmarks, and that's what we did here. I have never been one to overreact to criticism. It comes with the territory.

As of New Year's Day 2011, ESPN had signed agreements for coverage with the NFL (through 2013), Major League Baseball (also through 2013), the NBA (through 2016), and NASCAR (through 2013), in addition to BCS championships and twelve hundred college men's basketball games via NCAA basketball and football. The World Cup was added, with tremendous fanfare, in 2010, and ESPN also got the rights to air games from England's Barclays Premier League. Ever at one with "the curve," if not well ahead of it, the company added ESPN3 (originally called ESPN360) for broadband users, and as of October 2010, the only stand-alone news site to elicit more clicks was the BBC. When ESPN introduced a SportsCenter iPad *app in 2010, it was quickly downloaded by ten million users, 95 percent of whom personally customized it.*

And while the broadcast networks suffered and strained under a brutally tough economy and a sluggish ad-sales environment, ESPN was pulling in over $8 billion of revenue, and still had the best ratings of any basic cable network.

One of the most ambitious and auspicious original projects in ESPN's history—second only to SportsCentury—*began as a brief memo e-mailed to John Skipper and John Walsh in 2007 from dot-com columnist Bill*

*Simmons. He saw ESPN's thirtieth anniversary loom-
ing and envisioned a massive and promising venture: 30
for 30, a series of documentaries each dealing with some
theme, team, personality, rivalry, trend, or event—or
any other phenomenon—that had played an important
role in sports during the three decades that ESPN had
been in operation.*

*Despite the fact that, as Simmons said, "ESPN loves
celebrating ourselves," the films were conceived not as
baldly promotional pieces but as a collection of independent cinematic essays about people, places, and things
adjudged "too dramatic not to be real." Press releases
dubbed the project "unprecedented," and it was. It was
also one of ESPN's classiest undertakings.*

*Simmons thought each film should include at least
one appearance by its director—an introduction and
an interstitial element—explaining why the film's subject deserved greater, more comprehensive treatment
than it had so far received. But, who were these directors
going to be, and where would they come from? Simmons's friend Connor Schell suggested that outsiders, not
ESPN staff, should make the films; Simmons agreed,
and the dragnet was on.*

*What surprised Simmons was that finding enthusias-
tic filmmakers with a strong interest in sports wasn't
nearly as hard as he thought it would be. In fact, he
said, "These people had been waiting for us. They had
stories to tell. They just never thought they'd have a*

chance to tell them." It turned out, for instance, that actor turned director Peter Berg was "obsessed" with hockey great Wayne Gretzky. Rap star turned actor and director Ice Cube was devoted to the peripatetic Raiders. And it also turned out that the great, Oscar-winning director Barry Levinson (Rain Man, The Natural) *still mourned his beloved Baltimore's loss of the Colts, the pro football team that in 1984 literally stole away in the night and moved to Indianapolis. Having never quite gotten over it, he all but jumped at the chance to make a film about it.*

Once a few directors signed up, what Simmons dubbed "the domino effect" kicked in; big names attracted other big names, and they attracted still more. Morgan Freeman wanted to make a film about the 1995 South African rugby championships, and Spike Jonze, teamed with Johnny "Jackass" Knoxville, wanted to immortalize Mat Hoffman and the world of BMX racing on film. And on and on they came.

Controversial subjects were no liability. Steve James said he wanted to make a film about the part that racism played in the Virginia trial of basketball great Allen Iverson, charged at the age of seventeen with "maiming" a woman during a so-called race riot in a small Virginia town (his conviction was later overturned). 30 for 30 was a bold idea and a big risk, but it brought prestige, honor, and a new respectability to ESPN virtually from the outset.

JOHN SKIPPER:

My recollection is that *30 for 30* came out of a number of discussions afterward. As they say, success has many fathers and there were a number of people who contributed a lot, including Connor Schell, John Doll, and Keith. But I think without Bill Simmons, *30 for 30* could not have happened the same way. He was in the initial meetings, and he sent a seminal memo in which he suggested that we do thirty films.

However, a number of folks were critical to this initiative, including Keith Clinkscales, John Walsh, Joan Lynch, Connor Schell, Mike Tomlin, and the great unsung John Dahl. No one has been more influential in the final product than John Dahl, who is himself a documentary filmmaker and who clearly has the best connection to the filmmakers. Any suggestion of singular paternity here is an embellishment.

SPIKE LEE, *Filmmaker:*

Keith is a good friend of mine, and I really like John Skipper. It's a great company. They do great work, and for me, it's an ideal situation. They had been trying to get me to do something for them for a while, but I didn't really know what it should be. Then I saw this documentary on that soccer great on the French team, Zidane, where they had all these cameras on him only, and I thought, that might work even better for basketball. So I went to Kobe, who also happens to be a huge soccer fan, and he said, "Let's do it." We had, I think, more than twenty-five cameras on him, and I think it turned out really great. I still have people stop me all the time to tell me how much they liked it.

The people at ESPN enjoy and love sports. That's what comes through. I'm looking to do more for them.

CONNOR SCHELL, *Executive Producer, ESPN Films:*

Bill and I had been talking a lot about the different things we could be doing in the documentary space. Bill's got a real love for documentaries, as do I, Joan Lynch, John Dahl, John Skipper, and John Walsh. We all felt at the time like we could be doing more in the documentary space because it was consistent with the way ESPN wants to present content, and that we were in a better spot producing a high-end documentary about a great story in sports than we were producing a fictionalized, scripted version. And we believed there were real high-end Hollywood filmmakers who had such a passion for sports that, if you let them tell the story they wanted to tell, and if you gave them a platform to get that story out to the world and to the right audience, which ESPN can provide, that something like this project was possible.

So we went after great storytellers who were passionate about a particular story. In the back of our minds, we wanted to create a kind of mosaic to tell a larger story of what sports have meant to America over these thirty years. Once we got going, we knew within forty-five seconds of sitting down with someone whether or not they were going to do this. Either they had something they wanted to explore and we would help them find the angle, or they didn't and just looked at us like, "Why would I do a documentary for almost no money?"

We had great conversations with Barry Levinson, who came alive as he talked about the Colts. When we sat down with Steve Nash, the first thing he said was "I've never made a film before" but that when he was six years old, his teacher would tell him every day about where Terry Fox had run the previous day and that Terry was one of the most meaningful figures in his life; we just knew we had to let him tell that story.

STEVE NASH, *Basketball Player:*

Maura Mandt bribed me. I'm not kidding. She knew my love of film, and she told me she'd get me a meeting to pitch an idea for the *30 for 30* series if I came to the ESPYs. That was too great an opportunity to miss, so I went to the awards show, and actually had a good time. Terry Fox was one of the most remarkable human beings I had ever heard of, and I couldn't get his story out of my mind. His strength, courage, and vulnerability were so impressive, and the fact that he was so young was inspiring to me. It was a great honor to bring his journey to film, and I learned a great deal about filmmaking. I was particularly struck by what a difficult process editing can be, and the important influence it has on storytelling. In the end, making this film cemented for me the human potential. Terry was as compelling a person as I've ever come across—a seemingly normal, ordinary individual who had the strength to do the extraordinary and create a movement of epic proportion.

In the middle of the 2010 U.S. Open, Mary Carillo, considered one of the best analysts in television sports, abruptly walked off her job at ESPN. She had the grace to go quietly, without a word to the press or any kind of commotion—but her departure was a real setback for the network, though they were hardly about to admit it. They thought they had plenty of tennis personnel as it was, and that Mary Carillo was too opinionated—not on, but off the air.

MARY CARILLO, *Tennis Analyst:*
ESPN is very graphics oriented, and [it] was explained to me—because I was having a hard time watching the screen get smaller and smaller—that all that wizardry is there because there's a lot of places where the sound is off. ESPN is shown in bars or people have it on in the background. They're watch-

ing out of the corner of their eye. They're doing something else but they're still keeping an eye on the game. So they want to give them a lot of graphics. I got some really big issues with that. In this world of high-def, amazing camera work, and mics on the courts, I want everything else out of the way.

I would absolutely speak up in meetings, and I had a very definite idea about what good television looks like and sounds like. I have a strong sense of what we should be leaving the viewer with. I felt like we were smothering the product, that we weren't trusting it at all. People just want to see the tennis match and they don't really give that big a rip about all this other stuff that we're bringing in. I would say these things in production meetings a lot. I'd go into one of my rants about us being more of a minimalist. Sometimes there would be changes. Sometimes.

PATRICK McENROE, *Tennis Analyst:*

You turn on basketball, baseball, football, or any other big-time sport ESPN does and you've got the studio setup with the host and two or three people. Then you go out to the game and you've got the courtside person and another two or three people in the booth. I think they're taking that same tack with tennis now. We have a lot of great people, and that means I get to chill out a bit during the second week, but it is crowded.

ESPN had my brother and me broadcast officially

together for the first time, you know, as a team. They had the balls to do it, while others, who shall remain nameless, didn't. The first time we shared a booth calling a match I was obviously very excited. They actually had to do some major mixing of the voice levels between me and my brother because we sound so similar.

JOHN McENROE, *Tennis Analyst:*

It was great because we had talked about it for many years, and obviously, being brothers, the trick was I didn't really want to step on his toes and take anything away from him. But fortunately, the last couple of years he's been sort of working more toward doing sort of play-by-play stuff, so that enabled us to do the same match together. The only problem was we sound pretty similar. He used to take my phone calls for me when I was younger.

Meanwhile, progress made by women rising through the ranks and shattering the glass ceiling at ESPN had been pokey and plodding, but it did happen. Changes of late seemed especially noteworthy if compared to ESPN's earliest days, when the number of women in positions above production assistant could be counted on one hand; when women were being followed home by male staffers looking for action; and when bad boys in the newsroom let the Playboy Channel play as perpetually as Muzak.

By the first decade of the new century, however, women occupied key positions on the air and even in the company's once all-male executive suites. Times had—slowly—changed.

A milestone of sorts was marked on September 28, 2010. Not only was the day's 9:00 a.m. first edition of SportsCenter *anchored by two women—Hannah Storm and Linda Cohn—but so was the second installment, which followed immediately at noon, with Chris McKendry and Sage Steele helming.*

The pairings were remarkably appropriate. Since her arrival in 2007, Hannah Storm was among the network's most ubiquitous on-air talents, second only to Erin Andrews. She popped up everywhere—anchoring at Wimbledon and the NBA finals; hosting an event at the ESPYs; even producing one of the prestigious 30 for 30 *films, a documentary about the legendary rivalry between Martina Navratilova and Chris Evert.*

Perhaps not surprisingly, Storm engendered a good deal of jealousy, with coworkers shocked at how much she did and how management favored her. Erin Andrews's power came from outside the company; Storm's came from inside. Perhaps one of the most prolific Facebookers at the network, Cohn was also the author of a book where she talked candidly about her personal life, including her devotion to the Mets, Rangers, and Giants.

The tremendously popular McKendry and Steele, meanwhile, couldn't be more different than Storm and

Cohn. Both are understated, in terms of dress and temperament.

Cohn was ebullient as that first show came to an end and the time for the handoff drew nigh. "Never in my eighteen years here," said a near-giddy Cohn, "have there been back-to-back sets of woman anchors hosting SportsCenter." She and Storm made room on the set for McKendry and Steele. "Well done," Storm said, laughing—and adding, "by—us!" The occasion was jovial rather than solemn. The four women knew that their achievement was accomplished on behalf of all the women who had preceded them at ESPN—here, at the little corner store that had grown into an empire.

No one was ready to say its days as an all-boy network were gone forever, but in terms of symbolism, "Four Women's Day" was one helluva photo op.

CHRIS McKENDRY, *Anchor:*

I had a signature moment after one of my *SportsCenter* shows that I'll never forget. When Barry Bonds was indicted on perjury charges, they rushed Jay Harris and me onto the air an hour early, and we did an extended live broadcast with lots of breaking news and interviews. The next day, I got a letter from George Grande, on his Cincinnati Reds notepad— you know, because he was the voice of the Reds. He wrote, "Chris, that was a great job on *SportsCenter* Thursday night. You brought the perfect blend of reporting and knowledge, insight, and personality to one of the true special days for any reporter. The most fulfilling days I spent on *SportsCenter* were days like you experienced and I'm sure you had a great feeling of accomplishment when the day was done. As one who sat in that chair, I for one was proud to watch the way you carried the show. I've always enjoyed and admired your work. It's clear you would have been a star on *SportsCenter* in any year. Keep up the great work. — George Grande." I'm not sentimental. If you came through my office, I don't have credentials showing everything I've been to; I'm not one of those types. But I will save this letter forever.

SAGE STEELE, *Anchor:*

Maybe I'm naïve, but I have no proof of women being treated badly here at ESPN. I feel like I am treated just fine. I thought about this a lot because, honestly, I'm asked this all the time. My priority is my family. And the people who work here know that I have three small children, and I come to work, have a blast when I'm there, do my job, and leave. I leave pretty much immediately.

I think that has really helped me—that people realize I love my career, but I'd also leave my career in a heartbeat if I needed to. This is my lifelong goal as far as career is concerned, to be at ESPN, and yet nothing will ever come between me and my family. And if it doesn't work out, then I'm gone. I think that's really helped me and that they respect me for it.

Because there are so many women in this business, news or sports, that have put their personal lives on hold. And then they're forty years old and they say, "Oh, my gosh, I'm single," or, "Wow, I'm married and I have no kids. What do I do now?" And I just refuse to let that happen to me. I got pretty fortunate with a good husband. I think that's helped me, I really do. I am so lucky I can't even tell you. I thank God every day.

Robin Roberts is the person who made me realize what I wanted to do. She was one of the few females when I started watching ESPN who was constantly doing it. So in 1998, I was working at the ABC affiliate in Tampa, Florida, and coming up to visit my parents in Connecticut. I had a résumé paper and tape with me to show them my work. I was getting on the plane and I looked over and saw Robin Roberts. I was with my husband—my fiancé at the time—and I said, "Oh, my god, it's Robin Roberts. She's my hero." So I had this one tape with me, and for the whole flight I kept going back and forth— "Should I ask Robin to look at my tape and get back to me, give her my card and maybe get some constructive criticism from this woman I've admired for years? Or should I bring it home?" Because I had promised my parents. So I went back and forth, and finally I gave it to Robin. I said, "Excuse me" and woke her up. And she said she'd be glad to take a look at it. And then half an hour later we got off the plane.

She had been sitting up front, I was way in the back. And when I got off, she was standing out there, she'd waited a good five or six minutes for the whole plane to empty and for this kid to come off, then walked the whole way down to baggage claim to tell me she'd get back to me. And two weeks later, she did. She took the time for some nobody kid who threw a VHS tape at her and gave me this awesome feedback.

Then, at the National Association of Black Journalists convention in 2009, toward the end of this big breakfast with about five hundred people there, Robin Roberts was thanking everybody, and out of the blue she looked at me and said, "Sage, keep it up." And she got choked up and she said, "I can't believe I'm getting choked up right now. But when I watch you every morning, I see so much of me in you. You are amazing. You're setting a great example for young women everywhere, especially young black women who don't know if there's a chance of getting into this business." And she said, "You're fabulous. I am so proud of you." And I just couldn't *believe* it! Because this is the woman I strive to be like. I don't even really know her, and in front of all these people she called me out. She got emotional talking about me and how I reminded her of herself, and it just floored me.

I'm not impressed by very many people. Athletes, politicians, I really don't care. But because of the way she handled herself as a professional—and I had really studied her through the years, and when I got to ESPN I watched how she handled herself through the good and the bad there, how she carried herself on the air to this day, how she battled breast cancer, how her father was a Tuskegee airman, so she had the military connection, too, military brat—it had just meant more to me than anything in the world, more than anything anyone had ever said to me in this business. I still doubt myself. On days when maybe that doubt creeps in for a second, I think back to Robin Roberts on the podium that day and what she said to me.

JOHN ANDERSON:

I wouldn't have a career here, I don't think, without Linda Cohn. She's been instrumental, because when I went to *SportsCenter,* I wound up sitting next to her. Now, she had been here for a while. She's a made guy at that point. And she could have very well gone to her bosses and said, "Who's this guy who nobody knows that you stuck me with?" But she was just the opposite. She couldn't have been more helpful and more welcoming, and she's great to anchor with because she pays attention. I'm really grateful because she accepted me right off the bat and treated me like an equal from day one, and she didn't have to do that. There have been a lot of times when we ended shows where she said, "Good night, I'm Linda Cohn," and I'd go, "I'm the guy next to Linda."

DONNA ORENDER, *President, WNBA:*

What would I change about our relationship with ESPN? For one, I would like the perception out there to be that we are a prioritized partner of theirs. I'd like to see more of us on *SportsCenter.* I think our fans would like to see that too. I think young girls would like to see that. I think the daughters of the people who are putting on the coverage would like to see that. *SportsCenter* is a litmus test of what's important. It's a validater. And athletes want to be validated. We've spent a lot of time talking about taking the big voices — meaning the big guys with a lot of presence — and having them call WNBA games. Why? Because that's an indicator of importance and relevance. And ESPN's been very open to doing that. I think you'll see a lot more of that coming up. Dick Vitale covered a Connecticut–Notre Dame game, and I was thrilled. I was *thrilled.* Candace Parker was on the cover of the magazine, and that made a huge statement. We're getting there.

STAN VERRETT:

Neil [Everett] and I carried the *SportsCenter* flag to the West Coast. And Chris Berman left both of us a voice mail that said, "I watched the whole *SportsCenter* last night for the first time in I don't know how long, and I really enjoyed it 'cause you guys took me back to the old days when guys just got out there, did the stories, and had fun with it. It was really good to see. You guys are doing it the right way. Keep up the good work." That was a wide-eyed moment for me, like, wow. Neil had the same look. I'm keeping that message forever.

I was raised by a couple that's been married for almost fifty years, so I see how it works and it works when both people want it to work, when they're both invested not just in the "I's" but in the "we's." They look at it as joint ownership of something that's bigger than both of them. And that's how I've always looked at *SportsCenter*. "Hey, look, I have my little chair over here and you have your little chair over there, but when we come together at this table, this table's bigger than either chair separately, and it's bigger than both chairs together ultimately. So we have to respect that."

RUSSELL WOLFF, *Executive Vice President and Managing Director, ESPN International:*
Our first attempt at *SportsCenter* outside the U.S. was one of our least best moments. We were a struggling international division that wasn't doing great, but we knew we wanted to have a *SportsCenter* and so we created a *SportsCenter* produced out of London that we used around the world. We had the music and the graphics, but since we were trying to use it across the whole world, it had the NFL in it, cricket, ice hockey, soccer, and rugby. It was meant to be for

everybody, but it didn't hew to the origins and DNA of *SportsCenter,* which is sports authority and personality. And because we had to dub it into nine languages, we couldn't put any person, any faces, on it. So you had a faceless, nameless *SportsCenter,* which really didn't work. It was so not what *SportsCenter* is here and so not what *SportsCenter* should have been around the world.

With forty-six networks, you can't micromanage each network. I think the most important thing for us to focus on is the ESPN mission statement; when you do that, you almost never get it wrong. We're hardly going to be doing a great *SportsCenter* in Argentina if we're trying to force-feed something the American way. And so over the last nine years, we have created local versions of *SportsCenter,* and if you watch *SportsCenter* in Argentina or if you watch *SportsCenter* out of Mexico or you watch *SportsCenter* out of Singapore or India or Malaysia, they're local *SportsCenters* and they're speaking to fans in their language about their sports with personality. It still has the same music, and it still has the same set and still has the same look and feel as *SportsCenter,* but now you've got a *SportsCenter* show that remembers its roots, which is actually talking to fans and having a personality.

In the earliest days of ESPN — in fact, in the earliest years of ESPN — not many people wanted to go to

Bristol. It might well have been among the "Least Likely Places from Which to Run an Empire" if such a list were ever compiled. But Bristol is the seat of an empire now, and it has seemed to undergo a miracle cure for its undesirability: success.

Part of the change could probably be traced to the ingenious and star-studded promotional spots created for the network and SportsCenter by Wieden + Kennedy, creating a mock myth: that ESPN's Bristol headquarters serves as some sort of centralized high-tech playground, a sprawling twenty-first-century playhouse, a manly Mecca where athletes and even mascots meet, romp, and roughhouse with the journalists and technicians who cover them—all part of one big happy prank-playing family. The Sports Community.

In addition to that mythic image, there's the simple respectability that tremendous financial success confers. Bristol may not be much at all, but ESPN is the rose in the desert, a palace of practical pleasures amid some of the ugliest property in the otherwise verdant state of Connecticut—a Las Vegas of Sports.

Now not only sports stars come to Bristol. In the past decade, entertainment celebrities have become increasingly frequent guests. A trip to Bristol can, and often does, plug both ways.

BOB LEY:

I'll take credit for the term "Bristol car wash," and it's only gotten crazier since I came up with it. Let's say you're a sports celebrity and you're coming to Bristol for an interview. Okay, you've got radio in the early morning, then from 9:00 to 12:00 some guest appearances on *SportsCenter,* then *First Take.* At some point, you'll do a chat session on ESPN.com and probably visit Colin Cowherd along with some other afternoon radio shows. *Outside the Lines* will want you in the afternoon, and I'm sure there will be a couple more hits before dinner. It's a car wash. You'll get some underside protection, detailing, whatever, and you may look good, but you'll be exhausted.

JEFF BURTON:

It was a long day—"the car wash." They keep you busy the whole time, keep you humping, and it's good to do a whole lot in one day, you feel like you're being productive. But it's overwhelming, to be quite honest. Interview to interview and show to show, and of course all of them are on at different times so you actually spend a fair amount of time waiting to do something. It's a heck of a facility when you go up there, and you think about that deal being just to cover sports. And when you look at how big it is, and at the number of people it takes to do it, you really start to get a perspective of how important sports are to our country, that that much effort's put into covering sports. Pretty amazing, really.

CAROL MAYER, *Manager of Talent:*

A lot more people want to come and see ESPN now. I think what's happened is "the car wash" has gotten some cachet, and people are understanding that when they come up here, it's almost like going to a little "ESPN: The Amusement Park," or "ESPN: The Campus." You see all the people you see on TV every day, it's got a nice cafeteria, we treat them well when they come in and we're with them the entire day, so we really provide them with a great ESPN experience.

Say we're doing a John Smith Car Wash. What I would have done beforehand is reach out to all the different entities—we have a car wash distribution list that's probably up to about 130 people now—so that goes to ESPN Radio, all the ESPN television entities, *ESPN: The Magazine,* Page Two, ESPN.com, Visual Media, Podcast, the International, a bunch of different people. I'll send out a list like, "Hey, John Smith's thinking about coming on June 23, which shows would have interest if he were here?" Typically if people are interested, they'll respond in the first twenty minutes of getting that e-mail.

The main concern used to be that we weren't going to be able to get people here because it's Bristol. But I think as word spread, and as we started getting a sort of cachet, the name—I mean, now I can throw out that Pelé has been here. Pelé came up on his own dime, so, you know, Joe Shmoe football player, if you don't want to come, it's really no skin off our backs.

STEVE BERTHIAUME:

Scott Van Pelt and I had a conversation once and I said, "You know this place is really like an Island of Misfit Toys, like who else would employ these people? What else would they do?" We look around at some of the producers and the CPs [coordinating producers] and some of the talent, and they are just sort of social oddballs—where else would they find gainful employment but here, and here they thrive and they succeed.

MITCH ALBOM:

I think you just have to look at ESPN as a university, and there are some radical professors and some conservative professors, and there's the big classrooms with the four hundred people in a lecture hall, and there's the tiny little seminars with eight people in a room. That's what ESPN is. So it has programs like ours, which have stood the test of time and have a certain intelligence to them and pedigree, and you know, the people on it are older and have been around a long time. And then you'll have *Around the Horn*, that is young and splashy and noisy and gimmicky and all the rest, and you say, "How can this all be the same network?" Well, twenty-four hours a day, seven days a week is a lot to fill. And for a guy who started ESPN2 and said, "How can you have a second ESPN?" so now look and see ESPN Ocho is not that weird a reality, that may happen one day, so you just have to accept it. The landscape is huge and this is like flypaper and it catches a lot of different types of programs, and I'm just glad they haven't bounced *Sports Reporters*. They say, "You're not as angry as the rest of them." But I also think Sunday morning at 9:30 is not the time to be doing an *Around the Horn* sensibility. It's a different mood. Seven days a week there's a lot of different moods at different times.

DICK EBERSOL:

Every one of us would give our eyeteeth to have even a small piece of those subsidies that are just float-ing in to them, but for all that power, they don't do a lot of special things with it, other than a couple of studio shows. Their *Baseball Tonight* is beautiful tele-vision. The college football show with Fowler and those guys, beautiful television. But there's very little that they do anymore that's much better than some local cable operation. That's hard to believe with all the resources they have and the army of people and all that, but nobody seems to care. That's what I mean when I say they lost their way in terms of qual-ity and everything else.

FRED GAUDELLI:

When you work at ESPN, you work inside this tunnel, and you don't know it while you're there—I certainly didn't—but when you get out, you realize that "wow, we were very insular in our thinking, and there's a whole other way of doing things around here." But you never get to that level while working at ESPN, mainly because there's so much volume that you're overwhelmed by it and it's all you can do just to stay afloat.

CHRIS CONNELLY:

The competitiveness that you would assume with people who love sports comes out at ESPN not in people wishing others ill or in backbiting, but in the next producer wanting to do a piece that's even better than the piece that he saw on Sunday. And the sense that the organization is there to support him or her in those desires, that there's a sense on behalf of the entity that they want this next piece to be even better than the last one or the one before—tighter, smarter, more creative. And that's an invigorating thing to be around.

JOHN WALSH:

Moneyball is the most important sports business book written in the last quarter century. Few recognize it. I went down to Baltimore on a train last year, and I am watching the guy next to me read this number-cruncher book. I asked him what he did, and he said, "I'm the chief analytics officer for CVS drugstores," then went on to tell me there were three books that were required if you're in analytics in any business. *Moneyball* is one of them. The city of Boston has won six championships during the last decade, and if you really want to know what's going on, you need to realize that the Red Sox, Celtics, and Patriots are going into Harvard Business School, MIT Sloan School of Management, and Boston University to hire the smartest people. These new young analytic minds are looking at the way their teams do business, the way they sell tickets, the way they evaluate players, and it's a whole new way of looking at the way sports are played. So I went in and I talked to our guy who's doing our hiring. Sure enough, he says he was trying to hire this terrific candidate from BU, but it turned out the competition to get him was fierce as hell. We wanted him to be at ESPN as one of our top guys with numbers, but the Celtics and the Red Sox were battling for him too.

DAVID STERN:

I saw a poll which said that Walmart is the most successful symbol of American business, and in some way, I think ESPN is the most successful symbol of sports. What they do is spectacular. I mean, I'm in awe of it. It is the most monumental undertaking in the history of the world of television, and they do it day in and day out. And I understand that the time they can spend dealing with any one product as a production matter, or even one commissioner, is necessarily limited, and the amount of attention one gets sometimes may relate to how—what's the right word, what gets the most oil? The squeaky wheel. Okay. And so there's some combination of the two. We're respectful of what they do and we let them know how we feel. And each year, when the finals come around and you realize they're going to win the night for ABC—five games and five ratings wins—you feel pretty good, even if it happens to be an ESPN time buy on ABC.

BOB IGER:

We are very confident that ESPN will remain a vibrant company in every way. The reason is quite simple: they have proven to be very adept at marrying new technologies with unparalleled content to serve fans. ESPN has a very simple but powerful mission—serve sports fans. Everyone who works there starts their day with that in mind. You can't just issue a mission statement one day and have it become ingrained in the minds of nearly six thousand employees the next. It is a part of ESPN's culture that has developed over many years, which again goes to the competitive advantage ESPN has created for itself. And as we've seen, it works quite well.

Incredibly, sports—and sports media—continue to rapidly evolve in ways we could not have anticipated, and as a result, everything surrounding sports has become a much more integral part of the cultural landscape, both in the U.S. and in many ways around the world. We have new technologies, new mediums, paradigm shifts, global expansion, and the number of new ideas we see each day is truly amazing.

You tell me what fans will want in the next five years and ESPN will be there. If past is prologue, we know that will be true. Certainly there is room for growth in the digital arena, and in international markets. There is room for growth creatively on ESPN's biggest engine, domestic television. I could go on, but here's all you need to know about this topic: ESPN has deals with several leagues that call for content distribution on platforms that have yet to be invented.

JOHN SKIPPER:
George defines the culture now. Steve Bornstein was respected, admired, followed—and feared. George Bodenheimer is respected, admired, followed—and loved. George has been at his job since 1998. At some point, 1999 or 2000, he created this once-a-year strategy meeting. He gathers the top people, and what does he do? He says we as a group are going to decide our priorities as a company. And we now have this

annual thing we do about shared success—it's team-team-team. By nature, I'm a cynic and even a slight elitist—I moved to New York, I studied satire. That's what I was studying at Columbia—eighteenth-century satire—so I'm of a sardonic turn, and I can tell you this culture is not cynical. It's "team." It's complete enthusiasm, Moonie-ism in a positive sense. People believe in it. And that priorities thing, which you can make fun of—it's a little goofy, a little corny—we go together, we say the following four, five things are our priority. One year our priority is "Make ratings go up." One year it was "we have to make dot com work." So the whole company has been told, you might work in event production and operating camera and traveling around the country, but we're also looking to you to help us figure out how to make ESPN.com work.

You get a little card. We print cards with the priorities on them. You carry your card around. On the back is the mission and the company values. Really simple stuff, easy for a smarty-pants cynic who likes living in New York. But you can't make fun of it, because it works.

There is a cult of George in our company. George would hate that. George is the most influential person in sports; he actually doesn't care and actually doesn't like it—he'd be happy if it went away. To the rank and file, George walks on water.

You have to access the special features on the DVD release of Will Ferrell's Anchorman: The Legend of Ron Burgundy *to see Ferrell as Burgundy supposedly being interviewed for a job at ESPN in 1979, the year the network signed on. A twenty-four-hour sports network? Burgundy dismisses the whole idea as "ludicrous."*

Well, it's a big deal. Literally: The total number of different sports now aired by ESPN is 65. The number of countries receiving ESPN is 200. And the number of languages in which ESPN telecasts is 16.

ESPN has more than 6,000 employees and airs roughly 70,000 hours of programming annually, at least 25,000 of those live, on eight networks. ESPN Radio delivers 10,000 audio hours annually in more than 450 markets, and ESPN.com generates more than 600 original pieces each day of sports news, features, columns, video, and blog fare. When ESPN3D signed on in 2010, it was the first full-time 3D network in the country, airing more than 85 live events in 3D its first year.

Not to be forgotten: approximately $4 of every monthly cable bill in the U.S. goes to ESPN, obviously including viewers who've never watched a single ESPN telecast in their lives.

Today ESPN is worth more than the entire NFL; worth more than Major League Baseball, the NBA, and the NHL combined.

GEORGE BODENHEIMER:

The biggest tool I have for doing this job is that I am an optimist. I believe in this company's ability to continue to grow by sticking to our mission of serving sports fans and looking for ways to do that better tomorrow than we do it today. I believe that if we stick to our knitting, as they say, we'll always find ways to grow because interest in sports continues to grow. Do we have a strategic plan? Sure we do. But what I remind people constantly is that's only a piece of paper with ink on it. It's not a guarantee. So we need to be prepared, and we need to be able to try and do things differently all the time. Our announcements about local websites in 2010 were a great example. They didn't even exist in our strategic plan eight months before that. Were we talking about them? Of course. We've been talking about local sports since we discussed developing a regional sports network twenty years ago. Was Bob Iger exhorting me on a regular basis to think about how to expand that local business? Absolutely. So the notion had been here, and now we've developed what we think is another excellent opportunity for growth.

As for leading this company, I expect that if we are unsuccessful there will be other managers in here asked to do the job — that's the name of the game we operate in. Everybody here understands that, relishes it, and thrives on it.

I love it when someone says we're a niche business, because if sports is a niche business, I'm real happy to be in that niche. Whether you're watching your kids on the Little League or soccer fields, or watching Tom Watson holding an 8-iron on the 18th fairway challenging for the British Open at age fifty-nine, it's all self-renewing. And beautiful.

If you don't belong there, you may resent that one place has such power and influence; you may hate the hubris and self-promotion; you might think that others are more proficient at the same tasks yet make less of a production about them. But chances are, if you love sports and if you had the opportunity to join up, you'd do so. In a heartbeat.

Tour the headquarters of Johnson & Johnson and you probably won't be able to tell they do drugs; drop in at Sears corporate offices and it won't be readily evident they're in retail. But everything here at ESPN's Bristol campus reeks of sports. Walk from one building to another and you'll pass over yard markers; near the pizza roster in the café you'll notice a quip from the oft-quoted Yogi Berra: "Better cut it into six slices, I'm not hungry enough for eight." Pictures of athletes and games and balls and team logos and trophies are everywhere.

And there's Karl Ravech and John Kruk walking briskly along together, no doubt discussing a small gem of a baseball idea that will come to life on Baseball

Tonight; *a few steps away, Chris McKendry followed by Rece Davis, neither receiving much fanfare, but neither needing much, either—just doing their jobs well, on good days and bad. Inside Building 4 and all but chained to her desk is super assistant Denise Pelligrini, confirming details for yet another of John Skipper's or John Walsh's countless trips. John Wildhack is coming off the campus shuttle, carrying around in his head sought-after secrets for the next acquisition. In the elevator is Rich Feinberg, whose love for racing informs every mile of ESPN's coverage. Stephanie Druley and Carol Pandiscia, at opposite ends of the café, also work at opposite ends of the firm, two young standard-bearers of the culture, both looming large in the company's future.*

Earlier, quietly, Bill Creasy walked these halls— despite his rapscallion ways, one of the greatest executive starmakers in media, relentlessly supporting one young Turk or another who'd take the culture and flip it around like it was some Cirque du Soleil act. And before that, a cadre of SportsCenter *anchors, not fully realizing how popular they were because they so seldom got out into the real world. And a deceptively innocent-looking utility closet, memorial hideaway over the years for disparate yet like-minded couples expanding on the definition of "utility." Once, after their favorite team had won, a contented couple got so excited they summarily dumped colleagues and spouses and ducked into the closet to make love.*

And there's the old original newsroom, where in a different era propositions got proffered and porn was unreeled.

Going back in time, if we could, we'd zero in on a pair of thick glasses, a mane of Kringle-white hair, and a furry white beard, their owner caught in mid-rant as he insists that what this daft factory can produce is not just information but journalism, not mere sequences of numbers but artfully articulated thoughts, the mock-professorial sage holding court in an office filled with books, Rolodexes, and albino memorabilia.

And the legends, some of them ghostly: Bill Fitts, the veteran quarterback of an all-rookie squad that still managed to play proud; Scotty Connal, leaving behind a generation of protégées to carry on the work; the deeply adored and still-mourned Tom Mees, like Connal gone way too soon.

And Stu Evey washing blood off his hands, literally, after desperately trying to forestall the death of a magnate's son and then keep "the media" from learning about it. Not all his duties had been spelled out in his job description.

Further back, and further still, to a steamy summer afternoon in the middle of 1978, a drab, old, sputtering Mazda trapped on one of the jam-packed lanes of Route 84 outside Waterbury, Connecticut, its air conditioning horribly dead, a sweltering father and son, driver and passenger, arguing passionately over a bold idea that to this day has not been improved upon. The exasperated "don't knows" and "don't likes" and "can be dones" vol-ley back and forth, tensions tightening with every moment until the son says, half-defeatedly, "Show foot-ball all day and all night, for all I care"—the ensuing mutual exhilaration almost transcendent.

Acknowledgments

Thanks a lot for all your help. "No problem; let me know if there's anything else you need." I will. Appreciate it. "Oh, and can you do me one favor?" Of course. What is it? "Please don't mention my name in the acknowledgments. I don't want to get into trouble because somebody thinks I was a source."

That conversation, or one close to it, took place dozens of times with ESPN employees. Perhaps never before have so many been so helpful and yet so desirous of not being thanked. That being understood, let these few words serve as a general if inadequate "thank you" to all those at ESPN who were incredibly generous with their time, assistance, and, most of all, candor.

To ESPN management, who originally elected not to participate in the book, then changed their minds, we offer equal parts gratitude and empathy. Clearly this effort would not have been the same without your cooperation and without your allowing others to talk. But it can't have been easy to open your campus to inquisitive intruders without knowing what would come of it.

Gratitude also goes to those at other networks, league offices, and, most significantly, former ESPN employees for their openness. We are no less grateful to those who were interviewed but chose not to be quoted by name and those who, only because of space limitations, did not make the final cut. To them go apologies as well as thanks. To those who were not interviewed, it wasn't personal. There are literally thousands who could have made compelling contributions to this book; there just wasn't enough time and space to include everyone.

Maura Mandt's army of ESPY professionals, particularly Jennifer Aiello, were selflessly helpful, as were many publicists, agents, and others representing those who participated.

All the interviews were recorded on old-fashioned cassette tapes, because the one and only Harriet Schnitzer, who started transcribing tapes more than twenty-five years ago for *Running in Place: Inside the Senate,* prefers tapes. She is a marvel. However, the workload would have been unmanageable without an incredible lineup helping out as well: Katie Andrew, Martin Beiser, Lila Blaylock, Jennifer Haubrich, Bari Laskow, Oliver Miller-Farrell, Ryan Mitchell, Victoria Rosner, Alex Shapiro, and Avi Zenilman all provided invaluable support. To push the sports metaphor further: what a team.

Steve Skaggs, a dear friend, took time to read the manuscript and thus make the work journey more stimulating. Michael Ferman, a brother in spirit, makes the *life* journey more stimulating.

This book has been published at Little, Brown because that's where their extraordinary editor in chief Geoff Shandler resides. The world would be a smarter place if he could take a look at everything before its final version. Gratitude extends to his colleagues at Little, Brown — Karen Andrews, Amanda Brown, Nicole Dewey, Heather Fain, Peggy Freudenthal, Holly Hartman, Keith Hayes, Laura Keefe, Karen Landry, Pamela Marshall, Liese Mayer, Amanda Tobier, Mary Tondorf-Dick, and Betsy Uhrig — and their gifted, gracious leader, Michael Pietsch.

If Sloan Harris were to leave the agency business and become, say, a dentist, we would be his willing and even eager patients; were he to become an architect, we'd be at his office door asking him to design our houses. He is tireless in his devotion and deserves our warm professional — and personal — indebtedness.

Finally: loving appreciation to Chloe Tess Miller, humanitarian and artist; to Sophie Alexandra Miller, athlete and scholar; and to Zachary Samuel

Miller, idealist and visionary, for their incredible patience and heartfelt encouragement. These three gifts from G-d are the children of one coauthor and the G-dchildren of the other. In both roles, in their exuberance and delight, they put us to shame.